CADOGAN GUIDES

"Cadogan Guides really need no introduction and are mini-encyclopaedic on the countries covered... they give the explorer, the intellectual or cultural buff – indeed any visitor – all they need to know to get the very best from their visit... it makes a good read too by the many inveterate armchair travellers."
— *The Book Journal*

"Rochelle Jaffe, owner and manager of Travel Books Unlimited in Bethesda, Maryland, attributes [Cadogan Guides'] popularity to both their good, clean-looking format and the fact that they include 'information about everything for everyone'.... These guides are one of the most exciting series available on European travel."
— *American Bookseller*

"More entertaining companions, with sharp insights, local gossip and far more of a feeling of a living author.... The series has received plaudits worldwide for intelligence, originality and a slightly irreverent sense of fun."
— *The Daily Telegraph*

"Cadogan Guides are literate and agreeably idiosyncratic."
— *The Independent*

Other titles in the Cadogan Guides series:

AMSTERDAM
AUSTRALIA
BALI
BERLIN
THE CARIBBEAN
ECUADOR, THE GALÁPAGOS
   & COLOMBIA
GREEK ISLANDS
INDIA
IRELAND
ITALIAN ISLANDS
ITALY
MEXICO
MOROCCO
NEW YORK
NORTHEAST ITALY
NORTHWEST ITALY
PORTUGAL
PRAGUE
ROME
SCOTLAND

SOUTH ITALY
SOUTHERN SPAIN: ANDALUCÍA
   & GIBRALTAR
SPAIN
THAILAND
TUNISIA
TUSCANY, UMBRIA AND
   THE MARCHES
TURKEY
VENICE

Forthcoming:

CENTRAL AMERICA
CENTRAL ASIA
CYPRUS
GERMANY
MADRID & BARCELONA
MOSCOW & ST PETERSBURG
PARIS

ABOUT THE AUTHORS

Professional travel writers Dana Facaros and Michael Pauls have contributed eight books on Italy (among others) to the Cadogan Guides Series. Currently installed in the Midi, they offer this book as the first of the Cadogan France series. Dana and Michael are fitfully restoring an old farmhouse, where the rain patters through the roof, through the ceiling and into their word processors. Their children have already mastered several excruciating French verb tenses, and are patiently attempting to pass them on to their parents.

ACKNOWLEDGEMENTS

We would like to thank the many tourist offices whose advice and knowledge were of great help in preparing this book. Also a big thank you to Bill for arranging a car; to Rachel, our editorial godmother and mother confessor; to all the hitchhikers, vintners, old ladies and Catalans who gave us the lowdown on the Midi; and to everyone who came to boost our morale during this rather massive undertaking: George and Joanne, Dennis, Michael and Brian, Deborah, Ada, and Natasha, Mike and Judy, Paula, Carolyn, Chris, and even Robin.

Our particular thanks go to Simon Farr, wine buyer for Bibendum Wine Ltd (winner of the 1992 *Sunday Telegraph Good Wine Guide/Wine Magazine Wine Merchants of The Year* award in the specialist merchant category for Rhône wines) for editing the wine sections as well as contributing his own recommendations and wonderful stories. We would also like to thank copy-editors Louise Rogers and Louisa McDonnell and indexer Joe Britton for all their hard work.

CADOGAN GUIDES

THE SOUTH OF FRANCE

PROVENCE, CÔTE D'AZUR, LANGUEDOC-ROUSSILLON

DANA FACAROS and MICHAEL PAULS

CADOGAN BOOKS
London

THE GLOBE PEQUOT PRESS
Chester, Connecticut

Cadogan Books Ltd
Mercury House, 195 Knightsbridge, London SW7 IRE

The Globe Pequot Press
138 West Main Street, Chester, Connecticut 06412, USA

Cover design by Keith Pointing
Cover illustration by Povl Webb
Maps drawn by Thames Cartographic Services
Index by A. B. Britton

Series Editor: Rachel Fielding

First published 1992

British Library Cataloguing in Publication Data

Facaros, Dana
  South of France.
  I. Title   II. Pauls, Michael
  914.4804838
  ISBN 0–947754–30–X

Library of Congress Cataloging-in-Publication Data

Facaros, Dana
  The South of France: Provence, Côte d'Azur, and Languedoc-Roussillon /
by Dana Facaros and Michael Pauls: illustrations by Pauline Pears.
    p.   cm.—(Cadogan guides)
  "A Voyager Book."
  Includes bibliographical references (p.   ) and index.
  ISBN 0–87106–153–8
    1. France, Southern—Description and travel—Guide-books.
  I. Pauls, Michael.   II. Title.   III. Series.
  DC607.3.M36 1992   91–36767
  914.4′804838—dc20   CIP

Photoset in Ehrhardt on a Linotron 202
Printed and bound in Great Britain by
Redwood Press Limited, Melksham, Wiltshire

CONTENTS

Part V: Côte d'Azur: L'Esterel to Bandol *Pages 131–62*

Part VI: Metropolitan Provence: La Ciotat to Martigues, Marseille and Aix *Pages 163–99*

Part VII: The Provençal Alps *Pages 200–28*

Part VIII: Northern Provence: the Vaucluse *Pages 229–59*

Part IX: Down the Rhône: Orange to Beaucaire *Pages 260–90*

Part X: Down the Rhône: the Alpilles, Crau and Carmague *Pages 291–324*

Part XI: Nîmes, The Gard and Montpellier *Pages 325–57*

LIST OF MAPS

INTRODUCTION

'Our nights are more beautiful than your days,' Racine boasted to his Parisian friends, writing home from Uzès in the Gard. The nights are indeed thrilling, dry and clear and boiling with stars. After dawn, the southern sun quickens landscapes of sculpted hills and purple mountains, cypresses and lavender. Vincent Van Gogh, who saw more clearly into the heart of this extravagant world than anyone else, painted those landscapes, and especially those cypresses, as if they were moving and alive, with a lyrical and passionate intensity. Come to the hills around St-Rémy when the mistral is up, and you will see nature immitating art.

We outsiders have had an on-again off-again love affair with the south of France ever since the Romans colonized it and spent their decline lounging around their heated pools. Even the medieval popes and cardinals in Avignon succumbed to its worldly temptations, its wines and the scents of its *maquis*, its roses and violets, the droning hum of the cicadas. The popes' court painters, some of the greatest artists of the 14th century, lent their radiant Madonnas something of the voluptuous Mediterranean light and colour that would one day inspire Van Gogh, Cézanne, Renoir, Matisse and the Fauves, painters whose works have changed the way our eyes see not only the south of France, but the rest of our world as well.

These days, our world has decided on Provence as its possible paradise. Millions of people come here every year, hoping to catch a glimpse of it, wishing it didn't have so many second homes, holiday flats, trinket shops and traffic jams. To see the region at its best the delicate question of *when* to go becomes as important as where; in August, the worst month, even the dullest town on the coast of Provence can be as frantic as the monkey-pit in a zoo. One reason why we've included Languedoc-Roussillon, the 'other', western half of Mediterranean France is not only for its own considerable and un-deservedly little-known merits, but because much more of it is unspoiled. Within this larger territory, extending from the Alps to the Pyrenees, there's something for every taste: relics and monuments of a past that goes back a million years; medieval villages, some all but abandoned Brigadoons and others immaculately restored; world-class collections of art; mountain wildernesses and national parks; lively music and theatre festivals; ski resorts and wine roads; casinos and nightclubs; superb markets and restaurants that rival Paris' finest. Of course you can simply do as the Romans did and lounge around the pool, idly dreaming about what's for lunch. No wonder that Pope Gregory XI, who returned the papacy to Rome in 1377, took one look at the Eternal City and immediately decided to pack his bags to return to the comforts and delights of Avignon. Much to the relief of the Italians, he died before he could go.

A Guide to the Guide

Never think that this nebulous Anglo-Saxon concept 'the South of France' has any definite boundaries. Every writer who has ever covered the subject draws the line where he or she sees fit, and we must do the same. We definitely think we've given you the best

MAIN FEATURES

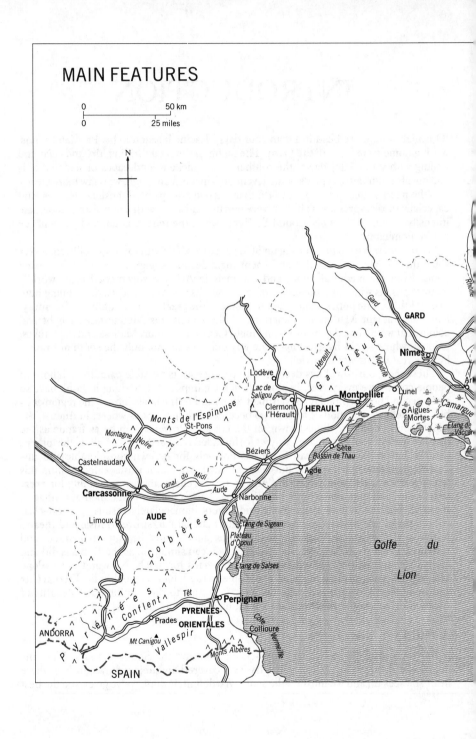

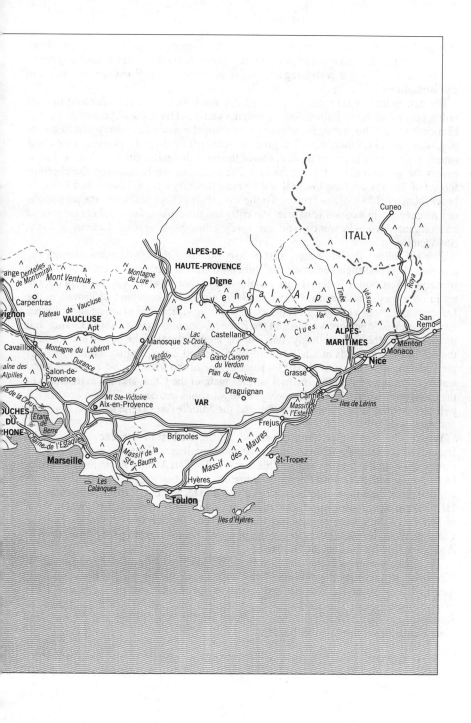

of it, pushing as far into such inland regions as the Provençal Alps if there is something worth the trip. The real innovation is that this book covers the entire French Mediterranean coast, offering a surprising alternative to overcrowded Provence—Languedoc and Roussillon.

For convenience's sake, the contents of this book follow a fairly strict east to west order, beginning on the Italian frontier with the section of the Côte d'Azur known as the French Riviera. This is *Part IV*, with dramatic corniche roads and outrageous fleshpots like Monaco and Cannes, as well as great museums of modern art, music festivals, and superb restaurants; here too is Nice, one of the most delightful cities in France. *Part V* covers the western Côte d'Azur: the blood-red cliffs of the Esterel and the chestnut forests of the Maures, the lovely Iles d'Hyères, the navy city of Toulon and France's beach-blanket Babylon, St-Tropez. To the west (*Part VI*) lies Marseille, the metropolis of Provence, set in a coastline of dramatic cliffs and fjord-like *calanques*; here too is staid and elegant Aix-en-Provence, and the lovely countryside around Cézanne's Mont Ste-Victoire.

Part VII follows the same east–west course, but takes the inland route through the maritime Alps and their secret valleys, difficult of access but worth the trouble for the scenery—Mercantour National Park and the Grand Canyon of the Verdon—and for the art in their medieval chapels. Next (*Part VIII*) comes the heartland of Provence: the Lubéron and Mont Ventoux, and pockets of exquisite villages full of artists and refugees from the coast. From here we descend the Rhône, beginning in *Part IX* with Orange and its Roman theatre, through lively Avignon, the medieval city of the popes, and through the celebrated vineyards of Châteauneuf-du-Pape and Tavel, France's finest rosé. As the Rhône continues south (*Part X*) it passes some of the south's most curious natural features: the jagged Alpilles, the rock-strewn plain of the Crau, and the marshlands of the Camargue, where Provençal cowboys herd wild bulls and horses. Roman Provence is well represented in St-Rémy and Arles, and the Middle Ages come to life in St-Gilles and Aigues-Mortes.

West of the Rhône lies Languedoc, with all the interest of Provence and only the fraction of the tourists—except perhaps at the magnificent Pont du Gard, one of the three most visited sights in France. This is covered in *Part XI*, along with the art town of Uzès, Nîmes with its famous Roman monuments, and dynamic Montpellier, a university city that rivals Paris in its enthusiasm for culture and technology. *Part XII* introduces the Hérault, the biggest wine-producing region of France, with rural delights equal to those of Provence—little wine regions like the Minervois, and the serendipitous tree-lined Canal du Midi. Its coast offers long miles of open beaches and the pretty resort town of Agde, founded by the ancient Greeks.

The next *département* is the Aude, in *Part XIII*; here you'll find the surprising city of Narbonne, with its magnificent cathedral; Carcassonne, the biggest and best-preserved medieval fortress city in Europe; and scores of spectacular castles hanging over the lonely landscapes of the Corbières. Last but not least, there are the Catalans of Roussillon, in *Part XIV*: sweet wines, medieval art, Pyrenean valleys and the delicious Côte Vermeille on the Spanish border.

THE BEST OF
THE SOUTH OF FRANCE

Aquariums: Musée Océanographique, Monaco; Banyuls-sur-Mer; Aquarium del Prado, Marseille.

Castles: Carcassonne, the biggest in Europe; Peyrepertuse; Salses; Château du Roi René, Tarascon.

Curiosities: mushroom art in Sérignan-du-Comtat and the Musée Barla, Nice; Rennes-le-Château; world's first concrete canoe, Musée du Pays Brignolais, Brignoles; the original dictaphone, in the Musée du Phonographie, Ste-Maxime; Cathedral, Vaison-la-Romaine; two-headed lamb, Musée d'Histoire Naturelle, Nîmes; *Danse Macabre*, Bar-sur-Loup.

Follies: Château de l'Anglais, Nice; Fondation Henry Clews, La Napoule; Institute of Marine Biology, Toulon; Château de Castille, Argilliers; the château-follies of Montpellier; Mausoleum Sec, Aix.

Gardens: Jardin des Plantes, Montpellier; Villa Ephrussi, St-Jean-Cap-Ferrat; Jardin des Colombières, Menton; Jardin de la Fontaine, Nîmes; Parc Phoenix, Nice; Jardin Thuret, Antibes.

Hotels: La Voile d'Or, St-Jean-Cap-Ferrat, Le Prieuré, Villeneuve-lès-Avignon; La Colombe d'Or, St-Paul-de-Vence; Hôtel de la Cité, Carcassonne.

Markets: Arles, Apt, Cannes, Nice, Carpentras; fish market of Marseille.

Medieval art and architecture: Avignon; Narbonne; St-Michel-de-Cuxa and environs; Aigues-Mortes; St-Guilhem-le-Désert; Abbaye de Valmagne, near Sète.

Natural Wonders: Grand Canyon du Verdon, Gargaï chasm on Mte Ste-Victoire; ochre quarries of Roussillon; Fontaine-de-Vaucluse; musical stalactites in the Grottes de St Cézaire near Grasse; the Falaises de Soubeyran, highest cliffs in France, La Ciotat.

Regions of picturesque villages: Eastern Lubéron, country north of Draguignan; Val de Peillon, near Nice; Val de Roya; La Cerdagne; lower Canal du Midi; Comtat Venaissin.

Restaurants: Jacques Maximin, Nice; Royal Gray, Cannes; La Reverbère, Narbonne; Moulin de Mougins, Mougins.

Roman monuments: Nîmes, Pont du Gard, Orange, St-Rémy, Vaison-la-Romaine, Arles.

Scenic areas: upper reaches of the Alpes-Maritimes *département*, around the Parc National de Mercantour; Pic du Canigou in the Pyrenees; the Alpilles; western Corbières.

Seaside resorts: Collioure; Agay; Juan-les-Pins; Ile de Porquerolles; Gruissan.

Traditional festivals: Gipsy pilgrimage, Stes-Maries-de-la-Mer; *Procession de la Sanch*, Perpignan.

Wine touring: Châteauneuf-du-Pape; Dentelles de Montmirail (Gigondas); east of Draguignan (Côtes de Provence); Minervois.

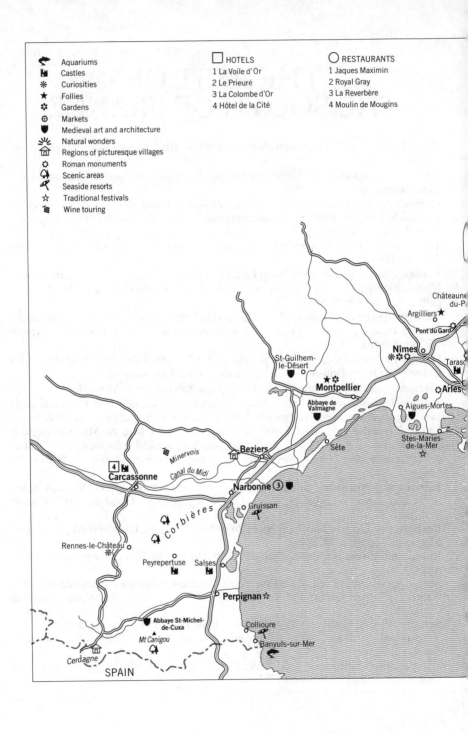

Aquariums
Castles
Curiosities
Follies
Gardens
Markets
Medieval art and architecture
Natural wonders
Regions of picturesque villages
Roman monuments
Scenic areas
Seaside resorts
Traditional festivals
Wine touring

HOTELS
1 La Voile d'Or
2 Le Prieuré
3 La Colombe d'Or
4 Hôtel de la Cité

RESTAURANTS
1 Jaques Maximin
2 Royal Gray
3 La Reverbère
4 Moulin de Mougins

Châteauneuf-
du-Pe
Argilliers
Pont du Gard
Nîmes
Tarasc
St-Guilhem-
le-Désert
Montpellier
Arles
Abbaye de
Valmagne
Aigues-Mortes
Stes-Maries-
de-la-Mer
Minervois
Beziers
Sète
Carcassonne
Canal du Midi
Narbonne
Gruissan
Corbières
Rennes-le-Château
Peyrepertuse
Salses
Perpignan
Abbaye St-Michel-
de-Cuxa
Collioure
Mt Canigou
Banyuls-sur-Mer
Cerdagne
SPAIN

THE BEST OF PROVENCE, COTE D'AZUR AND LANGUEDOC-ROUSSILLON

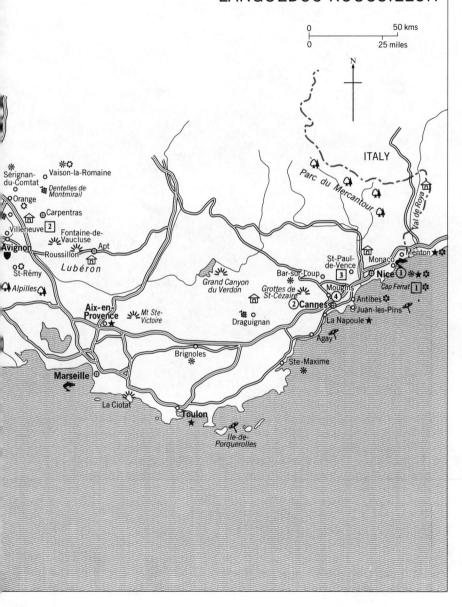

Part I

GENERAL INFORMATION

Grand Prix, Monaco

Before You Go

A little preparation will help you get much more out of your holiday in the south of France. Check the list of festivals (p. 22) to help you decide where you want to be and when, and book accommodation early: if you plan to base yourself in one area, write ahead to the local tourist offices listed in the text for complete lists of self-catering accommodation, hotels, and campsites in their areas, or else contact one of the many companies in the UK or USA (p. 21). For more general information and a complete list of tour operators, get in touch with a French Government Tourist Office:

UK: 178 Piccadilly, London, W1V OAL, tel (071) 491 7622
Ireland: 35 Lower Abbey St, Dublin 1, tel (010 353) 30 07 77.
Australia: BWP House, 12 Castlereigh St, Sydney NSW 2000, tel (612) 213 5244.
USA: 610 Fifth Av., New York, NY, 10020, tel (212) 757 1125; 645 N. Michigan Av., Chicago, IL 60611; 9454 Wiltshire Blvd, No. 303, Beverly Hills, CA 90212. Nationwide information tel (900) 420 2003.

Canada: 1981 Av. McGill College, No. 490, Montreal, Que. H3A 2W9, tel (514) 288 4264; 1 Dundas St W., No. 2405 Box 8, Toronto, Ont M5G 1Z3, tel (416) 593 4717.

Climate

Provence and Languedoc have a basically Mediterranean climate, one wafted by winds that give it a special character. The most notorious is the **mistral** (from the Provençal *mistrau*, or master) supposedly sent by northerners jealous of the south's climate—rushing down the Rhône and gusting east as far as Toulon and west to Narbonne, sparing the hot-house of the Côte d'Azur. On average the mistral blows 100 to 150 days a year, nearly always in multiples of three, except when it begins at night. It is responsible for the dryness in the air and soil (hence its nickname, *mangio fango*, or mud-eater). Houses in its line of fire are built *pointes en avant*, at an angle, the north side blank and in the shade, protected by cypresses, while on the south side plane trees protect the house from the strong sun. It blows so hard that it can drive people mad: an old law in Provence acquitted a murderer if it could be proved that he killed his victim while the mistral was blowing. But the mistral has its good points: it blows away harmful miasmas and pollution from the Rhône and makes the stars radiantly clear, as alive as Van Gogh's *Starry Night*.

Besides the Master, there are other winds: the east wind, or **Levant**, or southeasterly 'Greek' wind which brings the much desired rain; the **Pounent**, or west wind; and the suffocatingly hot **sirocco** from Africa. The region from the Spanish border to Montpellier is occasionally bulldozed by the **Tramontane**, the 'Catalan wind' from the northwest.

Rainfall varies widely across the south. The Pyrenees get more rain than most places on this planet—over two metres a year (Prats de Mollo, with 838 mm in 16 hours, holds the local record) while the Camargue barely gets 500 mm a year, the least rainfall in France. In the average year, it rains as much in Nice (750 mm per year) as Brest and more in Marseille than Paris. In the heart of Provence it rains much less frequently—not at all in the summer, and violently in spring and autumn (up to 135 mm in an hour)—hence the *restanques* or terraces carved in the hills by the farmers to prevent erosion. Recent years have been even drier than average, turning the forests of the south into tinder-boxes.

Each season has its pros and cons. In January all the tourists are in the Alps or Pyrenees; in February the mimosa and almonds bloom on the Côte d'Azur. In April and May you can sit outside at restaurants and swim, and in an hour's drive ski at Auron or Isola 2000. By June, the mistral slows down and the resorts begin to fill up; walking is safe in the highest mountains. July and August are bad months, when everything is crowded, temperatures and prices soar (Perpignan has the highest average summer temperatures in France) and tempers flare, but it's also the season of the great festivals in Avignon, Aix, Juan-les-Pins and Nice. Things quieten down considerably once French school holidays end in mid-September; in October the weather is comfortable and mild on the coast, as the first snows fall in the Pyrenees and Alps. November is another bad month; the rains begin and many museums, hotels, and restaurants close down. December brings Christmas holiday tourists and the first skiers.

Average Temperature Chart in °C (°F)

	Jan	*Feb*	*Mar*	*Apr*	*May*	*June*	*July*	*Aug*	*Sept*	*Oct*	*Nov*	*Dec*
Nice	11(52)	12(54)	14(56)	17(62)	20(69)	22(72)	24(75)	26(79)	25(77)	20(69)	16(61)	13(55)
Avignon	7(44)	7(44)	11(52)	15(59)	17(62)	21(70)	23(73)	25(77)	23(73)	16(61)	10(50)	8(45)
Perpignan	12(54)	12(54)	13(55)	17(62)	20(69)	23(73)	28(82)	28(82)	26(79)	20(69)	16(61)	14(56)
Font-Romeu	-2(28)	-2(28)	1(34)	4(39)	7(44)	10(50)	14(56)	15(59)	11(52)	7(44)	2(36)	0(32)

Getting There

By Air

The main international airports in the south are at Nice, Marseille, Montpellier, and Toulouse. Unfortunately, with the exception of Nice, these airports serve mainly business travellers and don't get enough holiday volume to make international fares competitive. Prices are highest in the summer and during the Easter holidays, but those who book several months in advance can usually save money. Check with your travel agent or your major Sunday newspaper for bargains or packages. There are a number of charters from London to Nice, but from most other points of departure—the rest of the UK, Ireland, North America, Australia, etc.—it's usually cheaper to fly to Paris and from there catch a cheap Air Inter flight or TGV train to the south. Check out Air France's Air and Rail scheme, which may save you money.

From Orly Airport in Paris, there are Air Inter flights to Nice, Cannes, Toulon, Marseille, Nîmes, Perpignan or Montpellier; discounts exist if you fly in low 'blue' periods (in the UK, Nouvelles Frontières, 1–2 Hanover St, London W1, tel (071) 629 7772 have all the Air Inter details). Students who equip themselves with the relevant ID cards are eligible for considerable reductions, not only on flights, but on trains and admission fees to museums, concerts, and more. Agencies specializing in student and youth travel can help in applying for the cards, as well as filling you in on the best deals. Try STA (071) 937 9921 and Campus Travel (071) 730 3402 in London or branches throughout the UK; STA tel (03) 347 6911 in Australia; Council Travel tel (800) 223 7402 and STA tel (800) 777 0112 in the US; CUTS tel (416) 979 2406 in Canada.

By Train

Air prices and airport hassles make France's highspeed TGVs (*trains à grande vitesse*) a very attractive alternative. TGVs shoot along at the average of 170 mph when they're not breaking world records, and the journey from Paris' Gare de Lyon to Marseille takes only 4 hours and 44 minutes; to Avignon 3 hours and 45 minutes; to Montpellier 5 hours; to Nice 7 hours. Costs are only minimally higher on a TGV. Some weekday departures require a supplement (30–40 F) and seat reservations (20 F), which you can make when you buy your ticket or at the station before departure. Another pleasant way of getting there is by overnight sleeper after dinner in Paris, although a recent spate of robberies in the compartments at night suggests that you should take extra precautions. People under 26 are eligible for a 30 per cent discount on fares (see the travel agencies listed above) and there are other discounts if you're over 65 available from major travel agents.

3

If you plan on some long train journeys, look into the variety of rail passes: France's national railway, the SNCF offers a *France Railpass* that gives you either four days (they don't have to be consecutive) of unlimited travel in a 15-day period, or nine days of travel within 30 days. It includes extras like a day's free travel in Paris (from the airport, the métro, etc.), TGV supplements (except the seat reservation), and discounts on car rentals and channel crossings. Get it before you leave from travel agents or SNCF offices: at 179 Piccadilly, London W1, tel (071) 834 2345 or 610 Fifth Av., New York, NY 10020 tel (212) 582 2816 (or tel (800) 848 7245). Other alternatives include the well-known InterRail pass for European residents under age 26, which offers a month's unlimited travel in Europe and 50 per cent reductions on Channel ferries, and various Eurail passes for non-Europeans, valid for 15 days to three months.

By Coach

The cheapest way to get from London to the south of France is by National Express Eurolines coach (tel (071) 730 0202; tickets available from any National Express office). There are at least three journeys a week: to Aix and Marseille (24 hours); Cannes and Nice (27 hours) by way of Grenoble; and other routes via Avignon and Nîmes stop at Perpignan (24 hours) en route to Spain.

By Car

A car entering France must have its registration and insurance papers. If you're coming from the UK or Ireland, the dip of the headlights must be adjusted to the right. Carrying a warning triangle is mandatory, and this should be placed 50 m behind the car if you have a breakdown. Drivers with a valid licence from an EC country, Canada, the USA or Australia don't need an international licence. If you're driving down from the UK, going through or around Paris is almost inevitable, a task best tackled on either side of rush hour. The various *autoroutes* will get you south the fastest but be prepared to pay some 500 F in tolls; the N7 south of Paris may take longer, but costs nothing and has better scenery.

A comfortable but costly option is to put your car on the train. Motorail services run from both Boulogne and Dieppe to Avignon and Fréjus/St Raphaël and from Boulogne to Nice and also to Narbonne.

If you plan to hire a car, look into air and holiday package deals as well as combination 'Train and Auto' rates to save money, or consider leasing a car if you mean to stay three weeks or more. Prices vary widely from firm to firm, and beware the small print about service charges and taxes: a couple of firms to try in the US are France Auto Vacances, tel (800) 234 1426 and Europe by Car Inc, tel (800) 223 1516 or Renault, tel (800) 221 1052.

Border Formalities and Visas

Holders of EC, US, and Canadian passports do not need a visa to enter France for stays of up to three months, but everyone else still does. Apply at your nearest French Consulate: the most convenient visa is the *visa de circulation*, allowing for multiple stays of

4

three months over a three-year period. If you intend on **staying longer**, the law says you need a *carte de séjour*, a requirement EC citizens can easily get around as passports are rarely stamped. On the other hand, non-EC citizens had best apply for an extended visa at home, a complicated procedure requiring proof of income, etc. You can't get a *carte de séjour* without this visa, and obtaining this is a trial run in the *ennuis* you'll undergo in applying for a *carte de séjour* at your local *mairie*.

Health and Travel Insurance

Citizens of the EC, who bring along their E-111 forms are entitled to the same health services as French citizens. This means paying up front for medical care and prescriptions, of which costs 75–80 per cent are reimbursed later—a complex procedure for the non-French. As an alternative, consider a travel insurance policy, covering theft and losses and offering 100 per cent medical refund; check to see if it covers your extra expenses in case you get bogged down in airport or train strikes. Beware that accidents resulting from sports are rarely covered by ordinary insurance. Canadians are usually covered in France by their provincial health coverage; Americans and others should check their individual policies.

Money and Banks

The franc (abbreviated with an F) consists of a 100 centimes. Banknotes come in denominations of 500, 200, 100, 50 and 20 F; coins in 10, 5, 2, 1 and ½ F, and 20, 10, and 5 centimes. You can bring in as much currency as you like, but by law are only allowed to take out 5000 F in cash. Travellers' cheques or Eurocheques are the safest way of carrying money; the most widely recognized credit card is *Visa* (*Carte Bleue* in French) which is accepted almost everywhere and will allow you to draw from most cash dispensers. If you plan to spend a lot of time in rural areas, where banks are few and far between, you may want to opt for International Giro Cheques, exchangeable at any post office.

Banks are generally open from 8:30–12:30 and 1:30–4; they close Sunday, and most close either on Saturday or Monday as well. Exchange rates vary, and nearly all take a commission of varying proportions. *Bureaux de change* that do nothing but exchange money (and exchanges in hotels and train stations) usually have the worst rates or take out the heftiest commissions, so be careful. It's always a good bet to purchase some francs before you go, especially if you arrive during the weekend.

On Arrival

Getting Around the South

By Train

The SNCF runs a decent and efficent network of trains through the major cities of the south, with an added service called the *Métrazur* that links all the resorts of the Côte d'Azur from Menton to St-Raphaël as often as every half-hour in the peak summer season. There are two narrow-gauge trains worth taking for their mountain scenery: the Nice to Digne *Train des Pignes* operated by the **Chemin de Fer de la Provence** (French rail passes are valid, other passes are granted a 50 per cent discount) and the SNCF's *Le Petit Train Jaune* from Villefranche-de-Conflent to Latour-de-Carol in the Pyrenees, with bus connections at either end to Perpignan and Andorra.

Prices have recently gone up but are still reasonable. If you plan on making only a few long hauls the France Railpass (see above) will save you money. Other possible discounts hinge on the day of your departure. The SNCF has divided the year into blue, white, and red days, based on demand. If you depart in a *Période Bleue* (off-peak) with a return ticket and travel over 1000 km you'll get a 25 per cent discount (*Billet Séjour*). Married couples are eligible for a free *Carte Couple* which entitles one to pay half-fare when travelling together on blue days. People over 65 can purchase a *Carte Vermeille*, valid for a year of half-price blue period travel; under 26-year-olds can buy a *Carte Jeune* for half-price blue-day travel from June to September. The more children you have, the more economical an expensive *Carte Kiwi* becomes: the card is in the name of one child, and family members each purchase complimentary cards. The child then pays full fare, and everyone else half.

Tickets must be stamped in the little orange machines by the entrance to the lines that say *Compostez votre billet* (this puts the date on the ticket, to keep you from using the same one over and over again). Any time you interrupt a journey until another day, you have to re-compost your ticket. Long-distance trains (**Trains Corails**) have snack trolleys and bar/cafeteria cars; some have play areas for small children. Nearly every station has large computerized lockers (*consigne automatique*) which take about half an hour to puzzle out the first time you use them, so plan accordingly.

By Bus

Do not count on seeing any part of rural France by public transport. The bus network is barely adequate between major cities and towns (places often already well-served by rail) and rotten in rural areas, where the one bus a day fits the school schedule, leaving at the crack of dawn and returning in the afternoon; more remote villages are linked to civilization only once a week or not at all. Buses are run either by the SNCF (replacing discontinued rail routes) or private firms. Rail passes are valid on SNCF lines and they generally coincide with trains. Private bus firms, especially when they have a monopoly, tend to be a bit more expensive than trains; some towns have a *Gare Routière* (coach station), usually near the train stations, though many lines start from any place that catches their fancy. The posted schedules are not to be trusted. The tourist office or shopkeepers near the bus stop have a more accurate inkling of when a bus is likely to appear.

By Car

Unless you plan to stick to the major cities or the coast, a car is regrettably the only way to see most of Provence and Languedoc. This too has its drawbacks: high rental car rates and petrol, and an accident rate double that of the UK (and much higher than the US). The vaunted French logic and clarity breaks down completely on the asphalt. Go slow and be careful; in Carcassonne, for example, there is an intersection where traffic converges from five directions, regulated by a signal that gives the green light simultaneously to three of them. Never expect any French driver to be aware of the possibility of a collision.

Roads are generally excellently maintained, but anything of less status than a departmental route (D-road) may be uncomfortably narrow. Mountain roads are reasonable except in the vertical department of Alpes-Maritimes, where they inevitably follow old mule tracks. Shrines to St Eloi, patron of muleteers, are common here, and a quick prayer is a wise precaution. Conditions vary widely; in rural Languedoc you may catch up on your sleep while you drive; traffic in the Côte d'Azur, the 'California of Europe', can be diabolically Californian—hectic enough on a winter Sunday, and a guaranteed holiday-spoiler in July and August. Petrol stations are rare in rural areas, so consider your fuel supply while planning any forays into the mountains—especially if you use unleaded. If you come across a garage with petrol-pump attendants, they will expect a tip for oil, windscreen-cleaning or air. The French have one delightfully civilized custom of the road; if oncoming drivers unaccountably flash their headlights at you, it means the *gendarmes* are lurking just up the way.

Always give *priority to the right* (*priorité à droite*) at any intersection—anywhere, unless you're on a motorway or on a road with a yellow diamond 'priority route' sign. This French anachronism is a major cause of accidents; most people only follow the rule when they're feeling generous. If you are new to France, think of every intersection as a new and perilous experience.

Parking on the Côte d'Azur is a permanent nightmare to which there is no solution. Everywhere else , the blue 'P' signs will infallibly direct you to a village or town's car park. Watch out, though, for the tiny signs that indicate which streets are meant for pedestrians only (with complicated schedules in even tinier print); and for Byzantine street parking rules (which would take pages to explain—do as the natives do, and especially be careful about village centres on market days).

Unless sweetened in an air or holiday package deal, car hire in France is an expensive proposition (350–400 F a day, without mileage for the cheapest cars; see p. 4 for leasing a car). Petrol (*essence*) at the time of writing is 5 F 30 a litre. Speed limits are 130 km/80 mph on the *autoroutes* (toll motorways); 110 km/69 mph on dual carriageways (divided highways); 90 km/55 mph on other roads; 60 km/37 mph in an 'urbanized area' as soon as you pass a white sign with a town's name on it and until you pass another sign with the town's name barred. Fines for speeding, payable on the spot, begin at 1300 F and can be astronomical if you fail the breathalyser.

If you wind up in an accident, the procedure is to fill out and sign a *constat aimable*. If your French isn't sufficient to deal with this, hold off until you find someone to translate for you so you don't accidentally incriminate yourself. If you have a breakdown and are a member of a motoring club affiliated with the Touring Club de France, ring the latter; if not, ring the police.

By Water

The major towns, as well as the islands, along the Côte d'Azur are linked by regular boat services. These come in handy especially in the summer when travelling by road is hot purgatory. Most are included in the text; just look for signs near the port for the Gare

Maritime. In Languedoc, see the Getting Around sections for Narbonne and Béziers for cruises and boat rentals on the Canal du Midi and the lagoons.

Yacht, motorboat, and sailboat charters are big business, especially along the Riviera. Companies and individual owners hire them out by the hour or day, or in the case of yachts, by the week or fortnight. Average cost per week for a 16-metre yacht that sleeps six, including food, drink, and all expenses is 90,000 F—about what six people would pay for a week in a luxury hotel. If things are slow you may dicker the price down. Contact individual tourist offices for lists of firms. Books on sailing in the area include *Reeds' Mediterranean Navigator* (Thomas Reed Publications) and *South France Pilot* by Robin Brandon (Imray Laurie); these and other nautical books and maps in English may be found at Le Silmar, 10 Rue Jean Braco, 06310 Beaulieu-sur-Mer, tel 93 01 30 00. For canal-boats, see Special Interest Holidays, below.

By Bicycle

Cycling spells more pain than pleasure in most French minds; and one of the hazards of driving in the foothills of the Alps and Pyrenees is suddenly coming upon bands of uniformed cyclists pumping up the kinds of inclines that most people require escalators for. If you mean to cycle in the summer, start early and stop early to avoid heatstroke. French drivers, not always courteous to fellow motorists, usually give cyclists a wide berth; and yet on any given summer day, half the patients in a French hospital are from accidents on two-wheeled transport. Consider a helmet. Also beware that bike thefts are fairly common, especially along the Côte d'Azur, so make sure your insurance covers your bike—or the one you hire.

Getting your own bike to France is fairly easy: Air France and British Airways carry them free from Britain. From the US or Australia most airlines will carry them as long as they're boxed and are included in your total baggage weight. In all cases, telephone ahead. Certain French trains (called *Autotrains*, with a bicycle symbol in the timetable) carry bikes for free; otherwise you have to send it as registered lugguage, and pay 40 F fee, with delivery guaranteed within 5 days. The best maps, based on ordnance surveys are put out by the Institut Géographique National (1:50,000 or 1:100,000), available in most French bookshops.

You can hire bikes of varying quality (most of them 10-speed) at most SNCF stations and in major towns. The advantage of hiring from a station means that you can drop it off at another, as long as you specify where when you hire it. Rates run at around 50 F a day, with a deposit of 300–400 F or credit card number. Private firms hire mountain-bikes and racing-bikes.

By Foot

A network of long-distance paths or *Grandes Randonnées*, GRs for short (marked by distinctive red and white signs), take in some of the most beautiful scenery in the south of France. Each GR is described in a *Topoguide*, with maps and details about camping-sites, *refuges*, and so on, available in area bookshops or from the Comité National des Sentiers de Grande Randonnée, 8 Av. Marceau, 75008 Paris, tel (1 16) 47 23 62 32. An English

translation covering several GRs in the region, *Walks in Provence* is available from Robertson McCarta, 122 King's Cross Rd, London WC1.
There are 5000 km of marked paths in the Alpes Maritimes alone. Of special interest are: **GR 5** from Nice to Aspremont, the Gorges de la Vésubie and St-Dalmas-Valdeblore—and thence to Amsterdam; **GR 52** from Menton up to Sospel, the Vallee des Merveilles to St-Dalmas-Valdeblore; **GR 52a** and **GR 5** through Mercantour National Park, both of which are open only from the end of June to the beginning of October. **GR 51**, nicknamed 'the balcony of the Côte d'Azur', from Castellar (near Menton) takes in the Esterel and Maures before ending at Bormes-les-Mimosas.

In Provence, **GR 9** begins in St-Tropez and crosses over the region's most famous mountains: Ste-Baume, Ste-Victoire, the Lubéron and Ventoux. **GR 4** crosses the Dentelles de Montmirail and Mont Ventoux en route to Grasse, **GR 6** crosses much of the area in this book, from the Alps through the Vaucluse and Alpilles, to Beaucaire and the Pont du Gard before veering north up the river Gard on to its final destination by the Atlantic. **GR 42** descends the west bank of the Rhône from near Bagnols-sur-Cèze to Beaucaire.

The Pyrenees are magnificent walking country, and the ideal way to take in the beauties of the Corbières and famous citadels of the Cathars from Padern, Peyrepertuse and Puilaurens to Montségur is by way of **Le Sentier Cathare** (described in French in Louis Salavy's *Le Sentier Cathare*), well-marked and endowed with places to eat and stay en route. **GR 10** (with a *Topoguide* translated as *Walking in the Pyrenees* by Robertson McCarta, see above) begins in Banyuls-sur-Mer and sticks to the French side of the mountains—in this book as far as Lac Bouillouses, the source of the River Têt. It, and other walks in the mountains are covered in the excellent *Randonnées Pyrénéennes* by J. L. Sarret.

Tourist Information

Every city and town, and most villages have a tourist information office, usually called a *Syndicat d'Initiative* or an *Office de Tourisme*. In smaller villages this service is provided by the town hall (*mairie*). They distribute free maps and town-plans, hotel, camping, and self-catering accommodation lists for their area, and can inform you on sporting events, leisure activities, wine estates open for visits and festivals. Addresses and telephones are listed in the text, and if you write to them, they'll post you their booklets to help you plan your holiday before you leave.

Disabled Travellers

When it comes to providing access for all, France is not exactly in the vanguard of nations; many Americans who come over are appalled. But things are beginning to change, especially in newer buildings. Access and facilities in 90 towns in France are covered in *Touristes quand même! Promenades en France pour les voyageurs handicapés*, a booklet usually available in the tourist offices of large cities, or write ahead to the Comité National Français de Liaison pour la Réadaptation des Handicapés, 30–32 Quai de la Loire, 75019 Paris. Hotels with facilities for the handicapped are listed in Michelin's *Red Guide to France*.

9

Health and Emergencies

Local hospitals are the place to go in an emergency (*urgence*). If you need an ambulance (SAMU) dial 15; police and ambulance, tel 17; fire, tel 18. Doctors take turns going on duty at night and on holidays even in rural areas: *pharmacies* will know who to contact or telephone *SOS Médecins*—if you don't have access to a phone book or Minitel, dial directory enquiries, tel 12. To be on the safe side, always carry a phone card (see telephones, below). If it's not an emergency, the *pharmacies* have addresses (f local doctors, or visit the clinic at a *Centre Hospitalier*. Pharmacists are also tra 1ed to administer first aid, and dispense free advice for minor problems. *Pharmacies* themselves open on a rotating basis. Addresses are posted in their windows and in the local newspaper.

Doctors will give you a brown and white *feuille de soins* with your prescription; take both to the pharamacy and keep the *feuille* for insurance purposes at home. British subjects who are hospitalized and can produce their E-111 forms (see Before You Go) will be billed later at home for 20 per cent of the costs that French social insurance doesn't cover.

Crime and Police Business

> Everyone in Marseille seemed most dishonest. They all tried to
> swindle me, mostly with complete success.   —*Evelyn Waugh*

There is a fair chance that you will be had in the south of France, though probably not in Marseille; thieves and pickpockets go for the flashier fish on the Côte d'Azur. Road pirates prey on motorists blocked in traffic, train pirates prowl the overnight compartments looking for handbags and cameras, car bandits just love the ripe pickings in cars parked in isolated scenic areas or tourist sight car parks; and try always to leave bicycles inside and out of sight. Although violence is rare, the moral of the story is to leave anything you'd really really miss at home, carry travellers' cheques and insure your property, especially if you're driving. Report thefts to the nearest *gendarmerie*, not a pleasant task but the reward is the bit of paper you need for an insurance claim. If your passport is stolen, contact the police and your nearest consulate for emergency travel documents. By law, the police in France can stop anyone anywhere and demand an ID; in practice, they only tend to do it to harass minorities, the homeless, and scruffy hippy types. If they really don't like the look of you they can salt you away for a long time without any reason.

The drug situation is the same in France as anywhere in the west: soft and hard drugs are widely available, and the police only make an issue of victimless crime when it suits them (your being a foreigner just may rouse them to action). Smuggling any amount of marijuana into the country can mean a prison term, and there's not much your consulate can or will do about it.

Consulates

UK
Nice: 12 Rue de France, tel 93 82 32 04

10

Marseille: 24 Av. du Prado 6ᵉ, tel 91 53 43 32
US
Nice: Rue Maréchal Joffre, tel 93 88 89 55
Marseille: 12 Blvd Paul Peytral, near the Préfecture, tel 91 54 92 00
Canada
Marseille: 24 Av. du Prado 6ᵉ, tel 91 37 19 37
Ireland
Marseille: 148 Rue Sainte 1ᵉʳ, tel 91 54 92 29
Antibes: Villa les Chênes Verts, 152 Blvd Kennedy, Antibes, tel 93 61 50 63

Post Offices and Telephones

Known as the *PTT* or *Bureau de Poste*, easily discernible by a blue bird on a yellow background, French post offices are open in the cities Mon–Fri 8 am–7 pm, and Saturdays 8 am until 12 noon. In villages offices may not open until 9 am, break for lunch, and close at 4:30 or 5 pm. You can receive mail *poste restante* at any of them; the postal codes in this book should help your mail get there in a timely fashion. To collect it, bring some ID. You can purchase stamps in tobacconists as well as post offices.

Post offices have telephone directories for all of France, offer free use of a Minitel electronic directory, and they usually have at least one telephone booth with a meter— the easiest way to phone overseas. Most other public telephones have switched over from coins to *télécartes*, which you can purchase at any post office for 40 F for 50 *unités* or 96 F for 120 *unités*. The French have eliminated area codes, giving everyone an eight-digit telephone number, which is all you have to dial within France, except when phoning Paris, where the prefix is 16 1 before the eight-digit number. For international calls, first dial 19, wait for the change in the dial tone, then dial the country code (UK 44; US and Canada 1; Ireland 353; Australia 61; New Zealand 64), and then the local code (minus the 0 for UK numbers) and number. The easiest way to reverse the charges is to spend a few francs ringing the number you want to call and giving them your number in France, which is always posted in the box; alternatively ring your national operator and tell him or her that you want to call reverse charges (for the UK dial 19 00 44; for the US 19 00 11). France's international dialling code is 33. For directory enquiries, dial 12; international directory enquiries is 19 33 12 followed by the country code, but note that you'll have to wait around the telephone for them to ring you back with your requested number.

Opening Hours, Museums and National Holidays

While many shops and supermarkets in Marseille, Nice and other large cities are now open continuously Tuesday–Saturday from 9 or 10 am to 7 or 7:30 pm, businesses in smaller towns still close down for lunch from 12 or 12:30 to 2 or 3 pm or in the summer 4 in the afternoon. There are local exceptions, but nearly everything closes down on Mondays, except for grocers and *supermarchés* that open in the afternoon. In many towns Sunday morning is a big shopping period. Markets (daily in the cities, weekly in villages) are usually open mornings only, although clothes, flea and antique markets run into the afternoon.

Most museums close for lunch as well, and often on Mondays or Tuesdays, and sometimes for all of November or the entire winter. Hours change with the season:

11

longer summer hours begin in May or June and last until the end of September—usually. Some change their hours every darn month. We've done our best to include them in the text, but don't sue us if they're not exactly right. Most close on national holidays and give discounts if you have a student ID card, or are an EC citizen under 18 or over 65 years old; most charge admissions ranging from 10–30 F. Churches are usually open all day, or closed all day and only open for mass. Sometimes notes on the door direct you to the *mairie* or priest's house (*presbytère*) where you can pick up the key. There are often admission fees for cloisters, crypts, and special chapels.

On French **national holidays**, banks, shops, and businesses close; some museums do, but most restaurants stay open. They are: January 1, Easter Sunday, Easter Monday, May 1, May 8 (VE Day), Ascension Day, Pentecost and the following Monday, July 14 (Bastille Day), August 15 (Assumption of the BVM), November 1 (All Saints'), November 11 (World War I Armistice), and Christmas Day.

Shopping

All in all, this is not a brilliant region for the holiday shopper. Traditional handicrafts have died out completely, and attempts to revive them—inevitably in the tourist areas of Provence—produce little you'd be proud to show the neighbours. Typical items are the *santons*, terracotta Christmas crib figures dressed in 18th-century Provençal costumes, usually as artful as the concrete statues of the Seven Dwarfs sold at your neighbourhood garden centre.

Every town east of the Rhône has at least one boutique specializing in Provençal skirts, bags, pillows and scarves, printed in intense colours (madder red, sunflower yellow, pine green) with floral, paisley or geometric designs. Block-print fabrics were first made in Provence after Louis XIV, wanting to protect the French silk industry, banned the import of popular Indian prints. Clever entrepreneurs in the papal-owned Comtat Venaissin responded by producing cheap imitations still known in French today as *indiennes*. The same shops usually sell the other essential bric-à-brac of the South— dried lavender pot-pourris, sachets of *herbes de Provence* (nothing but thyme and bay leaves), perfumed soaps.

Big name French and Italian designers and purveyors of luxury goods have boutiques at Cannes, Monaco, and Nice; fine chocolates have become very fashionable. Moustiers, Vallauris, and Biot have hand-made ceramics, and in Provence at least a million artists wait to sell you their productions. Fontaine-de-Vaucluse has a traditional paper and stationery industry; Cogolin specializes in pipes and saxophone-reeds; Grasse sells perfumes and essential oils.

Candy junkies will find western Provence heaven. Nearly every town has its own speciality: candied fruits in Apt, the chocolates and *calissons* (almond biscuits) of Aix, *berlingots* (mint-flavoured caramels) in Carpentras, *nougats* in Vence, *marrons glacés* in Collobrières, and orange-flavoured chocolates called *papalines* in Avignon.

Sport and Leisure Activities

Bicycling: (see Getting Around).

Bullfights: The Roman amphitheatres at Nîmes and Arles had hardly been restored in the early 1800s when they once again became venues for *tauromachie*. Attempts to abolish the sport in the 1900s fell flat when the poet Frédéric Mistral, the self-appointed watchdog of all things Provençal intervened; and if anything, bullfights are now more popular than ever.

Provence and Languedoc are so long in the tooth that not only do they put on regular bullfights with picadors and matadors, ultimately derived from the amphitheatres of ancient Rome, but also *Courses Provençales* (or *Courses Libres*), a sport descending from the bull games of ancient Thessaly as described by Heliodorus. Played by daring young men dressed in white called *razeteurs*, the sport demands grace, daring, and dexterity, especially in leaping over the barriers. The object is to remove a round cockade from between the horns of the bull by cutting its ribbons with a blunt razor comb—a sport far more dangerous to the human players than the animals. The bulls used for the *Courses Provençales* are the small, lithe, high-horned breed from the Camargue; good sporty ones retire with fat pensions.

You will see three other types of bullfight advertised: the *Corrida*, or traditional Spanish bullfight where the bull is put to death (*mise á morte*). The bullfighters are usually Spanish as well, and the major festivals, or Ferias, bring some of the top *toreros* to France, although beware that the already expensive tickets tend to be snapped up by touts. A *Novillada*, pitting younger bulls against apprentice *toreros* (*Novilleros*) is less expensive, but much more likely to be a butchery void of *arte*. In a *Corrida Portuguaise* the bullfighter (*rejoneador*) fights from horseback, but doesn't kill the bull.

Canoeing and Kayaking: Fédération Française de Canoe-Kayak, BP 58 Joinville Le Pont 94340, tel 48 89 39 89, is the national centre for information. Some of the most dramatic rafting and canoeing in this book is down the Grand Canyon du Verdon, but the journey requires considerable experience and considerable portage. Another disadvantage is that the electric company may be playing with the water. Contact the Association Verdon Animation Nature, Le Couvert, Moustiers-Ste-Marie, tel 92 74 60 03, for group excursions. Other good rivers are the Cèze, the Têt and the Aude, or the Gard for easier paddling.

Fishing: You can fish in the sea without a permit as long as your catch is for local consumption; along the Riviera captains offer expeditions for tuna and other denizens of the deep. Freshwater fishing requires an easily-obtained permit from a local club; tourist offices can tell you where to find them.

Football: Professional football in the south is dominated by the three Ms: Marseille Olympique, run by the charismatic Bernard Tapie, who has just entered politics, followed by Monaco, which is almost as wealthy, and Montpellier, the bright star in Languedoc—other first-division teams are in Toulon and Nîmes. Although *le foot* is the most popular spectator sport east of the Rhône, to the west it comes in heavy competition with rugby (see below).

Gambling: If you're over 21, every big resort along the coast comes equipped with a **casino** ready to take your hard-earned money. Scandals have plagued a few—Nice, especially, which now gets by without. Even if you aren't a gambler, a few are worth a visit: Monte Carlo, for its cynical mix of the voluptuous and the crass; Beaulieu, for its pickled retro charm; or Cannes, for high-fashion vice. Or you can do as the locals do and play for a side of beef, a lamb, or a VCR in a **Loto**, in a local café or municipal *salle de fête*. Loto is just like bingo, although some of the numbers have names: 11 is *las cambas de ma grand* (my grandmother's legs) and 75, the number of the *département* of Paris, is

13

los envaïssurs (the invaders). Everybody plays the horses, at the local bar with the *PMU* (off-track betting) outlet.

Golf: Increasingly popular in France, there are courses near most of the major resorts on the Côte d'Azur, and almost as many under construction. Cannes offers golfers the most choice, with three courses in Mandelieu and three in Le Cannet. The most spectacular course is Monaco's, which was laid out around the turn of the century, high over Monte Carlo.

Horse-riding: Every tourist office has a list of *Centres Hippiques* or *Centres Equestres* that hire out horses. Most offer group excursions, although if you prove yourself an experienced rider you can usually head down the trails on your own. The Camargue, with its many ranches, cowboy traditions and open spaces, is the most popular place to ride, and there are an increasing number of stables in the Alps, Corbières, Espinouse and Pyrenees for those who want to follow lonesome mountain trails. Most of the posher country inns can also find you a horse.

Pétanque: Like pastis and olive oil, *pétanque* is one of the essential ingredients of the Midi, and even the smallest village has a rough, hard court under the plane trees for its practitioners—nearly all male, although women are welcome to join in. Similar to *boules*, the special rules of *pétanque* were, according to tradition developed in La Ciotat (see p. 166). The object is to get your metal ball closest to the marker (*bouchon* or *cochonnet*). Tournaments are frequent and well attended.

Rugby: the national sport of Languedoc and the southwest, and the cradle of most of the players on the national team (although movements to change one of the Five Nations from France to Occitania have so far fallen flat). Although the best teams lately have been Toulouse, Agen, and Bordeaux, you can still see fiery matches in Béziers, longtime champions (the town has three rugby schools) and Carcassonne. In some places they play 'Cathar rugby'—13 to a side instead of 15.

Sailing: Most of the resorts have sailing schools and boats to hire. Get the complete list from the Fédération Française de Voile, 55 Av. Kléber, 75084 Paris Cedex 16, tel (16 1) 45 53 68 00.

Skiing: If the weather ever decides to settle down to what's expected of it (in 1990–91 Nice had as much snow as some of the Alps!) you can do as in California: ski in the morning and bake on the beach in the afternoon. The biggest resorts in the Alpes Maritimes are Isola 2000, Auron, and Valberg, and closest to Nice, Gréolières-les-Neiges. On the Mediterranean end of the Pyrenees, there's Font-Romeu, although snowfall has been just as unreliable there in recent years. Hence there are practically no package deals going from abroad. For the Alpes Maritimes, contact the Comité Régional Ski Côte d'Azur, 39 Rue Pastorelli 06000 Nice, tel 93 80 65 77. For the Pyrenees, write to the Comité Regional de Tourisme, 20 Rue de la République, 34000 Montpellier, tel 67 92 67 92.

Walking: (see Getting Around).

Water Sports: In 1763, the consumptive English writer and doctor, Tobias 'Smell-fungus' Smollett tried something for his health that shocked the doctors in Nice: he went bathing in the sea. Most extraordinary of all, it made him feel better, and he recommended that people follow his example, though it would be difficult for women 'unless they laid aside all regards to decorum'—as they so often do in the most fashionable resorts. There are scores of fine, sandy beaches along the coast, although *not*

14

on the Riviera east of Juan-les-Pins, and anyone who arrives with any ideas about access to the sea being a natural God-given right will be appalled to learn that paying concessions occupy most of the Provençal shore; free, quiet beaches require more effort (the Calanques west of Cassis, the coves below the Esterel and the Maures, the Hyères islands).

Languedoc-Roussillon is a completely different story: less glamour, but more miles of free sandy beaches than anywhere in the Western Mediterranean, stetching into the horizon on either side of its scores of small resorts—until you reach the rocky Côte Vermeille at any rate. Areas are always set aside for *les naturistes*, or nudists: Cap d'Agde and the Ile du Levant are two of Europe's biggest nudist resorts.

Every town on the coast hires out equipment for water-sports, often for hefty prices. Juan-les-Pins claims to have invented water skiing. If you're an experienced windsurfer, the biggest thrill this shore offers is Brutal Beach off Cap Sicié west of Toulon. The best diving is off Ile Port-Cros National Park (for a list of diving clubs, contact the Fédération Française d'Etudes et de Sports Sous-Marins, 24 Quai de Rive Neuve, 13007 Marseille). Or if you're genuinely jaded and have a weakness for medical-psychobabble, you can indulge in *thalassotherapie* to make you thin, fit, stress-free or a laid-back non-smoker.

Environment

'Come to the Côte d'Azur for a change of pollution' they say. Constantly threatened by frequent oil spills, a suffocating algae mistakenly released into the sea at the Oceanographic Institute of Monte Carlo, too many cars and too many people, the well-named 'California of Europe', from Marseille to Menton, may be the first place in southern Europe to achieve total ecological breakdown.

As elsewhere in the Mediterranean, a sad litany of forest fires heads the television news in summer. Especially in Provence, most of the herbs and trees are *xerophytes*, able to thrive in dry hot conditions on poor rocky soils. Most forests are pine—Aleppo pines in limestone, maritime pines in the Maures and Esterel. Here they often close roads in summer to decrease the chance of fires. Most are caused by twits with matches (*you'll* be more careful, won't you?), though many fires are deliberately instigated by speculators who burn off protected forests to build more holiday villas and suchlike. Fires often lead to erosion and flooding, though the local governments now do a good job of re-forestation. The weird wasteland of Blausasc, in a valley north of Nice (caused by greedy logging in the 1800s), shows what Provence would soon look like if they didn't.

The most spectacular environmental non-issue continues to be the overbuilding of the Côte d'Azur. The damage is done; one of the most exceptional parts of the Mediterranean coast has been thoroughly, thoughtlessly, irreparably ruined. Since the war there has simply been too much money involved for governments to act responsibly; most of the buildings you'll see were put up illegally—but there they are. Though this is changing—a politically connected developer near St-Tropez was recently forced to demolish an illegal, half-built project—local governments continue to promote industrial and tourist growth in areas where there is absolutely no room to grow. Paris bureaucrats are as responsible as local politicians; in public transport, for example, they insist on pushing a new TGV route around the coast, bringing down even more people instead of improving local transport that might cut down on the ferocious traffic they already have. The new route is a monster, cutting across scores of scenic areas and wine regions; citizen groups from the Corbières to Provence are fighting it tooth and nail.

Other enemies of the Midi include: the army, which has commandeered enormous sections of wilderness (Plan de Canjuers and parts of the Crau, Ile du Levant, Roussillon's Plateau d'Opoul) and regularly blows them to smithereens in manoeuvres and target practice; the nuclear industry, with France's nuclear research centre at Cadarache and most of its nuclear missiles hidden away on the Plateau de Vaucluse; the *chancre coloré*, a fungus that, like phylloxera, came from the US (on wooden crates during World War II) and now threatens the lovely plane trees of Provence; and finally the truly villainous national electric company, EDF, which once tried to flood the Grand Canyon du Verdon. The one genuine contemporary ecological disaster is the Etang de Berre, now entirely surrounded by the industrial and suburban sprawl of Marseille, a ghastly horror of power pylons, pollution and speculative development. Here too the EDF is involved; heated water, pumped from their giant power plant into the lagoon, is killing off the few remaining fish; local groups are fighting hard to make them stop.

In August, ecological dysfunction reaches its apogee on the sands of St-Tropez's crowded beaches, laced with trash, condoms, and human excrement. But there's another side to the story—over a hundred miles of clean, underpopulated beaches in Languedoc and Roussillon, and a mountainous hinterland from the Italian border to the Spanish that is still mostly pristine and delightful. Nature lovers can find everything they desire, and much that is new and strange—as long as they avoid the Côte d'Azur.

Special Interest Holidays

There are a number of ways to combine a holiday with study or a special interest. For information, contact the French Centre on (071) 792 0337 or the Cultural Services of the French Embassy: 22 Wilton Crescent, London SW1 tel (071) 235 8080, or at 972 Fifth Av., New York, NY 10021, tel (212) 439 1400. French universities—Aix for the humanities, Marseille for the sciences, Montpellier for law, agriculture and medicine—are easy to enter if you're already enrolled in a similar institution at home; tuition fees are nominal but room and board are up to you. The Cultural Services can send a prospectus and tell you what paperwork is required.

Accents Language and Leisure, BP 17, 01510 Artemare, France, tel 79 87 33 96: improve your French by the pool in the centre at Forcalquier in Provence.

Alliance Française, 1 Rue Vernier, 06000 Nice, tel 93 87 42 11: French classes on all levels.

Association Neige et Merveilles, La Minière de Vallauria, 06430 St-Dalmas-de-Tende, tel 93 04 62 40: offers photography and film courses for beginner and advanced from the end of March to mid-November.

Atelier du Safranier, 2 bis Rue du Cannet, 06600 Viel Antibes, tel 93 34 53 72: year-round courses in painting, engraving, lithography, etc.

Centre International de Formation Musicale, 24 Blvd de Cimiez 06000 Nice, tel 93 81 01 23: advanced courses in vocal and instrumental music in July.

Centre International de Recherche et d'Etudes, 35 Rue Joseph Vernet, Avignon, tel 90 82 68 10: for French courses at all levels.

16

Direction des Antiquités Préhistoriques et Historiques of each *département* has summer openings for volunteers who are invited to assist at archaeology digs. Write to them in early spring. The address in Provence, 21–23 Blvd du Roy René, 13617 Aix-en-Provence; in Languedoc, 5 bis Rue de la Salle l'Evêque, 24000 Montpellier.
L'Ecole de Moulin, Restaurant L'Amandier, Mougins 06250, tel 93 75 35 70, and Hôtel Beau Rivage, Rue Brea, 06300, Nice, tel 93 75 35 70: year-round *Cuisine du Soleil* cookery courses lasting a week under the auspices of Roger Vergé Inc.
Etudes Françaises pour L'Etranger, 98 Blvd Edouard Herriot, 06007 Nice, tel 93 37 53 89: classes in French literature and culture.
Institut de Paléontologie Humaine, 1 Rue René Panhard, 75013 Paris, tel (16 1) 43 32 62 91: has places for palaeontology students or fans who can spend a minimum of 15 or 30 days excavating caves in southeast France (address your letter to M. Henry de Lumley).
Organisation Scolaire Franco-Britannique, 29 Av. de la Trillade, Avignon, tel 90 82 70 56: French classes.
Space Camp Patrick Baudry, in Mandelieu 06210, tel 93 47 68 02 (in France): kids between 10 and 18 who suspect space is the place can undergo a week of real astronaut training in July and August.

From the UK

Allez France, 27 West St, Storrington, West Sussex, RH20 4DZ, tel (0903) 742 345: city breaks in Nice, golf holidays in Cannes, wine tours, short breaks in Antibes, Juan-les-Pins and Gorges du Verdon.
Alternative Travel Group, 69–71 Banbury Road, Oxford OX1 6PE, tel (0865) 310 399: walking holidays in Provence.
Andrew Brock, 10 Barley Mow Passage, London W4 4PH, tel (081) 995 3642: trips down the Canal du Midi and through the Camargue.
Artscape Painting Holidays, Units 40 and 41 Temple Farm Industrial Estate, Southend-on-Sea, Essex SS2 5RZ, tel (0702) 617 900: painting courses in Provence.
Belle France, Bayham Abbey, Lamberhurst TN3 8BG, tel (0892) 890 885: cycling and walking holidays in Provence.
DB Jazz Tours 37 Wood Street, Stratford upon Avon CV37 6ES, tel (07892) 67 532: jazz festival tours and tickets.
Headwater Holidays, 146 London Road, Northwich CW9 5HH, tel (0606) 48 699: cycling tours in southern Languedoc.
Hoseasons Holidays, Sunway House, Lowestoft NR32 3LT, tel (0502) 500 505: canal tours of the Midi and Camargue.
La France des Activités, Model Farm, Rattlesden, Bury St Edmunds IP30 0SY, tel (0449) 737 678: canal cruising Camargue and Canal du Midi, golfing holidays and riding treks along the Cathar trail.
LSG Theme Holidays, 201 Main Street, Thornton LE6 1AH, tel (0509) 231 713: a French-run company offering language classes at all levels; painting courses; photography; horseriding, cycling or mountain biking in Provence; rambling and nature-watch in Languedoc.
Par-Tee Tours, Fairway House, North Road, Chorleywood WD3 5LE, tel (0923) 284558: self-catering or hotel golf holidays on the Côte d'Azur.

Riviera Sailing Holidays, 45 Bath Road, Emsworth PO10 7ER, tel (0243) 374 376: sailing holidays based at Golfe Juan and canal boats down the Canal du Midi.
Serenissima Travel, 21 Dorset Square, London NW1 6QG, tel (071) 730 9841: art and architecture tour of Cézanne's Provence; painting holidays at Odeillo, near Font-Roman.
Susi Madron's Cycling for Softies, 2 and 4 Birch Polygon, Rusholme, Manchester M14 5HX, tel (061) 248 8282: easy cycling in Provence and the Camargue.
Waymark Holidays, 44 Windsor Road, Slough SL1 2EJ, tel (0753) 516 477: walking tours in Provence and Languedoc-Roussillon.
World Wine Tours, 69–71 Banbury Road, Oxford OX2 6PE, tel (0865) 310 344: Rhône valley wine tours.

From the USA
Abercrombie & Kent, 1520 Kensington Road, Oakbrook, IL 60521, tel (708) 954 2944: barge for cruising the Rhône into Provence and yacht charters on the Côte d'Azur.
Adventure Center, 1311 63rd Street, Suite 200, Emeryville, CA 94608, tel (415) 654 1879: walking and camping in Provence.
Baumeler Tours, 10 Grand Avenue, Rockville Centre, NY 11570, tel (516) 766 6160: cycling in Provence.
Eagle Yacht Charter Inc., 150 Main Street, Port Washington, NY 11050, tel (516) 944 6760: canal boats down the Canal du Midi and in the Camargue; sailing on the Riviera.
Int'l Curtain Call, 3313 Patricia Avenue, Los Angeles, LA 90064, tel (213) 204 4934: opera and music tours, e.g. Paris–Avignon–Aix-en-Provence–Cannes.
Le Boat Inc., PO Box E, Maywood, NJ 07607, tel (201) 342 1838, crewed motor or sailing yacht and bareboats from Côte d'Azur ports.
The Holiday Emporium—French Riviera Golf Tours, 12044 Ventura Boulevard, PO Box 1505, Studio City, CA 91604, tel (818) 985 2814: hotel golf holidays on Riviera.
Progressive Travels Inc., 1932 First Avenue, Suite 1100, Seattle, WA 98101, tel (206) 443 4225: luxury cycling and walking tours in Provence. Ballooning available.
XO Travel Consultants Inc., 231 E. Fifth Street, New York, NY 10003, tel (212) 979 0177: food, wine and horticultural tour specialists in Provence, Rhône valley, Riviera.

Where to Stay

Hotels
In the south of France you can find some of the most splendid hotels in Europe and some genuine scruffy fleabags of dubious clientele, with the majority of establishments falling somewhere between. Like most countries in Europe, the tourist authorities grade them by their facilities (not by charm or location) with stars from four (or four with an L for luxury—a bit confusing, so in the text luxury places are given five stars) to one, and there are even some cheap but adequate places undignified by any stars at all.

We would have liked to put the exact prices in the text, but in France this is not possible. Almost every establishment has a wide range of rooms and prices—a very useful and logical way of doing things, once you're used to it; in some hotels, every single room has its own personality and the difference in quality and price can be enormous; a large room with antique furniture, a television or a balcony over the sea and a complete bathroom will cost much more than a poky back room in the same hotel, with a window overlooking a car park, no antiques, and the WC down the hall. Some proprietors will drag out a sort of menu for you to choose the level of price and facilities you would like. Most two-star hotel rooms have their own showers and WCs; most one stars offer rooms with or without. The following guide will give you an idea of what prices to expect. The first numbers give the range you'll encounter from 90 per cent of the hotels (there are always exceptions); the second, in parentheses, is an average. **Note: all prices listed here and elsewhere in this book are for a double room.**

	Côte d'Azur	Elsewhere in Provence	Languedoc-Roussillon
***** average	650–3000 F (1750 F)	1400–1800 F (only one, in Avignon)	none
**** average	600–1500 F (850 F)	480–1600 F (780 F)	360–800 F (560 F)
*** average	300–620 F (460 F)	300–650 F (420 F)[1]	250–550 F (350 F)[2]
** average	190–400 F (260 F)	140–350 F (260 F)	140–320 F (180, 230 F in resorts)
* average	100–210 F (160 F)	110–260 F (130 F)	70–210 F (120, 160 F in resorts)

[1] Note that here is the widest range of difference; there are luxury rooms that can go as high as 900 F.
[2] Resort prices in Languedoc all vary widely all across the range: the new resorts—La Grande Motte and Cap d'Agde—are the most expensive.

Hotels with *no stars* are not necessarily dives; their owners probably never bothered filling out a form for the tourist authorities. Their prices are usually the same as one-star places.

Alas, although it's impossible to be more precise, we can add a few more generalizations. **Single rooms** are relatively rare, and usually two-thirds the price of a double, and rarely will a hotelier give you a discount if only doubles are available (again, because each room has its own price); on the other hand, if there are three or four of you, **triples or quads** or adding extra beds to a double room is usually cheaper than staying in two rooms. Prices are posted at the reception desk and in the rooms to keep the management honest. Flowered wallpaper, usually beige, comes in all rooms with no extra charge—it's an essential part of the French experience. **Breakfast** (usually coffee, a croissant, bread and jam for 20 F or 30 F) is nearly always optional: you'll do as well for less in a bar. As usual rates rise in the busy season (holidays and summer, and in the winter around ski resorts), when many hotels with restaurants will require that you take **half-board** (*demi-pension*—breakfast and a set lunch or dinner). Many hotel restaurants are superb and described in the text; non-residents are welcome. At worst the food will be boring, and it can be monotonous eating in the same place every night when there are so many tempting restaurants around. Don't be put off by obligatory dining. It's traditional; French hoteliers think of themselves as innkeepers, in the old-fashioned way. In the off-season board requirements vanish into thin air.

Your holiday will be much sweeter if you **book ahead**, especially anywhere near the Côte d'Azur from May to October. The few reasonably priced rooms are snapped up very early across the board. In Provence and Languedoc, July and August are the only really impossible months; otherwise it usually isn't too difficult to find something. Phoning a day or two ahead is always a good policy, although beware that hotels will only confirm a room with the receipt of a cheque covering the first night (not a credit card number). Tourist offices have complete lists of accommodation in their given areas or even *département*, which come in handy during the peak season; many will even call around and book a room for you on the spot for free or a nominal fee.

Chain hotels (Sofitel, Formula One, etc.) are in most cities, but always dreary and geared to the business traveller more than the tourist, so you won't find them in this book. Don't confuse chains with the various **umbrella organizations** like *Logis et Auberges de France*, *Relais de Silence*, or the prestigious *Relais et Châteaux* which promote and guarantee the quality of independently-owned hotels and their restaurants. Many are recommended in the text. Larger tourist offices usually stock their booklets, or you can pick them up before you leave from the French National Tourist Office. If you plan to do a lot of driving, you may want to pick the English translation of the French truckers' bible, *Les Routiers*, an annual guide with maps listing reasonably priced lodgings and food along the highways and byways of France (£7.99, Routiers Limited, 354 Fulham Rd, London SW10).

Bed and breakfast: In rural areas, there are plenty of opportunities for a stay in a private home or farm. *Chambres d'hôtes*, in the tourist office brochures, are listed separately from hotels with the various *gîtes* (see below). Some are connected to restaurants, others to wine estates or a château; prices tend to be moderate to inexpensive. *Friendly Home* (Les Amaryllis, 16 Rue Gazan, 06600 Antibes, tel 93 34 63 32) is a bed and breakfast society offering rooms, villas, and apartments along the Côte d'Azur from Nice to Mandelieu, all within 10 km of the coast. Prices range from 200 to 400 F for two people with breakfast.

Youth Hostels, *Gîtes d'Etape*, and *Refuges*

Most cities and resort areas have youth hostels (*Auberges de Jeunesse*) which offer simple dormitory accommodation and breakfast to people of any age for around 40–70 F a night. Most offer kitchen facilities as well, or inexpensive meals. They are the best deal going for people travelling on their own; for people travelling together a one-star hotel can be just as cheap. Another down-side is that many are in the most ungodly locations—in the suburbs where the last bus goes by at 7 pm, or miles from any transport at all in the country. In the summer the only way to be sure of a room is to arrive early in the day. Most require a Youth Hostels Association membership card, which you can usually purchase on the spot, although regulations say you should buy them in your home country (UK: from YHA, 14 Southampton Street, London WC2; USA: from AYH, P.O. Box 37613, Washington DC 20013; Canada: from CHA, 1600 James Maysmyth Dr, 6th floor, Gloucester Ottawa, Ont K1B 5N4; Australia: from AYHA, 60 Mary St, Surrey Hills, Sydney, New South Wales 2010.) Another option in cities are the single-sex dormitories for young workers (*Foyers de Jeunes Travaillers et de Jeunes Travailleuses*) which will rent out individual rooms if any are available, for slightly more than a youth hostel.

A *Gîte d'Etape* is a simple shelter with bunk beds and a rudimentary kitchen set up by a village along GR walking paths or a scenic bike route. Again, lists are available for each *département*; the detailed maps listed under 'Walking' above mark them as well. In the mountains similar rough shelters along the GR paths are called *refuges*, most of them open summer only. Both charge around 40 or 50 F a night.

Camping

Camping is a very popular way to travel, especially among the French themselves, and there's at least one camp-site in every town, often an inexpensive, no-frills place run by the town itself (*Camping Municipal*). Other camp-sites are graded with stars like hotels from four to one: at the top of the line you can expect lots of trees and grass, hot showers, a pool or beach, sports facilities, and a grocer's, bar and/or restaurant, and on the coast, prices rather similar to one star hotels (although these, of course, never have all the extras). But beware that July and August are terrible months to camp on the Côte d'Azur, when sites become so overcrowded (St-Tropez is notorious) that the authorities have begun to worry about health problems. You'll find more *lebensraum* in Languedoc and off the coast. If you want to camp outside official sites, it's imperative to ask permission from the landowner first, or risk a furious farmer, his dog and perhaps even the police.

Tourist offices have complete lists of camp-sites in their regions, or if you plan to move around a lot the *Guide Officiel Camping/Caravanning* available in most French book shops. A number of UK holiday firms book camping holidays and offer discounts on Channel ferries: Canvas Holidays, tel (0992) 553 535; Eurocamp Travel, tel (0565) 55 399; Keycamp Holidays tel (081) 661 1836. The French National Tourist Office has complete lists.

Gîtes de France and Other Self-catering Accommodation

The south of France offers a vast range of self-catering: inexpensive farm cottages, history-laden châteaux with gourmet frills, sprawling villas on the Riviera, flats in modern beach resorts or even on board canal boats. The *Fédération Nationale des Gîtes de France* is a French government service offering inexpensive accommodation by the week in rural areas. Lists with photos arranged by *département* are available from the French National Tourist office, or in the UK from the official rep: **Gîtes de France**, 178 Piccadilly, London W1V 9DB, tel (071) 493 3480. Prices range from 1000 to 2000 F a week. Other options are advertised in the Sunday papers or contact one of the firms listed below. The accommodation they offer will nearly always be more comfortable and costly than a *gîte*, but the discounts holiday firms can offer on the ferries, plane tickets, or car rentals can make up for the price difference.

UK

Allez France, 27 West Street, Storrington, West Sussex RH20 4DZ, tel (0903) 742 345: wide variety of accommodation from cottages to châteaux.
Angel Travel, 34 High Street, Borough Green, Sevenoaks TN15 8BJ, tel (0732) 884 109: villas, gîtes and flats in Provence, Languedoc-Roussillon and the Côte.
Beach Villas, 8 Market Passage, Cambridge CB2 3QR, tel (0223) 350 777, self-catering by the sea, especially for families.
Belvedere Holiday Apartments, 5 Bartholomews, Brighton BN1 1HG, tel (0273) 23 404: studio flats and apartments along the coast from Menton to Cap d'Agde.

21

CV Travel, 43 Cadogan Street, London SW3 2PR, tel (071) 581 0851: luxurious villas on the Riviera and near St-Tropez.

Crystal Holidays, The Courtyard, Arlington Road, Surbiton KT6 6BW, tel (081) 390 8033: villas in Languedoc-Roussillon and the Côte.

Dominque's Villas, 13 Park House, 140 Battersea Park Road, London SW11 4NB, tel (071) 738 8772: large villas and châteaux with pools etc. in Provence and on the Côte.

French Life Holidays, 26 Church Street, Hosforth, Leeds LS18 5LG, tel (0532) 390 077: apartments and gîtes in the south of France.

French Villa Centre, 175 Selsdon Park Road, South Croydon CR2 8JJ, tel (081) 651 5109: gîtes, villages de vacances, and villas near the coast and in the Var and Vaucluse.

International Chapters, 126 St Johns Wood High St, London NW8 7ST, tel (071) 586 9451: farmhouses, châteaux, and villas in Provence and the Côte.

Jet Tours and French Travel Service, Georgian House, 69 Boston Manor Road, Brentford TW8 9JQ, tel (081) 568 6981: modern flats along the coast and in Provence.

La France des Villages, Model Farm, Rattlesden, Bury St Edmunds IP30 0SY, tel (0449) 737 678: châteaux and manoirs in Provence and the Pyrenees.

Palmer and Parker Villa Holidays, 63 Grosvenor Street, London W1X OAJ, tel (071) 493 5725: upmarket villas with pool.

Vacances France, 14 Bowthorpe Road, Wisbech PE13 2DX, tel (0945) 581 479: simple accommodation to luxury villas on the Côte d'Azur.

Westbury Travel, 1 Belmont, Lansdown Road, Bath, BA1 5DZ, tel (0225) 445 732: apartments, villas, and gîtes inland and by the sea.

USA

At Home Abroad, 405 East 56th St, New York, NY 10022, tel (212) 421 9165: châteaux and farmhouses, Provence and Côte.

Four Star Living, 964 Third Avenue, New York, NY 10022, tel (212) 603 4128.

Hideaways International, P.O. Box 1464, Littleton, MA 01460, tel (508) 486 8955: farmhouses and châteaux.

Overseas Connections, 70 West 71 St, Suite 1C, New York, NY 10023, tel (516) 725 9303.

RAVE (Rent-a-Vacation-Everywhere), 328 East Main St, Suite 526, Rochester, NY 14604, tel (716) 965 0260.

Festivals

The south of France offers everything from the Cannes Film Festival to the village fête, with a pilgrimage or religious procession, bumper cars, a *pétanque* tournament, a feast (anything from sardines to *cassoulet* to paella) and an all-night dance, sometimes to a local band but often a travelling troupe playing 'Hot Music' or some other electrified cacophony. Bullfights (see p. 12) play a part in many fêtes from Spain to the Rhône; a *feria* is centred around them. A *bravade* entails some pistol- or musket-shots, usually in honour of a saint; a *corso* is a parade with carts or floats. St John's Day (24 June) is one of the big days and often features bonfires and fireworks.

At Catalan *festas* you're bound to see the national dance, the *sardana*, a complex, circular dance that alternates 16 long steps with 8 short ones, properly accompanied by a *cobla*, a band of a dozen instruments, some unique to Catalunya. In the southern Rhône valley people still like to celebrate with a *farandole*, a dance in 6/8 time with held hands or a handkerchief, which may be as old as the ancient Greeks. One-man musical accompaniment is provided by a little three-holed flute called a *galoubet* played with left hand, and a *tambourin*, a drum played with the right. Both *farandoles* and flamenco enliven the proceedings of the 24 May pilgrimage at Saintes-Maries-de-la Mer, by far the best attended of all popular festivities in the south.

Note: Dates change every year. For complete listings and precise dates of events in Provence, pick up a copy of the annual lists, available in most tourist offices.

Calendar of Events

January

Sunday nearest the 17th	*Fête de St-Marcel*, folkdancing and singing at **Barjols**; every four years (next 1994) Barjols does an ox roast as well
27	*Fête de Ste-Dévote*, **Monaco**
End of month	**Monte Carlo** rally

February

2	*Fête des Chandelles*, **Marseille**
3	Festival of olives and late golden Servan grapes, **Valbonne**
First week	International Circus Festival, **Monaco**; *Fête des Oursins*, sea urchin festival at **Carry-le-Rouet**
10 days at Carnival	*Fête du Citron*, **Menton**; *Feria du Carnaval*, at **Nîmes**
Carnival	**Nice** has the most famous festivities in France; during the school break in **Prats-de-Mollo**, traditional celebrations
Ash Wednesday	*Les Pailhasses* at **Cournonterral**, a 14th-century parade of boys in straw and turkey feathers, who try to squirt wine on passers-by
10	*Corso du Mimosa*, **Bormes-les-Mimosas**
End of month	*Fête de l'Ours*, ancient bear festival in **Arles-sur Tech**

March

25	*Festin es Courgourdons*, folklore and dried sculpted gourds, and folklore, **Nice**
Sunday before Palm Sunday	Traditional Carnival at **Limoux**

April

Throughout month	International Tennis Tournaments, **Monaco** and **Nice**
Maundy Thursday/Good Friday	*Procession de La Sanch*, in **Perpiganan**, **Collioure**, and **Arles-sur-Tech**; Procession of the Dead Christ, **Roquebrune-Cap-Martin**
Good Friday–Easter	Bullfights in **Arles**
Easter	Flower and sweets fair, **Villefranche-de-Conflent**

23

| 25 | Winegrowers' festival and blessing of the vines, Châteauneuf-du-Pape; *Fête de St-Marc*, Villeneuve-lès-Avignon |
| Last Sunday | *Fête des Gardians*, traditional rodeo in Arles |

May

Third week after Easter	*Bravade St-François*, Fréjus
Second week	Cannes Film Festival
Second weekend	*Fête de la Rose*, Grasse
Sunday after the 15th	*Fête de St-Gens*, costumes, pistol shots, etc, at Monteaux
16–17	*Bravade de St-Torpes*, St-Tropez
Third Sunday	Cherry Festival, Le Luc-en-Provence
Ascension weekend	Festival of ochre and colour, Roussillon; Monaco International Grand Prix
24–25	Gypsy pilgrimage at Saintes-Maries-de-la-Mer
Late May–mid July	International music festival, Toulon
10 days at Pentecost	Bullfights at Nîmes; *Cavalcade*, music festival at Apt

June

June–September	Music events in the Arènes, Nîmes; *Mirondela dels Arts*, with folklore, crafts, concerts, etc., at Pézenas
Throughout month	*Festival de la Danse et de l'Image*, Toulon
Early June	*Printemps des Comédiens*, theatre festival in Montpellier
1	*Cérémonie du St-Vinage*, Boulbon
15	*Bravade des Espagnols*, St-Tropez
Last half of June	Jazz and chamber music, in Aix; *Nuits Musicales*, music festival in Uzès
Corpus Christi	*Procession dai limaça*, Gorbio
Sunday before St John's Day	*Fête de St-Eloi*, blessing of the mules at Arles-sur-Tech
23–24	*Fête de St-Jean*, with processions, Entrevaux; with bonfires, dancing, and fireworks in Perpignan, Céret and Villefranche-de-Conflent
Sunday after the 24	*Fête Provençal*, with blessings of animals, in Allauch (near Marseille)
Late June–early July	*Festival International de Danse*, in Montpellier

July

| Last Saturday | Folklore festival of St Jean, Les Baux; *Fête de la Tradition*, Arles |
| Last Sunday | *Fête de la Tarasque*, Tarascon |

24

July

July–August	International Fireworks Festival, **Monaco**; Festival of Early Music, **Entrevaux**; *Nuits de l'Empéri*, theatre festival in **Salon**; modern music festival, **St-Paul-de-Vence**; Festival of Dance, Music, and Theatre, **Vaison-la-Romaine**; *Nuits de la Citadelle*, music and theatre at **Sisteron**; Côtes du Roussillon wine festival, **Perpignan**; *Rencontres Internationales d'Eté à la Chartreuse*, concerts, dance and theatre at **Villeneuve-lès-Avignon**; *Joutes nautiques*, **Agde**
Throughout month	International Music Festival, **Vence**; music festival, **Carcassonne**; *Rencontres Internationales de la Photographie*, **Arles**; *Festival de la Côte Languedocienne*, with concerts in **Béziers**; *Festival de la Sorgue*, music, theatre and dance at **Fontaine-de-Vaucluse** and around
4–14	*Festival Américain*, **Cannes**
First Sunday	*Fête de St Eloi*, bullfights and a decorated cart pulled by 40 horses in **Châteaurenard**
First two weeks	Dance Festival, **Aix**; International Folklore Festival, **Marseille**
Second Sunday	*Fête de St-Pierre*, with water jousts, etc., **Cap d'Antibes**
Mid-July	Jazz Festivals in **Nice** and **Toulon**; *Corso de nuit* for Notre-Dame-de-Santé, **Carpentras**; *Soirées Musicales*, **St-Maximin-la-Ste-Baume**; film festival, **La Ciotat**
14	Fireworks in many places for Bastille Day; **Avignon** and **Carcassonne** put on excellent shows
Last three weeks	Music Festival, **Aix**; *Festival de Radio France*, classical music and jazz in **Montpellier**
Mid-July–mid-Aug	International Theatre Festival, **Avignon**; Festival Pablo Casals, **Prades**; *Festival Passion*, operettas, ballet, and music at **Carpentras**
21–22	*Fête de Ste-Madeleine*, **St-Maximin-la-Ste-Baume**
Last two weeks	International Jazz Festival, **Juan-les-Pins**; music festival, **Orange**; fête in **Martigues**, with theatre, seafood, music and dancing; music festival, **Béziers**; *Festival de la Mer*, **Sète**; *Rencontres cinématographiques*, meet top film directors at **Prades**
Last Sunday	Donkey races and village fête, **Lacoste**
30	*Festa Major*, processions and distribution of Ste-Tombe's water, **Arles-sur-Tech**
End July	Folklore Festival and *Batailles des Fleurs*, **Nice**

August

All month	Chamber Music Festival, **Menton**; Music and Dance Festival, **Arles**; *Tournoise de joutes*, nautical jousts at **Sète**, culminating around the 25th
First two weeks	*Médiévales*, jousts and medieval crafts and costumes, **Carcassonne**; Music and Theatre festival, **Gordes**

25

First Tuesday	*Journées du Terroir*, flea markets and bullfights, **Sommières**
First Sunday	Lavender Festival, **Digne**; *Fête de la Madeleine*, with parade of flowered carts, **Châteaurenard**; Jasmine festival, **Grasse**
5	Passion procession, **Roquebrune**
9 and 11	**Fête de St-Laurent**, with bullfights, at **Eygalières**
14–18	*Feria* at **Collioure**, with fireworks
15	Village *fête* and operettas, **Le Thor**; *Feria* in **Béziers** with fireworks, parades, and fountains of wine
Third week	*Provençal festival* with processions, *bravades* and drama, **Séguret**
First Sunday after the 20th	*Fête du Traou*, dancing and polenta feasts at **Tende**
Second last Sunday	*Festival International de Sardanes*, Catalan dance festival, **Céret**
Third week	Provençal wine festival, **Séguret**
End of August	Bullfights at **Béziers**; *Fête de St-Louis*, with historical re-enactment, at **Aigues-Mortes**
29–29	*Fête de Notre-Dame-de-Grace*, **Maillane**

September

First week	*Fête de Musique in Catalogne*, **Elne**
First Sunday	*Festin des baguettes*, **Peille**
8	Village fête and pilgrimage to Notre-Dame-des-Fontaines, **Brigue**
Mid-month	*Festival du Cinéma méditerranéen*, **Montpellier**
Third week	*Feria des Vendanges*, bullfights at **Nîmes**
Last week–first week in October	*Nioulargue*, yacht race in **St-Tropez**

October

Mid-October	*Fête-Votive*, with Provençal bullfights, at **Aigues-Mortes**
22	*Fête de Ste-Marie-Jacobé*, **Saintes-Maries-de-la-Mer**
Third Sunday	*Fête du vin nouveau*, **Béziers**

November

Last Friday	*Foire St-Siffrein*, with truffle market, **Carpentras**
Last Sunday	*Foire des Santons*, until Epiphany, at **Marseille**

December

All month	Festival of Italian Cinema, **Nice**; Music festival, **Marseille**
24	Provençal midnight mass at **Ste-Baume**, **Séguret** and **Fontvieille**, with shepherds at **Allauch** (near Marseille); midnight mass in the Arènes at **Nîmes**; *Fête des bergers* and midnight mass, **Les Baux**; torchlight and Provençal wake, **Séguret**

Eating and Drinking

... and south of Valence, Provincia Romana, the Roman Provence, lies beneath the sun. There there is no more any evil, for there the apple will not flourish and the Brussels sprout will not grow at all.'

—Ford Madox Ford, *Provence*

Eating is a pleasure in the south, where seafood, herbs, fruit and vegetables are often within plucking distance of the kitchen and table. The high quality of these fresh native ingredients demands minimal preparation—Provençal cooking is perhaps the least fussy of any regional French cuisine, and as an added plus neatly fits the modern definition of a healthy diet. For not only is the south a Brussels sprout-free zone, but the artery-hardening delights of the north—the rich creamy sauces, butter, cheese and egg dishes, mega-calorie desserts—are rare birds in the land of olives, apricots, and almonds.

Some of the most celebrated restaurants in the world grace the south of France, but there are plenty of stinkers, too. The most tolerable are humble in their mediocrity (Languedoc is full of these) while others are oily with pretentions, staffed by folks posing as Grand Dukes and Duchesses fallen on hard times, whose exalted airs are somehow supposed to make their clients feel better about paying an obscene amount of money for the eight *petits pois à la graisse de yak* that the chef has so beautifully arranged on a plate. These places never last more than a year or two, but may just be in business as you happen by.

Just as intimidating for the hungry traveller are France's much ballyhooed gourmet bibles, whose annual awarding or removing of a star here, a chef's hat there, grade food the way a French teacher grades a *dictée* in school. Woe to the chef who leaves a lump in the sauce when those incognito pedants of the perfect palate are dining, and whose guillotine pens will ruthlessly chop off percentage points from the restaurant's final score. The less attention you pay them, the more you'll enjoy your dinner.

Restaurant Basics

Restaurants generally serve food between 12 noon and 2 pm and in the evening from 7 to 10 pm, with later summer hours; *brasseries* in the cities generally stay open continuously. All post menus outside the door so you know what to expect; if prices aren't listed, you can bet it's not because they're a bargain. If you have the appetite to eat the biggest meal of the day at noon, you'll spend a lot less money. Almost all restaurants have a choice of set-price menus; many offer a cheaper lunch special—the best way to experience some of the finer gourmet temples. Eating *à la carte* will always be much more expensive, in many cases twice as much; in most average spots no one ever does it. A few expensive places on the Côte d'Azur have no menus at all.

Menus in inexpensive places sometimes include the house wine (*vin compris*); if you choose a better wine anywhere, expect a scandalous mark-up. Don't be dismayed, it's a long-established custom (as in many other lands); the French wouldn't dream of a meal without wine, and the arrangement is a simple device to make food prices seem lower. If service is included it will say *service compris* or *s.c.*, if not *service non compris* or *s.n.c.*

27

Some restaurants offer a set-price gourmet *menu dégustation*—a selection of chef's specialities, which can be a great treat. At the other end of the scale, in the bars and brasseries, is the *plat du jour* (daily special) and the no-choice *formule*, which is more often than not steak and *frites*.

A full French meal may begin with an *apéritif*, hors d'oeuvres, a starter or two, followed by the *entrée*, cheese, dessert, coffee and chocolates, and perhaps a *digestif* to finish things off. If you order a salad it may come before or after, but never with your main course. In everyday eating, most people condense this feast to a starter, main course, and cheese or dessert. Vegetarians will have a hard time in France, but most establishments will try to accommodate them somehow.

When looking for a restaurant, homing in on the one place crowded with locals is as sound a policy in France as anywhere. Don't overlook hotel restaurants, some of which are absolutely top notch even if a certain red book refuses on some obscure principle to give them more than two stars. To avoid disappointment, call ahead in the morning to reserve a table, especially at the smarter restaurants, and especially in the summer. One thing you'll soon notice is that there's a wide choice of ethnic restaurants, mostly North African (a favourite for their economical *couscous*—spicy meat and vegetables served with a side dish of *harisa*, a hot red pepper sauce on a bed of steamed semolina); Asian (usually Vietnamese, sometimes Chinese, Cambodian, or Thai); and Italian, the latter sometimes combined with a pizzeria, although beware, quality very much depends on proximity to Italy, ie. the pasta and pizza are superb in Nice, tolerably good in Marseille, and often a pasty mess in Languedoc.

Don't expect to find many of these outside the Côte and the big cities; country cooking is French only (though often very inventive). But in the cosmopolitan centres, you'll find not only foreign cuisine, but specialities from all over France. There are Breton *crêperies* or *galetteries* (with whole-wheat pancakes), restaurants from Alsace serving *choucroute* (sauerkraut and sausage) , Périgord restaurants featuring *foie gras* and truffles, Lyonnaise *haute cuisine* and *les fast foods* offering *basse cuisine* of chips, hot dogs, and cheese sandwiches.

There are still a few traditional French restaurants that would meet the approval of Auguste Escoffier, the legendary chef (and a native of Provence); quite a few serve regional specialities (see below) and many feature *nouvelle cuisine*, which isn't so *nouvelle* any more, and has come under attack by devoted foodies for its expense (only the finest, freshest and rarest ingredients are used), portions (minute compared to usual restaurant helpings, because the object is to feel good, not full), and especially because many *nouvelle cuisine* practitioners have been quacks. For it is a subtle art, to emphasize the natural flavour and goodness of a carrot by contrasting or complementing it with other flavours and scents; disappointments are inevitable when a chef is more concerned with appearance than taste, or takes a walk on the wild side, combining oysters, kiwis and cashews or some other abomination. But *nouvelle cuisine* has had a strong influence on attitudes towards food in France, and it's hard to imagine anyone going back full time to smothering everything in a *béchamel* sauce.

The Cuisine of Provence
Thanks to the trail-blazing work of writers and chefs like Elizabeth David and Roger Vergé, Provençal cooking no longer sends the average Anglo-Saxon into

paroxysms of garlic paranoia as it did a hundred years ago. Many traditional dishes presage *nouvelle cuisine*, and their success hangs on the quality of the ingredients and fragrant olive oil, like the well-known *ratatouille*—aubergines (eggplant), tomatoes, garlic and courgettes (zucchini) cooked separately to preserve their individual flavour, before being mixed together in olive oil—or *bagna cauda*, a dish of the southern Alps, consisting of raw vegetables dipped in a hot fondue of garlic, anchovies and olive oil.

Among the starters, a refreshing summertime favourite is *salade niçoise*, interpreted in a hundred different ways even in Nice. Most versions contain most of the following: tomatoes, cucumbers, hard-boiled eggs, black olives, onions, anchovies, radishes, artichokes, green peppers, croutons, green beans, and sometimes tuna and even potatoes. In Nice pasta dishes come in all sorts of shapes, but the favourites are *ravioli* and *gnocchi* (potato dumplings), two forms served throughout Italy and invented here when Nice was still *Nizza* (the city has many other special dishes: see p. 104). Another dish that tastes best in the summer, *soupe de pistou* is a thick minestrone served with a fresh basil, garlic, and pine-nut sauce similar to Italian *pesto*. *Tian* is a casserole of rice, spring vegetables and grated cheese baked in the oven; *tourta de blea* is a sweet-savoury Swiss chard pie. *Mesclum* is a salad of dandelion and other green leaves, and a favourite hors d'oeuvre is *tapenade*, a purée of olives, olive oil and capers.

Aïoli, a kind of mayonnaise made from garlic, olive oil, lemon juice and egg yolks, served with codfish, snails, potatoes or soup is for many the essence of the region; Mistral even named his nationalist Provençal magazine after it. In the same spirit Marseille named its magazine *Bouillabaisse*, for its world-famous soup of five to twelve kinds of Mediterranean fish, flavoured with saffron; the fish is removed and served with *rouille*, a sauce of fresh red chilli peppers crushed with garlic, olive oil, and the soup broth. Because good saffron costs money and the fish, especially the gruesome *racasse* are rare, a proper *bouillabaisse* will run to at least 200 F. A less expensive but delicious alternative is *bourride*, a soup made from white-fleshed fish served with *aïoli*, or down a gastronomical notch or two, *baudroie*, a fish soup with vegetables and garlic. A very different kettle of fish is the indigestible Niçoise favourite, *estocaficada*, stockfish (and stockfish guts) stewed with tomatoes, olives, garlic, and eau-de-vie. Less adventurous, and absolutely delicious is *loup aux fenouille*, sea bass grilled over fennel stalks.

Lamb is the most common meat dish; real Provençal lamb (becoming increasingly rare) grazes on herbs and on special salt-marsh grasses from the Camargue and Crau. Beef usually comes in the form of a *daube*, slowly stewed in red wine and often served with ravioli. A Provençal cook's prize possession is the *daube* pan, which is never washed, but wiped clean and baked to form a crust that flavours all subsequent stews. Rabbit, or *lapin à la Provençal* is simmered in white wine with garlic, mustard, tomatoes and herbs. A more daunting dish, *pieds et paquets* is tripe stuffed with garlic, onions and salt pork, traditionally (although rarely in practice) served with calf's trotters. Stuffed courgette (zucchini) flowers, tarts of Swiss chard, and grilled tomatoes with garlic and breadcrumbs are popular vegetable dishes. Local cheeses are invariably goat—*chèvres*—little roundlets flavoured with thyme, bay, and other herbs. *Lou Pevre*, *Banon* and *Poivre d'Ain* are among the best.

Specialities of Languedoc-Roussillon

In France's 'culinary desert' as the region of Languedoc-Roussillon is unkindly known, they have the expression *Manjar força estofat* (to eat lots of stew), describing a masochist or someone who suffers martyrdom without complaint. What more can you say about a region that goes into raptures over *cassoulet*—beans, pork, *confits* and sausage stewed in goose fat? It is quite possible, as the Languedociens claim, that theirs is a subtle and complex cuisine—but at home; you can't confirm it from the restaurants. A poor and introverted region for 700 years, Languedoc does not much go out for dinner, and only recently has tourism been an influence on the few restaurants available.

Stay away from the dreary-looking places in the towns; some of these offer cuisine on the level of the average London sandwich bar. But out in the villages, in a growing number of new hotel-restaurants with younger owners, and in scores of *fermes-auberges*, you'll find something more to your liking, an honest, earthy cuisine entirely based on traditional local ingredients: game dishes, rabbit, pigeon, morels and cèpes, foie gras, occasionaly truffles, Corbières wine, and plenty of duck, usually in the form of a *confit* (cooked and preserved in its own fat—much better than it sounds). The eternal bean stew, *cassoulet* (see Castelnaudary) is still the king of the Languedocien table, along with regional variations like the *fricasée* of Limoux. Seafood, though simply prepared, is always good and fresh along the coast; there are plenty of mussels and oysters, raised in the coastal lagoons.

Some Languedocien basics have relatives in Provence. *Aïoli* is a favourite sauce, and seafood dishes like *bouillabaisse* are similar, although here you may find ham and leeks involved. Sète is famous for its delicious *bourride*, as Nîmes is known for its *brandade*, a cod purée with garlic. Then there's *bourboulhade*, a kind of poor man's *bouillabaisse* made of salt cod and garlic, or yet another B-soup, *boullinade*, a thicker fish soup with Banyuls wine. Sète specializes in *seiches farcies*, cuttlefish stuffed with the meat of its tentacles mixed with sausage. *Escargots*, or snails, come at you in all directions, with anchovies, as in Nîmes, or grilled (*cargolade*) or even in *bouillabaisse*. Land dishes you may encounter include *mourtayrol*, a delicious chicken *pot-au-feu* flavoured with saffron, and *rouzoles*, crêpes filled with ham and bacon. When the cheese platter comes around, it may have *pelardons*, the favourite *chèvre* from the Cévennes.

The Catalans in Roussillon have many sterling qualities, but display only the most modest ones in their restaurants. The totem fish of the *département* is the little anchovy of Collioure, which hardy souls from Spain to Marseille pulverize with garlic, onion, basil and oil to make *anchoïade*, a favourite apéritif spread on raw celery or toast. A popular starter is *gambas à la planxa*, prawns grilled and served on a plank. Main courses include *roussillonnade*, a dish of *bolet* mushrooms and sausages grilled over a pine-cone fire, and *boles de Picolat*, Catalan meatballs cooked in a thick sauce. And the classic dessert is *crème catalane*, a caramel-covered trifle flavoured with anis and cinnamon.

Markets, Picnic Food and Snacks

The food markets, especially in Provence, are justly celebrated for the colour and perfumes of their produce and flowers. They are fun to visit, and become even more interesting if you're cooking for yourself or are just gathering the ingredients for a picnic. In the larger cities they take place every day, while smaller towns and villages have

30

markets on one day a week, which double as a social occasion for the locals. Most markets finish up around noon.

Other good sources for picnic food are the *charcuteries* or *traiteurs*, both of which sell prepared dishes sold by weight in cartons or tubs. You can also find counters at larger supermarkets. Cities are snack-food wonderlands, with outdoor counters selling pastries, crêpes, pizza slices, *frites*, *croque-monsieurs* (toasted ham and cheese sandwiches) and a wide variety of sandwiches made from *baguettes* (long thin loaves of bread).

Drinking

You can order any kind of drink at any bar or café—except cocktails, unless it has a certain cosmopolitan savoir-faire or stays open into the night. Cafés are also a home away from home, places to read the papers, play cards, meet friends, and just unwind, sit back, and watch the world go by. You can sit hours over one coffee and no one will try to hurry you along. Prices are listed on the *Tarif des Consommations*: note they are progressively more expensive depending on whether you're served at the bar (*comptoir*), at a table (*la salle*) or outside (*la terrasse*).

French coffee is strong and black, but lacklustre next to the aromatic brews of Italy or Spain (you'll notice an improvement in the coffee near their respective frontiers). If you order *un café* you'll get a small black *express*; if you want milk, order *un crème*. If you want more than a few drops of caffeine, ask them to make it *grand*. For decaffeinated, the word is *déca*. Some bars offer *cappuccinos*, but again they're only really good near the Italian border; in the summer try a *frappé* (iced coffee). The French only order *café au lait* (a small coffee topped off with lots of hot milk) when they stop in for **breakfast**, and if what your hotel offers is expensive or boring, consider joining them. There are baskets of *croissants* and pastries, and some bars will make you a *baguette* with butter, jam or honey. If you want to go native, try the Frenchman's Breakfast of Champions: a pastis or two, and five non-filter *Gauloises*. *Chocolat chaud* (hot chocolate) is usually good; if you order *thé* (tea), you'll get an ordinary bag. An *infusion* is a herbal tea—*camomile*, *menthe* (mint), *tilleul* (lime or linden blossom), or *verveine* (verbena). These are kind to the all-precious *foie*, or liver, after you've over-indulged at the table.

Mineral water (*eau minérale*) can be addictive, and comes either sparkling (*gazeuse* or *pétillante*) or still (*non-gazeuse* or *plate*). If you feel run down, *Badoit* has lots of peppy magnesium in it—it's the current trendy favourite, even though Perrier comes from Languedoc. The usual international corporate soft drinks are available, and all kinds of bottled fruit juices (*jus de fruits*). Some bars also do fresh lemon and orange juices (*citron pressé* or *orange pressée*). The French are also fond of fruit syrups—red *grenadine* and ghastly green *diabolo menthe*.

Beer (*bière*) in most bars and cafés is run-of-the-mill big brands from Alsace, Germany, and Belgium. Draft (*à la pression*) is cheaper than bottled beer. Nearly all resorts have bars or pubs offering wider selections of drafts, lagers, and bottles.

The strong spirit of the Midi comes in a liquid form called *pastis*, first made popular in Marseille as a plague remedy; its name comes from the Latin *passe-sitis*, or thirst quencher. A pale yellow, 90 per cent nectar flavoured with anis, vanilla, and cinnamon, pastis is drunk as an apéritif before lunch and in rounds after work. The three major brands, *Ricard*, *Pernod*, and *Pastis 51* all taste slightly different; most people drink their '*pastaga*' with lots of water and ice (*glaçons*), which help make the taste more tolerable. A thimble-sized *pastis* is a *momie*, and you may want to try it mixed: a *tomate* is with grenadine, a *mauresque* with orgeat (almond and orange flower syrup), and a *perroquet* is with mint.

Other popular apéritifs come from Languedoc-Roussillon, including *Byrrh* 'from the world's largest barrel', a sweet wine mixed with quinine and orange peel, similar to *Dubonnet*. Spirits include the familiar Cognac and Armagnac brandies, liqueurs and *digestifs* made from walnuts, cherries, pears, and herbs (these are a specialty of the Alps), and fiery *marc*, the grape spirit that is the same as Italian grappa (but usually better).

Wine

One of the pleasures of travelling in France is drinking great wines for a fraction of what you pay at home, and discovering excellent labels you've never seen in your local shop. The south holds a special place in the saga of French wines, with a tradition dating back to the Greeks, who are said to have introduced an essential Côtes-du-Rhône grape variety called *syrah*, originally grown in Shiraz, in Persia. Nurtured back in the Dark and Middle Ages by popes and kings, the vineyards of Provence and Languedoc-Roussillon still produce most of France's wine—certainly most of its plonk, graded only by its alcohol content.

Some of Provence's best-known wines grow in the ancient places near the coast, especially its quartet of tiny AOC districts *Bellet, Bandol, Cassis* and *Palette*. But the best-known wines of the region come from the Rhône valley, under the general heading of *Côtes-du-Rhône*, including *Châteauneuf-du-Pape, Gigondas*, the famous rosé *Tavel*, and the sweet muscat *apéritif* wine, *Beaumes-de-Venise*. Elsewhere, winemakers have made great strides in boosting quality in the past 30 years, recognized in new AOC districts. Even greater strides have been made in Languedoc-Roussillon, the rising star on the French wine charts. Corbières, the fourth AOC district in France, and Minervois are only the two best known, while seldom-exported delights like *La Clape* and *Faugères* await the wine explorer. Languedoc is also the home of *Blanquette de Limoux*, the world's oldest sparkling wine, and *Banyuls*, France's answer to port, and *Rivesaltes*, a sweet muscat good Catalans drink all the live long day.

'If rules inhibit your enjoyment of wines, there should be no rules', Alexis Lichine wrote in the 1950s, and it still holds true today. The innocent drinker has to put up with even more words and snootery than the beleaguered eater. Confronting a wine list makes a lot of people nervous, while an obsequious *sommelier* can ruin their entire meal. Equally ruinous is the way some smart restaurants mark up AOC wines to triple or quadruple the retail price. If you love wine but have to watch expenses (and who doesn't these days?) buy it direct from the producers, or *vignerons*. In the text we've included a few addresses for each wine to get you started.

If a wine is labelled AOC (*Appellation d'Origine Contrôlée*) it means that the wine comes from a certain defined area and is made from certain varieties of grapes, guaranteeing a standard of quality. *Cru* on the label means vintage; a *grand cru* is a great, noble vintage. Down the list in the vinous hierarchy are those labelled VDQS (*Vin de Qualité Supérieure*), followed by *Vin de Pays* (guaranteed to at least originate in a certain region), with *Vin Ordinaire* (or *Vin de Table*) at the bottom, which may not send you to seventh heaven but is usually drinkable and cheap. In a restaurant if you order a *rouge* (red) or *blanc* (white) or *rosé* (pink), this is what you'll get, either by the glass (*un verre*), by the quarter-litre (*un pichet*) or bottle (*une bouteille*). *Brut* is very dry, *sec* dry, *demi-sec* and *moelleux* are sweetish, *doux* sweet, and *méthode champenoise*, sparkling.

If you're buying direct from the producer (or a wine co-operative, or *syndicat*, a group of producers), you'll be offered glasses to taste, each wine older than the previous one until you are feeling quite jolly and ready to buy the oldest (and most expensive) vintage. On the other hand, some sell loose wine à la petrol pump, *en vrac*; many *caves* even sell the little plastic barrels to put it in.

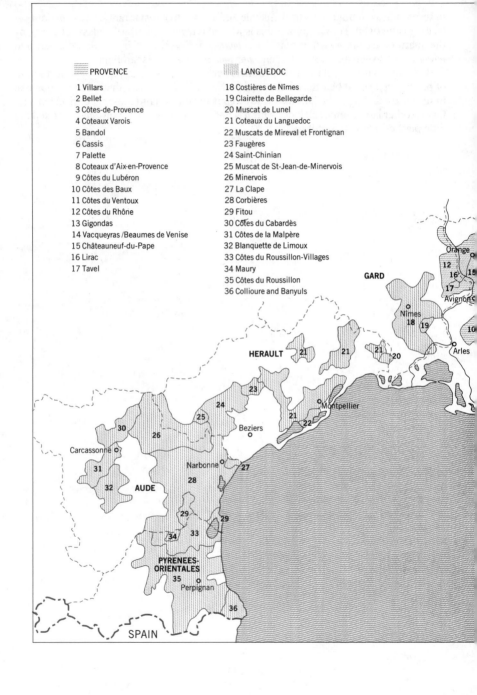

PROVENCE

1 Villars
2 Bellet
3 Côtes-de-Provence
4 Coteaux Varois
5 Bandol
6 Cassis
7 Palette
8 Coteaux d'Aix-en-Provence
9 Côtes du Lubéron
10 Côtes des Baux
11 Côtes du Ventoux
12 Côtes du Rhône
13 Gigondas
14 Vacqueyras /Beaumes de Venise
15 Châteauneuf-du-Pape
16 Lirac
17 Tavel

LANGUEDOC

18 Costières de Nîmes
19 Clairette de Bellegarde
20 Muscat de Lunel
21 Coteaux du Languedoc
22 Muscats de Mireval et Frontignan
23 Faugères
24 Saint-Chinian
25 Muscat de St-Jean-de-Minervois
26 Minervois
27 La Clape
28 Corbières
29 Fitou
30 Côtes du Cabardès
31 Côtes de la Malpère
32 Blanquette de Limoux
33 Côtes du Roussillon-Villages
34 Maury
35 Côtes du Roussillon
36 Collioure and Banyuls

GARD

Orange

Avignon

Nîmes

HERAULT

Montpellier

Béziers

Carcassonne

Narbonne

AUDE

PYRENEES-
ORIENTALES

Perpignan

SPAIN

Arles

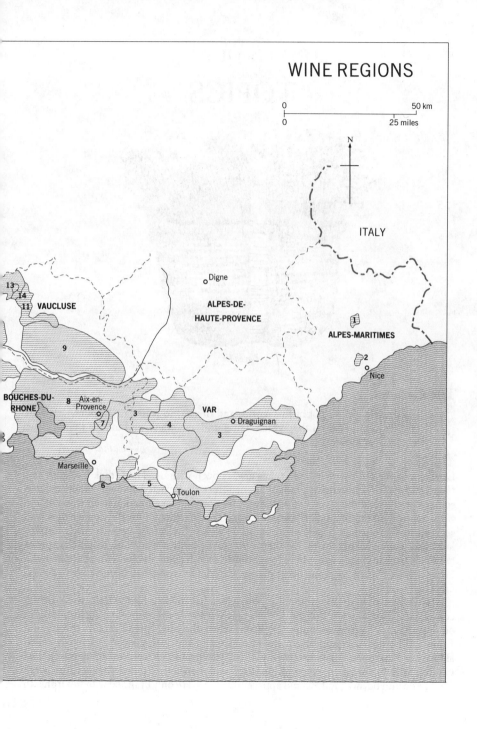

WINE REGIONS

0   50 km

0   25 miles

N

ITALY

Digne

**ALPES-DE-
HAUTE-PROVENCE**

13

14

11 **VAUCLUSE**

1

ALPES-MARITIMES

9

2

Nice

**BOUCHES-DU-
RHONE** 8 Aix-en-
Provence

3

VAR

7

4

Draguignan

3

Marseille

6

5

Toulon

Part II

TOPICS

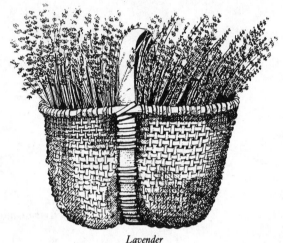

Lavender

The Cathars

> ...because we are not of this world, and this world is nought of ours,
> give us to understand that which Thou understandest, and to love that
> which Thou lovest.
>
> —*Cathar prayer*

Dualism, as the philosophers call it, has always been with us. The Greek Gnostics saw Good and Evil as contending, independent forces that existed forever. Good resided somewhere beyond the stars; Evil was here and now—in fact creation itself was evil, the work not of God but of a fallen spirit, identifiable with Satan. Our duty on earth was to seek purity by refusing to have anything to do with it. In the 3rd century AD, a Persian holy man named Mani took up the theme and made quite a splash; his teachings spread gradually back into the west, where the earliest Church councils condemned them as the 'Manichaean Heresy'. Among other places, the Manichaeans had been active in southern Gaul.

Always present in the Byzantine Empire, Manichaean ideas hit the Balkans in the 9th century; the 'Bogomil' or 'Bulgar' dualists reached a wide following, leaving hundreds of oddly-carved crosses as monuments. From there, the idea spread rapidly throughout Europe. The new sect appears in the chronicles of the 11th century, variously called Bulgars or Patarenes, Albigensians or Cathars (from a Greek word meaning pure). The Church was not slow to respond. In Italy and northern France the heretics were massacred and burned; in England apparently, they were only branded with hot irons. In

36

worldly and open Occitania, however they gained a foothold and kept it. The new faith was popular among peasants, townspeople and even many nobles; Occitan Catharism was organized into a proper church at a council at St-Felix-de-Caraman in 1167, presided over by a prelate named Nicetas, or Nikita, from Dragovici in the Balkans. The Cathars probably believed their faith was a return to the virtue and simplicity of the early Church. Their teaching encouraged complete separation with the Devil's world; feudal oaths, for example, were forbidden, and believers solved differences between themselves by arbitration rather than go to law. Some features were quite modern. Cathars promoted vegetarianism and non-violence; marriage was by simple agreement, not a sacrament—enhancing the freedom and status of women by doing away with the old Roman paternalist tradition and laws. Two other points made Catharism especially attractive to an increasingly modern society. It had a much more mature attitude towards money and capitalism than the Roman church—no condemnation of loans as usury, and no church tithes. This earned it support in the growing cities; like the later Protestants, many Cathars were involved in the textile trades. And Cathar simplicity, and its lack of a big church organization made a very favourable contrast with the bloated, bullying and thoroughly corrupt machinery of the Church of Rome.

Best of all, Catharism had a very forgiving attitude towards sinners. If creation itself was the Devil's work, how could we not err? Cathars were divided into two levels: the mass of simple believers, upon whom the religion was a light yoke indeed—no mass and few ceremonies, no money-grubbing, easy absolution—and the few *perfecti*, those who had received the sacrament called the *consolament*, and were thenceforth required to lead a totally ascetic life devoted to faith and prayer. Most Cathars conveniently took the *consolament* on their deathbeds.

Catharism was a strong and growing force when the Albigensian Crusade began in 1209; the papacy, the behaviour of which has always been a strong argument for the basic tenet of dualism, saw enough of a threat to its power to require a policy of genocide. The terror, enforced by French arms and overseen by the Dominicans and Cistercians, was vicious and successful. Its climax came in 1244, with the fall of the Cathar holy-of-holies, the temple fortress at Montségur in the Pyrenees (*département* of Ariège). Cathars who survived the mass exterminations were hunted down ruthlessly by the new Inquisition; Guillaume Bélibaste, the last of the *perfecti*, was burned at Villerouge-Termenès in the Aude in 1321. Nevertheless, doctrines are always more difficult to kill than human beings, and Catharism survived its persecutors in a number of forms, especially in its influence on the later southern Protestants, and on the Catholic Jansenists of the 1600s.

There are practising Cathars today; if you want to seek them out, the village of Arques, in the Aude, might be a good place to start, or else consult the worthy books (in French) of a modern-day sympathizer named René Nelli. There are probably fewer actual Cathars than books about them. Catharism did have a strong esoteric tinge to it, reserved for the *perfecti*. In the past few decades, this angle has been explored in every sort of work, from the serious to the pathetically inane, speculating on various 'treasures', real or metaphysical, that the last *perfecti* may have hidden, or connecting the sect with other favourite occult themes: the Templars (who in fact were their enemies), the Holy Grail (said to have been kept at Montségur), the Illuminati and Rosicrucians of the 15th century and onwards, or the body and possible descendants of Jesus Christ (see Rennes-le-Château, p. 419). Nelli and other authors have some provocative things to say about the greatest and most mysterious of all the Arthurian epics, Wolfram von Eschenbach's *Parzifal*—they see the poem as a sweeping Cathar allegory, confirming Montségur as the Grail castle, and identifying Parzifal with the Cathars' protector, Raymond Trencavel of Carcassonne. Trencavel's chroniclers also have an uncanny habit of comparing the Viscount to Christ, especially after his betrayal and death at the hands of Simon de Montfort; his dynasty, like that of the Counts of Toulouse, was quite a vortex for this sort of weirdness.

The weirdest of all modern Europe's occultist sects, the Nazis, were obsessed with the Cathars and the legends that have grown up around them. After their occupation of the south in 1942, they sealed off all the important Cathar sites and cave refuges in the Pyrenees, and Nazi high-priest Alfred Rosenberg sent teams of archaeologists to dig them up amidst the utmost secrecy. In 1944, not long before liberation, a group of local Cathars sneaked up to Montségur for an observance to commemorate the 700th anniversary of their forebears' last stand. A small German plane, with a pilot and one passenger, appeared and circled the castle. The Cathars, expecting the police, watched in amazement as the plane, by means of skywriting equipment, traced a strange, eight-branched cross over their heads, and then disappeared beyond the horizon.

A Country Calendar

Beyond the glamorous life in the villas and *résidences secondaires*, the cycle of the seasons goes on in the south of France as it has since Hector was a pup. A few crops have changed—silk, madder and a dozen different varieties of wheat have vanished, while flowers and early garden vegetables have become more important. Some corners are warm enough to produce three crops a year.

The calendar begins with two months of repose: *l'ivèr a ges d'ouro*, 'winter has no hours' is an old saying in the country. The mistral and tramontane winds howl away, and it snows, sometimes even in Nice. In **January** the Three Kings are feted with crown-shaped brioches studded with candied fruit. Fattened geese and ducks are turned into *confits* and pigs into sausages and raw ham. In early **February** the mimosas bloom and olives are squeezed into oil; traditional presses are still used in Contes and La Tour, both north of Nice. Flaky tarts filled with jam or cream are baked for Carnival. By the end of February the almonds burst into lacy bloom. The real work begins in **March**, when farmers prune their olives and vines and sow wheat and oats, and plant potatoes and melons.

In **April** two things must be cut: hay and fleece, much of the work done by itinerant sheep shearers who travel from farm to farm. Plums, apricots, cherries, and pears spring into blossom; and everyone prays the mistral doesn't blow the flowers and buds off the trees. Good Friday is traditionally celebrated with an *aïoli*, or dried cod and garlic mayonnaise feast; for Easter the first roast lamb of the year is served with a salad of *romaine* lettuce, fresh onions and hard boiled eggs. In **May** the flocks are driven to the greener pastures in the hills, following transhumance trails that date back to the Neolithic era. Early vegetables are abundant in the markets—little green artichokes called *mourre de gat* for omelettes, *fèves* (broad beans), garlic, spring onions and peas.

June brings the wheat harvest, once the most colourful event on the calendar as mountaineers descended by the thousands to provide the labour, fuelled on five meals and a barrel of wine a day. Asparagus, cherries and apricots ripen, and gourmets poke around in the woods for delectable morel mushrooms. The summer solstice and end of the harvest (St John's Day) are given a good old-fashioned Celtic send off with bonfires and fireworks, especially in Roussillon where holy Pic du Canigou is encircled with fires lit in every village; the sun itself is said to dance and jump three times over the Alpilles. Almonds are ready to be picked in **July**, but now and throughout **August** it's too hot to work except in the early morning. Melons and peaches are everywhere, and the lavender is ready to be cut. The evenings are alive with village fêtes, for this has always been the time to eat, drink and make merry, to horde strength for hard tasks ahead.

September brings fresh figs, and the rice is ready to be harvested in the Camargue. With the first rains mushrooms begin to poke up in the woods, especially the fragrant cèpes; these are tracked down with a relentlessness matched only by the hunters whose blasting advent is marked by a noticeable decline in birdsong. But the most important event of the month is the *vendange*, or grape harvest. **October**, too, is very much occupied with winemaking. The stripped vines turn red, wild boar meat appears in the markets, walnuts and chestnuts are gathered in the hills.

November marks the beginning of a new agricultural year, with the planting of wheat. Cold weather forces the shepherds and their flocks down from the mountains. Olives wait to be picked, and truffle hounds (the picturesque but uncontrollably greedy pigs have been retired) seek out the elusive *rabasso*, the black gold of the Vaucluse and Hérault. **December** brings Christmas, or *Calendo* in Provençal, a word resulting from an early confusion of Christ's birth with the Roman Calends. On Christmas Eve, the grandfather of each family blesses the *cacho-fiô* (a Yule log from a fruit tree) and the youngest in the family lays it in the hearth; a lavish meal of fish and vegetables traditionally followed by thirteen desserts precedes midnight mass. And this being France, the stomach dominates Christmas day as well: oysters, *foie gras*, black truffles, stuffed capon, goose with pears, and champagne, by necessity punctuated by frequent *trous provençaux*—frozen glasses of *marc* that magically make it possible to eat as much as Gargantua.

Mistral and the Félibrige

The attitude of the French was best expressed by Paul Morand's speech upon being admitted to the Académie Française: 'To write in French is to see flowing the waters of a mountain stream, next to which all languages are muddy rivers; it is to live in a crystal palace'. To someone like Morand, master of *pointu* or 'proper' French with all its mushy slushy vowel sounds, one of the muddiest rivers was *langue d'Oc*. Its demise became a priority in the 19th century; after subjugating the south politically and religiously, Paris decided to finish up the job linguistically and decreed French the sole legal language in the schools, military, government, and press.

One of the strategies of the *Franchimands* (as the southerners call French speakers) was to divide and conquer: *langue d'Oc*, claimed the central Frenchifyers, was actually thousands of dialects and could never constitute a language. Even the southerners admit to seven 'grand dialects' of Occitan, three of which fall into the confines of this book: the

Dauphinois of the Alpine valleys, Provençal, and Languedocien, the descendant of the troubadours' language. But it was in Provence that the reaction to the *Franchimands'* linguistic imperialism took its most curious form—in a sentimental, artificially contrived literary movement called the Félibrige.

According to legend, the idea for the Félibres was 'born of a mother's tear' when the mother of the poet Joseph Roumanille wept because she couldn't understand the French verses of her son. Not long after, on 21 May 1854, at the Château de Font Ségugne near Avignon, Roumanille, Frédéric Mistral and five other poets proclaimed the formation of a literary school to 'safeguard indefinitely for Provence its language, its colour, its easy liberty, its national honour, and its fine level of intelligence, for such as it is, we like Provence'. It was the 24-year-old Mistral who came up with the name for the school when he quoted a folk rhyme on the Seven Sorrows of Mary from his native village Maillane: *li sett felibre de la Lèi*—the seven doctors or sages of the law. As 21 May (the day when the sun is in the constellation of the Pleiades, or seven sisters) was the feast day of Santo Estello, the seven-pointed star of the Cathars was adopted as one of the Félibres' symbols. In later years, after Mistral's epic *Miréio* gave the movement its lustre, 21 May would be celebrated with a Grand Félibre Banquet when all the fifty members or *Majoraux* and their leader, the *capoulié* (Mistral, naturally) would pass around the *Coupo Santo*, the Félibres' Holy Grail.

The Félibres' greatest moment came in 1904, when Mistral won the Nobel Prize for literature, the only writer in a minority language ever to be awarded a Nobel Prize. Thanks to him and the other Félibres Provence became conscious and proud of its separate identity; the richness of the language charmed even foreigners like Ezra Pound, who wrote and translated Provençal. But in spite of these successes, the Félibrige best serves as a lesson on how *not* to revive a language. Today only a few people in their 80s in remote areas still use Provençal as a daily tool, a sorry record compared to the subsequent revivals of Irish, Catalan, Basque, Welsh, and most successful of all, Hebrew.

Where did the Félibres go wrong? Not for lack of trying: unlike the courtly troubadours, they purposely wrote in a simple style to appeal to the *paysans*. Slipshod grammar and spelling were codified in Mistral's labour of love, the *Trésor du Félibrige* (a work accused by some of passing off the rustic dialect of Maillane as the last word in Provençal). But the Félibres' biggest mistake was confusing language and time, associating Provençal with folklore and the past, and shunning the necessary political fight with Paris in a romantic illusion that their poetry was powerful enough to revive a dying tongue. Mistral's powerful, mystical evocation of western Provence (the real hero of all his epics) was more of a swansong to a dying culture, not the foundation for a Renaissance of new troubadours.

For nearly everything Mistral celebrated in his poetry was undergoing a sea change—Italians, Corsicans, and Spaniards were moving in by the thousands, and helping to build new roads and railroads, while old farming practices, rural customs, traditions, and even villages were rapidly being abandoned. Mistral for all his art, energy, charm and influence could not turn the clock back. He had the unique honour of attending the unveiling of his own statue in Arles—a melancholy recognition that he was dead in his own lifetime.

Hocus Pocus Popes

Filling the lifeless shell of the papal palace in Avignon with the lost trappings of the medieval popes is not an easy task for the imagination. And the more you learn, the harder it gets, for besides all the harlots, speculators, gluttons, and cheats that Petrarch railed against, there seems to have been a shocking amount of voodoo. Accusations of sorcery had already sullied the name of one Occitan pope, Sylvester II (Gerbert of the Auvergne) who reigned from 999–1003 after studying in the Islamic schools in Toledo, where he acquired a prophetic bronze head that advised him in sticky moments. Even today, his tombstone in St John Lateran sweats and rattles before the death of each pope.

In 1309, the French pope Clement V moved the papacy from Rome to Avignon, then died from eating a plate of ground emeralds (prescribed by his doctor for a stomach ache). He was succeeded by John XXII, a native of Cahors, who owed his election to a magic knife that enchanted the conclave of cardinals. This John was also a famous alchemist, and he filled the papal treasury with gold, while King Philip V gave him a pair of *languiers*, or amulets shaped like serpents' tongues, encrusted with gems that changed colour on contact with poison. They served the pope in good stead, as plenty of rivals in the Church were trying to do him in. The most notable culprits were the Bishop of Cahors, who was burned at the stake for trying to bewitch him with wax dolls, and Clement V's doctor, caught manufacturing a diabolical homunculus.

The next pope, Benedict XII, spent hundreds of thousands of florins on a new palace, and still had enough gold and precious stones left over to top up his treasury—thanks, it is said, to an elderly woman residing in Avignon's ghetto, who told him where to find the 'treasure of the Jews' buried under her hovel. And in the bitter end, just before the Anti-pope Benedict XIII was forced to flee Avignon, he sealed up a secret room in the palace with a cache of solid gold statues, confiding the secret to his friend, the Venetian ambassador. They were never found, although in Mistral's epic *Poème du Rhône*, three Venetian ladies who inherited the secret come to the palace and remove the flagstones that cover up the secret room—only to discover a bottomless abyss.

Occitans, Catalans and Related Species

The place is Verdun, the date 843 AD, and a fellow named Lothair is about to ball up European history for good. The three contentious grandsons of Charlemagne, unable to peaceably manage the Carolingian Empire, were deciding how to carve it up between them. The resulting Treaty of Verdun would be a linguistic landmark—one of the first documents issued in two new-fangled languages, later called French and German. It would also determine the future map of Europe. Lothair's two brothers were more sensible; Louis took the east, the future Germany, and Charles the Bald got the western half, most of what is now France. Lothair must have thought he was the clever one. Besides the imperial title (of dubious value) and the imperial capital, Aachen, he took away the richest lands of the Empire: northern Italy, Provence, Lorraine and Burgundy, along with Switzerland and the Low Countries.

If Lothair had considered what he would be leaving to his descendants, he might have noticed that this random collection of territories could never be held together for long. If he had had any sense of historical necessity, he might have said: 'You two can keep all the northern bits; just let me have what we Franks know as Aquitania, the land that folks in a thousand years are going to call southern France and Catalunya'. It would have made sense even then, a more coherent posession both culturally and politically. In the later Middle Ages, it would have seemed the obvious choice. This is Western Europe's nation that never was.

The nation would have been called Provence, most likely, as that was the name in the later Middle Ages for the Occitan-speaking lands that stretched from the Atlantic to the Alps. Its capital would probably have been Toulouse. Instead, after the speedy collapse of Lothair's and his brothers' kingdoms, the Occitan-speaking peoples south of the Loire and their Catalan cousins got centuries of a balanced feudal anarchy with no real overlord. Real power became fatally divided between two ambitious rivals, the County of Toulouse, and the new Catalan County of Barcelona, later the Kingdom of Aragon.

The Occitans didn't mind; the relative freedom gave them the chance to create their open, advanced civilization of poetry and tolerance, a March crocus heralding the blossoming of medieval Europe. The Catalans learned to sail and trade, and built themselves a maritime empire in the Mediterranean. Unfortunately, their lack of cooperation doomed the former to a brutal French military conquest, followed by the near-extinction of their language and culture. The Catalans, at least those south of the Pyrenees, would later suffer the same fate at the hands of Spain.

The great castles of Languedoc and Roussillon—Quéribus, Carcassonne, Salses and the rest—are the gravestones of the Lost Nation, the sites of defeats that marked its gradual, inexorable assimilation by the power of Paris and the north. Today, if you visit them in the off season the only other car in the car park will be likely to have a white Spanish tag with a 'B' for Barcelona. You may see the inscrutable Catalans—culturally much more alive than the poor Languedociens—picnicking in the snow at Peyrepertuse in December, or at Salses furtively taking voluminous notes on the guided tour. Catalans abroad, even when encumbered by children and small dogs, often have the raffish air of spies or infiltrating *provocateurs*; it's part of their charm. Here, they're on a real mission, piecing together the memorials and cultural survivals of a forgotten world—forgotten by everyone else, maybe, but a dream that the Catalans and France's Occitanian malcontents will never let die.

Troubadours

Lyric poetry in the modern Western world was born around the year 1095 with the rhymes of Count William (1071–1127), grandfather of Eleanor of Aquitaine. William wrote in the courtly language called Old Provençal (or Occitan) although his subject matter was hardly courtly ('Do you know how many times I screwed them? / One hundred and eighty-eight to be precise; / so much so that I almost broke my girth and harness...'). A descendant of the royal house of Aragon, William had Spanish-Arab blood in his lusty veins and had battled against the Moors in Spain on several occasions; but at the same time he found inspiration (for his form, if not his content) from a civilization that was centuries ahead of Christian Europe in culture.

The word *troubadour* may be derived from the Arabic root for lutenist (trb), and the ideal of courtly love makes its first appearance in the writings of the spiritual Islamic Sufis. The Sufis believed that true understanding could not be expressed in doctrines, but could be suggested obliquely in poetry and fables. Much of what they wrote was love poetry addressed to an ideal if unkind and irrational Muse, whom the poet hopes will reward his merit and devotion with enlightenment and inspiration. Christians who encountered this poetry in the Crusades converted this ideal Muse into the Virgin, giving birth to the great 12th-century cult of Mary. But in Occitania this mystic strain was reinterpreted in a more worldly fashion by troubadours, whose muses became flesh and blood women, although these darlings were equally unattainable in the literary conventions of courtly love. The lady in question could only be addressed by a pseudonym. She had to be married to someone else. The poet's hopeless suit to her hinged, not on his rank, but on his virtue and worthiness. The greatest novelty of all was that this love had to go unrequited.

Art songs of courtly love were known as *cansos*, and rarely translate well, as their merit was in the poet's skill in inventing new forms in his rhyming schemes, metres, melodies, and images. But the troubadours wrote many other songs as well, called *sirventes*, which followed established forms but took for their subjects politics, war, miserly patrons, and even satires on courtly love itself.

The golden age of the troubadours began in the 1150s, when the feudal lords of Occitania warred amongst each other with so little success that behind the sound and fury the land enjoyed a rare political stability. Courts indulged in new luxuries and the arts flourished, and troubadours found ready audiences, travelling from castle to castle. One of their great patrons was En Barral, Viscount of Marseille, who was especially fond of the reputedly mad but charming Peire Vidal. Vidal not only wrote of his love for En Barral's beautiful wife, but in a famous incident even went beyond the bounds of convention by stealing a kiss from her while she slept (her husband, who thought it was funny, had to plead with her to forgive him). Vidal travelled widely, especially after the death of En Barral in 1192, and wrote a rare nostalgic poem for the homeland of his lady fair:

> With each breath I draw in the air
> I feel coming from Provence;
> I so love everything from there
> that when people speak well of it,
> I listen smiling, and with each
> word ask for a hundred more,
> so much does the hearing please me.

> (trans. by Anthony Bonner, in *Songs of the Troubadours*)

Up Your Nose

If nothing else, Provence and Languedoc will make you more aware of that sense we only remember when something stinks. The perfumeries of Grasse will correct this 'scentual' ignorance with a hundred different potions; every *village perché* has shops overflowing with scented soaps, pot-pourris and bundles of *herbes de Provence*; every kitchen emits intoxicating scents of garlic and thyme; every cellar wants to you to breathe in the bouquets of its wines. And when you begin to almost crave the more usual French smells of *Gauloise* butts, *pipi* and *pommes frites*, you discover that this nasal obsession is not only profitable to some, but healthy for all.

Aromathérapie, a name coined in the 1920s for the method of natural healing through fragrances, is taken very seriously in the land where one word *sentir* does double duty for 'feel' and 'smell'. French medical students study it, and its prescriptions are covered by the national social security. For as an aromatherapist will tell you, smells play games with your psyche; the nose is hooked up not only to primitive drives like sex and hunger, but also to your emotions and memory. The consequences can be monumental. Just the scent of a madeleine cake dipped in tea was enough to set Proust off to write *Remembrance of Things Past*.

Aromatherapy is really just a fashionable name for old medicine. The Romans had a saying *Cur moriatur homo, cui salvia crescit in horto?* (Why should he die, who grows sage in his garden?) about a herb still heralded for its youth-giving properties. Essential oils distilled from plants were the secret of Egyptian healing and embalming, and were so powerful that there was a bullish market in 17th-century Europe for mummies, which were boiled down to make medicine.

Essential oils are created by the sun and the most useful aromatic plants grow in hot and dry climates—as in the south of France, the spiritual heartland of aromatherapy. Lavender, the totem plant of the Midi, has been in high demand for its mellow soothing qualities ever since the Romans used it to scent their baths (hence its name from the Latin *lavare*, to wash). Up until the 1900s, nearly every farm in Provence had a small lavender distillery, and you can still find a few kicking about today. Most precious of all is the oil of *lavande fine*, a species that grows only above 3000 feet on the sunny side of the Alps; 150 pounds of flowers are needed for every pound of oil.

For centuries in Provence, shepherds were regarded as magicians for their plant cures, involving considerable mumbo-jumbo about picking their herbs in certain places and certain times—and indeed, modern analysis has shown that the chemical composition of a herb like thyme varies widely, depending on where it grows and when it's picked. When the sun is in Leo, shepherds make *millepertuis*, or red oil (a sovereign anaesthetic and remedy for burns and wounds) by soaking the flowers of St John's wort in a mixture of white wine and olive oil that has been exposed to the hottest sun. After three days, they boil the wine off, and let the flowers distill for another month; the oil is then sealed into tiny bottles, good for one dose each, to maintain the oil's healing properties.

Still awaiting a fashionable revival are other traditional Provençal cures: baked ground magpie brains for epilepsy, marmot fat for rheumatism, dried fox testicles rubbed on the chest for uterine disease and mouse excrement for bedwetting.

Wide Open Spaces

Gertrude Stein, a great fan of Provence who spent a lot of time in St-Rémy thinking inscrutable thoughts, once dropped a famous line about Oakland, California: 'There's no *there* there', she concluded after a brief visit. Take an equally inscrutable modern-day rapper from Oakland out to the exact centre of Provence, around the Lac de Castillon, and you will get a neatly symmetrical opinion. Lac de Castillon, a big artificial lake behind a concrete dam, is a special place, surrounded by wrinkled hills of a grey so immaculately grey that it is hard to see them at all. Outside of a few dam workers and an occasional trendy hang-gliding above, the whole gigantic grey place will be eerily deserted. The Lac de Castillon is *nowhere*, and all the towns and villages for thirty miles or more in any direction are only variations on the theme. We like to imagine an advert in a London paper: '*Delightful farmhouse half-restored in the heart of the Provençal mountains, near mountain lake; 1½ hr from Cannes. Must sell.*'

When you visit, take a look at the sort of Frenchman who lives in such a place: no poodles, no shades, no attitudes; even in summer, he may well be wearing a flannel shirt, which under the big moustaches will make him look entirely like one of the jolly Gaulish villagers in *Asterix*. Some of these are real frontiersmen, rough-edged, self-sufficient types whose lives revolve around hunting, gathering mushrooms and getting in wood for the winter; they grumble laconically in a tongue that is still more Provençal than French. But we once met a picture-perfect example on the way to Draguignan. He was the baker in a village near the lake, hitch-hiking to the city with a jerrican of petrol to buy a used car (in France one never expects a used car to have any in the tank). His brother had gone off to the Harvard Business School and made it big. The baker, with his degree in cultural anthropology, preferred less stress and yeastier dough; having an asssistant allowed him enough time for long scholarly vacations in the darker corners of South America and Asia.

The moral seems to be: rural France provides some of the world's most interesting hitch-hikers. It does, but the point was that the English shibboleth the 'South of France' is not always what one might expect. The toadstool growth of the Côte d'Azur in the last century has entirely eclipsed the real Provence: lonely expanses of mountain and introverted villages, shepherds who still drive their flocks up to the mountains in summer on the old transhumance paths, and a traditional rural culture that, despite a great loss of population in the last century, is not yet prepared to compromise entirely with the modern world. One wild snapshot among many sticks in the mind: two Indian chiefs, Iron Tail and Lone Bear, sipping champagne with the Marquis de Baroncelli-Javon in 1889, while watching Camargue *gardians* and the cowboys of Buffalo Bill's Wild West Show compare their skills at a Provençal rodeo. The men of two worlds had a great time together, and seemed to understand one another perfectly. One young Sioux, whom the French called *Pan Perdu*, chose to stay behind in Provence; Frédéric Mistral met him, and thought he might be the reincarnated soul of a troubadour.

Part III

HISTORY AND ART

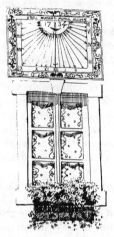

The most serene hours are marked with a shadow
—*on an old sundial in Riez*

Historical Outline

Before starting, a little political geography might help to relieve some major confusions. In France, almost all regional names are maddeningly fluid. First of all, there is **Provence** which has never had any fixed boundaries. The Romans called the southern coast their dear 'province', one of their first and most delectable conquests outside Italy. Specifically, this was the province of *Gallia Narbonnensis*, stretching from Toulouse to Geneva, though its rich heartland was always the coastal area from Narbonne to Marseille. In the early Middle Ages, ancient Gaul was evolving its linguistic north-south distinction between the *langue d'oc* and the *langue d'oeil* (two words for saying 'yes', from the Latin *hoc* and *hoc ille*). 'Provence' came to mean the *oc* domain, the southern third of what is now France, from the Dordogne to Lyon; both troubadour poets and noblemen's secretaries enjoyed making a connection with the classical civilization that built the Pont du Gard, the arch of Orange and the amphitheatres of Nîmes and Arles.

At the same time, the political boundary of the Rhône, between lands subject to the Holy Roman Emperors and those claimed by the kings of France, was redefining the terminology. 'Provence' took on the political meaning of the semi-independent county east of the Rhône, while the rest, as far as Toulouse and Aquitaine, was grabbed by force by the French in the 13th century and took the name of **Languedoc**. Provence held out longer, until its union with the French crown in 1486. Today, southern regionalists call the entire Midi **Occitania** (a word only invented in the 17th century).

Roussillon, the modern *département* of Pyrenées-Orientales, followed an entirely different history; part of the Catalan nation since the 10th century, it was an essential part of the County of Barcelona and later the Catalan Kingdom of Aragon, until the French annexed it in 1559.

Under the *ancien régime*, under the Revolution and all the regimes that followed it, these areas were smothered, politically and culturally, by imperialist France. The turning of the tide has come only in our own time, with the election of the 1981 Socialist government, and the beginnings of regional autonomy. The five *départements* east of the Rhône are now the artificially designed region of *Provence-Côte d'Azur*, those to the west (along with Lozère, in the Cévennes), are in **Languedoc-Roussillon**, still cut off from its traditional capital, Toulouse, by the intent of the Paris planners.

The First Million Years Or So

The first inhabitants, with all of the Midi to choose from, not surprisingly seem to have picked the Côte d'Azur for their residence. Tools and traces of habitation around Monaco go back as far as 1,000,000 BC. The first identifiable personality on the stage, however, is 'Tautavel Man'; a recent remarkable find in the small Roussillon village of that name has unearthed hundreds of thousands of bones of a people who rate among the very first Europeans yet discovered—at least 450, 000 BC, and perhaps as old as 680,000. Someone may have been around through all the millennia that followed, but evidence is rare; more bones have been found in caves around Nice, from about 200,000 BC. Neanderthal Man turns up about 60,000 BC (at Ganges, in the Hérault, and other places). The first evidence of the Neanderthalers' nemesis, that quarrelsome and unlovable species *Homo Sapiens*, appears some 20,000 years later.

Neolithic civilization arrived as early as 3500 BC, and endured throughout the region for the next 2000 years. People knew agriculture and raised sheep, traded for scarce goods (obsidian from the islands around Sicily, for example), and built dry-stone houses; one of these has been reconstructed by archaeologists at Cambous, in the Hérault. The Neolithic era left few important monuments: an impressive but little-known temple complex at Castellet, near Arles, and some large dolmens in the Minervois, the northern Hérault, and the Massif des Maures. Of succeeding ages we know more about technology than culture and changes in population: the use of copper began about 2000 BC, iron *c.* 800 BC. In both cases the region was one of the last parts of the Mediterranean basin to catch on.

By now, at least, the inhabitants have a name, even if it is a questionable one applied by later Greek and Roman writers: the Ligurians on the east coast and the Iberians in the west. There is plenty of room for confusion here; culturally and racially there may have been little difference between the two. From about 800 BC, they begin building their first settled villages, today called by the Latin name *oppidum*, a word you will see often in the south; it even survives in village names, such as Oppèdette in Provence. An *oppidum* is a small, fortified village, usually on a hilltop, built around a religious sanctuary or trading centre. Already, more advanced outsiders were coming to make deals with the natives: the Phoenicians, Etruscans, and most importantly the Greeks.

A major event of this same era was the arrival of the Celts, Indo-European cousins of the Ligurians and Iberians from the north. Beginning in coastal Languedoc in the 8th century BC, they gradually spread their conquests eastwards until the 4th at the expense of the Ligurians. At the same time, Greek merchant activity was turning into full-scale colonization. The Ionian city-states of Asia Minor had become over-populated, agriculturally exhausted and politically precarious, and their citizens sought to reproduce them in new lands. The first was *Massalia*—Marseille, *c.* 600 BC. Soon Massalia was founding colonies of its own: Nice, Hyères and Agde were among the most important. Greek influence over the indigenous peoples was strong from the start; as with everywhere else they went, they brought the vine (wild stocks were already present, but the Celts hadn't worked out what to do with them) and the olive, and also their art. The Celts loved Greek vases, and had metals and other raw materials to offer in return. Increased trade turned some of the native *oppida* into genuine cities, such as Ensérune, near Béziers, and Arles.

Roman Provincia

From the start, the Greeks were natural allies of the young city of Rome—if only because they had common enemies. Besides the strong Etruscan federation, occupying the lands in between the two, there were their trade rivals,the Phoenicians (later Carthaginians) and occasionally the Celts and Ligurians. As Rome gobbled up Etruria and the rest of Italy, the area became of increasing importance; a fact Hannibal demonstrated when he marched his armies along the coast towards Italy in 218 BC, with the full support of the Celts (historians still argue over how and where he got the elephants across the Rhône).

When the Romans took control of Spain in the Second Punic War (206), the coasts of what they called Gaul became a logical next step. In 125, Roman troops saved Marseille from a Celtic attack. This time, though, they had come to stay. The reorganization of the new province—'*Provincia*'—was quick and methodical. Domitius Ahenobarbus, the vanquisher of the Celts, began the great Italy-Spain highway that bears his name, the Via Domitia, in 121. New cities were founded, most importantly Aix (122) and Narbonne (118), which became the capital of what was now officially called Gallia Narbonnensis. Dozens of other new foundations followed over the next century, many of them planned colonies with land grants for veterans of the legions. The Celts were not through yet, though. Two northern tribes, the Cimbri and Teutones, mounted a serious invasion of Gaul and Italy in 115. They raided those areas continuously until 102, when they were destroyed by a Roman army under Marius near Mte-Ste-Victoire, near Aix. Marius, later populist dictator in Rome, became a folk hero and the subject of Provençal legends ever after. Celtic-Ligurian resistance continued intermittently until 14 BC; the great monument at La Turbie, on the border of Gaul, commemorates the defeat of the last hold-outs in the Alps.

The downfall of Marseille, still the metropolis of Provence and still thoroughly Greek in culture and sympathies, came in 49 BC. Always famed for its careful diplomacy, the city made the fatal mistake of supporting Pompey over Julius Caesar in the Roman civil wars. A vengeful Caesar crippled its trade and stripped it of nearly all its colonies and dependencies. Thereafter, the influence of Marseille gave way to newer, more Romanized towns: Aix, Narbonne, Nîmes, Arles, Fréjus.

Throughout all this, Provence had been easily assimilated into the Roman economy, supplying food and raw materials for the insatiable metropolis. With Caesar's conquest of the rest of Gaul, the Rhône trade route (which had always managed to bring down a little Baltic amber and tin from Cornwall) became a busy river highway and military route. Under the good government and peace bestowed by Augustus (27 BC–14 AD) and his successors, Provence blossomed into an opulence never before seen. The cities, especially those of the Rhône valley, acquired theatres, amphitheatres for the games, aqueducts, bridges and temples. Provence participated in the political and cultural life of the Empire, even contributing one of the better emperors, Antoninus Pius (from Nîmes, 138–161 AD), only obscure because his reign was so peaceful and prosperous.

Large areas of Roman towns have been excavated at Glanum and Vaison-la-Romaine, and both have turned up a preponderance of wealthy villas. This is the dark side of Roman Provence; from the beginning of Roman rule, wealthy Romans were able to grab up much of the land, forming large estates and exploiting the indigenous population. This trend was magnified in the decadent, totalitarian and economically chaotic late Empire, when, throughout Roman territory, the few remaining free farmers were forced to sell themselves into virtual serfdom to escape crushing taxes. After 200 AD, in fact, everything was going wrong: trade and the cities stagnated while art and culture decayed; the first of the barbarian raids brought Germans into Provence in the 250s, when they destroyed Glanum.

Constantine, while yet Emperor of only the western half of the empire (312–323), often resided at Arles and favoured that city; his baths there were probably the last big Roman building project in Provence. His pro-Christian policy gave the cult its first real influence in Gaul, at least in the cities; under his auspices, the first state-sponsored Church council was held at Arles in 314. Before that Christianity does not seem to have made much of an impression (later, to make up for it elaborate mythologies were constructed to place Mary Magdalene and other early saints in Provence after the Crucifixion; cf. the towns of Stes-Maries-de-la-Mer and St-Maximin-la-Ste-Baume).

600 Years of Uninvited Guests

French historians always blame the barbarian invaders of the 5th century for destroying the cities of Provence—as if Teutonic warriors enjoyed pulling down temple colonnades on their days off. In fact, few armies passed through Provence; the Visigoths, in the early 400s, were the most notable. Though government collapsed in chaos, business went on much as usual, with the Roman landowners (and their new German colleagues) gradually making their transition to feudal nobles. Arles, untouched by the troubles, became the most important city of the west, and briefly the capital, under Constantius III in 412. The weakness of the central power brought some long-due upheavals in the countryside, with guerrilla bands and vigilante justice against the landlords. The old and new rulers soon found common cause. For a while, a clique of a hundred of the biggest landowners took over administration in Gaul, even declaring one of their own as 'emperor' in Arles (455), with the support of the Visigoths.

The Visigoths soon tired of such games, and assumed total control in 476, the year the Western Empire formally expired. They had to share it, however, with the Ostrogoths, who had established a strong kingdom in Italy and seized all of Provence east of the Rhône—the beginnings of a political boundary that would last in various forms for a thousand years. When the Eastern Empire under Justinian invaded Italy, the Franks were able to snatch the Ostrogoths' half (535). They were never able to hold it effectively, and the area gradually slipped into virtual independence.

The Visigoths kept their part, a distant zone of their Spanish kingdom, until the Arab invasion of the early 700s rolled over the Pyrenees. In 719 the Arabs took Narbonne. The next two centuries are as wonderfully confused as anything in prehistory. There is the legend of the great Spanish Caliph Abd ar-Rahman, defeated in battle and leaving a treasure buried somewhere in the Alpilles. And a document survives, in which the bishops of Agde are rebuked by the Pope for minting coins with the image of Muhammad. Charles Martel, the celebrated Frankish generalissimo who stopped the Arab wave at Poitiers, made an expedition to the southern coast in 737–39, brutally sacking Agde, Marseille, Avignon and Aix. His mission was hardly a religious crusade—rather taking advantage of the Visigothic defeat to increase Frankish hegemony in the south; the cities of Provence are recorded as petitioning the Arabs at Cordoba to help them keep the nasty Franks out.

The Arabs couldn't help; the climate was too eccentric and the pickings too slim for them to mount a serious effort in Gaul. The nascent Franks gained control everywhere, and the entire coast was absorbed by Charlemagne's father, Pépin the Short, in 759. Under Charlemagne (768–814), Occitania seems to have shared little in the Carolingian revival of trade and culture, and after the break-up of the empire (at the Treaty of Verdun in 843) its misery was complete. The 9th- and 10th-century invasions were the real Dark Age in many parts of Europe. Provence suffered constant and destructive raids by the Normans, the Arabs again, who held the Massif des Maures and St-Tropez until the 970s, and even the Hungarians, who sacked what was left of Nîmes in 924.

The Beginnings of the Middle Ages

Even in this sorry period, the foundations were being laid for recovery. Monastic reformers in Charlemagne's time, men such as Benedict of Aniane (in the Hérault) helped start a huge expansion of Church institutions. The Abbey of St-Victor in Marseille took the lead in this, founding hundreds of new monasteries around Occitania; hard-working monks reclaimed land from forests and swamps—later they sat back and enjoyed the rents, while always keeping up the holy work of education and copying books. Pilgrimages became an important activity, especially to Arles (St-Trophime) and St-Guilhem, near Aniane; getting a sleepy and locally-bound society moving again and providing an impetus to trade.

The Treaty of Verdun (see above) had confirmed the Rhône as a boundary, and politically Provence and Languedoc went their separate ways. The Kingdom of Provence (or 'Kingdom of Arles'), proclaimed by a great-grandson of Charlemagne in 879, was little more than a façade for a feudal anarchy. Though the Kingdom was united with the Kingdom of Burgundy in 949, and formally passed to the Holy Roman Empire in 1032, the tapestry of battling barons and shifting local alliances continued without effective interference from the overlords. Across the Rhône it was much the same; Frankish control was almost non-existent, and the biggest power in Languedoc was that of the County of Toulouse.

The most important result of the Carolingian collapse was the birth of a new nation in the eastern Pyrenees—Catalunya. The Catalans, who spoke a language closely related to the Occitan of Languedoc and Provence, coalesced around the County of the Cerdagne, deep in the mountains. In the 10th century this dynasty became Counts of Barcelona, and expanded their control into what is now Roussillon.

Occitan and Catalan Medieval Civilization

As elsewhere in Europe, the year 1000 is the rough milestone for the sudden and spectacular development of the medieval world. Towns and villages found the money and energy to build impressive new churches. The end of the foreign raiders made the seas safe for merchants, from Genoa, Pisa and Barcelona mostly, but also a few from Marseille. New cities were founded, notably Montpellier, in 985. In 1002, the first written document in Occitan appears. The great pilgrimage to Santiago de Compostela, in Spain, made what was left of the old Roman roads into busy highways once more; along the main southern route the first of the medieval trade fairs appeared, at the new town of St-Gilles-du-Gard.

Things were on the upswing throughout the 11th century, and the trend was given another boost by the Crusades, which began in 1095. With increased prosperity and contact with a wider world, better manners and the rudiments of personal hygiene were not slow to follow. Feudal anarchy began to look quite genteel—maintaining a delicate balance of power, with feudal ties and blood relations keeping the political appetites of rulers from ever really getting out of hand. From the more civilized east, and from nearby Muslim Spain, came new ideas, new technologies and a taste for luxury and art. As an indication of how far Occitania had come, there are the troubadours (see p. 42), with modern Europe's first lyric poetry. Almost every court of the south was refined enough to welcome and patronize them.

The growing cities began to assert themselves in the 12th century, often achieving a substantial independence in *communes* governed by consuls: Avignon in 1129, Arles in 1132, Perpignan and Nîmes in 1198. In the countryside, successive waves of monastic reform spawned a huge number of new institutions: first the movement led from Cluny, in the 11th century, and in the 12th the Cistercians, who started a score of important monasteries. Efficiently exploiting the lands bequeathed by noblemen made them rich, and also did much to improve the agricultural economy all round.

Probably the richest corner of the south was the Catalan Pyrenees; substantial iron deposits, and the most advanced methods of smelting them, provided the capital for a Catalan trading empire based in Barcelona and Perpignan. From then on Catalunya's rise was dramatic. By 1125 the Counts of Barcelona controlled much of Provence south of the Durance; in 1137 they became Kings of Aragon, which included much of western Spain as well as Roussillon. Besides its wealth, Catalunya was characterized by its unique constitution, recognizing the interests of the new middle class as well as nobles, and writing down elaborate codes of rights called *fueros* as a check on royal absolutism. The Catalan oath of allegiance to the King went like this: 'We, who are as good as you, swear to you, who are no better than we, to accept you as our king and sovereign lord, provided you observe all our liberties and laws; but if not, not.'

The other leading power in the region, Toulouse, contended with the Catalans for Provence while being overlords of all Languedoc, excepting Carcassonne and Béziers, ruled by the Trencavel family, and Narbonne, with its independent Viscounts.

The Cathars and the Rape of Languedoc

It was a great age for culture, producing not only the troubadours but an impressive display of Romanesque architecture, and original schools of sculpture in Roussillon and at Arles. Perhaps the most remarkable phenomenon of the times was a widespread religious tolerance, shared by rulers, the common people and even many among the clergy. A long and fruitful exposure to the culture of Muslim Spain, as well as the presence of a large Jewish community, an important element in the towns since Roman times, must have helped. Still, such goodwill is hard to account for in medieval Europe. Like the troubadour poetry it is an indication of just how advanced Occitan society was, at its height in the 12th century. Unfortunately, this tolerance was also to bring about the fall of the Occitan nation. Religious dissenters of various persuasions sprang up everywhere. Most of the new sects soon died out, and are little known today—like the extremist 'Petrobrusians' of St-Gilles, who didn't fancy churches, sacraments, relics or priests, and who even had their doubts about the crucifixion of Jesus.

One sect, however, made startling inroads into every sector of society in 11th- and 12th-century Languedoc—the Cathars, or Albigensians. This Manichaean doctrine (see p. 36), obsessed with Good and Evil, had in its upright simplicity a powerful attraction for industrious townspeople and peasants. In many ways it was the very picture of 17th-century English Puritanism, though without any of the Puritans' noxious belligerence towards the less perfect; this kept it in good standing with the worldly nobility, and also allowed Cathar and Catholic villagers to live peacefully side by side.

The Cathars were never a majority in any part of the south; in most places they never made up more than 10% of the population. They might have passed on as only a curious footnote to history, had they not provided the excuse for the biggest and most flagrant land grab of the Middle Ages. The 'Albigensian Crusade', arranged after the 1208 murder of a papal legate, was a cynical marriage of convenience between two old piratical enemies, the papacy and the crown of France. One wanted the religious competition stifled, the other sought to assert its old Carolingian claim to the lands of the Counts of Toulouse. Diplomacy forced King Philip Augustus to disclaim any part in the affair, but nevertheless a big army of knights from the Ile-de-France went south in 1209 to burn some heretics and snatch what they might. Their leader made the difference: too smart, too brutal and too lucky, the sort of devil that changes history—Simon de Montfort. His vicious massacres at Béziers, where the Catholic population tried to defend the heretics and were incinerated along with them inside the churches, and his taking of the impregnable fortress town of Carcassonne put the fear of God into the southerners; Montfort won battle after battle and took every town he attacked, save only Beaucaire.

In a last attempt to save their fortunes, Count Raymond VI of Toulouse and King Peter II of Aragon combined to meet the northerners. With an overwhelmingly superior force, they blundered their way to crushing defeat at the Battle of Muret in 1213. Montfort soon claimed the titles of Count of Toulouse and Viscount of Carcassonne and Béziers for himself. The Languedociens continued to resist after his death in 1218; six years later, again under the pretence of a 'crusade', King Louis VIII took the matter in his own hands. Coming south with another army he forced the annexation of all eastern Languedoc and Carcassonne, the fortress key to the Midi, in 1229. The remainder of the century saw the inexorable consolidation of French power; the building or rebuilding of gigantic fortifications, as at Carcassonne and Peyrepertuse, begun by St Louis (King Louis IX, 1226–70), and the new port of Aigues-Mortes, used by Louis as base for his two Crusades (1249 and 1270).

Four centuries after the fall of the Carolingian Empire, the French once again had their foothold in the south. Languedoc was through, its distinctive culture quickly snuffed out. If Montfort's men had been Paris' shock troops, the occupying force would be made up of French bureaucrats and monks. The monks took charge of many village churches, replacing parish priests to keep an eye on the population. The Inquisition arrived to take care of the heretics—and of course anyone the northerners found politically suspect, or whose property they coveted. The last Cathar stronghold, the Château de Quéribus, fell to royal troops in 1255. The troubadours found less and less around them worthy of a song. One of the most famous, Folquet de Marseille, had already gone over to the side of France and bigotry; as Bishop of Toulouse he became a ferocious oppressor of the few surviving Cathars.

The Turn of Provence

Provence was still free, enjoying a prosperous era under its Catalan counts though still troubled by incessant feudal struggles, waged by such local powers as the *seigneurs* of Les Baux and Forcalquier. Count Raymond Berenger V (1209–45) was usually strong enough to keep them in check; under him Provence did very well, and developed a constitutional government on the Catalan model. Provence managed to temporarily avert French aggression in a roundabout way. In 1246, Raymond Berenger's daughter and heir married Charles of Anjou—St Louis' brother. The ambitious Angevin used Provence as a springboard to create a Mediterranean empire that at its height, in the 1280s, included southern Italy and parts of Greece.

The city of Avignon and its hinterlands, the Comtat Venaissin, loyal possessions of Toulouse, had suffered greatly at the hands of Louis VIII after the Albigensian Crusade. In 1274 Charles and Louis arranged to give the Comtat to the Papacy—its discreetly delayed share of the Albigensian booty. In 1309 Pope Clement V, fleeing anarchy in Rome, installed himself at Carpentras in the Comtat. Politically, the popes found Provence a convenient new home and decided to stay—the 'Babylonian Captivity' (as jealous Italians called it) that would last over a century. They soon moved to Avignon, purchasing the city in 1348 and conducting a worldly court that seemed a Babylon indeed to many.

The late 14th century brought hard times to Provence: first the Black Death in 1348, and then political instability under the hapless Queen Jeanne (1343–82). Once more the Seigneurs of Les Baux and their imitators raged over the land, with bands of unscrupulous mercenaries (the *Grandes Compagnies*) to help them ravage town and country. The Popes returned to Rome in 1377; they kept control of Avignon and the Comtat, though French-supported Antipopes held Avignon as late as 1403. After 1434, peace had returned and Provence was ruled by Good King René (Count of Provence, and only 'king' from his claim to Sicily, in which the Angevins had been replaced by the Aragonese after the 'Sicilian Vespers' revolution of 1282). The 'Good' is equally spurious. René was open-handed to courtiers, and a patron of artists, but his futile dream of recapturing Sicily and Naples led him to wring the last penny out of everyone else.

René's successor, Charles III, lasted only a year and died without an heir (1481), bequeathing Provence to the French crown. It was intended to be a union of equals, maintaining Provençal liberties and institutions. As such, the Provençal Estates-General ratified the agreement. The French immediately went back on their word, attempting to govern through royal commissioners, but their attempts to swallow Provence whole had to wait. Louis XI and Charles XII needed a peaceful Provence as a bridge for their invasions of Italy; the region paid for this, with two destructive invasions in the 1520s and 30s by France's arch-enemy Charles V, Holy Roman Emperor and King of Spain. This era also saw a landmark in the cultural effacement of Occitania, the 1539 Edict of Villars-Cotterets that decreed French as the official language throughout the kingdom.

The Wars of Religion

Meanwhile, a big dose of the new Protestant heresy was floating down the Rhône from Calvin's Geneva. The Occitans received it more than warmly, and soon there were large Protestant communities in all the towns. Though this seems a repeat of the Cathar story, the geographical distribution is fascinating—the old Cathar areas (like the Aude), now were loyally Catholic, while the orthodox regions of the 1300s now came out strongly for the dissenters; in eastern Languedoc (the Hérault and Gard) they attracted about half the population. Tolerance was still out of fashion, and the opening round of a pointless half-century of religious wars came with the 1542 massacres in the Lubéron mountains. The perpetrator was the *Parlement* in Aix (pre-Revolution *parlements* were not parliaments, but powerful judicial bodies appointed by and responsible to the King); the victims mostly Waldensians (Vaudois), pre-Reformation heretics who had migrated to Provence before the union with France, to escape oppression there.

In the open warfare that followed across the south, there were massacres and atrocities enough on both sides. Protestants distinguished themselves by the wholesale destruction of churches and their art (as at St-Gilles); churches were often converted into fortresses, as can be seen throughout Languedoc. Henry IV's 1598 Edict of Nantes acknowledged Protestant control of certain areas (Nîmes, Montpellier, Uzès, Gignac, Clermont-l'Hérault, Aigues-Mortes, Sommières, Orange, Lourmarin). The French monarchy had been weakened by the wars, but as soon as it recovered new measures were introduced to keep the south in line. Under Cardinal Richelieu in the 1630s, the laws and traditions of local autonomy were swept away; after 1639 the Etats-Généraux of Provence was not allowed to meet until the eve of the Revolution. As insurance, scores of feudal castles (such as Beaucaire and Les Baux) were demolished to eliminate possible points of resistance.

Louis XIV's revocation of the Edict in 1685 caused more troubles. Thousands of Protestants, the south's most productive citizens, simply left; most of the community in Orange went off to colonize new lands in Prussia. Louis' long and oppressive reign continued the impoverishment of the south, despite well-intentioned economic measures by his brilliant minister Colbert: starting new manufactures (Villeneuvette, near Clermont l'Hérault); founding the port of Sète; and helping Paul Riquet build the Canal du Midi. In the 18th century, things picked up considerably in Languedoc, with the beginnings of an important textile industry—usually promoted by the remaining Protestants: silk around Nîmes and parts of Provence (where farmers gave up their bedrooms to raise the delicate silkworms in them), and linen and cotton goods in Montpellier, Carcassonne and Orange. It was a great start, though unfortunately the English and their machines would come along to ruin Languedoc's cloth trade after 1800. In Provence, the century told a miserable tale; economic stagnation, deforestation of mountain areas that has still not been entirely repaired today, and plagues: the biggest, in 1720, carried off almost half the population of Marseille. The one bright spot was the growing naval town of Toulon.

The Partitions of Catalunya

Roussillon had followed a quite different history. though the result was the same. Under Jaume I the Conqueror (1213–76), Aragon reached the height of its merchant empire, while keeping the French at bay along the castle-strewn Roussillon–Languedoc border. Before his death, Jaume decided to divide the kingdom between his two sons, leading to the brief but exotic interlude of the 'Kingdom of Majorca' and a brief golden age for Perpignan, its capital. The French tried to take advantage of the split, again shamelessly proclaiming a 'crusade' against the piously orthodox Catalans (the pope, who wanted the Aragonese out of Italy, had given his approval), but they were thrown back across the border in 1285.

Aragon was reunited in 1344, but its troubles were just beginning. After the Black Death in 1348, recessions and political strife led to a long and disastrous decline in Catalan commerce. The union of Aragon and Castile to form the Kingdom of Spain in 1492 was a disaster for the Catalans, meaning the introduction of the Inquisition, the gradual destruction of the *fueros* and a total ruin of their commerce. The long series of wars between France and Spain resulted in the ceding of Roussillon to France in 1659. Immediately, that province suffered systematic and heavy-handed Frenchification, leading to revolts in the mountain valleys that were violently suppressed. The southern angle of France's mystic hexagon was now substantially complete; Provence, Languedoc and Roussillon would continue to be treated as conquered provinces until 1981.

The Joys of Being French

There has never been a north-south discussion, on territory currently French, except in terms of kicks in the ass: invasions, police raids, financial extortion and the squeezing of brains into the form of the Hexagon.

Yves Roquette, National Secretary of the *Institut d'Etudes Occitanes*

The French Revolution was largely a Parisian affair, though southerners often played important roles (the Abbé de Sieyés and Mirabeau), while bourgeois delegates from the manufacturing towns fought along with the Girondins in the National Assembly for a respectable, liberal republic. Unfortunately, the winning Jacobin ideology was more centralist and more dedicated to destroying any taint of regional difference than the *ancien régime* had ever dreamed of being. Whatever was left of local rights and privileges was soon decreed out of existence, and when the Revolution divided France into homogenous departments in 1790, terms like 'Provence' and 'Languedoc' ceased to have any political meaning.

In 1792 volunteers from Marseille had brought the *Marseillaise* to Paris, while local mobs wrecked and looted hundreds of southern churches and châteaux. Soon, however, the betrayed south became violently counter-revolutionary. Incidents occurred like the one in the village of Bédoin, near Carpentras, in 1793; when someone cut down the 'liberty tree', French soldiers burned the town and shot 63 villagers to 'set an example'. The Catalans raised regiments of volunteers against the Revolution. The royalists and the English occupied Toulon after a popular revolt, and were only dislodged by the brilliant tactics of a young commander named Bonaparte in 1793.

The south managed little enthusiasm for Napoleon or his wars. The Emperor called the Provençaux cowards, and said theirs was the only part of France that never gave him a decent regiment. Today the tourist offices promote the 'Route Napoléonienne', where Napoleon passed through from Elba in 1815 to start the Hundred Days—but at the time he had to sneak along those roads in an Austrian uniform, to protect himself from the Provençaux.

After Waterloo, the restored monarchy started off with a grisly White Terror in Nîmes and elsewhere. After the Revolution of 1830, the 'July Monarchy' of King Louis Philippe brought significant changes. The old industrious, Protestant strain of the south finally got its chance with a Protestant Prime Minister from Nîmes, François Guizot (1840–48); his liberal policies and his slogan—*enrichissez-vous!*—opened an age where there would be a little Protestant in every Frenchman. Guizot's countrymen were rapidly demanding more; radicalism and anti-clericalism (except in the lower Rhône and Vaucluse) increased throughout the century.

Southerners supported the Revolution of 1848 and the Second Republic, and many areas, especially in the Provençal Alps, put up armed resistance to Louis Napoleon's 1851 coup. Under the Second Empire (1852–70), France picked up yet another territory: Nice and its hinterlands (now the *département* of Alpes-Maritimes), with a mixed population of Provençaux and Italians. This was the price exacted by Napoleon III in 1860 for French aid to Vittorio Emanuele II in Italy's War of Independence.

Oppression and Resistance

The second half of the century saw the beginnings of a national revival in Occitania. In Provence it was all cultural and apolitical: a linguistic and literary revival bound up with Nobel Prize-winning poet Frédéric Mistral and the cultural group called the *Félibrige* (see p. 39), founded in 1854. In Languedoc it was all political and unconcerned with culture, focusing on the first of modern France's agricultural movements. Markets since the 1800s had encouraged Languedoc to become one vast vineyard. Phylloxera hit in 1875, but the quick recovery favoured the biggest producers who could afford the new American stocks. A huge wine boom in the 1880s was followed by an even huger bust; with competition from Algeria and Italy, prices by 1904 dropped to one-third of their 1890 levels. In 1907 the farmers went on the warpath, led by a charismatic café-keeper from the Aude named Marcellin Albert. Monster meetings in Narbonne and Montpellier attracted over 100,000 each; Paris sent troops to occupy the region, but some of the conscript regiments came close to mutiny. Finallly Albert was tricked into calling off a general strike by leftist Prime Minister Clemenceau. The movement dwindled, but farmers devoted their attention to building a strong cooperative system and keeping the political pressure on by more orthodox means; French politics would never be quite the same.

To counter these advances, the post-1870 Third Republic pursued French cultural oppression to its wildest extremes. History was re-written to make Occitania and Roussillon seem eternal parts of the 'French nation.' The Occitan languages were lyingly derided as mere *patois*, bastard 'dialects' of French; children were punished for speaking their own language in school, a practice that lasted until the 1970s. Roussillon was not even permitted political participation—the government and parties arranged to have outsiders stand for its seats in the National Assembly.

After 1910, economic factors conspired to defeat both the political and cultural aspirations of the Midi; rural depopulation, caused by the breakup of the pre-industrial agricultural society, drained the life out of the villages—and decreased the percentage of people who spoke the native languages. World War I decimated a generation—go into any village church in the south and look at the war memorial plaques; from a total population of a few hundred, you'll see maybe 30 names of villagers who died for the 'Glory of France'. By 1950, most villages had lost at least half their population; some died out altogether.

After the French débâcle of 1940, the south found itself under the Vichy government. German occupation came in November 1942, after the American landings in North Africa, provoking the scuttling of the French fleet in Toulon to keep it out of German hands. After 1942, the Resistance was active and effective in the Provençal Alps, the Vaucluse and the Catalan Pyrenees—not to mention Marseille, where the Germans felt constrained to blow up the entire Vieux Port area. Liberation began two months after D-Day, in August 1944. American and French troops hit the beaches around St Tropez, and in a remarkably successful (and little-noticed) operation they had most of Provence liberated in two weeks. In the rugged mountains behind Nice, some bypassed German outposts held out until the end of the war.

The California of Europe

The post-war era was all sweetness and ice-cream and reinforced concrete, a series of increasingly passionless snapshots: the Côte d'Azur become a myth of the masses— Grace Kelly with Cary Grant in *To Catch a Thief*, later with Rainier the Third in *Monaco*; socialist Languedoc farmers on a demonstration, wondering why someone couldn't sell all the goddamned wine they grow; grey and effective political machine bosses like Gaston Defferre of Marseille (socialist), or Jacques Médecin of Nice (gastronome-fascist); Paris bureaucrats expounding the glories of the Durance hydro-electrical scheme, meant to make Provence the Ruhr Valley of Tomorrow.

The changes have in fact been momentous. The overdeveloped, ever more schizo-phrenic Côte d'Azur has become the heart of Provence—the tail that wags the dog. Besides its resorts it has the likes of IBM and the techno-paradise of Sophia-Antipolis. Above all, the self-proclaimed 'California of Europe' has money, and will acquire more; in two or three decades it will be the first province in centuries to start telling Paris where to get off. Meanwhile, the increasingly posh Vaucluse has the highest rural crime and suicide rates in France. Those Languedoc farmers have learned their lesson; they make less wine, and much better. Their region, which stopped losing population about 1955, is changing fast. A typically French planning effort of 1968 has made its coastline into a growing tourist region, with new resorts like Cap d'Agde and La Grande Motte. Montpellier, under its dynamic mayor Georges Frêche, strives to become the futuristic metropolis of the Midi; jealous Nîmes bestirs itself to keep pace.

The greatest political event has been the election of the Socialist Mitterrand govern-ment in 1981, followed by the creation of regional governments across France. Though their powers and budgets are extremely limited, this represents a major turning point, the first reversal of a thousand years of increasing Parisian centralism. Its lasting effects will not be known for decades, perhaps centuries; already the revival of Occitan language and culture is resuming; indicators include such things as new school courses in the language, and some towns and villages changing the street signs to Languedocien, Provençal or Catalan. Roussillon is just beginning to feel the great upsurge of Catalan culture that began after the restoration of democracy in Spain.

Politics, quietly Socialist in most of the south, can still be primeval in Provence. Jean-Marie Le Pen and his tawdry pack of adolescent bigots find their biggest following here, riding a wave of resentment against immigrants (200,000 North Africans since 1945—but this is a Provençal tradition; there were anti-Italian pogroms in Marseille, Aigues-Mortes and other towns in the 1870s). At the time of writing Le Pen is engaged in a battle for Provence's soul, an electoral contest with a liberal Marseille industrialist, Bernard Tapie, for control of the Provence-Côte d'Azur regional government. The results will be in by the time you read this, and maybe they will offer some clues to the future.

Art and Architecture, and Where to Find It

Great art and architecture in the south coincides neatly with its three periods of prosperity: the Roman, the Middle Ages, and the mid-19th and early 20th centuries, when railways opened up the coast not only to aristocrats, but to artists as well.

Prehistoric

Early dwellers on the Riviera made the lumpy fertility goddesses, sea-shell bonnets and necklaces on display at the prehistory museums of **Monaco, Nice,** and **Menton.** Their Neolithic descendants left few but tantalizing traces of their passing: dolmens and a few menhirs (especially in the Hérault and Gard) and a tomb-temple complex at **Castellet** near Arles. **Cambous,** north of Montpellier, has a reconstructed communal Neolithic house, with low walls and a thatched roof that resembles the traditional cowboy dwellings (*cabanes des gardians*) in the Camargue. The first shepherds may well have put up the dry-stone, corbel-roofed huts called *bories*, rebuilt since countless times and still a feature of the landscape (especially at the 18th-century '*village des bories*' outside **Gordes**).

In the Iron Age (1800–1500 BC), the Ligurians or their predecessors covered the **Vallée des Merveilles** under Mont Bégo with extraordinary rock incisions of warriors, bulls, masked figures and inexplicable symbols. In a similar style are the statue-steles— menhirs with faces—found in Tuscany and Corsica as well as around **Nîmes** (in the Musée de la Préhistoire) and at **St-Pons** in the Espinouse mountains of Hérault.

Celto–Ligurian: 8th–3rd Centuries BC

The arrival of the Celts around 800 BC coincided with an increase in trade; Greek, Etruscan and Celtic influences can be seen in the artefacts of this age (as at the Oppidum of Ensérune near Béziers). The Celts had talents for jewellery and ironwork—and a bizarre habit of decapitating enemies and making images of the heads (atavistically surviving in the little grotesque heads that pop up all over Romanesque buildings).

The best of the originals are in the archaeology museum in **Nîmes**, in the Musée Granet in **Aix**, the Musée d'Archéologie Méditerranée in **Marseille** and in the Lapidary Museum of **Avignon**.

Gallo-Roman: 3rd Century BC–4th Century AD

Archaeologically the Greeks are the big disappointment of Provence—the only remains of their towns are bits of wall at **Marseille** and at **St-Blaise** on the Etang de Berre. But what the Romans left behind in their beloved *Provincia* makes up for the Greek: the **Pont du Gard**; the theatre of **Orange**, with the only intact stage building in the West; the Maison Carrée and amphitheatre at **Nîmes**; the amphitheatre and cryptoporticus in **Arles**; the elegant 'Antiques' of **St-Rémy**; the Pont Flavien at **St-Chamas**; the trophy at **La Turbie**; the excavated towns at **Vaison-la-Romaine** and **Glanum** (St-Rémy). Thanks to the Celts, Provence was the one province of the Western Roman empire that developed a definite style of its own, characterized by vigorous, barbaric reliefs emboldened by deeply incised outlines. Battle scenes were the most popular subject, or shields and trophies arranged in the exotic, uncouth style you see on the triumphal arches of **Orange** and **Carpentras**, or in the Musée de l'Art Païen (Museum of Pagan Art) in **Arles**. Roman landowners lived in two-storey stone houses, with their farm buildings forming an enclosed rectangular courtyard known as a *mansio*, the ancestor of the modern Provençal farmhouse, the *mas*.

Early Christian and Dark Ages: 5th–10th Centuries

Very few places had the resources to create any art at all during this period; the meagre attempts were nearly always rebuilt later. The oldest Christian relics are a remarkable sarcophagus from the 2nd century in **Brignoles**, and a large collection of 4th-century sarcophagi in the Musée d'Art Chrétien, at **Arles**, both close to Roman pagan models. Octagonal baptistries from the 5th and 6th centuries survive in **Fréjus**, **Aix**, **Riez** and **Six-Fours-les-Plages**, which also has an 8th-century Syrian-style church. Many church crypts are really the foundations of original Dark Age churches, and fragments of Merovingian-era reliefs will often be found set in a later church's wall.

Romanesque: 11th–14th Centuries

When good times returned in the 11th century, people began to build again, inspired by the ancient buildings they saw around them. There is not only a great stylistic continuity from Roman to Romanesque (rounded arches, barrel vaults, rounded apses), but also in the vigorous Celtic-inspired decoration of Roman Provence. The south has four distinct varieties of Romanesque: Provençal, Lombard, Languedocien, and Catalan, although the terms must be applied loosely; the enduring charm of Romanesque is in its very lack of restrictions and codes, giving architects the freedom to improvise and solve problems in highly original and sophisticated ways. Although parish and monastic churches were usually in the basilican form (invented for Roman law courts, and used in Rome's first churches), masons also created extremely esoteric works, often built as funeral chapels in pre-Christian holy sites: **Notre-Dame-de-Grosseau** and **Montmajour** are two in

Provence, and in Languedoc, there's an even odder seven-sided church at **Rieux Minervois** and a triangular one at **Planès** in the Pyrenees.

Of the four styles, the Provençal is the most austere and heaviest, characterized by simple floor plans, thick-set proportions, few if any windows, minimal if any decoration, and façades that are often blank. Churches that could double as fortresses were built along the pirate-plagued coast in the 11th and 12th century: St-Honorat in the **Iles-Lérins**, and the church of **Stes-Maries-de-la-Mer**. In the mid-12th-century, the Cistercians founded three important new abbeys in a sombre and austere style, the 'Three Sisters': **Le Thoronet, Sénanque**, and **Silvacane**. An octagonal dome at the transept crossing is a common feature of more elaborate churches, especially **Avignon** cathedral, the Ancienne-Major in **Marseille, Vaison-la-Romaine, Le Thor** and **Carpentras** (the ruined original). The finest of the few paintings that survive from this epoque is the 13th-century fresco cycle at the Tour Ferrande, in **Pernes-Les-Fontaines. Ganagobie** has the only floor mosaics from the period, as well as good sculpture.

In general, churches in the Rhône valley are more ornate, thanks to a talented group of sculptors known as the school of Arles. The wealth of ruins inspired them to adapt Roman forms and decorations to the new religion, complete with triumphal arches, gabled pediments, and Corinthian columns. The saints on the façade of St-Trophime in **Arles** seem direct descendants of Gallo-Roman warriors. Arlésien artists also created the remarkable façade of **St-Gilles du Gard**, portraying the New Testament—the true dogma in stone for all to see, perhaps meant as a refutation of the Cathar and other current heresies. Yet other Romanesque sculpture in the area, as at **Vaison-le-Romaine**, seems nothing but heretical.

As you move west into Languedoc, Romanesque becomes more decorative and fanciful, befitting the land of troubadours (**St-Martin-de-Londres** and the frescoed **Chapelle de Centeille** in the Minervois). Even when the austere Cistercians built here, as at **Fontfroide**, the mood is much less sombre. Itinerant Lombard masons in the 12th century built Italian Romanesque churches, characterized by blind arcading and bands of decorative stonework, especially around the apse (as at **St-Guilhem-le-Désert**). The Lombard campanile, pierced with patterns of windows, was adapted by the Catalans, especially in the Pyrenees (**Elne**). But **Uzès** has something even rarer in its Tour Fenestrelle: a round, arcaded six-storey campanile, typical of Byzantine Italy.

Along with the Arles craftsmen, the Catalans produced the finest medieval sculpture in the south, with the school of sculptors at the magnificent 11th-century abbey of **St-Michel-de-Cuxa**. Their work is characterized by precise and fanciful detail, arabesques and floral patterns, supremely elegant without the classicizing of the Arles school; more of their best sculpture may be seen at **Serrabonne** and **Elne**, the most beautiful cloister in the Midi. Catalunya also produced the vigorous and original Master of Cabestany, who in the early 12th century even went to Tuscany to teach the Italians how to sculpt. His best works in France are the tympanum at **Cabestany**, at **St Papoul**, near Castelnaudary, and the sculpture at **Rieux Minervois**. Catalans could paint, too; there are rare medieval frescoes at **St-Martin-de-Fenollar** south of Perpignan

Although examples of medieval palaces still stand in **Brignoles, St-Gilles**, and **Villemagne** in the Hérault, the greatest secular architecture of the period is military, often done with surprising originality. The vertiginous castle of **Peyrepertuse** is only the most enormous example of the scores of imposing works around the Languedoc and Roussillon border—one of the very best regions in Europe for castles. St Louis built the walls and towers of **Carcassonne** in a romantic fairy-tale style that has few equals, while the king's other project, **Aigues-Mortes** (1270s) is a grid-planned, square and functional modern town encased in a perfect set of walls.

Gothic and Early Renaissance: 14th and 15th Centuries

Although Gothic elements first appear in Provence in 1150 (the façade of St-Victor in **Marseille**) and in Languedoc around 1250 in the **Abbaye St-Martin-du-Vignogoul**, ogival vaulting and pointy arches belonged to a foreign, northern style that failed to touch southern hearts. Builders stuck to their Romanesque guns longer than anyone in France, and when Gothic made its final triumph it was usually a pale reflection of the soaring cathedrals of the Ile-de-France. The exceptions were built by northerners after the French conquest: the cathedrals of **Béziers**, **Carcassonne** and especially **Narbonne**, an unfinished, spectacular work that is the third-tallest Gothic church in France.

Gothic also found a home in **Avignon**, when the 14th-century popes summoned architects from the north to design the flamboyant Papal Palace, St-Pierre, the Convent des Célestines and St-Didier (other isolated examples are the **Abbaye de Valmagne** near Sète, the basilica of **St-Maximin-la-Ste-Baume**, and **Clermont-l'Hérault**). The Catalans, as ever marching to a different drummer, developed their own brand of Gothic, where width and strength counted more than height. The master of the genre, Guillermo Sagrera, designed **Perpignan**'s cathedral and the complex vaulting in its Salle Capitulaire (his best work is in Spain, at Palma de Mallorca).

Painting in the south of France took a giant leap forward when the papal court in Avignon attracted some of Italy's finest *trecento* artists, especially Simone Martini of Siena and Matteo Giovanetti of Viterbo, whose frescoes inspired the graceful fairy-tale style known as International Gothic (see **Avignon** and its Petit Palais museum). A new local style developed from International Gothic, and from the precise style of the Flemish painters favoured by the last popes: the early 15th-century *School of Avignon*. The school's greatest masters were from the north: the exquisite Enguerrand Quarton (*c.* 1415–66) from Laon (**Villeneuve-lès-Avignon**), and Nicolas Froment (Cathedral, **Aix**); also see Aix's church of the Madeleine and the Petit Palais museum in **Avignon**. King René, the great patron of the artists, built himself a fine chivalric castle in **Tarascon** and had a hand in the evolution of French sculpture when he invited the Italian Renaissance master Francesco Laurana to Provence (see artists' directory, below).

At the same time the *School of Nice*, led by the prolific Ludovico Brea, produced scores of altarpieces typical of northern Italian provincial styles—charming and luminous, if a good hundred years behind the Renaissance revolution going on in Tuscany. The Brea gang had some stiff competition in the early 15th century from a pair of little known Piedmontese painters, Giovanni Canavesio and Giovanni Baleison, who would be much better known had they left their charming pastel fresco cycles in less remote churches (**Notre-Dame-des-Fontaines** in the Roya Valley, others in the nearby valleys of the Vésubie and Tinée).

High Renaissance: Late 15th and 16th Centuries

Despite its promising start, subjugation by the French and the Wars of Religion made the Renaissance a non-event in Occitania. The few buildings of the day are imitative, mostly of the heavy, classicizing Roman style, as in the palace of the Cardinal Legate in **Avignon**. The best Renaissance building, the once delightful **Château La Tour d'Aigue** in the Lubéron is only a burnt-out shell. **Narbonne** has some exquisite Flemish Renaissance tapestries. Locally, the best work of this period is minute—in the carved wooden doors and choir stalls in **Vence, Bar-sur-Loup** and **Fréjus**.

The Age of Bad Taste: 17th-18th Centuries

The French prefer to call this their *époque classique* and even in the poor, benighted south admittedly many fine things were done. Towns laid out elegant squares, fountains and promenades (**Pernes-les-Fontaines, Aix, Barjols**); trees were planted on a grand scale, on market squares, along the Canal du Midi, and on the roads, especially in the western Aude, crossed with 18th-century avenues of plane trees. **Montpellier** and **Moustiers** have collections from their thriving faïence industries of the day (as does **Narbonne's** art museum and **Marseille's** Musée Cantini). Southerners went ape for organs, gargantuan works sheathed in ornate carved wood. The mother of them all is in **Narbonne** Cathedral; others adorn the churches in **Béziers** and **Uzès**.

But nearly everything else is all wrong. People took the lovely churches left to them by their ancestors and tricked them out like cat-houses in pink and purple and tinkered so much with the architecture that it's often difficult to tell the real age of anything. Aix, the capital of Provence and self-proclaimed arbiter of taste, knocked over its magnificently preserved Roman mausoleum and medieval palace of the counts of Provence just before the Revolution. The 17th- and 18th-century palaces of **Aix, Pézenas** and **Montpellier**, while lending a distinctive urbanity and ostentation to these cities, are rarely first-rate works of architecture in their own right, but rather eclectic jumbles with touches from Gothic, Renaissance, and Baroque style-books. The one great sculptor and architect the south produced in the period, Pierre Puget, suffered the usual fate of a prophet in his own land (Vieille Charité, **Marseille**). In painting, the south produced two virtuoso court painters, Hyacinthe Rigaud and Fragonard, whose portrayals of happily spoiled, rosy-cheeked aristocrats hide the side of their personalities that provoked the Revolution. The most sincere paintings of the age are the naive ex votos in many churches (some of the best are from sailors, as at Notre-Dame-de-la-Garde, in **Marseille**, in **Notre-Dame-de-Bon-Port** at **Cap d'Antibes** and Notre-Dames-des-Auzils, near **Gruissan**).

One architect who (unlike Puget) never lacked for work was Louis XIV's Maréchal Sébastien Vauban, whose forts and fortress-towns crop up everywhere; **Villefranche-de-Conflent** is a perfectly preserved example of 17th-century urban design. The next generation after Vauban produced the streamlined, modern Baroque fortresses near the Spanish border around **Collioure**. The best Baroque churches are Italian: St-Michel in **Menton** and the Chapelle de la Miséricorde in **Nice**.

France's Little Ice Age: Late 18th–mid 19th Centuries

If the last era lacked vision, taste in the neoclassical/Napoleonic era had all the charm of embalming fluid. The Revolution destroyed more than it built; the wanton devastation of the region's greatest Romanesque art (begun in the Wars of Religion) was a loss matched only by the mania for selling it off in the next century to the Americans. The greatest monuments of the Napoleonic era include the cold, funereal Musée Masséna in **Nice** and the paintings in many museums by David, Ingres, and Hubert Robert, the latter of whom specialized in scenes of melancholy Roman ruins in Provence and Italy, capturing the taste of the day (it was also a great age for cemeteries).

For the first time, however, there was a reaction to purposeful destruction of the past. Ruskin's contemporary, Viollet-le-Duc (1814–79), restored architecture, rather than just wrote about it (the walls of **Carcassonne** and **Avignon**, and the archbishop's palace of **Narbonne**). Thanks to the Suez Canal, **Marseille** suddenly had money to burn and tried to revive the past in its own way, with monstrous neo-Byzantine basilicas and the overripe Baroque Palais Longchamps.

Revolutions in Seeing: 1850–1939

A lady once came to see Matisse's paintings and was horrified to see a woman with a green face. 'Wouldn't it be horrible to see a woman walking down the street with a green face?' she asked him. 'It certainly would!' Matisse agreed. 'Thank God it's only a painting!'

In the 1850 Paris Salon, hanging amongst the stilted historical, religious, and mythological academic paintings were three large canvases of everyday, contemporary scenes by Gustav Courbet. Today it's hard to imagine how audacious his contemporaries found Courbet's new style, which came to be called Realism—almost as if it took the invention of photography by Louis Daguerre (1837) to make the eye see what was 'really' there. 'Do what you see, what you want, what you feel,' was Courbet's proto-hippy advice to his pupils. One thing he felt like doing was painting in the south, where his art revelled in the bright colour and light (especially his *Bonjour, Monsieur Courbet* of 1854 in **Montpellier**'s Musée Fabre). Courbet's visit was a major influence on the 19th-century painters of Provence, especially Paul Guigou and Frédéric Bazille, who painted Realist subjects drenched in southern sunlight. In the 1860s, as physicists made new discoveries in the field of optics, learning that colour derives from light, not form, the Impressionists made it their goal to strip Courbet's new-found visual reality of all subjectivity and to simply record on canvas the atmosphere, light, and colour the eye saw, all according to the latest scientific theories. Although many of the great Impressionists spent time in the south, only the sensuous Renoir moved down permanently, and then only on doctor's orders (to **Cagnes-sur-Mer**, in 1895).

The crucial role the south was to play in modern art dates from the 1880s, thanks to the careers of the two painters most closely associated with Provence today, Vincent Van Gogh and Paul Cézanne. Van Gogh, one the greatest innovators in art history, was influenced by the Impressionists and Japanese prints in Paris, but the most astonishing revolution in his art occurred when he moved to Arles in 1888, where he responded to the heightened colour and light on such an intense, personal level that colour came less and less to represent form in his art (as it did for the Impressionists), but instead took on a symbolic value, as the only medium Van Gogh found powerful enough to express his extraordinary moods and visions.

This revolutionary independence of colour from form was taken to an extreme by a group of painters that the critic Louis Vauxcelles nicknamed the Fauves ('wild beasts') for the violence of their colours. The Fauves used colour to express moods and rhythms to the detriment of detail and recognizable subject matter. As a movement the Fauves lasted from 1904 until 1908, but in those few years revolutionized centuries of European art. 'Fauve painting is not everything,' Matisse explained. 'But it is the foundation of everything.' Nearly all the Fauves—André Derain, Matisse, Maurice Vlaminck, Raoul Dufy, Kees Von Dongen—painted in St-Tropez as guests of the hospitable painter Paul Signac, and at La Ciotat, Cassis, L'Estaque, and Collioure. The results paved the way for Expressionism, Cubism, and Abstraction—avenues few of the Fauvists themselves ever explored. For after 1908 the collective new vision these young men had shared in the south of France vanished as if they had awoken from a mass hypnosis; all went their separate ways, leaving others to carry their ideas on to their logical conclusions. The Musée de l'Annonciade in **St-Tropez** has the best collection of Fauvist painting in the south, although anyone lucky enough to have attended the Royal Academy's Fauve exhibition in 1991 will know that two-thirds of the greatest Fauves are hidden in private collections.

Cézanne's innovations were as important as Van Gogh's, although his response to Provence was analytical rather than emotional, perhaps because he was born in the south. Loosely associated with the Impressionists in the 1860s and 1870s, Cézanne stood apart; his interest was not so much in depicting what he saw, but in the contradiction between the eye and mind, between the permanence of nature and the ephemeral qualities of light and movement. 'Nature is always the same, but none of it lasts beyond what we perceive', he wrote, and by the 1880s he had undertaken his stated task of 'making Impressionism solid and enduring, like the art of the museums', exploring underlying volumes, planes and structure, not through perspective, but through amazingly subtle variations of colour. In 1908, Georges Braque and the Fauvist Dufy went to paint together at L'Estaque in homage to Cézanne. The beginnings of the prismatic splitting of forms are in their respective works, and when the same critic Vauxcelles saw Braque's paintings, he came up with a new name: Cubism. In 1912 Braque and Picasso worked together in Sorgues, near Avignon, and produced canvases that verge on abstraction. Matisse, one of the Fauves who settled permanently in Provence, kept apart from subsequent schools, and was the most important among hundreds of artists who now flocked to the south. Even Picasso, another lone genius who moved permanently to Provence after World War II and to whom modesty was a stranger, acknowledged Matisse as his equal, and in many ways his master.

In architecture, this was the opulent age of the Côte d'Azur's Belle Epoque confections, its Russian Orthodox cathedrals, grand hotels, villas, and casinos, all done in a lavish, imaginative holiday spirit that often trod lightheartedly over contemporary rules of good taste and decorum. Only a few buildings survive, which, along with old photographs, give a hint of what **Nice**, **Cannes**, **Monaco** and **Menton** looked like at the turn of the century. The Moorish, Bengali, Norman, Tuscan and troubadour follies that went up (nearly all built by extravagant foreigners) caused outrage when they were built and are sorely missed now that all but a handful have been demolished.

Post-war

After the war, artists from many lands continued to pour into the hill villages of Provence: Bonnard, Léger, Chagall, Nicholas de Staël, Max Ernst, André Masson, Vasarély to name only the most prominent. The 1960s saw a reaction to the often precious art world in the 'second' School of Nice, led by often amusing multi-media iconoclasts like César, Arman and Ben, all displayed in a spanking new contemporary art museum in **Nice**, one of several giant projects built by the ambitious mayors of the south—led by Georges Frêche, the human dynamo who runs **Montpellier**. The most influential post-war building in the south has been Le Corbusier's *Unité d'Habitation* in **Marseille** (1952); if you don't care for warmed-over Bauhaus on stilts, there's the futuristic planned resort of **La Grande Motte** in Languedoc, begun in 1968 as the first post-modernist building ensemble in the south. The most artful, delightful building in recent years is the Catalan architect José-Luis Sert's Fondation Maeght, in **St-Paul-de-Vence**.

Artists' Directory

Bazille, Frédéric (1841–70). A native of Montpellier, who linked up with Monet in Paris in 1862 and with him was the first to paint the human figure and even nudes out of doors, inspired by the spontaneity of photography. His career was cut short in the Franco-Prussian war of 1870 (Musée Fabre, **Montpellier**).

Bonnard, Pierre (1867–1947). Although his early career is closely associated with the Nabis (a group of painters who rejected naturalism and natural colour), Bonnard changed gear in 1900 to become one of the 20th century's chief impressionists, painting colour-saturated landscapes and domestic scenes, after 1939 around his villa in Le Cannet, near Cannes (**Bagnols-sur-Cèze**, Musée de l'Annonciade, **St-Tropez**).

Braque, Georges (1882–1963). One of Cubism's founding fathers, Braque worked so closely with Picasso (in Céret in 1911, in Borgues in 1912, and elsewhere) that their early works are practically indistinguishable (Musée de l'Annonciade, **St-Tropez**).

Brea, Ludovico (active 1475–1544). Leader of the International Gothic Nice School, influenced by the Renaissance in his later career; although commissioned to do hieratical medieval-style subjects, his precise line and beautiful sense of light and shadow stand out—still, to call him the 'Fra Angelico of Provence' like some French critics is going too far. He invented a shade of wine-red French artists still call *rouge brea* (Franciscan church in Cimiez, **Nice**; Palais Carnolès, **Menton**; **Lucéram**, and **Monaco** cathedral).

Canavesio, Giovanni (*c.* 1425–1500). Of Piedmont, collaborated with **Giovanni Baleison** to paint the finest Renaissance frescoes in Provence; the style is typical of North Italian early Renaissance, colourful and precise, without much of the intellectuality of Tuscan painting (**Notre-Dame-des-Fontaines**, near La Brigue, retables at **Lucéram** and many chapels in the Valleys of the Vésubie and Tinée).

Cézanne, Paul (1839–1906). Born and died in Aix-en-Provence, where fellow schooolmate Emile Zola was his best friend, until Zola published his autobiographical

L'Oeuvre that thinly disguised Cézanne as the failed painter Lantier. Cézanne's painting went through several distinct periods: a sombre romantic stage (1861–71); an Impressionistic manner, inspired by Pisarro (1872–82); a period of synthesis (1883–95), combining elements of Impressionism with an interest in volume, surface planes, and the desire to represent perspective by colour only; and lastly, his lyric period (1896–1906), where singing rhythms of colour and form are intellectually supported by the basic tenets of Cubism, splitting the planes and volumes into prisms, expressing the tension between seeing and knowing (Musée Granet, **Aix**).

Chagall, Marc (1887–1985). Highly indvidualistic and spiritual painter and illustrator who drew many themes from Jewish-Russian folklore and the Old Testament; he spent his last years in Vence (Musée National Message Biblique Marc Chagall, **Nice**; Maeght Foundation, **St-Paul-de-Vence**).

Cocteau, Jean (1889–1963). Writer, surrealist film director, and illustrator, who painted pastel mural decorations in a number of chapels and town halls in the south (Mairie and Museum, in **Menton**; Chapelle de St-Pierre, **Villefranche-sur-Mer**).

Corot, Jean Baptiste Camille (1796–1875). Landscape painter of ineffable charm, made the typical French sojourn in Rome to discover the calm and tranquillity of classical landscapes; in his smaller, spontaneous sketches and private portraits his modern techniques make him a precusor of the Impressionists; painted with Ziem in Martigues (Musée Calvet, **Avignon**; Musée des Beaux-Arts, **Marseille**).

Courbet, Gustave (1819–77). High prince of the 19th-century Realist school, and a keen student of luminosity in nature. His journey to Montpellier in 1854 brought about a considerable lightening of his palette; his seacapes are awash in atmosphere, and his studies of skies, light, and shadows inspired Monet and Bazille (Musée Fabre, **Montpellier**; Musée des Beaux Arts, **Marseille**).

Daumier, Honoré (1808–79). Born in Marseille, began his career as a political caricaturist (occasionally jailed) for a magazine. But Daumier was also a highly original pre-expressionist painter in the Goya mould, best known for his hypnotic, violently-lit scenes based on the inherent tragedy of the human condition—a precursor of Toulouse-Lautrec, Degas, and Picasso (Musée des Beaux Arts, **Marseille**).

David, Jacques-Louis (1748–1825). Napoleon's favourite neoclassical painter, as cold and perfect as ice, portrayed the Frenchies of his day in kitsch-Roman heroic attitudes and costumes (Musée Granet, **Aix**; Musée Fabre, **Montpellier**; Musée Calvet, **Avignon**).

Delacroix, Eugène (1798–1863). Had little truck with the neoclassicism of David, and instead based his art on the chromatics and lighting of Constable. 'In painting, all is reflection' he said; many of his landscapes and North African watercolours presaged Impressionism (Musée Fabre, **Montpellier**).

Derain, André (1880–1954). Along with Vlaminck, key Fauvist painter of extraordinary innovation and originality, who took Fauvism and Expressionism to the limit before World War I (Musée de l'Annonciade, **St-Tropez**).

Dufy, Raoul (1877–1953). Dufy's most original and energetic painting was as a Fauve. After flirting with Cubism with Georges Braque in L'Estaque, his style took on its characteristic graphic quality, and he spent much of his remaining life in Nice, painting pleasing lightweight decorative interiors (Musée Dufy, **Nice**).

Fragonard, Jean Honoré (1732–1806). Native of Grasse and student of Boucher, Fragonard painted frivolous rococo scenes in anaemic pastels but with a verve and erotic wit that found favour with France's spiritually bankrupt nobility, who longed to escape into his canvases (Villa-Musée Fragonard, **Grasse**).

Granet, François Marius (1775–1849). Native of Aix and a pupil of David; although his canvases are run-of-the-mill academic, his watercolours and sketches reveal a poetic observation of nature that became the hallmark of the Provençal school (Musée Granet, **Aix**; Musée d'Art et d'Histoire, **Grasse**).

Guigou, Paul (1834–71). Landscape painter born in Villars, in the Vaucluse. Influenced by Corot's landscapes, Guigou sought out the most arid parts of Provence, especially the banks of the Durance, for his subjects, illuminating them with scintillating light and colour. Unable to make a living in the south, he took teaching jobs in the north, where he died at age 37, just as his career began to take off (Musée des Beaux Arts, **Marseille**; Musée Granet, **Aix**).

Ingres, Jean Auguste Dominique (1780–1867). As the most important neoclassical pupil of David, Ingres was acclaimed the master of official academic art, where he was capable of producing enormous mythological howlers. In his more appealing intimate subjects, especially his female nudes, he distorted proportions to achieve a sinuous eroticism and line that inspired Picasso, among other artists (Musée Granet, **Aix**; Musée Fabre, **Montpellier**).

Laurana, Francesco (*c.* 1430–1502). Itinerant Istrian sculptor trained in Tuscany, best known for his vivid, realistic style (St-Didier, **Avignon**; Ancienne Major, **Marseille**; Cathedral, **Aix**).

Léger, Fernand (1881–1955). Went from an early figurative manner to Cubism. Wounded in World War I, Léger attempted to create an art that interpreted the experiences of ordinary people in war, work and play, culminating in his colourful, geometric highly-stylized figures of workers and factories. He worked in many media, especially mosaics and ceramics (Musée National Fernand Léger, **Biot**; Fondation Maeght, **St-Paul-de-Vence**).

Maillol, Aristide (1861–1944). Sculptor from Banyuls who spent much of his career in Paris, though he never forgot his hometown, returning each summer to model female nudes on the pulchritude of the local nymphets (Hôtel de Ville, **Perpignan**, war memorials in **Banyuls** and **Céret**; Musée de l'Annonciade, **St-Tropez**).

Matisse, Henri (1869–1954). A trip to the south in the 1890s converted Matisse to the vivid colours that are a hallmark of his work. After he became one of the leading Fauves, the hot colours of the south continued to saturate his ever sensuous, serene, and boldly drawn works, qualities apparent even in the paper cut-outs of his last bedridden years. After 1917 he settled in Nice (Musée Matisse, **Nice**; Chapel of the Rosary, **Vence**; Musée de l'Annociade, **St-Tropez**).

Monticelli, Adolphe (1824–86). A native of Marseille, a student of Ziem and one of Van Gogh's great inspirations. Obsessed with light ('La lumière, c'est le ténor' he claimed), he conveyed its effects with pure unmixed colour applied with hard brushes;

subjects dissolve into strokes and blobs of paint (Musée des Beaux Arts and Musée Cantini, **Marseille**).

Picasso, Pablo (1881–1973). Born in Málaga, Spain, the 20th century's most endlessly inventive artist is especially celebrated for his mastery of line and his great expressive power. In 1948 Picasso abandoned Paris and moved to Provence, settling first in Vallauris, then Cannes, and finally at Mougins, where he died. Living in Provence heightened the Mediterranean and pagan aspects of his extraordinarily wide-ranging work; he also loved to attend the bullfights at Arles (Musée Picasso, **Antibes**; castle chapel at **Vallauris**; Musée Réattu, **Arles**).

Puget, Pierre (1620–94). Baroque sculptor, painter, and architect who began his career painting ships' figureheads before he went on to study in Rome under Bernini; unappreciated at home, he spent much of his career sculpting enormous saints in Genoa (Vieille Charité and Musée des Beaux Arts, all in his native **Marseille**; also the *Atlantes* of **Toulon**'s old Hôtel de Ville).

Renoir, Pierre-Auguste (1841–1919). Was as joyful as Van Gogh was tormented. Renoir combined Impressionism with the traditional 'gallant' themes of Fragonard, updated to the 19th century: pretty girls, dances, fêtes, children, nudes, bathers, pastorals. Wracked by rheumatism, he spent his last years in Cagnes, painting warm voluptuous nudes and landscapes (Musée Renoir, **Cagnes-sur-Mer**).

Rigaud, Hyacinthe (1659–1743). Born in Perpignan, painter of sumptuous royal portraits, in great demand for his ability to make his subjects look lofty yet amiable as well as for his accurate depiction of their swell get-ups (museums in **Perpignan**, **Narbonne** and **Aix**).

Seurat, Georges (1859–91). Theorist and founder of neo-Impressionism, with his technique of *pointillisme* (juxtaposing dots of pure colour to achieve a greater luminosity); although he was highly influential, none of his followers could match his precision and vision (Musée de l'Annonciade, **St-Tropez**).

Signac, Paul (1863–1935). Georges Seurat's most faithful follower down the path of *pointillisme*, the science of reducing a scene into dots of colour. When Seurat died, Signac left Paris and discovered St-Tropez in 1892, where influenced by the Fauves he gradually abandoned his dots for a freer style (Musée de l'Annonciade, **St-Tropez**).

Van Dongen, Kees (1877–1968). A Fauve painter of verve and elegance, who after Fauvism became the chief chronicler of Riviera society and mores of the 1920s and 30s (Musée Chervet, **Nice**; Musée de l'Annonciade, **St-Tropez**).

Van Gogh, Vincent (1853–90). Along with Cézanne, is most responsible for the images the outside world has of Provence—an unforgettable visionary, brilliantly-hued land, palpitating with energy. Coming from the cold, wet climes of the Netherlands and Paris, Van Gogh sought in the south, 'a different light, in the belief that to look at nature under a clearer sky could give us a better idea of the way the Japanese see and draw; finally, I seek a stronger sun'. Instead he found in the landscapes an underlying violence, tragedy and madness, which he painted with an intense lyricism that has never been equalled, in a 'research into the infinite' that ended with suicide. He sold but one painting in his short life, and ironically not a single one of the 800 or so canvases he painted around Arles remains in the south of France today.

Van Loo, Carle (1705–65). Native of Nice and younger brother of the less successful Jean-Baptiste van Loo, Carle was a Rococo painter in the 'grand style' and a keen rival of Boucher, painting hunt scenes, religious paintings, and designing Gobelin tapestries for the kings of France and Savoy (Ste-Marthe, **Tarascon**; Musée Chéret, **Nice**).

Vernet, Claude Joseph (1714–89). Born in Avignon, a landscape painter best known for his seascapes and ports; one of the first French painters interested in the play of light and water, if in a picturesque manner (Musée Calvet, **Avignon**; Musée des Beaux Arts, **Marseille**).

Vuillard, Edouard (1868–1940). Like his good friend, Bonnard, Vuillard began as a Nabis and later became better known for his Impressionistic, intimate, domestic scenes (Musée de l'Annonciade, **St-Tropez**).

Ziem, Félix (1821–1911). Started off illuminating canvases with a sense of light audacious for the period. Having found a successful formula, he repeated himself from then on. Much admired by Van Gogh, Ziem's favourite subjects were Venice and Martigues, whre he founded an art colony with Corot (Musée Ziem, **Martigues**; Musée Jules Chéret, **Nice**).

Part IV
THE CÔTE D'AZUR: MENTON TO CANNES

St-Paul-de-Vence

A calcined, scalped, rasped, scraped, flayed, broiled, powdered, leprous, blotched, mangy, grimy, parboiled, country, *without* trees, water, grass, fields—*with* blank, beastly, senseless olives and orange-trees like a mad cabbage gone indigestible.

—*Swinburne*

Just west of Italy begins that 70-km patch of Mediterranean hyperbole known as the French Riviera, or as the French have preferred to call it since 1887, the east end of the Côte d'Azur. Whatever charms its senseless olives once had are now endangered by a thick layer of cement and conga-lines of cars crawling between Menton and Cannes. '... the South of France, as far as I am concerned, has had it' declared Noel Coward in 1960, adding sour grapes to Swinburne's list of horrors. Or as the great Sam Goldwyn said: 'Nobody goes there anymore. It's too crowded.'

Despite its self-inflicted Californisation, certain pockets of the Côte, like Cap Ferrat and Menton, still recall the days when they were the winter playgrounds of English milords and Russian Grand Dukes. This first aristo trickle turned into a boom after 1860, when Nice was returned to France, railroads were built and the impoverished Grimaldis opened their casino at Monte Carlo. World War I put an end to the Riviera's Belle Epoque follies, and the future looked uncertain until the Roaring Twenties when writers, artists and rich Americans, in Paris for fun and booze, set the trend for spending

70

summers on the coast, cranking the whole fun machine up again until World War II. In the 1950s mass tourism began in earnest, inaugurated by an orgy of building that only began to be regulated in the 1970s, when it was already far too late. But just as the Riviera's obituaries as a resort were being written, it changed gear again, and would now like you to look at it as an international business centre, Europe's answer to America's Sunbelt, with offshore banking in Monaco, corporate offices in Sophia-Antipolis, and conference centres in Nice and Cannes. After all, New York, London and Tokyo are only a fax away.

So, dear traveller, why go? The climate is still as perfect as ever; the scenery, especially inland around Menton, Vence and Grasse, is voluptuous with flowers destined for the perfume bottle, in colours rivalled only by the Riviera's rich hoards of modern art. The restaurants equal the gourmet bastions in Paris, Nice is one of France's most urbane cities, and with a little extra effort you can even find charming villages in the coastal mountains that have not been hyper-restored into glossy Disneylands hawking artsy malarkey. And even in July and August, when the Côte seems more like hell than paradise, it tempts with its excellent jazz and art festivals.

Menton

The Côte d'Azur starts halfway between the fleshpots of Paris and Rome at Menton, right on the Italian frontier. Its history begins here as well, with the earliest traces of Riviera humans—folk who a million years ago already had the good sense to settle where a wall of mountains, still crowned with snow in April, blocks out the cold so that lemons can blossom all year.

Despite this early start, the Menton area wasn't inhabited again until the 10th century, when settlers clustered around the Annonciade hill, where they felt safe from Saracen pirates. The town first belonged to the Counts of Ventimiglia—little better than pirates themselves—then briefly joined Provence before it was sold to Charles Grimaldi of Monaco in 1346. The Grimaldis became rich from taxing Menton's citrus fruit up to 1848, when the town and its neighbour Roquebrune declared their independence. Unlike most of the revolts in Europe that fateful year, this puny one succeeded, and the Free Towns of Menton and Roquebrune endured until 1860, when the people voted to unite with France, and Charles III of Monaco sold his claim on the towns to Napoleon III for 4 million gold francs. The following year a Dr J. Henry Bennet wrote *Mentone and the Riviera as a Winter Climate*, a book that soon attracted a community of 5000 Brits, led by Queen Victoria herself in 1883. In World War II, the Germans wrecked Menton's port, and when they were chased out, lobbed bombs onto it from the Italian side of the border. The damage wasn't repaired until 1956.

Nattering nabobs of negativism claim Menton has a poor beach (true) and as much atmosphere as your grandmother's antimacassar, where 30 per cent of the population are retirees (the highest percentage in France) and most of the rest are miniature poodles. On the other hand, Menton is one of the prettiest towns on the coast, magnificently situated, low on craft shops but high on relaxation compared to the hard-edged glamour-pusses to the west.

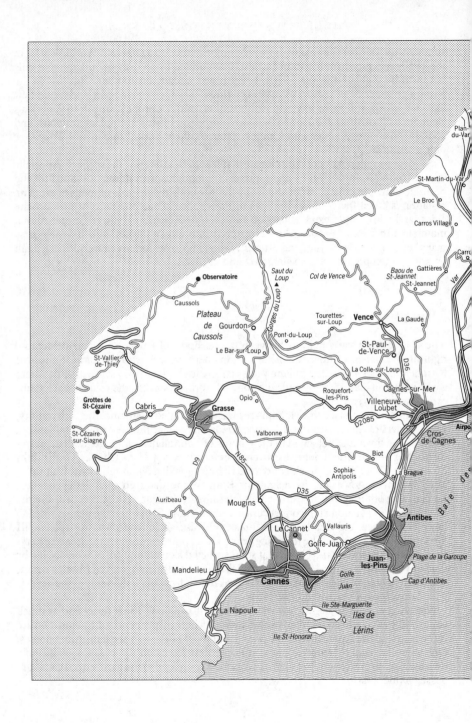

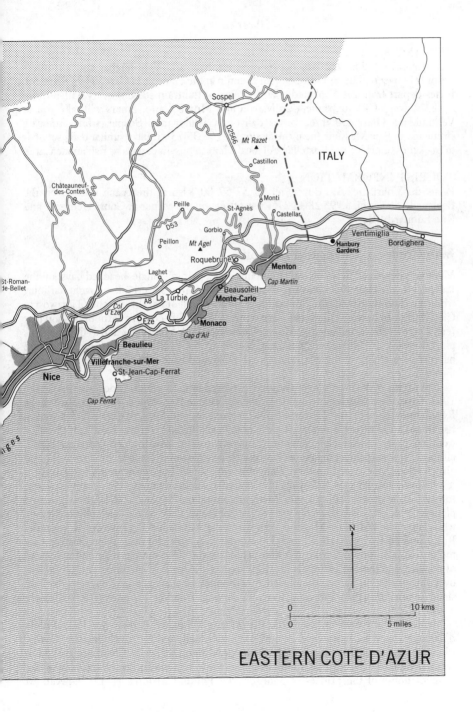

Sospel

D2566

Mt Razet ▲

Castillon

ITALY

Châteauneuf-
des-Contes

Monti

Peille   St-Agnès

Castellar

D53

Gorbio

Ventimiglia

Peillon   Mt Agel ▲

Hanbury
Gardens

Bordighera

Roquebrune

Menton

Laghet

Cap Martin

St-Roman-
de-Bellet

Beausoleil

Col
d'Eze

A8   La Turbie

Monte-Carlo

Eze

Monaco

Beaulieu

Cap d'Ail

Villefranche-sur-Mer

St-Jean-Cap-Ferrat

Nice

Cap Ferrat

N

0   10 kms

0   5 miles

EASTERN COTE D'AZUR

GETTING AROUND

The *Métrazur* trains that run between St-Raphaël and Ventimiglia, and all others running between Nice and Italy, stop in Menton at the Place de la Gare, tel 93 87 50 50. Buses depart from the Esplanade Careï (north of the train station) every half-hour to Nice, by way of Roquebrune-Cap Martin and Monte Carlo; others will take you to Ventimiglia. There are three buses daily to Castillon and Sospel, while Autocars Breuleux, in Rue Masséna (near the station), tel 93 35 73 51, have similar daily services to St-Agnès, Gorbio, and Castellar. All local Menton bus-lines pass by Esplanade Careï.

TOURIST INFORMATION

Palais du Tourisme, Av. Boyer, tel 93 57 57 00; also at the coach station, on the Esplanade du Careï, tel 93 28 43 27. **Post office:** on the corner of Cours George V and Rue Edouard VII.

Jean Cocteau, Love, and Lemons

Menton is squeezed between the mountains and a pair of shingle-beached bays: on the Italian side, the **Baie de Garavan**, where villas and gardens overlook the yacht harbour, while the **Baie du Soleil** (the Roman *Pacis Sinus* or Gulf of Peace) stretches 3 km west to Cap Martin. In between these two bays stands a little 17th-century harbour bastion that Jean Cocteau converted into the **Musée Cocteau** (Wed–Sun 10–12 and 3–6) to hold his playful series of *Animaux Fantastiques*, a tapestry of *Judith et Holopherne*, while the happier love affairs of the Mentonnais are portrayed in the *Innamorati* series, also on display.

This theme of Menton's lovers was first explored by Cocteau in his decorations for the 1957 **Salle des Mariages** in the Hôtel de Ville, three streets back in Rue de la République (open 8:30–12:30 and 1:30–5, closed Sat and Sun). A lemon-picker weds a fisherman amid rather discouraging mythological allusions: on the right wall there's a wedding-party in Saracen costume, referring to the Mentonnais' Saracen blood, although amongst the company we see the bride's frowning mother, the groom's jilted girlfriend and her armed brother. The other wall shows Orpheus turning back to see if his beloved Eurydice is following him out of hell, condemning her to return there forever; while on the ceiling Love, Poetry (mounted on Pegasus) and Science (juggling planets) look on. Love was also a favourite theme of the original Riviera inhabitants, who carved the little Cro-Magnon Venuses in the **Musée de Préhistoire Regionale**, Rue Lorédan Larchey (10–12 and 3–7, winter 2–6; closed Tues). Dioramas recreate the area's cave interiors from the time when people lived among mammoths instead of poodles, but the star exhibit is the 30,000-year-old skull of Menton man (found just over the border in Grimaldi) buried in a bonnet of seashells and deer teeth, long since calcified into the bone; note, too, rock carvings from the Vallée des Merveilles(see p. 206).

Menton's third museum is to the the west, a kilometre beyond the 1909 **Palais d'Europe** (once the casino and now an exhibition hall) and the exotic **Jardin Biovès**, where the fantastical lemon-studded floats of Menton's *Fête du Citron* are parked at carnival time. The trees that supply some of these lemons adorn the gardens of the summer home of the princes of Monaco, the **Palais Carnolès** (1717), now an art museum (3 Av. de la Madone, bus 3; same hours as the prehistory museum). It holds a Byzantine-inspired *Virgin and Child* from 13th-century Tuscany; Ludovico Brea's luminous *Madonna and Child with St Francis*, and all of the previous winners from Menton's very own Biennale of painting, some of which are so godawful you can only wonder what the losers were like. Other works were donated by English artist Graham Sutherland, who spent his last years in Menton.

The Vieille Ville, and the Gardens of Garavan

The tall, narrow 17th-century houses of Menton's Vieille Ville are reminiscent of the old quarter of Genoa, knitted together by anti-earthquake arches that span stepped lanes named after old pirate captains and saints. It's hard to believe that the quiet main street, **Rue Longue** (the Roman Via Julia Augusta) was, until the 19th century, the main route between France and Italy. According to legend, the lady at the Palais Princier (at No. 123) received a secret nocturnal visit from Casanova, who crept in through the sewers. Nowadays the street's chief thrill rests in a gimlet-eyed house cat sitting in a basket labelled *Chat Méchant* who guards the carrots and *haricots verts* at a grocer's.

From Rue Longue a ramp that leads up to the *parvis* of the ice-cream-coloured church of **St-Michel** (1675), and its equally charming Baroque neighbour, the **Chapelle des Pénitents Blancs**, headquarters of one of the old Riviera's many religious confraternities (see Nice). The *parvis* itself has a pebble mosaic of the Grimaldi arms, used as the setting for Menton's megastar chamber music festival in August.

The Montée du Souvenir leads to the top of the Vieille Ville, where the citadel was replaced in the 19th century by the romantic, panoramic **Cimetière du Vieux Château** 'the most aristocratic in Europe' according to Guy de Maupassant—the venerable names inscribed on the tombs include William Webb-Ellis, the 'inventor of rugby'. Many were consumptives in their teens and twenties who, like Aubrey Beardsley, only came to Menton to die.

From the cemetery, Boulevard de Garavan leads into the neighbourhood where this dead elite would reside if they were alive today, and to the **Jardin Botanique Val Rameh,** planted with 700 species from around the world (10–12 and 2–5, 4 in winter, closed Tues, adm). One road off the boulevard, Av. Blasco-Ibáñez, was named after the author of *The Four Horsemen of the Apocalypse* (1867–1928) who lived here in the **Villa Fontana Rosa** and decorated his garden with colourful ceramic tiles from his native Valencia; but now the house is private and it is not easy to worm a discreet peek. On the other side of the Garavan station is **Villa Isola Bella**, where the ailing Katherine Mansfield spent her happiest years which were fictionalized in a number of short stories.

To the north of Boulevard Garavan is the romantically overgrown **Jardin des Colombières**, the 40-year project of French artist and writer Ferdinand Bac (1859–1952), the flamboyant illegitimate son of Napoleon III (bus 7, open 9–12 and 2–6, closed Oct–Dec, adm). You can have a cup of tea in Bac's neo-Graeco-Roman villa (or stay overnight: see below) then wander amid the cypresses, the weed-covered Italianate stairs and broken pavilions, and muse on the ruins of time.

Market Days: Daily, opposite the Cocteau Museum, in a pretty building with ceramic decorations; flea market on Friday.

WHERE TO STAY   (postal code 06500)
Menton's once grand hotels are now converted into flats, and no sparkling new ones have
been built to take up the slack. But if you're travelling with your beloved and have 500 F
to rub together for bed and breakfast, you can pass an unforgettable night at Ferdinand
Bac's **Les Colombières** (see above), tel 93 41 62 48. First-comers can choose between
the Venetian, Persian, Spanish, or Greek bedrooms, then sit out in the gardens at night
overlooking Menton and its bay, bathed in golden light. Meals are available in the
splendiferous dining room (120F–200F). For more up-to-date luxury, ***Napoléon**,
29 Porte de France, tel 93 35 89 50, has a heated pool covered in the winter and
soundproofed, air-conditioned rooms. If you have a car, the English-owned **Auberge
Les Santons**, Colline de L'Annonciade, tel 93 35 94 10, offers a modern retreat far
from the noise (dinner obligatory). In the centre of Menton, **Du Pin Doré**, 16 Av.
Félix Faure, tel 93 28 31 00 is a charming white and blue villa by the sea, with a pool and
garden, or try the equally welcoming **Bristol**, 24 Av. Carnot, tel 93 57 54 32, with high
ceilings and seafront rooms (cheaper ones are at the back). Good bargains include
*Beauregard**, 10 Rue Albert I, below the station, tel 93 35 74 08, a sweet place with a
quiet garden; or *Magenta**, 8 bis Rue Guyau, tel 93 35 85 71, not on the sea, but with a
garden terrace under the palms.

EATING OUT
Menton is gastronomically a humble place, content to boast of its lemonade and
marzipan bonbons shaped like olives, lemons or oranges. If those don't fill you up, try the
plentiful and well-prepared seafood at flashy **Chez Germaine**, 46 Promenade du
Maréchal-Leclerc, tel 93 35 66 90, with menus at 115 F and 180 F. Homemade ravioli
filled with spinach and other Italian delights are the speciality at central **De la Poste**, on
Impasse Bellecour, tel 93 57 13 79, with 55 F and 65 F menus (open for lunch all year ,
and for dinner in July and August). Up at Monti, on the Rte de Sospel, the panoramic
Pierrot-Pierrette, tel 93 35 79 76, complements the views with delicious fresh blue
trout (130 F).

North of Menton

Four narrow mountain valleys converge at Menton, their slopes encrusted by villages,
linked by bus from Menton and to each other by mule-tracks. Above the easternmost
valley is **Castellar** (7 km from Menton), laid out on a grid plan in 1435 to replace the
original 1258 village, built by the counts of Ventimiglia high on a rocky peg. An hour's
walk will take you to its ghostly ruins; or take the less strenuous walk up the Sospel road
as far as the waterfall at the **Gourg de l'Oura**. Up the second valley, the Val du Carei, the
medieval monastery of **L'Annonciade** (5.5 km from Menton) has gone through countless transformations over the years; best of all are its grand views and its ex votos dating
back to the 1600s, including an unusual one—a piece of a zeppelin. Further up the Val
du Carei, amid the viaducts of the old Menton-Sospel railway, you can wander through
the scented **Forêt de Monti**, then continue up to **Castillon**, happily into its third
incarnation as 'the most beautiful new village in France' after being flattened by an
earthquake in 1887 and bombed in 1944. From here it's a 14-km zigzag on the scenic
D 2566 to Sospel (see p. 204).

From Menton a narrow, winding road noodles up to **Ste-Agnès**, at 650 m the loftiest village on the entire coast. It was founded in the 900s, they say, by a Saracen who fell in love with a local girl and converted to Christianity for her sake. It certainly looks old enough—a crazy quilt of vaulted passageways and tiny squares that have unfortunately succumbed to trinketshopitis. When you can't look at another smirking *santon*, head up Rue Longue for a view that stretches to Corsica on a clear day. A path descends to Menton in two hours, or better still, take the one-hour shortcut called the *Balcon de la Côte d'Azur* to **Gorbio** (from Menton it's 8 km). Gorbio is just as picturesquely medieval as Ste-Agnès but has somehow been spared the trinkets. The best time to visit is at *Fête Dieu* (Corpus Christi) in June, when the village maintains a medieval rite called the *Procession dai limaça* when its lanes are lit by thousands of flickering lamps made from snail shells filled with olive oil, set in beds of sand.

A Dip into Italy

Just over the border, in the village of Grimaldi, the beachside **Balzi Rossi** (red caves) were the centre of a sophisticated Neanderthal society that flourished *c.*100,000 to 40,000 BC and produced some of Europe's first art, displayed in the **Museo Preistorico** (museum and caves open 1–12:30 and 2:30–6, closed Mon, adm). Also, outside Ventimiglia at Mortola Inferiore, you can visit the extraordinary **Hanbury Gardens**, a botanical paradise of acclimatized plants from around the world, founded in 1867 by Sir Thomas Hanbury (open 10–4, closed Wed, adm). If you plan to go deeper into Italy, you can save literally thousands of *lire* by filling up with petrol in Menton (that's what all those Italians are doing).

WHERE TO STAY/EATING OUT (postal code 06500)
Up in **Castellar**, the only place to sleep and eat is the tranquil *Les Alpes*, Place Clémenceau, tel 93 35 82 83, with tidy little rooms and good food. Or you can go upmarket in **Castillon** at the ***Bergerie**, tel 93 04 00 39 with rustic but very comfortable rooms and more elaborate food. There are more choices at **Ste-Agnès**, *Le Saint-Yves**, tel 93 35 91 45, for sweet dreams and dreamy views, or in July, Aug, and Sept only, *La Vieille Auberge**, just before the entrance to the village, with a delightful garden—full board is mandatory, or just stop by for a gargantuan 140 F feast. In **Gorbio**, dine on the seasonal offerings at the **Auberge du Village** in Rue Gambetta, tel 93 35 87 83 (100 F).

Menton to Nice: the Three Corniches

When most people hear 'Riviera', they mentally picture this 20-km stretch of coast, where mighty mountains plummet drunkenly into the sea, and hairpinning *corniche* roads zigzag on ledges over vertiginous drops; where continental hormones go into overdrive as film stars in dark glasses race sporty convertibles down to 'Monte' to gamble their residuals away. A lot of that holds true, although the only racing that really happens is the Monaco Grand Prix. Traffic is nearly always slow and heavy—a fact that doesn't prevent some would-be James Bonds from contributing to an appalling accident rate.

The worst traffic jams inch along the lowest road, the **Corniche Inférieure** (N 98) through the seaside resorts; most of the frequent buses that ply the coast use this road, which runs parallel to the railway. To relieve the traffic, already choking in the 1920s, the most dramatic of the roads, the **Moyenne Corniche** (N 7) was drilled through the rock and hung sheerly through the hills—which makes it the favourite for car chase scenes. Higher up, along the route of the Roman Via Aurelia (also called Via Julia Appia), Napoleon built the **Grande Corniche** (D 2564) with the most panoramic views of all.

The Grande Corniche and Corniche Inférieure: Roquebrune-Cap-Martin

Nearly every potential building site in the lush mountain shore between Menton and Monaco is occupied by Roquebrune-Cap-Martin—from old Roquebrune just beside the Grande Corniche down to the exclusive garden cape of Cap Martin. Purchased by the Grimaldis in 1355 for 1000 florins, Roquebrune (like Menton) later revolted against Monaco and became a free town until it became French in 1861. The medieval village is all steep, winding, arcaded streets and over-restored houses, culminating at the top in the **Château** (9–12 and 2–7, 2–5 winter, closed Fri and Nov), with the oldest surviving *donjon* in France, erected in the 10th century by the Counts of Ventimiglia against the Saracen threat. In the 1400s, Lambert of Monaco built much of what stands today; in 1911, Sir William Ingram purchased the castle, and planted the mock medieval *tour anglais* by the gate. The antique-furnished rooms in the 3.5-m thick walls are surprisingly poky—most people have bathrooms bigger than this lordling's reception hall. But the view from the top floor is huge enough for any ego. The castle guards lived below the castle in picturesque **Rue Moncollet**, carved out of the living rock; another street under the castle, Rue du Château leads to Rue de la Fontaine and Chemin de St-Roch and a remarkable contemporary of the castle: a **1000-year-old olive tree** measuring 10 m in circumference.

In 1467, as plague decimated the coast, the Roquebrunois vowed to the Virgin that if they were spared they would, in thanksgiving, annually re-enact tableaux of the Passion. The Virgin apparently liked the offer, and the villagers have faithfully kept their side of the pact every year on 5 August. The best of the 500 roles involved in the colourful processions are jealously 'owned' by the oldest families, who pass them down to their descendants like the family silver.

Cap Martin

In the 1890s a pair of empresses, Eugénie of France and Elisabeth (the famous 'Sissi') of Austria, made Roquebrune's little peninsula of Cap Martin an aristocratic enclave, 'whispering of old kings come here to dine or die', as F. Scott Fitzgerald wrote. Churchill did the dining and Yeats, King Nikola of Montenegro, and Le Courbusier the dying, the latter drowning in 1965 while swimming off the white rocks beside what is now **Promenade Le Corbusier**—a lovely walk around the cape, past villas immersed in luxuriant pines, olives, cypress and mimosas.

Another spectacular path leads in an hour and a half from Cap Martin to Monte-Carlo Beach. If you walk it, look back towards the Cap to see the ruined tower of the long gone convent of St-Martin. The story goes that the men of Roquebrune had vowed to protect the nuns from pirates, and one night in the late 1300s the tower's bell sounded the alarm; the Roquebrunois piled out of bed and down the hill to defend the good sisters, who laughingly confessed that they were just testing the bell's efficiency. A few nights later, pirates really did appear, and although the nuns rang like mad, their defenders only rolled over in bed. Next morning in the smouldering ruins, the older nuns were found with their throats slit, while the prettier ones were carted off to the slave markets of Barbary.

WHERE TO STAY/EATING OUT   (postal code 06190)
Affordable hotels are scarce along the **Corniches**, but if money's no object there's the ****Vista Palace**, tel 93 34 01 50, the ultimate in luxury, hanging on a 305-m cliff along the Grande Corniche, with a God's-eye view over Monaco straight below. Its leisure centre includes a heated pool, squash, gym, and sauna. Down on the poor sinners' level, the **Westminster**, 14 Av. Louis Laurens, tel 93 35 00 68, has a pretty garden terrace near the junction of the lower and middle Corniches.

Near **Roquebrune's** castle, in a former sheepfold cut into the rock, **Le Grand Inquisiteur**, 18 Rue du Château, tel 93 35 05 37, offers well-prepared Provençal dishes like *pieds et paquets* (menus at 125 F and 200 F). A cheaper troglodyte choice, **Le Grotte** also has tables outside in Place des Deux-Frères at the entrance to the Vieille Ville in Roquebrune, and offers a 50 F *plat du jour* and bargain menus. Next to the water by Cap Martin, **Sporting du Cap**, 48 Av. W. Churchill, tel 93 35 63 07, has a delicious 150 F menu with spiced codfish and exotic desserts.

Monaco

In 1297, an ambitious member of Genoa's Guelph party named Francesco Grimaldi the Spiteful dressed up like a friar and knocked at the door of the Ghibelline fortress at Monaco, asking for hospitality. The soldiers sleepily admitted him; the phoney friar pulled a knife from his robe, killed the soldiers, and admitted his men. Although Francesco was the first Grimaldi to get into Monaco, the family only became lords of their rock when they purchased it outright from Genoa in 1308. Once rulers of a mini-empire including Antibes and Menton, the ambitions of others have reduced the Grimaldis' sovereign Ruritania to a sea-hugging 194 hectares (slightly larger than half of Central Park) under the looming mountain, Tête de Chien. Here Rainier III presides as the living representative of the oldest ruling family in the world, and Europe's last constitutional autocrat.

Over the centuries the Grimaldis' main income came from a tax levied on Menton's lemons and olives, and when Menton revolted in 1848, they faced bankruptcy. In desperation, Prince Charles III looked to the Duke of Baden-Baden, whose casino lured in Europe's big-spending aristocrats every summer. Monaco, Charles decided, would be the winter Baden-Baden, and he founded the *Société des Bains de Mer* (SBM) to operate a casino and tourist industry, with the principality as the chief shareholder. Success beyond anyone's wildest dreams arrived with the new railway from Nice in 1868; by 1870 the coffers were so full that Charles abolished direct taxation in Monaco. In gratitude his subjects renamed the hill under the casino Monte Carlo.

But gone are those fond days when the Monégasques could live entirely off the folly of others. France and Italy legalized gaming in 1933, ending the principality's Riviera monopoly; the proportion of its revenue that Monaco gleans from the tables has declined from 95 per cent to a mere 4 per cent. But under Rainier III and the omnipresent SBM, Monaco has found new ways to keep its 5000 citizens and 20,000 residents from paying income tax, especially in offshore banking (some 30 do business here), in the media (Télé and Radio Monte Carlo), and 'business tourism' (the construction of Monte Carlo's new ultra-modern congress hall). Foolish gambling pales before the deadly sin of greed: 'The promise of a penthouse, a place to park their Mercedes, and they'll sign away anything,' sighed an elderly Monégasque to *The Riviera Reporter*. Property speculation has joined tax evasion as the chief topic of conversation; owing to lack of space building is now mostly vertical, transforming this striking 3 km of coast into a Lilliputian Manhattan. Security grows tighter all the time, and now Big Brother's closed circuit cameras spy over every corner. The rich and their money feel safe in this tidy suburb of reality, where a calendar of car races, circuses, fireworks, First Division football and operas put a glittering mask over its ghoulish face.

GETTING AROUND

There are no customs formalities; you can just drive into Monaco along the Corniche Inférieure, or take the helicopter from Nice airport if you're in a hurry, or the minibus (a 50-min drive). The Monaco/Monte Carlo station is in Av. Prince Pierre, tel 93 87 50 50; buses every 30 min between Menton and Nice stop at several points along the Corniche.

Small as it is, Monaco is divided into several towns: Monte Carlo to the east, Fontvieille by the port, Monaco-Ville on the rock, and La Condamine below, and there's a public bus network to save you some legwork. More importantly, free public lifts and escalators operate between its tiers of streets.

TOURIST INFORMATION

2a Boulevard des Moulins, Monte Carlo, tel 93 30 87 01.

Monte Carlo

Set back in the sculpture-filled gardens of Place du Casino rises the most famous building on the whole Côte d'Azur: the 1878 **Casino de Monte Carlo**, a fascinating period piece known in its heyday as the 'cathedral of hell'. Anyone over 21 with a passport can visit the American room for free (open from 10 am) where one-armed bandits, American roulette, craps and blackjack tables click and clatter away just as in Las Vegas or Atlantic City—only the gilt, over-the-top rococo 1880s ceilings betray the surroundings as having Old World pretensions. In the Pink Salon Bar, where naked cigar-chomping nymphs float on the ceiling, Charles Deville Wells celebrated his three-day gambling spree in 1891 that turned $400 into $40,000 and inspired the popular tune *The*

Man who Broke the Bank at Monte Carlo. For 50 F (or 100 F to get into the *salons privés*, open from 3 pm) you can visit the quieter, more intense and greedy European rooms where oily croupiers accept bets on roulette and *chemin de fer* up to 500,000 francs a go.

The casino's bijou theatre, the **Salle Garnier** (open only for performances), was designed by Charles Garnier of Paris Opera House fame. Backed by pots of SBM money, it became one of the most exciting in Europe, commissioning operas from composers like Saint-Saëns and Massenet, and after 1911, ballets from the Ballets Russes de Monte Carlo. Its gods—Diaghilev, Nijinksy, Stravinsky, and set designers Picasso, Derain and Cocteau—held court among the dukes and flukes in the café of SBM's frothy **Hôtel de Paris**, next to the casino. Or as Katherine Mansfield put it: 'the famous Café de Paris with *real* devils with tails under their aprons cursing each other as they hand out the drinks. There at those tables sit the damned.'

If smug displays of wealth give you the misanthropic jitters, you can take comfort in the porcelain, metal, wood, and plastic people in the **National Museum and Collection of Dolls and Automata** in a pretty villa designed by Charles Garnier (17 Av. Princess Grace; daily Easter–12 Sept 10–6:30; other times 10–12:15 and 2:30–6:30, adm). Jolliest among them is an enormous 18th-century Neapolitan *presepio* or Christmas crib, with 250 figurines from Virgin to sausage-vendor; a smaller room holds a Josephine Baker automaton in a grass skirt and Princess Caroline's Barbie and Ken. Further east are beaches of imported sand, resort hotels, and that elite summertime rendez-vous, the Monte Carlo Sporting Club.

La Condamine and Fontvieille

The natural amphitheatre of La Condamine, the port quarter between Monte Carlo and Monaco-Ville, has suffered the most from the speculators, their big cement brutes dwarfing the votive chapel dedicated to Monaco's patron saint, **Ste-Dévote**. After her martyrdom in Corsica in 305, Dévote's body was put in a boat that sailed by itself to Monaco (still known then as *Portus Herculis Monoeci*, after Hercules). In the 11th century some relic pirates snatched her bones, only to be foiled when the Monégasques set their boat on fire—an event re-enacted every 26 January amid the armada of yachts.

From Place Ste-Dévote Rue Grimaldi leads west to Place du Canton and the **Jardin Zoologique**, used to acclimatize animals imported from the tropics (June–Sept 9–12 and 2–7, other times shorter hours, adm). More unusual are the prickly contents of another garden near the Moyenne Corniche, the **Jardin Exotique** (bus 2, open 9–7, until 6 in the winter, adm) where 7000 succulents planted in 1933 range from the absurd to the obscene. The same ticket admits you to the adjacent **Grottes de l'Observatoire**, one of the few places in Provence inhabited in the Palaeolithic era, and curiously, the only cave in Europe that gets warmer instead of cooler as you descend. Here too is the **Musée d'Anthropologie Préhistorique**, with bones of reindeer, mammoths and hippopotami, along with some from early editions of humankind.

To the south, between the sea and the ultra-modern **Stade Louis II**, where *AS Monaco* regularly punish the rest of the French football league, stretches new **Font-vieille Park** where the charming **Princess Grace Rose Garden** is the chief memorial to Monaco's beloved late princess, film actress, and daughter of an Irish-American brick magnate.

Up on the Rock: Monaco-Ville

In 1860 the principality of Monaco consisted of 2000 people living in this old Italian town, clinging spectacularly to a promontory 300 m above the sea; they never dreamt it would turn into a shopping centre for Prince Rainier ashtrays or Princess Grace dolls. As scrubbed and cute as any town in Legoland, it offers devilries that in comparison make the casino seem like an honest proposition: the **Wax Museum of the Princes of Monaco**, running the gamut from Francesco the Spiteful to Caroline and Stephanie; the **Multi-vision Monte Carlo Story**, a **Museum of Old Monaco** and a **Museum of Napoleonic Souvenirs** (with over a 1000 items connected to the little Corsican including 'garments and toys belonging to the King of Rome!'—his ill-fated son). From June to October you can yawn your way through the plush **Prince's Palace** itself, which, with its 19th-century 'medieval towers', is built around the Genoese fortress of 1215; at other times when Rainier's at home you'll have to be content with the rooty-toot-toot 11:55 am Changing of the Monégasque guard.

Here, too, is Monaco's unattractive **Cathedral**, built in the 19th century at the expense of a Romanesque chapel. From the chapel it inherited two lovely retables by Ludovico Brea from the early 1500s: *La Pietà* (over the sacristy door) and the grand *St-Nicolas* with 18 panels in the ambulatory. The more recent princes of Monaco are buried here, including Princess Grace, whose simple tomb is often bedecked with nosegays from admirers, all waiting for the miracle that will sway the Vatican to beatify her.

Monaco's most compelling attraction is nearby: the remarkable **Oceanographic Museum** in Av. St-Martin (open July and Aug 9–9, other times 9–7, adm exp), founded in 1910 by Prince Albert I, who sank all of his casino profits into a passion for deep-sea exploration. To house the treasures he accumulated in his 24 voyages, he built into the cliff this museum with an 85-m sheer stone façade, filling it with instruments, shells, whale skeletons, and on the ground floor a fascinating aquarium where 90 tanks hold some of the most surreal fish ever netted from the briny deep. The rest of the building is taken up with reseach laboratories headed by Jacques Cousteau that specialize in the study of ocean pollution and radioactivity.

Besides the aforementioned path east to Cap Martin, there's a path beginning at Fontvieille's Plage Marquet that heads west along the crashing sea to the train station at **Cap d'Ail**, 'Cape Garlic'. A third trail begins on the D 53 in **Beausoleil**, Monaco's French suburb, and ascends to the top of **Mont des Mules** in half an hour; an orientation table at the belvedere points out the sights, spread out like a map below.

ACTIVITIES

Thanks to the SBM, there's always something to do in Monaco, especially if you have a few oil wells to back up your credit cards: a mountaintop 18-hole golf course high above the town at La Turbie, tennis and every imaginable water sport (but no free beaches), deep-sea tuna-fishing and cruises, helicopter tours of the coast. In January there's the **Monte Carlo Rally**—the first one in 1902 occasioned the world's first tarmac road, designed to keep the spectators from being sprayed with dust. In April you can watch a tennis championship; the second week of May sees the famous **Monte Carlo Grand Prix** (when even the pavements charge a hefty admission).

WHERE TO STAY   (postal code 98030)
Monaco's hotels have nearly as many stars as the Milky Way, so if you'd like one of
the few more reasonably priced rooms in the summer, you can't reserve early
enough. Tycoons can check in at the palatial *****Hôtel de Paris, Place du Casino,
tel 93 50 80 80, opened in 1865 by the SBM for gambling czars and duchesses, or
the beautiful Belle Epoque *****Hermitage, perched high on its rock in Square
Beaumarchais, tel 93 50 67 31. For a third of the price, and a view of the sea, the top
choice is the old ***Balmoral, 12 Av. de la Costa, tel 93 50 62 37. All of the above
are in Monte Carlo; in Monaco-Ville, there's the new air-conditioned ***Abela, 23 Av.
des Papalins, tel 92 05 90 00, with a swimming-pool, garden, and sea view. Cheaper
choices are all here, too: the modern, air-conditioned **Terminus, 9 Av. Prince-
Pierre, tel 93 30 20 70; *De France, 6 Rue de la Turbie (near the station), tel 93 30 24
64; *Cosmopolite, 4 Rue de la Turbie, tel 93 30 16 95; or *Hôtel Helvetia, 1 bis Rue
Grimaldi, tel 93 30 21 71, all of which are adequate even if they don't bubble over with
charm.

EATING OUT
In Monte Carlo, those who make it big at the tables, or have simply made it big at life in
general, dine in the incredible golden setting of the Louis XV, in the Hôtel de Paris, tel
93 50 80 80. This was a favourite of Edward VII as Prince of Wales, who once while
dining here with his mistress was served a crêpe smothered in kirsch, curaçao and
maraschino that its 14-year-old maker, Henri Charpentier (who went on to fame as a
chef in America), accidently set alight, only to discover that it made the dish taste much
better. The Prince himself suggested that they name the new dessert after his companion, hence *crêpes Suzette*. Under Alain Ducasse, elected the '1990 Chef of the Year' by his
peers, the cuisine is once again kingly—made from the finest and freshest ingredients
Italy and France can offer, as sumptuous and spectacular as the setting (menus at around
550 F and 700 F). The dining room of the Hermitage's Belle Epoque (tel 93 50 67 31)
is a riotous pink and silver period piece, and a historical monument to boot; the food
(*feuilleté aux langoustines*, etc.) is equally classic (menus at 280 F and 380 F). For delicious
pasta dishes, there's Polpetta, 2 Rue Paradis, tel 93 50 67 84, with a terrace and a 115 F
menu; and for delicious duck dishes straight out of the Dordogne, try Le Périgordin, 4
Rue de la Turbie, tel 93 30 06 02 (menus at 75 F and 120 F).

NIGHTLIFE
Nightlife in Monaco is a glitzy, bejewelled fashion parade catered for by the omnipresent
SBM at the Monte Carlo Sporting Club, on Av. Princess Grace, with its summer
discotheque, Las Vegas-style floor shows, dancing, restaurants, and casino, or the
similar offerings at SBM/Loews Monte Carlo, 12 Av. des Spélugues, or at the American
Bar at the Hôtel de Paris. More affordably, the Cinema d'été in Av. Princesse Grace,
shows a different film in its original language every evening at 9:30pm, from 15 May–30
Sept. In January the opera and theatre season begins; in February an excellent Circus
Festival; in July and August a spectacular Fireworks Festival and concerts at the
palace; in December there's ballet. Or you can let the dandies get on with it and curl up
with a good book in English from Scruples, 9 Rue Princesse Caroline.

North of Monaco

From Monaco, the D 53 ascends to the Grande Corniche, a road the Romans called Via Julia Augusta, built to link up the Urbs to its conquests in Gaul and Spain. Several hard campaigns had to be fought (25–14 BC) before the fierce Ligurians finally let the road builders through, and in 6 BC the Roman Senate voted to erect a mighty commemorative monument known as the Trophy of the Alps (the Romans called it *Tropea Augusti* or 'Augustus's Trophy') at the base of Mont Agel. The views are precipitous, and you can escape the crowds by venturing even further inland to Peille and Peillon, two of the most beautiful villages on the Côte d'Azur.

GETTING AROUND
There are four daily buses from Nice to La Turbie that continue up to Peille, but never on Sundays; and one a day to La Turbie from Menton. Both Peillon and Peille have train stations, but they lie several steep kilometres below their respective villages.

TOURIST INFORMATION
In La Turbie, at the Mairie, tel 93 41 10 10.
In Peille, also at the Mairie, tel 93 79 30 32.

La Turbie and its Trophy

Though hemmed in by upstart mini-villas and second homes, La Turbie (a corruption of *Tropea*) still retains its old core of narrow vaulted alleys, typical of the area. Unlike its neighbours, however, it earned a mention by Dante in *The Divine Comedy*, and has the relevant immortal lines proudly engraved on its tower. La Turbie also has an elliptical 18th-century church, **St-Michel-Archange** with a sumptuous Baroque interior of marble and agate and paintings that are attributed to, or by the schools of Raphael, Veronese, Rembrandt, Ludovico Brea, Murillo and Ribera—not bad for a village of 2000 souls!

The old Via Julia Augusta (Rue Comte-de-Cessole) passes through town on its way to the **Trophy of the Alps**. This monument originally stood 45 m high, supporting a 6-m statue of Augustus; on its wall were listed the 44 conquered Ligurian tribes, and stairs throughout allowed passers-by to enjoy the view. When St Honorat saw the local people worshipping this marvel in the 4th century, he vandalized it; in the Dark Ages it was converted into a fort; Louis XIV ordered it to be blown up in 1705, and the stone was quarried to build St-Michel-Archange. The still formidable pile of rubble that remained in the 1930s was resurrected to 35 m and its inscription replaced thanks to a rich American, Edward Tuck. The only other such trophy to survive in situ is in Romania; a small museum on the site has models and drawings (April–Sept 9–6; otherwise 9–12 and 2–4:30 other times, adm). From the trophy's terrace it's a dizzy 400-m drop down to Monaco's skyscrapers.

Peillon and Peille

The two villages are tiny and lovely; balanced atop adjacent hilltops, both require a wearying climb to reach. But Peille and Peillon aren't quite the Tweedledee and

Tweedledum of the Côte. **Peillon**, most easily reached on the D 53 from Nice, is a bit more posh, complete with a foyer—a cobbled square with a pretty fountain at the village entrance. Inside are peaceful medieval stairs and arches, and the restored Baroque parish church, but Peillon's big attraction is right at the entrance: the **Chapelle des Pénitents Blancs** (open Thurs only) adorned with a cycle of Renaissance frescoes by Giovanni Canavesio (c. 1485) on the *Passion of Christ*, a bit faded but a good preparation for Canavesio's later and better treatment of this subject at La Brigue (see p. 207). From Peillon, marked trails lead you to some steep but delightful rambles in the surrounding countryside.

One of those walks follows the Roman road in two hours to **Peille**, further up the D 53. More isolated, Peille has more character, and its very own dialect, called *Pelhasc*. There's an ensemble of medieval streets like Peillon's and a church begun in the 12th century, with an interesting medieval portrait of Peille and its now ruined castle. Once during a drought, Peille asked for help from a shepherd (in Provence shepherds often moonlight as sorcerers), and he made it rain on condition that the lord of this castle give him his daughter to wed—an event remembered in a fête on the first Sunday in September. The Church may frown at such goings-on, but Peille often had its own ideas on religion, preferring twice in the Middle Ages to be excommunicated rather than pay the bishop's tithes.

WHERE TO STAY/EATING OUT

In **La Turbie** (06320), stay and eat at the ****Napoléon**, Av. de la Victoire, tel 93 41 00 54, closed annually in March. Try to get a room on the top floor, with views of the Trophy. Most rooms have baths and TVs (good food, with menus at 110 F and 190 F). In **Peillon** (06440), *****Auberge de la Madone**, tel 93 79 91 17, has comfortable rooms with traditional Provençal decor and views over the valley. Inside its excellent restaurant, or out on a terrace among the olive trees, you'll find seasonal dishes like red mullet with parsley and asparagus and *tourton des pénitents* with almonds, pine nuts and herbs (menus at 115 F and 180 F). ***La Braisière**, tel 93 79 91 06, has six simple rooms in the village and an adequate restaurant with stuffed mussels, rabbit dishes, and Provençal lasagne (menus from 95 F). At **Peille** (06440), ***Belvédère**, tel 93 79 90 45, the only hotel in the village, has five simple rooms with grand mountain views but you had better write ahead to book one. The restaurant does good ravioli and other Niçoise dishes (menus from 70 F).

The Moyenne Corniche: Eze

Between Monaco and Nice, the main reason for taking the middle road has long been the extraordinary village of Eze, the most perched, perhaps, of any *village perché* in France, squeezed on to a cone of a hill 430 m over the sea. It barely avoided being poached as well as perched in a catastrophic fire in 1986 that ravaged the landscape and destroyed the pine forest that once surrounded it. Now the poaching is done on tourists; nearly every house is a shop.

Eze, they say, is named after a temple the Phoenicians built to Isis. It then passed to the Romans, to the Saracens, and changed lords several times after. But on the whole, as you can see once inside its 14th-century gate, Eze was eminently self-reliant. Even if an enemy penetrated the walls, its tight little maze of stairs and alleys would cause confusion, the better to ambush or spill boiling oil on attackers. If they got so far as to assault what remains of the castle these days, they would run into the needles of the cacti in the **Jardin Exotique** (open 9–12 and 2–6:30, summer 8–8, adm). Nor did the views from the castle ruins allow for any sneak attacks. The other non-commercial attraction in Eze is the **Chapelle des Pénitents blancs** with a 13th-century Catalan crucifix, the *Christ of the Black Death* (typical of medieval Catalan art, the sculptor emphasized Christ's divine nature, and he smiles even on the Cross); here too is a 14th-century Virgin and Child called the *Madone des Forêts*, owing to the pine-cone in Jesus' hand.

A scenic path descending to Eze-bord-de-Mer is called the **Sentier Frédéric-Nietzsche** after the philosopher. Nietzsche, however, walked up instead of down, an arduous trek that made his head spin and inspired the third part of his *Thus spake Zarathustra*.

WHERE TO STAY/EATING OUT   (postal code 06360)

A road links the three Corniches at Eze, and there are hotels on each level. ****L'Hermitage**, at Col d'Eze on the Grande Corniche, tel 93 41 00 68, offers priceless views, but mundane food to go with its mundane rooms. Along the Moyenne Corniche two luxurious inns have only a handful of rooms but superb kitchens: the *******Château Eza** (closed Nov–Mar), actually a collection of medieval houses linked together to form an eagle's nest, all sharing an extraordinary terrace, with Niçois and other Provençal specialities to match (Rue de la Pise, tel 93 41 12 24, menus at 260 F and 500 F). In a medieval castle rebuilt in the 1920s, ******Château de la Chèvre d'Or** (Rue du Barri, tel 93 41 12 12) has a small park, a pool, and more ravishing views; its restaurant serves refined, light versions of the French classics, accompanied by one of the Riviera's best wine cellars (lunch menus 340 F; closed Nov–Feb). More modest choices in Eze include ****Golf**, Place de la Colette, tel 93 41 18 50 (closed Nov–Mar), and ***Auberge des Deux Corniches**, open all year, tel 93 01 19 54. Turbot or *filet de boeuf aux cèpes* go down nicely at the **Auberge du Troubadour**, Rue du Brec, tel 93 41 19 03, and the price is nice too (menus 110 F and 160 F). Down at Eze-bord-de-Mer, there's the ultra-luxurious Riviera dream *******Cap Estel**, tel 93 01 50 44, complete with heated pool (open Mar–Oct) or ****Le Soleil**, tel 93 01 51 46 (open all year).

The Corniche Infériure:
Beaulieu, St-Jean-Cap-Ferrat and Villefranche

To the west of Eze-bord-de-Mer another wooded promontory, Cap Ferrat, protrudes into the sea to form today's most fashionable address on the Côte d'Azur. The awful Leopold II, King of the Belgians, Otto Preminger, and Somerset Maugham have had sanctuaries here, along with a Rothschild heiress, whose eclectic villa and garden is one of the highlights of the coast. To the east, the promontory and steep mountain backdrop keep Beaulieu so sheltered that it shares with Menton the distinction of being the hottest town in France, while to the west the Corniche skirts the top of the fine old village of Villefranche-sur-Mer, with a port deep enough for battleships—grey tokens from the grey world beyond the Riviera.

TOURIST INFORMATION
Beaulieu (06310): Place Georges Clemenceau, tel 93 01 02 21.
St-Jean-Cap-Ferrat (06290): 59 Av. Denis-Séméria, tel 93 76 08 90.
Villefranche-sur-Mer (06230): Jardins François-Binon, near the Corniche Inférieure, tel 93 01 73 68.

Beaulieu

'O qual bel luogo!' exclaimed Napoleon in his Corsican mother tongue, and the bland name stuck to this lush banana-growing town overlooking the Baie des Fourmis, 'the Bay of Ants' so called for the black boulders in the sea. Beaulieu admits to a mere four days of frost a year and calls its easternmost suburb La Petite Afrique, while most of its affluent population are trying to imitate Gustav Eiffel, who retired here and lived to be 90. Beaulieu's vintage casino and *thés dansants* are a retro attraction, but the *real* magnet is a place so retro that even Socrates would feel at home there: the **Villa Kerylos** (open 2–6, summer 2:30–6:30, closed Mon and Nov, adm), a striking reproduction of a wealthy 5th-century BC Athenian's abode, furnishings, and garden, built in 1908 by archaeologist Theodore Reinach. Reinach spared no expense on the marbles, ivories, bronzes, mosaic and fresco reproductions, to help his genuine antiquities feel at home; glass windows, plumbing, and a hidden piano are the only modern anachronisms. And here, on a shore that reminded him of the Aegean, this ultimate philhellene lived himself like an Athenian, holding symposia, exercising and bathing with his male buddies, and keeping the womenfolk out of the way.

Cap Ferrat

Another retro-repro fantasy, the **Villa Ephrussi de Rothschild**, also known as the Musée Ile de France crowns the narrow isthmus of bucolic Cap Ferrat, enjoying spectacular views over both the Baie des Fourmis and the harbour of Villefranche (a 10-min walk from the Corniche Inférieure, or catch the irregular bus to St-Jean, guided tours at 10–12 and 2–6; 10–12 and 3–7 July and Aug; closed Mon, Sun am and Nov, adm). The flamboyant Béatrice de Rothschild, who never went anywhere without her trunk of fifty wigs, was a compulsive art collector, and after marrying the banker Baron Ephrussi, had this Italianate villa specially built to house her treasures—a Venetian rococo room was designed for Béatrice's Tiepolo ceiling, while other rooms set off her Renaissance furniture, Florentine bridal chests, paintings by Boucher, rare Chinese screens and furniture, Flemish and Beauvais tapestries, Sèvres porcelain, Louis-Quinze and Louis-Seize furniture, a covered Andalusian patio (a favourite location shot for James Bond and other films), a hidden bathroom and a collection of porcelain vases that ladies of yore discreetly slipped under their skirts when nature called. To create the equally eclectic gardens, the isthmus was given a crew cut, and terraced into different levels. There's a French garden with a copy of the *Amour* fountain from the Petit Trianon; a Florentine garden, with a white marble ephebe; a Spanish garden, with papyrus, dates and pomegranates; also Exotic, Japanese and English gardens, and a lapidary garden decorated with Romanesque capitals, arches, and gargoyles.

Cap Ferrat, with its lush greenery, secret villas and little azure coves is ripe territory for strolls or swims—there's even a rare sandy beach, **Plage de Passable** along Chemin du Roy, west of Villa Ephrussi. The 'Roy' in question was bad old King Leopold II of the Belgians, whose merciless exploitation of the Congo (see Conrad's *Heart of Darkness*) helped pay for his luxurious life here, where it was rumoured that he made his valet iron his morning newspapers. The villa (Les Cèdres) is now more democratically used for a delightful **zoo** with a chimp's tea party that kids find hysterical (open daily, adm).

If you have fortitude you can climb up and up the steep stair for the tremendous view from the **Phare** (the lighthouse at the south tip of the promontory, near the Sun Beach swimming pool; open 9–12 and 3–6 summer; otherwise till 4); if you need fortitude, you can find a *pastis* in the former-fishing-now-yacht-port of **St-Jean-Cap-Ferrat**. Jean Cocteau painted the village's *Salle des Mariages*, but with hardly the same vigour as in Menton. A walking path circles around the dew-claw of land south of the port called **Pointe St-Hospice** where, in the 6th century, the Niçois saint Hospice had a hermitage (now marked by a 19th-century chapel). With one arm chained to the wall, Hospice lived off algae brought to him by pious souls, and uttered dire prophesies about barbarian invasions that came true, recorded by the Merovingian historian, Gregory of Tours. Another path, the **Promenade Maurice Rouvier** leads from St-Jean's beach to Beaulieu in an hour.

Villefranche-sur-Mer

In the 14th century, the deep, wooded bay between Cap Ferrat and Nice was a duty-free port, and hence Villefranche's name. It became an important military port for the Savoys in the 18th century, a period that saw Villefranche take on the appearance it has today: tall, brightly coloured houses, narrow lanes and stairs, some so overhung with houses that they're actually tunnels like **Rue Obscure**, which came in handy as a bomb shelter in the last war. The streets open up to the wide quay, given over to bars and restaurants. Fishermen stored their nets in the portside Romanesque **Chapelle de St-Pierre** until 1957, when Jean Cocteau frescoed it in 'ghosts of colours' with scenes from the Life of St Peter (walking on the water with an angel's help, which astounds the fish but makes Christ smile), plus images of the fishergirls of Villefranche, the gypsies at Saintes-Maries-de-la-Mer, and angels from Cocteau's private heaven (9:30–12 and 2–4:30, until 6 in the summer, closed Fri, adm). The Duke of Savoy's **Citadelle St-Elme** has been put back to work as the Hôtel de Ville and three marginal museums: the **Musée Volti**, with sculptures of women by a native of Villefranche; the **Musée Goetz-Boumeester**, with works donated to the city by Henri Goetz and his wife Christine Boumeester, and one with items from a 16th-century shipwreck (all open June–Sept 10–12 and 3–7; Oct–May 10–12 and 2–5, closed Sun am, Tues and Nov).

Market Days: Beaulieu, daily exc Sunday. St-Jean-Cap-Ferrat, Tuesday, above the Centre Denis-Séméria. Villefranche, Sunday antique market.

WHERE TO STAY/EATING OUT
Beaulieu-sur-Mer (06310): in the 1870s, Gordon Bennett, flamboyant owner of the *New York Herald* (the man who sent Stanley to find Livingstone) built *******La Réserve**,

5 Blvd Maréchal-Leclerc, tel 93 01 00 01, one of the most exclusive hotels on the Riviera, and if a touch old-fashioned, still offering its guests grand sea views, a beach and marina, heated pool and more. The neo-Renaissance restaurant has had rave reviews for its new, exciting dishes by chef Joël Garault that vary with the season (menus 360–480 F). Its equally elegant *fin-de-siècle* Italianate neighbour, *****Métropole, Blvd Maréchal-Leclerc, tel 93 01 00 08, has similar amenities, but a more relaxed atmosphere and a superb master chef, Pierre Estival (perfect *bouillabaisse* for 400 F; menus 380 F and 460 F). Near the station, ***Don Gregorio, 3 Av. Maréchal-Joffre, has rooms with balconies and a pool at the back; on the same street at No. 29 **Le Havre Bleu, tel 93 01 01 40, is an attractive hotel, with pleasant rooms, many with terraces. The small, simple *Sélect, Place Général de Gaulle, tel 93 01 05 42, also near the station is the best of the lone-star choices. If it's time to eat and you're not a Rothschild, join the crowd in the garden at La Pignatelle, 10 Rue Quincenet, tel 93 01 03 37, which does delicious fish soup, and a lunch menu at 75 F (dinner menus 110F and 170 F).

St-Jean-Cap-Ferrat (06290): Even though its villas are the most exclusive on the Riviera, Cap Ferrat has hotels in all price ranges, beginning with one of the most beautiful of the entire Côte: a charming, voluptuous Italian villa, overlooking the pleasure port, *****Voile d'Or, tel 93 01 13 13. An ideal first or second honeymoon hotel, it has a laid-back atmosphere, a garden hanging over the port, a heated pool, and rooms with every luxury a hotel could have. Its equally exceptional restaurant, favoured by the yachting set, uses only fish caught off St-Jean, giving them traditional and more exotic treatments—such as shellfish jambalaya à la Key West. The grand wine cellar is managed by an *Ancien Premier Sommelier de France* (menus 320 F and 420 F; closed Nov–Feb). At the Belle Epoque *****Grand Hôtel du Cap-Ferrat, Blvd Général de Gaulle, tel 93 76 00 21, the already luxurious rooms have been restored in a more airy, comfortable Riviera style, all set in acres of gardens, lawns, and palms. A funicular railway lowers guests down to an Olympic-size pool just over the sea. The restaurant, on a terrace shaded by parasol pines, serves delicious meals, though decidedly unhealthy for your wallet (600–900 F).

More down-to-earth choices include **Brise Marine, Av. Jean-Mermoz, tel 93 76 04 36, with a garden, terrace, and large rooms, half with sea views; or **Clair Logis, near the centre of the Cap on quiet Allée des Brises, a villa set in an enclosed garden; or the relaxing *La Costière, Av. Albert I, tel 93 76 03 89, with lovely views across the cape and a garden. If you can splash out 165 F on an exquisite lunch menu, get a table at Jean-Jacques Jouteaux, 2 Av. D. Séméria, tel 93 76 03 97. Here, you can also eat *à la carte*, for considerably more, and try delicacies like violet asparagus *au jus de truffes* or thin slices of raw *daurade* (sea-bream) in balsamic vinegar. Another tempting, innovative 160 F menu is served at Le Sloop overlooking the bobbing yachts in the Port de Plaisance, tel 93 01 48 63; try their fresh pasta (cannelloni filled with crab-meat and ricotta), fresh fish in olive oil, and delectable chocolate and apricot desserts.

Villefranche-sur-Mer (06230): Just beside the port, ***Welcome, Quai Amiral-Courbet, tel 93 76 76 93, has recently been renovated, and all of its pretty rooms are air-conditioned; those on the 5th floor are ravishing (closed mid-Nov–mid-Dec, half-board in season). Or try the unpretentious, family-run **Provençal, 4 Av. du Maréchal Joffre, tel 93 01 71 42 (closed Nov–mid-Jan). For dinner, the delightful turn-of-the-century villa Le Massoury, Av. Léopold II, tel 93 01 03 66, has a grand terrace and views over the port to go with its succulent roast duck with garlic (menus 200 F with wine—400 F without). At **Langoustine's**, 10 Rue du May, tel 93 01 91 86, the English owner whips up half-a-dozen variations on *langoustines* alone as well as other tasty denizens of the deep (menu 130 F).

NICE

The capital of the French Riviera and France's fifth city, with 400,000 inhabitants, Nice is the Hexagon's most visited city after Paris—the English have been coming for well over 200 years, back to when 'Nizza la Bella' still belonged to Savoy. It was the presence of so many rich, idle foreigners that formed the city's character, its reactionary politics and unsavoury links with the Mafia, its culture (it has 17 museums and nearly all are free), its high density of poodles and frown-faced poodle ladies, and its ornate holiday-villa architecture. It is the one town on the Côte that doesn't seem to need tourists, the one that stays open through the winter.

Despite the megalomanic edifice-complex of disgraced mayor Jacques Médecin—the right wing's answer to Mitterand's neo-Louis XIV building programme in Paris—Nice is still surprisingly as nice as ever. The delights of Vieux Nice haven't been totally spoiled by its recent gentrification, and you could go for the food alone, a wonderful mix of the best of France and Italy. The public transport is excellent, making Nice the ideal base for exploring the Riviera.

History

Nice was a hot-spot even 400,000 years ago, when hunters who tracked mammoths and learnt how to make fires to grill their prey frequented the caves of Terra Amata. The Ligurians, around 1000 BC, were the first to move in permanently, constructing their *oppida* at the mouth of the Paillon river, and on the hill overlooking the valley. Greeks from Marseille founded a commercial colony near the seaside *oppidum* that they named Nikaïa after an obscure military victory, or perhaps after the nymph Nikaia. Beset by Ligurian pirates, the Nikaïans asked the Romans for aid. The Romans duly came, and stayed, but preferred to live near the hilltop *oppidum*, because it was closer to the Via Julia Augusta. They named this town *Cemenelum* (modern Cimiez), and made it the capital of the province of *Alpes Maritimae*. By the 3rd century AD Cemenelum had 20,000 inhabitants, all quickly going soft amid swimming pools and central heating.

But by the 6th century, luxury-loving Cemenelum had collapsed with the rest of the Roman empire while Greek Nikaïa struggled on and regrouped itself in the 10th century around a cathedral. By the 1340s, with a population of 13,000, Nice was the third city in Provence after Marseille and Arles. The Black Death and civil wars of the period soon cut it down to size, and in 1388 the city's leaders voted to hitch their wagon to a brighter star than Louis d'Anjou, and pledged allegiance to Amadeus VII, Count of Savoy.

The Savoys fortified Nice and it grew rich trading with Italy. It had its own little Renaissance, thanks to Ludovico Brea and the other members of the mid-15th-century Ecole Niçoise—Antoine and François Brea, Jean Miralhet, and Jacques Durandi—

noted for their uncluttered, simple compositions and firm sense of line. The 17th century saw the first expansion of Nice outside its medieval walls, and in 1696 and 1705 came the first of several French interludes that interrupted Savoy rule—interludes that Louis XIV took advantage of to blow up Nice's fortifications.

Cold Brits, and Absorbtion into the Mystic Hexagon

Although relations remained sour with France, the Savoys became firm allies with the English, and by 1755 the first trickle of milords began to discover the sunny charms of a Riviera winter. Doctor and novelist Tobias Smollett spent a year in Nice in 1763, and in his singularly grouchy *Travels through France and Italy* (1766) did what Peter Mayle has since done for Provence: made the Côte, because of, or in spite of, its quaint local characters, irresistible to the British. Even though it took at least two weeks to reach Nice from Calais, by 1787 there were enough Brits wintering here to support a casino (then a fashionable Venetian novelty), an English theatre, estate agent, and newspaper. In 1830, when a frost killed all the orange trees, the English community raised funds to give the unemployed a job: building a seafront promenade along the Baie des Anges known to this day as the Promenade des Anglais. Part of its purpose was to keep English girls away from the riff-raff, or more particularly the Niçois—the British brought with their money attitudes so arrogant that as early as the 1780s, sensitive locals left town each winter to avoid being humiliated by their visitors.

In 1860, as Napoleon III's reward for promising to help Vittorio Emanuele II of Savoy create the future kingdom of Italy, a secret treaty was signed ceding Nice and Savoy to France. To keep up appearances, a plebiscite was held. Vittorio Emanuele encouraged his subjects to vote for French union, but even more encouraging was the presence of the French army marching through Nice, and French agents bullying the majority Italian-speaking population. The final result (24,449 pro-France to 160 against), stinks even to this day. But the railway arrived shortly thereafter, and Nice settled down to its chosen vocation as the winter haven for Europe's elite. Sumptuous neo-Moorish-Gothic-Baroque follies were built to house some 20,000 wintering Britons and Russians by 1890; 20 years later the numbers of foreigners had increased to over 150,000. Queen Victoria preferred the suburb of Cimiez; her haemophiliac son, Prince Leopold, introduced croquet to Nice before dying after slipping on the marble floor in the casino.

Nice Today

Since the 30s, many of Nice's hotels and villas have been converted into furnished flats while the concrete mixers of destiny march further and further west and up the valleys. But there's still a lopsided amount of money floating around this town, where astronomical rents and property values are rivalled today in France only by Paris and Cannes; wealthy, politically conservative retirees help support an equally right-wing *rentier* population.

All this money floating about has attracted the corruption and underworld activities of the *milieu*, previously associated only with Marseille. For decades Nice was ruled as the personal fiefdom of the right-wing Médecin family. Jean Médecin was mayor from 1928 until 1965, and was succeeded by his flamboyant son Jacques, writer of cookbooks and lover of culture, an anti-Semite who hosted a National Front congress no other city would have, and who twinned Nice with Cape Town, South Africa. He was lambasted

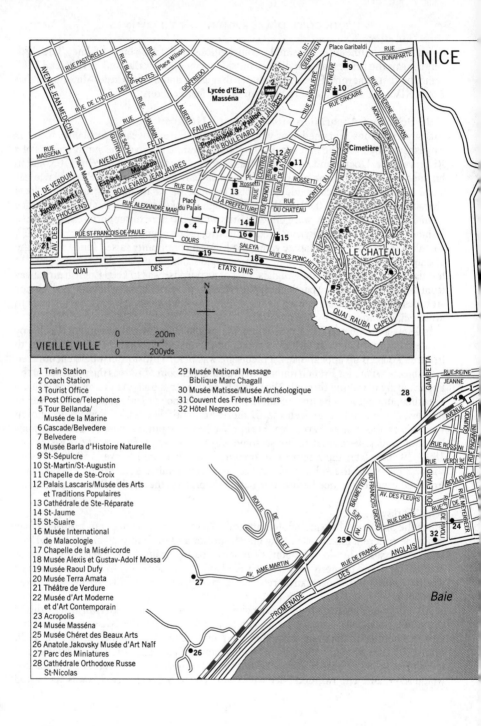

NICE

VIEILLE VILLE

0 ——— 200m
0 ——— 200yds

1 Train Station
2 Coach Station
3 Tourist Office
4 Post Office/Telephones
5 Tour Bellanda/
   Musée de la Marine
6 Cascade/Belvedere
7 Belvedere
8 Musée Barla d'Histoire Naturelle
9 St-Sépulcre
10 St-Martin/St-Augustin
11 Chapelle de Ste-Croix
12 Palais Lascaris/Musée des Arts
   et Traditions Populaires
13 Cathédrale de Ste-Réparate
14 St-Jaume
15 St-Suaire
16 Musée International
   de Malacologie
17 Chapelle de la Miséricorde
18 Musée Alexis et Gustav-Adolf Mossa
19 Musée Raoul Dufy
20 Musée Terra Amata
21 Théâtre de Verdure
22 Musée d'Art Moderne
   et d'Art Contemporain
23 Acropolis
24 Musée Masséna
25 Musée Chéret des Beaux Arts
26 Anatole Jakovsky Musée d'Art Naïf
27 Parc des Miniatures
28 Cathédrale Orthodoxe Russe
   St-Nicolas

29 Musée National Message
   Biblique Marc Chagall
30 Musée Matisse/Musée Archéologique
31 Couvent des Frères Mineurs
32 Hôtel Negresco

Baie

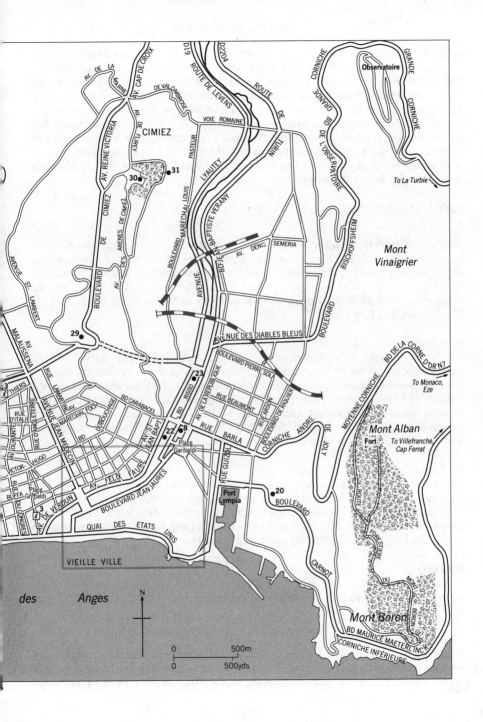

for his links with the Mafia in Graham Greene's 1982 booklet *J' accuse: The Dark Side of Nice*, which you still won't find in the city bookshops. In 1990 the slow, grinding wheels of French justice began to catch up with him, when it was discovered, among other things, that money for the Nice Opera was being diverted into the mayor's bank account. Médecin took to his heels and now resides in Punta del Este, Uruguay—a country that has no extradition treaty with France—where he has just requested citizenship. His sister, Geneviève, barely defeated the National Front candidate in local government elections, and took his old seat on the Conseil Général of the Alpes Maritimes *département*; meanwhile, Jean-Marie Le Pen hovers, considering how to best fill the right-wing void left by Médecin's departure.

GETTING AROUND

By Air

Nice's large, modern **Aéroport Nice-Côte d'Azur** is the third busiest in France, served by a wide variety of flights from around the world. Buses run every 20 min between the airport and coach station, while bus 23 provides links with the train station. Flights to or from Paris go through Aérogare 2; all others through Aérogare 1. Airline numbers are Air France, tel 93 83 91 00; British Airways, tel 93 83 19 61; Air Inter, tel 93 31 55 55, Dan-Air, tel 93 21 34 34.

By Train

Nice's train station is in Av. Thiers, not far from the centre (information tel 93 87 50 50, reservations tel 93 88 89 93). Besides *Métrazur* trains between Ventimiglia and St-Raphaël, Nice has frequent connections to Marseille and its TGV to Paris. The **Gare du Sud**, tel 93 84 89 71, served by the little *Train des Pignes* (so called for the pine-cones that the crew used stop to collect for pine-nuts, see p. 213) is currently at 33 Av. Malausséna, the upper extension of Av. Jean-Médecin, but a new station is under construction to the west, and the old one has been earmarked to become a shopping centre.

By Coach

The *gare routière* is on the Promenade du Paillon, on the edge of Vieux Nice, tel 93 85 61 81. There are frequent buses to Grasse, Vence, Cannes, Marseille, Aix-en-Provence, Avignon, Brignoles, St-Raphaël, Le Muy, Cagnes, Antibes, Menton and Monte Carlo, as well as one a day for Plan-du-Var, Puget-Théniers and Entrevaux (on the route to Gap). City buses 5 and 17 link the coach and train stations.

By Ferry

In the summer SNCM has frequent sailings to Corsica. For information and reservations contact them at 3 Av. Gustave V, off the western end of the Quai des Etats-Unis, tel 93 13 66 66.

City Buses

Buses run by the *Transports Urbains de Nice*, or TUN, are more than nice: nearly every stop has little lights telling you how far away your bus is. Pick up a free *Guide Horaire du Réseau Bus* with maps and schedules, at the tourist office or from TUN's information centre, 10 Av. Félix Faure, tel 93 62 08 08. Several tourist tickets are available, offering limitless rides for one, five or seven days. For **taxis**, tel 93 80 70.

Car, Bicycle and Scooter Hire
Among the cheapest car hire places, with special weekend discounts, are Loveo at 3 Rue Bonaparte, tel 93 89 71 10, and in the *gare routière*, tel 93 62 66 67. Try also Thrifty, at the train station, tel 93 21 00 25; Avis, at 2 Av. des Phocéens at the end of Blvd Jean Jaurès, tel 93 80 63 52; and Hertz at the airport, tel 93 21 36 72 and 12 Av. de Suède, tel 93 87 11 87. For **bike/moped/scooter hire**, contact Cycles Arnaud, 4 Place Grimaldi, tel 93 87 88 55; or Nicea Location Rent, 9 Av. Thiers, tel 93 82 42 71.

TOURIST INFORMATION
Av. Thiers, next to the train station, tel 93 87 07 07. Other offices are in the airport (tel 93 83 32 64) and at 5 Av. Gustave V, near Place Masséna, tel 93 87 60 60. A new office, Chalet Info Montagne in the Jardin Albert I, tel 93 87 30 24, will tell you all about ski holidays and mountain activities in the Alpes-Maritimes. Or avoid humans and ring up a computer called *Com'Azur*, which spouts data on hotels, museum hours and so on, tel 92 96 06 06. Information on lodgings, jobs, entertainment etc. for young people is available at **CIJ**, 19 Rue Gioffredo, tel 93 80 93 93. **Main Post Office**: near the station at 23 Av. Thiers, tel 93 88 55 41, although Nice's Poste Restante is in Place Wilson, tel 93 85 98 63.
Police: tel 17.
Medical: S.O.S. doctors and ambulance, tel 93 85 01 01. Casualty ward, Hôpital St-Roch, 5 Rue Pierre Dérolny, tel 93 13 33 00.

Vieux Nice

Dismissed as a dangerous slum in the 1970s, this piquant quarter east of Place Masséna is busy becoming the trendiest part of Nice, brimful with cafés, bistros, night-clubs, designer boutiques and galleries. And the population, once poor and ethnically mixed, is now more than half French and upwardly mobile. But the shock of the new is mitigated by the tenacity of the old-grandmotherly underwear, paint and stationery shops, and no-name working-men's bars have so far refused to budge. Picasso liked to walk here because it reminded him of the Barrì Chino in Barcelona.

'Vieux' in Vieux Nice means Genoese seaside Baroque—tall, steep *palazzi*, many with opulent 17th- and 18th-century portals and windows, turning the narrow streets and steps below into chasms that suddenly open up into tiny squares, each with its chapel. For the old Niçois are among the most religious people on the coast, and still join the confraternities of Penitents—lay organizations dedicated to public demonstrations of penitence, founded in Italy in the 14th century during the great Franciscan and Dominican revivals. Of the city's original seven confraternities, four still survive, all in this neighbourhood.

At its eastern end, Vieux Nice is closed by **Colline du Château**, the ancient acropolis of Nikaïa and site of the 10th- to 12th-century town and cathedral. Of the latter, a few ruins remain—the Savoyards demolished it to make way for their citadel, which was in turn blown up by Louis XIV. You can walk up the steps or pay a few *sous* to take the lift at the east end of the Quai des Etats-Unis near **Tour Bellanda** (where Berlioz composed his *King Lear Overture*) and the little **Musée de la Marine**, with ships' models (10–12 and 2–5, in summer until 7). Among the gardens at the top of the hill are two cemeteries, one Jewish and one grandiose Italian, where you can find the tombs of Garibaldi's mum and Mercedes Jellinek, who gained immortality in 1902 when her father chose her name for a new line of Daimlers. From the belvedere by the artificial cascade the real boats down below don't look much bigger than the models in the museum, while the shimmering, tiled, glazed roof-tops of Nice curl into the distance around the Baie des Anges.

If you descend by way of the east flank of the hill, down Montée Eberlé and Rue Catherine Ségurane, you'll end up in the arcaded, 18th-century **Place Garibaldi**, named after its glowering statue of the hero of Italy's unification, who was born near the port in 1806. The Blue Penitents (all Penitents are named by the colour of their hooded robes) have their neoclassical chapel of **St-Sépulcre** on this square, while just around the corner, facing the esplanade on Av. St-Sébastien, is the **Musée Barla d'Histoire Naturelle** (9–12 and 2–6, closed Tues, holidays, and mid-Aug to mid-Sept), where you can ponder, among other things, a 19th-century collection of 7000 painted plaster mushrooms.

South of Place Garibaldi off Rue Neuve is the city's oldest parish church, **St-Martin-St-Auguste**, where a monk named Martin Luther said a mass during his momentous pilgrimage to Rome. The interior was Baroqued in the 17th century; its treasures include a fine *Pietà* (*c.* 1500) by a follower of Ludovico Brea and a photocopy of Garibaldi's baptismal certificate. Further south, Rue Pairolièrie leads into 'Babazouck', the curious nickname for the heart of Vieux Nice, and **Place St-François**, where a pungent fish market takes place every morning except Monday. Continuing south, the **Chapelle de Ste-Croix** in Rue de la Croix is the headquarters of the Peñitents Blancs, the oldest confraternity (founded in 1306) and the most popular, perhaps because they were still into public self-flagellation in the 1750s.

A block to the west, at 15 Rue Droit, the **Palais Lascaris** is a grand 1648 Genoese-style mansion, converted by the city into the **Musée des Arts et Traditions Populaires** (9:30–12 and 2:30–6, closed Mon—and Tues in winter—and all Nov). The ground floor contains a reconstructed pharmacy of 1738; the first floor or *piano nobile*, where guests would be received, is saturated with elaborate Genoese 'quadratura' (architectural *trompe-l'oeil*) frescoes, Flemish tapestries, ornate woodwork, and a 1578 Italian precursor of the pianoforte. The next floor is devoted to popular traditions, furnishings, and manufacturing. Contemporary exhibitions take place at the corner of Rue Droite and Rue de la Loge, at the **Galerie Municipale Renoir** (10:30–6, closed Mon and Sun).

Take Rue Rossetti west to the cafés of pretty Place Rossetti, dominated by Nice's 17th-century **Cathédral de Ste-Réparate**, crowned with a joyful dome and lantern of glazed tiles in emerald bands. The uncorrupted body of Réparate, a 15-year-old virgin martyred in Cesarea in the 300s, arrived in Nice in a boat of flowers towed by a pair of angels (hence Baie des Anges). This same Réparate was the first patron saint of Florence before the city adopted intermediaries with greater heavenly clout, and here, too, in Nice, the young virgin is currently losing a popularity contest with St Rita of Cascia, whose cult has already usurped the 17th-century church of **St-Jaume** in Rue Benoît-Bunico. Here, her altar gets nearly all the business, possibly because her speciality is unhappy middle-aged housewives—Rita herself was burdened in the 14th century with a rotten husband, ungrateful children, and a smelly sore on her forehead that just wouldn't heal.

Rita's compatriot, Paganini, who died nearby in 1840 at 23 Rue de la Préfecture, had his share of troubles, too, but most of them were posthumous. Ste-Réparate's bishop was convinced that the sounds Paganini made on his violin could only have been produced by the devil incarnate (the maestro liked to startle the neighbours by making it howl like a tom cat) and refused him a Christian burial. He even wanted to toss Paganini's body into the Paillon. In the end, however, the dead fiddler was shunted to Cannes and then to Genoa and Parma, where he was finally buried in 1896.

Cours Saleya

After the dark lanes of Vieux Nice, the sun pops back into the sky over Cours Saleya, an elongated little gem of urban planning, where bars and restaurants line up along the famous outdoor market, overflowing with flowers and sumptuous food displays worthy of the Riviera's gourmet vortex. The Cours is closed at one end by the 17th-century Palais du Sénat and **St-Suaire**, home of the Red Penitents, who assisted pilgrims. But the principal focal point of the Cours is the Black Penitents' **Chapelle de la Miséricorde**, designed in 1740 by Bernardo Vittone, a disciple of Turin's extraordinary Baroque architects Guarino Guarini and Juvarra. Inside (unfortunately locked except for special tours: ask at the tourist office), it's all virtuoso Baroque geometry, a gold and stucco confection with vertiginous *trompe-l'oeil* paintings in the vault. A fine early Renaissance *Polyptyque de la Miséricorde* (1430) by Jean Mirailhet hangs in the sacristy, painted for the confraternity, whose mission was to assure the dead a dignified burial. The Cours also has the **Musée International de Malacologie** (at No. 3, open May–Sept, Tues–Sat 10:30–1 and 2–6). *Malakos* in Greek means soft, which describes the texture of the residents of the museum's 15,000 seashells, a few of whom are still quick in the aquarium, the rest dead on the shelf.

A double row of one-storey buildings separates Cours Saleya from the Quai des Etats-Unis, where you'll find a pair of little museums (both open Tues–Sat 10:30–12 and 2–6, Sun 2–6): the **Musée Alexis et Gustav-Adolf Mossa** at 59 Quai des Etats-Unis, featuring landscapes by Alexis, a native of Nice, and the exquisitely drawn mytho-morbid Symbolist works of his son Gustav-Adolf Mossa (1883–1971), who painted between 1903 and 1917 and then just stopped. At No. 77 the **Musée Raoul Dufy** has a large collection of paintings by a much cheerier soul who spent his latter years in Nice, producing colourful 'café-society' art. Far more compelling are the handful of Dufy's early Fauve works, especially the remarkable 1908 *Bateaux à l'Estaque*, a Cubist painting predating Cubism itself, although Dufy like many of the Fauves never followed the direction he mapped out for others.

The Port, Terra Amata, and Hilltop Follies

To the east, Quai des Etats-Unis circles around the wind-punched hill of the Château, where it's known as Quai Rauba-Capéu ('hat thief') before it meets placid **Port**

Lympia, the departure point for ferries to Corsica. Among the 18th-century buildings overlooking the port, is the **Musée Terra Amata** (25 Blvd Carnot, buses 1,2, 9, 10, 14, 10, 38; open 10–12 and 2–6, closed Mon), built into the cave holding one of the world's oldest 'households', a pebble-walled wind-shelter built by hunters 400 millennia ago. A fascinating set of models, bones and tools helps evoke life in Nice at the dawn of time. Nor had things changed radically 200,000 years later, judging by the palaeolithic relics left in the nearby **Grotte du Lazaret** (to visit, ask at Terra Amata).

Boulevard Carnot (the Corniche Inférieure) continues east past some extravagant Belle Epoque villas, culminating in eccentricity in the pink, turreted **Château de l'Anglais**. Built in 1858 by Colonel Robert Smith, a military engineer in India, the result weds English Perpendicular with mock-Mogul Palace to produce one of the best follies on the Riviera. Behind this rise the forested slopes of **Mont Boron**; off Route Forestière du Mont Boron, a magnificent path, the **Sentier Bellevue**, meanders to the top, capped by a fort of 1880.

A far more delightful piece of military architecture, **Fort Alban**, is just off the Moyenne Corniche, above the Youth Hostel (take bus 14 to Chemin du Fort, or if you're driving, turn right off Rte Forestière du Mont Boron, onto Chemin du Fort du Mont Alban). Built in 1570, it bristles with four toy turrets roofed with glazed Niçois tiles, from which the guards could see all the way to Menton. To the north, off the Grande Corniche, is an elegant **Observatoire**, designed in part by Charles Garnier with a dome by Gustav Eiffel (bus 74 from Blvd Pierre Sola).

Up the Paillon

Nice's torrential river, the Paillon, began to vanish under the pavements in the 1830s, and now secretly gushes or trickles below some of Nice's proudest showcases and gardens. Nearest the sea, Jardin Albert I is the site of the open-air **Théâtre du Verdure**, while upstream, as it were, vast **Place Masséna** is generously endowed with flower-beds and benches for Nice's sun-loving retirees. Further up, the Promenade du Paillon is dominated by the hanging gardens of the bus station/multi-storey car park, a mini-Babylon with an unsavoury reputation for small time vice—vice that pales in the face of ex-mayor Jacques Médecin's pair of dreadnoughts looming beyond.

The first of these, reached by sets of Aztec temple steps, is Nice's answer to the Pompidou Centre in Paris: the 282-million-franc **Théâtre de Nice** and the **Musée d'Art Moderne et d'Art Contemporaine** (or MAMAC, open 11–6 except Tues; Fri until 10). Inauspiciously inaugurated in June 1990, as the public revelations of Médecin's sins reached a pitch, the ceremony was boycotted by the Niçois art community, who convinced culture minister Jack Lang to stay away as well. But the building—four concrete towers, linked by glass walkways that seem to smile and frown and afford pleasant views over the city (never mind that the roof was already leaking four months after it was finished)—is an admirable setting for the works of Christo, Niki de Sainte-Phalle, Warhol, Dine, Oldenburg, Rauschenberg, and other influential figures of the 1960s and 70s. But the primary focus is on the artists of the 'Second Nice school': Yves Klein, Martial Rayasse, César, Arman, Ben, and Swiss-born Jean Tinguely, whose concoctions of plastic consumer junk, broken machinery, musical intruments and exploding suicide machines spoof not only society, but the artificial, rarefied and wordy world of contemporary art—especially the push-button fun house called the *Little Shop of Ben*.

The view up the Paillon is blocked by Médecin's 1985 congress and art centre and *cinemathèque* called **Acropolis**, a gruesome megalithic bunker of concrete slabs and smoked glass. No design could be more diametrically opposed (stylistically and philosophically) to the acropolis in Athens, and the mass of guitars in Arman's *Music Power* at the entrance hardly redeems it. Beyond this are more mastodons: a *Palais des Expositions* and a *Palais des Sports*,

West of Place Masséna and the Promenade des Anglais

The Paillon neatly divides Vieux Nice from the boom city of 19th-century tourism, full of ornate, debonair apartments and hotels. Important streets fan out from Place Masséna and the adjacent Jardin Albert I: Nice's main shopping street, **Av. Jean Médecin**, leads up to the train station; **Rue Masséna**, the centre of a lively pedestrian-only restaurant and shopping zone; and the fabled, palm-lined **Promenade des Anglais**, still a-glitter through the fumes of the traffic, which is usually as strangled as poor Isadora Duncan was when her scarf caught the wheel of her Bugatti here in 1927. The long pebble beach is crowded day and night in the summer, when parties spontaneously erupt among the many illegal but tolerated campers. Visitors from the opposite end of the economic spectrum check into the fabled Belle Epoque **Hôtel Négresco**, vintage 1906, although they no longer roll snake eyes in the casino of American millionaire Frank Jay Gould's 1929 **Palais de la Méditerranée**, a masterpiece of French Art Deco that was nevertheless recently destined for the wrecking-ball. The speculators gave in to the protests at the last minute, on the condition that the building had all its original innards removed like an Egyptian mummy. Another gem clinging tenaciously to the Promenade among the new buildings is at No. 139, a flowery Art Nouveau-style villa of 1910 built by a Finnish engineer.

Next to the Négresco is the garden of the **Musée Masséna** (daily except Mon, Oct–Apr 10–12 and 2–5; otherwise 10–12 and 3–6; closed Nov). Built in the Empire style in 1901 for Prince Victor Masséna, the grandson of Napoleon's marshal, it was left to Nice on the condition that it become a museum of history. At the entrance, a solemn statue of Napoleon tarted up in a toga sets the tone for the ground-floor salons—heavy and pompous and stylistically co-ordinated from ceiling stucco to chair leg. The atmosphere lightens upstairs with a pair of fine retables from the 1450s by Jacques Durandi, panels from a polyptych attributed to Ludovico Brea, ceramics, armour, and a curious 16th-century Flemish painting, the *Vierge à la Fleur* with a fly in the flower, 'a symbol of death and vanity'. The top floor displays statues of the Ten Incarnations of Vishnu, Spanish earrings, views of Nice, and rooms dedicated to hometown boys Garibaldi and the cruel and wicked Marshal Masséna, the military genius Napoleon called 'l'enfant gâté de la victoire' whose appetite for atrocities was matched only by his greedy plundering. Then there's the obligatory Napoleonana: a billiard-ball from St Helena and Josephine's bed, with a big N on the coverlet.

Fine and *Naïf* Arts, and a Russian Cathedral

From the Masséna museum, a brisk ten-minute walk or bus 22 (get off at the foot of Rue Bassenetts and walk 100m up the path) leads to the handsome 1880 villa built by a Ukranian princess, enlarged by an American millionaire, and now home of the **Musée Chéret des Beaux Arts** (33 Av. des Baumettes; 10–12 and 2–5, summer 3–6, closed Mon and Nov). With the Matisses, Chagalls and Dufys in Nice's other museums, the Chéret is left with 'old masters of the 19th century'—a euphemism for tired, flabby academic paintings and portraits of Madame this and Madame that, a *Portrait of an old man* by Fragonard and works by Carle Van Loo, a native of Nice. But there are a few meatier paintings: a 1615 *David* attributed to Tanzio da Varallo, a Lombard follower of Caravaggio; an self-portrait by Russian aristocrat Marie Bashkirtseff; and a roomful of her contemporary, Kees Van Dongen, including his entertaining 1927 *Tango of the Archangel*, which perhaps more than any painting evokes the Roaring Twenties on the Riviera—even the archangel, in his dinner-jacket, is wearing high-heels. One room is devoted to Félix Ziem, and another to the Belle Epoque's favourite lithographist, Jules Chéret, who introduced colour posters to France in 1866, most of them decorated with dancing doll-women caught in swirling pastel tornadoes of silly *putti*.

To the west, the perfume magnate Coty built the pink Château de Ste-Hélène, a building now used as the **Anatole Jakovsky Musée d'Art Naïf** (Av. du Val Marie, bus 8, 10,12, to Av. de la Californie, and walk or take little bus 34; open 10–12 and 2–5, 3–6 summer, closed Tues and Nov). The museum is formed around 600 paintings spanning the 17th to the 20th centuries, donated by Jakovsky, a tireless promoter of naïve art. The Yugoslavs are especially well-represented, with an enthusiasm for the genre that perhaps in some way counterbalances the unsolvable, nightmarish imbroglio of their politics. But even among the scenes of jolly village fêtes and fairs the surreal is never far, especially in *The Clock* by Jules Lefranc, and in the funny *Sodom and Gomorrah*, where the columns go flying every which way.

Two new commercial attractions have sprouted at the western end of Nice: the **Parc des Miniatures**, on Blvd Impératrice Eugénie, where Côte landmarks, from the Terra Amata caves up to Nice's Museum of Contemporary Art have been shrunk down to a 1:25 scale (bus 22, open every day; adm exp). Near the airport you may already have noticed the mega-greenhouse of **Parc Phoenix**, a Disneyland for botanists or garden lovers: its diamond dome supports 2,500 different plants in 7 different tropical climates (405 Promenade des Anglais: bus 9, 10, 23, 24, 26. Open 10 until sunset, closed Mon, adm exp).

In 1865, the young Tsarevich Nicholas was brought to Nice, and like so many consumptives who arrived in search of health he met the grim reaper instead. The luxurious villa where he died was demolished to construct, in his memory, the great **Cathédrale Orthodoxe Russe St-Nicolas**, modelled on the five-domed church of Jaroslavl near Moscow. Paid for by Tsar Nicolas II and completed only five years before the Bolshevik Revolution, its five onion domes shine with a colourful coating of glazed Niçois tiles; inside are lavish frescoes, woodwork and icons (located a few blocks from the west of the train station at 17 Blvd du Tzaréwitch, just off Blvd Gambetta (Mon–Sat 9–12 and 2:30–6, no shorts or sleeveless shirts, adm).

Cimiez: Chagall, Matisse, and Roman Ruins

On the low hills west of the Paillon, where wealthy Romans lived the good life in *Cemenelum*, modern Niçois do the same in Cimiez, a luxurious 19th-century suburb dotted with the grand hotels of yesteryear. Bus 15 or 15a from the *gare routière* will take you to the main attractions, beginning with the **Musée National Message biblique Marc Chagall**, at the foot of Cimiez hill on Rue du Docteur Ménard, west of Blvd de Cimiez (Oct–June 10–12:30 and 2–5:30; July–Sept 1–7, adm). Opened in 1971, the airy, specially-designed building incorporates stained-glass windows and mosaics by Chagall while 17 large canvases on Old Testament subjects glow on the walls, especially the red, red, red series of the *Song of Songs*. There are often temporary exhibits on Jewish art and studies, and a suitably biblical garden of olives and cypresses with an outdoor café.

Cimiez owed much of its original cachet to Queen Victoria, and she's gratefully remembered with a statue in front of her favourite lodging, the Hôtel Excelsior Regina Palace on Av. Regina, off Av. Reine Victoria. After World War II, the same hotel became headquarters for Henri Matisse, who died here in 1954, leaving the city a priceless collection of his works, displayed in the newly remodelled **Musée Matisse** (in a late 17th-century Genoese villa at 164 Av. des Arènes-de-Cimiez; 10–12 and 2:30–6:30: Oct–April 10–12 and 2–5, closed Sun morning and Mon). It contains all the bronzes Matisse ever made, and other works of every period—from one of his first oil-paintings, done in 1890 to his paper cut-outs of the 1950s; among the best known works are *Nature Morte aux Grenades*, *Rococo armchair*, designs for the chapel in Vence (see p. 112), illustrations made for Joyce's *Ulysses*, and the world's largest collection of his drawings.

Adjacent to the Matisse Museum is the new **Musée Archéologique** (10–12 and 2–6, closed Sun morn and Mon, adm), entered through the excavations of *Cemenelum*. These include the baths, with a marble summer pool, and the amphitheatre, with seating for 4000 (unusually small for a population of 20,000, but perhaps the posh Romans here were too couth for gladiators). The museum houses vases, coins, statues, jewels, and models of what Cimiez looked like 2000 years ago.

The Franciscan **Couvent des Frères Mineurs** is a short walk across the Jardin Publique. The Franciscans have been here since the 1500s, but their church was heavily restored in 1850, although it still has two beautiful altarpieces by Ludovico Brea: the *Vierge de Piété* and a *Crucifixion* on a gold background, together with other less explicable 17th-century paintings in the cloister that some scholars think may have alchemical meanings. Dufy and Matisse are buried in the adjacent cemetery, and there are fine views over the valley of the Paillon.

FESTIVALS

Nice is famous for its **carnival** in the two weeks before Lent, first mentioned in the 13th century. It died out in the early 1800s, and subsequent attempts to revive it to amuse the tourists only succeeded in 1873, when the painters Alexis and Gustav-Adolf Mossa took over the show. They initiated a burlesque royal cortège to escort the figure of King Carnival *Sa Majesté Carnaval* down Av. Jean-Médecin, accompanied by comical *grosses têtes*—masqueraders with giant papier-mâché heads. During the subsequent parades, dances and battles of flowers and sweets, King Carnival reigns from Place Masséna, only to be immolated on the night of Mardi Gras to the explosive barrage of fireworks. As mayor, Jacques Médecin was a big supporter of the carnival, much to the annoyance of many residents, especially since it cost more money to put on than it brought in, and was generally agreed to be a commercial rip-off; future carnivals will, it seems, be on a smaller scale. The second and third weeks of July see the excellent **Parade du Jazz** in the Jardin Publique de Cimiez; from the end of July to the beginning of August there are the **Festival de Folklore International** and more *Batailles des Fleurs*; and in December, a **Festival du Cinéma Italien**. The Comité des Fêtes handles all festival information at 5 Promenade des Anglais, tel 93 87 16 28.

ENTERTAINMENT AND ACTIVITIES
You can find out what's happening in Nice in the daily *Nice-Matin*, though it's not much good for anything else except lining the canary's cage. Other sources, covering the entire Côte are *7 jours/7 nuits*, distributed free in the tourist offices, or the *Semaine des Spectacles*, which appears Wednesdays in the news-stands. Local news, hours of religious services in English and more are in the monthly English-language *Riviera Reporter*, distributed free in English bookshops (in Nice, at **The Riviera Bookshop**, 10 Rue Blacas Chauvain and **The Cat's Whiskers**, 26 Rue Lamartine). If you need a **babysitter**, contact Association Niçoise de Services, 1 Rue Cavendish, tel 93 98 60 98.

Films in their original language unreel at the **Mercury Cinema**, 12 Place Garibaldi, tel 93 55 32 31, and at the **cinemathèque** in Acropolis, with special cartoons for children on Wednesday afternoons (tel 93 92 81 81). The Belle Epoque **Nice Opéra**, 4 Rue St-François-de-Paule, tel 93 85 67 31, puts on operas, concerts and recitals. Chamber and sacred music concerts are held at the **Musée d'Art Naïf** and the **Cathédrale Ste-Réparate**. Music, from ancient to avant-garde, and art videos are the fare in the auditorium of the **Musée d'Art Moderne et d'Art Contemporaine** (tel 93 62 61 62). Big-league musicians and dancers perform at **CEDAC de Cimiez** (49 Av. de la Marne, tel 93 81 09 09), while **Forum Nice Nord**, 10 Blvd Comte de Falicon, just off the A8 at Nice-Nord, tel 93 84 24 37, is a major venue for modern dance. From April onwards rock, jazz, and other concerts take place in the outdoor **Théâtre de Verdure** in Jardin Albert I. There are several small theatres in Vieux Nice with imaginative productions, such as **Théâtre du Cours**, in Cours Saleya, tel 93 80 12 67, and **Théâtre de La Sémeuse**, Rue du Château, tel 93 62 31 00. Molière and other classics are showcased at **Théâtre de l'Alphabet**, 10 Blvd Carabacel, tel 93 13 08 88, and in the new **Théâtre de Nice**, by the contemporary art museum, tel 93 80 52 60. For kids, there's **Zygoparc**, a vast amusement park west of town off the A8, open daily 10 am–8 pm in the summer (tel 93 18 36 36).

SHOPPING
Vieux Nice is the most attractive place to shop, for art, cheap clothes and glorious food at the outdoor markets and local shops. In Cours Saleya, the morning food and flower **market** (daily exc Mon) is supplemented on Monday, with old books, clothes, and bric-à-brac; arts and crafts appear on Wednesday afternoon, and paintings on Sunday afternoons. Jacques Médecin and many Niçois gourmets swear that the olive oil from **Alziari**, 14 Rue St-François-de-Paule is the best in the world; on the same street at No. 7, **Henri Auer** is famous for its chocolates and crystallized fruits. In Place du Gesù,

Espuno makes a wide variety of delicious breads. The pedestrian zone around Place Masséna has scores of clothes shops and boutiques, while in Av. Jean Médecin you'll find Nice's two biggest department stores, Galeries Lafayette and La Riviera, as well as *Nice Etoile*, a centre with useful shops like FNAC (which sells tickets to concerts and other events), The Body Shop and so on. For antiques, try the shops around Rue Antoine Gauthier (by the port) or the antique market, **Village Ségurane**, at 28 Rue Catherine Ségurane.

WHERE TO STAY   (postal code 06000)
Nice is packed with hotels of all categories, and in the summer most are just as tightly packed inside. If you arrive without a reservation, the tourist office next to the station will book rooms for 10 F. Get there by 10 am in the summer, or risk joining the nightly slumber parties on the beach or in front of the station, where you'll encounter giant cockroaches from hell. Come instead in the off season, when many of the best hotels offer the kind of rates the French call *très interessant*.

Expensive
Nice has luxury grand hotels galore, but for panache none can top the fabulous green-domed *******Négresco**, 37 Promenade des Anglais, tel 93 88 39 51. A national historic monument, it was designed for Romanian hotelier Henri Négresco (who started his career as a gypsy violinist) by Edouard Niermans, architect of the Moulin Rouge and the Folies Bergères. The one hotel in Nice where a Grand Duke would still feel at home, its 150 chambers and apartments have all recently been redecorated with Edwardian furnishings and paintings by the likes of Picasso and Léger. Most spectacular of all is the *salon royal*, lit by a Baccarat chandelier made for the Tsar.
    If hobnobbing with the rich and famous in the Négresco is out, there's the elegant Art Deco ******Beau Rivage**, 24 Rue St-François-de-Paule, tel 93 80 80 70, on a pedestrian street in Vieux Nice overlooking the sea and Beau Rivage beach; Matisse spent two years here and Chekhov, during his stay, wrote *The Seagull*. The rooms are as luminous and beautiful as a Matisse and there's direct access to the beach. Or you can choose the modern comforts, roof-top pool, sauna, and many other amenities of the artsy, stylish ******Elysée Palace**, 59 Promenade des Anglais, tel 93 86 06 06, with a façade dominated by an enormous bronze silhouette of a woman.

Moderate
Best among the tri-star choices is the idiosyncratic *****Windsor**, 11 Rue Dalpozzo Royale (behind the Négresco) tel 93 88 59 35, in the midst of a tropical garden, featuring a pool, an English-style pub, a Turkish hammam, a Thai sitting room and dreamy frescoes in the rooms. Another choice with character, *****Vendôme**, in the centre of town at 26 Rue Pastorelli, tel 93 62 00 77, has prettily-renovated, air-conditioned rooms, a superb stairway, and a garden. The Belle Epoque *****Gounod**, 3 Rue Gounod, tel 93 88 26 20 (four blocks back from the sea), another renovated choice, has the added plus of sharing the pool and sauna of its luxurious neighbour, the Sofitel Splendid. More reasonable but still stylish choices include the handsome ****Nouvel Hôtel**, 19 bis Blvd Victor-Hugo, tel 93 87 15 00, Belle Epoque in style, but with air-conditioned rooms,

103

each with its own bath. Up in quiet Cimiez, **Le Floride**, 52 Blvd de Cimiez, tel 93 53 11 02, is in an attractive old villa with a shady garden, and each immaculate blue room has a colour TV and bath (there's a good restaurant, too—see below).

Inexpensive
There are plenty of cheaper choices; perhaps the one most likely to bring happiness is the 11-room **Porte Bonheur**, with its little garden at 146 Av. St-Lambert, tel 93 84 66 10, undignified even by a star but the only cheap hotel in this list to be featured on French TV for its charm. Double rooms with bath are 120F–150F, but book well in advance to get one (it's north of the station near the interesting 1930s church of Ste-Jeanne d'Arc). A stone's throw from the station the friendly *La Belle Meunière, 21 Av. Durante, tel 93 88 66 15, is a long-time favourite of budget travellers in Nice—it even has parking and a little garden for breakfast. Another choice near the station, *Drouot, 24 Rue d'Angleterre, tel 93 88 02 03, is more modern, comfortable (with private bathrooms and colour TVs), and more expensive. In Vieux Nice, near the coach station, *Au Picardy, 10 Blvd Jean-Jaurès, tel 93 85 75 51, has pleasant soundproof rooms in a family pension atmosphere.

The **Auberge de Jeunesse** is 4 km east of town (bus 14, stop *L'Auberge*) on Rte Forestière du Mont-Alban, tel 93 89 23 64, but beware that the last bus leaves at 7 pm. Even further afield is Cimiez's **Clairvallon Relais International de la Jeunesse**, 26 Av. Scudéri, tel 93 81 27 63 (bus 15 or 15a), although it has the added plus of a pool. There are dormitory rooms in the **Centre Hébergement Jeunesse Magnan**, west of the centre at 31 Rue Louis-de-Coppet (bus 3, 9, 10, 12, 22 stop: *Rosa Bonheur*), tel 93 86 28 75; or individual ones in the university residence halls at **Les Collinettes** during July and August (3 Av. Robert-Schuman, tel 93 97 06 64 (bus 14 or 17, stop: *Châteauneuf*).

EATING OUT
Although now a solidly French-speaking corner of the Hexagon, Nice's cuisine still has a heavy Ligurian accent, with a fondness for seafood, olive oil and olives, chick peas, fresh basil, and pine-nuts. A typical first course consists of pasta—Nice, after all, invented ravioli (try it with a walnut sauce) or, in the summer, *soupe au pistou*, a hearty soup of courgettes (zucchini), tomatoes, beans, potatoes, onions and vermicelli, served with *pistou*, a sauce based on basil, pine-nuts, and garlic. Another Niçoise favourite is *bourride*, a fish soup served with *aïoli* that many prefer to the more elaborate *bouillabaisse*, and teeny-tiny fish called *poutines*, by law only caught between Beaulieu and Cagnes, and which local cooks fry in omelettes or pile on top of pasta.

Another popular first course is the world-famous *salade niçoise*, which even in Nice is made in as many 'true and genuine' ways as *bouillabaisse* in Marseille—with quartered tomatoes, capers, black olives, spring onions, anchovies or tuna, green beans, and with or without hard-boiled eggs and potatoes. Main courses are often from the sea: grilled fish with herbs or, more of an acquired taste, *estocaficada*, a stew made of stockfish, guts and all, stewed in *eau-de-vie*, with potatoes, garlic, onions, and peppers. Favourite side dishes include *ratatouille* (another famous dish of Niçois origin) or boiled Swiss chard (*blette*) in vinaigrette.

Nice is a happy hunting ground for nibblers, with a wide variety of snacks that can easily be combined for a light, inexpensive meal. Put the ingredients of a *salade niçoise* in between bread and you have a delicious, messy *pan-bagnat*. If you're dressed up, there are less gooey treats like *socca*, a kind of thin cake popular throughout the Ligurian coast, made of ground chick peas and water, baked, and sold by the slice; and *fougasse*, another Ligurian speciality, a flat bread baked with bits of bacon, or in a sweet version with sugar. Nice is also the home of a pungent kind of pizza called *pissaladière*, baked with onions, olives and anchovies (from *pissala*, a condiment made of anchovies and spices); and of sandwiches made from *porchetta*, roast suckling pig filled with herbs and spices, more commonly wolfed down in Umbria.

Expensive

Looming like a giant over culinary Nice is one of France's top chefs, Jacques Maximin, who worked for many years at the Négresco's Chantecler restaurant, and who, in 1989, at age 40, opened his own place in the former casino, **Jacques Maximin**, 2–4 Rue Sacha-Guitry, (near Place Masséna), tel 93 80 70 10. This has stupendously operatic decor, and if you can't afford one of the four menus (380–600 F—*à la carte* prices can easily go a lot higher), you can eat in the adjacent **Bistrot de Nice** for a mere 150–200 F or buy prepared food or sauces in the *boutique traiteur*. Meanwhile, Dominique Le Stanc, the new chef at the **Chantecler** (37 Promenade des Anglais, tel 93 88 39 51) is raking in the laurels with fabulous dishes like ravioli bursting at the seams with *langoustines*, asparagus tips, and artichokes, *homard au stockfish*, and a melt-in-your mouth *tarte au vin* (lunch menus from 275 F).

Moderate

Outside of these gourmet citadels, the best restaurant-hunting territory is Vieux Nice and around the port. **Atmosphère**, a new restaurant at 36 Cours Saleya, tel 93 80 52 50, offers seafood dishes that taste as good as they are beautiful on the plate (menus from 99 to 350 F). **Don Camillo**, 5 Rue des Ponchettes, tel 93 85 67 95, is another newish restaurant, opened by a former pupil of Maximin and Paul Ducasse, already celebrated for its homemade ravioli filled with Swiss chard *à la daube* and fabulous Italian desserts (*à la carte* only, around 270 F). Also in Vieux Nice, at 1 Rue Moulin, **Au Chapon Fin**, tel 93 80 56 92, specializes in delicious ravioli, this time filled with red mullet, and stockfish (menus from 110 F, more at dinner). Behind the port, in a little street off Rue Arson, is one of the culinary meccas of Nice: **Barale** (36 Rue Beaumont, reservations mandatory, tel 93 89 17 94), where in a vast dining-theatre decorated with enough bric-à-brac to fill a barn, hungry diners (and you'd better arrive hungry) indulge in a set menu of *socca*, *pissaladière*, ravioli with *cèpes*, *sauté de veau* and scrumptious *tourte* (170 F, wine included).

Inexpensive/Cheap

Less expensive choices abound. A couple of the best are up in Cimiez: **L'Auberge de Théo**, 52 Av. Cap de Croix, tel 93 81 26 19, where on a large terrace overlooking Nice, you'll find genuine Italian pizzas, salads with *mesclun* (Nice's special lettuce), and Venetian *tiramisù* for dessert (90–120 F); the second, **Le Floride**, 52 Blvd de Cimiez, tel 93 53 11 02, offers a delicious menu at a delicious price: 85 F. Best near the station is

Aux Voyageurs Nissart, 19 Rue d'Alsace-Lorraine, between the station and Av. Jean-Médecin, tel 93 82 19 60, which has a wide-ranging 55F menu. For snacks, Vieux Nice's **René Socca**, 2 Rue Miralhéti offers *socca*, *pissaladière*, pizza by the slice and much more, which you can down with a beer or wine at the bar across the street. If you want to sit, try **Caves Ricord**, 2 Rue Neuve, near Place Garibaldi, a funny old-fashioned wine bar with *socca*, pizza, and *pan-bagnats* and other inexpensive dishes; or the popular **La Taverne**, 3 Rue St-François (the north extension of Rue Droite), tel 93 80 67 89, with excellent *socca* and other delights, plus jazz on Friday nights (60 F).

NIGHTLIFE

Nice's nightlife, now void of casinos after a wave of scandals, is concentrated in expensive clubs and bland hotel piano bars, and in the livelier bars and clubs of Vieux Nice, which come and go like ships in the night. Some of the most jumping joints are the ex-pat havens in Vieux Nice, noisiest of which is the British-owned **Chez Wayne**, a pub and restaurant with live music every night (15 Rue de la Préfecture, open 10 am–midnight, reservations obligatory on weekends, tel 93 13 46 99). The Irish in Nice, and their French friends, bend elbows to fiddle music at the **Scarlett O'Hara**, 22 Rue Droite (before the Guinness, start with a few 5 F take-away *blinis* at the Russian restaurant across the street). The Dutch go boozing at the funky **Le Klomp**, 6 Rue Mascoïnat, near Place Rossetti. Other night music in Vieux Nice is Brazilian, at **Ship de Ipanema**, 5 Rue Barillerie (tel 93 80 46 76), accompanied by cuisine from the Americas (135 F menu) and Californian wines, of all things. **La Brocherie**, 25 Rue Benoît Bunico has jazz on Friday and Saturday nights and drinks from 35 F. Nightclubs have at least a 50 F cover charge and tend to be all corporate-produced synthetic rock, but for reggae and calypso try **Ruby's**, 8 Déscent Croh (Blvd Jean Jaurès, tel 93 62 59 60). **Quartz's**, 18 Rue Congrès, tel 93 88 88 87, is Nice's most popular gay/straight disco.

Other tempting places for a drink or snack include the 19th-century **Grand-Café de Turin** in Place Garibaldi, serving some of the best, cheapest oysters in town (and other shellfish in non-R months, open until 11); trendy **Pauline Tapas**, 14 Rue Emma Tiranty, off Av. Jean-Médecin in the centre, with drinks, snacks, and music (till 2 am), and the bird-filled **L'Hermitage**, 9 Rue St-Vincent, just north of the Palais de Justice in Vieux Nice, with drinks and sandwiches.

Vin de Bellet AOC

'The wine-merchants of Nice brew a balderdash, and even mix it with pigeon's dung and quick-lime' wrote Tobias Smollett. But they never dared to mess with Vin de Bellet, the rare and costly elixir produced in the steep, sun-soaked hills west of Nice. The vineyards owe their special quality to the alternating currents of sea and mountain air and to their original varieties of grapes: braquet, folle noire and negrette de Nice, all of which combine to create a noble wine with a bouquet of wild cherry that can be aged up to 30 years. The rosés, from the same grapes, are one of the best accompaniments to *loup*, the most delicate Mediterranean fish. Vin de Bellet blanc, reminiscent of chablis, is a blend of rolle, spagnou, roussan and mayorquin.

Only 1200 hectalitres are produced each year, and most of it never gets much further than the cellars of the Riviera's top restaurants. Alternatively, pick up a bottle of your own by ringing ahead and following the Route de Bellet north of Rue de France (parallel to the Promenade des Anglais) to St-Roman-de-Bellet and the 18th-century **Château de Bellet** (tel 93 37 81 57). The second estate, **Château de Crémat** (just south of the *autoroute* A 8, off Av. Durandy) is a fantasy castle, built in 1850 in a pseudo-medieval style called *style troubadour* (tel 93 37 80 30).

Cagnes

West of Nice runs the river Var, the wet but politically prickly border between France and Savoy, whose dukes were usually allied to France's rivals—England, Spain, or Austria. As bridges over the Var were periodically blown up, for centuries people crossed the water sitting on the shoulders of two strong men. Nowadays in the maelstrom of traffic and overbuilding it's hard even to notice the Var at all. Across the river lies the bloated amoeba of Cagnes, divided into three cells—overbuilt Cros-de-Cagnes by the sea with a Hippodrome; Cagnes-sur-Mer, further up, site of Renoir's house, the happiest of all artists' shrines in the south, and medieval Haut-de-Cagnes on the hill, notorious in the 17th and 18th centuries for the indecorous pastimes and the brilliant parties held in its castle before the Revolution—beginning a long tradition of artsy decadence satirized in Cyril Connolly's *The Rock Pool* (1936).

GETTING AROUND

There are train stations in both Cagnes-sur-Mer and Cros-de-Cagnes (for information, tel 93 22 46 47) and eight minibuses a day from Cagnes-sur-Mer station up the steep hill to Haut-de-Cagnes. No cars are allowed in Haut-de-Cagnes, but there's a massive underground car park just outside the village entrance. Buses from Nice to Vence stop in Cagnes-sur-Mer, where you can also **hire a bike** at Location 2 Roux at 3 Rue du Logis, tel 93 22 55 85.

Renoir's House, Cagnes

107

TOURIST INFORMATION
Cagnes-sur-Mer (06800): 6 Blvd du Maréchal-Juin, tel 93 20 61 64.
Cros-de-Cagnes (06800): 20 Av. des Oliviers, tel 93 07 67 08.

Cagnes-sur-Mer: Musée Renoir

There is only one thing to do in sprawling Cagnes-sur-Mer: from central Place Général de Gaulle follow Av. Auguste Renoir up to Chemin des Colettes, to Les Colettes, where Renoir spent the last 12 years of his life (10–12 and 2–5, summer 2:30–6, closed Tues and 15 Oct–15 Nov, adm). Stricken with rheumatoid arthritis, Renoir followed his doctor's advice to move to warmer climes and chose Cagnes, where 'one's nose is not stuck in the mountains'; in 1903 he purchased an ancient olive grove to build a villa. Rejuvenated by the climate, Renoir produced paintings even more sensuous and voluptuous than before, and there's no contrast more poignant than that of colour-saturated *Grandes Baigneuses* (in the Louvre) and the photograph in the museum of the painter's hands, so bent and crippled that they're painful even to look at. 'I pay dearly for the pleasure I get from this canvas,' he said of one portrait that he especially liked, painting with brushes strapped to his hands. It was also in Cagnes that Renoir first experimented with sculpture, by proxy, dictating detailed instructions to a young sculptor.

In 1989, the museum's collection of portraits of Renoir by his friends was supplemented with ten canvases the master himself painted in Cagnes. The north studio, with his wheelchair, palette, and easel, looks as if Renoir might return any minute—even the chicken wire he put over the window to keep out the children's tennis-balls is in place. You can wander freely through the venerable olive grove; the only drastic change from Renoir's day is the view down to the sea.

Haut-de-Cagnes

Spared the worst of the tourist shops, intricate, medieval Haut-de-Cagnes has become instead the fiefdom of contemporary artists, thanks to the UNESCO-sponsored *Festival International de la Peinture*. The show takes place each summer in the crenellated **Château-Musée de Cagnes** (daily exc Tues, 10–12 and 2–5 winter, summer 10–12 and 2:30–7, adm). This was built by Rainier Grimaldi in the 1300s, at a time when there were a hundred excess male Grimaldis prowling the coast, looking for a castle to call home. This particular branch of the family held onto Cagnes until the Revolution; its most famous twig was Henri, a good friend of Louis XIII who convinced his cousin in Monaco to put himself under the protection of France rather than Spain.

A handsome inner courtyard tiered with galleries provided all the castle's light and air. In the vaulted halls on the ground floor there's an **olive museum**, where among the presses you may find a small machine for pressing coins, not olives, used by the Marquis to counterfeit the king's coin (he was arrested in 1710, by the Comte d'Artagnan). Upstairs are Henri Grimaldi's ornate reception rooms, topped by *The Fall of Phaeton* (1624) by the Genoese Giovanni Andrea Carlone, one of those hysterical *trompe-l'oeil* ceiling paintings of floating horse stomachs and testicles that the Italians were so fond of. In another room, the **Donation Suzy Solidor** contains 40 paintings donated by the chanteuse and cabaret star, each a portrait of herself, each by a different artist—Van Dongen, Dufy, Friesz, Cocteau, and so on. On the next floor, the **Musée d'Art Moderne Méditerranéen** is dedicated to painters who have worked on the coast.

Besides the château, Henri hired the Genoese to fresco the walls of the **Chapelle Notre-Dame-de-Protection**, just below (2:30–6:30, winter 2–5, closed Tues and Fri). Later whitewashed over, the frescoes were only rediscovered by accident in 1936, and are full of quirky perspective tricks that make the babies as big as some of the mothers in the *Massacre of the Innocents*. Haut-de-Cagnes also sees the region's most fashionable nightlife, in the hallowed halls of **Jimmy's**, rendez-vous of artists and trendsetters.

Villeneuve-Loubet and Escoffier

To the southwest of Cagnes, on another hill dominated by another medieval castle, is Villeneuve-Loubet, a small village known for its fishing, visited by François I (where he signed a ten-year peace treaty with Charles V in 1538) and Marshal Pétain. In 1846 Auguste Escoffier came into the world here to become 'the chef of kings and the king of chefs'—the king in question being Edward VII, who encouraged Escoffier and the hotelier César Ritz to move to London, thus making the Savoy and the Carlton citadels of class and cuisine. Escoffier's birthplace is now the **Musée de l'Art Culinaire** (2–6, closed Mon, holidays, and Nov), but don't come looking for nibbles or scratch-and-sniff exhibits of his creations. Instead there's a 19th-century Provençal kitchen; an autographed photo of soprano Nellie Melba, thanking Escoffier for calling his new peach dessert after her; a collection of the chef's radical, light menus which seem incredibly elaborate nowadays; and the sugar sculptures Escoffier loved, still prepared by local *pâtissiers* for saccharine competitions that put kitsch back in the kitchen.

Villeneuve-Loubet-Plage is another kettle of fish, home of those concrete ziggurats you may have already noticed, looming over the Bay of Angels with all the charm of totalitarian Mesopotamia. They are part of the **Marina Baie des Anges** built in the 1970s, before the French regulated building on the coast—too late indeed for the once beautiful stretch between here and Cannes.

Market Days: Cagnes-sur-Mer, daily.

WHERE TO STAY/EATING OUT   (postal code 06800)
The luxury choice for this niche of the coast is **Haut-de-Cagnes' ***Le Cagnard**, Rue du Pontis-Long, tel 93 20 73 21, with sumptuous comforts discreetly arranged to fit in with the 12th-century architecture. Nearly every room has a private terrace, but the largest and most magical belongs to the hotel's excellent restaurant, serving delicacies such as pigeon stuffed with morels and *foie gras* (but for a price—menus begin at 300 F). You can dine for less at **Des Peintres**, 71 Montée de la Bourgade, Haut-de-Cagnes, tel 93 20 83 08, where the walls are covered with paintings and the tables with warm homemade bread and Provençal dishes (menus from 120 F). The nearby **La Comédie**, 85 Montée de la Bourgade, tel 93 73 44 64, does gourmet vegetarian dishes—a rarity in this part of the world (menus from 100 F). In **Cagnes-sur-Mer**, modern ****Les Collettes**, Av. des Collettes, tel 93 20 80 66, is the best choice, with a pool, balconies, and kitchenettes in most rooms. None of the restaurants in Cagnes-sur-Mer stand out, but the 40 different kinds of fresh chocolates do at **L'Oiseau d'Or**, 2 Place Général de Gaulle, including *grimaldines*, flavoured with fresh orange juice.

St-Paul-de-Vence and Vence

Inland from Cagnes are two towns as bound up with contemporary art as any in France. St-Paul-de-Vence is the site of the wonderful Fondation Maeght, while Vence has a unique chapel painted by Matisse **open only on Tuesdays and Thursdays**. D.H. Lawrence and Marc Chagall died in Vence, a pleasant enough old town where real people still live amongst the writers, artists, and perfectly tanned Martians with faces lifted, stretched, and moulded into permanent supercilious frowns.

GETTING AROUND
There are frequent buses from Cagnes-sur-Mer to La Colle-sur-Loup, St-Paul-de-Vence and Vence, and connections nearly every hour from Nice. La Gaude can be reached by bus from St-Jeannet and Cagnes-sur-Mer (but not from Vence); Tourettes-sur-Loup and Le Bar-sur-Loup are on the Vence to Grasse bus route.

TOURIST INFORMATION
St-Paul-de-Vence (06570): 2 Rue Grande, tel 93 32 86 95.
Vence (06140) : Place du Grand Jardin, tel 93 58 06 38.

St-Paul-de-Vence

Between Cagnes and St-Paul the D 6 winds above the river Loup, passing through **La Colle-sur-Loup**, a village once famous for its roses, that now earns its keep from the overspill of tourists from St-Paul-de-Vence, its mother town. For La Colle was founded in 1540, when François I showed his gratitude to St-Paul-de-Vence for standing up to the assaults of his arch-rival, Emperor Charles V, by financing a rampart. Some 700 houses had to be demolished, obliging the displaced populace to move elsewhere.

Reduced in size **St-Paul-de-Vence** became the *'ville de guerre'* and still preserves a *donjon* watchtower dating from the 12th century, as well as François's costly ramparts. A cannon captured from Charles V is embedded near the town gate, a gate much more accessible these days than the simple wooden door of the restaurant **La Colombe d'Or**, down in the square. Its first owner, an unschooled farmer named Paul Roux, fell in love with modern art and for 40 years accepted paintings in exchange for hospitality from the impoverished artists who flocked here after World War I—including Picasso, Derain, Matisse, Braque, Vlaminck, Léger, Dufy, and Bonnard. By the time he died he had accumulated one of France's greatest private collections—but strictly for the viewing by those who can at least afford a meal.

If you're prone to claustrophobia, visit St-Paul early, before its little lanes are clogged with visitors and baskets of artsy trinkets. From its ramparts, to the north, you can see the odd, sphinx-shaped rock called the **Baou de St-Jeannet**, that was painted into the uncanny landscape of Nicolas Poussin's *Polyphème*. There's a handsome fountain along Rue Grande, and the church of the **Conversion de St-Paul**, sumptuously furnished with Baroque stuccoes, woodwork and paintings—including one of St Catherine of Alexandria in the left aisle, attributed in part to Tintoretto.

Fondation Maeght

Here is an attempt at something never before undertaken: creating a world with which modern art can both find its place and that otherworldliness which used to be called supernatural.

—*the Foundation's inaugural speech by André Malraux, 1964*

Set back in the woods up on a hill along the Cagnes road, the Fondation Maeght is the main reason for visiting St-Paul (open 10–12:30 and 2:30–6, July–Sept 10–7, adm exp). The creators, Aimé and Marguerite Maeght, were art dealers and friends of Matisse and Bonnard who decided, in the early 60s, to create an ideal environment for contemporary art, and for its creators. They hired Catalan architect José-Luis Sert, a pupil of Le Corbusier, to design the setting—'building' seems too confining a term for these walls that are 'a play between the rhythms of the interior and exterior spaces', as Sert himself described them. The various levels of the building follow the changes in ground level; the white 'sails' on top collect rainwater for the fountains; 'light traps' in the roof are designed to distribute natural light evenly, although the quality of light varies from room to room.

The permanent collection, which includes nearly every major artist of the past 50 years, is removed during the Fondation's frequent exhibitions of young artists and retrospectives of established ones. But you'll always see the works incorporated into the walls, windows and gardens—Miró's *Labyrinth*, a garden path lined with delightful sculptures and a ceramic half-submerged Egg; a wet and wobbling tubular fountain by Pol Bury, a mobile by Calder, mosaics by Chagall, Tal-Coat, Braque and Ubac, Léger's *Flowers, Birds and Bench*, and Giacometti's stick-figured cat and elongated people, reminiscent of Etruscan bronzes at their quirkiest. The Fondation also has a cinema and a studio for making films, art workshops, and one of the world's most extensive art libraries.

WHERE TO STAY/EATING OUT   (postal code 06570)

To stay in St-Paul-de-Vence, have buckets of money and book months in advance in the summer, especially to sleep among the 20th-century art in *****La Colombe d'Or**, Place des Ormeaux, tel 93 32 80 02. The rooms are full of character, the pool is heated, the terrace lovely. The restaurant, where Yves Montand and Simone Signoret celebrated their wedding, is more a feast for the eyes than for the stomach, but you won't go wrong with its traditional groaning platters of hors d'oeuvres and grilled meats (*à la carte* only, around 400 F). In the centre, in the 16th-century *****Le St-Paul**, 86 Rue Grande, tel 93 32 65 25, the interior designers let their hair down to create unusual but delightful juxtapositions of medieval, surreal, Egyptian, and Art Deco elements. Its equally attractive restaurant, **La Baronie** has a summer terrace, where you can try delicacies such as *sashimi de saumon* with ginger and citrus fruits (lunch menus from 150 F). The more moderately-priced *****Le Hameau**, 528 Rte de La Colle, tel 93 32 80 24, has lovely views over the orange groves and a swimming-pool (no restaurant). Cheapest of all is ****Les Remparts**, 72 Rue Grande, tel 93 32 80 64: pleasant rooms with baths, and a good affordable restaurant with a superb terrace (menus from 90 F).

Vence

Sister city of Ouahigouya in Burkina Faso, Vence lies 3 km from St-Paul and 10 km from the coast, sufficiently far to seem more like a town in Provence than a Riviera fleshpot. Roman *Vintium*, it kept up its regional prestige in the Middle Ages as the seat of a bishopric (albeit the smallest in France) with a series of remarkable bishops. Two are now Vence's patron saints: Véran (449–481), from the seminary of St-Honorat near Cannes, and Lambert (1114–54). Lambert had to confront the claims of the new baron of Vence, Romée de Villeneuve, appointed by Raymond Berenger V of Provence after Romée arranged for Berenger's daughters the four most strategic marriages of all time—to the kings of England, France (St Louis) and Naples, and the German emperor. Although Romée earned a mention in Dante's *Paradiso* (an apocryphal story telling how he began and ended his career as an impoverished pilgrim), as baron he set a precedent of quarrelling with the bishop that lasted until the Revolution abolished both titles. Alessandro Farnese was head of Vence's see from 1508 to 1511—one of the 16 absentee bishoprics he accumulated thanks to his beautiful sister Giulia, the mistress of Pope Alexander IV, who slept with enough cardinals to get her brother elected Paul III. But best-loved of Vence's bishops was Antoine Godeau (1639–72), a dwarf famed for his ugliness, a gallant poet and 'the wittiest man in France'. Appointed the first member of the Académie Française by Cardinal Richelieu, Godeau tired of it all by the time he was 30, took holy orders and devoted himself to reforming his see—rebuilding the cathedral, and founding tanneries and scent industries.

Although a fair amount of villa sprawl extends on all sides, the **Vieille Ville** has kept most of its medieval integrity. Enter the walls by way of the west gate, the fortified **Porte du Peyra**: the **Place du Peyra**, just inside, was the Roman forum and is still the site of the daily market. Roman tombstones are incorporated in the walls of the **Ancienne Cathédrale**, a rococoed church full of little treasures— the pre-Christian sarcophagus of St Véran; the tomb of Bishop Godeau; Merovingian and Romanesque fragments of stones and birds, especially in the chapel under the belfry; a mosaic by Chagall; reliquaries donated by Alessandro Farnese; and best of all, the stalls with lace-fine carvings satirizing Renaissance customs and mores, sculpted by Jacques Bellot in the 1450s.

West, outside the walls, **Place du Frêne** is named in honour of a majestic ash tree planted here in 1538 to commemorate visits by François I and Pope Paul III; the 17th-century château built here by Vence's plucky barons is now used for exhibitions. But perhaps the best show in town is the one-man French and English nougat-making demonstration at **Chez Moraldo**, 28 Av. Colonel-Meyère (Wed and Sat at 11 am).

Matisse's Chapelle du Rosaire

Matisse arrived in Vence in 1941 to escape the bombing along the coast, and fell seriously ill. The 'White' Dominican sisters nursed him back to health, and as a gift he built and decorated the simple **Chapelle du Rosaire** for them (from Vence, follow Av. des Poilus to the route for St-Jeannet/La Gaude; open Tues and Thurs 10–11:30 and 2:30–5:30). Matisse worked on the project well into his 80s, from 1946 to 1951, using long bamboo poles to hold his brushes when he was forced to keep to his bed. He considered the result his masterpiece, the fruit 'of a life consecrated to the search for truth'. The truth he sought, however, was not in Christianity, but in the essentials of line and light.

Probably the most extraordinary thing about these decorations by the most sensual of Fauves is their lack of colour, except in the geometrically-patterned stained glass windows that occupy two walls and which give the interior an uncanny glow. The other walls are of white faïence, on which Matisse drew black line drawings of St Dominic holding a Bible, and the Virgin and Child, the Crucifixion and the fourteen Stations of the Cross. None of the figures have faces, but they're powerfully drawn and compelling in their simplicity. Still, Matisse's judgement of his own work is hardly shared by all.

Market Days: Vence, Tuesday and Friday.

WHERE TO STAY/EATING OUT   (postal code 06140)
Vence has more choice and lower prices than St-Paul—unless you check into the opulentissimo *****__Château du Domaine St-Martin__, a set of villa-bastides built around a ruined Templar fortress (3 km from Vence on Rte de Coursegoules, tel 93 58 02 02). The 12-hectare park has facilities for riding, fishing, tennis and a heart-shaped pool installed at the request of Harry Truman, who never had such luxuries back in Independence, Missouri. The restaurant is equally august, with prices to match (lunch menu 380 F). ****__Relais Cantermerle__, 258 Chemin Cantermerle, tel 93 58 08 18, is decorated with Art Deco bits and pieces from the gutted Palais de la Méditerranée in Nice. Set in its piney garden, with terraces and a pool, the Cantermerle's restaurant serves some of the finest food in Vence (try the *terrine de rascasse aux pointes d'asperges*; menu 220 F). **__La Roseraie__, 14 Av. H.-Giraud, tel 93 58 02 20, offers comfortable rooms, a pool, and a garden of magnolias and cedars, plus a restaurant that regales diners with specialities from the southwest of France—*confits*, *magret de canard* and sumptuous red wines from Cahors and Bergerac (menu 140 F). In the centre of Vence, the *__Closerie des Genets__ has quiet rooms, a garden and a decent 100 F menu in its restaurant. For a delicious *soupe de poissons* and other Provençal dishes, get yourself a table at **La Farigoule**, 15 Rue H.-Isnard, tel 93 58 01 27 (menus 100 F and 130 F). Also, check out **Le Pêcheur**, in Place Godeau, offering 300 different kinds of pizza.

Excursions around Vence, and the Gorges du Loup

Vence makes an excellent base for exploring the countryside, especially if you have your own car—otherwise the only connections are the once- or twice-daily buses from Nice to St-Jeannet and Gattières.

Ten km beyond the Chapelle du Rosaire, the wine-making village of **St-Jeannet** balances on a terrace beneath the distinctive *Baou*, a sheer 400-m rock that dominates the surrounding countryside. A 2-hour path from the Auberge de St-Jeannet leads to the summit, with views stretching to the Alps. A narrow road continues south to the unspoiled *village perché* of **La Gaude**, despite the giant Y-shaped IBM research centre along the way. Alternatively, continuing east on D 2210, are three other *villages perchés* that have yet to sell their souls to Mammon: **Gattières**, **Carros** on a 300-m rock over the

Var crowned by a 13th-century château, and **Le Broc**, 4 km up the Var on D 2209, with a Canavesio in its church. Another excursion from Vence takes you through the austerely beautiful **Clues de Haute Provence** (see p. 214) by way of the **Col de Vence**, 975 m up and affording an incomparable view of the coast from Cap Ferrat to L'Esterel (take D 2 north).

The most popular excursion of all is to loop-the-Loup, so to speak, around the upper valley of the Loup river, starting on D 2210. On the way you can call at the **Château Notre-Dame des Fleurs** (2.5 km from Vence), a 19th-century castle built over the ruins of an 11th-century Benedictine abbey, and now home to a **Musée du Parfum et de la Liqueur** (10–12:30 and 2–5:30, closed Sun am). You can learn about distilling essential oils, especially those that end up in the perfume or liqueur bottle. The château also has a very fragrant vegetarian restaurant that employs its most delectable aromas (tel 93 58 70 24).

Some of these essential oils, especially of violets, originate in **Tourrettes-sur-Loup**, 2.5 km further on. Its medieval core of rosy golden stone has often been compared to an Algerian town, the houses knitted together so that their backs form a wall defended by the three small towers that give the village its name. Tourrettes grows more violets than any town in France, and in March, all the façades are covered with bouquets for the *Fête des Violettes*. But in the summer Tourrettes turns into a veritable *souk*, where you can purchase handmade fabrics, jewellery, marionnettes, ceramics, household items and more. The village **church** has a triptych by the school of Ludovico Brea and a Gallo-Roman altar dedicated to Mercury, while the **Chapelle St-Jean**, at the village entrance, is painted with naïf frescoes mixing biblical tales with local rural life, painted by Ralph Souplaut in 1959.

Before heading into the Gorges du Loup, take a short detour south at **Pont-du-Loup** to **Le Bar-sur-Loup**, scented by its plantations of oranges, jasmine, roses, and violets. The village surrounds the château of the lords of Bar, a branch office of the counts of Grasse (one of whom grew up here to become the Admiral de Grasse, who chased the British out of Chesapeake Bay, so Washington could blockade Yorktown and win the American War of Independence). Legend has it that one of his 15th-century ancestors held a wild party here in the middle of Lent, during which the guests all dropped dead. Mortified, the lord commissioned an itinerant artist from Nice to commemorate the event by painting a curious little *Danse Macabre*, now in the tribune of the church of **St-Jacques**: the elegant noblity dance to a drum, unaware that tiny demons of doom echo the dance on their heads. Death, grinning, mows them down, while busy devils extract their souls in the form of newborn babies and pop them into the mouth of Hell. The church also has a retable by Ludovico Brea and on the door, beautiful Gothic/Renaissance panels representing St Jacques, carved by Jacques Bellot of Vence.

North of Pont-du-Loup, D 6 leads into the steep, fantastical cliffs of the **Gorges du Loup**, cooled by waterfalls—one next to the road falls a sheer 45 m—and is pocked by giant *marmites*, or glacial potholes. The largest of these is up at **Saut du Loup**, and in spring the river broils through it like a witch's cauldron. At Pont de Bramafan you can cross the gorge and head back south. Looming ahead is **Gourdon** 'the Saracen', a brooding eagle's nest converted into yet another rural shopping-mall of crafts and goodies. Its massive rectangular **château** was built in the 1200s over the Saracen citadel, and heavily restored in 1610. Inside are a pair of museums (June–Sept 10–12 and 2–5; Oct–May 2–5 only, closed Tues, adm): the **Musée Historique** with antique arms and armour, the odd torture instrument in the dungeon, a Rembrandt self-portrait, and Marie-Antoinette's writing-desk, while upstairs, a **Musée de Peinture Naïve**, features a small portrait by the Douanier Rousseau and works by his French and Yugoslav imitators. The panoramic three-tiered castle gardens were laid out by Le Nôtre, although now most of the plants are alpine. You can take a spectacular two-hour walk on the **Sentier du Paradis** from Gourdon to Pont-du-Loup, or sneak in a preview of lunar travel by driving up the D 12 (or walk along the GR 4 from Grasse) onto the desolate **Plateau de Caussols**, boasting the driest, clearest air in France—hence an important observatory. French film directors often use it for Western or desert scenes, the very kind used these days for selling French cars and blue jeans.

WHERE TO STAY/EATING OUT

In **Gattières** (06510): small ****Beau Site**, Rte de Vence, tel 93 08 60 06, has a lovely view down the Var, a garden, and a pleasant restaurant with a 100 F menu. **L'Hostellerie Provençale**, at the entrance of the old town, tel 93 08 60 40, offers excellent value for hungry travellers with its 120 F and 140 F menus—masses of hors d'oeuvres, homemade ravioli, *daube* and much more.

In **Tourrettes-sur-Loup** (06140): ****Auberge des Belles Terrasses**, 1315 Rte de Vence, tel 93 59 30 03, has comfortable rooms with views from its terraces and a good little restaurant (menus 75 F and up). On an even loftier terrace, at **Le Chantecler**, Rte de Vence, tel 93 59 34 22, you can flavour the views with Lyonnaise specialities like *gratin Dauphinois*, homemade bread, and kind prices (menus at 95 F and 190 F—but reserve). In **Le Bar-sur-Loup**, stop for lunch at **L'Amiral**, 8 Pl Francis-Paulet, tel 93 42 44 09, in an impressive 18th-century house that belonged to Admiral de Grasse. The dishes on the menu change daily, and are always spot on for freshness and value (menus at 80, 90 and 150 F). Dinner by reservation only.

Back on the Coast: Biot

Between Cagnes and Cannes, the *résidences secondaires* battle for space with huge commercial greenhouses and fields of flowers destined for the scent distilleries of Grasse, a paroxym of fragrance and colour powerful enough to make a sensitive soul swoon. Set in a couple of miles from the sea, Biot (rhymes with yacht) is a handsome village endowed with first-rate clay—in Roman times it specialized in the kind of wine and oil jars large enough to contain Ali Baba's forty thieves. In 1955, Fernand Léger purchased some land in order to construct a sculpture garden of monumental ceramics—then died 15 days later. In 1960 his widow used the land to build a superb museum and garden to display the works he left her in his will. Come late in the day if you want to see more of Biot and less of the human race.

GETTING AROUND

Biot's train station is down by the sea at La Brague, and you will have a steep 4-km walk from here up to the village. However, buses every other hour from Antibes stop at the station en route to Biot.

TOURIST INFORMATION
Place de la Chapelle, tel 93 65 05 85.

Musée Fernand Léger
To the right of the entrance to Biot, Léger's museum is hard to mistake behind its giant, sporty ceramic-mosaic designed for the Olympic stadium of Hannover (10–12 and 2–6, adm exp). Opened in 1960, the museum was enlarged in 1989 to provide more space for the 348 paintings, tapestries, mosaics and ceramics that trace Léger's career from his first flirtations with Impressionism. After being gassed in World War I, he recovered to paint scenes of soldiers and machines, and evolved his trademark style of brightly coloured geometric forms depicting workers, factories, and their pastimes. The new wing of the museum contains Léger's ceramics, mosaics and other works—most notably a tapestry of 1922 (*La Création*) and the *Liberté* tapestry illustrating the eponymous poem by his friend Paul Eluard. The presence of the museum has boosted the local ceramic and glass industry; across from the museum at the **Verrerie de Biot** you can watch workers make glass suffused with tiny bubbles (*verre à bulles*).

Guarded by 16th-century gates, Biot itself has retained much of its character, especially around central **Place des Arcades**. A hundred years ago, the accents in this charming square would be Genoese—Biot's original population was entirely decimated by the Black Death, and the village was only resettled in 1460, when the Bishop of Grasse invited in 50 families from Genoa. The church they built among the arcades has two excellent 15th-century altarpieces: the red and gold *Retable du Rosaire* by Ludovico Brea and the recently-restored *Christ aux Plaies* by Canavesio, who was married to a Biotoise.

With his bright colours and often playful forms, Léger is one artist kids usually like. Afterwards you can take them to **La Brague** by the sea, to watch the performing dolphins and other sea creatures at **Marineland**, the oldest of its kind in Europe (open daily from 11 am, with nocturnal performances at 9:30 pm in July and Aug, adm exp). Next door to it at **Aquasplash** you can play otter yourself on the slides (daily in summer), or watch the silent pretty creatures at **Le Jungle des Papillons**, a live butterfly zoo.

WHERE TO STAY/EATING OUT   (postal code 06410)
There aren't many choices in Biot, but on the other hand there aren't many nicer places in which to escape the maddening Riviera crowds than *****Hostellerie du Bois Fleuri**, 199 Blvd de la Source, tel 93 65 68 74, in the forest between Biot and Valbonne, offering tranquillity, views, swimming, tennis and large rooms in a rose-coloured castle. In the medieval centre of Biot, ***Arcades**, 16 Place des Arcades, tel 93 65 01 04, is a delightful old hotel in a 15th-century building, furnished with antiques. The amiable restaurant below does a genuine *soupe au pistou* and other Provençal favourites (140 F); but for a special feast, reserve a table at least a week in advance at ****Auberge du Jarrier**, 30 Passage de la Bourgade, tel 93 65 11 68, in an old jar-works, with a magical terrace, friendly service and a superb four-course seasonal 180 F menu that puts the Côte's *haute cuisine* budget-busters to shame.

116

Antibes, Juan-Les-Pins and Vaullauris

Set on the largest of the Côte's peninsulas, Antibes started out as the Greek trading colony of *Antipolis* 'the city opposite' Nice. The Greeks who live in Antibes these days are also mostly traders—although the gleaming white frigates they park in its port are for their own personal use, equipped with jacuzzis and helicopter pads. On the other side of luxurious Cap d'Antibes are the sandy beaches of Juan-les-Pins, where you can swing all night, especially to the tunes of the Riviera's top jazz festival. Inland from here is Vallauris, another ceramics village, this one synonymous with Picasso.

GETTING AROUND
Antibes' **train station** is near the edge of town, on the road to Nice at Av. Robert-Soleau, and has frequent trains to Nice and Cannes. Buses for Cannes, Nice, Nice airport, Cagnes-sur-Mer, and Juan-les-Pins depart from Place Général-de-Gaulle; others leave from Rue de la République. From Golfe-Juan buses leave every half hour for Antibes.

TOURIST INFORMATION
Antibes (06600): 11 Place du Général-de-Gaulle, tel 93 33 95 64.
Juan-Les-Pins (06160): 51 Blvd Gaillaumont, tel 93 61 04 98 (write them to book tickets for the jazz festival).
Golfe-Juan: 84 Av. de la Liberté, tel 93 63 73 12.
Vallauris (06220): Square du 8-Mai-45, tel 93 63 82 58.

Antibes and the Musée Picasso

> Now all the gay decorative people have left, taking with them the sense of carnival and impending disaster that colored this summer...'
>
> —*Zelda Fitzgerald, 1925*

Antibes has been a quieter place since the Fitzgeralds and their self-destructive high jinks set a precedent no alcoholic writer or artist has been able to match. The frolicking now takes place over at Juan-les-Pins, which took off as a resort shortly after F. Scott and Zelda's holiday, leaving Antibes to tend its rose nurseries. After the war, when developers cast an eye over to Antibes, there were enough building restrictions intact to keep out most of the concrete. Even so, inlanders regard the town with jaundiced eyes: instead of go to hell they say *'Vai-t'en-à-n-Antibo!'*

A relic of Antibes' earlier incarnation as France's bulwark against Savoyard Nice are its sea-walls, especially Vauban's massive **Fort Carré**. It provides a decorative backdrop for Antibes' pleasure port, big enough to moor even the 90-m behemoths of the ridiculously rich. The handsome 17th- and 18th-century houses of Vieil Antibes look over their neighbours' shoulders towards the sea, obscuring it from **Cours Masséna**, the main street of Greek Antipolis. Here the morning **market** (daily exc Mon) sells a cornucopia of local produce, from *fromages de chèvres aux olives* to a profusion of cut flowers that leave the paintings in Antibes' galleries pale by comparison. From the

117

Picasso Museum, Antibes

Cours, Rue Georges Clemenceau leads back to café-filled Place Nationale and the **Musée Peynet** (10–12 and 2–6, closed Tues), offering an uncomfortable journey back to the 1960s paved with the love postcards drawn by Raymond Peynet, the father of the genre.

The best sea views are monopolized by the **Château Grimaldi**—a seaside castle built by the same family who ran most of this coast at one time or another, and who had possession of Antibes from 1385 to 1608. It became a history museum in the 1920s, and for six months in 1946, the curator let Picasso use it as a studio. Picasso returned the kindness by leaving behind everything he made to form the excellent **Musée Picasso** (10–12 and 3–7, winter 2–6 closed Tues and Nov, adm). Despite a post-war lack of canvases and oil paint, he was exuberantly happy and feverishly creative, inspired by his love of the time, Françoise Gillot and the mythological roots of the Mediterranean, expressed in *La Joie de Vivre, Ulysses et ses Sirènes* and 220 other paintings, ceramics, and drawings. Among the other artists represented, note the eight striking works that Nicolas de Staël painted in Antibes shortly before he committed suicide (or merely fell out of the upstairs window) in 1955. Further south, in Promenade Amiral de Grasse, the Bastion St-André houses the **Musée d'Histoire et d'Archéologie** (9–12 and 2–6, summer 2–7, closed Tues and Nov, adm), where Greek and Etruscan objects dredged up from the sea and soil trace the history of Antibes.

Cap d'Antibes

Further south along the peninsula (follow the scenic, coastal D 2599) the beautiful, free, sandy beach of **La Salis** marks the beginning of Cap d'Antibes, scented with roses, jasmine and the smell of money—there's more concentrated here than almost anywhere else in France. Jules Verne was among the first to retreat here, where he found the inspiration for *Twenty Thousand Leagues under the Sea*; nowadays, to maintain the kind of solitude and high-tech luxury enjoyed by Captain Nemo aboard the *Nautilus*, the owners of the Cap's villas need James Bond security systems and slavering Dobermans. In Boulevard du Cap is the lovely **Jardin Thuret** (open daily, free) laid out in 1866 as an acclimatization station, where the first eucalyptus was transplanted to Europe (the park now contains over 100 varieties). It is said that one out of three roses sold in the world originated in the **Roseraies Meilland** at 134 Blvd du Cap, and if you want a preview of their newest blooms, you can arrange a visit (tel 93 61 30 30).

The **Plateau de la Garoupe** is the highest point of the headland, with a lighthouse, a grandiose view stretching from Bordighera to St-Tropez, and the ancient seamen's **Sanctuaire de la Garoupe**. Its two naves, one 13th-century and one 16th-century hold a fascinating collection of ex votos, the oldest one commemorating a surprise attack on Antibes by Saracen pirates. At the tip of the peninsula, a 12th-century tower holds the **Musée Naval et Napoléonien** (9–12 and 2–5, summer 10–12 and 3–7, closed Tues and Nov), with ships' models and items relating to Napoleon's connections with Antibes—he left Madame Mère and his sisters here during the siege of Toulon (they were so poor that the girls had to steal figs) and began 'The Hundred Days' at nearby Golfe-Juan.

Juan-les-Pins

The story goes that in 1921 a restaurateur in Nice saw a film about Miami Beach and was inspired to recreate it on the Côte. He found his location here, amongst the silver sands and pines, and with the revolutionary idea that people might like to come in the summer instead of the winter, he bought some land and opened a restaurant and nightclub. This attracted the attention of Frank Jay Gould, son of a notorious New York financier, who injected the essential money and publicity to help Juan-les-Pins take off. By 1930 it was the most fashionable and scandal-ridden resort on the Riviera, where women first dared to bathe in skirtless suits. The presence of Edith Piaf and Sidney Bechet boosted its popularity in the 50s, and it's still going strong, with nightclubs and an all-star jazz festival in the last two weeks of July.

Golfe-Juan

Next up the coast is **Golfe-Juan**, with its pines, sandy beach and pleasure port, famous as the very spot where Napoleon disembarked from Elba on 1 March 1815, proclaiming that 'the eagle with his national colours will fly from bell tower to bell tower all the way to the towers of Notre-Dame'. The locals responded by arresting a few of his men, a cold reception that decided the eagle to sneak along the back roads to Paris. In one of many Napoleonic coincidences, Bonaparte, as he landed, met the Prince of Monaco, who informed him that he was on his way to reclaim his tiny realm after being removed during the Revolution. 'Then, Monsieur, we are in the same business', Napoleon told him, and each continued on his way.

Vallauris

Two km inland from Golfe-Juan, **Vallauris** has two things in common with Biot: it was given an injection of Genoese in the 1400s and was famous for its pottery, in this case useful household wares. Because of competition with aluminium, the industry was on its last legs in 1946 when Picasso rented a small villa in town and met Georges and Suzanne Ramié, owners of the Poterie Madoura. Playing with the clay in their shop, Picasso discovered a new passion, and spent the next few years working with the medium. He gave the Ramiés the exclusive right to sell copies of his ceramics, and you can still buy them, for a price, at **Madoura**, just off Rue 19 Mars 1962. Thanks to Picasso, 200 other potters now work in Vallauris, some talented, others mind-boggling.

In 1951 the village asked Picasso if he would decorate a deconsecrated chapel next to the castle. The result is the famous plywood paintings of *La Guerre et la Paix*, said to have taken Picasso less time to do than if a house-painter had painted the wall. They are as spontaneous as *Guernica* was planned, and every bit as sincere (the **Musée National Picasso**; 10–12 and 2–6, or 5 in winter, closed Tues, adm). The same ticket admits you to the **Musée Municipal** up in the castle, which used to have many of Picasso's original pieces until art thieves struck in 1989; now to be seen are the winners of the ceramic Biennale and paintings by Alberto Magnelli. There's more Picasso in Place Paul-Isnard: a rather grumpy bronze man with a sheep.

Sophia-Antipolis

Meanwhile, as all this modern art appreciation and night-clubbing goes on around Antibes, 8000 international business people are punching away on their new generation computers in 'France's answer to Silicon Valley', the spooky ultra-modern complex of Sophia-Antipolis off D 103 north of Vallauris. Funded in part by Nice's chamber of commerce, executives seem to like it: Air-France's international reservations network is here, and at the time of writing Sophia-Antipolis is doubling in size.

Market Days: Antibes, daily exc Monday.

WHERE TO STAY AND EATING OUT

A short walk from central **Antibes** (postal code 06600) *****Mas Djoliba**, 29 Av. de Provence, tel 93 33 33 78, is a serendipitous *mas* in a small park with a heated pool. You can combine pleasure with thalassotherapy and beauty treatments at *****Thalazur**, 770 Chemin des Moyennes Bréguières, tel 93 74 78 82, with four heated pools, saunas, and a doctor on duty. ****L'Auberge Provençale**, 61 Place Nationale, tel 93 34 13 24, is a cosy house under the plane trees, with Provençal furniture and canopied beds. There are only 6 rooms, so reserve long in advance. Right in the middle of Antibes the ****Belle Epoque**, 10 Av. du 24 Août, tel 93 34 53 00, has rooms with or without bath, and a good restaurant downstairs.

The original of the hotel in F. Scott Fitzgerald's *Tender is the Night* was Cap d'Antibes' *******Hotel du Cap**, Blvd Kennedy, tel 93 61 39 01. Built in 1870, the hotel is set in an idyllic park overlooking the Iles Lérins, where the rest of the world seems very far away. No hotel on the Riviera has hosted more celebrities, film stars or plutocrats; you could easily drop 1000 F at the exalted restaurant, the Pavillon Eden Roc (closed Nov-Apr). A more reasonable choice in Cap d'Antibes is *****La Gardiole**, Chemin de La Garoupe, tel 93 61 35 03, with large, luminous rooms set in a pine wood and a magnificent wisteria over the terrace. Rooms vary greatly in price; half-board is obligatory in season (closed Nov–Feb). If you're young and come outside July and August, you may find a room at the **Relais International de la Jeunesse**, Blvd da La Garoupe, tel 93 61 34 40, set in the pinewoods; 100 F a head, half-board.

In Roman times, Antibes was famous for its *garum*—a sauce made of salted tuna guts left to dry in the sun. You can eat nearly anything else that was once seaworthy at **Bacon**, in Cap d'Antibes, on Blvd de Bacon, tel 93 61 50 02, as stylish and elegant as its perfectly prepared seafood and *bouillabaisse*, at classy prices: lunch menus at 350 F and 450 F. In the same price range, try some of the Côte's finest *nouvelle cuisine* at the renowned **La Bonne Auberge**, on the N 7 near La Brague, tel 93 33 36 65. Chef Jo Rostang's son Philippe has inherited the kitchen, and has already made a name for his *saint-pierre au pistou* and *soufflé glacé de lavande au miel de Provence*; the lunch menu is good value at 285 F. More reasonable choices abound in Antibes: **La Clafoutis**, 18 Rue Thuret, tel 93 34 66 70, with an excellent 125 F menu; **La Tour Chez Laurent**, 6 Cours Masséna, tel 93 34 59 28, for delicious fresh fish (100 F), and **Du Bastion**, 1 Av. Général Maizière, tel 93 34 13 88, with a terrace on the town ramparts, and well prepared fish and lamb dishes (menus at 120 and 180 F, wine included).

Juan-les-Pins (06160): Juan isn't exactly made for sleeping, but it makes sense to stay if you want to join in the late-night revelry. Unlike Antibes, everything closes tight from November to Easter. There are two grand survivors from the 20s: the beautiful Art Deco *********Juana**, not on the sea but in a lovely garden facing the pines on Av. G. Gallice, tel 93 61 08 70, with a private beach and heated pool, and the resort's top restaurant, the luxurious **La Terrasse** (tel 93 61 20 37), with delicate dishes imbued with all the freshness and colour of Provence, and excellent wines to match from the region's best vineyards (lunch menu at 350 F, dinner considerably more). The second palace, *********Belles Rives**, Blvd du Littoral, tel 93 61 02 79, offers de luxe rooms, vintage 1930, facing the sea. There's a private beach and jetty, and a good restaurant with a fine view over the gulf, serving more *nouvelle cuisine* delights (menus from 280 F).

More reasonably-priced beds may be found at *******Les Mimosas**, in quiet Rue Pauline, 500 m from the sea, tel 93 61 04 16, where the rooms have balconies overlooking the pool and garden; or at ******Pré Catelan**, set among the palms at 22 Av. des Lauriers, tel 93 61 05 11, with a private beach only a short walk away. There are doubles at all prices in the charming ******Auberge de l'Esterel**, 21 Chemin des Iles, tel 93 61 08 67, tucked in a garden, where the hotel's restaurant (tel 93 61 86 55) serves an excellent 160 F menu with aïoli and other Provençal dishes. Cheaper meals can be found at the aptly named **Le Cheap**, 21 Rue Dautheville, tel 93 61 05 66, where pizza and grills are served until the wee hours of the morn on the shady terrace (around 60 F), or **Lou Capitole**, 26 Av. Amiral-Courbet, tel 93 61 22 44, with generous menus at 75 F and 110 F.

ENTERTAINMENT AND NIGHTLIFE

In Antibes the famous **La Siesta** (on the road to Nice, tel 93 33 31 31) operates as a luxury beach concession by day, with special activities for your kids and a restaurant for your dog, and at night turns into an over-the-top nightclub where thousands of people flock every summer evening to get down on the seven dance floors, between the fiery torches and waterfalls (drinks start at 110 F). In Juan-les Pins, where everything stays open in the summer until 3 or 4 am, the two most popular bars are **Pam-Pam** in Blvd Wilson, tel 93 61 11 05, and **Le Festival** across the street, both with Brazilian or Caribbean music and delightful exotic fruit cocktails (get there by 9 or 10). Jazz bands often perform at **Le Madison**, 1 Av. Alexandre III. There are two shops in the area with books in English: **Old Antibes Books**, 10 Rue Sade in Antibes, and **Sophia English Bookshop**, 26 Rue du la Vigne Haute, in Sophia-Antipolis.

Grasse

It was Catherine de Medici who introduced artichokes to the French and the scent trade to Grasse. Although it may seem obvious that a town so profuse in flowers should be a Mecca for perfume-making, Grasse's most important industry throughout the Middle Ages was tanning imported sheep-skins from the mountains of Provence and buffalo-hides from her Italian allies, Genoa and Tuscany. Part of the tanning process made use of the aromatic herbs that grew nearby, especially powdered myrtle which gave the leather a greenish lustre.

In Renaissance Italy, one of the most important status symbols an aristocrat could flaunt were fine, perfumed gloves. When Catherine asked Grasse, Tuscany's old trading partner, to start supplying them, the Grassois left the buffalo hides behind to become *gantiers parfumeurs*. When gloves fell out of fashion after the Revolution they became simply *parfumeurs*, and when Paris co-opted the business in the 1800s, the townspeople concentrated on what has been their speciality ever since—distilling the essences that go into that final costly tiny bottle. And in that, this picturesque but unglamorous hilltown, with its 30 *parfumeries*, leads the world.

GETTING AROUND
There are frequent buses from Cannes to Grasse. The *gare routière* is on the north side of town, at the Parking Notre-Dame-des-Fleurs. Leave your car here or in one of the other places just outside the centre: Grasse's steep narrow streets are hell for motorists.

TOURIST INFORMATION
3 Place de la Foux, tel 93 36 03 56.

Vieille Ville
Grasse's name may sound like the French for fat, but it comes from *Grace*—the state in which its original Jewish inhabitants found themselves once they converted to Christianity. In the Middle Ages, it was an independent city-state on the Italian model, with close ties to the republics of Genoa and Pisa—a relationship witnessed these days by the austere Italian style of its architecture. During the 13th-century turmoil between the Guelphs and the Ghibellines, the town put itself under the protection of the Count of Provence. Today, a large percentage of the population hails from North Africa: the perfume magnates themselves live in Mougins and surrounding villages.

The one place where they often meet is at the morning food and flower market in arcaded **Place aux Aires** near the top of the town, where the handsome Hôtel Isnard (1781) with its wrought-iron balcony looks like it escaped from New Orleans. From here Rue des Moulinets and Rue Mougins-Roquefort lead to the Romanesque **Cathédrale Notre-Dame du Puy**, its spartan façade similar to churches around Genoa, matched by

122

its spartan nave. The art is to the right: the *Crown of Thorns* and *Crucifixion*, by Rubens at the age of 24, before he hit the big time; a rare religious subject by Fragonard, the *Washing of the Feet*; and most sincere of all, a triptych by Ludovico Brea. Across the Place du Petit-Puy, a plaque on the **Tour de Guet** (the former *évêché*) commemorates the Grassois poet Bellaud de la Bellaudière, whose songs of wine and women, the *Obras et Rimos Provençalos* (1585) are the high point in Provençal literature between the troubadours and Mistral. But then as now, it's a rare poet who can live off his verse: Bellaud supplemented his income by joining a band of brigands and sang his swan-song on a scaffold.

Place du Cours and Four Museums
The Cannes road leads into Grasse's promenade, **Place du Cours**, with pretty views over the countryside. Close by, at 23 Blvd Fragonard is the **Musée Villa Fragonard** (10–1 and 2–7; winter 10–12 and 2–5, closed Mon, Tues, and Nov), in a 17th-century home belonging to a cousin of Grasse's most famous citizen, Jean-Honoré Fragonard (1732–1806). Son of a *gantier parfumeur*, Fragonard expressed the inherent family sweetness in chocolate-box pastel portraits and genre scenes of French royals trying their best to look like frivolous poodles. Some of these are on display, along with copies of *Le Progrès de l'Amour dans la Coeur d'une Jeune Fille*, which even Mme du Barry, who commissioned them, rejected as too friovolous (the originals are in the Frick collection in New York). Fragonard lost most of his clients to the guillotine and in 1790, he ended up in Grasse feeling very out of sorts, until one very hot day in 1806 he died from a cerebral haemorrhage induced by eating an ice-cream.

Just north of the Cours, at 2 Rue Mirabeau, the **Musée d'Art et d'Histoire de Provence** (same hours as Villa Fragonard) has its home in the 1770 Italianate mansion built by the frisky sister of Count Mirabeau of Aix (see pp. 190–91); this lady was married to one of several degenerate Marquis who pepper the history of Provence—this one, the Marquis de Cabris, is remembered in Grasse for having covered the walls of the city with obscene graffiti about the local women. Besides Gallo-Roman funerary objects, *santons* and furniture in all the Louis styles, there's Count Mirabeau's death mask, his sister's original *bidets*, an exceptional collection of faïence from Moustiers and Apt, and paintings by Granet. At 8 Place du Cours, the **Musée International de la Parfumerie** (Wed–Sun 10–6, winter 10–12 and 2–5, closed Nov), displays lots of precious little bottles from Roman times to the present, plus Bergamot boxes of the 1700s and Marie-Antoinette's travel case, while around the corner in Blvd du Jeu-de-Ballon, the **Musée de la Marine** (Mon–Sat 10–12 and 2–6) is devoted to the career of the intrepid Admiral de Grasse, hero of the American War of Independence.

Parfumeries
It's hard to miss these in Grasse, and if you've read Patrick Süsskind's novel *Perfume*, the free tours may seem a bit bland. The alchemical processes of extracting essences from freshly cut mimosa, jasmine, roses, bitter orange etc. are explained—you learn that it takes 900,000 rosebuds to make a kilo of rose essence, which then goes to the *haute-couture* perfume-bottlers and hype-merchants of Paris. Even more alarming are some of the other ingredients that arouse human hormones: the genital secretions of Ethopian cats, whale vomit, and Tibetan goat musk.

Tours in English are offered by **Parfumerie Fragonard** at 20 Blvd Fragonard and at Les 4 Chemins, on the Route de Cannes; **Molinard**, 60 Blvd Victor-Hugo, and **Gallimard**, 73 Rte de Cannes (N 85). And they don't seem to mind too much if you don't buy something at the end. Across the road from Gallimard, the kids may prefer the miniature TGV and engines in the **Musée des Trains Miniatures** (daily 9–7, adm).

Around Grasse: Dolmens and Musical Caves

The Route Napoléon (N 85), laid out in the 1930s to follow the little emperor's path to Paris, threads through miles of empty space on either side of medieval **St-Vallier-de-Thiey** (12 km). Things were busier here around 800 BC, when the people built elliptical walls with stones as much as 2 m high. An alignment of 12 small **dolmens**, most of them buried under stone tumuli, stands between St-Vallier and St-Cézaire-sur-Siagne; a balanced flat rock nearby is known as the *pierre druidique* (St-Vallier's tourist office in Place du Tour has a map). Just to the southwest, signposted on the D 5, there's a subterranean lake in the **Grotte de la Baume Obscure** (Easter–Oct daily 10–6, weekends only the rest of the year, adm). **Cabris**, 6 km west of Grasse, a *village perché* once favoured by Camus, Sartre and Antoine de Saint-Exupéry, is now a town of artisans and perfume executives. The D 11 and D 13 to the west lead to more caves: the red **Grottes de St-Cézaire**, where the iron-rich stalactites, when struck by the guide, make uncanny music (2:30–5; in summer 10:30–12 and 2:30–6, closed Nov–Feb, adm). **St-Cézaire-sur-Siagne** itself is an unspoiled medieval town; its white 13th-century cemetery-chapel built on pure, sober lines, is one of the best examples of Provençal Romanesque near the coast.

Market Days: Grasse, daily exc Monday.

WHERE TO STAY   (postal code 06130)
In **Grasse** ***Hotel des Parfums**, Blvd Eugène Charabot, tel 93 36 10 10, has not only pretty views, a pool and a jacuzzi, but from 1 Jan–31 July offers an 'Introduction to Perfume' package that takes you into the secret heart of the smell biz, lending you a 'nose' to help create your own perfume. Modern ***du Patti**, in the centre of medieval Grasse on Place du Patti, tel 93 36 01 00, has very comfortable rooms, all with air-conditioning and TV. ***Le Printania**, Rue des Roses (in easy walking distance of the centre), tel 93 36 95 00, offers a room with a view and a garden plus an inexpensive restaurant.

In **St-Vallier-de-Thiey** (06460) there's a charming choice: ***Le Préjoly**, Place Rougière, tel 93 42 60 86, with 20 rooms in a large garden, most with terraces, and an excellent restaurant frequented by film stars up from Cannes (menus at 100, 160, and 200 F). In Cabris (06530), the friendly ***Hôtel l'Horizon**, tel 93 60 51 69, is a well-situated Provençal-style hotel far from the crowds.

EATING OUT
Grasse's culinary specialities are if anything, *grasse*, especially *sous fassoun* (cabbage stuffed with pig's liver, sausage, bacon, peas and rice and cooked with turnips, beef, carrots, etc.) or *tripes à la mode de Grasse*. Both dishes appear frequently on the menu at

Maître Boscq, 13 Rue de la Fontette, tel 93 36 45 76, the local master of traditional cuisine, with a 100 F menu. Orange-blossom essence goes into the delicious sweet *fougassettes* sold at **Maison Venturini**, 1 Rue Marcel Journet. In Cabris, **Le Petit Prince**, 15 Rue F. Mistral, tel 93 60 51 40, has a lovely terrace, with delicious *filets de boeuf aux morilles* and *rascasse* (menus begin at 110 F).

Mougins

Cooking, that most ephemeral of arts, is the main reason most people make a pilgrimage to Mougins, a luxurious, fastidiously flawless village of *résidences secondaires*, with more gastronomy per square inch than any place in France, thanks to the magnetic presence of Roger Vergé (see below). But there are a few sights to whet your appetite before surrendering to the table: a **Photography Museum**, near the Porte Sarrasine, with changing exhibitions, often featuring the work of Jacques Lartigue, who lived in nearby Opio (open 1–7; July and Aug 2–11 pm, closed Tues). Other exhibitions take place in the old village *lavoir* (wash-house) in the pretty-as-a-picture Place de la Mairie. Two km southeast of Mougins, Picasso spent the last 12 years of his life in a villa next to the exquisite hilltop **Chapelle de Notre-Dame-de-Vie**, a 12th-century priory founded by monks from St-Honorat, and rebuilt in 1646. Until 1730, when the practice was banned, people would bring stillborn babies here to be brought back to life, just long enough for them to be baptized and avoid limbo.

Appropriately located just off the *autoroute* to Cannes, at the Aire des Bréguières, the de luxe **Musée de l'Automobiliste** is a modernistic cathedral to the car, from its first faltering steps as an 1882 Grand Bi, to Bugattis and Mercedes (with their perfectly-reconstructed garages *circa* 1939), to recent winners of the murderous Paris-Dakar rally (10–6, adm exp).

PEUGEOT 302 DARL'MAT, LE MANS
Musée de l'Automobiliste, Mougins

WHERE TO STAY/EATING OUT   (postal code 06250)

In 1969 chef Roger Vergé bought a 16th-century olive mill near Notre-Dame-de-Vie and made it into the internationally famous **Le Moulin de Mougins** (Chemin du Moulin, tel 93 75 78 24). Of late France's gourmet bibles have been sniffing that the mild-mannered celebrity chef, author of *The Cuisine of the Sun* (1979) has lost a bit of his touch—and little faults seem big when you shell out 1000 F for a meal. But it's still a once-in-a-lifetime experience for most, in the most enchanting setting on the Côte (closed end of Jan–Mar; reserve *now* if you want a table in two or three months). If you can't get a table, Vergé's shop in central Place du Com.-Lamy, with tableware and a selection of the master's sauces, may offer some consolation. Another gourmet temple, **Le Relais à Mougins**, run by André Surmain at Pl. de la Mairie, tel 93 90 03 47, serves exquisite, classic French cuisine (*gelée de saumon fumé au caviar* etc.) on a delicious garden terrace (menus 280 and 380 F; closed mid-Nov–mid-Dec and mid-Feb–mid-Mar). The *nouvelle cuisine* and chocolate desserts at the hotel-restaurant ******Les Muscadins**, at the village entrance (18 Blvd Courteline, tel 93 90 00 43) have received excellent reviews (menus 200 F and up), and the hotel has sumptuous bedrooms of charm and character (closed mid-Jan–mid-Mar). Mougins even has affordable restaurants like **Feu Follet**, Place du Com.-Lamy, tel 93 90 15 78, owned by André Surmain's daughter, offering excellent menus (*selle d'agneau en croûte*) for 130 and 160 F (closed Mar and Nov).

Cannes

In 1834, the 3000 fisherfolk and farmers of Cannes were going about their business when Lord Brougham, retired Lord Chancellor, and his ailing daughter checked into its one and only hotel, stuck in the village because a cholera epidemic in France had closed the border with Savoy. As they waited, Lord Brougham was so seduced by the climate and scenery that he built a villa, where he spent every winter. English milords and the Tsar's family played follow-my-leader, and flocked down to build their own villas nearby. 'Menton's dowdy. Monte's brass. Nice is rowdy. Cannes is class!' was the byword of the 20s. Less enthusiastic commentators mention the dust, the bad roads, the uncontrolled building, and turds bobbing in the sea.

If nothing else, the Riviera ends with a bang at Cannes. The spunky sister city of Beverly Hills, France's Hollywood, a major year-round convention city, and home of Haiti's ex-dictator, 'Baby Doc' Duvalier, Cannes offers a moveable feast of high fashion, show-biz trendiness, overripe boutiques, and glittering nightlife. Depending on your mood, and perhaps on the thickness of your wallet, you may find it appalling or amusing, or just plain dizzy. You can always catch the next boat to the offshore Îles de Lérins, some of the most serene antidotes to any city.

GETTING AROUND

The frequent *Métrazur* between St-Raphaël and Menton, and every other train whipping along the coast, calls into the station at Rue Jean-Jaurès (information tel 93 99 50 50). More confusingly, there are two **bus stations**: the one next to the train station (tel 93 39 31 37) is good for Golfe-Juan, Vallauris, Grasse, Mougins and Nice airport.

The second, in Place de l'Hôtel de Ville, tel 93 39 11 39, has buses for Juan-les-Pins, Antibes, Grasse, Vallauris, Nice, and St-Raphaël. The 11 city bus lines depart from Place l'Hôtel de Ville, where there's a bus information office; a handy minibus plies the seafront between Place F.-Mistral and the Palm Beach Casino. You can rent **bikes** at the train station or at 5 Rue Alliés, tel 93 39 46 15, between Rue d'Antibes and Parking Gambetta.

Boat trips out to the Iles de Lérins (tel 93 39 11 82)depart from the *gare maritime*, the Allées de la Liberté, from 7:30–3:30 in the summer, and much less frequently between October and June, when the last sailing is at 2:45.

TOURIST INFORMATION
Palais des Festivals, Esplanade du Président Georges Pompidou, tel 93 39 01 01; another office is in the SNCF station, tel 93 99 19 77. **Cannes Information Jeunesse**, 5 Quai St-Pierre, tel 93 68 50 50, has listings of events, jobs, etc. **Post office**: 22 Bivouac Napoléon, tel 93 39 14 11.

La Croisette and Le Suquet

Besides ogling the shops, the shoppers, and their dogs there isn't much to see in Cannes. Characterless luxury apartment buildings and boutiques have replaced the gaudy Belle Epoque confections along the fabled promenade **La Croisette**, its glitter now clogged by incessant traffic in the summer, its lovely sands covered by the sun-beds and parasols of the beach concessions. One rare public beach is in front of the fan-shaped **Palais des Festivals** a 1982 construction that may have been the prototype for one of Saddam Hussein's cosier bunkers. Hand-prints of film celebrities line the 'Allée des Étoiles' by the 'escalier d'Honneur' where the limos pull up for the festival. Outside of May, this orange monster engorges conventioneers attending events such as the Festival of Hairdressing or Dentistry.

The **Vieux Port**, with its bobbing fishing-boats and plush, luxury craft is on the other side of the Palais des Festivals. Plane trees line the **Allées de la Liberté**, where the flower market takes place. Two streets further back, narrow pedestrian **Rue Meynadier** is the best place to buy cheese (*Ferme Savoyarde*), bread (*Jacky Carletto*), and fresh pasta (*Aux Bons Raviolis*), near the sumptuous **Forville** covered market (every morning exc Mon). Cannes' cramped old quarter, **Le Suquet**, rises up on the other side of the port, where the usual renovation and displacement of the not-so-rich is just beginning. At the city's highest point, the monks of St-Honorat built the square watchtower, the **Tour du Mont Chevalier** in 1088, and their priory is now the **Musée de la Castre** (10–12 and 2–5, summer 3–7), an archaeological and ethnographic collection donated by a Dutch Baron in 1873, with everything from Etruscan vases to pre-Columbian art and a 40-armed Buddah.

Everything else worth seeing in Cannes is a long walk from the centre—including the unabashedly eccentric **Casino de Palm Beach** (1929) at the far end of La Croisette, where you can disco, eat, swim, and watch a floorshow as well as empty your wallet at the tables. Check at the tourist office to see if the **Observatoire de Super-Cannes** has re-opened in the northeast suburbs, where a lift whisks you up for a panorama stretching to Corsica and Italy.

127

Les Iles de Lérins: St-Honorat

When Babylon begins to pall, you can take refuge (and a picnic, for the island restaurants are dear) on a delightful pair of green, wooded, traffic-free islets just off the coast. Known in antiquity as Lero and Lerina, they are now named after two saints who founded religious houses on them at the end of the 4th century: little **St-Honorat** and the larger **Ste-Marguerite**. According to legend, when St Honorat landed on the islet that bears his name in 375, he found it swarming with noxious snakes and prayed to be delivered of them. They immediately dropped dead but the stench of the cadavers was so hideous that Honorat climbed a palm tree and prayed again, asking the bodies be washed away. God obliged again, and in memory the symbol of the island became two palm trees intertwined with a snake.

St Honorat shares with Jean Cassien of St-Victor in Marseille the distinction of introducing monasticism to France. The island became a beacon of light and learning in the Dark Ages; by the 7th century, St-Honorat had 4000 monks, and 100 priories and lordships on the mainland (including Cannes, which belonged to the monastery until 1788). Its alumni numbered 20 saints, including St Patrick, who, before going to Ireland, trained here and picked up some tips on dealing with pesky snakes.

The monastery was also a big boon to local sinners: a journey to St-Honorat could earn a pilgrim an indulgence equal to a journey to the Holy Land. Other visitors, especially Saracen pirates, were not as welcome. To protect themselves, the monks built a fortress, connected to the abbey by means of an underground tunnel. Although the abbey is long gone, the evocative, crenellated **donjon** remains strong, lapped by the wavelets on three sides, mellowed by sea and time; within there's a vaulted cloister and chapel, and a terrace with views that stretch to the Alps. In 1869 Cistercians from Sénanque purchased St-Honorat, rebuilt the abbey (men only are admitted on weekdays, but there's not much to see) and have done all they could to preserve the islet's natural beauty and serenity, so close to, and yet so far from the sound and fury of Cannes.

Ste-Marguerite, and the Man in the Iron Mask

Legend has it that Marguerite, sister of St-Honorat, founded a convent for holy Christian women on this larger island, but it broke her heart that her austere brother would only come to visit her when a certain almond tree blossomed. Marguerite asked God to make him come more often, a prayer answered when the almond tree miraculously began to bloom every month.

Ste-Marguerite has nicer beaches than St-Honorat, especially on the south end of Chemin de la Chasse. On the north end stands the gloomy **Fort Royal**, built by Richelieu as a defence against the Spaniards (who got it anyway) and improved by Vauban in 1712. By then the fortress mainly served as a prison, especially for the mysterious Man in the Iron Mask, who was transferred here from Pigneroles in 1687, and then ended up in the Bastille, in 1698. Speculation about the man's identity continues to at least amuse historians (who insist that the mask was actually leather): was he Louis XIV's twin, as Voltaire suggested, or according to a more recent theory, the gossiping son-in-law of the doctor who performed the autopsy on Louis XIII and discovered that the king was incapable of producing children? Later prisoners included six Huguenot pastors who dared to return to France after Louis XIV's revocation of the Edict of Nantes, and were kept in solitary confinement until all but one of them went mad.

Market Days: Marché Forville, daily exc Monday; Saturday flea market in the Allées de la Liberté.

FESTIVALS

Since 1946, the **Festival International du Film** has erupted in Cannes around the second week of May with a hurricane of hype, *paparazzi*, journalists, and gawking fans climbing over one another for a view of their movie idols. There are some 350 screenings, but most of the tickets are reserved for the cinema people themselves, while 10 per cent go to the Cannois, who bestow the *prix populaire* on their favourite film. The few seats left over go on sale at the Palais' box-office a week before the festival. From 4–14 July, the **Festival Américain** brings in jazz and country music.

WHERE TO STAY   (postal code 06400)

Expensive

Although there are sizeable discounts if you come to Flash City in the off-season, you can't book too early for the film festival or for July and August. Cannes' two tourist offices offer a free reservation service, but they won't be much help at that time of year if you want a room that costs less than a king's ransom; if, however, you possess one of those, you can drop a considerable lump of it at the *******Carlton**, 58 La Croisette, tel 93 68 91 68, one of the great landmarks of the Riviera, with its two black cupolas, said to be shaped like the breasts of the notorious Belle Otéro, the Andalusian flamenco dancer and courtesan of kings. Given a thorough renovation by its new Japanese owners, the seventh floor has been endowed with a pool, casino, beauty centre, and more. In the same category, the traditional *******Majestic**, 14 La Croisette, tel 93 68 91 00, is the movie stars' favourite with its classic French decor, heated pool, private beach etc. A third, the *******Martinez**, 73 La Croisette, tel 93 94 30 30, has kept its Roaring Twenties character, but with all imaginable modern comforts, including tennis-courts, a heated pool and, from the seventh floor, grand views over the city.

Moderate/Inexpensive

If you aren't in Cannes on an MGM expense account, there are other alternatives, such as *****Bleu Rivage**, 61 La Croisette, tel 93 94 24 25, a renovated older hotel amidst the big daddies on the beach where rooms overlook the sea, or the garden at the back. The kosher *****Acapulco**, 16 Blvd d'Alsace, tel 93 99 16 16, inspected by the regional rabbi, has a heated pool on the roof, a back terrace and comfortable rooms. The 19th-century ****Molière**, 5–7 Rue Molière, tel 93 38 16 16, sits in the midst of a garden, with bright rooms and terraces. Another quiet choice, the modern ****Sélect**, 16 Rue Hélène Vagliano, tel 93 99 51 00, has air-conditioned rooms, all with bath, while ***Le Chante-clair**, 12 Rue Fortville, tel 93 39 68 88, has decent doubles with showers.

EATING OUT

Expensive

Good food follows money, and Cannes is well-endowed with opportunities for gastro-nomic indulgence. Two of the top restaurants on the whole Riviera are here: the **Royal**

Gray, by the luxurious Lebanese hyper-mall at 6 Rue des Etats-Unis, tel 93 99 04 59, is the citadel presided over by young chef Jaques Chibois, who combines ingredients such as fresh shrimp from Tunisia and tiny morels from Canada to create the extraordinarily rare and delightful dishes, at rarefied prices—although there's a tempting 200 F weekday lunch menu that definitely bears thinking about. **Le Palme d'Or** in the Martinez hotel (see above), has a fabulous Art Deco dining room, the Alsacian cook, Christian Willer, prepares dishes including a succulent *filet d'agneau aux farcis provençaux* which you can enjoy at lunch for as little as 260 F, wine included.

Moderate/Inexpensive
For well-prepared versions of the French classics, try **Le Rescator,** 7 Rue du Maréchal-Joffre, tel 93 39 44 57, a favourite with its generous 150 and 190 F menus. For affordable seafood and fine views of its original habitat, try the 100 F menu at the nautical **Lou Souléou,** 16 Blvd Jean Hibert, tel 93 39 85 55. There's only one 180 F menu at **La Brouette de chez Grand-Mère,** 9 Rue d'Oran, tel 93 39 12 10, and it's only served in the evenings, but it will fill you up, with everything that could possibly be crammed between an apéritif and coffee, with as much *vin du pays* as you want—but be sure to reserve. **Le Bec Fin,** 12 Rue du 24-Août, near the station, tel 93 38 35 86, serves good food and plenty of it, with a wide selection of *plats du jour* for 75 or 95 F. Spread out over the Vieux Port, **La Pizza,** 3 Quai St-Pierre, tel 93 39 22 56, has fine pizzas, pasta, and a congenial atmosphere—until 4 am in the summer.

ENTERTAINMENT AND NIGHTLIFE
Cannes the fleshpot will keep you entertained if you have the wherewithal to afford it. Its casinos draw in some of the highest rollers on the Riviera, although the adjoining casino discos are fairly staid. To get into the most fashionable clubs (those with no signs on the door) you need to look like you've just stepped off a 30-m yacht to get past the sour-faced bouncers. There's usually live music to go with the food at **La Chunga,** 24 Rue Latour-Maubourg, tel 93 94 07 31 (open til 2:30 am; meals about 300 F). **Le Whiskey à Gogo** has a well-heeled crowd grinding away to the top of the pops. **Le Blitz,** 22 Rue Massé (open 11 pm–7 am, 60 F cover) attracts a young crowd of every possible sexual persuasion. Cannes also has two gay bars of long standing: **Le Bar Basque,** 14 Rue Macé (open 7 pm–7 am) and the noiser **Zanzi-Bar,** 85 Rue Félix-Faure (2 pm–4 am); newer on the scene, the **Club 7 Disco** at 7 Rue Rouguière has dancing and a transvestite show (open 11 pm–7 am, 90 F cover charge).

For something tamer, every hour in the summer, the glass-bottomed boat, *Nautilus,* departs for tours of the port and its sea creatures (tel 93 99 62 01; tickets 60 F). **The English Bookshop,** 11 Rue Bivouac Napoléon, has a wide selection.

Part V

CÔTE D'AZUR:
L'ESTEREL TO BANDOL

St-Tropez

Where the shores of the fabled Riviera tend be all shingle, the beaches of the western Côte d'Azur are mostly soft sand. The crowds, cars, art, yachts, boutiques and prices are less intense as well, with the outrageous exception of St-Tropez, the playground of dry-martini louts. But just behind these careless seaside pleasures bulge two of the world's most ancient chunks of land, the prodigious porphyry Esterel and the dark, forested Maures, while tucked in between are museums of Post-Impressionism, music boxes, ships' figureheads and booze; Roman ruins and a tortoise reserve; an island national park and the oldest baptistry in France; and to begin with, the most Gothic of follies, Henry Clews' little house of horrors in La Napoule.

The Esterel

> The Esterel is supposed to receive its name from the fairy Esterelle, who intoxicates and deceives her ardent lovers and thus fittingly makes her home on the Coast of Illusion.
>
> —Douglas Goldring, *The South of France* (1952)

Between Cannes and St-Raphaël this fairy Coast of Illusion provides one of nature's strangest but most magnificent interludes: a wild *massif* of blood-red cliffs and promontories, with sandy or shingle beaches amid dishevelled porphyry boulders tumbling into

131

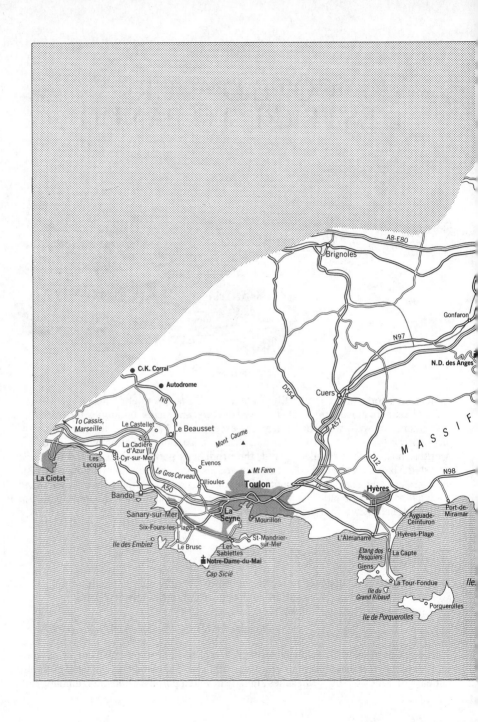

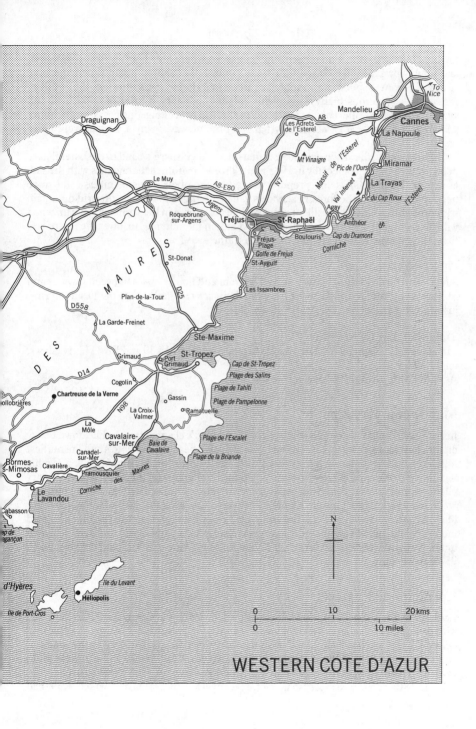

WESTERN COTE D'AZUR

the blue blue sea—the kind of romantic landscape where holy hermits like St Honorat, and unholy brigands like Gaspard de Besse, once felt equally at home. The handsome Gaspard, from a bourgeois family of Besse-sur-Issole, was himself the stuff of romance—a generous highwayman with knightly manners, a lover of good food and wine, a man able to entertain the jury at his trial in Aix by reciting long passages of Homer and Anacreon in Greek. When they hanged him anyway, many a woman wept bitter tears.

Unfortunately, the virgin cork forests that once hid Gaspard's band in the Esterel have been ravaged by fire (especially in 1985 and 1986)—enviromental tragedies with the side effects of clearing sites for property brigands and their cement-mixers, who race neck-and-neck with the forestry service's gallant attempts to reforest the arid mountain with drought and disease resilient pines and ilexes. Come in the spring if you can, when wild flowers ignite this Fauvist volcanic fairyland; in the summer, to lower the risk of real fires, the internal roads are often closed to traffic.

GETTING AROUND
The Corniche de l'Esterel is well served by train and hourly buses between Cannes and St-Raphaël. From Mandelieu-La Napoule there are regular boats to the Iles de Lérins, just off Cannes (see p. 128), tel 93 49 15 88).

TOURIST INFORMATION
Mandelieu-La Napoule (06210): Av. de Cannes, tel 93 49 14 39 and Blvd Henry Clews, tel 93 49 95 31.
Agay (83700): Blvd de la Mer, tel 94 82 01 85.

Mandelieu-La Napoule

Just west of Cannes, three golf courses are Mandelieu's claim to fame, while down below on the coast its sister town, La Napoule, has the usual beaches and hotels and the nuttiest folly ever built by a foreigner on this shore, the **Fondation Henry Clews**, a Gothic nightmare castle appropriately located on Pointe des Pendus (of the hanged men). Henry Clews, from a wealthy American banking family, fancied himself a sculptor, and between 1917 and 1934 made it his life's work to convert a medieval fort into a fantasy palace of the gross and grotesque; from the front gate right through into the parlour distorted monsters and animals writhe next to cryptic inscriptions and Clews' own self-designed tomb. Now an American art school, it's open for tours Mon–Fri 3:15 and 4:45 (tel 94 49 95 05 to be sure).

Corniche de l'Esterel

Laid out by the French Touring Club way back in 1903, the Corniche (N 98) is dotted with panoramic belvederes overlooking the extraordinary red, blue, and green seascapes below. The largest beaches of sand or shingle are served by snack wagons in the summer, and in between, with a bit of climbing, are rocky coves and nooks you can have all to yourself. Heading west from La Napoule, **Théoule-sur-Mer** has three small beaches and an 18th-century seaside soap factory converted into a castle, which isn't bad

134

compared to **La Galère** (the next town west on the same road), infected in the 1970s by a private housing estate seemily modelled on cancer cells. This is a suburb of fashionable **Miramar**, where the best thing to do is walk out along **Pointe de l'Esquillon** for the view of the sheer cliffs of **Cap Roux** plunging into the sea. The nearby slopes and jagged shore, pierced with inlets and secret coves belong to the villas and hotel of **Le Trayas**.

Beyond Le Trayas, a road at **Pointe de l'Observatoire** ascends to the **Grotte de la Ste-Baume**, where St Honorat resided as a hermit when four-star views were free of charge. Meanwhile the Corniche road itself twists and turns towards **Anthéor** and the Esterel's biggest resort, **Agay**, a laid-back village dominated by porphyry cliffs, set around a perfect horseshoe bay rimmed with sand and pebble beaches. In 1944 the American 36th Division disembarked just to the west at the **Plage du Dramont**, where you can pick up the path to the **Sémaphore du Dramont**, with broad panoramas over the Gulf of Fréjus and the two porphyry sea rocks at its entrance called the *Lion de Mer* and *Lion de Terre*.

The Esterel: Inland Routes

From Cannes, the N 7 follows the path of the Roman Via Aurelia, passing through the bulk of the Esterel's surviving cork forest. The high point of the trip, both literally and figuratively, is **Mont Vinaigre**, rising to 600 m; from the road a short path leads to its summit and a fantastic viewing platform in an old watchtower. Other hairpinning roads begin in Agay and lead to within easy walking distance of the Esterel's most dramatic features: the hellish **Gorge du Mal-Infernet**, and the panoramic **Pic de l'Ours** and **Pic du Cap Roux**, where the wanton Esterelle is at her most ravishing, and the Coast of Illusion a flaming vision of colour and light.

WHERE TO STAY/EATING OUT

Mandelieu-La Napoule (06210): In **Mandelieu**, golf-enthusiasts can sleep near their favourite sport at the modern *****Hostellerie du Golf**, 780 Blvd de la Mer, 93 49 11 66, equipped with a pool and spacious rooms with terraces. La Napoule's ******Ermitage du Riou**, Av. Henry Clews, tel 93 49 95 56, is a luxurious refuge built like a Provençal bastide, with a garden and pool overlooking the sea. The much more affordable ****La Calanque**, Av. Henry Clews, tel 93 49 95 11, has a shady terrace and views of the sea and Clews' folly (closed Nov–Mar). For dinner, try the *soupe de poisson* and grilled fish at **La Boucanier**, by the Port de Plaisance, tel 93 38 80 51 (95 F menu).

Le Trayas (83700): The one hotel ****Le Relais des Calanques**, Corniche d'Or, tel 94 44 14 06, has 14 rooms plus a pool and a good fish restaurant (menus from 120 F). There's a superb **Auberge de Jeunesse** (Youth Hostel cards required), tel 93 75 40 23, but as usual it's hard to reach—a 2 km march uphill from the station, so ring ahead; and in summer, book.

Anthéor (83700): ****Les Flots Bleus**, tel 94 44 80 21, is the best place to sleep and eat; the rooms have views of the sea and the seafood served on the terrace is fresh and copious (menus from 85 F).

Agay (83700): There are mostly camp-sites here, and among the handful of hotels the most comfortable is the isolated *****Sol e Mar**, at Plage Le Dramont, tel 94 95 25 60, right on the sea, with two salt-water pools and a restaurant with adequate food but tremendous views (180 F). **France Soleil, tel 94 82 01 93, in Agay itself, is a reliable choice on the beach, open from Easter to October only.

Along the N7: The *Auberge des Adrets is a lonely inn (dating back to 1653), once notorious as a refuge for bandits. It now has 8 simple but bandit-less rooms just beyond Mt Vinaigre (tel 94 40 36 24).

St-Raphaël and Fréjus

Between the Esterel and the Massif des Maures, in the fertile little plain of the river Argens, are St-Raphaël and Fréjus, the largest towns on the coast between Cannes and Hyères. After the fireworks of the Esterel, St-Raphaël is all too predictable: more beaches, blocks of holiday flats, and yachts. It has swollen to merge imperceptibly with its venerable neighbour Fréjus (*Forum Julii*), a market town and naval port on the *Via Aurelia* founded by Julius Caesar himself to rival Greek Marseille. Octavian made it his chief naval arsenal, to build the ships that licked Cleopatra and Mark Antony at Actium. Even today, Fréjus is a garrison town, with France's largest naval air base.

GETTING AROUND

St-Raphaël is the terminus of the *Métrazur* trains that run along the coast to Menton. Other trains between Nice and Marseille call at both St-Raphaël and Fréjus stations, making it easy to hop between the two towns; St-Raphaël also has direct connections to Aix, Avignon, Nîmes, Montpellier and Carcassonne (train information, tel 93 99 50 50). Both have buses for Nice and Marseille (Cars Phocéens, tel 94 95 24 82), more expensive ones for St-Tropez and Toulon (Sodetrav, tel 94 95 24 82) and buses inland for Bagnols, Fayence, and Les Adrets (Gagnard, tel 93 36 27 97). Les Bateaux Bleus, tel 94 95 17 46, depart regularly from the Vieux Port of St-Raphaël to St-Tropez and St-Aygulf, and make day excursions to the Iles de Lérins and Ile de Port Cros, as well as jaunts around the Golfe de Fréjus and its *calanques* (creeks); be sure to reserve ahead in July and Aug. Bike hire: Cycles et Loisirs, 3 Rue Jean-Mermoz and Ideal Loisirs, 892 Blvd de la Mer, both in Fréjus-Plage.

TOURIST INFORMATION

St-Raphaël (83700): Place de la Gare, tel 94 95 16 87.
Fréjus (83600): 325 Rue Jean-Jaurès, tel 94 51 54 14; Fréjus-Plage: Blvd de la Libération, tel 94 51 48 42.

St-Raphaël

The fiefdom of right-wing politican François Léotard and his family, St-Raphaël has money if not much heart. Its once glittering turn-of-the-century follies and medieval centre were bombed out of it in the war, leaving only the 1150 church of St-Raphäel intact, with its Templar watchtower (just north of the station). This is the third church to occupy the site, re-using the same old Roman stones—one in the choir vault is carved with something you won't often see in church: a flying phallus, an ancient charm for averting evil (Pompeii has lots of them). If the church is closed, pick up the key at the adjacent **Musée d'Archéologie Sous-Marine** (Oct–May 11–12 and 2–4, closed Sun; June–Sept 10–12 and 3–6, closed Tues). For centuries there were rumours of a sunken city off St-Raphaël, apparently confirmed by the bricks that divers brought to shore. Jacques Cousteau went down to see and found, not a new Atlantis, but a Roman shipwreck full of building materials. Some are displayed here along with a fine collection of amphorae.

Fréjus: the Roman Town

Founded in 49 BC, *Forum Julii* was the first Roman town of Gaul, but not the most successful; the site was malarial and hard to defend, and eventually the river Argens silted up, creating the vast sandy beach of **Fréjus-Plage** but leaving the Roman harbour, once famous for its enormous size, high and dry a mile from the sea. A path tracing the ruined quay begins at Butte St-Antoine, south of central Fréjus, but even then it's hard to picture a hundred Roman galleys anchored in the weeds. The one monument still standing, the **Lanterne d'Auguste** isn't even Roman, but a medieval harbourmaster's lodge built on a Roman base.

Other fragments of *Forum Julii* are a long hike away across the modern town—Fréjus is one place where those ubiquitous little tourist trains make sense. Best preserved is the ungainly, greenish **Arènes** or amphitheatre, flat on its back with the rib-like arches of its *vomitoria* (entrance) exposed to the sky. Arches from a 40-km **aqueduct** still leapfrog alongside the road to Cannes; the **theatre**, north on Av. du Théâtre-Romain has had new seats installed for modern performances.

The Oldest Baptistry in France

On a map marked with walls that once contained *Forum Julii*, modern Fréjus looks like the last lamb-chop on a platter. The Saracens had much of the rest in the 10th century, coming back seven times to pillage and destroy the bits they missed. When the coast was clear, the Fréjussiens rebuilt their **Cathedral** in Place Formigé and made it the centre of a small *cité épiscopale* with a crenellated defence tower, a chapterhouse and a bishop's palace. Built from the 12th to the 16th centuries, the cathedral has a superb pair of **Renaissance doors** carved with sacred scenes, a Saracen massacre, and portraits of aristocratic ladies and gents, including King François I. Inside, over the sacristy door, there's a *retable de Ste-Marguerite* (*c.* 1450) by Jacques Durandi, of the School of Nice.

The rest of the *cité* is open June–Sept 9–7, other times 10–12 and 2–4:30, closed Tues, adm. The **Baptistry**, the one bit of Fréjus the Saracens missed, dates from the 4th or 5th century, and like most palaeo-Christian baptistries, it is octagonal, defined by eight black granite columns with white capitals borrowed from the Roman forum. Only adults were baptized in the early days, and they would enter the narrow door and have their feet washed at the terracotta basin; the bishop would then baptize them in the pool in the centre, and as new Christians, they would leave through the larger door to attend mass.

Fairest of all is the beguiling 12th-century **Cloister**, with slim marble columns and a 14th-century ceiling. This is coffered into 1200 little vignettes, of which a third still have curious paintings that compile a whole catalogue of monkish fancies: grotesques, mermaids, animals, portraits, and debaucheries. Upstairs, the **Archaeology Museum** has a collection of finds from *Forum Julii*, among them a perfectly preserved mosaic, a fine head of Jupiter, and a copy of the superb two-faced bust of Hermes discovered in 1970.

Just off Place Formigé, at 53 Rue Sieyes are two Atlantes, all that remains of the house of the Abbé Sieyes (1748–1836), pamphleteer of the Revolution, deputy at the Convention and mastermind of the 18th Brumaire coup that brought Napoleon to power. Later exiled as a regicide, he returned to Paris in 1830; and when asked to sum up his career in politics he gave the famous laconic reply: 'I survived.'

Around Fréjus

Just outside Fréjus stand a pair of remarkable monuments recalling the rotten days of World War I, when states supplemented their manpower by importing men from the colonies to fight wars that weren't theirs. The Vietnamese built a colourful **Buddhist pagoda** as a memorial to their 5000 dead (2 km from the centre on the N 7, daily 3–6), while the Sudanese sharpshooters at the local marine base built a concrete reproduction of the Missiri mosque at Djenne, Mali (5 km; take the N 7 to the D 4 towards Fayence). Futher along the D 4, the modern **Musée de Troupes de Marine** covers the history of the marines from 1622 to the present (2–5, closed Tues). Another mile futher on you can drive and walk through the **Parc Zoologique**, where parrots and yaks don't look too out of place under the parasol pines.

Ten km up the River Argens from St Aygulf (Fréjus' resort suburb to the west) offers a break from coastal craziness at the picturesque 16th-century village of **Roquebrune-sur-Argens**, a wine and orchid centre that boasts the largest mulberry tree in France. Along the road to Le Muy the **Rochers de Roquebrune** form a peculiar, red baby massif that toddled away from the Esterel.

Market Days: St-Raphaël, daily exc Monday. Fréjus, Wednesday and Saturday.

WHERE TO STAY/EATING OUT
St Raphaël (83700): This town is rich in pricey camp-sites, but few hotels stand out. St-Raphaël's best choices are outside the centre, like ***Le Chêneraie**, Blvd des Gondins (near the Valescure golf course, tel 94 83 65 03), with very comfortable rooms and stylish baths, pool and tennis. Its restaurant serves delicious salads on the terrace (menus from 180 F). In Boulouris, 5 km east, ***La Potinière**, tel 94 95 21 43, is a modern hotel dedicated to sports (pool, tennis, sailing) and R and R, set in a pretty park of mimosas and eucalyptus. In town, try **Des Pyramides**, 77 Av. P.-Doumer, tel 94 95 05 95, with a little garden; or in the old town, *Des Templiers, Place de la République, tel 94 95 38 93. There's a youth hostel, **Centre International du Manoir**, Chemin de l'Escale (near the Boulouris station), tel 94 95 20 58, more expensive than most, but fancier as well and close to the beach. For delicious seafood, **L'Ile Bleue** will fill you up with a 120 F menu (by the yachts in Port Santa-Lucia, tel 94 82 22 26). Fish dishes like *mousseline de sole* are the fare at **L'Orangerie**, Promenade R.-Coty, tel 94 83 19 50, along with fresh pasta (good value menus, beginning at 90 F). If it's Friday, go for the special 140 F aïoli menu at **Pastorel**, an excellent address with a garden terrace at 54 Rue de la Liberté, tel 94 95 02 36.

Fréjus (83600): ***Résidence du Colombier, Rte de Bagnols, tel 94 51 45 92, is perfect for families with modern rooms in bungalows, each with a private garden and terrace, spread out in a pine-wood, plus a heated pool, tennis, volley ball, etc. At Fréjus-Plage, **Il etait une fois, 254 Rue F.-Mistral, tel 94 51 21 26, is a charming reasonably-priced Provençal-style hotel in a garden near the sea. In Fréjus centre, the best of the cheapies is the quiet *Bellevue, a minute from the cathedral in Place P.-Vernet, tel 94 51 42 41. There's a pleasant but inconvenient Auberge de Jeunesse 2 km from Fréjus' historic centre (in a large park east on the N 7, tel 94 52 18 75, open all year): in the morning a special bus transports guests to and from the station. For dinner, Lou Calen near the cathedral at 9 Rue Désaugiers, tel 94 52 36 87, serves specialities based on fresh seasonal ingredients from the sea and garden (menu at 150 F). Or eat for less at the popular *crêperie* Cadet Rousselle, 25 Place Agricola, tel 94 53 36 92, or its pizzeria neighbour Lou Grilladou, tel 94 53 48 27 (both around 50 F). Beer-lovers can chug down one of a hundred varieties at Fréjus-Plage's Maison de la Bière, 461 Blvd de la Libération.

Massif des Maures

Between Fréjus and Hyères, the coast bulges out and up again to form the steep rolling hills and arcadian natural amphitheatres of the ancient Massif des Maures. Although it lacks the high drama of the Esterel, this mountain range (760 m at its highest point) is as much of a geological oddball, its granite, gneiss, and schist completely unrelated to the limestone that dominates the rest of Provence. The name Maures is derived from *maouro*, Provençal for black, describing its dark, deep forests of umbrella and Aleppo pines, chestnuts and cork. For centuries the latter two trees provided the main source of income of the few inland villages.

Until the 19th century this was the most dangerous coast in France. The Saracens made it their chief stronghold in the area in 846, building forts (*fraxinets*) on each hill to watch for ships to plunder, and to defend themselves from the Franks. They were finally forced out in the campaign of 972, led by William of Provence, who was greatly assisted by a knight from Genoa named Grimaldi, the first of that family to appear in what is now France. But although the pirates had to abandon their *fraxinets*, they hardly abandoned the coast, and maintained a reign of terror that continued until 1830, when the French captured Algiers. A hundred years later, the fashion for seaside bathing spread west from the Riviera, giving every crowded beach a holiday town to call its own.

Ste-Maxime

In the seaside conurbation spread between Fréjus and St-Tropez, the only place that may tempt a detour is Ste-Maxime, a modern resort town with a beach of golden sand facing St-Tropez. It willingly takes the overflow of fashionable and bankable holiday-makers from there, who can take the frequent boats back to the capital of see-and-be-seen. Far more interesting, both visibly and audibly, are the exhibits of the remarkable Musée du Phonographe et de la Musique Mécanique, in the unlikely setting of the wooded Parc de St-Donat (10 km north on the D 25, or take the the Le Muy bus from

Ste-Maxime; open Easter–15 Oct, 10–12 and 3–6:30, adm). About half of the music boxes, barrel organs, automata and player pianos still work, as well as some of the rare prizes: one of Edison's original phonographs of 1878, an accordion-like 'Melophone' of 1780, a 1903 dictaphone, and an audio-visual 'pathegraphe' to teach foreign languages, built in 1913.

From Ste-Maxime the road passes through **Port-Grimaud**, a posh private housing estate designed in 1968 by Alsatian architect François Spoerry, inspired by the lagoon pleasure complexes around St Petersburg, Florida, where wealthy home-owners, like Venetians, can park their boats by the front door. The traditionally-styled, colourful houses themselves are a preview of the real McCoys in St-Tropez and Martigues; the pseudo-Romanesque **church**, sitting on its own islet, has stained glass windows designed by Vasarely.

St-Tropez

It made the headlines in France when St-Tropez's mayor, Alain Spada, forced the discos to close at 2 am and declared the beaches off limits to dogs, inciting the fury of Brigitte Bardot, that crusading Joan of Arc of animal rights and the town's most famous citizen. For ever since BB starred in Roger Vadim's *Et Dieu Créa La Femme* in 1956 the French have kept close tabs on this little town, regarding it as the official throbbing showcase of the fun, sun and sex side of their national character, a showcase *naturellement* veneered with glamour and fashion and tainted with the pouts of spoiled grown-ups. Everyone who wants to be associated with fun and fashion tries to squeeze into St-Tropez in the summer, booking one of the few hotel rooms nearly a year in advance, or just coming down for the day for a gawk at the yachts.

The French fondly call this St-Trop (St Too Much) and in the summer it really is: too many people (100,000 on an average day) clogging the roads, lanes, and beaches; too much rubbish; too many artists hawking paintings around the port; too many crowded cafés and restaurants charging unholy prices. At other times of the year it's easier to understand what started all the commotion in the first place—although beware that in winter St-Tropez, the only town on the Côte d'Azur to face north, can be extremely blustery.

History

One of the strangest but somehow most fitting legends along the coast has it that St-Tropez's first incarnation, the Greek colony Athenopolis, was founded by Praxiteles' famous model Phryne, who had a face like a toad but the body of a goddess. Put on trial in Athens for unseemly behaviour, she lifted up her skirt, astonishing the jury with her charms, and was acquitted on condition that she left Athens. She ended up here, wedded to a Ligurian chieftain. Together they founded Athenopolis, although Phryne was later sacrificed to the Ligurian gods with the request that they please keep outsiders away in the future.

In 68 AD, Torpes, an officer of Nero, was beheaded in Pisa for his Christian beliefs. As anyone who knows the Lives of the Saints, the Romans had no lack of ingenuity in dealing with martyrs; in this case, they buried Torpes' head in Pisa, and put his body in a boat with a dog and a cock, who were to slowly devour it. But the animals had no appetite, and their boat floated safely to Athenopolis (the Roman *Heraclea Cacabria*) which eventually adopted St Torpes' name. The saintly body was hidden and lost during the Saracen attacks, one of which destroyed St-Tropez in 739.

St-Tropez was repopulated in 1470 with settlers imported from Genoa. Good King René of Provence exempted them from taxes in return for defending the coast, and until the 1600s the Tropéziens enjoyed a special autonomous status under their *Capitaines de Ville*. Their most glorious moment came on the 15 June 1637, when they courageously defended St-Tropez from an attack by 22 Spanish galleons, an event annually celebrated in the *Bravade des Espagnols*.

Later invaders were more successful. The first famous visitor from the outside world, Guy de Maupassant, drifted into the port in 1880s and in his pre-syphilitic madness was a preview of the 1960s. In 1892, the Post-Impressionist painter Paul Signac was sailing his yacht along the coast and was forced by the weather to call in at St-Tropez; enchanted, he bought a villa called La Hune and invited his friends down to paint in the summer. St-Tropez was a revelation to many: Matisse, who had previously painted in a rather dark style, came down in 1904 and produced his key, incandescent picture of nudes on a St-Tropez beach, *Luxe, Calme, et Volupté*, thereby joining the Fauvist revolution begun by Signac's friends Derain, Vlaminck, Van Dongen, and Dufy; today their hot-coloured scenes of St-Tropez illuminate the town's museum. Writers like Colette joined their 'Montparnasse on the Mediterranean' in the 30s; while a third wave, of show-biz types, far less talented but far more conspicuous than the previous two, began with Bardot. And despite the panting paparazzi it's still going strong; recent visitors include Dustin Hoffman, Elton John and Clint Eastwood.

GETTING AROUND

On its peninsula, St-Tropez is a dead end; the one road leading into it (D 98A), and the lanes leading off to the beaches, are packed solid with vehicles from June to August. Besides the St-Raphaël-Hyères coastal bus (for info tel 94 97 01 88 or 94 97 62 77), there's a regular bus in season linking Toulon to St-Tropez (tel 94 57 41 41). Note that there's no place at all to leave your luggage if you want to stop off en route. You may be better off catching a boat from St-Raphaël or Ste-Maxime. The ghastly traffic makes bike and moped hire an attractive alternative (Ets Mas-Louis, 5 Rue Quaranta, near Place Carnot, tel 94 97 00 60; open daily June–Sept 15).

TOURIST INFORMATION

Quai Jean-Jaurès, tel 94 97 45 21 and 23 Av. du Général-Leclerc, tel 94 97 41 21.

Musée de l'Annonciade

As godawful as St-Tropez can be, this port-side museum set in a 17th-century chapel is a compelling reason to visit (open Oct–May 10–12 and 2–6, June–Sept 10–12 and 3–7, closed Tues). The collection, mostly by the painters in Paul Signac's St-Tropez circle, are Post-Impressionists and Fauves who began where Van Gogh and Gauguin left off and blazed the trail for Cubism and abstract art—and blaze they do indeed, saturated with colour that takes on a life of its own with Vlaminck (*Le Pont de Chatou*) and Derain (*Westminster Palace* and *Waterloo Bridge*). Seurat's small but fascinating *Canal des*

141

Gravelines (1890) gives an idea of his mathematical, optical treatment of Impressionism, a style his disciple, Signac, moved away from while painting in St-Tropez. Other highlights include Braque's *Paysage de l'Estaque*, painted in homage to Cézanne; Matisse's *La Gitane* (1906); Vuillard's *Deux Femmes sous la Lampe*, Bonnard's *Nue devant la Cheminée*) and key paintings by Van Dongen, Freiz, Dufy, Marquet, and Cross.

From the Port to the Citadelle
Just outside the museum, the **port** is edged with the colourful pastel houses that inspired the Fauves, a scene that regains much of its original charm if you can get up before the trippers and the scores of hack painters who block the quay. The view is especially good from the **Môle Jean Réveille**. In the street above, the church of **St-Torpes** contains the gilt bust of St Torpes, used in processions, and ex votos (ships' models from sailors, and blunderbusses from the *bravades* that earned their place in the church because they never hurt anybody). Seek out Place de l'Ormeau, Rue de la Ponche, and Place aux Herbes, poetic corners of old St-Tropez that have refused to shift into top gear. You can look down on the shiny roof tiles from the 16th- to 18th-century **citadelle** at the top of town (or visit its little Musée de la Marine 10–6, closed Thurs). Another essential ingredient of St-Tropez is the charming **Place Carnot**, better known by its old name of Place des Lices, an archetypal slice of Provence with its plane trees, its Tuesday and Saturday market, its cafés and never-ending games of pétanque.

Market Days: Tuesday and Saturday.

Beaches, and St-Tropez's Peninsula

Although the beaches begin even before you enter St-Tropez, those famous sandy strands where girls first dared to bathe topless skirt the outer rim of the peninsula. In the summer minibuses link them with Place Carnot, a good idea as beach parking is as expensive as the beaches themselves. **Plage des Graniers** is within easy walking distance, but it's the most crowded. A path from here skirts Cap de St-Tropez and, in 12 km, passes **Plage des Salins** (4 km direct from St-Tropez) and ends up at the notoriously decadent **Plage de Tahiti**, the movie stars' favourite. Tahiti occupies the north end of the 5-km **Plage de Pampelonne**, lined with cafés, restaurants, and luxury concessions where any swimming-costumes at all are optional. On the other side of Cap Camarat, **Plage de l'Escalet** is hard to reach, but much less crowded and free (take the narrow road down from the D 93); from l'Escalet you can pick up the coastal path and walk in an hour and a half to the best and most tranquil beach of all, **Plage de la Briande**.

The centre of the peninsula, swathed with Côtes de Provence vineyards, is dominated by two villages of sinuous vaulted lanes and medieval houses, **Gassin**, up a dizzy series of hairpin turns, and below it the larger **Ramatuelle**. Both were Saracen *fraxinets*, and both have caught a hefty dose of fashion and artsy boutiques from St-Trop, but they still make refreshing escapes from the anarchy down below. In Ramatuelle's cemetery you can see the romantic tomb of actor Gérard Philipe (*Le Diable au Corps* and *Fanfan la Tulipe*), who was only 37 when he died in 1959.

FESTIVALS

The *Bravade des Espagnols* (15 June) when St-Tropez's finest lads parade in 18th-century uniforms and fire off nerve-shattering fusillades of blank cartridges. St Torpes himself is honoured with an even more important *bravade* in the middle of May that includes processions and a two-day shooting spree.

ENTERTAINMENT AND NIGHTLIFE

Besides the aforementioned *Bravades*, the most exciting annual event in St-Tropez is the **Nioulargue**, the last French yacht race of the season (last week of September and the first week of October), where you can watch the oldest and most beautiful yachts in the world take on the autumn billows. This being St-Tropez, you can also follow the course by sea in special boats, or by helicopter.

The bars in Place Carnot provide an entertaining side-show in which to pass the average evening, especially the resolutely old-fashioned **Café des Arts**, with its zinc bar and crowd of St-Germain-des-Prés habitués. By the port, **Sénéquier** is still *the* bar in which to order a coffee, but note that all the Joe Cools sit in the back.

WHERE TO STAY   (postal code 83990)

If you haven't already booked a hotel long ago, forget about arriving in St-Tropez on the off-chance between June and September. There are acres of camp-sites in the area, although in the summer they are about as relaxing as refugee camps; the tourist office keep tabs on which ones have a few inches to spare. As for prices, expect them to be about 20 per cent higher per category than anywhere else on the coast. And if you want to come in the off season, beware that most hotels close in the winter.

If money's no object, you can sleep in one of the most fashionable hotels on the entire Côte d'Azur, *****Le Byblos**, Av. Paul Signac, tel 94 97 00 04, built by a Lebanese millionaire, designed like a *village perché*, with rambling corridors, patios, and opulent rooms furnished with Middle Eastern arts. In the middle there's a magnificent pool, and the nightclub is one of most desirable to be seen in (closed Nov–mid-Dec). More discreet swells check in at the Relais et Châteaux *****Résidence de La Pinède**, Plage de la Bouillabaisse, tel 94 97 04 21, or at the ***Ermitage**, Av. Paul Signac, tel 94 97 52 33, a charming hotel set in a garden at the foot of the *citadelle* and 5 min from Place Carnot, and (by St-Tropez standards) reasonably priced for its category. As is ***La Ponche**, Place du Révelin, tel 94 97 02 53, located in a group of old fishermen's cottages—a romantic nook to bring your special darling (closed 15 Oct–Mar). Or you can sleep in the port overlooking the yachts at ***Le Sube Continental**, tel 94 97 30 04, the oldest hotel in town and an historic monument to boot (always open). Budget specials that must be reserved a light year in advance: the sweet and intimate garden-hotel *La Romana**, Chemin des Conquêtes, tel 94 97 18 50 (open Apr–Oct; with a good Italian restaurant as an added touch), and at the entrance of town *Les Chimères**, near Port-Grimaud, tel 94 97 02 90 (closed 15 Dec–30 Jan).

Ramatuelle (83350): This includes all the hotels along Tahiti and Pampelonne beaches, nearly all of which sport three stars and close mid-Oct–Easter. As does ***La Figuière**, Le Pinet, Rte de Tahiti, tel 94 97 18 21, an old farmhouse in the middle of a vineyard, with a relaxed atmosphere, tennis, and a pool and the less expensive ***Ferme d'Augustin**, Rte de Tahiti, tel 94 97 23 83, set in a garden a stone's throw from the sea.

The views are enchanting further up among the the vineyard terraces at ***Le Baou,
Av. G. Clemenceau, tel 94 79 20 48, which also has a heated pool and a good restaurant
(see below).

Gassin (83990): *Bello Visto, Place dei Barri, tel 94 56 17 30, offers simple,
inexpensive rooms next to Gassin's magnificent belvedere, but again, book early for a
chance of staying in one (open April to Oct).

EATING OUT
In this 21st *arrondissement* of Paris, you can bet there are some mighty good fills for some
mighty big *sous*. On the other hand, you can also indulge in the finest 260 F menu on the
coast, on the beautiful terrace of Le Chabichou, Av. Foch, tel 94 54 80 00 (superb *coulis
de crustacés* and *pieds et paquets à la tropezienne*). Note that it's only open between 12
May–10 Oct). Anther top choice for food and beauty, L'Olivier (1 km from town on Rte
des Carles, tel 94 97 58 16) is set in a lush garden serving a luscious, imaginative, and
perfectly-prepared array of seafood and land-food (menus 180 and 270 F). For affordable delights from the realm of Neptune, you can't do better than the 150 F menu in the
olive grove of Chez Madeleine, Rue de Tahiti, tel 94 97 15 74 (closed Jan–mid-Mar).
Or, if you're a confirmed culinary landlubber, an old favourite in the heart of town is
L'Eschalote, 35 Rue Allard, tel 94 54 83 26, famous for its grilled steak with shallots, on
a 170 F menu that includes wine, all to be partaken in a summer garden (closed 15
Nov–15 Dec). La Cascade, 5 Rue de l'Eglise, offers a lively atmosphere and a touch of
Antilles in the kitchen, with a 96 F menu (open evenings only).

Ramatuelle has two excellent restaurants: Le Terrasse du Baou (see above) with
delicious sunny Provençal treats like *daube de saint-pierre* and pasta with truffles from the
Haut Var (menus 260 F and up). Amid the vines at Quartier La Rouillère, Ferme
Ladouceur, tel 94 79 24 95, will fill you up with solid home cooking and the family's
home-brew wine (130 F menu, open evenings only, closed Nov–mid-Mar).

Into the Maures

Beckoning just a short drive from the coastal pandemonium are the quiet chestnut
woodlands of the Massif des Maures, penetrated by only a few roads, some of which may
be closed in dry summers. The main walking path through the hills, the GR 9, begins at
Port Grimaud and passes through La Garde-Freinet on its way west to Notre-Dame-
des-Anges; if you're going by road, the most rewarding route is the D 14, beginning at
Grimaud.

GETTING AROUND
Grimaud and Cogolin are stops on the St-Raphaël-Hyères bus routes. Other villages are
much harder to reach by public transport: two buses a day go from Le Lavandou to La
Garde-Freinet, and there's but one linking La Garde-Freinet and Grimaud to Toulon.

TOURIST INFORMATION
Cogolin (83310): Place de la République.
Grimaud: Place des Ecoles, tel 94 43 26 98.
La Garde-Freinet: Place de la Mairie, tel 94 43 67 40.

Cogolin and Grimaud

Perhaps by now you've noticed signs advertising pipes from **Cogolin** (6 km inland from Port Grimaud) not an especially pretty town but a busy one. But for once the craftsmen are not just loose ends from Paris and Picardy selling artsy gimcracks to tourists. The famous pipes of Cogolin are carved from the thick roots of a bush related to heather (*erica arbores*) that grows up to 6 m high in the Maures. Armenian immigrants in the 20s introduced their ancestral art of hand-knotted wool rugs, the origin of a local industry that now sells its *tapis de Cogolin* to the best addresses in Paris and the Arab-Emirates (you can watch the carpets being woven Mon–Fri at **Lauer**, Blvd Louis-Blanc). Another important industry harvests an ancient swamp to produce top-quality reeds for saxophones and clarinets. And Provence's only bamboo forest provides the raw material for Cogolin's cane furniture.

Unlike Cogolin, **Grimaud** is all aesthetics and boutiques. A former Saracen and Templar stronghold, it can hold its own among the most perfect *villages perchés* on the coast, crowned by the ruined castle of the Grimaldis, after whom the village is named. The Romanesque church of **St-Michel** is in surprisingly good nick; from here, Rue des Templiers (formerly Rue des Juifs) lined with arcades of 1555, passes the **House of the Templars**. This is one of the few surviving structures in Provence built by that religious and military order of knights founded in Jerusalem during the First Crusade in 1118. Before their wealth, influence and secret rites incited the deadly envy of King Philip the Fair of France and Pope Clement V, the Templars acquired extensive properties in exchange for their military services. They often built their castles and churches in Jewish or Saracen quarters, both to learn from their ancient wisdom and to protect them from the Christians—hence the damning charge of heresy raised against them by Pope and King, who conspired together to dissolve the order in 1307.

La Garde-Freinet

When Charles Martel defeated the Moorish invaders at Poitiers in 732 and pushed them back to Spain, a few managed to give the Franks the slip and escape into Provence, where they generally made a nuisance of themselves (but are also credited with introducing the tambourine, medicine, and flat roof tiles). Their stronghold, or *fraxinet*, gave its name to La Garde-Freinet, a large village full of medieval charm and British ex-pats. A path, past chestnuts said to be 1000 years old, ascends to the site of the Saracen fortress (the standing walls are from the 15th century); from here look-outs would signal the approach of fat merchant ships down to the pirates' cove of St-Tropez.

One of the arts brought to Provence by the Saracens was working in cork, which involves stripping the tree of its outer layer of bark during certain years when the tree can survive the loss; the bark is then boiled in water, cut into strips, boiled again, and set to dry and season for six months before it can be carved into bottle stoppers. This was the chief industry in the 19th century, and in 1851 the cork workers of La Garde-Freinet, both men and women, formed a co-operative that stood up to the bosses, beginning an experiment in socialism in the same dark year as Louis Napoleon declared himself emperor. Things are quieter these days in La Garde-Freinet; besides wandering through the medieval streets and trying the local wines at the **Caves des Vignerons** in

Rue St-Jacques, stop at the **Maison de La Garde-Freinet et Pays des Maures** (just south of town at the crossroads) for information on the Maures.

Collobrières and Around

Six kilometres off the D 14 from Grimaud to Collobrières stands the moody, ruined **Chartreuse de la Verne**, founded in 1170 in one of the most desolate corners of France. Rebuilt several times before it was abandoned and burned in the Revolution, the vast Carthusian complex (great and small cloisters, guest house, chuch, and porch) is mostly of interest for its use of local stone—a combination of reddish schist and hard greenish serpentine. Since 1983, restoration work has been carried out by the brothers of Bethlehem (open daily 10–7, closed Tues Oct–May). Near the crossroads for the Chartreuse, a minor road leads to the *maison forestière* Ferme Lambert, where you can ask permission to see the two largest **menhirs** in Provence (3.5 m and 3 m high) and the largest chestnut tree, the **Châtaignier de Madame** (10 m in circumference).

The air is sweet in the biggest settlement of the western Maures, **Collobrières**, an attractive old village scented with chestnuts being ground into paste and purée or undergoing their apotheosis into delectable *marrons glacés*. The village's name comes from *couleuvre* (grass snake), due the snake-like patterns in the prevalent serpentine stone. But the thick forests all around are known for other natural delights: boar and deer (and their hunters), not to mention a fabulous array of mushrooms.

Due north of Collobrières, narrow roads squiggle up through the forests to **Notre-Dames-des-Anges**, a sanctuary sitting on top of the highest point in the Var, with brave views over the Maures. Further squiggles north, just east of **Gonfaron** (on the N 97) will bring you to the **Village des Tortues** (daily 9–7), devoted to saving France's last native land tortoise, the yellow and black Hermann's tortoise of the Maures. Some 1200 tortoises live at this non-profit-making centre until they reach the age of three, when they are released into the Maures where the lucky ones will live to be 80. The best months to visit the centre are April and May when the tortoises mate, June when they lay their eggs, and September, when they hatch.

Market Days: Cogolin, Wednesday and Saturday. Grimaud, Thursday. La Garde-Freinet, Wednesday and Sunday. Collobrières, Sunday.

WHERE TO STAY/EATING OUT

Grimaud (83310): ***Côteau Fleuri**, Place des Pénitents, tel 94 43 20 17, is a comfortable inn built in the 30s on the quiet western outskirts of town, with grand views over the Massif des Maures; its restaurant serves reliably good Provençal dishes (*filet de rouget au pistou* and *carré d'agneau*); the lunch menu at 130 F is good value. For more great views and silence, but with a pool and tennis and a video library to boot, try the intimate ***La Boulangerie**, Rte de Collobrières, tel 94 43 23 16. In dining rooms full of *santons*, indulge in a gourmet spread of lobster salad, seafood, or thyme-scented *selle d'agneau* at **Les Santons**, Rte Nationale, tel 94 43 21 02 (menus 300 F and up).

Pennywise, the best bet for food is the **Café de France**, tel 94 43 29 05, an old stone house with a summer terrace and an average 105 F menu.

La Garde-Freinet (83310): In the centre, there's *Auberge La Sarrasine, tel 94 43 67 16, with simple, inexpensive rooms and a good restaurant with very filling menus (60 or 100 F for seafood).

Collobrières (83610) has just one hotel, *Notre-Dame, 13 Av. de la Libération, tel 94 48 07 13, with adequate rooms and a garden. Ring ahead to make sure there's a table at **La Petite Fontaine**, Place de la République, tel 94 48 00 12, where you can dine on ribsticking polenta, rabbit in wine, mushrooms in season and the local wine, amid quirky curios and antique tools (menus 90 and 120 F).

From the Corniche des Maures to Hyères

Outside of fashionable pockets like Bandol and Cassis, the Corniche des Maures is the last glamorous hurrah of the Côte d'Azur, where celebrities and other big money types have villas among the pines and flowers, by the silver sand. No railways come between the towns and the sea, but the main road in season is a slow purgatory of fed-up motorists and bus passengers.

GETTING AROUND
Besides the slow and expensive buses, there are summer boat connections from Cavalaire-sur-Mer and year-round services from Le Lavandou to the Iles d'Or. To explore the hinterlands, you can rent bicycles or motorcycles in Le Lavandou at **Holiday Bikes**, Av. des Ilaires, tel 94 64 86 03.

TOURIST INFORMATION
Cavalaire-sur-Mer (83240): Square Lattre-de-Tassigny, tel 94 64 08 28.
Le Lavandou (83980): Quai Gabriel-Péri, tel 94 71 00 61.
Bormes-les-Mimosas (83230): Rue J.-Aicard, tel 94 71 15 17.

Baie de Cavalaire

The bay on the underside of the St-Tropez peninsula, with its clear coves and large beaches of silken sand, has been given lock, stock and barrel to the property promoters. **La Croix-Valmer** is all new although the story of its name dates back to Emperor Constantine who, as mere co-emperor of Gaul, was on his way to his destiny in Rome when he saw a cross lit against the sky here, telling of his future destiny as the first Christian emperor. The longest beach in the bay is at **Cavalaire-sur-Mer** which, like La Croix-Valmer, is more popular with families than movie stars. For a quiet detour inland, take the narrow D 27 from Canadel-sur-Mer west of Cavalaire to **La Môle**, a tiny village of character with a two-towered château, where Antoine de Saint-Exupéry spent much of his youth.

Le Lavandou and Bormes-les-Mimosas

Persevering west past Cap Nègre and the exclusive villages of **Pramousquier** and **Cavalière** you find the big boys on the Corniche-des-Maures, the fishing port and resort of Le Lavandou and **Bormes-les-Mimosas**, a cute hyper-restored medieval enclave with a hyper-hideous pleasure port. Bormes added the mimosas to tart up its name in 1968, although the honour of first planting and commercializing these little yellow ball blooms goes to Cannes; in 1880 a gardener there carelessly tossed a branch someone had given him into a pile of manure and *voilà*, the next morning he had the lovely flowers that are now the totem plant of the Côte d'Azur. Le **Lavandou** is a good place in which to empty your wallet on seafood, watersports, boutiques, and nightclubs; for a freebie, take the walk out along the coast to Cap Bénat. If you have a car or bike, don't miss the little coastal wine road, beginning at **Port-de-Miramar**, west of Le Lavandou (take D 42 off the N 98); it passes Cap de Brégançon and its fortified château (Mitterand's private retreat) and leads to the delicious beach at **Cabasson**, with a camp-site and hotel. Although the beach is crowded in the summer, the most extraordinary thing of all is that this is the one corner of the Côte d'Azur free from the scourge of cement.

Market Days: Bormes-les-Mimosas, Wednesday, also flea-market on first and third Sunday of each month.

WHERE TO STAY/EATING OUT
Bormes-les-Mimosas (83230): The best hotel in the commune, ***Les Palmiers**, tel 94 64 81 94, is a steep drive south along the D 41 to Cabasson, and is only a few minutes from the sea; its restaurant serves solid classic food which is a good thing because board is obligatory in the summer (menus from 140 F). In Bormes itself ***Le Grand Hôtel**, Pavillon de l'Orangerie, tel 94 71 23 72, is splendidly located and very reasonably priced for its category. In the centre of the medieval town, the **Provençal** has pretty white-painted rooms, a pool and a restaurant with a 130 F menu and good views (open mid-Feb to mid-Nov); *La Terrasse**, at the top of Bormes in Place Gambetta, tel 94 71 15 22, offers simple but immaculate rooms and good meals based on regional delights (menus at 80 and 100 F). The finest *nouvelle cuisine* in the area is served at **La Tonnelle des Délices**, Place Gambetta, tel 94 71 34 84, where tables are set under a gallery of vines, and the food is made entirely from local ingredients with the finesse of a master and perfectionist. The prices are reasonable by Côte standards: menus from 150 F, *à la carte* around 300 F. **La Cassole**, Ruelle du Moulin, tel 94 71 14 86, serves delights like *bavarois de saumon* and *nougat glacé* with pistachio sauce (menus from 150 F).

    Le Lavandou (83980): For luxury and style, the new and extragavant *****Les Roches**, 1 Av. des Trois-Dauphins, tel 94 71 05 07, set magnificently over the *calanques* 4 km east of Le Lavandou at Aiguebelle, has lovely, bright rooms furnished with antiques, marble bathrooms, a private beach and pool, tennis plus a golf course a mile away. The restaurant (tel 94 71 05 05) is just as palatial, and presided over by an extremely talented young chef, who waves a magic spoon over the typical ingredients of Provence, followed by heavenly desserts (menus from 300 F). The less extravagant but charming ***Belle Vue**, at St-Clair, tel 94 71 01 06, is as good as its name, with views over the coast. The good value **L'Escapade**, 1 Chemin du Vannier, tel 94 71 11 52, is a small but very cosy hotel in a quiet lane, with air-conditioning and TVs. Even less expensive, **L'Oustaou**, 20 Av. de Gén.-de-Gaulle, tel 94 71 12 18, is one of the few hotels in Le Lavandou open all year, a cheerful place a stone's throw from the beach; the same holds true of its neighbour at No. 26, **Le Neptune**, tel 94 71 01 01. For imaginative versions of the day's catch, try **Au Vieux Port**, Quai G.-Péri, tel 94 71 00 21 (menus from 145 F). On the beach at St Clair, the summery **Le Tamaris**, tel 94 71 07 22, offers fresh grilled fish and *langoustines* that will warm the cockles of your heart for around 200 F.

Hyères and its Golden Isles

Known as Olbia by the Greeks from Marseille, who founded it in 350 BC, as Pomponiana by the Romans, and as *Castrum Arearum* ('town of threshing floors') during the Middle Ages, Hyères claims to be the original resort of the Côte d'Azur, with a pedigree that goes back to Charles IX and Catherine de' Medici, who wintered here in 1564. It knew its greatest fame in the early 19th century, when people like Empress Josephine, Pauline Borghese, Victor Hugo, Tolstoy, and Robert Louis Stevenson built villas here and invited one another to teas and soirées, before it faded genteelly from fashion in the 1880s. For despite its mild climate and lush gardens, Hyères was, unforgivably, three miles from the newly-popular seaside. But the town had more than one egg in its basket, and has since made the most of its salt pans on the peninsula, exploited since ancient times, and its nurseries of date palms (developed from a Californian species adaptable to sand and salinity) most of which are exported to Saudi Arabia and the Arab emirates.

GETTING AROUND
Hyères' **Aéroport du Palyvestre** is served mainly by Air Inter from Paris (for information, tel 94 57 41 41). By **train**, Hyères is a dead end, linked to Toulon but nowhere else; the railway station is 1.5 km south of town. The **bus** station, with coastal connections along the Corniche des Maures to St-Tropez and St-Raphaël, is in the centre at Place Clemenceau. City buses link the two, and Hyères to Hyères-Plage and the Giens peninsula. You can **hire bicycles** at 33 Av. Gambetta.

Boats for all three of Hyères islands—Porquerolles, Port-Cros, and Le Levant—depart at least twice a day, year-round, from Port d'Hyères (tel 94 57 44 07) and Le Lavandou (tel 94 71 01 02) with additional sailings in the summer. There are more frequent connections from La Tour-Fondue, at the tip of the Giens peninsula, to Porquerolles (tel 94 54 21 81) and in summer, boats also sail from Toulon to Porquerolles. But note that inter-island connections are more rare; check the schedules before setting out.

TOURIST INFORMATION
Rotonde Jean-Salusse, Av. de Belgique, tel 94 65 18 55.

Hyères

Mit Palmen und mit Ice-cream, ganz gewöhnlich, ganz gewöhnlich... (With palms and ice-cream, quite normal, quite normal...) so Bertolt Brecht, and so Hyères. There isn't much to do but take a brief wander into the Vieille Ville, beyond **Place Massillon**. Here stands the **Tour St-Blaise**, a remnant from a Templar's lodge, and on top of a monumental stair, the collegiate church of **St-Paul** (1599) with 400 ex votos dating back to the 1600s (Mon–Sat 2:30–5). The Renaissance house next to St-Paul doubles as a city gate, through which you can walk up to **Parc St-Bernard** with Mediterranean plants and flowers. At the upper part of the park, the so-called Château St-Bernard or **Villa de Noailles** was designed as a *château cubiste* by Robert Mallet-Stevens in 1924 for art patron Charles de Noailles, financier of Cocteau's first film, *Blood of the Poet* (1930) and Salvador Dali and Luis Buñuel's *L'Age d'Or*—which nearly got Noailles excommunicated. Austere cement on the outside, furnished with pieces commissioned from the Bauhaus, this vast villa was a busy hive of creativity between the wars—it even stars in Man Ray's murky 1929 film *Le Mystère du Château de Dé*. The city plans to convert it into a cultural centre. Further up the hill are the hollow walls and towers of the **Vieux Château** with an overview of Hyères' peninsula and jumble of hills.

In 1254, when Louis IX returned to France from the Crusades, he disembarked at Hyères and went to pray in the 13th-century Francsican church in Place de la République, now named **St Louis** in his honour. Inside the main thing to see is a set of *santons* too large to move (open 2:30–5). Below, in Place Th. Lefebvre, the heart of 19th-century Hyéres, a **Municipal Museum** (Mon–Fri 10–12 and 3–6, Sat and Sun 10–12, closed Tues) houses the the fragmentary remains of Hyères' Greek and Roman seaside predecessors, as well as two engraved menhirs and a Celto-Iberian figure holding two heads, similar to the statues at Roquepertuse in Aix (see p. 176). Further south, on Av. Gambetta, you can relax in the **Jardin Olbius-Riquier** amongst the palms and rare tropical and semi-tropical trees, cacti, a lake, and a small zoo for the kids. Two neo-Moorish villas from the 1880s remain in this part of town: the **Villa Tunisienne** in Av. Beauregard and the **Villa Mauresque** in Av. Jean Natte.

Market Days: Hyères, Place de la République, Tuesday and Thursday, Tuesday only in winter.

The Giens Peninsula

Over the centuries the island that was Giens has been anchored to the continent by two sand-bars whose arms embrace a salt marsh, the **Etang des Pesquiers**. Although the link has historically been dodgy—Giens became an island again in the storms of 1811—it hasn't stopped people from building villas and hotels, especially on the isthmus at **La Capte**. The barren west arm, dotted by shimmering white piles of salt, is traversed by the narrow *route du sel* beginning at **Plage de l'Almanarre**. In 1843, the archaeologist king, Frederick VII of Denmark, excavated the ruins of the Greek-Roman town at **Almanarre**, but most of it has since been reclaimed by the sand; there are curious Merovingian tombs in the village's 12th-century **Chapelle St-Pierre**. The salt road ends in **Giens**, a quiet little hamlet under a ruined castle that was the last home of the 1961 Nobel-prize-winning poet St-John Perse, who is buried in the cemetery; further up are extensive views from the ruined castle. To the south, **La Tour-Fondue** is the principal port for Porquerolles. But beware that the often violent seas around the peninsula have caused scores of shipwrecks. In 1967, an intact cargo ship dating from the

Roman republic was found in the Golfe de Giens, with sealed amphorae containing a clear liquid with reddish mud on the bottom—the ultimate fate of red wine aged too long.

Les Iles d'Hyères

Known as the *Stroechades* or 'chaplet' by the ancient Greeks, and in the Renaissance as the *Iles d'Or*, due to the shiny yellow colour of their rock, Hyères' three islands are voluptuous little greenhouses that have seen more than their share of trouble. In the Middle Ages, they belonged to the monastery of St-Honorat, and attracted pirates like moths to a flame; in 1160, after the Saracens carried off the entire population, the monks gave up and just let the pirates have the islands. The expansion of the Turkish Empire throughout the Mediterranean in the 16th century made the kings of France sit up and notice the Saracens, and in 1515 an attempt was made to preach a crusade against the Hyères pirates, but the crusading spirit was long past. François I had a golden opportunity to install the then homeless Knights of St John on Porquerolles, but the two parties couldn't agree on terms, and the Knights settled for Malta, then belonging to Spain, paying their famous rent of one golden falcon. François had to build his own forts and send settlers to man them against Charles V and every other sea predator, but again the pirates carried everyone off.

Henri II, successor to François, thought he had a good idea in populating the islands with criminals and malcontents. By this time, however, France had found the solution to her piracy problem: becoming allies with them and the Turks. On one memorable occasion in 1558, the French navy had a big party on Porquerolles to help the notorious Barbarossa and his cut-throats celebrate the end of Ramadan. Then the inhabitants of the islands spoiled Henri's plans by following their instincts and becoming pirates themselves, capturing numerous French ships and once even pillaging the naval base in Toulon. It took another century to eradicate them.

Later rulers rebuilt the island's forts. In the late 19th century, they were variously used to quarantine veterans of the colonial wars and as sanctuaries for homeless children: Le Levant and Porquerolles became Dickensian orphanages and juvenile penal colonies. In both cases the young inmates rebelled, and many were killed. Industrialists opened sulphur plants on the islands that no other place in France would have tolerated, and the navy bought Le Levant in 1892 and blew it to pieces as a firing range. In the 1890s fires burned most of the forests on Porquerolles and Port-Cros. Fortunately, in this century, the French government has moved decisively to protect the islands; strict laws protect them from the risks of fire and developers.

Porquerolles

Largest of the three, Porquerolles stretches 7 km by 3 km and has the largest permanent population, which in the summer explodes to 10,000. Its main village, also called Porquerolles, was founded in 1820 as a retirement village for Napoleon's finest soldiers and invalids. It still has a colonial air, especially around the central pine-planted **Places des Armes**, the address of most of Porquerolles' restaurants, bars, hotels and bicycle hire shops. Even the village church was built by orders of the Ministry of War, and has military symbols on the altar. Although the cliffs to the south are steep and dangerous for swimming, there are gentle beaches on either side of the village, especially **Plage**

Notre-Dame to the east and **Plage d'Argent** to the west. The previous owners of the island took a special interest in acclimatizing flora, such as the *bellombra*, a Mexican tree with huge roots and bark-like elephant-skin, but today green thumbs concentrate on vines, producing exquisite but rare AOC Côte des Iles. You can try some at **Domaine de la Courtade**, at La Courtade, open for visits by appointment, tel 94 58 31 44.

Between Porquerolles and Giens the now deserted little islet of **Grand Ribaud** was used in the early 1900s for 'spiritualist experiments' and other researches by one Dr Richet, who also imported kangaroos. The kangaroos liked the islet, we are told, but banged themselves to untimely deaths by jumping too exuberantly on the sharp rocks.

Port-Cros

Although barely measuring a square mile, Port-Cros rising to 195 m is the most mountainous of the three islands. Since 1963 it has been a national park, preserving not only its forests of pines and ilexes, recovered from a devastating fire in 1892, but nearly a hundred species of birds; brochures will help you identify them as you walk along the mandatory trails. There are a selection of these: the **sentier botanique** is for visitors pressed for time, while at the other end of the scale, there's a 10-km *circuit historique* for the lucky ones who have a packed lunch and all day. Two curiosities of the island are its abundant native catnip and its *euphorbe arborescente*, which loses all its leaves in the summer and grows new ones in the autumn.

Like the national park in the Florida Keys, Port-Cros also protects its surrounding waters, rich in colourful fish and plant life. There's even a 300-metre 'path' which divers can follow from Plage de la Palud to Rascas islet, clutching a plastic guide sheet that identifies the underwater flora. Of late some of the more fragile plants around the island have suffered as a result of Port-Cros' extraordinary popularity—from the emissions and anchors of the thousands of pleasure craft that call here each year.

Ile du Levant

The French navy still hogs almost all of this flowering island, but they no longer use it for target practice. Nowadays, they test aircraft engines and rockets, which are marginally quieter. The island's remaining quarter is occupied by **Héliopolis**, France's first nudist colony (1931). Anyone who's been to St-Tropez and other fashionable Côte beaches will find the ideal of a specially-reserved nudist area fairly quaint by now, but Héliopolis still has its determined Adams and Eves, especially because it's so warm: 60 members of the colony stick it out here all year.

WHERE TO STAY/EATING OUT   (postal code 83400)
Hyères town: The newly-opened ****Relais Bleu**, 45 Av. Victoria, tel 94 35 42 22, is the most comfortable in town, with TVs and air conditioning. Up in the Vieille Ville, ****Soleil**, Rue du Rampart, tel 94 65 05 55, is a pleasant quiet choice near Parc St-Bernard. In the centre, the immaculate ***Hôtel-Pension de la Poste**, Av. du Maréchal-Lyautey, tel 94 65 02 00, is the best of the cheapies, and open all year. Or if you'd rather be near the sea, try little ***La Reine Jane**, by the sea at Ayguade, tel 94 66 32 64, with good rooms and food at bargain prices. For a more elaborate dinner, try the delicious *soupe des poissons* at the dove-decorated **La Colombe**, at La Bayorre, tel 94 65 02 15 (menu 130 F). The liveliest bar in town is **L'Estaminet** in Rue de Limans.

Porquerolles: There are five hotels on the island, all priced a bit above the odds and all booked months in advance in the summer. All close in the winter. The most elegant, ***Mas du Langoustier**, tel 94 58 30 09, is a romantic old inn between the woods and a long sandy beach, with lovely rooms and a superb restaurant, where the chef imaginatively combines the best ingredients of Provence with a touch of the Far East—*lotte* in coconut sauce and *langouste* with black mushrooms. The wine list includes Porquerolles' famous rosé (menu 250 F). Of the other hotels, **Le Relais de la Poste**, Place d'Armes, tel 94 58 30 26, is the only one not requiring half-board. **Sainte-Anne**, tel 94 58 30 04, is a bit dilapidated but stays open longer than the rest, closing for the first half of December and January only. Among the tourist restaurants, the traditional favourite is the old **L'Arche de Noë**, Place d'Armes, tel 94 58 30 74, where most of the world's celebrities have dined on stuffed fish and *bouillabaisse* (à la carte only, 300–400 F). For more affordable but tasty fare, try **Oustau de la Mer**, tel 94 58 30 13, with fresh dishes using local market produce (menus from 85 F).

Port-Cros: There are only a couple of choices on paradise, and they need to be booked long in advance: the pricey but tranquil and casual ***Le Manoir**, tel 94 05 90 52, among the eucalyptus groves, has a fine little restaurant (closed Oct–April; menus from 200 F). The second choice, **Hostellerie Provençale** overlooks the port, tel 94 05 90 43, the hotel is open all year but the restaurant closes in the winter.

Ile du Levant: If you can bare it, Ile de Levant with a greater selection of hotels makes a good base for visiting Port-Cros. The best is **Héliotel**, tel 94 05 90 63, set in the mimosas and greenery, boasting a pool, a piano bar, a little beach down below and a restaurant with pretty views over the other islands (open Easter–Sept). In Place du Village, *La Brise Marine, tel 94 05 91 15, is at the summit of the islet, with pretty rooms situated around a patio with a pool (closed Oct–mid-April).

Toulon

Lauso la mar e ten-ten terro
(Praise the sea but stick to the land).
—*Provençal proverb*

If Provençal traditionalists (and they are landlubbers all) look upon the cosmopolitan Côte d'Azur as an alien presence, they feel equally ill-at-ease in the south's two great ports, Toulon and Marseille: to the Provençal they are dangerous, salty cities, populated by untrustworthy strangers and prostitutes. But while Marseille is essentially a city of merchants and trade, Toulon has always been the creature of the French navy, and whatever piquant charms its old port and quarter once had were bombed into oblivion in World War II. The brash new Toulon that rose from the ashes, with nearly 200,000 people, is still more concerned with entertaining sailors on shore-leave than with entertaining you—making it a lively, inexpensive place to go if the Côte d'Azur's wonderful world of tourism begins to drive you crazy.

History
For some reason the deepest, most majestic natural harbour in the Mediterranean tempted neither the Greeks nor the Romans. Instead Toulon (originally *Telo Martius*)

was from Phoenican times a centre for dyeing cloth, thanks to its abundant murex shells, (the source of royal purple) and the dried red corpses (*kermès*) of the *coccus illicis*, an insect that lived in the forests of oaks. Toulon's destiny began to change when Provence was annexed to France in 1481. The first towers and walls went up under Louis XII in 1514; Henri IV created the arsenal, but it was Louis XIV who changed Toulon forever, making it the chief port of France's Mediterranean fleet, greatly expanding the arsenal and assigning Vauban the task of protecting it with his star-shaped forts, built by forced labour. It was during this period that Toulon became the most popular tourist destination in Provence, when well-heeled visitors came to see not the new navy installations, but the miserable galley slaves—Turkish prisoners, African slaves, criminals and later, Protestants—chained four to an oar, where they worked, ate and slept in appalling conditions. The 17th century was such a rotten time that there were even volunteers for the galleys—distinguished by their moustaches and less likely to feel the cat o' nine tails.

Toulon's history is marked by three disasters. In 1720, nature's neutron bomb, the plague, killed 15,000 out of 26,000 inhabitants. The second disaster began after the execution of Louis XVI, when Toulon's royalists had confided the city to the English and their Spanish and Sardinian allies. In 1793, a ragamuffin Revolutionary army of volunteers and ruffians under the painter Carteaux, fresh from massacring 6000 people in Lyon, arrived at the gate of Toulon and began an ineffectual siege of two months. A young Napoleon Bonaparte came on the scene, and convinced the commissioners to put him in charge of the artillery. Bonaparte turned his guns to the west side of the harbour, on the English redoubt of Mulgrave, so well fortified that it was nicknamed 'Little Gibraltar' (now Fort Caire), and captured it by the 19 December. In spite of the opposition of the English commander Samuel Hood, the allies decided to abandon Toulon to its fate. The thousands who couldn't escape were mercilessly slaughtered by the Jacobins. 'We must guillotine others to save ourselves from being guillotined', commented Barras, one of the commissioners. The hitherto unknown Bonaparte, promoted to brigadier-general, became the darling of the Convention. But even after the Revolution, when the galley slaves were hailed as 'the only decent men of the infamous city', convicts (like Jean Valjean in *Les Misérables*) were sentenced to the *bagnes* (penal camps) in Toulon until the 1850s, where they were chained in pairs, had rats for pets, and envied the lucky few who made a fortune as executioners: 20 *livres* for breaking a nobleman (crushing all his bones, but not shedding a drop of his noble blood), 15 for a hanging or burning alive, down to 2 for cutting off a nose. In 1860 the convicts were packed off out of sight to Devil's Island in French Guyana.

The city's most recent sufferings began in 1942, when the Germans took the city by surprise, and the Vichy Admiral Laborde blocked up the harbour by scuttling the entire Mediterranean fleet to keep it from falling into the hands of the enemy. On 15 August 1944, after flattening the picturesque old port with aerial bombing raids, the allies landed, and the French army, under General de Lattre de Tassigny recaptured Toulon while the entrenched Germans blew up the citadel, the harbour and the dockyards. Toulon was rebuilt quickly, although without a great sense of design or beauty. Since then new dark clouds have begun rolling over Toulon's horizon: the principal shipbuilding yards in La Seyne are facing closure, and the ugly forces of reaction succeeded in electing France's first *Front National* deputy.

GETTING AROUND

Toulon is the major transport hub of the region, and any one dependent on public transport will find it hard to avoid. Toulon's **airport** is out near Hyères (for information, tel 94 38 60 60). Air Inter's number is 94 09 47 47. The **train station** is on the northern side of Toulon in Place Albert I, tel 94 91 50 50, with three daily TGVs to Nice and Marseille, and frequent connections up and down the coast and to Hyères; for St-Tropez and the coast between Hyères and St-Raphaël, catch a SODETRAV bus in the adjacent *gare routière*. Other buses will take you frequently to Hyères, Bandol, La Seyne, Six-Fours, and Sanary, and to inland cities like Brignoles, Draguignan, Aix, and St-Maximin. From Quai Stalingrad, sea-buses go to La Seyne, Les Sablettes and St-Mandrier.

From May to September there are daily sailings to Corsica and weekly sailings to Sardinia (tel 94 41 18 38). Companies departing from Quai Stalingrad offer tours of Toulon's harbour, the *grande rade* and *petite rade*), and the surrounding coasts and islands: **Les Bateliers de La Rade**, tel 94 31 21 36 (year-round tours of the *rades* and all three Iles d'Hyères); **Transport Maritime Toulonnais**, tel 94 75 27 34, (tours of the *rades*); **Vedette Alain I**, tel 94 46 29 89 (tours of the *rades* and their battleships); **SNRTM**, tel 94 62 41 41 (tours of the *rades* and mini-cruises, and from 15 June-15 Sept a regular service to the Iles d'Hyères).

TOURIST INFORMATION

8 Av. Colbert, tel 94 22 08 22; and in the train station, tel 94 62 73 87. The main **post office** is at the corner of Rue Ferrero and Rue Bertholet.

Central Toulon

From the train station, Av. Vauban descends to Av. Général-Leclerc; on the left at No. 113 are the **Musée de l'Histoire Naturelle**, with stuffed birds and beasts (daily 10–12 and 2–6) and **Musée de Toulon** (daily except Sun and holidays, 1–7), containing an above-average collection of paintings and sculptures, although there's only room to display a fraction of the works by Breughel, Annibale Carracci, Fragonard, Vernet and Pierre Puget; there's also an especially strong contemporary collection (Bacon, Arman, Yves Klein, Christo etc.). Avenue Vauban continues down to the large formal gardens of **Place d'Armes**, decorated with ordnance from the adjacent arsenal, one of the biggest single employers in southeast France with some 10,000 workers. Alongside the arsenal in Place Monsenergue are miniature versions of the ships that it once made, displayed in the **Musée Naval** (10–12 and 1:30–6, closed Tues, Sun, and holidays, adm). France's great Baroque sculptor and architect Puget started out in Toulon carving and painting figureheads for the ships, and the museum has works by his followers. The grand Baroque entrance to the building itself is the original Louis XIV arsenal gate.

The best surviving works of Puget in Toulon are the two **Atlantes** (1657) on Quai Stalingrad, *Force* and *Fatigue*, whose woe and exhaustion may well have been modelled on the galley slaves. They once supported the balcony of the old Hôtel de Ville, and were packed off to safety just before the bombings in the last war. Off the Quai, **Rue d'Alger**, now a popular evening promenade, used to be the most notorious street in Toulon's **Vieille Ville**, the pungent pocket of the pre-war town. Now blocked off from the sea by rows of new buildings, the Vieille Ville's narrow, dirty streets are still lit by the neon signs of bars, flophouses, greasy-spoons, sex shops, cheap clothes shops etc., that belong after dark to the sailors, prostitutes and pick-pockets. Unfortunately, the city and the landlords of the Vieille Ville have little sense of historic preservation, and are content not only to let its old buildings fall down, but even push them over in an attempt to destroy the last bit of genuine sleaze on the coast.

Come in the morning to take in the colourful fruit and vegetable market in Cours Lafayette, and the fish market in Place de la Poissonerie. At 63 Cours Lafayette there's the dingy **Musée du Vieux Toulon** (2–6, closed Sun and holidays) with sketches by Puget and historical odds and ends. Around the corner is the **Cathedral**, 17th-century on the outside and Romanesque-Gothic within, although its features are barely discernible in the gloomiest interior in the south of France; during the Revolution, an attempt to convert it into a stable failed when the horses threw their riders rather than enter it. At the top of the adjacent pedestrian quarter is Toulon's prettiest fountain, the 18th-century **Fontaine des Trois Dauphins**. North of this is Toulon's main street, Boulevard de Strasbourg, site of the **Opéra**, with an interior inspired by Charles Garnier.

Mont Faron
Toulon looks better when seen from a distance. Bus 40 will take you to Boulevard Amiral-Vence in Super-Toulon, site of the terminus of the little red *téléphérique* (funicular) that runs Tues–Sun 9:15–12 and 2:15–6 to the top of 535-m Mont Faron (there's a narrow hairpin road circuit as well, beginning in Av. E.-Fabre). Besides a tremendous view over the city and its harbours, there's the **Musée Mémorial du Débarquement** (9:30–11:30 and 2:30–4:30, closed Mon, adm), devoted to the August 1944 Allied landing in Provence, with models, uniforms and 1944 newsreels. It shares the summit with a large wooded park, two restaurants, and a **zoo** (daily 2 pm to dusk, adm) that specializes in breeding jaguars, tigers, lions, and monkeys.

Around the Harbour
Bus 3, from in front of the station or on Boulevard Leclerc, will take you to the **Plage du Mourillon**, Toulon's largest beach and site of the city's oldest fort, Louis XII's 1514 **Grosse Tour** or Tour Royale that once guarded the eastern approaches to Toulon with its rounded walls, some 5 to 7 m thick. In later years the lower part, excavated in the rock, was used as a prison and now contains an annex of the Musée Naval, with more figureheads in a baleful setting (closed at the time of writing). The west shore of the *La Petite Rade* is Toulon's business end, especially the yards and industry at **La Seyne**. To the south, at l'Aiguillette, stood 'Little Gibraltar', near **Fort Balaguier**, another English strongpoint that fell to Bonaparte; this now contains a museum of Napoleana (Wed–Sun 10–12 and 2–6, adm). Further south is the residential suburb of **Tamaris**, once the home of officers and their families, and where George Sand wrote her novel *Tamaris* in 1861. In the 1880s, the mayor of neaby Sanary purchased much of Tamaris in the hopes of turning it into a resort. This mayor had a more exciting career than most: born Michel Marius in Sanary in 1819, he was employed by the Ottoman Empire as a builder of lighthouses, a job he performed so well that the Sultan made him a pasha before sending him home in 1860 with a fat pension. Inspired by what he had seen in Turkey, Michel Pasha commissioned a number of fantasy neo-Moorish buildings in the area, especially Tamaris' **Institute of Marine Biology**. The resort was a flop, but a fad for

neo-Moorish confections swept across the Riviera at the turn of the century. Beyond the fine sands of **Les Sablettes** beach, the hilly **St-Mandrier peninsula** closes off the west end of the *Grande Rade*, and includes a naval air base, and the fishing village and pleasure port of **St-Mandrier-sur-Mer**, with wide-ranging views from the cemetery.

Market Days: Cours Lafayette, every morning except Monday.

WHERE TO STAY   (postal code 83000)
Prices are about a third less than on the fashionable Côte, and fall even lower in the off-season. The most elegant place to sleep and eat in Toulon is *****La Corniche**, 1 Littoral F.-Mistral, at Mourillon, tel 94 41 35 12, a cleverly designed modern, Provençal hotel, air-conditioned and near the beach. The resturant, **Le Bistrot**, built around the massive trunks of three maritime pines, not only serves refined seafood and dishes such as *selle d'agneau en rognonnade* but also has one of the best wine cellars for miles around (menus from 150 F). In the pedestrian zone, not far from the opera ****Du Dauphiné-Arcantis**, 10 Rue Berthelot, tel 94 92 20 28, is a comfortable older hotel. The brand new ****St-Nicolas**, in the centre at 49 Rue Jean Jaurès, tel 94 91 02 28, has 40 sound-proof rooms with colour TV, mini-bars etc. Nearby, the friendly ***Le Jaurès**, 11 Rue Jean-Jaurès, tel 94 92 83 04, is the top bargain choice; the rooms all have baths. If that's full, try ***Molière**, near the opera at 12 Rue Molière, tel 94 92 78 35.

EATING OUT
If they don't go to the aforementioned Bistrot at La Corniche, the Toulonnais in search of a special meal drive 20 km northeast to Cuers to eat at **Le Lingousto**, Rte de Pierrefeu, tel 94 28 69 10, located in an old bastide, where the freshest of fresh local ingredients are transformed into imaginative works of art—langoustines with fresh pasta, omelettes with *oursins* (sea urchins), cheeses that have 'worked' to perfection and divine chocolate desserts (menus from 190 F). Back in Toulon, in the Vieille Ville, **La Véranda**, 29 Rue A.-Dumas, tel 94 92 81 46, is one of the neighbourhood's most charming restaurants, with delicious fish and sorbets (lunch menu 80 F and up). In the same vicinity, **La Ferme**, 6 Place Louis Blanc, tel 94 41 43 74, serves classic dishes like *marmite du pêcheur* (menus at 95 and 140 F). Finally there are two worthy choices on Rue Jean Jaurès: **Le Galion**, No. 10, tel 94 93 02 52, has a fine and filling 130 F menu, and the jovial and friendly **Le Cellier**, No. 13, tel 94 92 64 35, with a good little 45 F menu, including wine.

ENTERTAINMENT AND NIGHTLIFE
Northwest of Toulon, a 17th-century tower was converted in 1966 into a handsome amphitheatre to host cultural events, especially the July **Festival de la Danse et de l'Image** (tel 94 24 11 76). From the end of May to mid-July, the **Festival International de Musique** puts on a wide range of classical and non-classical music, tel 94 93 52 84. There's opera and theatre in the winter. The **Femina Cinéma** shows films in their original language every night (20 Rue V.-Clappier, north of Blvd de Strasbourg, tel 94 92 39 31). There's no lack of bars, both straight and gay, especially around Rue Pierre Sémard, but they're not places where you'll feel comfortable alone. Smart Toulon

society prefers the bars and restaurants along Littoral Frédéric-Mistral on Mourillon beach, or the **Piano Crêperie**, 29 Rue V.-Clapier, which has jazz on Friday, 'polymusique' on Saturday, and videos to accompany your crêpes on other nights.

West Coast of the Var: Toulon to Les Lecques

West of Toulon, the coast tosses out the curious peninsula of Cap Sicié with the old town of Six-Fours before ending in a string of small towns with sandy beaches: Sanary, fashionable Bandol, one of the coast's great wine towns, and Les Lecques. Offshore you can be entertained on Paul Ricard's two little islets, or amuse yourself exploring the hills, woods, vineyards and gorges around Ollioules, La Cadière-d'Azur and Le Castellet.

GETTING AROUND
Six-Fours and Sanary are easiest reached by bus from Toulon. The **train station** of Ollioules is halfway between the town and Sanary, with bus connections to both. Bandol is a stop on the Toulon-Marseille TGV; for **bus** information tel 94 29 46 58 and 94 74 01 35. In Bandol, you can **hire a bike** to explore the beautiful hinterlands at Kit Provence, 118 Rue 11 Novembre.

TOURIST INFORMATION
Ollioules (83190): 16 Rue Nationale, tel 94 63 11 74.
Bandol (83150): at the port, tel 94 29 41 35.

Around Cap Sicié: Six-Fours

Cap Sicié, like a clenched fist punching the sea, takes the brunt of the wind and rough seas from the west. If you can, avoid the depressing main roads and urban sprawl that cut across the peninsula from Les Sablettes to Sanary, and take the **Corniche Varoise**, a minor road that circles the cliffs of the Cap (not recommended on windy days, however). The cliffs tower up to 335 m over the sea at **Notre-Dame-du-Mai**, named after a sanctuary much esteemed by sailors, who always approached it barefoot. On the west side of the peninsula, the little port of **Le Brusc**, set amid cliffs and pines, has two or three departures every hour for **Ile des Embiez**, owned by Paul Ricard, the pastis baron. Ricard has left the seaward side of the island alone, but facing the mainland he is busy developing what he calls 'the leisure centre of the future', a vast pleasure port and the **Fondation Océanographique Ricard** (daily 9–12 and 2–6), with 100 different species from the Mediterranean.

The rough winds and waves off Cap Sicié's west coast offer an exciting challenge to surfers and windsurfers who get their kicks at **Brutal Beach** and **Plage de Bonnegrâce**, part of the commune of **Six-Fours-les Plages** (from the Latin *sexfurni*). The village once stood on the isolated mountain nearby, but was destroyed in the 19th century to build the **fort** (no entry, but you can drive up to the barbed wire outside for the view). Two churches were spared: a 10th-century **oratory** on the road to Le Brusc, commemorating a victory over Saracen pirates, and the 12th-century Collegiate church of **St-Pierre-aux-Liens** (June–Sept 3–7, closed Fri and Mon; Oct–May 3–5, open Wed, Sat and Sun only), built in pure Provençal Romanesque over a 5th-century baptistry; Palaeo-Christian coins and gems found here are displayed in a case. The church has a number of medieval works of art, including a polyptych of Provence's favourite saints by Jean de Troyes (1520). The niche behind the altar, built to hold the Eucharist, was until 1914 (when the practice was banned) used by the faithful to deposit scraps of cloth taken from the clothes of dead relatives for whom they prayed. North of here, off the D 63, is the stone-built **Chapelle Notre-Dame-de-Pépiole** (usually open after 3), with its three little barrel-vaulted naves modelled after the earliest Syrian churches. It goes back to at least the 8th century, the date of fragments of Islamic ceramics found inside, and may even be Carolingian.

Sanary-Sur-Mer, Ollioules and the Big Brain

Provençal for St Nazaire, Sanary is a little resort of pink and white houses and with a sandy beach, one picked out by Aldous Huxley (among other writers) in 1930. After 1933, Huxley was joined by the cream of anti-Nazi German intelligentsia, led by Thomas and Heinrich Mann and Bertolt Brecht. But Sanary was not far enough away, and under the Vichy régime, many Germans were rounded up and imprisoned in an internment camp near Aix. On Sanary's promontory, the chapel **Notre-Dame-de Pitié** has a delightful collection of naïve ex votos.

Ollioules' funny name comes from olives, although these days it's better known for its wholesale Mediterranean flower market. The town itself has all the typical Provençal charms—arcaded lanes, a medieval castle and a Romanesque church—and numerous artisans who make barrels, bird-cages, nougat, olive woodwork, goats' cheese and the like, a welcome respite from trinkets and objets d'art. A kilometre north of town, just past the romantic ruins of an 18th-century oratory, is the Celto-Ligurian Iron Age *oppidum* of **La Courtine**, built on a basalt rock and covered with wild roses planted by two frustrated amateur archaeologists when they got tired of digging. You can still make out the dry-stone walls and wells. Over 300 Greek coins engraved with the features of Hercules and Hecate were discovered here, donated to a sanctuary destroyed by Romans in 123 BC.

Around **Evenos**, a restored *village perché* just to the north off the N 8, the romantic scenery makes for good walks, especially in the fantastical yellow-tinted **Gorges d'Ollioules**, a natural Gothic landscape much admired by Victor Hugo. The D 220 from Ollioules leads onto the wooded mountain ridge of **Le Gros Cerveau** or 'Big Brain', a curious name of uncertain derivation and site of another *oppidum*. It, too, has strange rock formations and is pitted with caves, where 'witches' hid in the time of Louis XIII—in 1616 three were sentenced to be strangled, hanged, and then burned.

Market Day: Sanary, Wednesday.

Bandol

Sheltered from the ravages of the mistral, travellers will find Bandol either a preview or a *déjà vu* of the typical Côte d'Azur town: pretty houses and lanes festooned with flowers, palm trees, boutiques, a casino, the morning market in Place de la Liberté, and an over-saturation of villas on the outskirts. But Bandol has something most of the Riviera hotspots lack—its own excellent wine and a little island, **Ile de Bendor**. A barren 6-hectare rock when Paul Ricard bought it with his pastis fortune in 1953, it is now a little adult playground, a masterpiece of architectural dissonance from the 50s and 60s—Ricard himself hopes that it will someday fall in ruins and become 'a 20th-century Delos'! There's a diving and windsurfing school, a nautical club that organizes yacht races, an art school and gallery, a business centre, hotels, and the **Exposition Universelle des Vins et Spiritueux** (Easter–Sept 10–12 and 2–6, closed Wed). The building is decorated with frescoes by art students and the displays of 7000 bottles and glasses from around the world will whet your thirst for some Bandol AOC.

Market Days: Daily except Wednesday.

Bandol
When a courtier asked Louis XV the secret of his eternal youth, the king replied 'the wines of Rouve (in Bandol), which give me their vigour and spirit'. They had to have a certain vigour to survive the journey to Versailles, sloshing about in barrels in slow boats from the Mediterranean to the Atlantic and up the Seine. Today Bandol still flexes its charming muscle; at 35 to 60 F a bottle, it gets top marks in Provence in value for money.

The arid, wine-coloured *restanques* (or terraces) cut into the mountain flanks in the eight communes around Bandol have produced wines since 600 BC. Dominated by small, dense mourvèdre grapes mixed with cinsault and grenache, the reds are sombre of tone, but require patience to reach their peak; the fabulous 87 or 88 vintages should stay corked until 1993. Bandol also comes in pale salmon-hued rosés, known for their delightful perfume, and dense whites that are to taste what wild roses are to the nose, and make the ideal accompaniment to grilled fish—1990 was a great year for both. Some Bandols have extraordinary pedigrees: **Domaine des Salettes**, at La Cadière-d'Azur (tel 94 90 06 06), has been in the same family since 1602. Other estates to visit are **Château Pradeaux**, in St-Cyr-sur-Mer, tel 94 26 10 74, producer of classic Bandol reds and rosés, and **Domaine Ray-Jane**, at Le-Plan-du-Castellet, tel 94 98 64 08, where besides wine, visitors can examine France's largest collection of cooper's tools. The Comte de Saint-Victor's estate of **Château de Pibarnon**, at La Cadière-d'Azur, tel 94 90 12 73, is sculpted into rugged limestone flanks geologically millions of years older than their neighbours, which give its spicy reds, charming rosés and fruity whites a personality all their own. **Domaine de la Laidière**, at Sainte-Anne d'Evenos, tel 94 90 37 07, is one of the most quality conscious estates of the area, producing red, white and rosé, but it is the red wine that is the finest. Next to Bandol's tourist office, the **Maison des Vins du Bandol** sells most of the labels and has a list of all the other estates open for visits.

Around Bandol

Besides wine, Bandol offers its visitors pink flamingos, toucans, cockatoos, and disgusting Vietnamese pigs in a lovely exotic garden of tropical flora at the **Jardin Exotique et Zoo de Sanary-Bandol**, 3 km east on the D 559 (open 8–12 and 2–7, closed Sun am). This is near the *Moulin de St-Côme*, where you can tour the most important olive press in the Var (or in December and January, watch it at work) and buy a bottle of *huile d'olive vierge extra* to take home.

North of Bandol are a pair of medieval wine-producing *villages perchés*, both restored, both lovely nonetheless, and neither as virgin as their olive oil. **La Cadière-d'Azur** sits on a hill with cliffs sliced sheer on the north side, with views out to the Massif de Ste-Baume. **Le Castellet** is perched even more precariously over its sea of vines. Much refurbished, it looks like a film set, and indeed has often been used as such (Pagnol got here first, for his *Femme du boulanger*); its 12th-century church is attractively austere, although the same cannot be said of the streets full of pseudo-arty shops. East of here (follow D 26 towards the N 8), the 16th-century agricultural villlage of **Le Beausset** sits in a plain 2.5 km from the 12th-century **Chapelle Notre-Dame-du-Beausset-Vieux** (daily July–Sept, Sat and Sun only other times), with a basalt altar that once served as a millstone in an olive press, *santons* from the 16th century, and ex votos. North, on N 8, is another Ricard installation, this time a race track and aerodrome. If all the above seems too staid, you can watch a cowboy and Indian shoot-out, have your face covered with war-paint, and ride the carousel at the **O.K. Corral**, a Wild West fantasyland owned by a Dutchman (on N 8, towards Cuges-les-Pins; daily 10 to sundown, May–Aug, and in school holidays between Mar–Nov, one adm for the works).

Les Lecques and St-Cyr-sur-Mer
West of Bandol, **Les Lecques** is an unpresuming family resort with a sandy beach, set in front of the old Bandol AOC town of **St-Cyr-sur-Mer**. It also offers the cool, wet delights of **Aqualand**, where you can dump the kids—or yourself—down the slides. Les Lecques itself is one of several places that claim to be ancient *Tauroentum*, a colony of Greek Marseille where Caesar defeated Pompey in a famous naval battle and gained control of Marseille. But most of the finds in Les Lecques so far have been Roman, as displayed in the **Musée de Tauroentum** on the road to La Madrague (June–Sept 4–7, closed Tues; other times weekends only 2–5). The museum protects the remains of two Roman villas built around the year 1, with mosaics and bits of fresco, vases and jewellery, and outside, an unusual two-storey tomb of a child. Ancient Tauroentum is supposed to be somewhere just off shore, lost under the sea. You can look for traces of it along a lonely coastal path (marked with yellow signs) that begins near the museum and continues to Bandol; along the way are little *calanques* for quiet swims.

WHERE TO STAY/EATING OUT
Le Brusc: Le Saint-Pierre, 47 Rue de la Citadelle, tel 94 34 02 52, will fill you to the brim with the offerings on its delicious menus, from 90 to 170 F (the latter with *bouillabaisse*).

Bandol (83150): The delightful pink ***La Ker Mocotte**, Rue Raimu, tel 94 29 46 53, once belonged to the Toulon-born actor Raimu, who starred in several Pagnol films. It has a seaside garden and private beach, and offers facilities for water sports. On Ile de Bendor there's Ricard's ***Délos**, tel 94 32 22 23, with big, comfortable rooms decorated in extravagant bad taste—but the views of the sea below and the many watersports make up for it. **La Brunière**, Av. Louis Lumière, tel 94 29 52 08, is near the centre of Bandol on a wooded headland, with rooms overlooking the sea or the gardens. Of the budget hotels, the villa *Coin d'Azur*, Rue Raimu, tel 94 29 40 93, has the added plus of its location directly over the beach, west of the port (closed Oct–Mar) while the exceptionally pleasant *L'Oasis*, 15 Rue des Ecoles, tel 94 29 41 69, is open all year, with a cool, shady garden, a short walk from the beach. **L'Auberge du Port**, 9 Allée J.-Moulin, tel 94 29 42 63, is Bandol's gourmet rendez-vous, specializing in seafood, where you can go the whole hog on a 300 F *menu dégustation* or try the 55 F platter of *aïoli*. Its rival, the pretty **Grotte Provençal**, 21 Rue Dr-Marçon, tel 94 29 41 52, offers classics like stuffed capon and *soufflé au Grand Marnier* (menus from 110 F).

Le Castellet (83330): Next to the medieval gate, *****Le Castel Lumière**, tel 94 32 62 20, has six rooms, and a good restaurant, with panoramic views, partially funished with antiques.

La Cadière-d'Azur (83740): The one hotel in the village, *****Hostellerie Bérard**, Rue Gabriel-Péri, tel 94 90 11 43, is charming and luxurious, in an old convent building, with a shady terrace, a heated pool, gardens, and a good restaurant with panoramic views, serving delicately perfumed dishes (try the *carré d'agneau* with basil, menus from 150 F).

Part VI

METROPOLITAN PROVENCE: LA CIOTAT TO MARTIGUES, MARSEILLE AND AIX

Although this is the business end of Provence, the most densely populated, hurly-burly, industrial and everything-else-you've-come-to-get-away-from part of Provence, the region holds several trump cards: the artistocratic city of Aix-en-Provence with its incredible markets and countryside synonymous with Cézanne; a tumultuous coastline ripped into the bones of the earth between La Ciotat and Marseille; and Marseille itself, every bit as good as its magnificent setting, as bad as any big port city, and as ugly as the fish in its heavenly *bouillabaisse*.

La Ciotat, Cassis and the Calanques

Before settling down and creating the broad, smooth bay that permits the existence of Marseille, the Provençal coast bucks and rears with the fury of wild horses. La Ciotat, halfway between Toulon and Marseille, is a shipbuilding, hard-nosed and gritty town, while well-heeled Cassis is endowed with a dramatic setting, a bijou harbour and delicate white wine.

GETTING AROUND
La Ciotat is a main stop for **trains** between Marseille and Toulon (tel 91 08 50 50); regular **buses** cover the 3 km from the station to the Vieux Port. Cassis' train station is just as far from the centre but has less frequent services; if you're coming from Marseille,

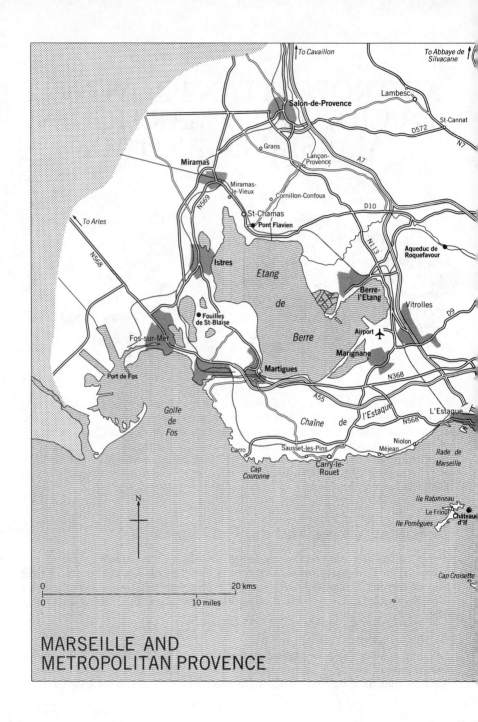

To Cavaillon

To Abbaye de Silvacane

Salon-de-Provence

Lambesc

St-Cannat

D572

N7

Grans

Lançon-Provence

A7

Miramas

Miramas-le-Vieux

Cornillon-Confoux

D10

To Arles

St-Chamas

Pont Flavien

N113

Aqueduc de Roquefavour

N568

N569

Istres

Etang

Berre-l'Etang

Vitrolles

D9

de

Fouilles de St-Blaise

Berre

Airport

Fos-sur-Mer

Marignane

Port de Fos

Martigues

N368

Golfe de Fos

A55

Chaîne de

l'Estaque

N568

L'Estaque

Niolon

Méjean

Rade de Marseille

Carro

Sausset-les-Pins

Carry-le-Rouet

Cap Couronne

N

Ile Ratonneau

Le Frioul

Château d'If

Ile Pomègues

Cap Croisette

0   20 kms

0   10 miles

MARSEILLE AND
METROPOLITAN PROVENCE

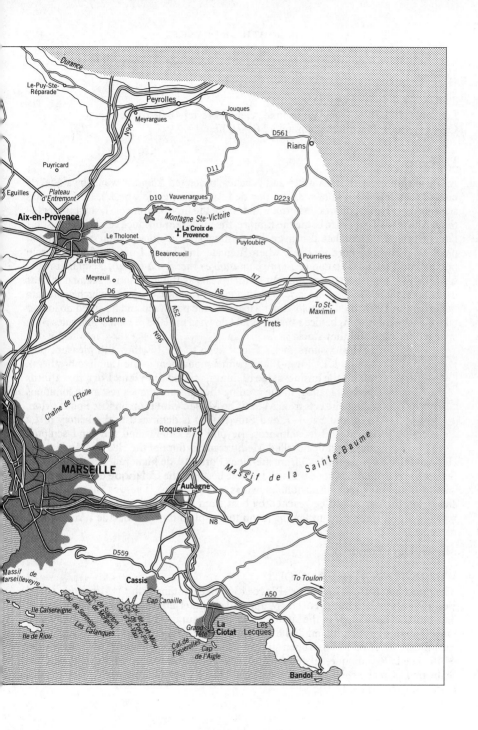

take one of the frequent coaches that drop you off in the central Place Montmorin (tel 42 73 18 00).

TOURIST INFORMATION
La Ciotat (13660): 2 Quai Ganteaume, Vieux Port, tel 42 08 61 32.
Cassis (13260): Place Baragnon, tel 42 01 71 17.

La Ciotat

A safe anchorage with fresh water and beaches, protected from the winds by a queerly eroded rock formation known as the Bec de l'Aigle (the 'eagle's beak'), La Ciotat has seen ancient Greeks, pirates, fishermen and, since the time of François I, shipbuilders—though instead of galleys to battle the Empire, the yards now produce vessels to transport liquefied gas. La Ciotat has also given the world two momentous pastimes: first, motion pictures, pioneered here in 1895, when Auguste and Louis Lumière filmed a train pulling into La Ciotat station (*L'Entrée d'un train en gare de La Ciotat*), a clip that made history's first film spectators jump out of their seats as the locomotive seemed to bear down upon them. And second, *pétanque*, that most Provençal of sports, which came into being here in 1907 when one old-timer's legs became paralyzed and he could no longer take the regulation steps before a throw, as laid down in the laws of *boules*. The rules were changed for him, and they stuck.

Most visitors to La Ciotat keep to the beaches and pleasure port around **La Ciotat-Plage** (with a monument to the Lumière brothers), but it's the business side of things, around the **Vieux Port**, that affords the best loafing; in the evening the shipyard cranes resemble luminous mutant insects from Mars. The **Musée Ciotaden** on Rue Polius (Mon, Wed and Sat 4–7, and Sun 10–12) is dedicated to the history of La Ciotat and its shipyards. Beyond the latter, amid the wind-sculpted rocks and dishevelled Mediterranean flora of the Bec de l'Aigle is the cliff-top **Parc du Mugel** (Bus 3 from the Vieux Port). Av. de Figuerolles continues from here to the red pudding-stone walls and pebble beach of the **Calanque de Figuerolles**, with its hunchback rock formation, known as 'le Capuchin'. The wee islet floating off shore, the **Ile Verte**, can be reached by boat from Quai Ganteaume; it has a simple restaurant and views back to the mainland that explain how the Bec de l'Aigle got its name.

Market Day: Tuesday.

WHERE TO STAY/EATING OUT
The nicest hotels are at **La Ciotat-Plage** (13600), beginning with *****Miramar**, 3 Blvd Beaurivage, tel 42 83 09 54, is a classy, updated old hotel amid pine groves, by the beach; half-board is mandatory in the summer, but its restaurant, **L'Orchidée**, is the best in town (menus at 100, 140 and 260 F). A good budget choice, the ***Beaurivage**, 1 Av. Beaurivage, tel 42 83 09 68, is open all year, while in La Ciotat town ****De La Rotonde**, 44 Blvd de la République, tel 42 08 67 50, is the best choice near the Vieux Port. Quai Stalingrad near the shipyards has the widest choice of restaurants with cheap menus, most featuring seafood.

Route des Crêtes
If you can sneer at vertigo and laugh in the face of tenuous hairpin turns, ignore the main road between La Ciotat and Cassis and twist and turn along the 17-km **Corniche des Crêtes**. Alternatively, a footpath cuts through the road loops and takes about 4 hours. Your pains will be amply rewarded with plunging views from the highest cliffs in France: the **Falaises de Soubeyran**, or 'Big Head' (399 m), and craggy **Cap Canaille**. From Pas de la Colle the road and path descend to the ancient Gallo-Roman *Portus Carcisis*, now known as Cassis.

Cassis and the Calanques

The old coral-fishing village of Cassis, with its fish-hook port, white cliffs, beaches, and quaint houses spilling down steep alleyways was a natural favourite of the Fauve painters. Since their day, the village has made the inevitable progression from fishing to artsy to chic, and beyond the purse of most fishermen and artists. The swanky modern Casino Municipal does a roaring trade thanks to its proximity to the gambling-mad Marseillais. When they're not counting wads of banknotes, the Cassidans bestir themselves to make one of the most delicious white wines of Provence and export their crystalline white stone. The latter is quarried in the sheer limestone cliffs between Cassis and Marseille, pierced by tongues of lapis lazuli called *calanques*.

In 1991 a member of a local diving club was exploring the *calanques* when he noticed that one of the many underwater fissures in the cliffs led up to a cave. He wiggled up the passageway into a half-submerged grotto, and found it painted with horses, birds, and bison that were believed to date back 12,000 years. Unfortunately, what could have been the greatest discovery in palaentology has now been revealed to be an elaborate hoax.

The **calanques** themselves are much more accessible: take a look at them by motor boat from Cassis port (but you cannot get off), or more strenuously, by walking along the path that first leads to **Port-Miou**, where the hard, white stone was hewn for the Suez Canal; another mile's hike will take you to **Port-Pin**, with a pretty beach, and **En-Vau**, its sheer cliffs a favourite challenge for daring human flies. Take a picnic, and spend a day skinny dipping in the exhilarating crystal water. Serious walkers can continue along GR 98 all the way to Marseille.

Market Days: Cassis, Wednesday and Friday.

Cassis AOC
In Cassis, they say their white wine obtained its divine quality when God came down the road from heaven and shed a tear at the plight of a family trying to scratch a living from the rocky amphitheatre overlooking the village. The divine tear fell on a vine and *voilà*, it gave birth to a dry wine of a pale green tint, with a bouquet of heather and rosemary.

The Cassis district is minute, but was one of the first to be granted AOC status (1936). Ugni blanc, marsanne, clairette and bourboulenc are the dominant grapes of this pale cocktail, popularized abroad by the late James Beard and considered by the Marseillais to be the only liquid worthy of washing down a *bouillabaisse*, a grilled red mullet, or lobster. Try some in the vast, ancient *caves* of **Clos Sainte-Magdeleine** (tel 42 01 70 28) and **Château de Fontcreuse**, Route de La Ciotat, tel 42 01 71 09, the district's only real château, which between the wars, was the property of a retired English colonel, who improved the stock and carved out new vineyards in the steep limestone hills.

WHERE TO STAY/EATING OUT

Don't expect any bargains in Cassis (13620). Most spectacular, perched on the promontory overlooking Cassis bay, is *****Les Roches Blanches**, Route des Calanques, tel 42 01 09 30. Rooms are a tad small, but very comfortable; there's a private beach and sun terraces, and as usual half-board is mandatory in season. Set amid lemon groves and bougainvillea, *****Les Jardins du Campanile**, Rue A. Favier, tel 42 01 84 85, is a lovely Provençal-style oasis, with a pool. Book months in advance for the more reasonable (and restaurant-less) ****Grand Jardin**, 2 Rue Pierre-Eydin, tel 42 01 70 10. To the west of Cassis, overlooking the *calanques*, France's most remote youth hostel, **La Fontasse** (tel 42 01 02 72) is an hour's walk from town or from the Marseille–Cassis bus stop *Les Calanques*. Open all year round, this hostel has a magnificent setting, but is not for sissies—beds, lights, and cold water are the only creature comforts. The local, rosy-pink sea-urchins, *oursins*, often crop up on the menu in the company of other tasty sea creatures at the excellent **La Presqu'île**, in Quartier de Port-Miou, tel 42 01 03 77, with menus at 180 and 280 F. Among the many places on the waterfront, **El Sol**, 28 Quai des Baux, tel 42 01 76 10, has the only reasonably priced food (menus from 80F); get there early.

MARSEILLE

Marseille is tired of being Marseille.

—*a current saying*

Amid Provence's carefully-nurtured image of lavender fields, rosé wine and *pétanque*, Marseille is the great anomaly, the second city of France and the world's eighth largest port. Like New York, it has been the gateway port to a new world for hundreds of thousands of new arrivals—especially Corsicans, Armenians, Jews, Greeks, Turks, Italians, Spaniards and Algerians. Many immigrants have gone no further, creating in Marseille perhaps the most varied mix of cultures and religions in Europe, 'the meeting place of the entire world' as Alexandre Dumas called it. The grateful Armenian community even talks about funding a Statue of Liberty for the harbour.

Unfortunately, Marseille also shares many of New York's less savoury traits: racial hostility towards whoever was the last off the boat, the petty crooks and hardened gangsters of the French mafia, or *milieu*, heroin and prostitution rings, political and financial scandals, and a godawful international reputation put about by films like *The French Connection*. It is the great anti-Paris, ever defiant of central authority and big-wigs be they Julius Caesar, Louis XIV, Napoleon, Hitler, or De Gaulle. These days a third of

Marseille votes for that blustering pathetic clown, Jean-Marie Le Pen, whose shrill politics are a reminder that the cultural diversity that can make New York so appealing is perceived with fear and loathing in Marseille.

'These Marseillais make Marseilles hymns, and Marseilles vests, and Marseilles soap for all the world; but they never sing their hymns, or wear their vests, or wash with their soap themselves', wrote Mark Twain. So what *do* they do? Marseille, with its million-strong population, must be the largest secret city in Europe, an extraordinary blank, a metropolis that in its 2600 years has contributed precious little to western civilization; it is the eternal capital of great expectations, 'a city that's been waiting for Godot', according to an editor in one of Marseille's young publishing houses. There are hints (in theatre, the plastic arts, in research) that its long bottled-up juices are ripe and ready to flow; if nothing else it comes as an unclogging shot of *pastis* to your blood after the mental cholesterol of the Côte d'Azur.

History

The story goes that in 600 BC Greek colonists from the Ionian city of Phocaea, having obtained the approval of the gods, loaded their ship with olive saplings and sailed towards Gaul. They found a perfect bay, and their handsome leader Protis went to the local king to obtain permission to found a city. That very day the king was hosting a banquet for the young men of his land, after which, according to tradition, his daughter Gyptis would select her husband. Protis was invited to join, and, thanks to his great beauty, was chosen by the princess. For his new wife's dowry, Protis asked for the land the Greeks coveted near the mouth of the Rhône, including the Lacydon (the *Vieux Port*). He named the new city Massalia.

Massalia boomed from the start; by 530 BC it had its own treasury at Delphi, and its own colonies, from Málaga to Nice; it traded for tin with Cornwall and its great astronomer Pytheas explored the Baltic and in 350 BC became the first scientist to accurately calculate latitudes. Rivalling Carthage, it allied itself with Rome, and profited from the latter's conquests in Spain and Gaul. By the 2nd century BC, Massalia had a population of 50,000, and was ruled by a merchant oligarchy whose political astuteness was admiringly described by Aristotle and Cicero. This astuteness failed them when they sided with Pompey, calling down the vengeance of Caesar, who conquered their city after a long siege and seized all of Massalia's colonies, with the exception of Nice and Hyéres. Yet even after the 2nd century AD, when Massalia adopted Roman law, it remained a city apart, the westernmost enclave of Hellenism, with famous schools of Greek rhetoric and medicine.

As the Pax Romana crumbled, Marseille nearly went out of business, taking hard knocks from Goths, Franks, Saracens and then more Franks again in the 700s, under Charles Martel. Plagued by pirates, business stayed bad until the 11th century, when the Crusaders showed up looking for transport to the Holy Land. This was the best get-rich-quick opportunity of the Middle Ages, and although Genoa and Venice grabbed the biggest trading concessions in the Levant, Marseille too grew fat on the proceeds. Briefly a republic, real power in the city soon passed to a merchant oligarchy; between 1178 and 1192 the big boss was the cultivated En Barral, patron of two of

Provence's greatest troubadours, the mad Piere Vidal and Folquet of Marseille (see p. 43).

Trumped by Kings: Charles d'Anjou to Louis XIV

When Charles d'Anjou acquired Provence in 1252, he confiscated Marseille's entire fleet to achieve his conquest of Sicily. Thanks to the monumental arrogance of the Angevins, the ships were annihilated in the revolt of the Sicilian Vespers (1282). With her legitimate commerce undermined by her own rulers, Marseille became a den for pirates and went into such a decline that it became an easy target for the Angevins' rival, Alfonso V of Aragon who destroyed as much of it as he could in 1423.

Coming under French rule in 1481 meant, for Marseille, tumbling headlong into the power-grasping scrum known as the Wars of Italy (1494–1559). The city's galleys went to war again, and attracted the fury of Emperor Charles V, who sent his henchman, the rebel Constable of Bourbon, to besiege the city. Marseille resisted heroically, and François I showed his gratitude by giving the city the freedom to trade at will in the eastern Mediterranean. Once again the money rolled in, to be pumped into new industries, especially soap and sugar.

Marseille's longing to be left alone to mind her own affairs put her squarely at odds with Louis XIV; for 40 years the city thumbed her nose at his Royal Sunniness while scrambling to retain her autonomy. By 1660, the King had had enough, and opened up a great breach in Marseille's walls, humiliating the city by turning its own cannons back on itself. The central authority installed by Louis was much more lax than the city had previously been about issues crucial to the running of a good port—like quarantine. The result, in 1720, was a devastating plague that spread throughout Provence.

Tunes, Booms and Busts

Marseille sprang back quickly. Trade with the Levant, North Africa, and the new markets in America made it Europe's greatest port. Its industries (soap, woollens, porcelain, *tarot* cards) blossomed, only to wither in the Revolution, which for ten years divided the proletariat and the oligarchs. Volunteers from Marseille contributed much to the upholding of the Revolution, however; as 500 of them set off for Paris in July 1792, someone suggested singing the new battle song of the Army of the Rhine, recently composed by Rouget de l'Isle. It caught on, and as the volunteers marched, they improved the rhythm and harmonies so that by the time they reached Paris, the 'song of the Marseillais' was perfected and became the hit tune of the Revolution, and subsequently, the most bloodcurdling of national anthems.

But as the Revolution evolved into the Terror, Marseille was found so wanting in proper politics that it was known as the *ville sans nom*, and any building that had sheltered an anti-Revolutionary was demolished, including the ancient monastery of St-Victor. The misery continued under Napoleon, another bugbear in Marseille's books for provoking the blockade by the British and ruining trade. Recovery came with the Second Empire, the conquest of Algeria in 1830, and the construction of the Suez Canal. Soon Marseille was more prosperous than ever before, and more populous, with some 60,000 new immigrants every decade between 1850 and 1930—Greeks and Armenians fleeing the Turks, Italians fleeing Fascism, and later, Spaniards fleeing Franco.

After becoming one of the first French cities to vote socialist (1890), Marseille's reputation took a nosedive. Corruption, rigged elections and an open link between the Hôtel de Ville and the bosses of the *milieu* were so rampant that in 1938 Paris dissolved the municipal government and ran the city at a distance. Yet the 30s also saw the release of Marcel Pagnol's classic Marseillais film trilogy *Marius*, *Fanny* and *César*, which helped create throughout France an insatiable appetite for *operette marseillaise*; even Josephine Baker sang the tunes of Marseille's great songwriter Vincent Scotto.

In 1953, Marseille elected a socialist mayor—Gaston Deferre, the antagonist of De Gaulle, who reigned until his death in 1986. Deferre oversaw rapid changes: the decline of Marseille's trade as France lost its colonies, and a population that exploded from 660,000 in 1955 to 960,000 in 1975. To accommodate the new arrivals (mostly *pieds noirs*—French refugees and Algerians) the city infested itself with the shoddy high-rise housing that still scars most quarters; unemployment rose as the traditional soap and fat industries plummeted, and new projects such as the steel-mills and port at Fos failed to provide as many jobs as expected—fuelling the racial tensions and organized crime that still give the city a rough reputation. Less well known is Marseille's re-orientation, for the first time in its history, away from the Mediterranean and towards Europe: it is now the most important research centre in France after Paris, home of a major science university, inventor of a new fifth-generation computer language, and site of COMEX, the world's leading developer of underwater technologies.

GETTING AROUND/ORIENTATION

Marseille's **airport** is to the west at Marignane; tel 42 89 90 10 for flight information. Air France is at 14 La Canebière (1er), tel 91 54 92 92; Air Inter at 8 Rue des Fabres (1er), tel 91 91 90 90; British Airways at 41 La Canebière (1er), tel 91 91 66 44. A bus links the airport with the train station, Gare St-Charles, every 20 minutes from 6:10 am to 9:50 pm.

Gare St-Charles is the main **train station**, and the only one in France that could star in a Busby Berkeley musical, with its big stagey staircase, draped with buxom statues representing Asia and Africa. There are connections to nearly every town in the south, and the TGV that will get you to Paris in just under 5 hours. For train information, tel 91 08 50 50; tickets also available from the SNCF office at 4 La Canebière, tel 91 95 14 31. The **coach station** is behind the train station, in Place Victor-Hugo (3e), tel 91 08 16 40, with connections to Cassis, Nice, Arles, Avignon, Toulon and Cannes. Some **car hire** firms, including Avis, are in the Gare St-Charles. Others include Hertz, at 16 Blvd Charles-Nédelec (1er), tel 91 90 19 77 and Mattei, 121 Av. du Prado (8e), tel 91 79 90 10. **Ferries** sail to Algeria, Corsica, or Tunisia, contact SNCM, 61 Blvd des Dames, tel 91 56 32 00.

City transport: Marseille runs an efficient bus network and two metro lines. Pick up the useful *plan du réseau* at the tourist office or at the RTM (Réseau de Transport Marseillais) information desk by the Bourse (6–8 Rue des Fabres, tel 91 91 92 10). Tickets are transferable between the bus and metro. RTM also has guided tour buses: the *Bus Pagnol*, for sites associated with Pagnol's childhood, and a *Histobus*, a tour of historic Marseille. If you need a **taxi**, tel 91 03 60 03 or 91 05 80 80, and make sure the meter is switched on at the start of your journey.

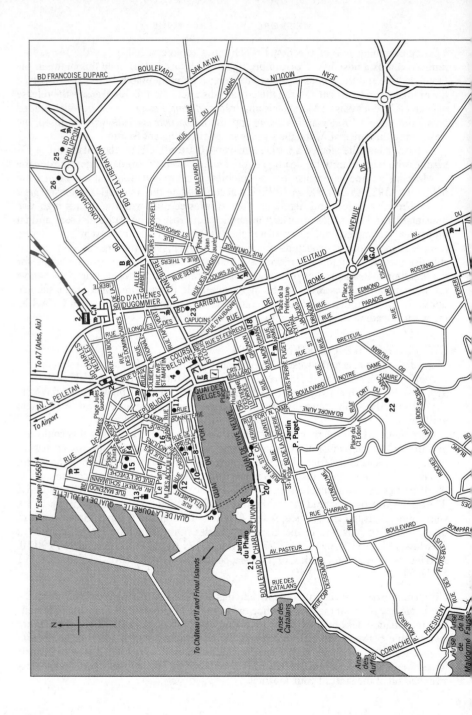

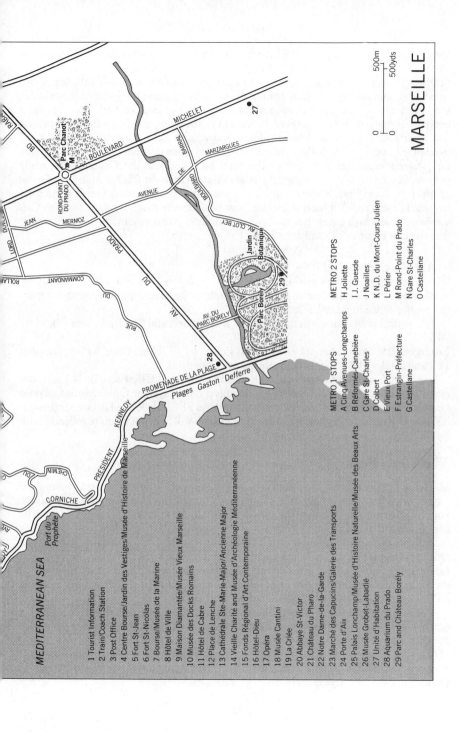

MARSEILLE

MEDITERRANEAN SEA

Port du Prophète

1 Tourist Information
2 Train/Coach Station
3 Post Office
4 Centre Bourse/Jardin des Vestiges/Musée d'Histoire de Marseille
5 Fort St-Jean
6 Fort St-Nicolas
7 Bourse/Musée de la Marine
8 Hôtel de Ville
9 Maison Diamantée/Musée Vieux Marseille
10 Musée des Docks Romains
11 Hôtel de Cabre
12 Place de Lenche
13 Cathédrale Ste-Marie-Major/Ancienne Major
14 Vieille Charité and Musée d'Archéologie Méditerranéenne
15 Fonds Régional d'Art Contemporaine
16 Hôtel-Dieu
17 Opéra
18 Musée Cantini
19 La Criée
20 Abbaye St-Victor
21 Château du Pharo
22 Notre Dame-de-la-Garde
23 Marché des Capucins/Galerie des Transports
24 Porte d'Aix
25 Palais Lonchamp/Musée d'Histoire Naturelle/Musée des Beaux Arts
26 Musée Grobet-Labadié
27 Unité d'Habitation
28 Aquarium du Prado
29 Parc and Château Borély

METRO 1 STOPS
A Cinq Avenues-Longchamps
B Réformés-Canebière
C Gare St-Charles
D Colbert
E Vieux Port
F Estrangin-Préfecture
G Castellane

METRO 2 STOPS
H Joliette
I J. Guesde
J Noailles
K N.D. du Mont-Cours Julien
L Périer
M Rond-Point du Prado
N Gare St-Charles
O Castellane

0   500m
0   500yds

Orientation: Marseille, with 110 neighbourhoods and 16 *arrondissements*, is one of Europe's largest cities, sprawling over twice as many acres as Paris. The northern neighbourhoods are the poorest, the first addresses of many new immigrants; the Panier (see below) and neighbourhoods around the station constitute the North African quarters, lively during the day but uncomfortable to wander in after dark. The southern neighbourhoods, with their parks and access to the beaches, are distinctly more monied and sanitized. A circle of hills divides the city from the mainland, physically and psychologically. The Vieux Port, the heart of the city since its founding, is now used only for pleasure craft and boats out to the islets of Frioul and the Château d'If, while commercial port activities are concentrated to the north in the *Rade de Marseille*. To the south of the Vieux Port, where the golden Virgin of Notre-Dame de la Garde is the chief landmark, the Parc du Pharo marks the start of a *corniche* road along the coast to Cap Croisette, lined with coves, beaches and restaurants, with a mountain, Marseilleveyre, that you can climb at the end for a view of all the above.

TOURIST INFORMATION
By the Vieux Port, at 4 La Canebière, tel 91 54 91 11 (open Mon–Sat 9–7:30, Sun 10–5), worth a visit for the hilarious 'drop-dead' attitude of the mannequins who run it. Or try the gentler office in the train station.

The central **post office** is at the corner of Rue Colbert and Rue Barbusse (1er), tel 91 90 31 33.

Emergencies: ambulance, tel 91 49 91 91. Police, tel 17. Hôtel Dieu, 6 Place David in Le Panier, tel 91 90 29 35 is the main casualty **hospital**.

Special Information Centres exist for **young people**, at CIJ, 4 Rue de la Visitation, near Palais Longchamp, tel 91 49 91 55; **disabled visitors**, at the Office Municipal pour Handicapés et Inadaptés, 128 Av. du Prado (8e), tel 91 81 58 80; and **crime victims**, at AVAD, 49 Rue Grignan (6e), tel 91 54 81 00, which will help out if you're robbed blind.

The Vieux Port

Marseille the urban mangrove entwines its aquatic roots around the neat, rectangular Vieux Port, where people have lived continuously for the past 2600 years. Now a pleasure port, its cafés have fine views of the sunset, though in the morning, the action and smells centre around the Quai des Belges and its boat-side **fish market**, where the key ingredients of *bouillabaisse* are touted in a racy *patois* as thick as the soup itself. From the Quai des Belges *vedettes* sail to the Château d'If and Frioul islands (see below), past the two bristling fortresses that still defend the harbour: to the north, **St-Jean**, first built in the 12th century by the Knights of St John, and to the south **St-Nicolas**, built by Louis XIV to keep a close eye on Marseille rather than the sea.

A bronze marker in the Quai des Belges pinpoints the spot where the Greeks first set foot in Gaul. And yet Marseille concealed its age until this century, when excavations for the glitzy new shopping mall, the Centre Bourse, revealed the eastern ramparts and gate of Massalia, dating back to the 3rd century BC, now enclosed in the **Jardin des Vestiges**. On the ground floor of the Centre Bourse, the new **Musée d'Histoire de Marseille** (Mon–Sat 12–7) displays models, everyday items, mosaics, and a 3rd-century BC wreck of a Roman ship, discovered in 1974. Built of 15 different kinds of pine, it had become so fragile that it had to be freeze-dried like instant coffee to prevent further deterioration. Elaborate antique models of later ships that sailed into the Vieux Port, and items related to Marseille's trading history are the main focus of the **Musée de la Marine et de l'Economie de Marseille** (10–12 and 2–6, closed Tues). This is housed in the 1860 **Palais de la Bourse,** France's oldest stock exchange, built under Napoleon III to obliterate an unrepentant democratic quarter that spilled much blood in the Revolution of 1848. But this corner, stock exchange or not, remained a vortex for violence: a plaque on the Canebière side of the Bourse recalls that King Alexander of Yugoslavia was assassinated here in 1934.

Le Panier

North of the Vieux Port, the Panier ('the Basket', named after a 17th-century cabaret) is Marseille's oldest quarter—an irregular weave of winding narrow streets and stairs dating from the ancient Greeks, many in the perpetual shadow of steep houses and flapping laundry. When the well-to-do moved out in the 18th century, the Panier was given over to fishermen and a romanticized underworld; guides were published to its 'private' hotels and the hourly rates of their residents. Before the war it was a lively Corsican and Italian neighbourhood, and later, its warren of secret ways absorbed hundreds of Jews and other refugees from the Nazis, hoping to escape to America. In January 1943, Hitler cottoned on and ordered the dynamiting of everything between the Vieux Port and halfway up the hill, to the Grand'Rue/Rue Caisserie. Given one day to evacuate, the 20,000 departing residents were screened by French and German police, who selected 3500 for the concentration camps.

Two buildings were protected from the dynamite: the 17th-century **Hôtel de Ville** on the quai, and behind it, in Rue de la Prison, the **Maison Diamantée,** Marseille's 16th-century Mannerist masterpiece, named for the pyramidical points of its façade. It holds the **Musée Vieux Marseille** (daily 10–5), a delightful attic where the city stashes its odds and ends—Provençal furniture; an extraordinary relief diorama made in 1850 by an iron merchant, depicting the uprising of 1848; 18th-century Neapolitan Christmas crib figures and *santons* made in Marseille; playing and tarot cards, long an important local industry; and poignant photos of the Panier before it was blown to smithereens.

The dynamite was responsible for revealing the contents of the **Musée des Docks Romains** (2 Place Vivaux, daily 10–5), built over a stretch of the vast 1st-century AD Roman quay, where wine and grains were stored in *dolia* or massive jars. Exhibits describe seafaring in the ancient Mediterranean. One last survivor of the pre-war Panier is the oldest house in Marseille, the **Hôtel de Cabre** (1535), a Gothic-Renaissance confection on Grand'Rue. The rest of the lower Panier was rebuilt on the cheap after the war, and still fulfils its traditional role as the first address of Marseille's most recent arrivals, now 80 per cent Arab.

Once you walk north of Rue Caisserie, the Panier retains some of its old character in the web of lanes atop the steps of **Montée des Accoules,** and around **Place de Lenche,** the former *agora* of the Greeks. Just to the north, looming over the tankers and cargo ships drowsing in Marseille's outer harbour basin, are the two 'majors': the striped neo-Byzantine **Cathédrale de-la-Major,** built in 1853 with the new money coming in

175

from the conquest of Algeria—enough to make it the largest church built in France since the Middle Ages, held up by 444 (count 'em) marble columns and with less bombast and more charm, its Romanesque predecessor, the **Ancienne-Major**. Although the transept was brutally amputated for the new cathedral, note the Ancienne-Major's crossing, a fantasy in brick that sets an octagonal dome on four stepped conical squinches, a typically Provençal conceit. One chapel has a *Descent from the Cross* (early 1500s), a late work from the Della Robbias' Florentine workshop, and an altar by one of their students, Francesco Laurana, of *SS. Lazarus, Martha, and Mary Magdalene*. What you don't get to see is the Ancienne-Major's old curiosity shop of locked-away relics, but it is said to include part of Jesus' cradle and one of His tears, St Peter's tooth, and best of all, the fishbones left over from the feast at the Sermon on the Mount.

Near the cathedral, at the top of Rue du Petit-Puits is a gem of a different cut, the Baroque **Vieille-Charité**, designed by Pierre Puget, a student of Bernini and court architect to Louis XIV—and a native of the Panier. Built by the city fathers between 1671 and 1745 to take in homeless migrants from the countryside, this is one of the world's most palatial workhouses: three storeys of arcaded ambulatories in pale pink stone, overlooking a court with a sumptuous elliptical chapel crowned by an oval dome—a curvaceous Baroque work forced into a straitlaced neo-Corinthian façade in 1863. Although the complex became a barracks after the Revolution, it returned to its original purpose in 1860, housing families displaced first by the construction of the Bourse and later by the Nazis' destruction of the Panier. By 1962, the Charité was in so precarious a state that everyone was evacuated, and in 1985 it reopened, all restored—no longer a shelter for the homeless but for art, photography, and video exhibitions as well as the **Musée d'Archéologie Méditerranéenne** (open Mon–Fri 10–5; Sat and Sun 12–7), featuring Egyptian art and mummies, finds from Cyprus, Susa, Mesopotamia and the reconstructed **Sanctuary of Roquepertuse** from Velaux, near Aix. Built by a head-hunting Celto-Ligurian tribe called the Salians, the sanctuary has pillars pierced with holes to hold skulls, a lintel incised with the outline of four horse heads (who symbolically transported the dead soul), and Buddah-like figures sitting in the lotus position. Similar temples found in Entremont (see p. 197) and Mouriès prove a common religion, perhaps a chthonic cult in which warriors went to commune with the spirits of their dead heroes. Living artists from Provence have a showcase in a former convent around the corner at the **Fonds Régional d'Art Contemporain**, 1 Place Francis-Chirat (daily 12–6 closed Tues).

South of the Vieux Port:
St-Victor and Notre-Dame de la Garde

The *filles*, they say, are more discreet on this side, especially around the **Opéra**, two blocks south of the Quai des Belges in Place Reyer. Built in 1924, it is graced with a pure Art Deco interior and a fine reputation for Italian opera. Two streets back, in the **Musée Cantini** at 29 Rue Grignan (Mon–Fri 10–5, Sat and Sun 12–7, adm) there are even more square yards of 20th-century art—by Picabia, Max Ernst, André Masson, Francis Bacon, Balthus, César, Niki de Saint-Phalle, Arman, Ben, and so many more that only a fraction can be displayed at a time. It also displays an exceptional collection of faïence made in Marseille and Moustiers, dating back to the 17th century.

Quai de Rive Neuve is lined with ship chandlers' shops and the new national theatre, **La Criée**, installed in a former fish auction house (see below). Among the salty Rive Neuve bars, the **Bar de la Marine** was the set for the famous card-playing scene in Marcel Pagnol's *Marius*, and has a mural of the same. Further along the *quai*, castle walls good enough for Hollywood hide one of the most intriguing Christian sites in Provence, the **Abbaye St-Victor** (open 8–12 and 2–6). St-Victor was founded *c.*416 BC by Jean Cassien, formerly an anchorite in the Egyptian Thebeaid. One account has it that he brought with him from Egypt the mummy of St Victor, though the more popular version says Victor was a Roman legionary who converted to Christianity, and slew at least one sea serpent before being ground to bits between a pair of millstones.

The first chapels of the fortified abbey were built into the flank of an ancient stone quarry, and near a Hellenistic necropolis, expanded for Christian use as a *martyrium* (rock-cut burials surrounding the tomb of a martyr). In the 11th and 12th centuries, when the monks adopted the Rule of St Benedict, they added the church on top, turning the old chapels into **crypts and catacombs** (small adm fee). These are strange and clammy with ancient mystery—the primitive bas-reliefs and sarcophagi date from the 3rd century AD, and some of the latter were found to contain seven or eight dead monks crowded like sardines, proof of the popularity of an abbey that founded 300 other monastic houses in Provence and even Sardinia. Then there's the 5th-century **Chapel of Notre-Dame-de-Confession**, enshrining one of Marseille's three Black Virgins (according to some students, they are Christian versions of Artemis, the patroness of Massalia). A primordial Candlemas rite takes place here every 2 February: the Archbishop comes to bless green candles before the black statue, and in the abbey's ancient bakery, small loaves are made in the shape of boats, or *navettes*—a similar custom, in the temple of Isis, used to herald the beginning of the navigation season. The faithful then take the green candles home to light at wakes as a symbol of rebirth.

Below St-Victor is Louis XIV's inaccessible Fort St-Nicolas, and beyond that, the **Château du Pharo** (bus 83 from the Vieux Port), built by Napoleon III as a gift for his wife, the Empress Eugénie, who never got around to seeing it. The gardens, with striking views over the port, are used for concerts and summer theatre under the stars; beyond are the Calanques (see p. 180). The prize 360-degree view, however, is from Marseille's watchtower hill—an isolated limestone outcrop towering 162 metres above the city, crowned by **Notre-Dame de la Garde**, a neo-Byzantine/ Romanesque pile with an unfortunate resemblance to a locomotive (a killer walk, and even fairly hair-raising to drive; let bus 60 do the work, from Place aux Huiles on Quai de Rive Neuve). This landmark supports France's largest golden mega-Madonna, 10-m high and shining like a beacon out to sea. In 1214 a monk of St-Victor built the first chapel here, and over the decades it gained a reputation for the miracles performed by a statue of the Virgin, Marseille's 'Bonne Mère'. The chapel's florid Second Empire architecture attracted some real bombs when the Nazis made it their headquarters and last stand, and you can still see some of the dents. But besides the view, the main attraction is the basilica's great **collection of ex-votos**, painted by fishermen and sailors.

La Canebière

Before La Canebière itself was laid out in Louis XIV's expansion scheme of 1666, this area was the ropemakers' quarter. The hemp they used has given its name to Marseille's most famous boulevard—*chanvre* in French, but in Provençal more like the Latin *cannabis*—a not entirely inappropriate allusion, for this was the high street of French *dolce-far-niente*, an essential ingredient of music-hall Marseille, which could swagger and boast that 'the Champs-Elysées is the Canebière of Paris.' In its day La Canebière sported grand cafés, toy shops and hotels where travellers of yore had their first thrills before sailing off to exotic lands, but these days La Canebière—or 'Can o' beer' as English sailors know it—has suffered the same fate as the Champs-Elysées: banks, airline offices and heavy traffic have chased out all but the seediest nightclubs and tourist traps. Some of the old flavour lingers in the lively streets to the south around 'Marseille's stomach' the **Marché des Capucins**. Here, too, is Noailles station, the last resting-place for the city's retired omnibuses and tramways (**Galérie des Transports**, Tues–Sat 10–5) although Marseille's last working tram still has its terminus here. Behind this hurly-burly stretches the **Cours Julien**, a favourite promenade and *pétanque* court, lined with antique shops, galleries, and restaurants.

North, and perpendicular to La Canebière, extends another tarnished grand boulevard, **Cours Belsunce**. Until 1964 No. 54 was the site of the famous neo-Moorish/Art Nouveau music-hall where Maurice Chevalier and Fernandel once starred, and where Tino Rossi and Yves Montand had their stage débuts. Now the Cours leads only to the **Porte d'Aix**, a fuzzy-minded Roman triumphal arch, vintage 1823, erected to Louis XVI or Liberty or both, adorned with statues of virtues such as Resignation and Prudence, whose heads (much like Louis XVI's) suddenly fell off in 1937 and rolled down the street. This quarter, like the Panier, is now mostly Arab: Marseille's mosque is just on the other side of the arch.

Palais Longchamp and Environs

In 1834 Marseille suffered a drought so severe that it dug a canal to bring in water from the Durance. This 80-km feat of aquatic engineering ends with a heroic splash at the **Palais Longchamp**, a delightfully overblown nymphaeum and cascade, populated with stone felines, bulls, and a buxom allegory of the Durance (metro: Longchamp-Cinq-Avenues; bus 80 from La Canebière). Behind the palace stretch the public gardens, an observatory (one of four in this city, which has been the home of many famous astronomers) and a little zoo; in the right wing of the palace itself, some of the same creatures are embalmed in the **Musée d'Histoire Naturelle** along with their fossilized ancestors (Thurs–Mon 10–12 and 2–6, closed Tues, Wed only).

The left wing of the Palais Longchamp houses the **Musée des Beaux Arts** (daily 10–5, adm). Formed around art 'conquered' by Napoleon's army, it has some second-rate canvases by Italian masters such as Perugino, and stagey burlesques like Rubens' violent *Boar Hunt* (in which ladies daintily watch the spurting blood) or Louis Finson's *Samson and Delilah* (1600), with a nasty Delilah tugging the ear of a very dirty-footed Samson. The mood changes with Michel Serre's scrupulously dire *Scenes of the Marseille Plague of 1720*, where a large percentage of the plague's 40,000 victims are shown dropping like flies while healthy rich men in suits prance by on horseback, looking politely sympathetic.

These same gentlemen never dismounted to assist Marseille's native artists, either— even an establishment figure like Baroque sculptor, architect, and painter Pierre Puget (1671–1745); the rooms devoted to him feature models for buildings and a lovely square that Marseille regretfully never built. Then there's Françoise Duparc, a follower of Chardin (1726–76) who worked most of her life in England; and the satirist Honoré Daumier (1808–97), who went to prison for his biting caricatures of Louis-Philippe's toadies, here represented by Spitting Image-style satirical busts modelled after his drawings. Here, too, is Van Gogh's roving, bohemian precursor, Adolphe Monticelli (1824–86), who sold his paint-encrusted canvasses of fragmented colour for a day's food and drink in the cafés along La Canebière. Also of note are paintings by Provençal pre-Impressionists, especially 18th-century scenes of Marseille's port by Joseph Vernet and sun-drenched landscapes by Paul Guigou.

Just across Boulevard Longchamp, the **Musée Grobet-Labadié** (10–5, Sun 12–7, adm) contains a private collection as interesting for its eclecticism as for any individual painting, table, plate, musical instrument, tapestry, or iron lock.

Heading South: Le Corbusier, Mazargues, and Parc Borély

The building that achieves speed will achieve success
—Le Corbusier

To pay your respects to Modular Man, take bus 21 from the Bourse down dreary Boulevard Michelet to the *Corbusier* stop. In 1945, at the height of Marseille's housing crisis, the French government commissioned Le Corbusier to build an experimental **Unité d'Habitation**, derived from his 1935 theory of 'La Cité Radieuse'. Le Corbusier thought the solution to urban anomie, transport, and housing was to put living-space, schools, shops, and recreational facilities all under one roof, in a building designed according to the human proportions of Leonardo da Vinci's Renaissance man-in-a-circle, reborn as Le Corbusier's wiggly Modular Man (he displays the proportions according to which the work was built). You can see the Man in relief on the huge rough concrete *pilotis*, or stilts, the most revolutionary aspect of the building, which lift it quite literally above the ground level of everyday human affairs.

For a city like Marseille, where people enjoy getting out and about at ground level, the building was a ghastly aberration, and they nicknamed it the *casa de fada* or 'house of the mentally deranged.' Plans for other *unités* were stifled and in 1952 the state sold the flats off as co-ops. But architects were entranced; for the next 30 years thousands of buildings in every city in the world went up on *pilotis*, before everyone realized that the Marseillais were right all along: it was madness to deprive a building of its most important asset, a ground floor. The Unité's good points, however, had few imitators—each of its 337 flats is built on two levels and designed for maximum privacy, with views over the mountains or sea. Of the original extras, only the school, the top-floor gym, and the communal hotel for residents' guests (see Where to Stay below) have survived.

Bus 21 continues towards **Mazargues**, a once-fashionable *banlieue* under the Massif de Marseilleveyre, famous in the 19th century for its climate. And when its residents

179

died, at a ripe old age, they often chose to be remembered in the local **cemetery** by a mini-monument to their life's work—there are stone hedge-clippers, fishing boats, hoes, and on the tomb of an omnibus driver, a tramway.

Marseille's Corniche and Calanques

Why go to the Riviera when Marseille has one of its very own? From the Vieux Port, you can catch bus 83, and pass the Parc du Pharo, to Corniche Président J. F. Kennedy, a dramatic road overlooking a dramatic coast that must have reminded the ancient Greek colonists of home—now improved with artificial beaches, bars, restaurants, villas, and nightclubs.

Amazingly, until the road was built in the 1850s, the first cove, the **Anse des Catalans,** was so isolated that the Catalan fisherfolk who lived there as squatters in the ruins of the old Lazaretto (or quarantine station) could hardly speak French. This now has the most popular (and the only real) sandy beach. From the bus stop *Vallon des Auffes* you can walk down to the fishing village **Anse des Auffes,** ('of the ropemakers') isolated from the corniche until after World War II and still determinedly intact. Other typical quarters with still more piquant names lie further on: **Anse de Maldormé** and **Anse de la Fausse Monnaie.**

The *corniche* then descends to the artificial **Plages Gaston Deferre,** where a copy of Michelangelo's *David* holds court at the corner of Av. du Prado, looking even more smugly ridiculous than he does in Florence. The big fellow stands near Marseille' excellent **Aquarium del Prado** (open Sun–Thurs 10–7, Fri and Sat 10 am–midnight, adm exp), featuring 350 different denizens of the deep. On the other side of David opens the cool green expanses of **Parc Borély,** with a botanical garden, duck ponds, and the **Château Borély,** an 18th-century palace built according to the strictest classical proportions for a wealthy merchant. Unique for its surviving interior decoration, the Château is to reopen soon as a museum of decorative arts.

To continue along the coast from the park, you'll need to change to bus 19, which poops out just after **Calanque du Mont Rose,** Marseille's nudist beach. Bus 20 from here continues to **Cap Croisette,** a miniature end-of-the-world at the base of the Massif de Marseilleveyre—forming a backdrop to the fishing hamlet in the **Calanque des Goudes**—and the pebble beach at **Calanque de Samena,** facing the islets of Maïre and Tiboulen. The road gives out at the narrow **Calanque de Callelongue,** where the GR 98 costal path to Cassis begins. Another path from here leads in two hours to the summit of Marseilleveyre (432 m), with grand views over Marseille, its industrial *rade,* and islands.

The more distant *calanques* can be most painlessly reached from Marseille by boat, operating mid-June to mid-September from the Quai des Belges (Société des Excursionnistes Marseillais, 16 Rue de la Rotonde, tel 91 84 75 52). Alternatively, take bus 21 from La Canebière to the end of the line (Luminy) and walk 40 min to **Calanque de Morgiou,** dotted with seaside *cabanons,* or to the wilder **Calanque de Sugiton.**

The Château d'If and Frioul islands

If in French means yew, a tree associated with death, and an appropriately sinister name for this gloomy precursor of Alcatraz built by François I in 1524 (GACM boats from the

Quai des Belges, departures hourly from 9 to 5 in the summer, in winter 9, 11, 2, 3:30 and 5). Even when Alexandre Dumas was still alive, visitors came to see the cell of the Count of Monte-Cristo, and a cell, complete with escape hole, was obligingly made to show to visitors. Real-life inmates included Mirabeau, imprisoned by his father-in-law for running up debts in Aix (see p. 191); a Monsieur de Niozelles, condemned to six years in solitary for not taking his hat off in front of Louis XIV; and after the revocation of the Edict of Nantes, thousands of Protestants who either died here or went on to die as galley slaves elsewhere.

The two other islands in the Archipel du Frioul, **Pomègues** and **Ratonneau** were originally hunting and fishing reserves that witnessed, in 1516, one of the first rhinoceri in Europe, who rambled here en route to Pope Leo X's menagerie in Rome. Later used as quarantine islands, they are now linked by a causeway at Port du Frioul, a pleasure port designed by Le Corbusier's pupil, José-Luis Sert; scores of swimming coves can be easily reached by foot, along paths lined with aromatic herbs that the Marseillais pick for their *bouquets garnis*. A 20-minute path leads to the **Hôpital Caroline**, built in the 1820s on Ratonneau, where the winds blow the strongest, on the theory that they would help 'purify' infectious diseases. Now used for a summer festival, the hospital has excellent views of Marseille—as Marseille was meant to be seen, from the sea—that must have been heartbreaking to the imprisoned patients.

SHOPPING

Marseille holds a remarkable market of clay Christmas crib figures, the *Foire aux Santons*, from the end of November to 6 January; at other times, you can find *santons* at **Marcel Carbonel**, near St-Victor at 47 Rue Neuve Ste Catherine (7e), tel 91 54 26 58 (on Mon from 10 am on, or Wed and Fri after 2:30 pm demonstrations show how they're made). Year-round markets include the daily old book, postcard, and record market in Place A. et F. Carli, near the Noailles métro, or the Sunday morning flea-market in Rue Frédéric-Sauvage (14e) (métro Bougainville, then bus 30). English books are sold at **Fuèri-Lamy**, 21 Rue Paradis (1er); for the best in Provençal food and wine, try **Bataille**, 18 Rue Fontange.

SPORT

France's champion **football** squad, **Olympique de Marseille** (OM) is also the most enthusiastically supported, and tickets often sell out (Stade Vélodrome Municipal, Blvd Michelet (8e), tel 91 76 56 09). **Windsurf boards and sailboats** can be hired at the Centre Municipal de Voile, Promenade de la Plage (8e), tel 91 76 31 60. On rainy days you can roll the rock or shoot some pool until 2 am at **Le Bowling Notre-Dame**, 107 Blvd Notre-Dame, (6e), tel 91 37 15 05.

WHERE TO STAY   (postal code 13000)

Marseille's top-notch hotels are the bastion of expense-account businessmen and women, while its downmarket numbers attract working girls of a different kind. In between, you can sleep where Chopin and George Sand canoodled—at the central, wood-panelled ****Hotel **Pullman Beauvau**, 4 Rue Beauvau (1er), tel 91 54 91 00, overlooking the Vieux Port and comfortable with air-conditioned, soundproof rooms (no restaurant). Up in the hills south of the Vieux Port, the modern ***Résidence

Bompard, 2 Rue des Flots-Bleus (7e), tel 91 52 10 93 (bus 61 from métro Joliette or St-Victor) seems remote from the city, set in its own peaceful grounds, with rooms overlooking a garden; those in bungalows have their own kitchenette. A special treat for students of architecture is the hotel incorporated into the Unité d'Habitation: ****Le Corbusier**, 280 Blvd Michelet (8e), tel 91 77 18 15; reserve one of its 24 rooms as early as possible. Near La Canebière, the ****Moderne**, 30 Rue Breteuil (6e), tel 91 53 29 93, has nice rooms, most with shower; other very palatable budget choices include ***Montgrand**, 50 Rue Montgrand (6e) (off Rue Paradis, behind the Opéra), tel 91 33 33 81, and ***Azur**, 24 Cours F. Roosevelt (1er), tel 91 42 74 38, with frills such as colour TV and garden views (métro: Réformés). Near the Gare St-Charles the most benign choice is ****D'Athènes-Little Palace** at the foot of the grand stair, 37 Blvd d'Athènes (1er), tel 91 90 12 93). The best of Marseille's two youth hostels is in a château overlooking the city at **Auberge de Jeunesse de Bois-Luzy**, 76 Av. de Bois-Luzy (bus 8 from La Canebière, or bus K after dark), tel 91 49 06 18.

There's a fair smattering of choices overlooking the sea: Marseille's most refined, exculsive hotel, ******Le Petit Nice**, 16 Rue des Braves; off Corniche Président J. F. Kennedy (7e), tel 91 52 14 39, is a former villa overlooking the Anse de Maldormé, with a fine restaurant, Le Passédat (see below). ****Peron**, 119 Corniche Président J. F. Kennedy (7e), tel 91 52 33 53, near the Plage des Catalans has an unusual cast-iron façade and good rooms. Or try the inexpensive ***Le Richelieu**, 52 Corniche Président J. F. Kennedy (7e), tel 91 31 01 92; best rooms here are Nos. 28, 29 and 30.

EATING OUT

The Marseillais claim an ancient Greek—even divine—origin for their ballyhooed *bouillabaisse*; one story claims that Aphrodite invented it to beguile her husband Hephastios to sleep so that she could dally with her lover Ares—seafood with saffron being a legendary soporific. Good chefs prepare it just as seriously, and display like a doctor's diploma their *Charte de la Bouillabaisse* guaranteeing that their formula more or less subscribes to tradition: a saffron and garlic-flavoured soup cooked on a low boil (hence its name), based on *rascasse* (otherwise notorious as the ugliest fish in the Mediterranean, and always cooked with its leering head attached) which lives under the cliffs, and has a bland taste that enhances the flavour of the other fish, especially conger eel, *grondin* and perhaps lobster. When served, the fish is presented on a side dish with *rouille*, a paste of Spanish peppers. The real McCoy does not come cheap; anything less than 200 F will probably be skimpy and disappointing. Reliable, traditional *bouillabaisse* may be had at **Michel-Brasserie des Catalans**, 6 Rue des Catalans (7e), tel 91 52 64 22 (full seafood meals 350 F and up; closed Tues and Wed); **Miramar**, by the Vieux Port at 12 Quai du Port (2e), tel 91 91 10 40 (350 F and up; closed Sun and Aug); **Chez Fonfon** prides itself on the freshness of its fish, at 140 Rue du Vallon des Auffes (7e), tel 91 52 14 38 (300 F and up, closed Sat and Sun, and Oct); **Le Chaudron Provençal**, 48 Rue Caisserie (2e), tel 91 91 02 37, presents a very serious version (300 F, closed Sun and Aug) while at the friendly **Le Faucigny**, near Ste-Marie-Major at 56 Rue de Mazenod (2e), tel 91 91 14 19, the dish is just as delicious and much more reasonable (220–275 F for a full meal, closed Sun and Aug).

But there's more than *bouillabaisse* in Marseille. For a genuine Provençal spread try **Marcel Brun: Aux Mets de Provence**, 8 Quai Rive-Neuve (7e), tel 91 33 35 38, a

50-year-old restaurant with an overwhelming 290 F menu that starts with eight different hors-d'oeuvres. The haughty gourmet **Passédat**, Anse de Maldormé (7ᵉ), tel 91 59 25 92, offers ravishing food in its exotic garden (weekday lunch menu 300 F; otherwise 500 F and up). Overlooking the Jardin des Vestiges, **L'Oursinade** in Rue Neuve-St-Martin, tel 91 91 91 29, offers an irreproachable mix of *nouvelle cuisine* and tradition with menus at popular prices—185 F and up. The fare is much simpler (*daube*, etc.) but a delight at **Chez Madie**, 138 Quai du Port (2ᵉ), tel 91 90 40 87 (menu 120 F with wine). For less than a 100 F try the salad bar and menu at **Le Dent Creuse**, 14 Rue Sénac near La Canebière, opposite Square L. Blum, tel 91 42 05 67 (60 F); or the great, quick lunch fare at **Le Poussin Bleu**, near the Préfecture at 17 Rue Armény (6ᵉ), tel 91 33 34 83 (80 F).

For perfect oysters, look up **Coquillages Toinou**, 18 Cour St-Louis, tel 91 54 08 79, home of Francis Rouquier, France's champion *écailler* (oyster-shucker); or try Armenian dishes at **Ho'Kiss**, 3 Rue de la Prison (2ᵉ), for around 120 F (closed Sun and Mon). Fine chocolates, pastries, and *plats du jour* are the fare at **L'Artisan du Chocolat**, 43 Cours Estienne-d'Orves (1ᵉʳ), tel 91 35 55 99 (lunch only). Night owls can assuage their hunger pangs at **Le Mas**, by the Opéra at 4 Rue Lulli (1ᵉʳ), tel 91 33 25 90, open daily until 6 am offering good pasta dishes and grills for around 100 F. Then there's the even cheaper 24-hour **O'Stop**, Place de l'Opéra (no phone) with similar fill-ups whenever you need them.

ENTERTAINMENT AND NIGHTLIFE

Marseille may be going on 3000 years, but the old girl's still kicking—sometimes in the wrong places, especially after 10 in the back-streets between the station and the Vieux Port. But you don't have to be a brawny sailor to have a good time: Marseille has lively after-dark pockets, especially around Place Thiers, Cours d'Estienne-d'Orves and Cours Julien. You can find out what's happening in *Atout Marseille*, distributed free by the tourist office, or in the pages of *La Marseillaise*, *Le Provençal* or the Wednesday edition of *Le Méridional*. Or try the book and record chain **FNAC**, in the Centre Bourse, which not only has information on events, but sells tickets as well. If you need a **babysitter**, ring SOS Babysitting, tel 91 88 19 21, or Baby Service, tel 91 25 66 26.

The city has always had a special affinity for music: Berlioz claimed that Marseille understood Beethoven five years before Paris. At the **Opéra Municipal** in Place Reyer (1ᵉʳ), tel 91 54 70 54, the bill includes Italian opera and the National Ballet Company of Roland Petit. Music from around the world is performed at **La Maison de l'Etranger**, 16 Rue Antoine Zattara (3ᵉ), tel 91 95 90 15. Another concert venue, the **Abbaye de St-Victoire** hosts a chamber music festival in Oct–Dec (tel 91 33 25 86). Jazz, rock, dance and theatre are all on offer at **Espace Julien**, 33 Cours Julien (6ᵉ), tel 91 47 09 64; nearby at 10 Rue Vian, off Rue des Trois Mages, a wide variety of rock and R & B plays at the **Maison Hantée**, tel 91 92 09 40; more R & B happens on weekends at **May Be Blues**, 2 Rue Poggioli (6ᵉ).

In the last decade, most of the cultural excitement in Marseille has been generated in its theatres. Since 1981, **Théâtre National de Marseille la Criée**, directed by Marcel Maréchal, has put on performances to wide critical acclaim (30 Rue de Rive-Neuve (7ᵉ), tel 91 54 70 54). **Espace Massalia**, 60 Rue Grignan (1ᵉʳ), tel 91 55 66 06, is France's first all-marionnette theatre. **Bernadines** puts on experimental dance and theatre at 17 Blvd Garibaldi (1ᵉʳ), tel 91 42 45 33. Theatre, food, and exhibitions are combined in **L'Avant-Scène**, 59 Cours Julien (6ᵉ), tel 91 42 19 29. Modern dance and plays also crop up among the high-rises at **Théâtre du Merlan**, Av. Raimu (14ᵉ), tel 91 98 28 98, and **Système Friche Théâtre**, 31 Blvd Magallon (14ᵉ), tel 91 05 87 70.

Old and avant-garde films in their original language (*v.o.* for *version originale*) are shown in the **Institut National de l'Audiovisuel**, in the Vieille Charité. The three **Breteuil** cinemas also run *v.o.* films at 120 Blvd de Notre-Dame (6ᵉ), tel 91 37 88 18, as does the **Nouveau Paris**, 31 Rue Pavillon (1ᵉʳ), tel 91 33 15 59.

West of Marseille: Chaîne de l'Estaque and the Etang de Berre

Whatever personality of its own this region once had has been thoroughly chewed and swallowed by the metropolis next door. Once sheltering attractive, out-of-the-way retreats, the Estaque coast and the broad lagoon of Berre behind it have in the last three decades totally succumbed to creeping suburbia; isolated corners that once knew only hamlets of poor fishermen now suffer some of the biggest industrial complexes in France. Still, the 'Côte Bleue' as the tourist offices call the Estaque coast, is a very attractive piece of coastline, despite having a giant octopus for a neighbour. Especially in the east, the mountains plunge straight into the sea, with sheltered *calanques* between them; there is no road along the coast until Carry-le-Rouet.

Leaving Marseille on the N 568, you'll pass the industrial suburb, docks and marinas of **L'Estaque**—a favourite subject of Cézanne, whose vision of a new, classical Provence transformed the town's smokestacks into Doric columns. The road then crosses over the **Souterrain du Rove**, the world's longest ship tunnel. A partial collapse closed it in the 60s, and no one has found it worth repairing since. Tortuous side-roads from the N 568 will take you down to two pleasant enclaves harbouring old fishing villages, **Niolon** and **Méjean**. The reputation of **Carry-le-Rouet**, the biggest town on the coast, is based on the two very odd-looking gifts it has bestowed on the world: the horse-faced actor Fernandel and prickly-stickly sea-urchins; it celebrates the latter with a festival each February. There is a beach, often oversubscribed; Carry is fast being surrounded by the weekend villas of the Marseillais. **Sausset-les-Pins**, the next town, is much the same; if you press on further there are popular but not too crowded beaches around **Carro** and **Cap Couronne**.

Martigues

On the lagoon side of the Chaîne de l'Estaque, facing inland across the Etang de Berre, the distinguished old city of **Marignane** has been completely engulfed by Marseille's sprawl and airport. In the centre of the old town, you can visit its **château** (now the *mairie*), an eccentric 17th-century work with mythological frescoes. From here, making a clockwise tour around the Etang de Berre, the next stop is **Martigues**, a sweet little city (pop. 80,000 and growing) full of salt air and sailboats, not a compelling place to visit but probably a wonderful place to live. If Carry-le-Rouet serves up sea-urchins to visitors in February, Martigues can answer with its own speciality—fresh sardines—during their Sardine Festival in July and August.

Martigues sits astride the Canal de Caronte, linking the lagoon and the sea, lending it a slight but much-trumpeted resemblance to Venice. According to legend the city was founded by and named after the Roman General Marius; the oldest part of town is the Ile Brescon, at the head of the channel, with the Baroque church of the Madeleine and a number of 17th- and 18th-century buildings. One of its prettiest corners is a quay called the Miroir des Oiseaux, the 'mirror of birds'. On the mainland, the **Musée Ziem**, Blvd du 14 Juillet (10–12 and 2:30–6; afternoons only in winter; closed Mon and Tues) has paintings left to Martigues by landscapist Félix Ziem, and works by Provençal painters Guigou, Monticelli, and Loubon, as well as archaeology exhibits.

Fos

The French, fascinated with technology, actually come to visit this gigantic industrial complex. Fos has an information centre (on Av. Jean Jaurès) and there are guided tours (ring 91 91 90 66). You too might consider a drive through; in its way Fos is the most astounding, unsettling sight in Provence. Before 1965, when France's Mephistophelean economic planners commandeered it to replace the overcrowded port of Marseille, this corner of the Camargue was pristine marshland. Today it is the biggest oil port, and the biggest industrial complex, on the entire Mediterranean. In area, it is considerably larger than Marseille.

To a degree, it makes sense to concentrate unpleasant industry all in one place. But driving past its 19 km of chemical plants, steel-mills and power-lines, rising out of the void like a mirage, the senses rebel. Economically, the 'ZIP' (*zone industriel-portuaire*) is a failure; as planning, it is stupidly primitive, ecologically disastrous, and demeaning to the people who live and work in it, the perfect marriage of corporate gigantism and bureaucratic simple-mindedness.

West and North of the Etang de Berre

Along the west shore there is more of the same, engulfing ancient villages like **St-Blaise**, with a Romanesque church and a wealth of ruins currently being excavated, including a rare stretch of Greek wall. Of the two large towns **Istres** and **Miramas**, the latter is more attractive, with ruins of its medieval predecessor nearby at **Miramas-le-Vieux**. **St-Chamas**, to the southeast, has an impressive Baroque church. The Via Domitia passed this way, and over a small stream south of the village stands one of the finest and best-preserved Roman bridges anywhere, the **Pont Flavien**. Built in the 1st century AD, the single-arched span features a pair of very elegant triumphal arches at the approaches, decorated with Corinthian capitals, floral reliefs and stone lions.

North of the Etang, towards Salon, lie three attractive villages: **Cornillon-Confoux**, on a steep hill with a wide view, **Grans** and **Lançon-Provence**, the latter being home of some of the most exquisite AOC Coteaux-d'Aix-en-Provence wines (see below).

Salon-de-Provence

The home of Nostradamus should be a more interesting place. Aix-en-Provence's disagreeable little sister, Salon is quite well-off from processing olive oil and from being home to the French air force training school. The town seems aptly named: a tight little bourgeois parlour, smug and stuffy and neat as a pin. Its spirit is captured perfectly in the antiseptic, gentrified *vieille ville*, totally ruined by a hideous and insensitive restoration programme in the last few years.

TOURIST INFORMATION
56 Cours Gimon, tel 90 56 27 60.

The old quarter, surrounded by a ring of boulevards, is entered by the 18th-century **Porte de l'Horloge**, with an iron-work clock tower. In the centre, at the highest point of Salon, is the **Château de l'Empéri**, parts of which go back to the 10th century. Long a possession of the Archbishops of Arles, it now houses the **Musée de l'Art et d'Histoire Militaire**, (Museum of Military Art and History—daily exc Tues, 10–12, 2–6; adm), a substantial hoard of weapons, bric-à-brac and epauletted mannequins on horseback, covering France's army from Louis XIV to 1918, with an emphasis on Napoleon.

NOSTRADAMUS
Salon's most famous citizen was born in St-Rémy in 1503, of a family of converted Jews. Trained as a doctor in Montpellier, young Michel de Nostredame made a name for himself by successfully treating plague victims in Lyon and Aix. In 1547, he married a girl from Salon and settled down here, practising medicine and pursuing a score of other interests besides— studying astrology, publishing almanacs, and inventing new recipes for cosmetics and hair dyes. The first of his *Centuries*, ambiguous quatrains written in the future tense, were published in 1555, achieving celebrity for their author almost immediately.

Nostradamus himself said that his works came from 'natural instinct and poetic passion'; in form they are similar to some other poetry of the day, such as the *Visions* of du Bellay. It may be that he had never really intended to become an occult superstar—but when the peasants start bringing you two-headed sheep, asking for an explanation, and when the Queen Regent of France sends an invitation to court, what's a man to do? Nostradamus went to Paris, and later Charles IX and Catherine de' Medici came to visit him in Salon. The Salonnais didn't appreciate such notoriety; if it had not been for Nostradamus's royal favour, they might well have put him to the torch. Now they've made up, and you can visit **Nostradamus's House** just inside the Porte de l'Horloge (in summer, daily exc Mon 10–12 and 2:30–6:30, otherwise call 90 56 22 36; adm). On his death in 1566, Nostradamus was oddly buried inside the wall of the Cordeliers' church; tales spread that he was still alive in there, writing his final book of prophecies. After his tomb was desecrated in the Revolution, he was moved to the 14th-century Dominican church of **St-Laurent**, on Rue Maréchal Joffre, where he rests today.

Market Days: Martigues, Thursday and Sunday. Salon, Wednesday.

WHERE TO STAY/EATING OUT

In **Carry-le Rouet** (13620), there's plenty of seafood along the Promenade du Port; try the roast lobster or sea bass grilled with spices on the attractive seaside terraces of **L'Escale**, tel 42 45 00 47; menus 350–470 F. Since most people here have villas or day-trip from the city, accommodation is scarce and functional, as at ***La Tuilière**, on Blvd Draïo-de-la-Mer (tel 42 45 02 96). There's a wider choice, though equally simple, in **Martigues** (13500). In the centre, **Le Provençal** on Blvd 14 Juillet, (tel 42 80 49 16), or on the outskirts, the fancier *****Eden** (Blvd Emile Zola, tel 42 07 36 37).

Spending a night in **Salon** (13300) should be contemplated only if neccessity demands it. At the luxury end of the scale is the ******Abbaye de Ste-Croix**, 5 km out of town towards Val-de-Cuech on the D17, with expensive and lovely rooms overlooking a medieval cloister. There's a swimming-pool and horse-riding, an ultra-posh restaurant with shrimps flambéed in *pastis* and lamb in truffle sauce, and a big wine list (menus 400–550 F; closed Dec–Jan, tel 90 56 24 55). At the opposite end of the scale, try the gracefully mouldering ***Hôtel Wilson** on Rue des Kennedys (tel 90 56 31 92). For dinner, there's **Robin**, Blvd G. Clemenceau, tel 90 56 06 63; a truly dull-looking place with truly good cooking, but it is undergoing changes; with luck the food, that changes by the season, will stay as good (menus 190–320 F). In the centre of the old town on Place de la Révolution, **Bourg Neuf** is simple but good for fish, like grilled red mullet in saffron butter.

Aix-en-Provence

Elegant and honey-hued, the old capital of Provence is splashed by a score of fountains, a charming reminder that its very name comes from its waters, *Aquae Sextiae*— sweet water, mind you, with none of the saltiness of Marseille. For if tumultuous Marseille is the great anti-Paris, Aix-en-Provence is the stalwart anti-Marseille— bourgeois and homogeneous, reactionary and haughtily proud of its aristocratic grandeur and good taste. Since 1948 Aix has hosted France's most elite festival of music and opera, while its 580-year-old university not only teaches the arts and humanities to the French but instructs foreign students in the fine arts of French civilization (the more 'practical' science departments are in Marseille); a large percentage of Aix's 170,000 souls are doctors, lawyers, and professors, not to mention financial and underworld nabobs who commute to Marseille; and you can be sure that the National Front posters on reactionary Aix's walls remain unsullied by graffiti. But as much as Aix tries to out-poodle Paris, it can never quite live down having mocked and laughed at Cézanne, the one real genius it produced. The city and artist were at such loggerheads that whenever someone from Aix asked to see his paintings, Cézanne would tell them to get lost.

History

The first version of Aix, the *oppidum* of Entremont, was the capital of the Celto-Ligurian tribe, the Salyens, who liked to decapitate their enemies and tie their heads to the tails of their horses. By 123 BC they had pulled this trick once too often on the Greeks of

187

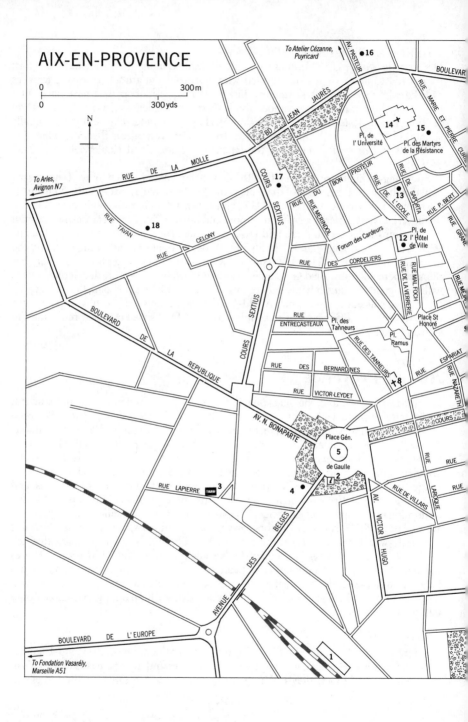

AIX-EN-PROVENCE

0 _____ 300 m
0 _____ 300 yds

N

To Arles,
Avignon N7

To Atelier Cézanne,
Puyricard

●16

BOULEVAR

RUE MARIE ET PIERRE CURIE

AV. PASTEUR

BD JEAN JAURÈS

Pl. de
l' Université

14 ✛

15 ●

Pl. des Martyrs
de la Résistance

RUE DE LA MOLLE

RUE DE

COURS SEXTIUS

17 ●

PASTEUR

RUE DU BON

RUE MERINDOL

RUE DE SABATTA

RUE DE L'ÉCOLE

13 ●

RUE P. BERT

RUE GRAND

RUE TAVAN

●18

CELONY

RUE

Forum des Cardeurs

Pl. de
12 l' Hôtel
● de Ville

RUE DES CORDELIERS

RUE DE LA VERRERIE

RUE MAL FOCH

RUE MER

RUE MÉR

BOULEVARD

DE

LA

RÉPUBLIQUE

SEXTIUS

COURS

RUE
ENTRECASTEAUX

Pl. des
Tanneurs

RUE DES TANNEURS

Place St
Honoré

Pl.
Ramus

ESPARIAT

RUE

RUE NAZARETH

RUE DES BERNARDINES

RUE

✛ 8

RUE VICTOR-LEYDET

AV. N. BONAPARTE

Place Gén.

5

de Gaulle

COURS

RUE

RUE

RUE LAPIERRE

3

4 ●

2

BELGES

AV. VICTOR HUGO

RUE DE VILLARS

LARQUE

RUE

1

BOULEVARD DE L'EUROPE

AVENUE DES

To Fondation Vasarély,
Marseille A51

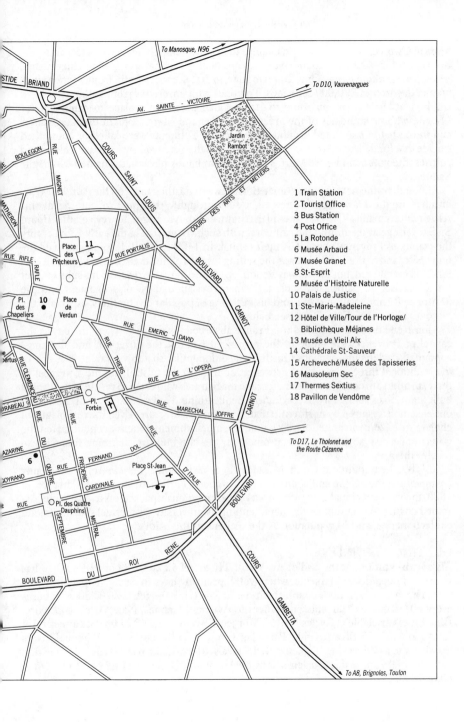

To Manosque, N96

To D10, Vauvenargues

STIDE - BRIAND

AV. SAINTE - VICTOIRE

Jardin Rambot

COURS SAINT - LOUIS

COURS DES ARTS ET METIERS

RUE BOULEGON

RUE MIGNET

MATHERON

RUE RIFLE

RAFLE

Place des Prêcheurs

11

RUE PORTALIS

BOULEVARD CARNOT

Pl. des Chapeliers

10

Place de Verdun

RUE EMERIC DAVID

RUE THIERS

RUE DE L'OPERA

pértus

RUE CLEMENCEAU

MIRABEAU

RUE DU

RUE

Pl. Forbin

RUE MARECHAL JOFFRE

CARNOT

To D17, Le Tholonet and the Route Cézanne

AZARINE

6

RUE DU QUATRE

RUE FREDERIC

FERNAND

DOL

Place St-Jean

D'ITALIE

BOULEVARD

GOYRAND

CARDINALE

7

RUE

Pl. des Quatre Dauphins

SEPTEMBRE

MISTRAL

RENE

ROI

BOULEVARD

DU

COURS

GAMBETTA

To A8, Brignoles, Toulon

1 Train Station
2 Tourist Office
3 Bus Station
4 Post Office
5 La Rotonde
6 Musée Arbaud
7 Musée Granet
8 St-Esprit
9 Musée d'Histoire Naturelle
10 Palais de Justice
11 Ste-Marie-Madeleine
12 Hôtel de Ville/Tour de l'Horloge/
   Bibliothèque Méjanes
13 Musée de Vieil Aix
14 Cathédrale St-Sauveur
15 Archeveché/Musée des Tapisseries
16 Mausoleum Sec
17 Thermes Sextius
18 Pavillon de Vendôme

Massalia, who called in their Roman allies to destoy them. Under Sextius Calvinus, the Romans did just that, and founded a camp at a nearby thermal spring which they named *Aquae Sextiae Salluviorum*. Only 20 years later, in 102 BC, these Latin frontiersmen woke up one day to find 200,000 ferocious Teutones with covered wagons full of wives and children at their door, on route to Italy—looking not for a place to camp but for *lebensraum*. The strategies of the great Roman general Marius caught them unawares, and in the battle that raged around Aix, so many Teutones were killed or committed suicide that for decades Aix enjoyed bumper crops thanks to soil enriched with blood and corpses; the mountain where Marius's final triumph took place was renamed Montagne Sainte-Victoire.

Although by the next century Aquae Sextiae was a bustling town on the Aurelian Way, invaders in the Dark Ages destroyed it so thoroughly that next to nothing of this settlement remains. Only in the 11th century did Aix begin to revive: the Bourg St-Sauveur grew up around the cathedral with such vigour that in the early 13th century the counts of Provence chose it as their capital. In 1409 Louis II d'Anjou endowed the university; and in the 1450s Aix was the setting for the refined court of Good King René, fondly remembered, not for the way he squeezed every possible *sou* from his subjects, but for the artists he patronized such as Francesco Laurana, Nicolas Froment and the Maître de l'Annonciation d'Aix, and his initiating of popular celebrations, especially the masquerades of the Fête-Dieu (see below).

After René died (at Aix, in 1486), France absorbed his realm and kept the city as the capital of Provence, the home of the provincial Estates, the governor, and the king-appointed Parlement—the latter institution so unpopular that it was counted as one of the traditional three 'plagues' of Provence, along with the mistral and the Durance. In the 17th and 18th centuries, the aristocratic magistrates who came to reside in the capital built themselves refined *hôtels particuliers*, bequeathing Aix a rare, stylistically harmonious ensemble inspired by northern Italian Baroque architecture. Even the real plague of cholera in 1720 contributed to Aix's unique embellishment, when it contaminated the water; once new sources had been piped in, the city built its charming fountains to receive them.

In 1789, the tumultuous Count Mirabeau became a popular hero in Aix by eloquently championing the people and condemning Provence's Parlement as unrepresentative; in 1800, the whole regional government was unceremoniously packed off to Marseille. Aix settled down to a venerable retirement, tending its university, its thermal spa, its almond confectioneries, and its reputation as the 'Athens of the Midi'.

GETTING AROUND

Aix's **train station**, at the end of Av. Victor-Hugo, tel 42 26 02 89 or 91 08 50 50 has hourly connections to Marseille, where you'll probably have to change to get anywhere else. The more tumultuous **coach station** is in Rue Lapierre, tel 42 26 01 50, with buses every 20/30 min to Marseille and others to Avignon, Cannes, Nice, Arles, and more. **Bike hire** is available at Cycles Nadéo, Montée d'Avignon, tel 42 21 06 93; **car rental** at Location ADA, 53 Blvd Aristide-Briand or Contrat, 33 Blvd de la République. Drivers should try to avoid playing chicken with the locals' Mercs in the narrow alleys of Vieil Aix, and park in the Place des Cardeurs or by the bus station. For a taxi ring 42 27 71 11 or at night 42 26 29 30.

TOURIST INFORMATION
Place du Général-de-Gaulle, tel 42 26 02 93; guided tours of Aix daily at 10, 3:30, and 9, in English Wed at 10 am (40 F). They also sponsor various *Promenades en Land Rover* (2 hours, half-days or whole days) through the beautiful Aixois countryside.

Cours Mirabeau

Canopied by its soaring plane trees, decked with fountains and flanked by cafés, banks, pâtisseries, and *hôtels particuliers* of the 17th and 18th centuries, **Cours Mirabeau**, 'the most satisfying street in France', is the centre stage for Aixois society. Laid out in 1649 to replace the south walls, it begins in Place Général de Gaulle, which takes the old roads from Marseille and Arles and spins them around the pompous Second Empire fountain **La Rotonde**. Other fountains punctuate the Cours itself, like the lumpy, mossy **Fontaine d'Eau Chaude**, oozing up its much esteemed 34° water, and at the far end, the **Fontaine du Roi René**, with a fairy-tale statue of the good monarch holding up a bunch of the muscat grapes he introduced to Provence (along with the turkey and silkworms, which the sculptor left out).

Of the fine mansions on the Cours, No. 12 is where Mirabeau wed the aristocratic Emilie de Covet-Marignane in 1772, after playing her a dastardly trick. When the young lady refused his marriage proposal, Mirabeau sneaked into her house and appeared in the morning on her balcony, clad only in his nightshirt and socks, publically compromising her virtue. In revenge, his new father-in-law refused the couple any money, and when Mirabeau ran up huge debts, he signed the order to have him imprisoned in the Château d'If. Mirabeau returned to Aix to plead in the subsequent divorce case, and despite his unparalleled eloquence, he lost the appeal. Thus rebuked by his noble peers, he returned to Aix in 1789 as a member of the Third Estate and proceeded to attack their privileges—a trial run for his major role in igniting the Revolution in Paris.

Cézanne grew up at 55 Cours Mirabeau, the son of a hatter who later turned banker (on the façade you can still make out the sign of the *chapelier*). Nearby, at No. 53, the elegant mirrored café **Les Deux Garçons** has been Aix's smartest place to see and be seen since World War II, with a reputation and price list similar to Paris's famous café-citadels of artsy existentialist mumbo-jumbo; until recently North Africans were not admitted to enjoy its rarefied air. It looks across towards the weighty façade of the 1647 **Hôtel Maurel de Pontevès** (No. 38), the building that was the inspiration for Aix's secular Baroque—still supported after all these years by two musclebound stone giants.

South of Cours Mirabeau lies the **Quartier Mazarin**, its straight lanes laid out according to the rules of Renaissance urban design by the archbishop brother of the famous cardinal. At 2a Rue du Quatre Septembre, the **Musée Paul Arbaud** (open daily 2–5, closed Sun, adm) is the city's overflow tank for odds and ends, especially Provençal ceramics and a few hundred portraits of Mirabeau's overlarge pockmarked head.

Musée Granet

Two streets south of the Musée Arnaud, and left at the Fountain of the Four Dolphins are the meatier archaeology and art collections of the **Musée Granet** in the former 1675

Priory of the Knights of Malta (Place St-Jean, open daily 10–12 and 2–6; closed Tues Sept–May only, adm). In the basement and ground floor sections there's a superb **statue of a Persian Warrior** (200 BC) of the Pergamon school, finds from Roman Aquae Sextiae, and unique **sculptures from the Salian sanctuary at Entremont**, believed to be the oldest in Gaul. Appropriately enough for residents of the land that would invent the guillotine, the overall theme is cult decapitation. The remains of 15 embalmed heads were found in the sanctuary, and the sculptures on display here, like death masks, may have been carved to replace real heads that mouldered away; according to Tertullian, the Celts would spend nights with their dead ancestors, seeking oracular advice. One head, with a hand on top, has the same face as the famous gold mask of Agamemnon from Mycenae (thanks to the proximity of Marseille, Greek stylistic influences are strong); another head resembles not a dead man, but a resurrected youth.

A far more insidious worship of death waits upstairs. The Aixois François Granet (1775–1849), after whom the museum is named, was a minor neoclassical artist and a crony of Ingres, enabling him to secure for Aix the latter's enormous *Jupiter and Thetis* (1811), arguably Ingres' most objectionable canvas. But the real culprit behind this smirking art is Napoleon, whose totalitarian approach to statecraft opened a Pandora's box of kitsch: art like this is born when cloying sentiment and a cynical manipulation of the classical past are evoked to serve political ends. The expression on Jupiter's magnificently stupid face not only sums up a whole era, but looks ahead to the even more cynical kitsch-mongers of the 20th century, who make Napoleon look like Little Red Riding Hood.

The museum also has Ingres's far more palatable and subtle *Portrait of Granet*, painted while the two artists sojourned at Rome's Villa Medici, and canvases by other neoclassical painters including David, Gros, and Granet himself. There is an extensive collection of Dutch and Italian Baroque paintings; flattering 17th-century artistocratic portraits of Aixois nobility by Largillère and Rigaud; and works by Provençal painters such as Guigou, Loubon, and Monticelli. But what of Cézanne, who took his first drawing-classes in this very building? For years he was represented by only three measly watercolours (no one in Aix would buy his works), until 1984 when the French government rectified the omission by depositing eight small canvases here that touch on the major themes of his work.

Vieil Aix

Shops, cafés, and sumptuous, overflowing outdoor markets of every kind fill the narrow lanes and squares of Vieil Aix, north of Cours Mirabeau. Enter by way of Rue Espariat from Place Général de Gaulle, and you'll come to a cast-iron Baroque campanile and the church of **St-Esprit**, where a 16th-century retable has portraits of 12 members of the first Provençal Parlement cast in the roles of the apostles. Further up, just beyond Aix's most elegant little square, the cobbled, fountained **Place d'Albertas**, you can pop into the lavish, Puget-inspired Hôtel Boyer d'Eguilles of 1675, now the **Musée d'Histoire Naturelle** at 6 Rue Espariat (10–12 and 2–6, closed Sun)—well worth it for an impressive 17th-century interior, a grand stair, and a notable clutch of petrified dinosaur eggs.

The street ends at the neoclassical **Palais de Justice**, a dull building of the 1760s that hardly merited the demolition of a well-preserved Roman mausoleum and the medieval palace of the counts of Provence. Aix's flea-market occupies the adjacent Place de Verdun; opposite, the **Place des Prêcheurs** was laid out in 1450 by King René for popular entertainments and all kinds of executions; in 1772 the Marquis de Sade and his valet were burned in effigy here after sodomizing some prostitutes in Marseille. Facing the square, the church of **Ste Marie-Madeleine** has paintings by Rubens and Van Loo, though the show-stopper is the central panel of the *Triptych of the Annunciation*, a luminous work of the 1440s painted for a local draper. The panel has provoked endless controversy over its attribution (it is perhaps by the same painter who illuminated King René's courtly allegories in the famous *Livre du Coeur d'Amour Epris* in Vienna's National Library), and over its singular iconography that would seem to detract from the pious message: the angel Gabriel with wings of owl feathers (a bird of evil omen) kneels in the porch of a Gothic church, decorated with a bat and a dragon. From on high, an unconventionally gesturing God the Father sends down a bizarre foetus in a golden ray, just missing a monkey's head; a vase of flowers holds poisonous belladonna.

The more orthodox blooms of Aix's flower market lend an intoxicating perfume to the square in the very heart of Vieil Aix, in front of the stately **Hôtel de Ville** (1671), a perfectly proportioned building decorated with stone flowers and fruits and intricate iron grilles. Upstairs, the **Bibliothèque Méjanes** has a rich collection of incunabula and illuminated manuscripts, some of which are usually on display, along with exhibits relating to the **Fondation St-John Perse**, a museum and study centre bequeathed to Aix by the French poet who won the Nobel Prize in 1960. Next to the town hall, the flamboyant **Tour de l'Horloge** (1510) has clocks telling the hour and the phase of the moon, as well as wooden statues that change with the season. From here, Rue de Saporta leads to the **Musée du Vieil Aix**, at No. 17 (10–12 and 2–5, closed Mon, adm), housed in another grand 17th-century hôtel with another magnificent staircase. It stores some quaint paintings on velvet, a bevy of *santons*, and marionettes made in the 19th century to represent the biblical, pagan, and local personages who figured in King René's Fête-Dieu processions, beginning with a figure representing Moses and someone tossing a cat up and down, and ending with Death swinging his scythe.

Cathédrale de St-Sauveur, the Tapestry Museum and Joseph Sec

Rue de Saporta continues north to the **Cathédrale de St-Sauveur**, a curious patch-work of periods and styles that houses a treasure trove of art. The statues that adorned the central flamboyant portal of 1340 were destroyed in the Revolution, except for the Virgin, who was spared when someone popped a red cap of Liberty on her head, and made Mary a Marianne. The interior has a central Gothic nave, a Baroque aisle on the left and a Romanesque aisle on the right; on the walls are 26 tapestries on the lives of Christ and the Virgin made in Brussels in 1510. These originally hung in Canterbury Cathedral, but were sold by the Commonwealth, and purchased by a cathedral canon in Paris for next to nothing in 1656.

The cathedral's most famous treasure, Nicolas Froment's Flemish-inspired **Trip-tyque du Buisson Ardent** (1476) is on the right wall of the Gothic nave, and opened only on request, by the eloquent sacristan (though usually not on Tues and Sun). On the two folding panels are portraits of King René, who commissioned the work, and his second wife, kneeling amongst saints, while the central scene depicts the vision of a monk of St-Victor of Marseille, who saw the Virgin and Child appear amidst the miraculous burning bush vouchsafed to Moses. The flames in the green bush symbolize her virginity, as does the unicorn; the mirror held by the Child symbolizes his incarnation. The meticulously-detailed castles in the background may have been inspired by the towers of Tarascon and Beaucaire. The sacristan will also unlock the covers over the fine walnut panels of the west door, carved in 1504 by Jean Guiramand of Toulon with figures of four Old Testament prophets and the twelve sibyls who were said to have predicted the coming of Christ to the pagans.

Another curious painting of the same period, the *Martyrdom of St Mitre* is behind the high altar, an illustration that Aix's ancient interest in decapitation still lingered into the 1400s. Mitre, a Christian accused of sorcery, had his head chopped off by Roman soldiers. His trunk then picked up the head (already adorned with a halo) and carried it into the cathedral. The sight scared the children but made the Romans, who had a modern sense of humour, laugh until they cried.

The Romanesque aisle on the right harbours the oldest section of St-Sauveur, the 5th-century octagonal **baptistry**, its pool encircled by recycled columns from the temple of Apollo that once stood on this site. Nearby, the 5th-century sarcophagus of St Mitre has a hole that emits an ooze collected by the faithful to heal eye diseases. In the Baroque aisle, the Chapelle de Ste-Anne has the **altar des Aygosi** (1470), attributed to the Istrian Francesco Laurana. The *Crucifixion* shows the skull of Adam at the base of the Cross, while above Christ's head is a pelican, who according to medieval legend, feeds her nestlings with her own blood. Below stand SS. Anne, Marcel, and Marguerite, the latter piously emerging from the shoulders of the dragon that swallowed her whole. Last, but not least, don't miss the light, airy, twin-columned, 12th-century **cloister**, with capitals daintily carved, though in an awful state of repair.

Cloister, St-Sauveur, Aix-en-Provence

194

To the right of the cathedral, the grand 17th–18th-century residence of Aix's archbishops, **L'Archevêché** is the setting for the festival's operas. It also houses the **Musée des Tapisseries** (Tapestry Museum—9:30–12 and 2:30–5:30, closed Tues, adm), containing three sets of lighthearted Beauvais tapestries, which were hidden under the roof during the Revolution and rediscovered only in the 1840s. The set known as the *Grotesques* (1689) features arabesques, animals, dancers, and musicians; there are nine rococo scenes from the story of *Don Quixote* (1740s), and four on the subject of *Jeux Russiens* (1769–93), inspired by the rustic frolics that the court of Louis XVI got up to in the backwoods of Versailles.

Just north of the cathedral on Av. Pasteur stands an eccentric relic, the 1792 **Mausoleum Sec**, believed to be a symbolic discourse on the Revolution that spoiled those pampered bucolic daydreams. Joseph Sec, the builder, was a Jacobin who made his fortune floating timber down the Durance, and no one has ever satisfactorily explained the meaning behind the reliefs and statues of biblical characters, allegories, and masonic and symbols he chose for his mausoleum.

Cézanne, Vasarély and the Pavillon de Vendôme

Paul Cézanne spent an idyllic childhood roaming Aix's countryside with his best friend, Emile Zola, and as an adult painted those same landscapes in a way landscapes had never been painted before. The **Atelier Cézanne**, the studio he built in 1897, a half-kilometre north of the cathedral (9 Av. Paul Cézanne; 10–12 and 2–5, summer 2:30–6, closed Tues, adm) has been grudgingly maintained as it was when the master died in 1906, with a few drawings, unfinished canvases, his smock, palette, pipe and some of the bottles and skulls used in his still-lifes. Which is all very well, though for a better understanding of Cézanne's art, pick up the *Itinéraires de Cézanne* (on sale here), a guide to his favourite landscapes around Aix.

Cézanne's family home at Jas de Bouffan is now dominated by the irritating black and white cubic forms of the **Fondation Vasarély**, 1 Av. Marcel Pagnol (a 25-minute walk southwest of town, or bus 12 from La Rotonde; open Wed–Sun 9:30–12:30 and 2–5:30, adm). Inaugurated in 1976 by the same op/geometric/kinetic artist who created Gordes' 'didactic' museum, it is just as pretentious, claiming as its goal the desire to promote 'more human' buildings, especially low income housing estates. A laudable goal surely, which Vasarély could have served better by spending his money on houses poor people could actually live in, instead of on cute capers like the *trompe-l'oeil* 'mural integrations' displayed here in hexagonally-shaped rooms. The foundation offers endless images to look at, and lots of words: pack an aspirin.

Along the boulevards west of Aix, you can find a cure for your aix and pains at the revived Roman spa, **Thermes Sextius** on Cours Sextius, or visit the lavish 1665 summer house and gardens built for a cardinal, the **Pavillon de Vendôme**, 34 Rue Célony (closed during lunch and on Tues); it has yet another impressive grand stair and patrician furnishings, and on the façade, a pair of Atlantes, who by their expressions have just been staring into one of Vasarély's more fiendish optical illusions.

195

Aix-urbia: Montagne Ste-Victoire, Puyricard and the Arc Valley

The serene, gently rolling countryside around Aix is the quintessence of Provence for those who love Cézanne: the ochre soil, the dusty green cypresses—as still and classical as Van Gogh's are possessed and writhing—the simple geometric forms of its houses and the pyramidal prow of the bluish-limestone **Montagne Ste-Victoire**. These landscapes east of Aix along the D 17 (the **Route Cézanne**) are so inextricably a part of Cézanne's art that one can only wonder who created what. What if this grouchy, lonely genius had been born in Manchester or New Jersey?

The Route Cézanne leads to the wooded park and Italianate château of **Le Tholonet**, where Cézanne often painted the view towards the Ste-Victoire, a mountain that appears in at least 60 of his canvases ('I am trying to get it right,' he explained). The château belongs to the local canal authority, while the park is used as a venue for Aix's music festival (bus from La Rotonde). The entire 60-km route around the mountain by way of Beaurecueil, Puyloubier and **Pourrières** is especially lovely, decked with the vineyards that produce Coteaux d'Aix-en-Provence. Pourrières is said to be named after *Campi putridi*, the field of putrefaction, where the unburied corpses of the Teutones rotted after Marius's victory; local farmers made vine trellises from their bones. A trophy was erected to Marius here, showing the victorious general carried shoulder-high on his shield by his soldiers. When it eroded away, parts of it were salvaged and reconstructed as a fountain.

The two-hour path (GR 9) to the top of the Ste-Victoire requires only a pair of sturdy shoes, water and stamina, and begins on the north side from Les Cabassols, near **Vauvenargues** in the Vallée de l'Infernet. At the summit, there's a 17th-century stone *refuge* with water and a fireplace if you want to spend a night, and the 17-m **Croix de Provence**, which Cézanne never painted, but has been here, in one form or another, since the 16th century. Legend has it that Marius stood on this precipice, watching his troops annihilate the Teutones, then, at the urging of his sybil Martha, had 300 defeated chieftains brought up and tossed into the celebrated chasm called the **Garagaï**. One legend claims the floor of the Garagaï is occupied by an enchanted lake and meadows, abode of the legendary Golden Goat of Provence; shepherds would lower their sick sheep and cows down on ropes to graze the therapeutic grass. Others speculated that it was the entrance to hell, or linked to the Fountain of Vaucluse (and indeed, fluoride released here surfaced there three months later). In the 17th century, curiosity reached such a pitch that the Parlement in Aix offered a condemned man his freedom if he would agree to be lowered into the Garagaï and tell what he found. Carefully trussed, the man went down, but was strangled in the ropes before he reached the bottom.

Vauvenargues' 14th-century château was the home of Luc de Clapiers (1715–47) Marquis de Vauvenargues and author of the *Introduction à la connaissance de l'esprit humain*, in which he wrote that 'the highest perfection of the human soul is to make it capable of pleasure.' In 1958, the château was purchased by Picasso, who probably would have agreed with him. Although the building is closed to the public you can see Picasso's grave and a few of his sculptures in the garden. One of the most idyllic roads in the area, the D 11 (parallel to GR 9) descends north of Vauvenargues for 13 kilometres to **Jouques**, sheltered in a cool, green valley.

Four kilometres to the north, overlooking modern Aix is the plateau where the city's story began, the Celto-Ligurian **Oppidum of Entremont** (9–12 and 2–6 exc Tues). Similar to the prehistoric Nages in Languedoc, its primitive stone houses were built in clusters along parallel streets, and you can trace the foundations of the large public building that produced the Granet museum's sculptures. You can get there on the bus to Puyricard, which continues north to the **Chocolaterie Puyricard** where some of the most delectable (and expensive) fresh chocolates you'll ever taste are made in the traditional pre-Willy Wonka manner.

To the west of Aix, the D 64 continues for 10 km from the Fondation Vasarély to the impressive three-tiered **Aqueduc de Roquefavour** (1847), twice as high as the Pont du Gard and built across the valley of the river Arc to bring the waters of the Durance to Marseille. The wooded setting is delightful—the Arc is the river where Cézanne painted his famous proto-Cubist scenes of bathers. The edge of the Arc valley is dotted with old farms and *villages perchés*: **Eguilles** north on the D 543, with fine views from its William Morris-style medieval château (now the *mairie*); and south, off the busy Aix-Marseille routes, lofty **Cabriès** and **Mimet**. **Gardanne**, an old village often painted by Cézanne, has remained unchanged, defended by an ugly ring of industry.

 ### Coteaux-d'Aix-en-Provence and La Palette

One of the hottest political potatoes in Provence is the route of the *TGV Provençal* planned for 1997, which would cut out the heart of this relatively recent AOC district just as it has begun to make a name for its red, rosé and white wines. Coteaux-d'Aix-en-Provence originates in 50 communes in the highlands stretching from the Durance to Marignane, and west to Salon and east to the flanks of Montagne Ste-Victoire, and consists of the region's traditional syrah, grenache, cinsault, mourvèdre, and carignan grapes, enhanced in the past 20 years with the addition of cabernet-sauvignon, a stock that has improved the wine's ageing ability. Coteaux-d'Aix's sunny whites are made from sauvignon, grenache blanc and ugni—but never from René's sweet muscat grapes, although these now grow merrily in Roussillon.

Many growers welcome visitors, such as Puyricard's **Château du Seuil**, a handsomely restored 13th-century bastide, where the 89 reds and 90 whites are an excellent buy (tel 42 92 15 99). Or head further north, 20 km from Aix, to Le Puy Ste-Réparade and the lush estate of **Château de Fonscolombe** on the banks of the Durance, where the Marquis de Saporta raises swans and produces classic, fragrant red, rosé, and white wines (tel 42 28 60 05). Further afield, another estate that welcomes visitors also supplies some of France's best restaurants: Denis Langue's 120-hectare **Château de Calissanne**, overlooking the Etang de Berre on the site of an ancient Celtic *oppidum* (on the D 10, near Lançon-Provence, tel 90 42 63 03). On the south bank of the lagoon, one of the sunniest corners of France, **Château St-Jean** produces prize-winning rosés (dominated by counoise, an old-fashioned stock, mixed with grenache and carignan) and reds full of old-fashioned finesse (at Gignac-la-Nerth near Marignane, tel 42 88 55 15).

La Palette is a venerable microscopic AOC region on a north-facing limestone scree east of Aix, on the left bank of the Arc; although fairly sheltered from the mistral, it has cooler summer and winter temperatures than its environs. La Palette's red, white, and rosé nectar has been served for the royal fêtes of such diverse monarchs as King René and Edward VII, but only two estates still produce this rare fine wine of the south, aged in small casks: the celebrated 150-year-old **Château Simone**, at Meyreuil (off the pretty D 58H, tel 42 66 92 58) where dark, violet-scented reds are kept for three years in caves carved out by 16th-century Carmelites, and **Château Crémade**, a 17th-century bastide in Le Tholonet, which bottles magnificent, well-structured red wines and a fruity blanc de blancs (tel 42 66 92 66).

FESTIVALS
Aix publishes a free monthly guide to events, *Le Mois à Aix*, which comes in especially handy during Aix's summer festivals. Headquarters and general booking office for these is the **Comité Officiel des Fêtes**, Complexe Forbin, Cours Gambetta, tel 42 63 06 75. The most famous is the **International Music Festival**, featuring celebrity opera and classical music during the last three weeks of July. This highbrow (and *very* expensive) affair is supplemented with lively alternative performances in the streets and smaller theatres. It is preceded by a less formal **Rock Festival**, an umbrella title that includes jazz, big band music, and chamber music during the second and third weeks of June. This is followed, in the first part of July, by the **International Dance Festival**, ranging from classical ballet to jazz and contemporary dance.

SHOPPING
You can pick up books in English at **Paradox**, 2 Rue Reine-Jeanne, tel 42 26 47 99, and the **Centre Franco-Américain de Provence**, 24 Place des Martyrs de la Résistance, which also organizes exchanges, au pair work, and courses. The traditional souvenirs of Aix are its almond sweets, *calissons*, which have been made here since the 1500s; buy them at Bechard, 12 Cours Mirabeau or Brémond Fils, 36 Cours Mirabeau. If you can't make it up to the chocolate factory at Puyricard, they have a shop at 7 Rue Rifle-Rafle, off Place des Prêcheurs.

Market Days: every morning in Place Richelme; flea-market and crafts Tuesday, Thursday and Saturday in Place du Palais de Justice; flower market in Place de l'Hôtel de Ville Tuesday, Thursday and Saturday.

WHERE TO STAY   (postal code 13100)
If you want to come in the summer during the festivals, you can't book early enough; Aix's few cheap hotels fill up especially fast. In the luxury category, there's the romantic ****Pullman Le Pigonnet**, on the outskirts at 5 Av. du Pigonnet, tel 42 59 02 90, with rose arbours, lovely rooms furnished with antiques, and views out over the Aix countryside. Or stay in the centre, in the renovated, elegant 18th-century *****Grand Hôtel Nègre-Coste**, 33 Cours Mirabeau, tel 42 27 74 22, still hoisting guests in its original elevator (no restaurant), or at the *****Mercure Paul Cézanne**, 40 Av. Victor Hugo (near the train station), tel 42 26 34 73, an exceptional little hotel, furnished with antiques and serving delicious breakfasts. Two of Aix's medieval religious buildings have been converted into hotels: the 12th-century convent of *****Les Augustins**, 3 Rue de la Masse, just off Cours Mirabeau, tel 42 27 28 59, which has soundproofed rooms and a breakfast garden and *****Le Manoir**, 8 Rue Entrecasteaux, tel 42 26 27 20, built around a 12th-century cloister. The home of composer Darius Milhaud (who grew up in Aix) has been restored as a hotel, ****La Renaissance**, 4 Blvd da la République,

tel 42 26 04 22. Outside of the centre, the most charming choice is the 17th-century *Le Prieuré, Rte de Sisteron, tel 42 21 05 23. Cheaper choices in town include *Pax, near Place d'Albertas, on 29 Rue Espariat, tel 42 26 24 79; *Du Casino, off Rue Espariat at 38 Rue Victor-Leydet, tel 42 26 06 88; and *Splendid, 69 Cours Mirabeau, tel 42 38 19 53, not so splendid, but an undeniably smart address. The modern **Auberge de Jeunesse** is by the Fondation Vasarély, at 3 Av. Marcel Pagnol (bus 12), tel 42 20 15 99.

There are two superb inns off the Route de Cézanne in **Beaurecueil** (13100): ***Mas de la Bertrande**, Chemin de la Plaine, tel 42 28 90 09 (closed mid-Feb to mid-Mar) and **Relais Ste-Victoire**, tel 42 66 94 98 (closed Feb) both with pools, plenty of Provence atmosphere, and delicious menus beginning around 200 F. Or sleep in a 12th-century château perched high over the village of **Meyrargues** (13650), north of Aix, near the Durance: ***Hostellerie du Château de Meyrargues**, tel 42 57 50 32, which does its best to fulfil whatever Hollywood castle fantasies you may have, down to the tapestries, log fires, and antique furniture.

EATING OUT

Unlike Marseille's, Aix's 400 restaurants aren't famous for their food, and the food they serve is not a bargain, though always remember a lunch menu costs a lot less than dinner. This is especially true at places like **Le Bistro Latin**, 18 Rue de la Couronne (just north of Place Général de Gaulle, tel 42 38 22 88), featuring imaginative variations on local themes such as leg of lamb with herbs, with refreshingly reasonable prices: lunch menu 85 F; dinner 100 F and up. **Le Clos de la Violette**, 10 Av. de la Violette, tel 42 23 30 71, has long been considered the best in Aix, and does wonderful things with crab and rabbit (lunch menu 180 F, dinner menus from 275 F). A favourite bistrot, **Chez Gu et Fils**, 3 Rue F. Mistral, tel 42 26 75 12, has Provençal dishes and fresh pasta (lunch menu 90 F).

Most of the cheaper choices have an ethnic twist. Especially good is the Egyptian, **Kéops**, 28 Rue de la Verrerie, tel 42 96 59 05 (menus 65 and 90 F); the Tunisian **Djerba**, 8 bis Rue Rifle-Rafle, tel 42 21 52 41, with couscous and a lot more for less than 100 F; the Italian **Amalfi**, 5 Rue d'Entrecasteaux, tel 42 38 30 01 (85 F menus); Spanish tapas and paella at **La Bodéga**, 8 Rue Campra (just south of the Archevêché) tel 42 96 05 85, with live flamenco on Fri and Sat nights (80–100 F), and least expensive of all, **L'Hacienda**, 7 Rue Mérindol (near Place des Cardeurs) tel 42 27 76 82, which has a 58 F menu including wine.

ENTERTAINMENT AND NIGHTLIFE

Outside the festival season, the large student population keeps a number of jazz clubs in business, such as **Hot Brass**, west of the centre on Rte d'Eguilles-Célony, tel 42 21 05 57, or **Le Scat**, 11 Rue de la Verrerie, tel 42 23 00 23. **La Chimère**, outside of town at Montée d'Avignon, tel 42 23 36 28, is Aix's main gay bar and disco. Films in their original language are shown at **Le Mazarin**, 6 Rue Laroque, tel 42 26 99 85.

Lastly, lovers of cornball roadside attractions can visit a concrete whale, Gulliver, and a giant caterpillar at the **Village des Automates**, on the N 7 towards St-Cannat (10–6 daily April–Sept, other times Wed and weekends only, adm).

Part VII
THE PROVENÇAL ALPS

Semper Virum

The Côte d'Azur has an admirably spacious back garden, rolling over mountains and plateaus from the Italian border to the valley of the Durance, and covering the better part of three *départements*. Yet it has only two towns of any size in it, Digne and Draguignan. Between them are plenty of wide open spaces, landscapes on an Arizonan scale including even a Grand Canyon worthy of the name.

But is there really anything up here to tempt you away from the fleshpots of the Côte d'Azur? The stars of the east, in this huge and diverse area are beyond doubt the spectacular mountains, Italianate villages and frescoed churches of the **Alpes-Maritimes**, inland from Monaco and Nice. Everything to the west is limestone, eroded into fantastically-shaped mountains and deep gorges, such as the *clues* north of Grasse and the canyons that run almost the entire length of the Verdon—including the Grand one, a sight not to be missed. Further south the landscapes become gentler and greener; you may find the Provence you're looking for in the amiable and relatively unspoiled villages and wine country around Draguignan.

Les Alpes-Maritimes

Lacet means a shoelace, or a hairpin-turn. It's a word you'll need to know if you try to drive up here, on the worst mountain roads in Europe, designed for mules and never improved. When you see a sign announcing '20 *lacets* ahead', prepare for ten minutes in second gear, close encounters with demented lorry drivers, and a bad case of nerves.

200

So, what do you get for your trouble, in this corrugated department where the Alps stretch down to the sea? For starters these are *real* Alps—arrogant crystalline giants, who make their contempt felt as we crawl through the valleys beneath. Up in Switzerland, they would have enough altitude to make the geography books. Close to the sea, their numbers aren't overwhelming—but if you think 2845-m Mt Bégo is a foothill, try climbing it. Bégo is a holy mountain, an Ararat or a Mount Meru, a prehistoric pilgrimage site for the ancient Ligurians.

The scenery defies any travel writer's verbiage, a jigsaw-puzzle panorama at the turn of every *lacet*. The best parts have been set aside as the **Parc National du Mercantour**. In the valleys of the Roya and the Tinée, there's another attraction—all those *lacets* will also take you to the some of the finest Renaissance painting in the Midi.

The Parc Mercantour

The highest regions of this *département* are contained in the **Parc National du Mercantour**, stretching along the Italian border for over 128 km, and joining with the adjacent Argentera National Park in Italy to make a unique preserve of Alpine and Mediterranean wildlife. Established only in 1979, it consists of a central 'protected zone', a narrow strip of the most inaccessible areas, including the Vallée des Merveilles with its prehistoric rock carvings (see below), and a much larger 'peripheral zone' that includes all the villages from Sospel to St-Etienne-de-Tinée and beyond. There are many excellent hiking trails, some of which allow you to cross over into Italy. The park rangers, all local people, have an excellent reputation for helpfulness and knowledge. They enforce some strict rules in the protected zone: no tents, dogs, or fires, no motor vehicles (though all-terrain vehicles have recently been allowed on trails only, as an experiment), and no collecting flowers, insects or anything else.

The most spectacular Alpine fauna, and the sort you're most likely to see, are the birds of prey: golden eagles, falcons and vultures; a recent addition, reintroduced from the Balkans after becoming extinct here, is the mighty *gypaète barbu* (lammergeyer), a 'bearded' vulture with a bizarre face, orange-red feathers, black wings and a reputation for carrying off lambs and children. On the ground, there's the ubiquitous stoat, or ermine, popping out of the snow in his white winter coat and looking entirely too cute to be made into royal coat linings, also his bulkier cousin the marmot, and plenty of boars, foxes, *mouflons* (wild mountain sheep), chamois and, in the more inaccessible places, *bouquetins* (ibex). All of these have been rapidly increasing in number since the establishment of the park.

As for wildflowers, the symbol of the park is the spiky *saxifrage multiflora*, one of 25 species found here and nowhere else. Edelweiss exists, but is as elusive as anywhere else. Beyond these exotic blooms, there is a tremendous wealth of everything that grows. Blue gentians and anemones are everywhere, plus hundreds of other species, in micro-climates that range from Mediterranean to Alpine. Half the flowers of the whole of France are represented here.

There are several **Park Information Centres**:

Tende (06430): Av. 16 Septembre, tel 93 04 67 00.
Casterino (Vallée des Merveilles): Maison de la Minière, tel 93 04 68 66.

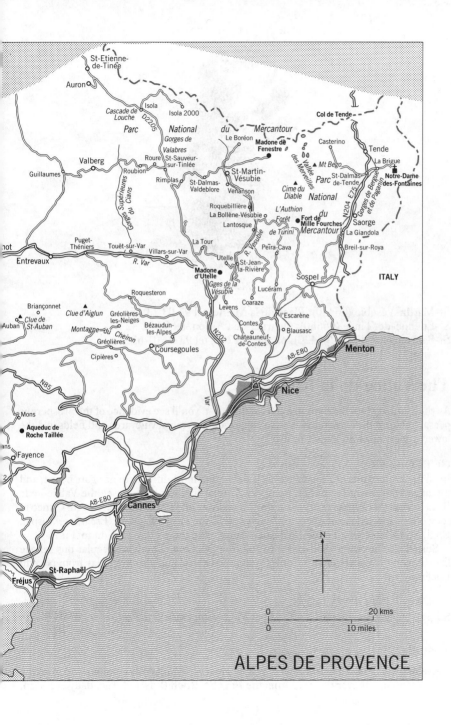

St-Etienne-
de-Tinée

Auron

Cascade de
Louche

Isola

Isola 2000

Col de Tende

Parc

National

du

Mercantour

Le Boréon

Casterino

Tende

Valberg

Gorges de
Valabres

Madone de
Fenestre

La Brigue

Guillaumes

Roure

Roubion

St-Sauveur-
sur-Tinlée

Mt Bego

St-Dalmas-
de-Tende

Notre-Dame
des-Fontaines

Rimplas

St-Martin-
Vésubie

Parc

St-Dalmas-
Valdeblore

Venanson

Cime du
Diable

National

Roquebillière

L'Authion

du

Saorge

La Bollène-Vésubie

Lantosque

Forêt

Fort de
Mille Fourches

La Giandola

Puget-
Théniers

Touët-sur-Var

La Tour

de Turini

Mercantour

Breil-sur-Roya

not

Entrevaux

Villars-sur-Var

R. Var

Utelle

Peïra-Cava

Madone
d'Utelle

St-Jean-
la-Rivière

Briançonnet

Roqueston

 Gges de la
Vésubie

Lucéram

Sospel

ITALY

Clue de
St-Auban

Clue d'Aiglun

Gréolières-
les-Neiges

Coaraze

l'Escarène

Auban

Montagne du Cheiron

Bézaudun-
les-Alpes

Levens

Contes

Blausasc

Gréolières

Châteauneuf-
de-Contes

Menton

Cipières

Coursegoules

Mons

Var

Nice

Aqueduc de
Roche Taillée

Fayence

A8-E80

Cannes

N

St-Raphaël

Fréjus

0   20 kms

0   10 miles

ALPES DE PROVENCE

Marmot

St-Martin-Vésubie (06450): Place de la Mairie, tel 93 03 23 15.
St-Etienne-de-Tinée (06660): Quartier de l'Ardon, tel 93 02 42 27.
St-Sauveur-sur-Tinée (06420): on the D 2205, tel 93 02 01 63.

The Vallée de la Roya

As you climb up into the mountains from the coast, you'll see evidence of the prosperous peasant culture these mountains once supported. Terraced vineyards and fields line the lower slopes, most no longer in use.

GETTING AROUND
In all the hinterlands of Provence, this is the region most difficult to navigate by car, and the most convenient for public transport. One of the best ways to see the Vallée de la Roya is from that Alpine rarity—a train. The railway line from Nice that runs to Cuneo in Italy offers spectacular scenery and serves all of the local villages: L'Escarène, Sospel, Breil, St-Dalmas and Tende (five each, daily). One train a day goes on to Turin.
    Sospel also has three daily buses to and from Menton. There is a regular bus service from Nice to L'Escarène and Contes—some 20 a day, and also five a day from Nice to Lucéram.

TOURIST INFORMATION
Sospel (06380): In summer, on the Pont Vieux, otherwise at the *mairie*, tel 93 04 00 19.

Sospel

Travelling along the road from Nice, Sospel greets you with rusty cannons and machine guns, pointing out over the road from the **Fort St-Roch** (July and Aug, daily exc Mon, otherwise Sat and Sun, 2–6). The fortress, almost entirely underground, shows only a few blockhouses, in a sort of military Art Deco; it dates from a 30s counterpart of the Maginot Line. Inside, exhibits show details of its short career. The fort was designed to keep the Italians out, which it did with ease until the French surrender in 1940. Four years later, in September 1944, Sospel found itself on the front line again—the vexing *sitzkrieg* of the Provençal front, where the Allies had no effort to spare for a serious advance. The Germans held out in Sospel until almost the end of the war.

Through all that, the town suffered considerable damage, now entirely, and lovingly, restored, including Sospel's landmark, the **Pont Vieux**, the base of which dates back to the 10th century; the tiny tower in the middle of the bridge has art exhibits and a tourist information office in the summer. The church of **St-Michel** retains its original 12th-century bell tower, but the rest has been Baroqued with charming tastelessness inside and out, including a wonderful circus-tent baldachin over the altar, dripping with gilt and tassels; a chapel to the left discreetly hides a fine *Annunciation* by Ludovico Brea, as well as another retable of the Virgin in a Gothic frame, possibly also by Brea or one of his followers.

Market Days: Sospel, Thursday.

Breil and Saorge

To the north, the D 2204 is the best route into the Vallée de la Roya, with only a few dozen *lacets* and one mountain pass; the other route, following D 93 and the N 204, is slightly shorter, but it passes two border crossings in and out of Italy. **Breil-sur-Roya**, the first town in the French part of the valley, has two peculiar attractions: the unidentifiable black pseudo-turkeys who live in the river Roya under the bridge, and the 18th-century church of **Sancta-Maria-in-Albis**, with large cracks in its ill-formed walls that seem ready to bring the place down around the ears of the faithful. Inside is another retable attributed to Brea, though not a very good one. Further north, the village of La Giandola sits among the olive groves that once were the valley's only resource, and beyond that come the **Gorges de Saorge**.

After the gorges, the village of **Saorge** is a magnificent sight—neat rows of Italianate slate-roofed, green-shuttered houses, perched on a height like some remote Byzantine monastery, punctuated by church steeples with cupolas of coloured tiles. Saorge guards the Roya valley, and the Piedmontese made it a key border stronghold. You won't see more than ruins of their fort today—it was destroyed after a young commander named Bonaparte took it during the wars of the Revolution. The town suffered during World War II, when its inhabitants were evacuated and forced to spend the duration in Antibes.

Saorge is just as attractive from close up, an ancient border village with customs and a dialect all its own, a little bit Occitan and a little bit Ligurian Italian; instead of *rue* or *via* on the street signs, you'll see *caréra* or *chu* or *ciassa*. The streets, stairways more often than not, climb and dive and duck under arches. The sights require a kilometre's hike to the outskirts: the 18th-century **Franciscan Monastery**, in elegant Piedmontese Baroque, and beyond that the 11th-century chapel of the **Madonna del Poggio**, with Renaissance frescoes including a *Marriage of the Virgin*. West of Saorge, you can penetrate into the southernmost corner of the Mercantour National Park, up the narrow D 40 into the **Fôret de Caïros**.

205

Vallée des Merveilles

Before going further, understand that the Roya is a *cul-de-sac*; there's no way out besides retracing your steps or continuing through the Tende tunnel to Cuneo, Italy. After Saorge, the mountains close in immediately, with the **Gorges de Bergue et de Paganin**; these end at the village of **St-Dalmas-de-Tende**, once the border post between France and Italy and now the gateway to the Vallée des Merveilles.

From about 1800 BC, the Ligurian natives of these mountains began scratching pictures and symbols on the rocks here. They kept at it for the next 800 years, until over 100,000 inscriptions decorated the valley: human figures, religious symbols (plenty of bulls, horns and serpents), weapons and tools. Most defy any conclusive interpretation—circles, spirals and ladders or chequerboard patterns of the kind found all over the Mediterranean; the Val Camonica in northern Italy has even more carvings, from the same era. Why they were made is an open question; one very appealing hypothesis is that this valley, beneath Mont Bégo, was a holy place and a pilgrimage site, and that the carvings can be taken as ex votos made by the pilgrims.

The presence of these symbols has brought the valley some notoriety—superstition gave the surroundings place names like Cime du Diable ('Devil's Peak') and Valmasque (*masco*, or mask, was an old local word for sorcerer). The first person to study the site systematically was an Englishman, Clarence Bicknell, in the early part of this century. As the prime attraction of the Parc Mercantour, the valley gets its share of visitors these days. Besides the carvings, the landscape itself is worth the hike, including a score of mountain lakes, mostly above the tree line, all in the shadow of the rugged, uncanny **Mont Bégo**, highest of the peaks around the Roya; the mountain's name, as far as anyone can tell, comes from an Etruscan god of storms.

Don't just wander up here like some fool tourist, looking for Neolithic etchings. Plan the trip out beforehand, with advice from the Park Information offices. They will probably recommend a guided tour; the symbols are plentiful, but nonetheless inconspicuous and hard to find; apart from the summer months, many will be covered in snow. To tour the valley is *at least* a 20-km round-trip trek from the *refuge* at Les Mesches, at the end of the road west from St-Dalmas; there are hotels in nearby Casterino (see below) and *refuges* within the park if you want to stay over; make arrangements at the park office. Jeep-taxis can also take you around (expensively) from St-Dalmas.

La Brigue and Notre-Dame-des-Fontaines

Vittorio Emanuele II, the last King of Piedmont-Sardinia and the first of unified Italy, may have been utterly useless at his job, but as a hunter few crowned heads could match him. When he arranged to give away the County of Nice in 1860, he stipulated only that the Upper Roya, above St-Dalmas-de-Tende, be left for him as a hunting reserve (to add to a few others he had, strung out across Italy, including the famous Isle of Monte Cristo). The few inhabitants had already voted (under French supervision) for union with France; suspiciously, 73 per cent of the electorate abstained. But this had to wait until 1947, when another plebiscite was held and the valley became France's latest territorial acquisition.

Tende, a dour slate-roofed village, is the only town. No longer a dead end since the road tunnel through to Italy was built, it has become a busy place by local standards. It has the ruined castle of the Lascaris, long-time feudal lords of the Roya, and a late Gothic church, **Ste-Marie-des-Bois**, with a painted façade and ceiling.

East of St-Dalmas-de-Tende, the D 43 takes you into La Brigue, a minute region (partly in Italy) that grows apples and pears and raises trout. **La Brigue**, the tiny capital, has some fine painting in its church of **St-Martin**, another late Gothic work of the 1400s: three altarpieces by Ludovico Brea and his followers, along with Italian paintings from the 17th and 18th centuries. The people who live in La Brigue seem to have an elevated opinion of tourists, since the only ones who pass through have come a long way to see their paintings and, more importantly, those by Giovanni Canavesio at **Notre-Dame-des-Fontaines**, 4 km from the village of La Brigue. The name comes from seven intermittent local springs, miniature versions of the Fontaine de Vaucluse, gushing out of the rock or stopping according to pressure and the water-table; these can still be seen, though now they are on the Italian side of the border.

The Upper Roya may not have been much of an economic or strategic gain for France, but artistically it was a real prize—the country's total number of good Renaissance frescoes went up considerably. Giovanni Canavesio, from Piedmont, is not well known in his own region, but he was a painter in the best North Italian Renaissance tradition: gay colours, exquisite, stylized draughtsmanship and an ability to put genuine religious feeling in his frescoes that recalls Fra Angelico. His works in this rural chapel, done in the 1490s, include 26 large scenes of the *Passion of Christ* in the nave, and on one of the side walls a tremendous **Last Judgement**, a gentle reminder that God wasn't joking. All the tortures of the damned are portrayed in intricate detail, as the devils sweep them into the gaping Mouth of Hell. Around the choir, on the triumphal arch, he painted scenes from the Life of Mary, from the *Birth of Mary* at the upper left to the *Presentation at the Temple* at the bottom right.

The frescoes in the choir itself are by another hand, Giovanni Baleison. Done in the 1470s, in a more old-fashioned style that still shows the influence of Byzantium, these include the *Four Evangelists* on the vaulted ceiling, the four Doctors of the Church (Ambrose, Jerome, Gregory and Augustine), under the arch, more scenes from the Life of Mary, including an *Assumption* on the back wall, over the *Reproach of Thomas* and the *Visit to the Tomb*.

WHERE TO STAY/EATING OUT

There's little choice between the four hotels in **Sospel** (06380); ****Des Etrangers**, is marginally the more expensive, and has a pool and a good restaurant (7 Blvd de Verdun, tel 93 00 04 09, closed Dec); the cheapest, and open all year is the ***Gare** near the station on the Route de Menton (tel 93 04 00 14).For a simple but satisfying lunch in Sospel, the popular **La Cabraia** on the village square has a 75 F menu and tables outside; around the corner, the **Auberge Pont Vieux**, overlooks the river and serves grilled chops, sole and trout on 65, 85 and 120 F menus.

Breil-sur-Roya (06540) is not the most enchanting place to stay in the Roya, but it has several hotels, including the comfortable modern ****Castel du Roy** (near the river on the Route de Tende, tel 93 04 43 66); and the slightly raggedy budget ***Napoléon**

also just north of town on the Route de Tende (tel 93 04 40 25). **La Stella** on Rue Pasteur offers pizzas and a simple 80 F menu.

There are unfortunately no hotels in **Saorge** (06540), but a simple and adequate inn on the N 204, 2 km to the north at Fontan: ***L'Auberge de la Roya** (tel 93 04 50 19), with a popular restaurant serving an 80 F menu. For lunch in Saorge, there are two spots just near the parish church. The **Bellevue** is run by a couple from Normandy who have brought plenty of Calvados for the *trou normand*; also calves' liver in Calvados and other northern fancies on a 100 F menu; while across the street, **Lou Pontin** makes excellent pizzas (70 F). The best choice of the three hotels in **La Brigue** (06430) is ****Le Mirval** on Rue St-Vincent Ferrier at the west end of the village; some rooms have good views, and the management can arrange a trip (expensive) into the Vallée des Merveilles (closed Jan through Mar; tel 93 04 63 71).

If you're doing the Merveilles on your own, it's convenient to start from **Casterino** (06430), a hamlet at the end of the D 91; the nicest of the three hotels here is ***Les Melèzes**; small but comfortable rooms and an unambitious restaurant (tel 93 04 64 95, closed Nov through Mar). Also with a restaurant is the ***Marie-Madeleine** (tel 93 04 65 93, closed Nov through April).

West of Sospel: the Paillon Valley

There is some painting here too, in the rugged mountains between Sospel and the valley of the Var. The Italian influence shows itself in another way—the road map looks like a plate of spaghetti, with more twists and bends than anywhere in the *département*. Lacking a mule, you'll need to return to Sospel to get out of the Roya. The D 2204 west will take you to **L'Escarène**, a lovely Italianate village with houses overhanging the river. Here, you can visit the **Chapelle des Pénitents-Blancs**, with spectacular rococo plaster decoration. There are some peculiar landscapes to the south: stone quarries on the road to Nice that have carved out a huge, nearly perfect ziggurat (perhaps the Médecins of Nice could tunnel inside and make it their family tomb); the road is sometimes closed in the mornings for blasting. In the hills above, around Blausasc, 19th-century deforestation has left a lunar wasteland of bare rock; the government is currently building water channels to keep the erosion from spreading.

Lucéram

North of L'Escarène, **Lucéram** is an old shoe of a village, well-worn and a bit out at the toes. Full of arches and tunnels like Saorge, it has some remains of walls and towers on the mountain-side, a steep but pleasant excursion if you want to circumnavigate them. The church of **Ste-Marguerite** is second only to Notre-Dame-des-Fontaines as an artistic attraction. Amidst the gaudy Baroque stucco of the interior, the altarpieces of the Nice school seem uncomfortably out of place. The best, with an innocence and spirituality matched by few other saintly portraits, is the *Retable de Ste-Marguerite* over the main altar, attributed to Ludovico Brea. Marguerite, a martyr of Antioch, is another popular Provençal dragon-slayer, often confused with St Martha (see Tarascon, p. 286).

Brea made her exceedingly lovely; the Tarasque-like demon at her feet obviously never stood a chance. The other retables around the church include *SS Peter and Paul* (with the keys and sword); *St Claude, St Lawrence* (with his gridiron, upon which he was barbecued) and *St Bernard*, all by unknown 15th-century artists; Giovanni Baleison contributed a good one of *St Anthony of Padua* (1480) in the Chapelle du Trésor, keeping company with a **Trésor** of awful clutter: reliquaries, monstrances and statuettes including a silver image containing relics of Ste Marguerite.

Outside the church, the **Chapelle St-Jean** was built by the Knights of St John—the Knights of Malta, who had a commandery here. Its beautiful exterior, painted to imitate precious marble, is currently under restoration (though the inside is still full of electricity generators).

If you have the time, there are some worthwhile digressions into the mountains around Lucéram, beginning just outside the village with two more chapels with frescoes by Giovanni Baleison, similar to his work at Notre-Dame-des-Fontaines: **St-Grat** (on the road towards L'Escarène) and **Notre-Dame-de-Bon-Coeur** (on the road for Coaraze; the sacristan in Lucéram has the keys for both). East of Lucéram, a half-hour climb up into the hills, there is a wild spot with a huge circular prehistoric wall, the site of a fortified village from the time of the inscriptions in the Vallée des Merveilles—a logical place for such a settlement, with a fine view of holy Mont Bégo.

North of Lucéram, the D 21 and D 2566 take you past Peïra-Cava, a resort for the French military and their families, to the **Forêt de Turini**, centered around a 1520-m mountain pass, the Col de Turini, at the tip of three river valleys. Up above the pass are several old forts, near the summit of Mont L'Authion, an eyrie that commands almost all the Alpes-Maritimes. These were one of the Germans' last redoubts in the war; signs of the battle are still evident, especially around the **Fort des Mille Fourches**, reduced, incredibly, by bombardment from the sea in 1945.

The Devil's Tail, and Other Tales

A long detour on the D 2566/D 15 west from Lucéram (7 km for the crow, 19 for you) will take you with some difficulty to **Coaraze**, a village that is a magnet for attracting stories. One is its name, *Caude Rase* in medieval times, or the 'cut tail'—of the Devil. The villagers back then somehow trapped Old Nick, who had to give up his tail like a lizard to get away. Coaraze has also attracted its share of artists lately; one has given the village centre a lizard mosaic to commemorate the event. Other artists, including Cocteau, have contributed a number of colourful ceramic **sundials** around the village. Another legend deals with the abandoned village of **Roccasparvière**, an hour's walk from Coaraze in the mountains. Queen Jeanne of Provence, the story goes, once took refuge from her enemies here. The plot differs in every version, but in most of them someone in the village kills Jeanne's twin sons, and serves them up for dinner. '*Roc, méchant roc,*' Jeanne cursed. '*Un jour viendra où plus ne chantera ni poule ni coq*'. No chickens indeed are singing in Roccasparvière today, but spoilsport historians say it was because the village well dried up.

Another tortuous 10 km south of here on the D 15, **Contes** has its stories too. One fine day in 1508, the village was attacked by a horde of caterpillars. Apparently it was not the first time; the area has a colourful species the French call *chenilles processionnaires*, who enjoy a promenade in town every now and then. This time, the Contois had had enough; they called in the Bishop of Nice, who brought inquisitors and exorcists, and made anathemas and proclamations until the caterpillars finally grew uncomfortable and went home. Such affairs were not uncommon, especially in old France. Animals, too, were considered subject to God's law; horses and dogs occasionally went on trial for their indiscretions when times were dull. Contes has another altarpiece in the Brea manner in its church, and down by the river a well-preserved **forge** with a water-powered hammer, near the communal olive oil press. Here, and in many villages in the mountains, the oil presses are still in use. Across the river, and 9 km up in the Ferion mountains, there is another abandoned village to explore, outside **Châteauneuf-de-Contes**.

WHERE TO STAY/EATING OUT
Chic sophistication goes only as far as the foothills. In these mountains, so close to Nice and Monte Carlo, you'll find both food and accommodation surprisingly basic and humble. In the centre of **Lucéram** (06440), the *Hotel-Restaurant de la Mediter-ranée is as well-worn as Lucéram itself, and doesn't care who notices; decent rooms and very satisfying home cooking on an honest 70 F menu (tel 93 91 54 54). At the top of Col de Turini, you can stop for the view and lunch at the **Trois Vallées**, roast boar and such, 160–250 F.

   Coaraze (06390), with its sundials and restored houses, seems to get more visitors than the other villages, and not entirely coincidentally it has the most attractive mountain hideaway in the area. Despite its single star, the *Auberge du Soleil** has a lot going for it: a dreamy location at the top of the village, a pool, and a fine restaurant with a memorable view from the terrace (tel 93 79 08 11); this end of the village is closed to traffic—call ahead if you need help with your baggage. The restaurant has an excellent 110 F menu; hotel prices correspond to a two-star place. There is a less expensive alternative in **Contes** (06390), the *Auberge du Cellier** (Blvd Charles-Olunni, tel 93 79 00 64), with only a few rooms and a simple restaurant on the road to Nice.

The Valleys of the Vésubie and the Tinée

The extensive valley of the river Vésubie is almost completely isolated from the regions to the east; from Lucéram the only ways across are the D 21 / D 2566 / D 70 through the Col de Turini, or the miserable D 2566 / D 73 directly over the mountains. There's an equally tortuous route from Contes—the D 815 / D 19.

GETTING AROUND
There are no trains in either the Vésubie or the Tinée valleys, and the coach service is sketchy. St-Martin-Vésubie can be reached by coach from the *gare routière* in Nice (Cars TRAM, tel 93 65 61 81); buses for St-Saveur and St-Etienne in the Tinée also leave from here, tel 93 23 15 15. Roads in this area are as difficult as those to the east; service stations are few so keep your tank full.

TOURIST INFORMATION
St-Martin-Vésubie (06450): Place Félix Faure, tel 93 03 21 28.
Venanson: At the *mairie*, tel 93 03 23 05.

Levens to Lantosque

The Vésubie flows into the Var near **Levens**, a big walled village on a small plain. Beneath it, the main road up the valley, D 2565, follows the scenic **Gorges de la Vésubie**. From St-Jean-la-Rivière, at the end of the gorge, a winding 15-km detour leads to the sanctuary of the **Madone d'Utelle**, one of the most popular pilgrimage sites in Provence, with a chapel full of naïve ex votos to Notre-Dame-des-Miracles, many from sailors, and a spectacular view as far as the sea. **Lantosque**, the next village up the valley from St-Jean, is a humble place, regularly shaken by landslides and earthquakes. Lantosque was occupied by the Austrians in the Revolution. One of them must have been *un bon coq*, as the French say; it's a joke in the other villages that you can always find someone in Lantosque named Otto.

St-Martin-Vésubie

At the top of the valley, St-Martin is the only town for a great distance in any direction, and a base for tackling the upper part of the Mercantour. It's as unaffectedly cute as a town can be, and once it was a spa of some repute. In the delightful and shady town square is an old fountain where the mineral waters used to flow, with inscriptions testifying to their 'organoleptic properties'. The medieval centre is traversed by a lovely street (Rue Dr Cagnoli) with a mountain spring flowing down a narrow channel in the middle, as in a garden of the Alhambra. On this street you'll see an impressive Gothic mansion, the **Maison des Contes de Gubernatis**, and the parish church, housing an altarpiece attributed to Brea and a polychrome wooden statue of the Virgin from the 1300s.

In the vicinity, **Venanson** is a beautiful village up in the mountains above St-Martin, with a small church full of frescoes by Giovanni Baleison. To the east, up into the Parc Mercantour on the D 94, the **Sanctuaire de la Madone de Fenestre** was an ancient holy site near the present Italian border; the name comes from a natural window in a nearby mountain peak. The chapel has burned four times. In the Middle Ages the Templars held the site; they were massacred in the 14th century, and their ghosts were often seen in the neighbourhood. Hiking trails from here can take you on a very scenic route to the Vallée des Merveilles. Another road from St-Martin, the D 89 leads northwest up a valley between the peaks of Mont Archas and Cime du Paigu, to the resort village of **Le Boréon**; this is a lovely area, with many hiking trails, a waterfall (near the village) and some mountain lakes near the Italian border.

The Valley of the Tinée

There's nothing splashy or spectacular about the Tinée. People who love the Mercantour follow the slow D 2205 along its length, from the N 202 out of Nice, up to the protected zone of the Parc; skiers flock in winter to the modern resorts of Isola 2000 and Valberg. But outside their punctual visitations, there is a sort of pious hush in this valley, serenely beautiful even by Alpine standards. In the lower part of the valley, the scenery is as much indoors as out; prosperity in the 15th and 16th centuries allowed the villages of the Lower Tinée to decorate their modest churches with fine Renaissance frescoes by artists of the Nice school.

The river flows into the Var with a climax, at the **gorges**, across the mountains from Utelle; beyond that, **La Tour** has frescoes of 1491 in its **Chapelle des Pénitents-Blancs**. The traditional subjects are represented: the *Passion* and a colourful *Last Judgement*, with Christ sitting on a rainbow and allegorical figures of the Seven Deadly Sins riding on fantastical animals, accompanying the damned to hell.

The next paintings are at **Clans**, in two chapels just outside the village: **St-Antoine** offers more Sins, from an unknown, late-fifteenth-century hand; they accompany some 20 rather peculiar scenes from the *Life of St Anthony*—cooking eggs and exorcizing female demons. **St-Michel** has frescoes by an Italian named Andrea de Cella, *c.* 1515, including St Michael 'fishing for souls', an odd conceit that goes back to Byzantine art. The parish church in the centre of the village has pictures too: surprisingly, a rare late medieval hunting scene. Next up the valley, there is a pleasant detour on D 2565 through Valdeblore, the only reasonable road through to the Vésubie. It begins at **Rimplas**, and the nearby **Chapelle de la Madeleine**, a conspicuous landmark occupying a gorgeous site overlooking the valley; and continues through **St-Dalmas-Valdeblore**, where there is a large and sophisticated Romanesque church: the **Eglise de l'Invention de la Sainte-Croix**, with fragments of its original frescoes.

Continuing up the Tinée, the next stop is **St-Sauveur-sur-Tinée**, throbbing metropolis of the valley, with its 496 souls. From here the D 30 follows the Vionène valley west, through the rugged and lovely villages of **Roure** and **Roubion**. The former, set amidst the biggest larch forest in Europe, has more painting: a Brea (attributed) altarpiece in the church of **St-Laurent**, and unusual frescoes of the lives of St Sebastian and St Bernard in the chapel outside the village—all these chapels outside villages, incidentally, are a regional peculiarity, set outside the gates as if to avert evil influences, and often dedicated to plague saints like Sebastian. Roubion has a Sebastian chapel too, with another frescoed set of Deadly Sins. Continuing in this direction, the next town is the modern ski resort of **Valberg**. There is Alpine scenery in these parts but little else; the best of it is in the long, lonely canyons stretching south off the D 30: the **Gorges Supérieures du Cians** and the **Gorges de Daluis**.

The uppermost part of the Tinée, following the D 2205, runs through the northern half of the Parc Mercantour, never more than a few kilometres from the Italian border. After St-Sauveur come the **Gorges de Valabres**, decorated with an EDF electric plant that somehow managed to sneak inside the park borders. **Isola**, on the other side of the river, has some more appealing sights, both just off the D 2205: a magnificently tall waterfall, the **Cascade de Louch**, and an impressive Romanesque bell tower, the only survival of an abbey washed away by a flood 300 years ago. A good road takes you up to the Italian border and **Isola 2000**, a British-built, modern, concrete ski resort that does good business due to its proximity to the coast. Everywhere else to the north is at ski level, and almost all the villages have learned to bend their lives and habits to the seasonal invasions of the ski-bunnies. If you haven't yet had enough Renaissance frescoes, you may also want to follow the Tinée to its source. In **Auron**, the 12th-century church of **St-Erige** has a sequence of paintings of that obscure Provençal saint, along with the Parisian St Denis, a stranger in these parts. **St-Etienne-de-Tinée** has two painted rural chapels: **St-Sébastien** with a cycle of works by Canavesio and Baleison, in very bad shape, and the chapel of the **Couvent des Trinitaires** where the subject is, of all things, the great naval victory of the Venetians and Spaniards over the Turks at Lepanto in 1571.

WHERE TO STAY/EATING OUT

On the way up to the Parc Mercantour, there's a gracious country hotel in **Lantosque** (06450): the ***Hostellerie de l'Ancienne Gendarmerie. The 'former police station' occupies a pretty hillside site, with garden-side rooms and a pool. The restaurant specializes in salmon and *escargots*; menus 160 and 180 F, also lunch at 120 F (closed Nov–Jan, tel 93 03 00 65).

**La Bonne Auberge in St-Martin-Vésubie (06450) is as good as its name, a welcoming and pretty place on the main Place Félix Faure, with nice inexpensive rooms and a cosy cellar restaurant with a boar's head over the chimneypiece—grilled chops, *escargots, civet du lapin* and profiteroles, menus at 90 and 130 F (tel 93 03 20 49). If they're full, settle for the modern and plain *Des Alpes across the square (tel 93 03 21 06). In St-Martin, you can step out for some of the best pizza this side of the border—in a proper pizza oven—at La Treille on Rue Dr Cagnoli, also pasta and a menu of more ambitious dishes, 90–150 F (tel 93 03 30 85).

Outside the town, *Le Boréon in the village of the same name is a chalet-style place with a few simple rooms and a good restaurant, serving 80–170 F menus including *truite aux amandes*, and homemade desserts (tel 93 03 20 35). At Valdeblore (06420) there is a *ferme-auberge* called Le Grand Chalet: four simple rooms in a modern chalet with Italian-Niçoise home cooking (D 2565 west of St-Dalmas, tel 93 02 83 50).

Don't expect anything out of the ordinary in the sparsely-populated, little-visited Tinée valley: simple country inns with restaurants are the rule, like the Auberge St-Jean in Clans (06420, tel 93 02 90 21); or in St-Etienne (06660), La Pinatelle, Blvd d'Auron, tel 93 02 40 36. These two, and most of the others, require half-board in the summer.

When in the mountains, look out for locally made liqueurs, an Alpine speciality: *myrtille* (bilberry), pear, or something called *Genépi Meunier*—made from an Alpine herb that is closely related to absinthe.

Alpes de Haute-Provence

GETTING AROUND

Buses are so rare they aren't worth the trouble, but it can be fun seeing this region by the scenic rail-line familiarly called the *Train des Pignes*, from Nice to Digne; it follows the Var, and a few trains stop at villages along the way: Villars, Puget-Théniers, Entrevaux and Annot—five a day at the most. This is not the SNCF, but a separate line called *Chemin de Fer de Provence* (see Nice, p. 94; in Digne, tel 92 31 01 58 for details). The *Train des Pignes* is currently being modernized—in the future it will be much quicker (2 hours instead of 4) if less fun.

TOURIST INFORMATION

Puget-Théniers: *mairie*, tel 93 05 02 81.
Entrevaux: at the village entrance, by the gate, tel 93 05 46 73.
Castellane: Rue Nationale, tel 92 83 61 14. Ask about the guided tours organized by the *mairie*, featuring local sights and country life.
Riez: Place des Quinconces; tel 92 74 80 13.
Digne: Place Tampinet, tel 92 31 42 73.

Villars to Entrevaux along the N 202

The N 202 is the east-west traffic chute, following the upper Var, and the only convenient way to get through the mountains north of Grasse. It isn't scenic, though the gravelly, impossibly blue Var makes a refreshing sight alongside; it may however be an antidote to claustrophobia after traversing too many gorges. The trip begins with a local novelty—wine—at **Villars-sur-Var**. The centre of the only, tiny AOC wine region in the mountains, Villars was almost abandoned before the awarding of the *dénomination* in the 70s. Production has vastly increased since then, and you'll occasionally see this variety of *Côtes-de-Provence* in trendy restaurants on the coast—perhaps more for its curiosity value than for anything else. The village church has a few Renaissance pieces: a retable of *St John the Baptist*, and an Italian fresco of the *Annunciation*, both anonymous works of the early 1500s.

Next comes a postcard shot: **Touët-sur-Var**, seemingly pasted up on the side of a cliff, with much of its medieval defences still intact in case anyone tries to storm the place. **Puget-Théniers**, the biggest village on this stretch of the Var, is more open and welcoming, a shady oasis after the stark mountain landscapes, where you may stop for lunch and look at more pictures—two genuine jewels among a number of altarpieces in the parish church: Antoine Ronzen's *Notre-Dame de Secours* and Mathieu d'Anvers' *Passion*, both done about 1525. A monument by Aristide Maillol in the town square commemorates Puget's pride: a local boy named Auguste Blanqui who became one of the leaders of the Paris commune in 1870.

Entrevaux is the strategic key to the valley. There has been a fort of some kind here since Roman times, and its present incarnation is particularly impressive—the work of Louis XIV's celebrated engineer Vauban, high up on the cliffs above the village; at the time it was built the French-Piedmontese border was only a few miles away (it is now the departmental boundary between Var and Alpes-Maritimes). The village, like many others in the area, is rundown to the point of ruin; today, with a little tourist money coming in, some restoration of its houses is under way and Entrevaux is beginning to pick itself back up. The entrance is a **fortified bridge**, rebuilt by Vauban on medieval foundations. Around the village, vestiges of its old garrison days can be seen: barracks and powderhouses, and an ancient **drawbridge**, still in working order, behind the 17th-century **cathedral**. The serious part of the fort is a long climb up; a 10-franc piece gets you throught the turnstile and after that you're on your own to explore the efficient and subtle military mind of Vauban, through the fortified path up to the towers and gun posts on top, with exceptional views around the valley.

The Clues and the Esteron Valley

South of the Var is a grim and lonely region; you can see Nice and Cannes from the summit of the **Montagne du Cheiron** in its centre; but from here the Riviera beaches seem a world away. A *clue*, or more properly *cluse*, is a transverse valley, formed between the limestone folds of the mountains; here the name is given to the many narrow gorges that make life and communications in the area difficult. Local villages are humble and crumbling and few, and the roads across are winding and exasperating. From Puget, the D 2211A/D 17 takes you to **Roquesteron**, a fortified village divided into two parts (before 1860 one was Piedmontese, one French); west of the village, a bad road, the

D 10, leads off into the isolated **Clue d'Aiglun**, perhaps the most dramatic of the *clues*, with a big waterfall. On the other side of the mountains, D 2211A leads to **Briançonnet**, a spectral village with great views and bits of Roman inscriptions built into the old houses; beyond here is the **Clue de St-Auban**.

The more southerly route—with a choice of roads running east-west, some conveniently reached from Vence or Nice—passes some lovely *villages perchés*: **Bézaudun-les-Alpes**, **Coursegoules**, **Gréolières** and **Cipières** (follow D 1/D 8/D 2, from Carros on the Var, north of Nice), all starting to be colonized by people from the Riviera. Gréolières, under the Montagne du Cheiron, has an enormous ruined castle; from here you can follow D 603 into the **Gorges du Loup** towards Grasse, or take D 2/D 802 onto the Cheiron and the new ski station of **Gréolières-les-Neiges**.

WHERE TO STAY/EATING OUT

Being the only good road across this region, the N 202 has the best selection of places to stay and eat, with a few rather better than the average *routier* and truck stop. In **Touët-sur-Var** (06710), the *Auberge des Chasseurs** has a few rooms, but does most of its business serving fish and game to appreciative locals; ravioli and rabbit stew figure on menus at 90–160 F (tel 93 05 71 11). The local favourite in **Puget-Théniers** (06260) is **La Guignette** on Rue 4 Septembre just off the main square; 80 and 100 F menus with an emphasis on seafood and trout. For a pizza, there's **L'Univers** on the square (also inexpensive rooms, tel 93 05 02 81). The only real hotel is the ****Auberge du Vieux Chêne** on Place Contil (tel 93 05 00 14).

Entrevaux (04320), with its castle, attracts a few tourists, though the only place to stay is the hotel-restaurant *Vauban** along the river (tel 93 05 42 40). A good stop for lunch, **L'Echauguette** has outside tables on the central Place de la Mairie, with 80 and 100 F menus, including some seafood and, for starters, a salad served with the local speciality, a beef sausage called *secca*.

The Grand Canyon of the Verdon

After Entrevaux, the Var turns northwards, while the main road continues west, past the modest mountain resort of **Annot** and the **Gorges du Galange**. Further west the country becomes even stranger and lonelier; long monotonous stretches lull you to sleep until suddenly the road sinks into a wild gorge, or confronts a patch of striated mountains that look like gigantic *millefeuille* pastries tumbled over the landscape. Grey is the predominant colour, making a startling contrast with the opaque blue sheet of the **Lac de Castillon**, backed up behind the Barrage de Castillon, a mighty, 90-m concrete dam begun in 1942 under the Vichy government, with a distinctly grim, wartime look about it. The D 955 passes over this on its way to **Castellane**, a village that has become the base for visiting one of the greatest natural wonders of Europe.

The most surprising thing about the **Grand Canyon du Verdon** is that it was not 'discovered' until 1905. That the most spectacular canyon on the continent could be so overlooked speaks volumes about the French—their long-held aversion to nature, which they are now working so enthusiastically to correct, and the traditional disdain of Parisian authorities for the Midi. The locals always knew about it, of course; agriculturally useless and almost inaccessible, the 21-km canyon had an evil reputation for centuries, as a haunt of devils and 'wild men'. Even after a famous speleologist named Martel brought it to the world's attention at the beginning of the century, many Frenchmen weren't impressed. In the 50s the government decided to flood the whole thing for another dam (the tunnels they dug are still visible in many places at the bottom); when the plan was finally abandoned, it was for reasons of cost, not natural preservation.

The name 'Grand Canyon' was a modern idea; when the French became aware of its existence, comparisons with that grand-daddy of all canyons in Arizona were inevitable. It does put on a grand show: sheer limestone cliffs as much as a half-km apart, snaking back and forth to follow the meandering course of the Verdon; in many places there are vast panoramas down the length of it. There are roads along both sides, though not for the entire distance. Most of the best views are from the so-called **Corniche Sublime** (D 71) on the southern side; if you want to explore the bottom, ask about trails and the best way to approach them (it's a long trek) at the tourist information office in Castellane.

The lands south of the Canyon are some of the most desolate in France; you will find them either romantic or tiresome depending on your mood. But either mood will be definitively broken when columns of tanks and missile-carriers come rattling up the road towards you. The Army has appropriated almost all of this area, the **Grand Plan de Canjuers** for manoeuvres and target practice; you'll see their base camp on the D 955 towards Draguignan.

Directly west of the Canyon, a less spectacular section of the Verdon has indeed been dammed up, forming the enormous **Lac de Ste-Croix**; there is yet another dam further

downstream, and the next 40 km of the river valley are under water too: the **Gorges du Verdon**, in parts as good as the Canyon, but sacrificed forever to the beaverish Paris planners. It's wild country on both sides, and access is limited since the roads are few. Beyond the dam on the way to Manosque and the Lubéron, **Gréoux-les-Bains** will treat your aching bones to a jolt of sulphurous, radioactive water. It was a fashionable resort in the early 1800s, when Napoleon's tearaway sister Pauline Borghese dropped by, but never since; it's a pleasant place, though, and does good business with the rheumatic set. The village sits under a ruined **castle**, built in the 12th century by the Templars.

Gréoux-les-Bains

Riez and Moustiers

The **Plateau de Valensole**, north of the Verdon and the Lac de Ste-Croix, is a hot, dry plain of olive and almond trees, and one of the big lavender-growing areas of Provence. **Riez**, at its centre, is an attractive village; an old centre for lavender-distilling, it has lately also become adapted to tourism. Ruined medieval houses are gradually being fixed up, and artists and potters line the narrow streets. Riez was an important Celtic religious site, though it isn't clear exactly which deity it honoured. Testimonies to later piety can be seen at the western edge of town, thought to have been the centre of Roman-era Riez: four standing columns of a Roman **Temple of Apollo**, and a 6th-century **Baptistry** that is one of the few surviving monuments in France from the Merovingian era; octagonal, like most early Christian baptistries (after the original, in the Lateran at Rome), it has eight recycled Roman columns and capitals; all the rest was heavily restored in the 1800s. Inside is a small museum of archaeological finds (ask for the key at the tourist information office). Inside the medieval gates are two pretty fountains recycled from Roman remains, and a number of modest palaces and chapels that recall Riez's prosperity in the 16th to 18th centuries. 14 km west of Riez, **Valensole** is an ancient village, built over the ruins of its Roman predecessor.

To the east, some 15 km on the D 952, **Moustiers-Ste-Marie** sits near the western end of the Grand Canyon du Verdon. Like Castellane on the other side, it is a popular base for visiting the Canyon, and busy in summer. The town will be familiar to any one who haunts the museums of the Midi, as Moustiers in the old days was Provence's famous centre for painted ceramics. The blue and yellow faiences, usually painted with country scenes or floral designs, were often works of art in their own right; first popular in the time of Louis XIV, they were made here as late as the 1870s. Today a large number of potters, some talented and some pretty awful, clutter the village streets, capitalizing on the perfect clay of the region (and on the tourists). You can compare their efforts with the originals at the **Musée de la Faïence**, a small collection on Place du Presbytère.

Moustiers' other distinction, as everyone in Provence knows, is the **Cadeno de Moustié**, a 225-m chain suspended between the tops of two peaks overlooking the village. A knight of the local Blacas family, while a prisoner of the Saracens during the Crusades, made a vow to put it up if he ever saw home again; the star in the middle comes from his coat-of-arms. The original (thought to be solid silver, but really plated) was stolen in the Wars of Religion, and a replacement didn't appear until 1957.

Also Worthy of Your Attention...

Riez in French is a singular or plural imperative: laugh! **Digne** means 'worthy', and one suspects a degree of deliberate etymological mutation in the gradual name change from the local Gaulish tribe, the *Bodiontici*, whose capital this was, to Roman *Dinia*, and finally to *Digne*. The capital of *département* number 04 (Alpes de Haute-Provence), and the only city in a long stretch of mountains between Orange and Turin, over in Italy, Digne is grey and provincial, but it has a modest boulevard, some cafés and a little action. In the miniscule medieval centre, the main attraction is not the crumbling, down-at-heel, 15th-century **Cathédrale de St-Jérome**, but something entirely unexpected: the **Fondation Alexandra David-Neel**, the former home of a truly remarkable French-woman who settled here in her 'Himalayas in miniature' after a lifetime exploring in Tibet (guided tours, daily in summer at 2, 3:30 and 5, otherwise at 10:30, 2 and 4; adm). Ms David-Neel called this house *Samtzen Dzong*, the 'castle of meditation', and Tibetan Buddhist monks attended her when she died here in 1969, at the age of 101. The Dalai Lama has since come to visit; there are exhibits of Tibetan art and culture, photographs, and also Tibetan crafts on sale.

Also in Digne, on Blvd Gassendi, the **Musée Municipal** has a collection of mostly 19th-century Provençal painters, archaeological finds and local curiosities (daily exc Mon 10–12 and 2–6, Sun until 5; adm). Follow Blvd Gassendi to the eastern edge of town, passing the peculiar neoclassical **Grande Fontaine** (1829), and you will find Digne's former cathedral, **Notre-Dame-du-Bourg**, a large Lombard-style Romanesque building of the 1100s, complete with a bell tower of that date, and inside some fragments of frescoes.

Market Days: Moustiers, Friday. Riez, Wednesday and Saturday. Digne, Wednesday and Saturday.

WHERE TO STAY/EATING OUT

This region isn't quite so wild as the badlands to the east; after a day's tramping through the Grand Canyon du Verdon you can splurge for a memorable dinner in **Moustiers-Ste-Marie** (04360) at **Les Santons**, serving classic cuisine quite rare in this *département* (tel 92 74 66 48; menus 150–300 F). Hotels in this village are basic; the best is the ****Belvédère** (tel 92 74 66 04). **Castellane**, on the opposite side of the canyon, is much the same; **La Petite Auberge** (closed Jan-Feb, tel 92 83 62 06) is inexpensive and acceptable for a short stay. The most stylish way to see the Canyon is from the glassed-in restaurant terrace of the ****Grand Hôtel du Verdon**, overlooking it from the D 71, 14 km east of the village of Aiguines (83114), at the Falaise des Cavaliers, tel 94 76 91 31 (closed Oct through April).

Digne (04000) can be an urban oasis in which to relax after too many empty spaces. There's a distinguished hotel in a restored monastery: *****Le Grand Paris**, with an excellent restaurant featuring truffles and seafood, menus 160–350 F (Blvd Thiers, tel 92 31 11 15, closed Jan–Feb). Less expensively, ***Le Petit St-Jean**, on Cours des Arès has attractive rooms and a good restaurant (70–130 F menus, tel 92 31 30 04).

From Grasse to Aix

GETTING AROUND

Driving in this southern half of the Provençal mountains will prove much less trouble than the areas to the north and east; roads are better and service facilities more common. You can take the A 8 motorway straight across and miss everything—but the villages to the east and west of Draguignan offer some of the most delightful opportunities for casual touring in Provence—good bicycling country too. Two possible itineraries for you: from Fayence (west of Grasse on D 562) to Le Muy, through the lovely villages along the D 19 and D 25 (the latter is the wine route). Or from Draguignan, travel west on the D 557, dipping into the mountains on the D 77 for Aups, then the D 22 for Sillans-la-Cascade and Cotignac, and west again (D 32) to Fox-Amphoux or Barjols.

The main Provençal railway follows the motorway from Aix and Marseille to Cannes; for Draguignan you'll usually have to change at Les Arcs. Draguignan and Brignoles are well-served, unlike almost everywhere else. Draguignan is also the hub for village buses, though as always these are few and generally inconvenient: several daily to Grasse, stopping at Bargemon, Seillans and Fayence along the way, and several daily in the other direction, to Tourtour and Aups, with at best one or two to the other villages.

TOURIST INFORMATION

Fayence (83440):Place Léon Roux, tel 94 76 20 08.
Draguignan (83300): 9 Blvd Clemenceau, tel 94 68 63 30.

Fayence, Mons and Seillans

The first leg of this journey, as far as Draguignan, is close enough to the coast to have become thoroughly colonized by the holiday-home set. **Fayence**, a large village of moderate cuteness, has plenty of Englishmen and estate agents. Built on a steep hillside like Grasse, its road winds back and forth up to the centre, which is pleasant enough (the *mairie* is perched on an arch over the main street) but with little to see. North of Fayence, there is some lovely, wild countryside; off the D 37, **Roche Taillée** has a Roman aqueduct still in use—but don't expect the Pont du Gard. This one is entirely carved out of the rock, along a steady descent of some 5 km. Also from the D 37, you'll see the towers of an impressive 17th-century castle, the **Château de Beaure-gard**, a private home. Further north, **Mons** is a beautiful and strange village of narrow streets overhung with arches. The language of its inhabitants still conserves some Ligurian Italian words; the people of Mons were totally wiped out in the Black Death of 1348, and colonists from the area around Genoa and Ventimiglia were brought in to replace them. There are a large numbers of **dolmens** in the area, some are inaccessible on the base of the Canjuers army camp, the borders of which are only 2 km away.

Mons

West of Fayence, the farmhouses may now all be bijoux holiday-homes, but the scenery is delicious; the main road, the D 562 to Draguignan is fine, but even better is the winding D 19/D 25, passing through three pretty villages. **Seillans** has been occupied since the time of the Ligurians, giving it some two-and-a-half millennia to perfect its charm, with cobbled streets leading up to the restored castle. The village lives on flowers, and was the last home of Max Ernst. **Bargemon**, further west, is just as old; behind its medieval gates are several fountains and a 15th-century church. Last before Draguignan is **Callas**, under a ruined castle. The D 25 south of Callas, as far as Le Muy, is a beautiful drive through forests, with the **Gorges de Pennafort** and a waterfall along the way; it is also one of the best wine roads in the region, with a few places to stop and sample *Côtes de Provence* along the way (see p. 224).

Draguignan

Draguignan gets a bad press, especially from the timid English: ugly, depraved, full of soldiers; *avoid it if you can* ... Under the garish Provençal sunlight, we watched a young fellow on the Boulevard de Maréchal Joffre being run in by a pair of municipal policemen—clean-shaven, brutishly intelligent, all dressed up, military-style, in black and silver like American cops. Beautiful women waltzed by, swinging their handbags and smiling at the unfortunate; flaccid shopkeepers squinted furtively through immaculately clean windows.

After the Casino at Monte Carlo, there's no better free theatre in Provence. Tough, sharp-edged Draguignan is not French so much as French colonial. The Army owns it—it's the biggest base in France—and its dusty palm-shaded boulevards pass the national schools of Artillery and Military Science. The town's symbol is the *drac*—yet another Provençal dragon, chased out by an early bishop, though its fire-spitting image can still be seen everywhere. Draguignan could be Saigon or Algiers or Dakar, a cinematic fantasy in a wreath of *Gauloise* smoke, waiting for the Warner Bros cameras to capture Bogart, Lorre and Greenstreet conspiring in some tawdry nightclub.

Anyhow, have your papers in order, and try not to exceed the speed limits. Touring in Provence you'll be bound to pass through here once or twice, and it's a pleasant stop, really. The Saturday market is especially good, and there are a few things to see: the 17th-century **Tour de l'Horloge**, Draguignan's architectural pride; a small **museum** on Rue de la République, with a picture gallery and faiences from Moustiers (also porcelain from China); and the **Musée des Arts et Traditions Populaires**, at 15 Rue de la Motte (daily exc Sun and Mon morning, 10–12, 2:30–6; adm). This is a complete, didactic overview of everything you'll never see in the real Provence any more—from mules to silk culture, along with reconstructions of country life, including kitchens, barns, festivals and, naturally, some antique *boules* and *tambourins*; a pretty old merry-go-round with painted horses steals the show. And just outside town, on the D 955 towards the Verdon Canyon, is one of the biggest dolmens in Provence, the **Pierre de la Fée**.

Market Days: Fayence, Tuesday, Thursday and Saturday. Draguignan, Wednesday and Saturday.

WHERE TO STAY/EATING OUT
After a hard day guzzling *Côtes de Provence* in the wine country east of Draguignan, **Les Gorges de Pennafort** on the D 25 offers a gratifying repast in a wonderful setting, with menus at 160–270 F including pigeon stuffed with *foie gras*—and more *Côtes de Provence*. In the centre of **Fayence** (83440), **Le Vieux Buffet** serves up an uncomplicated but satisfying lunch or dinner: *canard à la forestière*, steaks and chops on 75 and 110 F menus. Also **La France**, where you can dine on a balcony overlooking the town square; try the chicken with pine-nuts, menus at 82 and 130 F. Fayence has inexpensive hotels, including the **Auberge de la Fontaine* (Route de Fréjus, tel 94 76 07 79); but the only place you're likely to remember is the ****Moulin de la Camandoule*, a lovely old olive-oil mill, prettily restored (by a British couple) with all the amenities—pool, garden, TV in the rooms, also a restaurant (menu 180 F, Chemin Notre-Dame-des-Cyprès, tel 94 76 00 84).

   Bargemon (83620) is a good place to rest without breaking the bank. There are simple, inexpensive hotels, like the **Auberge des Arcades* on Av. Pasteur (tel 94 76 60 36), and one fine restaurant with an outside terrace: the **Auberge Pierrot** (Place Chauvier, tel 94 76 62 19, menus 70–260 F).

   Don't expect red-carpet treatment in military **Draguignan** (83300); the only really decent place is outside town, clean, modern and colourless—but with a view: the ****Col d'Ange* on the D 557 towards Lorgues (tel 94 68 23 01). In town, you'll do no better or worse than the stolid and plain ***Hôtel Dracénois* (14 Rue du Cros, tel 94 68 14 57). As for dining, also on Rue de Cros, **Le Brignolet** does a gratifying 95 F lunch: *daube à la provençale* and other filling specialities. The most unexpected and interesting place for dinner is Armenian, **Restaurant Ohaness**, on Av. du Maréchal Juin: the cuisine is reminiscent of Turkey, with plenty of aubergines and imaginative hors d'oeuvres (tel 94 47 18 88; menu 130 F).

Villages of the Central Var

Heading west from Draguignan, there are two choices; if aesthetics are a bigger consideration than time, don't bother with the A 8 motorway or the parallel road through

Brignoles and St-Maximin (for which, see below); instead, take the D 557 or 562 directly west for a leisurely tour through some of Provence's loveliest and most typical landscapes. Though this area gets its share of foreign and Parisian summer folk, it isn't quite chic—compared to similar but totally colonized places like the Lubéron. But there's enough lavender and blowing cypresses, plenty of wine, and a dozen relentlessly charming villages that won't trouble you with any strenuous sightseeing.

TOURIST INFORMATION
Aups (83630): Place de la Mairie, tel 94 70 00 80.
Barjols (83670): At the *mairie*, tel 94 77 07 15.

From Lorgues to Aups

Lorgues is the first village, with a complete ensemble of 18th-century municipal decorations, proof that the *ancien régime* wasn't quite so useless after all: a fountain, the dignified church of **St-Martin**, and the inevitable avenue of venerable plane trees, one of the longest and fairest in Provence. To the north, along the D 10, you'll pass the **Monastery of St-Michel**, a recently re-founded Russian Orthodox community; its handmade wooden chapel, a replica of a Russian church, may be visited. Further north, there are a number of pretty villages around the valley of the Nartuby: **Ampus**, **Tourtour**, up on a height with views down to the sea, and **Villecroze**. At the edge of the Plan de Canjuers, this last village is built up against a tufa cliff; there is an unusual park at the base of it, with a small waterfall and a cave-house dug into the rock in the 16th century.

Aups was a Ligurian settlement, and a Roman town; its name comes from the same ancient root as *Alps*. It has a reputation for being different; a monument in the town square records Aups' finest hour, when the citizens put up a doomed Republican resistance to Louis Napoleon's coup of 1851. The village is known in the region for its Thursday truffle market, held through the winter months. The village church seems oddly below surface level; the ground level around it was raised to avoid the frequent flooding of the old days. Aups, like the other villages, has not completely escaped Riviera modernism. The **Musée Segal**, founded by an eponymous Russian artist, has his and other 20th-century works and is on Av. Albert I. **Salernes**, south of Aups, has been known for over 200 years as a manufacturer of tiles: the small, hexagonal terracotta floor-tiles called *tomettes* that are as much a trademark of Provence as lavender. They still make them, and in a day when French factory-made tiles all come in insipid beige, they are at a premium. Lately Salernes' factories and individual artisans have been expanding into coloured ceramics and pottery; there are a few shops in the village and factory showrooms on the outskirts. With such a workmanlike background, the village itself is rather drab, with a medieval fountain and a simple 13th-century church in the centre.

Further west, **Sillans** has lately been calling itself Sillans-la-Cascade, to draw attention to the 36-m waterfall just south of the village (it dries up in summer); beyond that **Fox-Amphoux** is worth a visit just to hear the locals pronounce the name; this miniscule and well-restored village of stepped medieval alleys sits on a defensible height. There is a ruined castle, and on the trail to the hamlet of Amphoux, an odd cave-chapel, **Notre-Dame-de Secours**, hung with ex votos, many from sailors.

Thoronet Abbey

South of Salernes, **Entrecasteaux** is dominated by a 17th-century castle, completely restored in the 70s by a Scotsman named McGarvie-Munn; visitors are admitted, but there's nothing to see and the fee is exorbitant. Further south, the artificial **Lac de Carcès** has been a favourite with fishermen since the dam was built in the 30s. To the east are the biggest bauxite mines in France, which are playing hell with one of the most impressive medieval abbeys in Provence. The **Abbaye de Thoronet** (daily exc Tues, 10–12 and 2–5, adm), was the first Cistercian foundation in Provence, on land donated by Count Raymond Berenger of Toulouse in 1136; the present buildings were begun about 1160. Like most Cistercian houses, it was in utter decay by the 1400s; and like so many other medieval monuments in the Midi, it owes its restoration to Prosper Mérimée, Romantic novelist (*Carmen*, among others) and State Inspector of Historic Monuments under Napoleon III; he chanced upon it in 1873, when most of the roof was gone, the galleries were overgrown with bushes and the only beings dining in the refectory were cows.

It often seems as if the restoration is still under way; you may find it full of props, scaffolding and concrete piers, as its keepers experiment desperately to keep Thoronet from being shaken to pieces by the bauxite lorries rumbling past on the D 79. The mines themselves (nearby, but screened by trees) have caused some subsidence, and cracks are opening in the walls. Nevertheless, this purest and plainest of the Cistercian 'Three Sisters' of Provence (with Silvacane and Sénanque) is worth a detour. Following the stern austerity of Bernard of Clairvaux, it displays sophisticated Romanesque architecture stripped to its bare essentials, with no worldly splendour to distract a monkish mind, only grace of form and proportion. The elegant stone bell tower would have been forbidden in any other Cistercian house (to keep local barons from commandeering them for defence towers), but those in Provence got a special dispensation—thanks to the mistral, which would have blown a wooden one down with ease. There are no such compromises in the blank façade, but behind it is a marvellously elegant interior; note the slight point of the arches, a hint of the dawning Gothic—Thoronet was begun in the same year as France's first Gothic churches, in the north at St-Denis and Sens. The **cloister** with its heavy arcades is equally good, enclosing a delightful stone fountainhouse.

Cotignac and Barjols

Its inhabitants might be unaware of it, but **Cotignac** is one of the cutest of the cute, a Sunday supplement-quality Provençal village where everything is just right. There are no sights, but one looming peculiarity: the tufa cliffs that hang dramatically over it. In former times these were hollowed out for wine cellars, stables or even habitations; today there are trails up to them for anyone who wants to explore; at the base of the cliffs there is a meadow where Cotignac holds its summer music festival.

Westwards on the D 13/D 560, the landscapes are delicious and drowsy; **Pontevès** will startle you awake again, a castle with a remarkable setting atop a steep conical hill. Long the stronghold of the Pontevès family, feudal rulers of most of this region, the apparition loses some of its romantic charm after the climb up; there's nothing inside but a few houses, *La Poste* and a food shop. Three km further on, **Barjols** has little cuteness but much more character. This metropolis of 2000 souls owes its existence to leather tanning, an important industry here for the last 300 years. There is still one shoe factory left, but Barjols is now little more than a market town, although it retains an urban and somewhat sombre air: elegant rectangular squares of the 18th century, and moss-covered fountains in the form of stone trees, a brilliant idea inspired by the *Fontaine d'Eau Chaude* in Aix.

To see Barjols at its best, you'll have to come on 16–17 January, the feast of St Marcel (Marcellus, the 4th-century pope) whose gaudy relics, stolen in the Middle Ages from a Provençal monastery, can be seen in the 16th-century parish church. There'll be a bit of dancing and, equally unusual for Provence, the essentially pagan slaughter and roasting of an ox, accomplished to the sound of flutes and *tambourins*.

Market Days: Aups, Wednesday and Saturday.

WHERE TO STAY/EATING OUT

Lorgues (83510), 13 km from Draguignan, is a more pleasant place than Draguignan to stop over if you're passing through the area; the venerable, classy hotel in the centre, a bit down on its luck but still comfortable, is the **Hôtel du Parc**, with a restaurant with 90 and 150 F menus (Blvd Clemenceau, tel 94 73 70 01). For something different, there's **Nysios**, in the old town on Rue Four Neuf, serving Greek-French food, with *moussaka* but nothing more exotic; outside tables.

Tourtour (83690), easily the poshest of the villages in this region, also has the most luxurious accommodation: the ******Bastide de Tourtour**, a modern complex with pool, tennis and all the amenities, including a highly-reputed restaurant with a blend of Provençal cooking and *nouvelle cuisine*, menus 160–350 F (Route de Draguignan, tel 94 70 57 30). 3 km east of the village at **St-Pierre-de-Tourtour**, the ****Auberge St-Pierre** is a find—an up-to-date working farm built around a hotel; exceptional rooms in an 18th-century house and a fine restaurant, with authentic Provençal food (largely the farm's own produce) menus 160 and 200 F (swimming-pool, horse-riding and other activities, tel 94 70 57 17).

In **Salernes** (83690), the ***Grand Hôtel Allègre** is another old establishment, like the one in Lorgues, with a bit of faded grandeur and some of its 20s decor intact (20 Rue Rousseau, tel 94 70 60 30). The cooking's a bit faded too; you'll do better with a simple *magret* or stewed rabbit at **La Fontaine** on Place 8 Mai 1945 (outside tables; tel 94 70 64 51). If you're going to **Sillans** (83690), the first thing you'll see, right on the D 32, is the **Auberge des Pins**, a very popular restaurant in an old stone house, serving grilled meats with shrimps for openers on 125–165 F menus, also a few inexpensive rooms (closed Jan and Feb, tel 94 04 63 26). Nearby, off the D 560, is **La Dame d'Argent**, a restaurant in a beautiful setting by the river Bresque, from whence come the trout and *écrevisses* that figure prominently on the menus (120–250 F).

One of the most pleasant village inns in Provence is in **Fox-Amphoux** (83670): the ****Auberge du Vieux Fox**, with rooms overlooking the Place de l'Eglise, and a delightful restaurant; try the *carré d'agneau* (loin of lamb); menus 120–260 F (closed mid-Dec–mid-Feb, tel 94 80 71 69). *****Lou Calens** is an unexpectedly stylish hotel-restaurant in the centre of **Cotignac** (83850), with a lovely hidden garden and pool; only eight rooms, and as many (more expensive) suites; also a somewhat unexciting restaurant, menus 120–135 F and upwards (1 Cours Gambetta; tel 94 04 60 40). Less expensively, the ***Hotel du Cours** across the street is simple and friendly (tel 94 04 66 34).

Off the Motorway from Draguignan to Aix

With the Var's rocky coast, and the mountains behind it, the only easy route across the *département* is a narrow corridor through Brignoles and St-Maximin-la-Ste-Baume. The French have obligingly plonked down a motorway across it, successor to the Via Aurelia and the old St-Maximin pilgrims' route as the great high road of Provence.

TOURIST INFORMATION
St-Maximin-la-Ste-Baume (83470): Hôtel de Ville, tel 94 78 00 09.
Brignoles (83170): Place St-Louis, by the coach station, tel 94 69 01 78.

Les Arcs

Picking up the D 555 south of Draguignan, you'll pass through **Les Arcs**, a well-exploited village of stepped streets, pink stone and ivy. Next comes **Le Luc**, practically strangled by the motorway and the parallel national routes but a game town nevertheless, with another steep medieval centre, a castle on top, and a restored Romanesque church flanked by an unusual hexagonal tower from the 1500s. To entertain the hordes of coast-bound tourists there's a museum of philately, and another small museum in a 16th-century church, the **Musée Historique du Centre Var**, with a collection ranging from fossils and Neolithic finds to medieval art.

Côtes de Provence: La Vie en Rose

Half of all French rosés originate in the Republic's largest AOC region, the 18,000-hectare Côtes de Provence. The growing area stretches from St-Raphaël to Hyères, with separate patches around La Ciotat, Villars-sur-Var, and a wide swathe south and west of Aix. Based on grenache, mourvèdre, cinsault, tibouren, cabernet and syrah grapes, Côtes de Provence rosé is a dry, fruity, and elegant summer wine that doesn't have to worry about travelling well: more than enough eager oenophiles travel to it every holiday season. Unfortunately, its price in the past couple of years has travelled too, and there are no prizes for guessing which way. It is however possible to find good inexpensive alternatives since some estates produce a *vin de pays*. This is often as good as wines with full *appellation contrôlée* status. An excellent example is **Château d'Astros** at Vidauban, tel 94 73 00 25, which produces a wonderful range of Vin de Pays des Maures: red, white and rosé. The property is run by the charming Buisines for an absentee 'patron' banker from Marseille. A visit to this grand rambling house and estate in the forest is great fun. One can also buy *en vrac*—either supply your own containers or buy one from M. Buisine.

Côtes de Provence reds (20 per cent of the production) are much finer today than the rough plonk Caesar issued to his legions, most notably the special *cuvées* put out by the better estates. The whites, of clairette and ugni blanc grapes, are scarcer still, and account for only 5 per cent of the AOC label.

With 57 cooperatives and 350 private cellars, Côtes de Provence wine is easily sampled, especially along the signposted 400-km *Route des Vins*, which you can pick up at Le Luc or Le Muy from the A 8 or N 7 or at Fréjus, Les Arcs, and Puget-sur-Argens. Two of the best-known producers are at Trets, on D 56 east of Aix: **Château Ferry-Lacombe**, where the vines are planted on ancient Roman terraces, tel 42 29 33 69 (where, along with the pink stuff, you can find the excellent Cuvée Lou Cascaï); and the 1610 **Château Grand'Boise**, tel 42 29 22 95, where the subtle red Cuvée Mazarine and a flowery blanc des blancs are grown amidst a large forest. Near Le Luc, Hervé Goudard's **Domaine de St-Baillon**, on the N 7 at Flassans-sur-Issole, tel 94 69 74 60, mixes syrah and cabernet bordelais to produces its truffle-scented Cuvée du Roudaï. Just under the landmark cliffs of Mont Ste-Victoire, **Domaine Richeaume** at Puylou-bier, tel 42 66 31 27, is owned by German ex-pat Henning Hoesch, who combinines a love of modern abstract art with wine, in Provence's most modern and efficient *cave*, producing along with rosés an interesting selection of red wines, one of pure syrah and another of pure cabernet-sauvignon. At La Londe-les-Maures (west of Bormes-les-Mimosas) **Domaines Ott**, Clos Mireille, Route de Brégançon, tel 94 66 80 26, offers one of the appellation's top white wines, of ugni and sémillon grapes aged in wooden barrels.

A much higher percentage of red wine is produced in the cooler, drier **Coteaux Varois**, a region of 28 communes around Brignoles in the central Var, beginning a few miles north of the Bandol district and extending north as far as Tavernes. This old **vin de pays** has recently been elevated to the ranks of VDQS, and all the vinters along the N 7 and the other roads outside Brignoles hang out signs to lure you in. You can try a good (and completely organic) Coteaux Varois at the **Domaine de Bos Deffens**, on the Cotignac road just east of Barjols. Or sample both Cotes de Provence and Coteaux Varois (especially the 88, 89, and 90 reds) at **Château Thuerry**, set in a magnificent wooded landscape at Villecroze, tel 94 70 63 02.

Brignoles

The biggest date in Brignoles' history, perhaps, is 25 September 1973, when several thousand dead toads rained down from the sky, an event that does not seem to be commemorated in any way. Little else has ever happened here. This gritty but somehow likeable place earns its living mining bauxite. It has an attractive medieval centre, and a museum to remember.

Le Musée du Pays Brignolais (Regional Museum)

Situated at the top of the old town, on Place des Comtes de Provence in a palace that was those counts' summer residence, Brignoles' incredible curiosity shop has grown to fill the whole building since a local doctor began the collection in 1947 (daily exc Mon, Tues, 9–12, 2:30–6; adm). Amidst two big floors packed full of oil presses, fossils, cannon-balls, reliquaries and roof tiles, you'll see some things you never dreamed existed. In the place of honour, near the entrance, is the original model of a great invention by Brignoles' own Joseph Lambot (1814–87): the **steel-reinforced concrete canoe**. Contemporary accounts on display suggest the thing floated, though the idea somehow never caught on. Lambot probably never collected a *sou* for his revolutionary new construction technique, since found to be better adapted to skyscrapers.

Admittedly, a hard act to follow, but just across the room is a provocative **sarcophagus**, dated *c.* 175–225 AD, nothing less than the earliest Christian monument in France. Well-sculpted and well-preserved, the imagery is a remarkable testament to religious transition. The centre shows a familiar classical scene, a seated god receiving a soul into the underworld—but whether the god is Hades, Jesus, or another remains a mystery. Also present are Jesus as the 'Good Shepherd' (the most common early Christian symbol), a figure that may be St Peter (fishing, figuratively, for souls), another that seems to be a deified Sun, and another early Christian symbol, an anchor. The sarcophagus is believed to be Greek, possibly made in Antioch or Smyrna; how it got here no one knows.

Nearby is a rare but badly-worn Merovingian tombstone, and a part of the counts' palace, the **Chapel of St-Louis-d'Anjou**, a Provençal bishop who may be better known in California—the town of San Luis Obispo is named after him. The chapel houses a hoard of gaudy church clutter, with Louis' chasuble and rows of wax saints under glass. After that, you may inspect a **reconstructed Provençal farm kitchen**, and a **reconstructed mine tunnel**. Other prizes await on the second floor: a **plywood model of Milan Cathedral** by a local madman, a **stuffed weasel**, and large collections of **owls** and **moths**. Local painters are exhaustively represented: some of the finest works are 19th-century ex votos in the French tradition, with the Virgin Mary blessing people falling off wagons and out of windows. Even after all this, Gaston Huffman's *Allegory of Voluptuous Folly* takes the cake, a medieval conceit in a modern style, with a delicious lady in a little boat enjoying the caresses of a cigar-smoking pig.

Rue des Lanciers, the spine of old Brignoles, begins opposite the museum's front door, passing the 13th-century **Maison des Lanciers**, where the counts' guards stayed when they were visiting.

West of Brignoles, there are two sights of some interest off the main road, for both of which you'll need to talk your way in to visit: first the half-ruined **Abbaye de la Celle**, an ancient foundation (started in the 6th century) that made a reputation for itself due to the open licentiousness of its nuns, and which was dissolved in 1770; the buildings are now part of a farm. Second, also on a farm, off the D 205 6 km east of Tourves, is the **Chapelle de la Gayole**, an early Romanesque cemetery chapel in the shape of a Greek cross (built in 1029, though parts of it go back to the 700s).

St-Maximin-la-Ste-Baume

For proof that Provençal sunlight softens the Anglo-Saxon brain, consider St-Maximin. 'Considerable charm' gushes one guidebook; 'another pretty Provençal village' yawns another. Prosper Mérimée, back in 1834, got it right: 'Saint-Maximin is a miserable hole between Aix and Draguignan'. It hasn't changed. The general atmosphere of bricks and litter is reminiscent of some burnt-out inner-city in the Midlands or Midwest. It is hard to imagine a place remaining in such a state of total, lackadaisical decrepitude, in the midst of a prosperous region, without some effort of will on the part of its inhabitants.

But once upon a time, the Miserable Hole was a goal for the pious from all over France. According to legend, the site was the burial place of the Magdalene (see

Stes-Maries-de-la-Mer, p. 316) and her companions St Maximin, the martyred first bishop of Aix, and St Sidonius. Their bodies, supposedly hidden from Saracen raiders in a crypt, had disappeared, and were conveniently 'rediscovered' in 1279 by the efforts of Charles II of Anjou, Count of Provence. Inconveniently, the body of Magdalene was already on display at the famous church of Vézelay, in Burgundy. Nevertheless, an ambitious basilica and abbey complex was begun, and eventually the Pope was convinced or bribed into declaring St-Maximin's relics the real McCoy. The pilgrim trade made St-Maximin into a town; among the visitors' number were several kings of France, the last being Louis XIV. There were wild times during the Revolution; St-Maximin renamed itself 'Marathon', and was briefly under the command of Lucien Bonaparte, who was calling himself 'Brutus'. This most devoutly revolutionary of Bonapartes saved the basilica from a sacking. As the local legend tells it, an official from Paris came down to oversee its liquidation, but Brutus had him greeted with the *Marseillaise*, played all stops out on the church's great organ.

Basilica Ste-Marie-Madeleine
After its ramshackle, unfinished façade, on a desolate square decorated only by a faded Dubonnet sign, the interior seems an apparition: the only significant Gothic building in Provence. Despite the prevailing gloom, and the hosts of awful, neglected 18th- and 19th-century chapels and altars, the tall arches of the nave and the lovely apse, with its stained glass, leave an impression of dignity and grace. The original decoration is spare: coats-of-arms and effigies of Charles of Anjou and Queen Jeanne on some of its capitals. Among the later additions, the most impressive is the enormous, aforementioned **organ**, almost 3000 pipes and all the work of one man, a Dominican monk named Isnard (1773). Another Dominican, Vincent Funel, was responsible for the lovely choir screen (1691). To the left of the high altar, don't miss the retable of the *Passion of Christ* (1520) by an obscure Renaissance Fleming named Ronzen: 22 panels of the familiar scenes with some surprising backgrounds: the Papal Palace in Avignon, the Colosseum and Venice's Piazzetta San Marco. Stairs lead down to the **crypt**, a funeral vault from the 4th or 5th century AD, where the holy sarcophagi remain with a host of eerie reliquaries.

THE COUVENT ROYAL
The monastery attatched to Ste-Marie-Madeleine was a 'royal' convent because the Kings of France were its titular priors. After losing it in the Revolution, the Dominican Order bought back the monastery and church in 1859. Apparently St-Maximin proved too depressing even for Dominicans; they bolted for Toulouse in 1957, leaving the vast complex in a terrible state. Restorations have been going on fitfully since the 60s. The buildings include the imposing **hospice** from the 1750s (now the town hall), to the left of the basilica's façade; the rest, behind it, now houses an institute for cultural exchanges; they offer guided tours (Oct–April, daily 10–11:30 and 2:30–6; rest of the year Sat and Sun afternoons only; adm). The best part is the **cloister**, with Lebanon cedars and a charming subtropical garden in the centre. One of the arcades is a Gothic original of 1295.

The Massif de la Ste-Baume
If you're heading towards Marseille or the coast from here, you might consider a detour into this small but remarkable patch of mountains. Rising as high as 975 m, and offering

views over the sea and as far north as Mont Ventoux, the massif shelters a small forested plateau called the **Plan d'Aups**. This is a northern-style forest, including maple, beech and sycamore, as well as scores of species of wild flowers and other plants not often seen around the Mediterranean. They have remained in their primeval state because the massif is holy ground, the site of the cave (*Sainte-Baume*, or holy grotto) where according to legend the Magdalene spent the last years of her life as a hermit. The cave, furnished as a chapel, was part of the pilgrimage to St-Maximin since the Middle Ages, and can be seen today along the D 80. Monastic communities grew up around the site, and you may visit the 13th-century Cistercian **Abbaye de St-Pons**, near the loveliest part of the forests (the Parc de St-Pons).

Market Days: Brignoles, Saturday. St-Maximin, Wednesday.

WHERE TO STAY/EATING OUT

Les Arcs (83460), strategically located on the road to the Côte d'Azur, has spawned one exceptional hotel-restaurant. ****Le Logis du Guetteur** is located at the top of the old town; a lavishly restored castle dating in parts from the 11th century, with a garden and pool; some rooms have wonderful views. The restaurant serves ambitious *haute cuisine*: smoked salmon, stuffed sole, and elaborate desserts with menus at 165, 250 and 350 F (Place du Château, tel 94 73 30 82).

Brignoles has plenty of inexpensive hotels, most of them dives; try the centrally located ***Univers**, over a simple restaurant on Place Carami (tel 94 69 11 08). Something more elegant can be found outside town: the ****Château Brignoles-en-Provence** on the N 7, just on the eastern edge of Brignoles, offers peace and quiet in an old farm, with pool and tennis (tel 94 69 06 88). A little further east, at the village of **Flassans-sur-Issole** (83340), is a gracious and friendly farm hotel, ****La Grillade au Feu de Bois**, with nine rooms and a restaurant with admirable home cooking (on the N 7, tel 94 69 71 20).

Dining in Brignoles' medieval centre, the best bet is **L'Assiette Gourmande**, on Rue Gradalet; the cooking is both Italian and French—you can have *carpaccio* or pizza for starters, and there is a shady outdoor terrace (menus 85 and 150 F). Or else, try **Les Deux Platanes**, across from the church; above-average menus (even *escargots*) at 65 and 82 F. For a change, there is a good Vietnamese restaurant, the **Saigon** on Square St-Louis (110–150 F).

If you're compelled to stay in St-Maximin, head for the wild orange shutters of the ****Hôtel Plaisance** (Place Malherbe, tel 94 78 00 74). Dining in this town is an adventure; the local speciality is limp pizza; finding anything else can be difficult.

Part VIII

NORTHERN PROVENCE: THE VAUCLUSE

EAGLE OWL 'DUCAS'

BONELLI'S EAGLE

EGYPTIAN VULTURE

WILD BOAR

The 'Three Plagues of Provence', according to tradition, were the mistral, the Durance and the Parlement at Aix. The Parlement is ancient history, but the other two still serve to define the troublesome boundaries of this region: the long curve of the wicked, boat-sinking, valley-flooding River Durance to the south, and a line of long, ridge-like mountains, Mont Ventoux and the Montagne de Lure, to the north—folk wisdom has always credited these northern boundary-stones of Provence as the source of the terrible mistral. But the lands in between these natural prodigies are the eye of the hurricane, some of the most civilized countryside and loveliest villages to be found in the Midi. These have not passed without notice, of course, and the rural Vaucluse is now what the Côte d'Azur was forty years ago: the in-place for both Frenchmen and foreigners to find a bit of sun-splashed holiday paradise amongst the vineyards.

Not everything included in this section is actually in the *département* of Vaucluse (Manosque and Forcalquier are in Alpes-de-Haute-Provence); and the Vaucluse's two cities, Orange and Avignon, will be found in Part IX. The remainder divides neatly into three areas: the mountainous Lubéron, cradled in the Durance's arc, a *pays* of especially pretty villages; the old papal Comtat, nearer the Rhône, rich agricultural lands rightfully called the 'Garden of France', and Provence's definitive northern wall, including the dramatic Mont Ventoux and the Dentelles de Montmirail, along with the Roman city of Vaison.

229

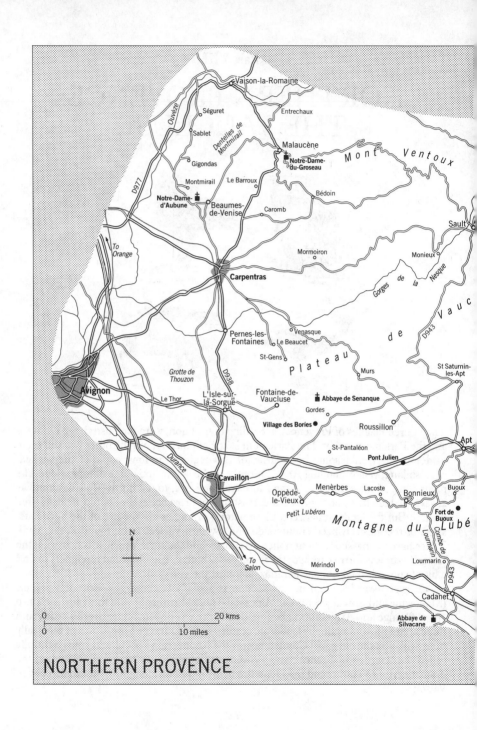

NORTHERN PROVENCE

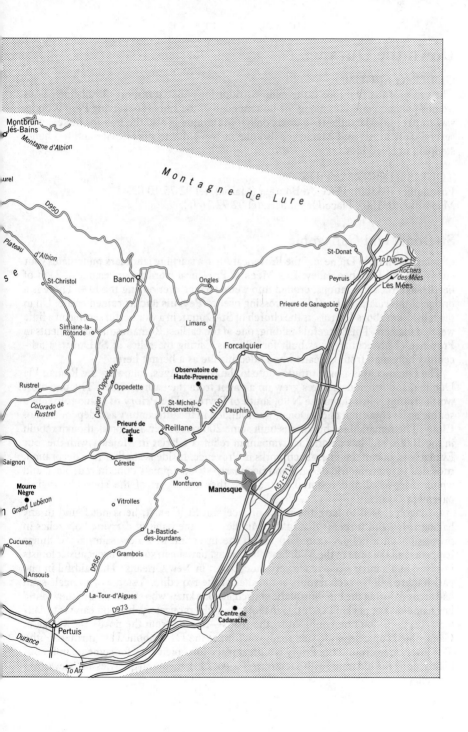

Down the Durance

GETTING AROUND
The valley of the Durance is the main corridor for public transport. A rail-line passes Manosque and continues along the bottom edge of the Lubéron, serving Pertuis on its way to Aix and Marseille (five or six daily). Manosque is also the hub for **buses**, with several daily to Aix and Marseille, also one or two a day to Forcalquier and to Digne, stopping in Les Mées.

TOURIST INFORMATION
Forcalquier (04300): Place du Bourget (Mairie), tel 92 75 10 02.
Manosque (04100): Place Dr Joubert, tel 92 72 16 00.

St-Donat and Ganagobie

Coming down from Digne and the Provençal Alps, a startling landmark punctuates your entry into the Durance valley: **Les Mées** (a Provençal word for milestones), 2 km of needle-like rock formations, eroded into weird shapes overlooking the D 4. There is a bridge at the village of Les Mées, crossing over to **Peyruis** and its ruined castle. Up in the hills, 5 km above Peyruis, is the church of **St-Donat**, in a wonderful setting on a little wooded plateau. This graceful building, one of the earliest Romanesque monuments in Provence (11th-century) was built for pilgrims visiting the relics of St Donat, a 5th-century holy man from Orléans who ended his life as a hermit here.

The Durance was a major trade route in the Middle Ages, following the Roman Via Domitia, and religious centres grew up along it from the earliest times. The one most worth visiting is just down the N 96, south of Peyruis. The **Priory of Ganagobie**, in a setting as lovely as that of St-Donat, was founded in the 9th century as a dependency of Cluny. The remarkable church was built some 200 years later. Its portal, though rebuilt in the 1600s, still has its original tympanum relief: a **Christ in Majesty** with the four Evangelists, one of the finest such works in Provence. Inside is another rare decoration, **mosaics** with geometric designs and peculiarly-styled animals done in red, black and white; discovered and restored in the 60s, they were part of the church's original pavement.

Ganagobie used to have the relics of a certain St Transit; he is not found in any hagiography, and it seems that in the Middle Ages the habit of carrying holy relics in procession on a holiday (a *transit*) led to the invention of a new saint. Such things happened all the time in the Midi (and there must have been some Provençaux colonists involved in a similar occurrence very much later, in New Orleans. The faithful in one parish there still beseech favours at the altar of Ste Expedite. A statue of a female saint had arrived during the building of the church; no one knew who she was—but they found her name on the packing crate). Ganagobie is still a monastery, but you can visit (daily 9:30–12, 2–5; don't be confused by the roads—coming from the north, the village of Ganagobie is up a separate side road; you'll want the D 30, about 3 km further south). The lovely area around the Priory is a great place for a picnic, or for some unambitious hiking along the old trails, with a few *bories* (see p. 244), medieval quarries and views over the valley.

232

Forcalquier

Nowadays a rather dull village that only comes to life for the Monday market, Forcalquier was once a miniature capital—in the 11th and 12th centuries, when its independent counts carved out a little mountain state for themselves, and often made life difficult for the counts of Provence. Alphonse II managed to swallow it up in 1209, by marriage, but later Provençal rulers like Raymond Berenger V made Forcalquier a favoured residence throughout the 1300s. They left few traces: a tower and other scanty remains of Forcalquier's **citadel**, overlooking the town; the well-restored 13th-century **Couvent des Cordeliers**, parts of which were originally the counts' palace, given to the Franciscans (called *cordeliers* in France because of their rope belts) by Raymond Berenger V. There is a small museum inside, and frequent concerts and exhibitions in summer.

The lands around Forcalquier are some of the most beautiful in this part of Provence, full of oak forests and sheep meadows, rustic and peaceful and not yet as touristy as the Lubéron to the south. Twelve km south of the town, the **Observatoire de Haute-Provence** was attracted to the area by a study that found (in the 30s) that the *pays de Forcalquier* had the cleanest, clearest air, and the least fog of anywhere in France; there are guided tours, sadly only during the day (June–Sept, 2:00–3:45). This is a region of *villages perchés*: **Dauphin**, just to the south; **Oppedette**, to the west, overlooking the scenic canyon of the River Calavon; **Limans** and **Banon** to the north, the first famous for its rather luxurious 16th-century *pigeonniers*, the second for sheep's cheese. Most impressive of all, perhaps, is **Simiane-la-Rotonde**, set high on a small plateau. The *'rotonde'* is a peculiarly-shaped *donjon* dominating the village, all that's left of a feudal castle. Simiane is by far the most chic of the villages in this area, with plenty of restored second homes; it's a charming place nevertheless, with a late Gothic church and an old **covered market-place**.

Manosque

By far the biggest town in this part of the Durance valley (pop. 18,000), Manosque is unavoidable. It isn't, however, a town to spend much time in. Once a drowsy place, with no other distinction than being the home town of Jean Giono, Manosque today presents the spectacle of a Provençal village out of control. Acres of concrete suburban sprawl press against the hilltop medieval centre, and the traffic can be as ferocious as Marseille's. The culprit is Cadarache, France's national nuclear research centre, a huge complex to the south across the Durance, begun in 1959; most of its workers live around Manosque.

Manosque's tidy, teardrop-shaped centre, an oasis amidst the sprawling disorder, is entered by two elegant 14th-century gates, the **Porte Saunerie** and the **Porte Soubeyran**, designed more for decoration than defence. Inside are two unremarkable churches on quiet squares: **St-Sauveur**, made in bits and pieces from the 1200s to the 1700s, but attractive nevertheless, and **Notre-Dame-de-Romigier**, with a Renaissance façade; the altar here is an early Christian sarcophagus with reliefs of the Apostles.

Market Days: Manosque, Saturday. Forcalquier, Monday. Banon, Tuesday.

WHERE TO STAY/EATING OUT

Lodgings can be hard to find in the thinly-settled region around **Forcalquier** (04300). The village itself is the best bet; the ****Hostellerie des Deux Lions** stands out, with lovely rooms and a justifiedly popular restaurant, with menus that change daily and the best local cheeses and wines (menus 100 F, weekdays, also 160–190 F, Place du Bourguet, tel 92 75 25 30). Less expensively, there is the not-so-grand but perfectly acceptable ****Grand Hôtel** at 10 Blvd Latourette (tel 92 75 00 35); also a bed-and-breakfast *ferme-auberge*, the **Ferme de Bas-Chalus**, 2 km from the village (tel 92 75 05 67).

Manosque has a good selection of hotels, though nothing really special, from the pleasant ****Rose de Provence** on the outskirts (570 Route de Sisteron, tel 92 87 56 28) to the budget **Artel**, in the centre on Place de l'Hôtel de Ville (tel 92 72 13 94). The only luxury hotel-restaurant in this area is outside Manosque, the *****Hostellerie de la Fuste**, across the Durance on the D 4, just north of the D 907. The rooms are fine, in a restored *bastide* with a covered pool, but the real attraction is an elegant, highly-rated restaurant: game dishes and truffles in season, marinated trout; menus go from 200 F up to a spectacular *menu dégustation* with a little bit of everything for 350 F (post code 04210, Valensole; tel 92 72 05 95).

Manosque really comes into its own at lunch-time; on Promenade Aubert-Millot, near the Porte Saunerie by the statue of a dog, look for a crowded hole-in-the-wall with no sign: **Le Petit Pascal**, a one-woman operation with delicious, filling home-cooking (menus 47, 75 F, lunch only); second choice is **Chez André**, on Place du Terreau (tel 92 72 03 09).

The Lubéron

As is the case with many a fair maiden, the Lubéron's charms are proving to be her undoing. This is Peter Mayle country, the stage set for his surprise bestseller *A Year in Provence*. Yes, this is that magical place where the natives are endlessly warm and human, the vineyards ever-so-lovely in autumn, and the lunch in the little bistro worth writing about for pages and pages. All true, in fact—but everybody knows it, and the trickle of outsiders who began settling here in the 50s, permanently or in holiday homes, has now become a flood.

How you experience the Lubéron will also depend on what time of year you come. Most of the year it's as quiet as a graveyard; in summer it can seem like St-Tropez-under-the-Poplars, with vast crowds of Brits, Yanks and Parisians milling about, waiting for lunch-time. It's hard to imagine why anyone would want to come here in August, but if you insist, make sure you have your hotel reservations months in advance.

The Regional Park

Like many parts of rural Provence, the Lubéron presents a puzzling contrast—how these villages became such eminently civilized places, set amidst a landscape (and a population) that is more than a little rough around the edges. The real Lubéron is a land of hunters stalking wild boar over Appalachian-like ridges, and weatherbeaten farmers in ancient Renaults full of rabbit cages and power tools. There are other regions of Provence, equally scenic and rustic, that merit being frozen into a nature preserve, but the Lubéron was the one most in danger of being destroyed by a rash of outsiders and unplanned holiday villas. The **Parc Régional du Lubéron** was founded in 1977, a cooperative arrangement between the towns and villages that covers most of the territory between Manosque and Cavaillon; quite a few (often where the mayor is an estate agent or a notary) have decided not to participate at all. The Lubéron is not an exceptional nature area like the Mercantour. Still, the Park is doing God's work, protecting rare species like the long-legged Bonelli's Eagle, a symbol of the Midi that needs plenty of room to roam and is nearing extinction; most of all, it is a reasonably effective legal barrier to keep the Lubéron from being totally overwhelmed by the kind of building madness that wrecked the Côte d'Azur.

Park Information: the **Maison des Pays du Lubéron**, Place Jean-Jaurès in Apt, with exhibits, slide shows and a gift shop; tel 90 74 08 55.

GETTING AROUND
Public transport is woefully inconvenient in the Lubéron; it's possible to get around the villages, but just barely. Apt is on an SNCF branch line, with a few **trains** daily to Cavaillon and Avignon. Buses from Apt leave from the Place de la Bouquerie by the river; there are one or two daily to Roussillon, to Avignon, to Aix, stopping at Bonnieux, Lourmarin, Cadenet and Pertuis; also one to Digne, stoping at Céreste. Cavaillon is on the main Avignon–Marseille rail line, and there are also buses to L'Isle-sur-la-Sorgue, Pernes-les-Fontaines and Carpentras (several daily), to Apt and Avignon, and very occasionally to Bonnieux and other western Lubéron villages.

There are some ways of getting around you may not have considered: for **helicopter tours** of the Lubéron, call Mme Emmanuelle in Lourmarin, tel 90 08 04 47. Finding a **horse** is no problem in most areas; in Cucuron, try the Gîte Equestre La Rasparine, tel 90 77 21 46; and in St-Martin (north of Pertuis), Randonnées Haras, tel 90 68 02 89.

TOURIST INFORMATION
La Tour d'Aigues (84240): In the château, tel 90 77 50 29.
Cadenet (84160): La Glaneuse, Av. Girard, tel 90 74 08 55; includes a shop for Cadenet's basket-weavers, the village's old craft speciality.
Lourmarin (84160): Av. Philippe de Girard, tel 90 68 10 77; summer only.
Bonnieux (84480): Place Carnot, tel 90 75 91 90.
Cavaillon (84300): 79 Rue Saunerie, tel 90 71 32 01.

The Pays d'Aigues
The southern end of the Park is the sleepier corner of the Lubéron, a rolling stretch of good farmland sheltered by the Grand Lubéron mountain to the north. **Pertuis**, along the D 973, is its modest capital, with a bit of an aristocratic air; prosperity in the 1600s has left it a number of fine buildings. Of the smaller villages, a few stand out: **Grambois** is a neatly rounded hilltop hamlet; the church of Notre-Dame-et-St-Christophe has both its patrons represented in art inside: a good Renaissance altarpiece of the Virgin,

Grambois

and an original 14th-century fresco of St Christopher. **Ansouis**, north of Pertuis on the D 56, is a *village perché* built around the sumptuously furnished **Château de Sabran**, still in the hands of the original family: a Henry IV monumental stair leads to Flemish tapestries, Italian Renaissance furniture, portraits and later Bourbon bric-à-brac. The atmosphere is wonderfully snooty, but they let us in to visit just the same (daily exc Tues, 2:30–6:30).

For an airier, pleasanter castle without the bric-à-brac, try **La Tour-d'Aigues**, just to the east. The **Château** here, in fact, doesn't even have a roof. The Baron of Cental was still making repairs to damage caused by a fire in 1782 when the Revolution came, and the local peasantry torched the place for good and all. What's left is a thoroughly elegant Renaissance shell, begun in 1555 by an Italian architect, Ercole Nigra, imitating the styles then fashionable in Paris. The entrance is a massive triumphal arch, carved with trophies, inspired by the Roman arch at Orange. One of the château's side towers has been rebuilt, and the Conseil de Vaucluse, who now own it, plan to restore the rest a little at a time as funds are available. There is a small **museum** down in the cellar, with exhibits on the history of the *pays d'Aigues* (daily exc Mon, 2:30–5:30, in summer daily, 10–12, 3–7; adm). La Tour also has an unusual Romanesque church, **Notre-Dame-de-Romegas**, with an apse at either end—originally built facing the east, it was turned around in the 1600s when some clerical stickler for the rules had a second apse built.

Lourmarin and Cadenet

Further west, into the heart of the Lubéron, **Lourmarin** was the last home of Albert Camus, who is buried in its cemetery. This is an unusual village, densely packed almost to the point of claustrophobia; many of its houses have tiny courtyards facing the street—too cute for its own good, as few villages even in the Lubéron are so beset by tourists. Its only attraction is another 16th-century **château**, well restored, now the property of the Académie of Aix, who use it for cultural programmes, concerts and exhibitions. **Cadenet**, a big village overlooking the rocky bed of the Durance, is only 5 km away, but the difference is like day and night. An ancient place, Cadenet began as a pre-Celtic *oppidum*; even older are some of the cave dwellings that can be seen in the cliffs behind the village (others were refuges for persecuted Waldensian Protestants in the 1500s). It's also a very attractive village. On the Place du Tambour, one of the focal points of the Monday market, is the bronze statue of Cadenet's favourite son, André Estienne, a 15-year-old drummer boy who once managed a difficult river crossing for Napoleon's troops—wading right in and beating the charge under direct Austrian fire. The embarrassed soldiers could only follow. Have a peek inside the parish church, **St-Etienne**, on the northern edge of town. The baptismal font has well-preserved reliefs of a Bacchic orgy; scholars call it 3rd-century, but disagree over whether it was originally a sarcophagus or a bathtub.

West of Cadenet, **Mérindol** isn't much to look at, but worth a mention as a symbol of a very dark page of the Lubéron's history. When plagues and war depopulated the region in the 1300s, immigrants from the Alps and from Italy came to work the land. Many were peaceful, hard-working Waldensian dissenters (see p. 59); when the Reformation began, the authorities could no longer tolerate them. In 1540, the Parlement of Aix oversaw the burning of 19 Waldensian villages in the Lubéron, including Mérindol, and Lourmarin as well. Over 3,000 innocents were butchered, and hundreds more were sent off to the King's galleys.

Abbaye de Silvacane

Life as a medieval Cistercian was no picnic. Besides the strict discipline and a curious prejudice against heating, there was always the chance the Order might send you to somewhere in the middle of a swamp. They built this, the first of the 'Three Sisters of Provence' (open daily exc Tues, 10–12, 2–6; adm), in just such a location because they meant to reclaim it—the 'forest of rushes' (*silva cana*), south of the Durance, 7 km from Cadenet. It took a century or two, but they did the job, as you can see today from the fertile farmlands around Silvacane. A Benedictine community had already been established here when the Cistercians arrived in 1147. Work began on the present buildings soon after, partially financed by the barons of Les Baux, and Silvacane became quite prosperous. Bad frosts in the 1300s killed all the olives and vines, starting Silvacane on its long decline. When the government bought the complex to restore it in 1949, it was being used as a barn.

The church is as chastely fair as its younger sisters at Sénanque and Thoronet, perhaps more austere and uncompromising still; even the apse is a plain rectangle. Of sculptural decoration there is hardly any (though scores of masons' marks on the columns and vaulting). The adjacent **cloister** now contains a herb garden, around a lovely broken fountain. Note the capitals on the arcades, carved, oddly, with maple leaves.

Market Days: Cadenet, Monday and Saturday mornings.

WHERE TO STAY/EATING OUT

Coming down from Manosque, there is a pleasant hotel at **La-Bastide-des-Jourdans** (84240), on the road to La Tour-d'Aigues: **Au Cheval Blanc**, with a restaurant that specializes in game dishes and trout and an outdoor terrace (**Le Cours**, tel 90 77 81 08). For lunch in **La Tour-d'Aigues** (84240), there's an honest 65 F menu at the **Antoine de Tres**, across from the church. If you're staying over, the best bet is ****Les Fenouillets,** just outside the village on the D 956. Rooms are simple, but there's a swimming-pool, and an inexpensive restaurant with outdoor tables (tel 90 07 48 22).

Lourmarin (84160), small as it is, has become the chic rendezvous in the southern Lubéron. One of the classy establishments to open here in recent years is a restored farmhouse on the Route de Vaugines, just east of the village: the *****Hôtel de Guilles**, beautifully restored and decorated, with lots of antiques and all the amenities: tennis court, pool and gardens (tel 90 68 30 55). For something less expensive, there's the ***Hostellerie le Paradou,** in a dreamy setting north of Lourmarin on the D 943, at the entrance to the Combe de Lourmarin, (tel 90 68 04 05). Lourmarin can also offer some of the best restaurants in the Lubéron. **La Fenière**, on Rue du Grand Pré in the centre, combines innovative cooking with old Provençal favourites: a menu might include Vietnamese spring rolls, batter-fried courgette flowers and a hearty *daube* (140, 240 and 400 F menus). For a budget lunch, try **Le Ratelier** on Rue Albert Camus—pizza and a beefsteak on an 80 F menu.

Cadenet (84160), less expensive and touristy than Lourmarin, is a good alternative for a stay in this region. The **Hôtel Aux Ombrelles** combines nice inexpensive rooms with a fine restaurant; the truffle omelettes and *magret de canard* are very popular with the locals; wide choice of menus from 80 to 200 F (tel 90 68 02 40, closed Dec through Jan). Even cheaper, but acceptable, is the old hotel-restaurant *Le **Commerce** on Av. Gambetta (tel 90 68 02 35). South of Cadenet, on the D 943 on the way to Silvacane, there's a good *routier* roadside inn, **Le Relais Fleuri** (lunch menu 55 F).

Northern Lubéron: Along the N 100

TOURIST INFORMATION
Apt (84400): Place Bouquerie, tel 90 74 03 18.
Roussillon (84220): Place de la Poste, tel 90 05 60 25.
Gordes (84220): Place du Château, tel 90 72 02 75.
Fontaine-de-Vaucluse (84800): Place de l'Eglise, tel 90 20 32 22.

Under the Grand Lubéron

Coming from Forcalquier, this route follows the northern slopes of the mountains, generally much more scenic country than the other side, with pretty villages like **Reillane**, almost deserted a century ago, but now making a comeback, even attracting a few artists; and **Céreste**. Between the two, you can make a excursion to the **Prieuré de Carluc**, with a Romanesque chapel and unique ruins of the original early Christian priory, partly carved out of a rocky outcrop; like Notre-Dame du Groseau on Mont Ventoux (see p. 253), this was an ancient religious site, built around a sacred spring; the ruins around the rock include a Gallo-Roman cemetery.

The narrow roads south of the N 100 are some of the most beautiful in the Lubéron, passing through **Vitrolles** or through **Montfuron**, with its lofty ruined castle, on their way to the Pays d'Aigues. There are also several hiking trails, from Vitrolles or from **Saignon** near Apt, leading up to the summit of the Grand Lubéron, the **Mourre Nègre**, with views that take in all of the Vaucluse and beyond. Saignon itself is a beautiful village between two crags, with a well-preserved 12th-century church.

Apt

The capital of the Lubéron (pop. 13,000 and growing) also claims to be the 'World Capital of Candied Fruits', with one big factory and plenty of smaller concerns that make these and every other sort of sweets. There is a certain stickiness about Apt; everyone in the Lubéron comes here for the huge, animated Saturday market, but no one has ever admitted to liking the place, at least not in print. Roman *Colonia Apta Julia*, a colony refounded over a Celtic village, was the capital of the area even then. Despite languishing for a few dark centuries, before being rebuilt in the 1100s, the streets still bear traces of a rectangular Roman plan, bent into kinks and curves through the ages.

The Cathedral, and More Dubious Provençal Saints

We can guess that the **Rue des Marchands**, the main shopping street, roughly follows the course of its Roman predecessor. It leads to the **Tour de l'Horologe** (1567), the bell tower of Apt's old cathedral of **Ste-Anne**. Begun in the late 12th century and tinkered with incessantly until the 18th, the ungainly exterior conceals a wealth of curiosities within. There is fine 14th-century stained glass in the apse, and an early Christian sarcophagus and an odd golden painting of John the Baptist in two chapels on the north side; also an interesting **trésor** with books of hours, reliquaries and some Islamic ivories. Another trophy from the east is a linen banner, brought back from the Crusades by a lord of Simiane; as its origin was forgotten, it came to be revered in Apt as the *Veil of St Anne*.

Few regions of Europe had such a longing for relics as Provence in the Dark Ages. Other peoples, the Germans and Venetians, had a kleptomanic urge to steal holy bones when no one was looking; the Provençaux, showing less initiative but greater imagination, simply invented them. We met St Transit at Ganagobie (see above), and the **crypt** here has two more, maybe three. According to legend the bones of St Anne, the mother of Mary, were miraculously discovered in this crypt in the 700s, occasioning the building of the first cathedral. In those days, any early Christian burial dug up was likely to be elevated to saint status; beyond that, scholars guess the Anne invented for the occasion was less the biblical figure than a dim memory of the primeval pan-European mother goddess, who was known as Ana, or Dana, to the Celts, the Romans (*Anna Perenna*), and nearly everyone else. Next to her are the bones of 'St Auspice', claimed to be Apt's first bishop—really the sacred auspices of pagan times (divination from bird flight or from the organs of sacrificed animals), another verbal confusion like St Transit. That leaves St Castor, another obscure early martyr. Who might he be? Well, *castor* in French is a beaver, but if the Aptestens were being imaginative again it's more likely this is a survival of the Roman *Dioscurii*, the Heavenly Twins—Castor and Pollux.

Fruits and Fossils
Apt also has a good, well-laid out **Museum**, on Rue de l'Amphithéâtre, with archaeological finds going back to the Palaeolithic period, late Roman sarcophagi, painted ex votos and a display of Apt's once flourishing craft of faience, which had its heyday in the 18th century (daily exc Sun, Mon; in winter 2:30–4:30, Sat mornings 10–12; in summer 10–12, 2:30–5:30; adm). The town's other attraction is the **Maison du Pays du Lubéron**, the headquarters and information centre of the Regional Park; it has exhibits on the region's natural life, including a push-button Palaeontology Museum for the children, an interesting gift shop, and all the information you'll ever need on the wild areas of the Lubéron (daily 8:30–12, 2–6). Finally, you can take a tour of the **Apt-Union factory**, west of town on the N 100, where they make most of those crystallized fruits. It's an interesting process; they suck the water out of the fruit and replace it with a sugar solution—a bit like embalming.

Market Day: Saturday morning.

WHERE TO STAY/EATING OUT
As rooms in the smaller villages are hard to come by, you'll probably find yourself staying in Apt (84400). Nothing special here; the most pleasant is outside town, the ****Relais de Roquefure**, an old stone-built inn with an inexpensive restaurant (on the N 100, 4 km west, tel 90 04 88 88, closed mid-Jan–mid Mar). In the town centre are the ****Auberge du Lubéron**, on the river at Quai Léon Sagy (tel 90 74 12 50), and ****Le Palais**, the most inexpensive in town, on Place Gabriel Péri, which includes a pizzeria with a 60 F

lunch menu (and other dishes apart from pizza, particularly a good *ratatouille*, tel 90 04 89 32). Restaurants are similarly undistinguished; top choice is **Le Platane** on Place Jules Ferry, off Rue Gambetta, serving lamb with garlic, a Lubéron favourite, in a pretty garden (tel 90 74 14 17). For something different, there's **L'Oasis**, on Rue du Sous-Préfecture, with couscous for 90 F (including wine).

Red Villages North of Apt

Technically this isn't part of the Lubéron, though it is within the boundaries of the Regional Park. Above Apt, on the southern slopes of the Plateau de Vaucluse, the geology changes abruptly. The plateau is mostly limestone, which erodes away to make caves and water tricks like the Fontaine-de-Vaucluse (see below). This particular part has sandy deposits full of iron oxides—ochre, the material used in prehistoric times as skin-paint, and lately to colour everything from soap to rugs. Centuries of mining have left some bizarre landscapes—cliffs and pits and peaks in what the locals claim are '17 shades of red', also yellow and cream and occasionally other hues besides.

Rustrel, northeast of Apt on the D 22, was one of the mining towns until 1890. The huge ruddy mess they left is called the **Colorado**; there are marked routes around it for tourists. From here, the D 179 west takes you to **St-Saturnin-lès-Apt** (St Saturnin is probably the Roman god Saturn, but let's not get started on that again). This village had little to do with mining, but it has always grown nice red cherries; there are plenty of ruins, including a castle and bits of three different sets of walls (13th- to 16th-century), also a simple Romanesque chapel from the 1050s. **Roussillon**, further west again, occupies a spectacular hilltop site, and well it should, for centuries of mining have removed nearly everything for miles around. The *Association Terre d'Ochres*, an organization that wants to get the business going again, has an information centre in the village, and can direct you on a tour through the old quarries, known locally as the *Sables de Roussillon*. Samuel Beckett spent the war years exiled in Roussillon; rural peace and quiet gave him a nervous breakdown.

South of Roussillon, near the meeting of the N 100 and D 149 is a well-preserved Roman bridge, the **Pont Julien**.

Villages of the Petit Lubéron

West of Apt, and south of the N 100, is a string of truly beautiful villages that have become the high-rent district of the Lubéron, one of the poshest rural areas in France. Don't come here looking for that little place in the country to fix up; it's all been done, as long as 40 years ago. The first to arrive were the Parisians, including many artists, intellectuals and eccentrics, giving the place a reputation as 'St-Germain-in-the Lubéron'. Since the 60s, a wave of outsiders looking for Provençal paradise, including many Americans, have transformed the place. None of this is readily apparent, apart from the infestations of swank villas on many hillsides outside the Regional Park boundaries. The villagers, a bit richer now, take it in their stride and carry on as they always have—separate worlds, existing side by side.

Biggest and busiest of the villages, **Bonnieux** is also one of the loveliest, a belvedere overlooking all the Petit Lubéron. The ungainly modern church at the bottom of the village contains four colourful 16th-century wood paintings of the *Passion of Christ*; the other attraction, so to speak, is the **Musée de la Boulangerie** on Rue de la République, which as the name suggests will tell you everything you wanted to know about Provençal bread. There are some wonderfully scenic excursions from here: take the D36/D943 south to Lourmarin (see above); this is the only good road across the spine of the Lubéron, and passes through a long and beautiful gorge called the **Combe de Lourmarin**, south of Bonnieux. East of Bonnieux off the D 943 a side road, the D 113, takes you up into the mountains, passing the slender, elegant Romanesque bell tower of the **Prieuré de St-Symphorien**, and up to the hamlet of **Buoux**; above it, the ruined medieval **Fort de Buoux** offers tremendous views over the heart of the Lubéron. Nearby is the beginning of a **nature trail** marked out by the Regional Park, with informative placards on the Lubéron's flora and fauna all along the way.

    Lacoste, west of Bonnieux on D109, is a trendy *village perché*, home to an American school run by the Cleveland Institute of Art. Overlooking the village is a gloomy ruined **castle**, the home of no less a personage than the Marquis de Sade (d. 1814). The French are a bit embarrassed by the author of *120 Journées de Sodome*, but he certainly wasn't insane, and he is a literary figure of some note, taking to extremes the urge for self-expression that came with the dawn of the Romantic movement. He did have his little weaknesses, which kept him in and out of the calaboose for decades, on charges such as pushing 'aphrodisiac bonbons' on servant girls, and worse. Scion of an old respectable Provençal family, he spent a lot of time here when Paris grew too hot for him. Oddly enough, the Marquis seems to have been a descendant of Petrarch's Laura—Laura de Sade (see Avignon, p. 269). The thought of it obsessed him for life, and he saw her in visions in the castle here. The castle, burned in the Revolution, is currently undergoing a slow, one-man restoration by its eccentric owner, M. Bouer, who occasionally gives tours (tel 90 75 80 39).

    Continuing along the D 109, you come to **Ménerbes**, honey-coloured, artsy and cuter than cute. Ménerbes is so narrow, from some angles it looks like a ship, cruising out of the Lubéron toward Avignon; at the top is a small square, about 6 m across, with balconies on either side. The D 188 from here takes you almost to the top of the Petit Lubéron, to **Oppède-le-Vieux**, with an even gloomier ruined castle, one that can be explored. Perhaps it has a curse on it; this was the home of the bloodthirsty Baron d'Oppède, leader of the genocide against the Waldensians in the 1540s.

WHERE TO STAY/EATING OUT

If you book ahead, you can find something in the villages. One of the few real luxury places is in **Roussillon** (84220). ***Mas de Garrigon** is a well-restored farmhouse with all the amenities, lovely rooms and a good restaurant; but both, unfortunately, are woefully overpriced (600–650 F for a double room; tel 90 05 63 22). **St-Saturnin** is a friendly village and though a bit out of the way it is a good choice for a base; stay at the delightfully old-fashioned *Hotel des Voyageurs, on Place Gambetta (closed Jan; tel 90 75 42 08), or at the *Saint Hubert on Place de la Fraternité, which has a slightly better restaurant (menus 120, 180 F, tel 90 75 42 02).

    Bonnieux (84480) has a real find, the ***Hostellerie du Prieuré**, a 17th-century priory in the village centre; rooms with a view and a garden (tel 90 75 80 78). Less expensively, there is the **Hotel César** on Place de la Liberté (tel 90 75 80 18). To really get away, there is an isolated hotel above **Buoux** (84880), near the Fort, the inexpensive *Auberge des Séguins*; simple rooms and home-cooking in a memorable setting (off the D 113, tel 90 74 16 37). You can dine well in **Ménerbes**, at **Le Calendal** on Place Roure; a fine *salmis de pigeon* and local goat's cheese, on menus of 90, 110 and 155 F.

Côtes-du-Lubéron

Between the mountains of the lower Durance and the Calavon Valley around Apt are the vineyards that produce AOC Côtes-du-Lubéron—mostly young ruby wines made from grenache, syrah, cinsault, mourvèdre and carignan; the whites come from bourboulenc and clairette. This is produced in an extraordinary, high-tech works at the **Château Val-Joanis**, in Pertuis (tel 90 79 20 73), where the red, with a high percentage of syrah (60 per cent) is both good and a good buy. On the other hand, **Château de l'Isolette**, on the main road between Bonnieux and Apt, tel 90 74 16 70, is run by the Pinatels, a family that has been making wine since the 1500s. Over the past decade the estate has won scores of medals, especially for its red wines aged in oak barrels, like the 82 *Grand Sélection*; they also do a fine *blanc de blancs* and rosé. In Bonnieux itself, look for **Château La Canorgue** (Rte du Pont-Julien, tel 90 75 81 01), a beautiful 16th-century château which won a gold medal at Blaye for its 88 red, which has a bouquet of violets.

Cavaillon

Lacking anything more compelling, Cavaillon is famous for its melons. As one of the biggest agricultural market towns in France, it ships a million tons or so of these and all the other rich produce of the surrounding plains to Paris every year. It also has a local market (on Mondays) that competes with Apt's as the most important in the Vaucluse. The town is old enough, built under a steep hill overlooking the Durance, the **Colline St-Jacques**, where a Neolithic settlement has been uncovered; it is a short climb from the centre of town, with a medieval chapel and great views over the river valley. Roman-era Cavaillon has left behind only a 1st-century AD **arch**, at the foot of the hill. Unlike the arches of Carpentras and Orange, this one probably doesn't mark any particular triumph; it is four-sided, a *quadroporticus*, and like the only similar construction, the Arch of Janus in Rome, it probably was a simple decoration for—appropriately enough—a market-place; its decorative reliefs, mostly fruits and flowers, are now too eroded to be seen very clearly.

Cavaillon's other attractions include a small **Archaeological Museum**, on Cours Gambetta; the Romanesque cathedral of **Notre-Dame et St-Véran**, with a tatterdemalion 17th-century interior; and an ornate 18th-century **synagogue**, similar to the one in Carpentras, with a small museum, on Place Castil-Blaze. Before the Revolution, Cavaillon had the biggest Jewish population in the Papal enclave; among them were the ancestors of the composer Darius Milhaud. Segregated in a tiny ghetto around the synagogue, the community prospered despite occasional gusts of Papal persecution; after the Revolution, most of Cavaillon's Jews moved to the larger cities of Provence, and there are hardly any living in the town today.

Market Day: Monday.

WHERE TO STAY/EATING OUT

In **Cavaillon** (84300), even though the *parc* has become a car park, the old ****Hôtel du Parc** is still a pleasant place to stay (Place du Clos, tel 90 71 57 78). Slightly more expensive, the equally venerable and well-kept ****Toppin**, 70 Cours Gambetta (tel 90 71 30 42). For lunch, the **Fin de Siècle**, on Place du Clos, by the Roman Arch, is a good bet, a café-restaurant that takes its name from its old-fashioned decor; menus 80–100 F and upwards, with treats like stuffed chicken breast and salmon cakes on even the cheaper menus (tel 90 71 12 27). On Place Philippe de Cabassole, in the centre, the eccentric **Le Pantagruel** lives up to its name with a Rabelaisian 118 F 'menu des ogres', more than you can eat, including a slab of ham with cèpes, or a *coquelet* (tel 90 76 11 30).

Gordes

The first thing you'll notice about this striking *village perché* is that it has a rock problem. They have it under control; the vast surplus has been put to use in houses and sheds, and also for the hundreds of thick stone walls that make Gordes seem more like a south Italian village than one in Provence. The stones made agriculture a bad bet here, so the Gordiens planted olives instead, and became famous for them—at least until the terrible frost of 1976 killed off most of the trees. But without ever asking for it, Gordes has found something easier and more profitable: art tourism, with exhibits and concerts in the summer, and two of the slickest artistic roadside attractions in Provence.

Gordes was a fierce resistance stronghold in the war and suffered for it, with wholesale massacres of citizens and the destruction of much of the village; after the war the village was awarded the Croix de Guerre. All the damage the Nazis did has been redeemed; the village centre, all steep, cobbled streets and arches, is extremely attractive. At the centre, you may see flocks of well-scrubbed art students lounging on the steps of the imposing **château** built by the lords of Simiane in the 1520s. They are making their pilgrimage to an avant-garde that no longer exists.

The Vasarély Didactic Museum

Hungarians are renowned for their cleverness; they say a man from Budapest can enter a revolving door behind you and come out in front. Victor Vasarély, a poster artist, arrived in France from Budapest in 1929; he always had his mind set on something a little more serious, and the abstract madness of the post-war era finally gave him a chance. With a modicum of talent and a tidal wave of verbal mystification about the 'plastic alphabet' and 'escaping the ephemerality' of figurative art, Vasarély became an op-art celebrity in the 60s, planting his little bulging circles and cubes in museums and corporate offices around the world. Few artists have ever managed to commandeer a castle as a personal monument; he convinced the village to allow it by paying for the restorations.

Unlike Vasarély's other self-celebration, at Aix, this one is meant to ensure we understand the various stages of his career (daily exc Tues, 10–12, 2–6). Early attempts at actually drawing are mostly self-portraits; the later works that made him famous are all very tidy and colourful; some have been turned into Aubusson tapestries, flanking a fine Renaissance fireplace, one of the few decorations that survives from the pre-Vasarély château.

To see what real art's all about, walk over to Gordes' parish church of **St-Fermin**, with a memorable 18th-century interior of purple, pink and gilded jiggumabobs, a lodge brother's fantasy seraglio. A statue of the Magdalene on the right looks down on it all with a jaundiced eye.

Around Gordes: Les Bories, and Another Bore

Across the Midi they are called *bories*, or *garriotes*, or *capitelles*, or a dozen other local names. In Provence there are some 3,000 of them, but the largest collection in one place is the **Village des Bories** south of Gordes, off the D 2. A *borie* is a small dry-stone hut, usually with a well-made corbelled dome or vault for a ceiling. From their resemblance to Neolithic works (like the *nuraghi* of Sardinia) they have always intrigued scholars. Recently it has been established, however, that though the method of building goes way back, none of the *bories* you see today are older than the 1600s. Elsewhere they are usually shepherds' huts, but these are believed to have been a refuge for the villagers in times of plague. This group of 12 *bories* has been restored as a rural museum (daily 9–sunset; adm). You'll see other *bories* all around Gordes; some have been restored as holiday homes, and one has even become an expensive restaurant. Determined *borie*-hunters should also tour the large concentrations in the countryside around Bonnieux, Apt, Buoux, St-Saturnin, and Saumane, north of Fontaine de Vaucluse.

South of Gordes, there is a beautiful, simple Romanesque church at the hamlet of **St-Pantaléon**. West of that, watch out for the well-publicized 'Musée du Vitrail Frédérique Duran', where another little Vasarély has set up shop. There are indeed exhibits on the history of stained glass, but their only purpose is to suck you into the adjacent gallery for a look at the high-priced and gruesome work of Duran and others.

Abbaye de Sénanque

The loveliest of the Cistercian Three Sisters lies 4 km north of Gordes on the D 177. The church may be almost a double of the one at Thoronet (see p. 222), but built in the warm golden stone of the Vaucluse and set among lavender fields and oak groves, it makes quite an impression. Now it is in the hands of the same cultural association that controls the abbey at St-Maximin-la-Ste-Baume; oddly enough they use the place for studies of Saharan nomads, and there is a room of exhibits on the subject. The Benedictine monks of Ile St-Honorat, who hold the title, seem interested in occupying it again, so Sénanque's status is uncertain. Meanwhile, it is a favourite venue for summer concerts, often of medieval music.

The **church**, (daily 10–12, 2–6, adm), begun about 1160, shows the same early Cistercian seriousness as Thoronet and Silvacane, and has been changed little over the centuries; even the original altar is present. Most of the monastic buildings have also survived, including a lovely **cloister**, the *chauffoir*, the only heated room, where the monks transcribed books, and a refectory with displays giving a fascinating introduction to Sénanque and the Cistercians .

Fontaine-de-Vaucluse

Over a century ago, explorers found the source of the Nile. They're still looking for the source of the little Vaucluse river called the Sorgue. It's underground; the best spelunkers in France have been combing the region's caves for decades without success, and in 1983 a tiny, specially-made submarine probe (the *Sorguonaute*) sent back data from some 250 m below the surface of the **Fontaine-de-Vaucluse**, where the Sorgue makes its daylight debut, through a dramatic gaping hole in a cliff in the beautiful narrow valley the Romans called *Vallis Clausa*—the origin of *Vaucluse*. A second probe, *Sorguonaute II*, was sent down in 1984, and imploded soon after immersion; finally, in 1985, a sophisticated device usually used in oil exploration—the *Modexa 350*—plunged to a sandy bed 312 m below the surface, though the passages that carry the stream into this remain unexplored.

Medieval legends record St Véran, patron of Cavaillon, dispatching a big snake near the source—a sure sign this was an ancient holy place, given the close connection between underground water and mythological serpents everywhere in Europe. The more prosaic Romans channelled the water into an aqueduct, remains of which can still be seen along the D 24 towards Cavaillon. In later times, among those attracted by Provence's greatest natural wonder was Petrarch, who spent many seasons in a villa by the river bank from 1327 to 1353, the year a band of brigands sacked the village and frightened him back to Italy.

The Fontaine is still an exquisite place, but the 600 or so residents of the town of Fontaine-de-Vaucluse have not been able to keep the place from being transformed into one of Provence's more garish tourist traps. To reach it, from the car park next to the church, you'll have to walk a noisy 2-km gauntlet of commerciality, everything from *frites* stands to a 'Museum of authentic Provençal *santons*'; soon to open is a museum of medieval torture instruments. Incredibly, many of the attractions are worthwhile. There is **Norbert Castaret's Subterranean World**, a museum of underground rarities and informational exhibits overseen by France's best-known cave explorer; and **Vallis Clausa**, a paper-mill powered by old wooden wheels in the river that keeps up an old craft tradition on the Sorgue, making paper the 15th-century way for art books and stationery (guided tours and sales). Most surprising of all, in a sharp modern building, is the **Musée de la Résistance**, a government-sponsored institution that recaptures the wartime years vividly with two floors of explanatory displays, vignettes of daily life under the Nazis, newsreels and magazines, weapons and other relics. As at Gordes, Resistance life around Fontaine-de-Vaucluse was no joke; among the exhibits is a tribute to Fontaine's own mayor, Robert Garcin, whose aid to the *maquis* earned him a one-way ticket to Buchenwald in 1944.

Finally, there is the source itself, well worth the trouble even in its off-season. In the spring, and occasionally in winter, it pours out at a rate of as much as 200 cubic metres per second, forming a small, intensely green lake under the cliff. From the late spring until autumn it is greatly diminished, and often stops overflowing altogether (the water appears slightly further down the cliff); its unpredictability is as much a mystery as its source. It is a beautiful spot; if you're ambitious, it is also the beginning of two excellent hiking trails (GR 6 and 97), leading up into some of the most scenic parts of the Plateau de Vaucluse. More easily, you can climb up to the romantically ruined 13th-century **château** overlooking the spring.

Before you leave, have a look at the village church, **Ste-Marie-et-St-Véran**. Begun in 1134, this lovely Romanesque building incorporates Roman and Carolingian fragments, including some bits of floral arabesques and the columns and capitals around the altar. The cornice outside is decorated with winsome rows of human and animal faces. Inside, there is the 6th-century Merovingian tomb of St Véran, and a good painted altarpiece of the *Crucifixion*, donated in 1654 by the village's *confrérie* of paper-makers.

WHERE TO STAY/EATING OUT

Gordes (84220) is big business; several fancy villa-hotels have sprung up on the outskirts, but the whole Gordes scene is expensive, over the top, and a bit exploitative of the credulous, who want it and deserve it. If you must, there's *****La Mayanelle**, just below the centre on the Cavaillon road; unpretentious, comfortable, and a good bargain, with an authentic Provençal kitchen to help you forget Vasarelian didacticism, and an outdoor terrace (some rooms with a grand view; tel 90 72 00 28; closed Jan–Feb). Another honest establishment, outside the village, the ****Auberge de Carcarille**, is a carefully restored *mas*, with pretty rooms, some with balconies, and a reasonable restaurant specializing in fish and game (menus 90–160 F; southwest of town on the D 2, tel 90 72 02 63). There's nothing lacking in Gordes' restaurants: the ***Hostellerie Provençale**, behind the château, guarantees a tasty dinner even if it's only a simple chicken or lamb chops; also a few inexpensive rooms (menus 90–100 F, 65 F at lunch, tel 90 72 03 95).

Fontaine-de-Vaucluse (84800), in spite of its touristic vocation, is a quite pleasant place in which to stay or to dine. The **Hostellerie Le Château**, in Fontaine's old *mairie*, overlooking the Sorgue, has an outdoor terrace (behind glass, so you won't get splashed by the water-wheel in front). Excellent cooking on menus from 90–175 F, includes delicate sautéed frogs' legs and *truite en papillotte*; also five nice inexpensive rooms (tel 90 20 31 54). The closest restaurant to the spring isn't a bad one: **Restaurant Philip**, mostly seafood, on 90, 120, 155 F menus, with an outside terrace by the river. There is also a popular pizzeria, **Les Bourgades**, on Rue Bourgades off the central square.

From Cavaillon to Carpentras

Until the Revolution, the western Vaucluse plains from Cavaillon north to Vaison-la-Romaine were known as the *Comtat Venaissin*, a county that was a part of the papal dominions in France, though legally separate from Avignon. St Louis had stolen the territory from the Counts of Toulouse in 1229, part of the French Kings' share of the booty after the Albigensian crusade, and Philip III passed it along to the popes in 1274 to settle an old dispute. It was a worthy prize—medieval irrigation schemes had already made the rich lands of the Comtat the 'Garden of France', an honorific it holds today as the most productive agricultural region in the country. Besides Cavaillon's famous melons, this small area has 5 per cent of all France's vineyards, including its best table grapes, and still finds room to grow tons of cherries, asparagus, apples and everything else a Frenchman could desire. All this intensive agriculture doesn't do the scenery any harm, and passing through it you'll find some fat, contented villages that make the trip worthwhile.

TOURIST INFORMATION
L'Isle-sur-la-Sorgue (84800): Place de l'Eglise, tel 90 38 04 78.
Pernes-les-Fontaines (84210): Pont de la Nesque, tel 90 61 31 04.

L'Isle-sur-la-Sorgue

The Sorgue, that singular river that jumps out of the ground at Fontaine-de-Vaucluse and makes fly fishermen happy all the way to the suburbs of Avignon (it's one of France's best trout streams), has one more trick to play before it reaches the Rhône. At L'Isle-sur-la-Sorgue, it briefly splits into two channels to make this Provençal Venice, a charming town of 15,000 souls, an island indeed. In the Middle Ages, as a scrappy semi-independent commune, L'Isle-sur-la-Sorgue dug two more channels, and put the water to work running mills and textile factories; when trouble came, as during the Wars of Religion, the town knew how to keep out invaders by flooding the surrounding plains and making itself even more of an island.

Today, L'Isle-sur-la-Sorgue still makes fabrics and carpets, but it is best known as the antiques centre of Provence, with a number of permanent shops on the southern edge of town, around Avenue des Quatre Otages, and a big 'Antiques Village' by the train station, open on Sundays (some booths open Sat and Mon also). Circumnavigating the town is a pleasant diversion, passing a number of old canals and wooden **mills**, some still in use. There are two along Rue Jean Théophile, a street that will also take you to the 18th-century **Hôtel-Dieu**, with a sumptuous chapel and a perfectly preserved pharmacy of that era that can be visited, an ensemble of Moustiers faience and ornate carved wood. There are frequent art exhibitions in an 18th-century palace, the **Hôtel Donadéi de Campredon**, on Rue Dr Tallet. And finally, right in the centre, is the town's beached whale of a church, 17th-century **Notre-Dame-des-Anges**, sprawling across Place de l'Eglise. Even in a region full of marvellously awful churches, this one is a jewel, a mouldering imitation of Roman Baroque outside and gilt everything within. Opposite the façade, note the old firm of Fauques-Beyret, the prettiest drapery shop in Provence, with a fine Art Nouveau front; inside and out, nothing seems to have changed since the turn of the century.

West of L'Isle-sur-la-Sorgue, the N 100 leads to Le Thor, with one of the best Romanesque churches in Provence, carrying the intriguing name of **Notre-Dame-du-Lac**. Begun about 1200, it is a work of transition, the Provençal Romanesque giving way to Gothic influences, as seen in the pointed vaulting of the nave. The sculptural decoration is spare but elegant, emphasizing the perfect symmetry of one of the last great medieval buildings in this region. Some 3 km north of Le Thor on the D 16 is the **Grotte de Thouzon** (daily in July and August, 9:30–7pm; Nov–Mar, Sun only 2–6; rest of year 10–12 and 2–6, adm). Of all the caves in Provence, this may be the one most worth seeing—weird and colourful, with rare needle-slender stalactites hanging down as much as 3 m.

Pernes-les-Fontaines

L'Isle-sur-la-Sorgue's tiny neighbour to the north, Pernes-les-Fontaines has only a single drowsy stream passing through it, the Nesque. In the 18th century, perhaps out of jealousy, the Pernois took it into their heads to build decorative fountains instead. They got a bit carried away, and now there are 37 of them, or one for every 190 inhabitants. The fountains contribute a lot to making Pernes-les-Fontaines the most thoroughly delightful town in the Vaucluse. It is an introspective place, still turning its back on the world, sheltering inside a circuit of walls that was demolished a hundred years ago, to be replaced by a ring of boulevards. Pernes-les-Fontaines is for walking; the Pernois have used the centuries to make their town an integrated work of art, looking exactly the way they want it to look; there's a surprise around every corner—or at least, a fountain.

Starting from the centre, the old **bridge** over the Nesque is embellished at both ends, with the 16th-century **Porte de Notre-Dame**, the **Cormorant Fountain** and the small chapel of **Notre-Dame-des-Graces**, from the same era. Behind it, the 12th-century church of **Notre-Dame-de-Nazareth** includes some Gothic chapels and reliefs of Old Testament scenes. The relative simplicity of its interior, in contrast to so many other Provençal churches, is a reminder of Pernes' earnest Catholicism through the centuries (one of its current economic mainstays, incidentally, is making the communion hosts for all the churches of France). Ask at the Tourist Office for a guide to take you around to the **Tour Ferrande**, on Rue Gambetta. This unassuming medieval tower, next to a fountain with carved grotesques, contains what are claimed to be the oldest frescoes in France (*c*. 1275): vigorous, primitive scriptural scenes, Charles of Anjou in Sicily, St Sebastian and St Christopher, and a certain Count William of Orange battling against a giant.

East of Pernes-les-Fontaines is a very odd place, **Le Beaucet** (on the D 39 south of St-Didier), where the people used to live in cave houses, some of which can still be seen, along with a ruined castle; above it, in the mountains, a source similar to Fontaine-de-Vaucluse has given rise to one of the biggest pilgrimage sites in Provence, a well-decorated chapel dedicated to the 12th-century **St-Gens**, a rain-maker and tamer of wolves. **Venasque**, further east, was the old capital of the Comtat Venaissin, and gave the county its name. Though a pretty village, and lately fashionable, nothing is left of its former distinction but the usual ruined fortifications and a venerable **baptistry**, really a 6th-century Merovingian funeral chapel reworked in the 1100s. The twisting D 4, connecting Carpentras and Apt, was the main road of the Vaucluse in medieval times; it is still an exceptionally lovely route, passing eastwards from Venasque through the **Forêt de Venasque** and some rocky gorges on the edge of the Plateau de Vaucluse.

Market Days: L'Isle-sur-la-Sorgue, Sunday mornings (antiques).

WHERE TO STAY/EATING OUT

Both L'Isle-sur-la-Sorgue and Pernes-les-Fontaines are delightful places for a stay, and accommodation in each is fine. Outside **L'Isle-sur-la-Sorgue** (84800), there is a restored inn from the 1700s, the ***Mas de Cure Bourse**, with a pool and extensive gardens, only a few rooms, and a restaurant where the Lubéron lamb in garlic sauce is a treat (menus 160–220 F, at Velorgues, 2 km south of town on the D 938, tel 90 38 16 58). In town, the ****Le Gueulardière** on Av. Charmasson, right in the centre, has cosy rooms and a garden terrace for dining; specialities of the house include salmon terrine and duck with olives (tel 90 38 10 52). The best budget hotel is ***Le Bassin** on the river, with a simple restaurant (tel 90 38 03 16). For lunch, two inexpensive local favourites are the

Pizzeria la Joute on Place Gambetta (70 F) and the **Saigon**, a Vietnamese place on Rue de la République, 70–75 F menus. **La Basilic 2**, also on Place Gambetta, offers a somewhat eccentric 85 F menu with things you won't often see in the Vaucluse—from chilli to *carpaccio*.

Pernes-les-Fontaines (84210), generally overlooked by the Vaucluse's tourist hordes, has only the unpretentious ****La Margelle** in the village itself (Place Giraud; tel 90 61 30 36); you're better off in the quiet and gardens of the ****Mas de la Bonoty**, on the Chemin de Bonoty outside the village, which also has a restaurant with a creditable *bouillabaisse* on a 120 F menu (closed Jan; tel 90 60 61 09). Another good restaurant, though only open weekends outside the summer months, is **La Pergola** on Place Aristide Briand, worth a splurge for the 170 F menu—stuffed haunch of rabbit with basil, after salmon *crêpes* (also 120 F menu, tel 90 66 43 43).

Carpentras

The average French town of 30,000 or so, unless it has some great historical importance or major monument, is likely to be a rather anonymous place. Carpentras isn't. Perhaps because of its long isolation from the rest of France, under papal rule but really run by its own bishops, Carpentras has character and a subtle but distinct sense of place. A bit unkempt, and unconcerned about it, immune to progress and to any sudden urges for urban renewal, it is nevertheless an interesting place to visit. There are some cock-eyed monuments, and some surprises. The rest of Provence pays Carpentras little mind; ask anyone, and they'll probably remember only that the town is famous for caramels, mint-flavoured ones called *berlingots*.

GETTING AROUND

Carpentras is the node for what little there is of coach transport in the northern Vaucluse, with good connections to Avignon (some going by way of Pernes-les-Fontaines and L'Isle-sur-la-Sorgue) and Orange, one to Marseille; also one or two a day to Vaison-la-Romaine and some villages of the Dentelles de Montmirail, including Beaumes-de-Venise and Gigondas. Almost all of these stop at Place Aristide-Briand, on the ring boulevard. There are also several daily SNCF trains to Orange and Avignon.

TOURIST INFORMATION

170 Allée Jean-Jaurès, tel 90 63 57 88.

As in so many other French towns, you'll have to cross a sort of motorway to get into the centre: a ring road of boulevards that was created when the town walls were knocked down in the last century (it's one-way and very fast; miss a turn and you'll have to go all the way around again; the French find these very entertaining). One part of the fortifications remains, the towering 14th-century **Porte d'Orange**, built in the 1360s under Pope Innocent IV.

If you can get in, you'll find an amiable and lively town, especially when the gorgeous produce of the Comtat farmers rolls in for Friday market. The stands fill half the town, but the centre is Rue des Halles, with the **Passage Boyer**, an imposing glass-roofed arcade, built by Carpentras' unemployed in the national public works programme started after the 1848 revolution.

Cathédrale St-Siffrein

Undoubtedly this is one of the most absurd cathedrals in Christendom. So many architects, in so many periods, and no one has ever been able to get it finished and get it right. Worst of all is the mongrel façade—Baroque on the bottom, a bit of Gothic and God knows what else above—like a mutt with a spot around its eye, likeable somehow, the kind that follows you home and you end up keeping him. Begun in the 1400s, remodellings and restorations proceeded in fits and starts until 1902. Some of the original intentions can be seen in the fine Flamboyant Gothic portal on the southern side, called the **Porte Juive** because Jewish converts were taken through it, in suitably humiliating ceremonies, to be baptized. Just above the centre of the arch is Carpentras' famous curio, the small sculpted *Boule aux Rats*—a globe covered with rats. The usual explanation is that this has something to do with the Jews, or heretics. But bigotry was never really fashionable among 15th-century artists, and more likely this is a joke on an old fanciful etymology of the town's name: *carpet ras*, or ' the rat nibbles'.

The interior, richly decorated in dubious taste, includes some stained glass of the 1500s (much restored) and an early 15th-century altarpiece (left of the high altar) by Enguerrand Quarton of the Avignon school. The sacred treasures are in a chapel on the left: the relics of St Siffrein, one of the most obscure of all saints, not even mentioned in any early hagiographies; and the *St-Mors*, the 'holy bridle bit', said to have been made by St Helen out of two nails of the Cross as a present for her son, Emperor Constantine. Next to the cathedral, the **Palais de Justice** (1640) is the former Archbishop's Palace, occupying the site of an earlier palace that, for the brief periods that popes like Innocent IV chose to stay in Carpentras, was the centre of the Christian world. The present building, modelled after the Farnese Palace in Rome, contains some interesting frescoes from the 17th and 18th centuries: mythological scenes, and also views of Comtat villages and towns (ask the concierge to be shown round).

The Triumphal Arch and the Secret Cathedral

Everyone knows that if you walk around a church widdershins (against the sun: counter-clockwise), you'll end up in fairyland, like Childe Harolde. Try it in Carpentras, and you'll find some strange business. The 9-m Roman **Triumphal Arch**, tucked in a corner between the Cathedral and the Palais de Justice, was built about the same time as that of Orange, in the early 1st century AD. Anyone who hasn't yet seen Orange's would hardly guess this one was Roman at all. Of all the ancient Provençal monuments, this shows the bizarre Celtic quality of Gallo-Roman art at its most stylized extreme, with its reliefs of enchained captives and trophies. In the 1300s, the arch was incorporated into the now-lost Episcopal Palace. By 1640, when it was cleared, it was serving an inglorious role separating the archbishop's kitchens from his prisons. Originally, it must have connected the palace with the Romanesque cathedral.

Now, look at the clumsily-built exterior wall of the present cathedral, opposite the arch. There are two large gaps, through which you can have a peek at something that few books mention, and that even the Carpentrassiens themselves seem to have forgotten: the **crossing and cupola** of the 12th-century cathedral, used in the rebuilt church to support a bell tower (later demolished) and neglected for centuries. In its time this must have been one of the greatest buildings of Provence, done in an ambitious, classicizing style—perhaps too ambitious, since its partial collapse in 1399 necessitated the rebuilding. The sculpted decoration, vine and acanthus-leaf patterns, along with winged creatures and scriptural scenes, is excellent work; some of it has been moved to the town museum.

The Synagogue and Museums
Behind the cathedral and palace, two streets north up Rue Barret, is the broad Place de l'Hôtel de Ville, marking the site of Carpentras' Jewish Ghetto. Before the Revolution, over 2000 Jews were forced to live here in unspeakable conditions, walled in and forced to pay a fee any time they wanted to leave. All that is left today is the **Synagogue** at the end of the square. Built in 1741, it has a glorious decorated interior in the best 18th-century secular taste (Mon-Fri, 10–12 and 2–5). Other attractions in town include the **Hôtel-Dieu** on Place Aristide Briand, an 18th-century hospital with another well-preserved pharmacy and an attractive chapel, containing the tomb of Carpentras' famous bishop (1735–73) and civic benefactor, the Monseigneur d'Inguimbert. This hospital is his monument, along with the important library he left to the town and the beginning of the collections in the **Musée Comtadin-Duplessis** on Blvd Albin-Durand (the ring road). Here are displayed artefacts and clutter from Carpentras' history, old views of the town, as well as 16th- and 17th-century paintings, many by local artists (daily exc Mon, 10–12 and 2–4, until 6 in summer; adm).

Market Days: Carpentras, Friday morning (truffles from Dec until Feb).

WHERE TO STAY/EATING OUT
Carpentras (84200) somehow manages to be left out of the annual tourist visitations, and accommodation here is limited. For the most luxurious the town can offer, work out with the travelling salesmen at the modern *****Safari Hôtel**, out in the suburbs on Av. J. H. Fabre, complete with health club, tennis, pool, and balconies and TV for most rooms (tel 90 63 35 35). For something cosier in the centre, there is the elegant old ****Le Fiacre** in an 18th-century building on Rue Vigne, near the Syndicat d'Initiative (tel 90 63 03 15). The budget choice is the ***Hôtel de Théâtre** on the ring boulevard, where the friendly proprietor may try to corner you into a game of chess (7 Av. Albin-Durand; tel 90 63 02 90).

You'll do well at dinner-time, even if there aren't a large number of choices. For original cooking, try **Le Galant Vert**, on Rue des Clapiès; 150–220 F for strictly fresh seafood. If the day's catch is unspectacular, you won't go wrong with their *suprême de pigeon* or grilled lamb either (also 80 F lunch menu; tel 90 67 15 50). L'Orangerie on Rue Duplessis is a similar place both in price and in its innovative tinkering with old local favourites; the lamb here, for example, comes flavoured with mint (unheard of!); also a memorable seafood platter, *délices aux fruits de mer*, menu 80 F (lunch only), otherwise 110, 130, 190 F (tel 90 67 27 23). For less than a 100 F note, you won't do better than the popular and friendly **Le Marijo** on Rue Raspail, sometimes serving genuine fresh seafood, or at least a well-cooked trout, 55–90 F.

East of Carpentras
If you plan to head north, for Mont Ventoux and Vaison-la-Romaine, you might consider a slight detour to the east, along the D 974; towards the village of **Bédoin**, a small resort

below Mont Ventoux, you will pass Carpentras' **aqueduct**—not Roman but a 17th-century work, and impressive nevertheless. **Caromb**, to the west of here, is an attractive village that has kept parts of its medieval fortifications, as well as a surprisingly grand church, **Notre-Dame-et-St-Maurice**, with a wealth of Renaissance decoration inside. From here the skyline is dominated by **Le Barroux**, a dramatically-perched village built around a 13th-century castle that belonged to the Seigneurs of Baux.

An even bigger detour can take you into the centre of the Plateau de Vaucluse on the D 942/D1. Few ever take it, though they miss the most spectacular scenery the Vaucluse has to offer: the dry, rugged **Gorges de la Nesque**, leading to Sault and the Plateau d'Albion (see below). **Monieux**, at the eastern end of the Gorges, is a strange and isolated village that seems to have grown out of the rocky cliffs. There are caves and underground streams in the neighbourhood; experiments with dyeing the water have suggested that one of the sources of the Fontaine-de-Vaucluse may be here.

Mont Ventoux

You can pick it out from almost anywhere on the plains around Carpentras, a commanding presence on the northern horizon. **Mont Ventoux**, a bald, massive humpbacked massif over 20 km across, is the northern boundary stone of Provence, and it has always loomed large in the Provençal consciousness. For the Celts, as for the peoples who came before them, it was a holy place, the Home of the Winds; excavations early this century at its summit brought to light hundreds of small terracotta trumpets, a sort of ex voto that has never been completely explained. Winds, in Provence, inevitably suggest the mistral, and as the source of that chilling blast Mont Ventoux has always had a somewhat evil reputation among the people; medieval Christians sought to exorcize it, perhaps, with the string of simple chapels that mark its slopes.

Mountain-climbers will find a special interest in Mont Ventoux, if only because the sport was invented here. Petrarch, that admirably modern soul, went up with his brother in 1336—this, according to historian Jacob Burckhardt, was the first recorded instance of anyone doing such an odd thing simply for pleasure. The experience had an unexpected effect on the poet. Reading a passage from his *Confessions of St Augustine* at the summit, he was seized with a vision of the folly of his past life, and resolved to return to Italy: ' . . . and men go forth, and admire lofty mountains and broad seas, and roaring torrents, and the course of the stars, and forget their own selves in doing so.' For us the trip will be easier, if perhaps less profound; Edouard Daladier, the Carpentrassien who became French Prime Minister in the 30s, had a road built to the top (the D 974).

TOURIST INFORMATION
Malaucène (84340): Place de la Mairie, tel 90 65 22 59.
Bédoin (84410): Portail Olivier, tel 90 65 63 95.

Malaucène and the Fountain of Groseau
The base for visiting the mountain is **Malaucène**, an open, friendly village on the road from Carpentras to Vaison; its landmark is the impressive church of **St-Michel-et-St-**

Pierre, built in 1309 by Pope Clement V. From here, the D 153 was the ancient route around Mont Ventoux, passing a pair of medieval chapels and a ruined defence tower around the village of Beaumont-du-Ventoux (it now peters out into a hiking trail, the GR 4). The D 974, into the heart of the massif, passes a pre-Celtic site dedicated not to wind, but water. **Notre-Dame-du-Groseau** marks the spot today, an unusual 11th-century octagonal chapel. Originally this was part of a large monastery, now completely disappeared. Pope Clement V used it as his summer home, and his escutcheon can be seen painted inside (the *curé* at Malaucène has the key). But this was also a holy spot in remotest antiquity; the iron cross outside the chapel is planted on a stone believed to have been a Celtic altar. *Groseau* comes from *Groselos*, a Celtic god of springs; the object of veneration is a short distance up the road, the *Source du Groseau*, pouring out of a cliff face. The Romans, as they did at Fontaine-de-Vaucluse, channelled the spring into an aqueduct for the city of Vaison; fragments of this can still be seen.

Further up the mountain, the almost permanent winds make themselves known and vegetation becomes more scarce (despite big reforestation programmes in this century). The D 974's big day comes, almost every summer, when the Tour de France puffs over it, probably the most tortuous part of the race; it was here that the English World Champion Tommy Simpson collapsed and died in 1967. The top of Ventoux (1890 m) is a gravelly wasteland, embellished with communications towers and a meteorological observatory. Coming down the eastern side of the mountain takes you into one of the least-visited backwaters of Provence, a land of shepherds, boar and *cèpes*. There are a few attractive villages: **Sault**, with a quirky museum of fossils, village curios and archaeology (even a mummy); and further north, two medieval *villages perchés*, **Aurel** and **Montbrun-les-Bains**. South of Sault, the lonely **Plateau d'Albion** takes its name (like the English Albion, the Alps and the Provençal village of Aups) from an ancient Indo-European root meaning white—from the odd limestone mountains around it, that seem to be covered in snow. The landscape can be a bit eerie, even more so when you consider that much of this territory, around the village of St-Christol, has been taken over for a complex of bases where France keeps most of its nuclear missiles.

Market Days: Malaucène, Wednesday.

Côtes du Ventoux

The vineyards of this little known AOC region are situated on the lower slopes of the Mont Ventoux. The area is known principally for its reds, which are similar in style to those Côtes du Rhone AOC. The best estates, such as that of Englishman Malcolm Swan at **Domaine des Anges**, make wines with a high proportion of syrah in the blend giving them depth and structure. A 15th-century glassworks, **Domaine La Verrière** at Goult, tel 90 72 20 88, has been transformed into another of the area's best sources of wine. M. Maubert produces a wine of unusual concentration, full of broad, spicy flavours which complement the local dishes perfectly. The Perrin brothers, famous for producing one of the finest and most sought-after Châteauneuf-du-Pape at Château de Beaucastel, also make a very fine Côtes du Ventoux at their purpose-built winery on the outskirts of Orange, **La Vieille Ferme**, tel 90 34 64 25.

Les Dentelles de Montmirail

Montmirail's 'lace' is a small crown of dolomitic limestone mountains, opposite Mont Ventoux on the other side of Malaucène. Eroded by the wind into a lace-like fantasy of columns and arches, they form an ever-changing pattern as you circle around them. You can do this easily from Malaucène, beginning with the D 938 north to Vaison, then down the D 977 west, following a counter-clockwise tour that ends up back in Malaucène.

TOURIST INFORMATION
Gigondas (81490): Place du Portail, tel 90 65 85 46.
Beaumes-de-Venise: Cours Jean-Jaurès, tel 90 62 94 39.

Wine and Antiques

The western slopes of the Dentelles are Côte-du-Rhône country (see below); the D 88 towards **Séguret** is the beginning of a great wine road, passing miles of immaculately-tended vineyards. Séguret is the prettiest of the Montmirail villages, and it has attracted a few artists and antique dealers. It is a good base for hiking; there are two trails (GR 4 and 7) and one village track that passes through a gap in the Dentelles to the eastern side. Further south come the wine villages of **Sablet** and **Gigondas**, little jewels in a setting of high Dentelle walls and cypresses, and **Montmirail**, a thriving thermal spa in the last century, now gone slightly to seed. Along the D 81, there is the Romanesque chapel of **Notre-Dame-d'Aubune**, on a height overlooking the Comtat plains, and **Beaumes-de-Venise**, with a ruined castle to explore, and a small archaeological museum.

Côtes-du-Rhône Sud
Wines called Côtes-du-Rhône originate in 263 communes within the 200 km between Vienne and Avignon. Because of the diversity of growing conditions in such a vast area, from hot rocky plains to steep green slopes, the district is a crazy quilt of local varieties, which as a general rule are better than wines merely labelled Côtes-du-Rhône. You may find any mix of 13 varieties of grapes in a bottle of southern Côtes-du-Rhône, but the dominant forces are, grenache, which gives its tanin and famous sturdy quality; while cinsault, counterbalances with its delicacy and finesse; and syrah, contributes fragrance and its ability to age.

The star of the Dentelles is Gigondas, its very name derived from 'joy', or *Jocunditas*, from a holiday camp for Roman soliders. Part of their delight, according to Pliny, was in the wine, one of the most subtle, noble, dark, and fragrant of all Côtes-du-Rhônes, the perfect match for pheasant, partridge, wild rabbit, or truffles. Two excellent wines to buy and keep around are the *Signature* 90 and *Pavillon de Beaumirail* 88, aged in oak barrels at the **Cave des Vignerons de Gigondas** (tel 90 65 86 27), responsible for 20 per cent of the total Gigondas production. As usual, for the finest wines, one has to go to the individual estates, where the best winemakers can concentrate on producing small quantities of wine from the very best vineyard sites. One of these, **Domaine les Pallières** in Gigondas, tel 90 65 85 07, is currently run by the latest generation of Roux. The label still bears the name of their late father, a former dynamo of the region largely responsible for encouraging his fellow producers to improve quality. The **Domaine Les**

254

Gouberts, tel 90 65 86 38, also in Gigondas offers the remarkably dense *Cuvée Florence 88* and, more unusual for the Dentelles, a *Sablet Blanc*, a fine white wine from ancient clairette vines. Vacqueyras, the minute region just to the south of Gigondas, produces sober and full-bodied wines; some of the finest are made by a Provençal-speaking Pole named Jocelyn Chudzikiewicz at the **Domaine des Amouriers**, Les Garrigues, Sarrians, tel 90 65 83 22 (the 87 has a fine truffle perfume, and the 88 is so dense that it's almost black). Try the **Château de Montmirail**, in Vacqueyras, tel 90 65 86 72, a long-established family vineyard which also does a delightfully mellow Gigondas. The small *appellation* of Beaumes de Venise produces good reds but is rightly famous for its rich sweet white wine made from the Muscat grape. The wine is made by partially fermenting very ripe grapes and arresting the fermentation by the addition of alcohol which kills off the yeasts, leaving much of the sugar and giving the wine an extra potency. The locals find the rather eccentric English habit of treating the wine as a desert wine highly amusing as they drink it as an aperitif! The local cooperative makes a very good example. The two leading estates are **Domaine Durban** which is owned by M. Leydier, 84190 Beaumes de Venise, tel 90 62 94 26 and the Perrin brothers of **La Vieille Ferme**, tel 90 34 64 25, on the outskirts of Orange.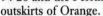

WHERE TO STAY/EATING OUT
Malaucène (84340), the best base for tackling Mont Ventoux, is well-equipped to make your stay a comfortable one. Among the hotels, the clean and shipshape **L'Origan** in the centre stands out; the restaurant offers some hearty cooking—dishes such as guineafowl with *morilles*, on menus of 80, 100 and 120 F (tel 90 65 27 08). If you make it to the other side of Ventoux, stop at Aurel (84390) and the **Relais du Mont Ventoux*; plain but comfortable rooms and a restaurant with no surprises on the menu, but the best you'll do in this little-visited region (tel 90 64 00 62). East of the summit of Ventoux, at the corner of the D 164 and D 974, the **Chalet-Reynard** is the only restaurant for miles, a cosy, wood-lined bar where the local lumberjacks tuck into boar and a *pichet de rouge* at lunch-time; menus 70–110 F.

In the **Dentelles de Montmirail**, the one special place to stay is in Séguret (84110), the *****Domaine de Cabasse**, part of a *Côtes-du-Rhône* estate on the D 23 towards Sablet; a few comfortable rooms with terraces, a pool, and an excellent restaurant that has truffles in season and other rather extravagant dishes year-round (menus 140–160 F, more on weekends, tel 90 46 91 12, closed mid-Oct–mid-Mar). The only inexpensive place is in Beaumes-de-Venise (84190), the **Auberge St-Roch*, with a modest restaurant that does seafood and local dishes (tel 90 62 94 29). One of the old spa establishments of Montmirail (84190) has recently been reopened, without the waters: the ****Hôtel de Montmirail** (pool and garden; and a restaurant with menus at 140–210 F; tel 90 65 84 01).

Vaison-la-Romaine

Some towns simply refuse to stay put. We can blame it on a difficult history, but Vaison, in all its 2400 years has never been able to make up its mind which side of the River Ouvèze it wanted to be on. Its peregrinations have left behind a host of monuments, including extensive Roman ruins that have tempted an otherwise reasonable town to transform itself into a tourist trap, change its name ('la Romaine' is a recent addition), and even bombastically declare itself the 'Pompeii of Provence'. Don't be put off, though. Vaison is a pleasant and beautiful place (with a good market if you are staying locally), and if you're interested in the Romans or the Middle Ages it will be a mandatory stop on your Provençal agenda.

TOURIST INFORMATION

Place du Chanoine Sautel, tel 90 36 02 11. The folks who run this ambitious Syndicat d'Initiative, in a modern pavilion near the ruins, have a modern approach to tourist information, and will consent to *sell* you some brochures. There is a vast car park across the street for visitors.

History

Vaison began on the heights south of the Ouvèze, as a Celtic *oppidum*. In the late 2nd century BC, the Romans took control and refounded it as *Vasio Vocontiorum*, a typical colony on the gentler slopes to the north of the river. For an out-of-the-way site, Vasio prospered spectacularly for the next five centuries, an *urbs opulentissima* with a large number of wealthy villas and as many inhabitants as it has today (about 10,000). Vaison survived the age of invasions better than many of its neighbours; church councils were held here in the 6th century, a time when the city could afford to begin its imposing cathedral.

For the following centuries, bishops ruled in Vaison as the city gradually declined. Perhaps in the 700s, the Counts of Toulouse acquired the site of the old Celtic *oppidum* and built a castle on it. They carried on a chronic quarrel with the bishops; meanwhile most of the people were abandoning the Roman town (and the bishops) for the freedom and safety of the heights, the beginnings of what is now the Haute-Ville. In the 1300s Vaison fell into the hands of the Pope, along with the rest of the Comtat Venaissin, and did not become part of France until the Revolution. In the 1900s, on the move once more, the Vaisonnais were abandoning the Haute-Ville for the river bank. In 1840, the first excavations were undertaken in the Roman city. Vaison nevertheless had to wait for a local cleric, the Abbé Sautel, to do the job seriously. He dug from 1907 until 1955, financed mostly by a local businessman.

The Ruins

The Abbé uncovered almost 11 hectares of Roman Vaison's foundations, while the modern town grew up around the digs. There are two separate areas, the **Quartier de la Villasse** and the **Quartier de Puymin**; their entrances are on either side of the central Place Abbé-Sautel, by the Tourist Information pavilion (daily 9–5 in winter, until 7 in summer; same adm for both, also includes cathedral cloister—see below). Vaison's ruins are an argument for leaving the archaeologists alone; with everything sanitized and tidy, interspersed with gardens and playgrounds, there is the unmistakable air of an archaeological theme park. The Villasse is the smaller of the two areas; from the entrance, a Roman street takes you past the city's **baths** (the best parts are still hidden under Vaison's post office) and the **Maison au Buste d'Argent**, a truly posh villa with two *atria* and some mosaic floors. It has its own baths, as does the adjacent **Maison au Dauphin**;

beyond this is a short stretch of a **colonnaded street**, a status embellishment in the most prosperous Roman towns.

The Puymin quarter has more of the same: another villa, the **Maison des Messii** near the entrance. Beyond that, however, is an *insula*, or block of flats for the common folk, as well as a large, partially excavated quadrangle called the **Portique de Pompée**, an enclosed public garden with statuary that was probably attatched to a temple. On the opposite side of the *insula* is a much-ruined *nymphaeum*, or monumental fountain. From here you can walk uphill to the **theatre**, restored and used for concerts in the summer, and the **museum**, displaying the best of the finds from the excavations. You'll learn more about Roman Vaison here than from the bare foundations around it; there is a model of one of the villas as it may have looked. All the items a Roman museum must have are present: restored mosaics and fragments of wall painting, some lead pipes, inscriptions, hairpins and bracelets, and of course statuary: municipal notables of Vaison, a wonderful monster *acroterion* (roof ornament) from a mausoleum, and a few marble gods and emperors—a startling family portrait with the gay Emperor Hadrian completely naked and evidently proud of it, next to his demurely clothed Empress Sabina, smiling wanly.

The Cathedral of Notre-Dame-de-Nazareth

The French, with their incurable adoration of anything Roman, go on forever about the ruins and neglect Vaison's real attraction, one of the most fascinating medieval monuments of the Midi. A treasure-house of oddities, it is a reminder that there is more to the art and religion of the Middle Ages than meets the eye, and much of significance that is lost to us forever. It stands a half-km west of the ruins, on Avenue Jules Ferry.

The church was begun in the 6th century. Its **apse** is the oldest part; looking at it from the outside, you'll see where excavations have uncovered the dressed Roman stones and drums of columns that were recycled to serve as a foundation. The rest of the structure dates from a rebuilding that began in the 1100s, including some handsome sculptural decoration around the portals, cornices and bell tower. The first clues to the mystery of this church can be seen near the top of the façade: a rectangular **maze**, and a triangular figure that may be a mystic representation of the Sun. Even with this, the exterior is subdued, and the muscular perfection of the columns and vaults inside comes as a surprise. The 12th-century nave is Romanesque at its best, but still the eye is drawn down it to the magnificent, arcaded interior of the apse. There is nothing like this apse in France; it is a place to muse on time and fate—the last surviving work of Roman Provence, the wistful farewell of a civilization that can be heard across the centuries. Almost incredibly, the 6th-century marble **altar** is still present, carved in a beautiful wave-like pattern. Also here are the original bishop's throne, and benches set around the semicircle of the apse where the monks would sit: the earliest form of a choir, as in the churches of Ravenna.

In the medieval nave, some of the decoration is as provocative as that on the façade. At the rear, near a column that survives from the original basilica, you'll notice the figure of an unidentifiable 'hairy person', extending a hand in a gesture of benediction. Elaborate masons' marks are everywhere. Odd figures of the Evangelists embellish the squinches of the fine octagonal cupola; behind one of them, high up, on the second column on the right side of the nave, is what appears to be a little *devil*. You'll meet his big brother in the cloister.

THE CLOISTER

Look around as you enter. Grinning over the ticket-booth to the cloister is Vaison's most famous citizen—Old Nick himself, with horns and goatee, carved into the stone as big as life. This is not a personage one usually sees portrayed in cathedral cloisters, and no one has ever come up with an explanation for his presence here—one unlikely guess is that it's really Jesus, superimposed over a crescent moon. This is a small but graceful cloister from the 1100s, with a number of finely carved capitals (one with a pair of entwined serpents) and architectural fragments displayed around the walls.

And if you think the Devil and all the other curiosities were simply fanciful decoration, look up from the cloister at the Latin verse inscription, running the entire length of the church's southern cornice:

> I exhort you, brothers, to triumph over the party of Aquilon *[the north]*, faithfully maintaining the rule of the cloister, for thus will you arrive at the south, in order that the divine triple fire shall not neglect to illuminate the quadrangular abode in such a way as to bring to life the arched stones, to the number of two times six. Peace to this house.

The medieval Latin is in parts obscure enough for other interpretations to be possible, but these tend to be even stranger. The twelve stones seem to be pillars of the cloister, the 'quadrangular abode'. The rest is lost in arcane, erudite medieval mysticism, wrapped up with the architecture and unique embellishments, and undoubtedly with a monastic community that was up to something not entirely orthodox. Like most medieval secrets, this one will never be completely understood.

Chapelle St-Quenin

A bit of a climb to the north, on Avenue de St-Quenin, you can continue in this same vein of medieval peculiarity. **St-Quenin**, a chapel dedicated to a 6th-century bishop who became Vaison's patron saint, fooled people for centuries into thinking it a Roman building. Its apse, unique in France, is triangular instead of the usual semicircle, and crowned with a cornice that includes fragments from Roman buildings as well as primitive reliefs that may date from Merovingian times. It is difficult to ascribe any special significance to this odd form. Probably built in the 11th or 12th century, it may be simply an architectural experiment, typical of the creative freedom of the early Romanesque. On the front of the chapel is a Merovingian-era relief of two vine shoots emerging from a vase, a piece of early Christian symbolism that has become the symbol of Vaison.

The Haute-Ville

From Roman and modern Vaison, the medieval version of the town is a splendid sight atop its cliff, a honey-coloured skyline of stone houses under the castle of the Counts of Toulouse. Almost abandoned at the turn of the century, the Haute-Ville is becoming quite chic now, with restorations everywhere and more than a few artists' studios. You reach it by crossing the Ouvèze on a **Roman bridge**, still in good nick after 18 centuries of service; then climb up to the gate of the 14th-century fortifications, next to the **Tour Beffroi**, the clock-tower which is the most prominent sight of the Haute-Ville's silhouette. The cobbled streets and the shady **Place du Vieux-Marché** with its fountain are lovely; trails lead higher up to the 12th- to 14th-century **castle**, half ruined but at least offering a view.

Market Days: Vaison-la-Romaine (the lower town), Tuesday.

WHERE TO STAY/EATING OUT

Vaison (84110) has plenty of room, and in the crowded summer months you might end up here even if you had preferred to be in one of the villages of the Dentelles—for a compromise, try the ****Hôtel les Aurics**, a modernized old farmhouse with a pool, west of Vaison on the D 977 and convenient to both (tel 90 36 03 15). In town, staying up in the Haute-Ville is not entirely convenient—but it can be very gratifying: *****Le Beffroi** is in a picturesque 16th-century house, furnished to match, inexpensive for its category (Rue de l'Evêché, tel 90 36 04 71). The budget choice is the old ***Théâtre Romain** in the centre, very accommodating, though some rooms can be a little noisy (Rue Abbé-Sautel, tel 90 36 05 87).

Despite the quantities of tourists, exceptional restaurants are few. All the hotel restaurants have rather unexciting offerings, and there are plenty of pizzerias and such. One place that stands out is in the Haute-Ville, **La Fête en Provence**; serving their own *foie gras de canard*, followed by a *magret* or lamb with olives, on a bargain 110 F menu (tel 90 36 36 43). For a change, there are West Indian specialities at **Le Colibri** on Cours Taulignan (menus 90, 110, 130 F).

Part IX

DOWN THE RHÔNE: ORANGE TO BEAUCAIRE

The Papal Mint, Avignon

Despite Frédéric Mistral's best efforts in the epic 1896 *Poème du Rhône*, this is not a lyrical river, neither fair of face nor full of grace. Its nickname *malabar*, the strongman, describes it well: deep and swift-flowing with muscular currents, its banks like bulging biceps, its secret depths hosting legendary man-eating monsters such as the Tarasque and Drac, the scourge of Beaucaire. For the Rhône is a Saturday's child and has to work for a living: after serving the industries and nuclear plants to the north, it does it all again in Provence, at France's biggest centre for the processing of nuclear waste, at Marcoule, at the hydroelectric plant and Satanic mills of Avignon's industrial quarter, and at the paper mills near Tarascon.

Historically most of the Rhône's traffic has come south with the current, ferrying the blond barbarians, the eaters of *frites* and drinkers of beer, down to the sultry Mediterranean. The river also divided the spoils: Provence, on the east bank, owed allegiance to the Emperor and Pope; Languedoc, on the west, belonged to the kingdom of France after the Albigensian crusade. Rhône boatmen called the banks not port and starboard, but Empire and Kingdom. On the Empire's side are Orange, with its famous Roman theatre, Châteauneuf-du-Pape and Avignon, where 14th-century popes spent what Petrarch called their 'Babylonian exile', and Tarascon, favoured home of Provence's Good King René. The Kingdom's bank bristles with the towers of Villeneuve-lès-Avignon, where cardinals escaped the profanity of Avignon, and Beaucaire, long famous for its international fair.

260

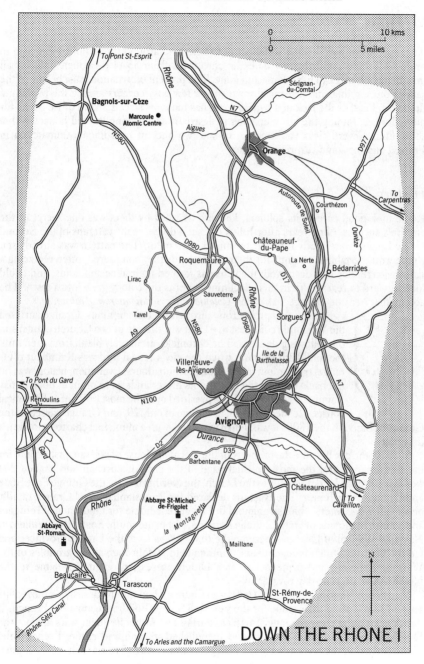

0   10 kms
0   5 miles

To Pont St-Esprit

Sérignan-
du-Comtal

Rhône

N7

Bagnols-sur-Cèze

Marcoule ●
Atomic Centre

Aigues

N580

Orange

D977

Autoroute de Soleil

Courthézon

To
Carpentras

Châteauneuf-
du-Pape

La Nerte

Bédarrides

D980

Roquemaure

Ouvèze

D17

Lirac

Sauveterre

Rhône

Sorgues

Tavel

N580

D980

A9

Ile de la
Barthelasse

A7

Villeneuve-
lès-Avignon

To Pont du Gard

Remoulins

N100

Avignon

Gard

D2

Durance

D35

Barbentane

Châteaurenard

To
Cavaillon

Rhône

Abbaye St-Michel-
de-Frigolet

la Montagnette

Abbaye
St-Roman

Maillane

N

Beaucaire

Tarascon

St-Rémy-de-
Provence

Rhône-Sète Canal

DOWN THE RHÔNE I

To Arles and the Camargue

261

Orange

There seems to have been a settlement of some kind around the hill of St-Eutrope in prehistoric times, and the city dates its chronicles from 35 BC—enough time for all imaginable Oranges to have come and gone. The present incarnation must be one of the sadder ones, a miasmic provincial town with a few cosy corners among the prevailing drabness. Fate, or the lack of a bypass road, has made its streets a kind of Le Mans for heavy lorries, fouling the air, menacing pedestrians and coating the old houses with a sooty film. Nevertheless you'll come, to see two ancient monuments unmatched in France, and for some surprises besides.

History

Rome took good care of its soldiers; keeping its word by them was one secret of the empire's success. Nine years after Julius Caesar's death, many veterans of the Second Gallic Legion were ready for their promised retirement. The pattern was already set. Rome would establish a colony for them in the lands they conquered, often replacing a native village they had destroyed; the veterans farmed their allocated lands, and could look forward to real wealth in their declining years as the colony grew into a town. The colony that became Orange was called *Colonia Julia Secundanorum Arausio*.

Exceedingly prosperous throughout Roman times, Orange survived the Visigothic conquest in 412; it was the site of two Church councils in the following decades. The chronicles are largely blank from then until the mid-12th century, when the city's feudal lord was Raimbaut d'O-range, troubadour and patron of troubadours. Even then, history was on the back-burner; the city and its hinterlands were often in hock to pay Raimbaut's debts, while he presided over the most brilliant of Provençal courts. He died in 1173, at the age of only 29, and Orange passed to the Counts of Baux. In the 1300s it was a thriving place, with a municipal charter and even a university.

In 1530, the city became the property of the German House of Nassau, just in time for the Reformation and the most unusual page of the city's history, an odd chance that would let Orange lend its colour to the Dutch, the Northern Irish, the Orange Free State and Orange, New Jersey. The Nassaus declared for Protestantism, and Orange rapidly became the dissenters' chief stronghold in Provence, a home for thousands of refugees and a thorn in the side of arch-Catholic Avignon, just to the south. Soon after, William of Nassau—William of Orange—became the first *stadhouder* of the United Provinces and led the fight for Dutch independence. Orange held fast through all the troubles of the Wars of Religion, and came out of it a Dutch possession, giving its name to the Netherlands' present-day royal family.

Maurice of Nassau, in the early 1600s, did Orange a bad turn by destroying most of its ancient ruins, using their stone for the new wall he was building against the French. It didn't keep them away for long. In 1672, during one of his frequent wars against the Dutch, Louis XIV seized the city and demolished its wall and castle. French rule, particularly after the revocation of the Edict of Nantes (see p. 54), was a disaster; Orange lost its prosperity and many of its best citizens. The city never really recovered, but it earns a fair living today from industry, and from the big army and air force bases that make it one of the most important military centres in France.

GETTING AROUND
The **train station** on Av. Frédéric Mistral, tel 90 82 50 50, has direct connections to Paris, Avignon, Arles, Marseille, and Cannes; **buses** depart from Cours Portoules, tel 90 34 15 59, several times a day for Carpentras, Vaison-la-Romaine, Avignon and twice daily for Séguret. You can hire a **bike** at Cycles Lurion, 48 Cours Aristide Briand, tel 90 34 08 77.

TOURIST INFORMATION
Cours Aristide Briand, tel 90 34 70 88.

The Best-preserved Theatre of Antiquity

Its architects might be distressed to hear it, but these days the most impressive part of this huge structure (the *Théâtre Antique*, daily 9–12 and 2–5; continuously in summer; adm, also valid for Municipal Museum) is its back wall. 'The best wall in my kingdom', Louis XIV is said to have called it. If the old prints in the municipal museum are accurate, this rugged, elegant sandstone cliff facing Place des Frères Mounet was originally adorned with low, temple-like façades. In its present state, it resembles a typical Florentine Renaissance palace, without the windows. The classically-minded architects of the 1400s all travelled in Provence, and perhaps this stately relic of Rome, at its best, had a hidden influence that would have made its architects proud.

Built in the early 1st century AD, the theatre is a testimony to the culture and wealth of Arausio. Like the Colosseum in Rome, it even had a massive awning (*velum*), a contraption of canvas and beams that could be raised to cover most of the spectators. All over the Mediterranean, theatres fell into disuse in the cultural degradation of the late empire. This one was probably already abandoned when it burned in the 4th or 5th century. In the Middle Ages other buildings grew up over the ruins; old prints show the semicircular tiers of seats (*cavea*) half filled-in and covered with ramshackle houses.

The site is typical for a Roman theatre, backed into the hill of St-Eutrope where the banks of seats could be built on the slope. These have been almost completely restored. Since 1869, Orange has used the theatre for a summer festival called *Les Chorégies*. Mistral and the Félibres (see p. 39) were active in its early years, when Greek and Roman plays were often on the bill; today contemporary drama and opera are more common.

Unlike Greek theatres, which always opened to a grand view behind the stage, those of the Romans featured large stage buildings, serious architectural compositions of columns, arches and sculptured friezes. This is what the great exterior wall is supporting; Orange's stage building (35 m high) is one of two complete specimens that remain to us (the other is at Aspendos, in Turkey), though the fragments of its decoration are mostly in the municipal museum across the street. A statue of Augustus remains, in the centre, over an inscription honouring the people of Arausio and welcoming them to the show. Outside the theatre, foundations of a temple have been excavated, along with a semi-circular ruin that may have been a nymphaeum, or a gymnasium.

The Musée Municipal

Save some time for this bulging curiosity shop, directly opposite the theatre on Place des Frères-Mounet; it is one of the most fascinating town museums in Provence (daily 9–12 and 2–6:30; adm, also valid for the Roman theatre). As expected, the main rooms are given over to Roman art, including an exceptional *frieze of satyrs and amazons* from the theatre. The *plan cadastral* (land survey) is unique: a stone tablet engraved with property records for the broad Roman grid of farmland between Orange and Montélimar. The first pieces of it were dicovered in 1856, though no one guessed what they were until the rest turned up, between 1927 and 1954; since then they have been a great aid to scholars in filling in some of the everyday details of Roman life and law.

Climbing the stairs into the upper levels of the museum, you'll pass rooms of Dutch portraits and relics of Nassau rule, and a collection of works by the Welsh Impressionist Frank Brangwyn (who was, in fact, born in Bruges): heroic compositions among wharves and factories, along with some lovely country scenes. The most unexpected exhibit is the **Salle des Wetters**, a remarkable relic of the Industrial Revolution in France. The Wetters were a family of mid-18th-century industrialists who produced *indiennes*, printed cotton cloth much in demand at the time. They commissioned an artist named G. M. Rossetti to paint a record of their business; this he did (1764) in incredible detail, on five huge, colourful naive canvases showing every aspect of the making of *indiennes*, from the stevedores unloading the cotton on the docks to the shy, serious factory girls in the great hall—the Wetters were among the first in France to stumble on the factory system, and employed over 500 people.

Old Orange and the Triumphal Arch

Touring old Orange does not handsomely reward the visitor; you may walk up the **Hill of St-Eutrope** for a view over the town and a look at the foundations of the castle destroyed by the French. In the city centre, there is only an utterly pathetic cathedral, begun in 529 over a Temple of Diana and rebuilt to death between 1561 and 1809. One thing Orange does have is original street names—sometimes unintentionally so, like the *Impasse de Parlement*.

Rue Victor-Hugo, roughly following the route of the ancient Roman main street, or *cardo major*, is the axis that leads to Orange's other Roman attraction. The **Triumphal Arch**, built around 20 AD, celebrates the conquests of the Second Gallic Legion with outlandish, almost abstract scenes of battling Romans and Celts. This is the epitome of the Provençal-Roman style: excellent, careful reliefs, especially in the upper frieze, portraying a naval battle, though with a touch of Celto-Ligurian strangeness in the details. Odd oval shields are a prominent feature, decorated with heraldic devices and thunderbolts. Seemingly random symbols at the upper left—a whip, a pitcher, something that looks like a bishop's crozier, and others—are in fact symbols of animal sacrifice and marine attributes (the 'crozier' is the prow of a ship). On the sides of the arch are heaps of arms—'triumphs'—that were to influence the militaristic art fostered by rulers such as Emperor Charles V in the Renaissance. A little over a half-century before this arch was built, Orange was still Rome's wild frontier, and art such as this evokes it vividly. Note the standards the legionaries are carrying: not the expected Roman eagle, but a boar.

When frontier days returned to Orange, in the Middle Ages, the arch was expanded into a castle by Raymond of Baux—typical of that haughty family. It is said that Raymond arranged it so that the battle reliefs would be a wall of his dining hall; we have his arrogance to thank for their relatively good state of preservation.

WHERE TO STAY/EATING OUT   (postal code 84100)
The best bet in the centre of Orange is the ***Hôtel Arène on Place de Langes: pleasant, with a good restaurant, on a quiet square where you can't hear the lorries, tel 90 34 10 95. There are a number of decent budget choices: the *St-Florent at 4 Rue du Mazeau, tel 90 34 18 53; or the dour old Hôtel Fréau, near the theatre on Rue Ancien Collège (tel 90 34 06 26).

For lunch after looking over Orange's theatre, try Rue du Pont Neuf, where there are a number of restaurants, including one Vietnamese and one couscous place, also L'Antre de Cybèle with 75–125 F menus and imaginative dishes like chicken *fricassée* with prunes, and a local favourite, beefsteak with roquefort sauce.

Sérignan-du-Comtat and the 'Virgil of Insects'

A short 8-km detour northeast of Orange on the D 976 will allow you to pay your respects to the great entomologist, botanist, scientist and poet Jean-Henri Fabre (1823–1915). Although born into poverty, the largely self-taught Fabre qualified as a *lycée* teacher of sciences in Avignon, only to be fired in 1870 for explicitly describing the sex life of flowers. In 1879 he bought an abandoned property here that he called L'Harmas, the 'fallow land' (daily except Tues 9–11:30 and 2–6, 2–4 winter). Fabre walled in the garden and planted a thousand species of flower and herb, which have run amok as he intended and are now part of a botanical preserve. Purchased by the state in 1922, the house strongly evokes Fabre's personality and work, most extraordinarily of all in his 700 watercolours of the fungi of the Vaucluse, so real that you can hardly believe they are only two-dimensional. You can also see the harmonium Fabre like to play and his study, where he wrote his passionate books on insects that have been translated into English (and made several children of our acquaintance into amateur entomologists) but are disgracefully out of print and hard to find, even in French.

South of Orange: Châteauneuf-du-Pape

> *Je veux vous chanter, mes amis,*
> *Ce vieux Châteauneuf que j'ai mis*
> *Pour vous seuls en bouteille:*
> *Il va faire merveille!*
>
> *Quand de ce vin nous serons gris,*
> *Vénus applaudira nos ris:*
> *Je prends à témoin Lise,*
> *La chose est bien permise!*

(My friends, I want to sing you / Of this old Châteauneuf that I've bottled just for you / It will work miracles! / For when this wine makes us tipsy / Venus will crown our mirth / I take Lise as my witness / No one will mind if I do!)

—Pope John XXII's drinking song

TOURIST INFORMATION
Place du Portail, tel 90 83 71 08.

You'll begin to understand why Châteauneuf's wines are so expensive when you pass through the vineyards, between Orange and Avignon. Blink, and you'll miss them. This pocket-sized wine region, tucked between the outskirts of Avignon and Orange, has become one of the most prosperous corners of France; every available square inch is covered with vineyards of a rare beauty, so immaculately precise and luxuriant they resemble bonsai trees. Such good fortune is not without its disadvantages. **Châteauneuf-du-Pape**, the very attractive village that gives the wine its name, has not resisted the temptation to become the Midi's foremost oenological tourist trap; along the main street, there are few grocers or boutiques, but plenty of wine shops. In places it is hard to see the buildings for the signs, advertising other shops, or the winemakers' estates in the hinterlands.

Legend has it that one of the first things Clement V did on leaving Rome was to inspect his vineyards north of Avignon. In 1316, his successor John XXII, a celebrated imbiber, did him one better by building a castle here, which the Avignon popes used as a summer residence—a 14th-century Castel Gandolfo. Sacked by the Protestants in the Wars of Religion, it was finally blown up by the retreating Germans in 1944; two crenellated walls still stand.

 Châteauneuf-du-Pape

An inspiration to both popes and lovers, Châteauneuf-du-Pape's reputation has remained strong through the ages; to safeguard it in 1923 its growers agreed to the guarantees and controls that formed the basis for France's modern *Appellation d'Origine* laws. Several factors combine to give the wine its unique character: the alluvial red clay and pebbly soil, brought down by a Rhône glacier in the ice age; the mistral which chases away the clouds and haze, letting the sun hit the grapes like an X-ray gun; and the wide palette of grapes that each winemaker can choose from: grenache, syrah, cinsault, mourvèdre, terret noir, vaccarèse, connoise, and muscardin for the reds; and clairette, bourboulenc, roussane, picpoul and picardan for the whites, 30 years ago dismissed as mere novelties and today celebrated as some of Provence's top wines—pale blond with greenish highlights and a fresh, floral bouquet. Because of the complex blends that give Châteauneuf its voluptuous qualities, the grapes are sorted by hand—unique among southern wines. The end result must have the highest alcoholic minimum of any great French wine (12.5%), a level achieved by spacing the vines a good 2 m apart to soak up the maximum amount of sun, and from the heat-absorbing pebbles underneath the vines that keep the grapes toasty after dark. Light, soft, and fast to mature, Châteauneuf-du-Pape red can be enjoyed much earlier (often in three years) than its Rhône rivals, and only gets better the longer you can bear to wait.

In its hometown, the wine is not exactly hard to find, and even in the cellars it's not cheap, as many of the *cuvées* of the 1980s promise to be superb. Perhaps the best known of the many excellent vineyards that welcome visitors are **Château Le Nerthe**, with its fascinating ancient cellars, tel 90 83 70 11, or the vaulted cellars of **Château de la Gardine**, tel 90 83 73 20, where the 1980 red, with its aroma of truffles and the lively, intense 1990 white are good examples. In Bédarrides, the vineyards of **Domaine du Vieux Télégraphe**, 3 Route de Châteauneuf, tel 90 33 00 31, occupy a rugged promontory topped by a tower once used for optic telegraphic experiments; the 88 red and 90 white are excellent buys. The three finest estates are in a class of their own and have such highly individual styles as to be unmistakable even tasted blind. **Clos des Papes**, tel 90 83 70 13, is run by the highly intelligent and innovative Paul Avril. Avril is alone in employing humidifiers in his cellar to alleviate the drying effects of the mistral wind in particular and the heat in general. As a consequence his wines have the best defined fruit of the region and are the most elegant. With age Avril's Châteauneuf-du-Pape can taste like expensive claret. The wines of **Château de Beaucastel**, in Courthézon, tel 90 70 70 60, have been consistently among the top wines of the *appellation*— lately the 88 and 89 reds, and a very classy 89 white. The most extraordinary source of Châteauneuf-du-Pape and possibly one of the country's most interesting wines is made by Jacques Raynaud at **Château Rayas**. Raynaud's cellar has been described as the most filthy and disorganized in France, and it is only fair to warn you he has a well-deserved reputation for being very inhospitable. One well-known wine merchant, and one not used to anything other than gracious hospitality when visiting growers, turned up on time for a pre-arranged rendezvous to find the place deserted. After nearly an hour's wait, the hapless fellow got back into his car and pulled out of the driveway. Looking back in his rearview mirror he caught a glimpse of Raynaud clambering out of the ditch in which he had been hiding! Raynaud may be difficult to visit but his wines are a must for all keen wine lovers. They are the product of a bygone era—wines of incredible concentration and depth with the capacity to age 20 years or more. Wines such as these are increasingly rare in an age when technology, which has helped to ensure that most wine is well made, also means that too many are sound but mediocre.

WHERE TO STAY AND EATING OUT (postal code 84320)

It's difficult to imagine how such a sweet old restaurant could survive in a tourist trap like Châteauneuf-du-Pape, but if you're passing through do stop at **La Mère Germaine**, in the centre on the D 17; simple, filling cooking like *coq au vin* and duck with olives (menus at 75, 115 and 135F). For a more ambitious repast, or a luxurious stay, there is the ****Hostellerie Château Fines Roches, an imposing but entirely fake crenellated castle (19th-century) with gardens, set among the vineyards south of Châteauneuf; elegant and quite expensive, the kitchen shines in seafood dishes and elaborate desserts (2 km south on the D 17; tel 90 83 70 23; menus 200 F, 260 F).

AVIGNON

Avignon has known more passions and art and power than any town in Provence, a mixture of excitement whipped to a frenzy by the mistral. But even the master of winds has never caused as much trouble as the papal court, a vortex of mischief that ruled Avignon for centuries, trailing violence, corruption and debauchery in its wake. 'In Paris one quarrels, in Avignon one kills', wrote Hugo. In Avignon Petrarch's platonic, courtly love for Laura was an aberration. 'Blood is hot there', wrote an anonymous writer in the 1600s, 'And the most serious occupation in the land is the search for pleasure ... even most of the husbands are accommodating in love, and allow their wives the same freedoms they enjoy themselves.'

Avignon still has a twinkle in its eye; it is alive, ebullient, and has been one of France's most innovative cities ever since the Italian Renaissance filtered through here to the rest of Europe. As the cultural and publishing centre of the south, it rocked the cradle of the Félibrige, the Provençal literary movement (see p. 39) and since the war it has been the stage for Europe's most exciting theatre festival. Charming it's not, but as an old Provençal proverb puts it: *Quau se lèvo d'Avignoun, se lèvo de la resoun* or 'He who takes leave of Avignon takes leave of his senses.'

History

Rome, *anno domini* 1303. Anarchy reigns: popular riots, regular visits from foreign armies, and clans waging medieval gang war in the streets, turning the tombs of the Caesars into urban fortressess. The papacy, though in the thick of it all, usually kept the papal person himself in places like Viterbo and Anagni for safety's sake—as it had the arrogant intriguer Boniface VIII, now fresh in his grave. Boniface's arch-enemy, Philip the Fair of France, has just bribed the conclave to elect a Frenchman, Clement V. Philip also suggested that the new Pope flee the inferno of Rome for the safer havens of the Comtat Venaissin in Provence—and Clement didn't have to be asked twice.

The Church had picked up this piece of Provence real estate as its spoils after the Albigensian Crusade. Isolated within it was the little city-republic of Avignon, belonging to the Angevin Counts of Provence—old papal allies, who welcomed their illustrious visitor. Clement V always intended to return to Rome, but when he died the French cardinals elected a former archbishop of Avignon, John XXII (1316–34), who moved the Curia into his old episcopal palace and greatly enriched the papacy (through alchemy, it was rumoured: see p. 41). Although he enlarged the palace with the proceeds, it still wasn't roomy enough for the his successor, Benedict XII (1334–42), who replaced it with another palace, or for Clement VI (1341–52), who added another. It seemed that the popes meant to stay forever, especially after 1348 when Clement purchased Avignon outright from the young Angevin Countess of Provence, Jeanne I of Naples, for the sale price of 80,000 florins and an absolution for her possible involvement in the suspicious strangulation of her husband.

Meanwhile all the profits that the 14th-century papal machine generated—from tithes and the sale of indulgences, pardons, offices, and the visits of pilgrims—went to Avignon instead of Rome. Overcrowding, debauchery, dirt, luxury, plague, blackmail, and crime came with the deal—troubles exasperated by papal tolerance that admitted outcasts from everywhere else into Avignon, as long as they could pay. Such refugees included not only common criminals but also Jews and, during the Schism, heretics. The Italians, mortified at losing their cash cow during this 'Babylonian captivity', expressed their self-righteous indignation through the longtime Avignon resident Petrarch: 'Avignon is the hell of living people, the thoroughfare of vice, the sewers of the earth ... Prostitutes swarm on the papal beds.' Yet these same popes summoned the best *trecento* artists from Italy, especially from Siena, who perfected in Avignon the elegant, courtly, fairy-tale style of painting known as International Gothic. And when he wasn't being outraged, Petrarch wrote incomparable love sonnets to his beloved Laura, a mysterious figure believed to have been an ancestress of the Marquis de Sade.

In 1377, Avignon's population rose to 30,000 souls, a third of them under religious orders. In that year St Catherine of Siena convinced the seventh Avignon pope, Gregory XI, to return to Rome. The Pope came, he saw, he sickened, but before he could pack his bags to return to Avignon, he died. The Roman mob seized their chance, and physically forced the Cardinals to elect an Italian pope who would re-establish the papacy in Rome. When the French cardinals escaped the Romans' clutches, they sparked off the Great Schism by electing a French anti-pope, Clement VII, and went back to Avignon. A Church council, held in Pisa 30 years later to resolve the conflict, only ended in the election of yet a third pope. In 1403 the French went over to the Rome faction and sent in an army to persuade Avignon's second Anti-Pope, Benedict XIII, to leave for his native Catalunya—from where he spent the rest of his life bitterly raining anathemas and excommunications on all and sundry.

When the Church finally settled on one pope, Avignon and the Comtat Venaissin settled in for three-and-a-half centuries of relaxed rule by cardinal legates, under whom the debauchery and violence continued, although on a more modest level. The party really ended when the Comtat Venaissin was incorporated into France during the Revolution in a blood rite of atrocities and the destruction of centuries' of art and architecture.

But even as part of France, Avignon has maintained its lively international character. Publishers who first set up shop with the popes stayed on under the cardinal legates, beyond the bounds of French censorship (there were 20 in town before the Revolution); in the 1850s they took on a new life publishing the works of the Félibrige. In 1946, Jean Vilar founded the Avignon Festival of Theatre and Film, the liveliest and most popular event on the entire Provençal calendar.

GETTING AROUND

Avignon's **airport** is at Caumont, tel 90 88 43 49. **Train** (tel 90 82 50 50) and **bus** stations (tel 90 82 07 35) are tête-à-tête outside the Porte de la République; Avignon is on the Paris–Marseille TGV line, and has frequent links to Arles, Montpellier, Nîmes, Orange, Toulon, and Carcassonne; buses go to St-Rémy, Fontaine-de-Vaucluse, the Pont du Gard, Uzès, Châteaurenard, Châteauneuf-du-Pape and Tarascon; for Ville-neuve-lès-Avignon take bus No. 10 from the train station. Travellers of yore always approached Avignon by boat, a thrill still possible on the **tourist excursion boat** *Le Cygne* from Beaucaire, tel 66 59 35 62, or with a **lunch or dinner cruise** on *Le Miréio*, based at Allées des Oulles, tel 90 85 62 25. Or, best yet, you can paddle on your own, from Pont d'Avignon **boat rentals**, tel 90 32 23 24.

Bike hire shops in Avignon include Dopieralski, 84 Rue Guillaume Puy, tel 90 86 32 49; Richard Masson, Place Pie, tel 90 82 32 19; and Transhumance (for all terrain and mountain bikes), tel 90 95 57 81. Inexpensive car hire firms are VEO, 5 Av. Pierre Sémard, tel 90 87 53 43, and Ardam, 14 Blvd Limbert, tel 90 82 10 31.

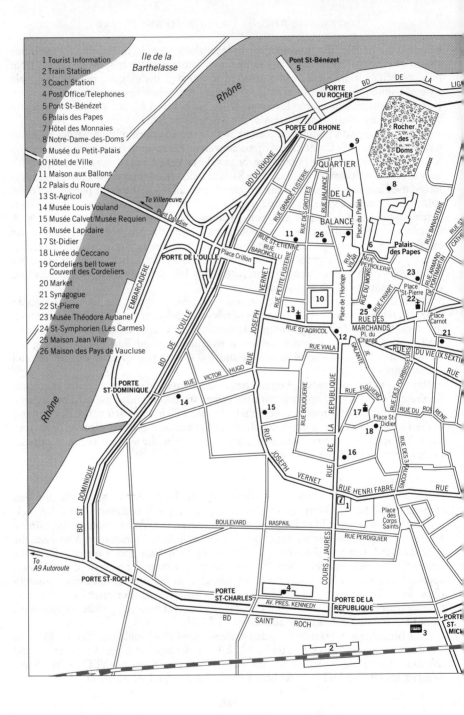

1 Tourist Information
2 Train Station
3 Coach Station
4 Post Office/Telephones
5 Pont St-Bénézet
6 Palais des Papes
7 Hôtel des Monnaies
8 Notre-Dame-des-Doms
9 Musée du Petit-Palais
10 Hôtel de Ville
11 Maison aux Ballons
12 Palais du Roure
13 St-Agricol
14 Musée Louis Vouland
15 Musée Calvet/Musée Requien
16 Musée Lapidaire
17 St-Didier
18 Livrée de Ceccano
19 Cordeliers bell tower
   Couvent des Cordeliers
20 Market
21 Synagogue
22 St-Pierre
23 Musée Théodore Aubanel
24 St-Symphorien (Les Carmes)
25 Maison Jean Vilar
26 Maison des Pays de Vaucluse

Ile de la
Barthelasse

Rhône

To Villeneuve
Pont Daladier

Pont St-Bénézet
5

PORTE
DU ROCHER

BD   DE   LA   LIG

PORTE DU RHONE

Rocher
des
Doms

9

8

BD DU RHONE

QUARTIER

DE LA

RUE GRANDE FUSTERIE

RUE DES GROTTES

RUE BALANCE

Place du Palais

BALANCE

RUE ST-ETIENNE
RUE BARONCELLI

11

26

7

6

Palais
des Papes

RUE BANASTERIE

RUE ST
CATHE

Place Crillon

PORTE DE L'OULLE

RUE VILAR

RUE PEYROLERIE

RUE DU MONS

23

Place
St-Pierre
22

RUE ARMAND
DE PONTMARTIN

EMBARCADERE

VERNET

RUE PETITE FUSTERIE

JOSEPH

Place de l'Horloge

13

10

RUE FAVART

25
RUE DES
MARCHANDS
Pl. du
Change

Place
Carnot

BD   DE   L'OULLE

RUE ST-AGRICOL

12

21

RUE VIALA

GALANTE

RUES   DU VIEUX SEXTI

RUE

PORTE
ST-DOMINIQUE

RUE   VICTOR   HUGO

14

RUE

15

RUE BOUQUERIE

RUE   DE   LA   REPUBLIQUE

RUE FIGUIER

17

RUE DES FOURBISSEURS

RUE DU   ROI   RENE

Place St-
Didier

18

RUE DES 3 FAUCONS

RUE

Rhône

JOSEPH VERNET

RUE

DE

16

RUE HENRI FABRE

RUE

BD   ST   DOMINIQUE

1

Place
des
Corps
Saints

To
A9 Autoroute

PORTE ST-ROCH

BOULEVARD

RASPAIL

COURS J. JAURES

RUE PERDIGUIER

PORTE
ST-CHARLES

4

AV. PRES. KENNEDY

PORTE DE LA
REPUBLIQUE

PORTE
ST-
MICI

BD   SAINT   ROCH

3

2

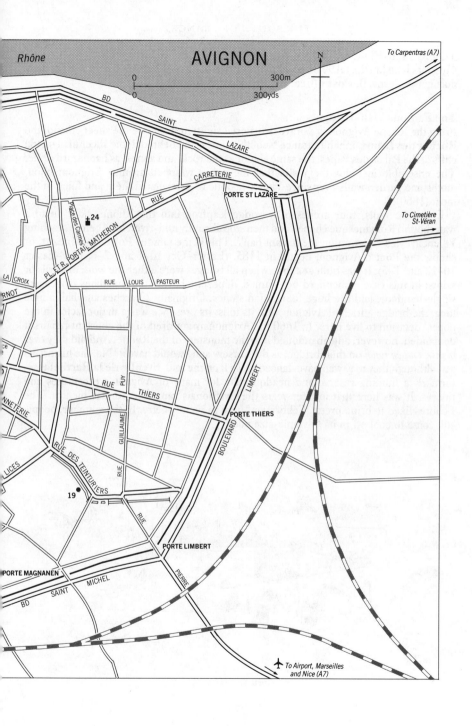

Rhône

AVIGNON

N

To Carpentras (A7)

0   300m
0   300yds

BD
SAINT
LAZARE
CARRETERIE
RUE
PORTE ST LAZARE

To Cimetière
St-Véran

Place des Carmes
PL. ET R. PORTAIL MATHERON
■ 24

LA CROIX
RNOT
RUE   LOUIS   PASTEUR

ce

RUE   PUY
THIERS
GUILLAUME
BOULEVARD
LIMBERT
PORTE THIERS

NNETERIE
RUE DES TEINTURIERS
RUE
LICES
19 ●

RUE

PORTE LIMBERT

PORTE MAGNANEN
SAINT   MICHEL
BD
PIERRE

✈ To Airport, Marseilles
and Nice (A7)

TOURIST INFORMATION
41 Cours Jean Jaurès, tel 90 82 65 11 (Mon–Fri 9–6; Sat 9–12 and 2–6; and 9–8 pm daily during the Festival). **Post office**: Av. Président-Kennedy.

The Famous Half-Bridge

From the Rhône Avignon is a brave two-tiered sight: in front rise the sheer cliffs of the **Rocher des Doms**, inhabited since Neolithic times, and behind it, the sheer man-made cliffs of the Palais des Papes, the same colour as the rock, and almost as haphazard a pile. The ensemble includes the **walls** that the popes wrapped around Avignon: bijou, toothsome garden walls ever since Viollet-le-Duc re-crenellated them and filled in the moat (1860).

From the walls, four arches of a bridge leapfrog into the Rhône, sidle up to a waterbound Romanesque chapel, and then stop abruptly mid-river, long before reaching Villeneuve-lès-Avignon on the distant bank. This is the famous **Pont St-Bénézet**, or simply the Pont d'Avignon, begun in 1185. (Easter–Oct 10–1 and 2–6, Nov–Easter 10–12 and 1–5). It was built at a time when all bridges were either the work of devils or saints; in this case a shepherd boy named Bénézet, obeying the mandates of heaven, single-handedly laid the huge foundation stones. Originally 22 arches and half a mile long, the bridge enriched Avignon with its tolls: its presence was a major factor in the popes' decision to live here. In 1660 the Avignonais got tired of the constant repairs it demanded, however, and abandoned it to the monsters of the Rhône. And did they ever *'danse, tout en rond'* on their bridge, as the nursery song would have it? No, the historians say, although they may well have danced *under* it on the mid-river **Ile de la Barthelasse**, formerly a hunting reserve and headquarters for many of Avignon's prostitutes and thieves. It was here that in later years the Avignonais came for Sunday picnics. The Félibres liked to bring pretty 'Félibresses' here to recite poetry. In the summer, people still come to cool off in its Olympic-size pool.

Pont St-Bénézet

The Palais des Papes

For a curious sensation, park directly under the popes' palace and take the lift up to the traffic-free **Place du Palais**. Once crowded with houses, the square was cleared by Anti-Pope Benedict XIII to emphasize the message of the Palace's vertical, impregnable walls: 'you would think it was an Asiatic tyrant's citadel rather than the abode of the vicar of the God of peace', wrote Mérimée. But the life of a 14th-century pope justified paranoia. The entrance is up the steps, in the centre of Clement VI's façade (open daily Mar–June 9–11:15 and 2–5:15; summer 9–6; 1 Oct–Mar 9–11:15 and 2–4:15, adm. Optional guided tours in English at 3).

What is harder to realize is that the life of a 14th-century pope and his cardinals, courtiers, mistresses and toadies, was also extremely luxurious. The palace was spared destruction in the Revolution only to end up serving as a prison and a barracks, and until 1920 its bored residents amused themselves by chipping off frescoes to sell to tourists, so that on most of the walls the only remaining decoration is an extraordinary variety of masons' marks.

OLD PALACE: GROUND FLOOR

After crossing the **Cour d'Honneur**, the great courtyard dividing Benedict XII's stern Cistercian Palais Vieux (1334–42) and Clement VI's flamboyant Palais Neuf (1342–52), the tour begins in the **Jesus Hall**, so called for its decorative monograms of Christ. Once used to house the pope's treasure and account books, it now contains a hoard of maps, views of Old Avignon and curios like a pair of 17th-century bell-ringing figures, or Jaquemarts. The most valuable loot would be stored behind walls 3 m thick in the windowless bowels of the **Angels' Tower**, its ceiling supported by a single stone pillar like an enormous palm tree.

Next, the **Consistory**, where the Cardinals met and received ambassadors; as its lavish frescoes and ceiling burned in 1413, it now displays 19th-century portraits of Avignon's popes and Simone Martini's fresco of the *Virgin of Humility*, detached from the cathedral porch in 1960. Under the fresco, the restorers found Martini's *sinopia*, or intial line sketch etched in the stone. As an artist could only paint a small patch of fresh, wet plaster a day, such *sinopie* were essential to maintain the composition, and these, as is often the case in Italy, give a clearer idea of the painter's intent than the damaged fresco itself. Traces of *sinopie* in situ are in the **Chapelle St-Jean**, dedicated to both Johns, the Baptist and the Evangelist. Matteo Giovannetti of Viterbo, a *trecento* charmer who left the bulk of his work in Avignon, did the frescoes for Clement VI; saints float overhead in starry blue landscapes (recall at the time that ultramarine blue paint was even more expensive than gold). On one wall, John's head is blissfully served to Herod at table, as if in a restaurant.

OLD PALACE: FIRST FLOOR

The tour continues to the first floor and the banqueting hall, or **Grand Tinel**, hung with 18th-century Gobelin tapestries. Although big enough for a football pitch, the Grand Tinel was too small to hold all the cardinal-electors who would gather in a conclave ten days after a pope's death. Masons were brought in to accommodate them: the arches on the far end were knocked down to give the cardinals more room to manoeuvre (in both senses of the word), while the doors and windows were bricked up to keep them from bringing in more food and endlessly prolonging the conclave. The trick always worked, for the appetites of the 14th-century Curia were Pantagruelian—the adjacent **Upper Kitchen** boasts a pyramidal chimney that could easily handle a roast elephant, or the menu of Clement VI's coronation feast: 1023 sheep, 118 cattle, 101 calves, 914 kids, 60 pigs, 10,471 hens, 1446 geese, 300 pike, topped off by 46,856 cheeses and 50,000 tarts, all consumed by just 3000 guests—some 16 tarts per person, with a few thousand left over for the Pope's midnight snack. Off the Grand Tinel, more delightful frescoes by Matteo Giovannetti decorate the **Chapelle St-Martial**, celebrating the French saint who came from the same Limousin village as Benedict XII.

THE NEW PALACE

The tour continues from the Grand Tinel to the pope's **Anti-chamber**, where he would hold private audiences, and continues to the **Pope's Bedroom** in the Tower of Angels, a room covered with murals of spiralling foliage, birds, and birdcages. It leads directly into the New Palace and the most delightful room in the entire palace, the **Chambre du Cerf**, Clement VI's study, where he would come 'to seek the freedom of forgetting he was pope'. In 1343 he had Matteo Giovannetti (probably) lead a group of French painters in depicting outdoor scenes of hunting, fishing, and peach-picking that not only quickened the papal gastric juices, but expressed what was then a revolutionary new interest in the natural world, where flowers and foliage were drawn from observation rather than copying a 'source'.

The arrows direct you next to the **Sacristy**, crowded with statues of kings, queens, and bishops escaped from Gargantua's chessboard, followed by Clement VI's **Great Chapel**, longer even than the Grand Tinel and just as empty, though the altar has recently been reconstructed. The **Robing Room** off the chapel contains casts of the Avignon popes' tombs. Revolutionaries bashed most of the figures that once adorned the elaborate **chapel gate**; through the bay window in front of this, the pope would bless and give indulgences to pilgrims. A grand stair leads down to the flamboyant **Great Audience Hall**, where a band of Matteo Giovannetti's *Prophets* remain intact, along with outline sketches of a *Crucifixion* that would have been splendid if it had ever been completed.

Around the Palace: Notre-Dame-des-Doms

Before spray paint, the posterity-minded had to record their passing with family emblems. None did it better than the Borghese of Rome (the family of Paul V); his nephew, legate in Avignon, produced the striking 1619 **Hôtel des Monnaies**, or mint, just across from the Palais des Papes, where reliefs of the Borghese dragon and eagle prance in garlands of fruit salad.

To the left of the palace is Avignon's cathedral, **Notre-Dame-des-Doms**, built in 1150, its landmark square bell tower ridiculously dwarfed by a massive gilt statue of the Virgin added in 1859, an unsuccessful attempt to make the church stand out next to the overwhelming papal pile. The interior has been fuzzily Baroqued like a soft-centre chocolate, but it's worth focusing on the good bits: the dome at the crossing, with an octagonal drum pierced with light, the masterpiece of this typically Provençal conceit; the 11th- or 12th-century marble bishop's chair in the choir; and in a chapel next to the sacristy, the flamboyant *Tomb of John XXII* (d. 1334) by English sculptor Hugh Wilfred, mutilated in the Revolution, and restored in the 19th century with a spare effigy of a bishop on top to replace the smashed Pope.

Next to the cathedral, ramps lead up to the oasis of the **Rocher-des-Doms**, now a garden enjoying panoramic views from the Rhône below to Mount Ventoux rising on the right. Peacocks squawk and preen in trees so crippled by the mistral they need crutches; you can tell the hour with your own shadow on a sundial called the *cadran solaire annalemmatique*, and admire a statue dedicated to an Armenian refugee named Jean Althen who 'introduced the cultivation of madder to the Midi'.

Musée du Petit Palais

Overlooking the Rhône at the end of the Place des Papes stands the **Petit Palais**, built in 1318 and modified in 1474 to suit the tastes of Cardinal Legate Giuliano delle Rovere—one day to become Michelangelo's patron and nemesis, as Pope Julius II. In 1958, the Petit Palace became a museum to hold all the medieval works remaining in Avignon (9:30–11:50 and 2–6, closed Tues, adm).

Although the scale of the Petit Palais can be daunting, it contains rare treats from the dawn of the Renaissance by artists hailing for the most part from Siena or Florence. But Avignon gets its say as well: the sculptures and pretty courtly frescoes from the 12th to the 14th century in the first two rooms demonstrate the city's role in creating and diffusing the late International Gothic style of the early 1400s. The third room contains some fascinating fragments of the 15-m, 8-storey **Tomb of Cardinal Jean de Lagrange** (1389), which stood in Avignon's church of St-Martial before the Revolution. One bit that survived was the *transi*, or relief of the decomposing corpse that occupied the lowest level of the tomb and was carved with morbid anatomical exactitude. Such *mementi mori* would soon become popular in northern France, always used to contrast with handsome effigy of the deceased while alive. The mouldering Cardinal Lagrange is one of the earliest, perhaps the prototype of the genre.

The next six rooms glow with the gold backgrounds (the better to show up in dim churches) of 14th- and early 15th-century Italian painting. Nearly all depict the Virgin and Child, a reflection of the cult of Mariolatry and chivalric ideals of womanhood that began where the troubadours left off. Although the subject matter is repetitive, it makes it easy to trace the medieval revolution in art and seeing, back in the good old days when art was content merely to imitate nature and not try to outdo her. The iconic, Byzantine flatness of the earliest paintings (see especially Paolo Veneziano's *Virgin* (1340), remarkably never restored in its 650 years), begins to give way to a more natural depiction of space, composition and human character after the innovations of Giotto in Italy (see especially Taddeo Gaddi, Pseudo Jacopino di Francesco, Lorenzo Monaco, and Gherardo Starnina). Meanwhile, Sienese artists, following the lead of the great Duccio di Buoninsegna, took up a more elegant, stylized line and richer colours (see Simone Martini and the many works by Taddeo di Bartolo).

The taste of Avignon's popes for Sienese art made the latter the strongest influence in the International Gothic style forged at the papal court (room 8), a style which the Sienese kept at long after the Florentines had moved on to new things—see Giovanni di Paolo's *Nativity* (1470), or Pietro di Domenico da Montepulciano's kinky *Vierge de Miséricorde* (1420), a delicate portrayal of a congregation sheltered under the Virgin's mantle, while a band of flagellants whip themselves in robes with custom-cut backs.

Bridal chests (*cassoni*) were often used to illustrate cautionary tales for women: in room 9, see Domenico de Michelino's *cassone* panels of 1450 on the story of Suzanna and the Elders.

RENAISSANCE GEMS, SACRED AND PROFANE

Beyond the *salon de repos* hangs the museum's best-known work, Botticelli's *Virgin and Child*, a tender, lyrical painting of his youth inspired by his (and Leonardo da Vinci's) master, Verrocchio. The next few rooms offer nothing as striking until room 15 and its four delightful narrative panels from bridal chests (*c.* 1510) by the Maestro dei Cassoni Campana. This unknown master's meticulous, miniaturist style is as rare as the subject of his cautionary tale: *The Minotaur*, beginning with Queen Pasiphae of Crete's love for a white bull, resulting in the birth of the Minotaur. The third panel shows Ariadne, her ball of twine, and Theseus slaying the Minotaur in an exquisite labyrinth of concentric circles.

The sacred equivalent of the *cassoni* is in room 16b: the *Sagra Conversazione* by Venetian Vittore Carpaccio, lyrical master of charm, colour and incidental detail. Such 'sacred conversations' portray the Virgin and saints meditating together on matters sublime, to the accompaniment of angelic music. To this, Carpaccio has added a landscape dominated by a natural rock bridge, where episodes from the lives of SS. Jerome, Augustine and Paul the Hermit take place.

Lastly, rooms 17–19 are devoted to works by French artists in Avignon, who after 1440 formed one of the most important schools of French Renaissance art. Influenced by the realism of Flemish oil painting (introduced to Avignon by Benedict XIII) and the almost abstract, decorative lines of the Italians, it concentrates on strong, simple images, as in the altarpiece *Virgin and Child between two Saints* (1450), by the school's greatest master, Enguerrand Quarton, with a pair of luminous shutters with SS. Michael and Catherine on the reverse by Jossé Lieferinxe. Or take two works by an accomplished but unknown hand: the striking *Jacob's Dream* and the lyrical *Adoration of the Child* (*c.* 1500), where the well-dressed donor seems to have stumbled unexpectedly onto the divine mystery.

Place de l'Horloge and Quartier des Fusteries

Just below the Place du Palais, an antique carousel spins gaily in the Place de l'Horloge, site of the old Roman forum, now full of buskers and holiday layabouts. The timepiece of its name is in the 1363 tower of the Hôtel de Ville; this originally belonged to a Benedictine monastery on the site, but was secularized with a clock and two **jacquemarts** who sound the hours. They aren't the only archaic figures here: many first-time visitors do a double-take when they notice the windows on the east side of the square filled with *trompe-l'oeil* paintings of historic personages, who all are linked in some way to the city.

Behind the Hôtel de Ville lies the **Quartier des Fusteries**, thus named for the wood merchants and carpenters, who had their workshops here in the Middle Ages, which were replaced in the 18th century with *hôtels*: in one, the **Maison aux Ballons** (with little iron balloons on the window sills) at 18 Rue St-Etienne, Joseph de Montgolfier discovered the principle of balloon flight in 1782, when he noticed how his shirt, drying by the fire, puffed up and floated in the hot air. From the Quartier des Fusteries, the steep picturesque lanes of the **Quartier de la Balance** wind back up to the Place des Papes.

Off Place de l'Horloge and Rue St-Agricol, Rue du Collège-du-Roure leads to the fine mid-15th-century **Palais du Roure**, marked by a flamboyant gate topped by intertwining mulberry branches in memory of the Taverne de Mûrier that it replaced. Equally flamboyant was the 19th-century descendant of the Florentine family who built it, the Félibre poet Marquis Baroncelli-Javon, who preferred to spend his time as a cowboy in the Camargue and lent this town-house to Mistral as a headquarters for his Provençal-language journal *Aïoli*. It now houses a study centre and exhibits on the language (guided tours Tues at 10 and 3). Rue St-Agricol is named after the recently restored Gothic church of **St-Agricol** (1326); its treasure is the *Doni Retable*, a rare Provençal work from the Renaissance. At No. 19 is the **Librairie Roumanille**, founded in 1855 by the Avignon poet Joseph Roumanille, father of the Félibrige (see p. 39). The bookshop published the movement's first masterpiece, Mistral's epic *Miréio* (1859) and continues to put out books in Provençal, while Avignon's literati chum around in the shop's atmospheric 19th-century salon.

Museums: Vouland, Calvet, Requien and Lapidaire

At the end of Rue St-Agricol curves Rue Joseph-Vernet, lined with 18th-century *hôtels*, antique shops, pricey restaurants and cafés. The kind of overly-ornate, spindly furniture, porcelains, and knick-knacks that originally embellished these mansions is on display nearby in Rue Victor Hugo's **Musée Louis Vouland** (open June–Sept 10–12 and 2–6, otherwise 2–6, closed Sun and Mon, free). More exciting are the contents of the handsome Hôtel de Villeneuve-Martignan, at 65 Rue Joseph-Vernet, first opened to the public as a 'cabinet of curiosities' in the late 1700s by collector Esprit Calvet. Now the **Musée Calvet** (open 10–12 and 2–6, closed Tues, adm), it offers something for every taste: 6000 pieces of wrought iron, Greek sculpture, 18th-century seascapes by Avignon native Joseph Vernet and paintings of ruins by Hubert Robert and Panini, mummies, a portrait of Diane de Baroncelli (grandmother of the Marquis de Sade), a bust of a boy by Renaissance sculptor Desiderio da Settignano, tapestries, prehistoric statue-steles, dizzy kitsch paintings of nude men (David's *Mort de Barra* and Horace Vernet's *Mazeppa and the Wolves*), as well as an excellent collection of 19th- and 20th-century paintings by Corot, Guigou, Soutine, Daumier, Dufy, Morisot, Utrillo, Seurat, Toulouse-Lautrec, Vlaminck, and Rouault. At the time of writing, the museum is undergoing a major restoration, due to be completed in 1992. Although the clean-up may well destroy its delightful faded charm, it may save some of the exhibits: one Egyptian mummy began to stink so badly in 1985 that it had to be buried in the local cemetery.

Adjacent to the Calvet museum, the **Musée Requien** is Avignon's fuddy-duddy natural history collection (Tues–Sat 9–12 and 2–6, free) where a 37-kilo beaver found in the Sorgue steals the show. Lastly, at 27 Rue de la République, in the chilly 17th-century chapel of a Jesuit College, are the sculptures of the **Musée Lapidaire** (10–12 and 2–6, closed Tues, free). It's worth popping in for the 2nd-century BC (or Merovingian) man-eating *Tarasque de Noves*, each hand gripping the head of a Gaul, while an arm dangles from its greedy jaws; or for its statues of Gallic warriors, looking much nattier in their mail than Asterix; or for the unlabelled masks in petal-like hoods. There is good Renaissance sculpture as well, but the best is in the nearby church of **St-Didier** (1359), just to the north in Place St-Didier: Francesco Laurana's polychrome **reredos** of Christ bearing the Cross, called *Notre-Dame du Spasme* for the spasm of pain on Mary's face; it was one of the first Renaissance sculptures to reach France, executed for Good King René in 1478. Opposite, in the first chapel on the left, are Florentine frescoes *c.* 1360, uncovered in 1952. More 14th-century frescoes have recently been restored opposite the church in the **Livrée de Ceccano**, now the town library.

The Eastern Quarters

From Place St-Didier, Rue du Roi René is lined with chiselled palaces, one built on the site of the church of Ste-Claire (No. 22) where Petrarch first saw his Laura on Good Friday 1327. ('It was the day when the sun darkened, as God/Himself vanished into death, when I was taken', he wrote). Laura died, probably of the plague, in 1348, and was buried nearby in the Franciscan **Couvent des Cordeliers**, by the corner of Rue des Lices and Rue des Teinturiers; only the Gothic bell tower survived the fury of the Revolution. In 1533, a humanist from Lyon claimed to have found her tomb in the church, and such was Petrarch's reputation that François I made a special trip to Avignon to see it.

    Rue des Teinturiers, the most picturesque street in Avignon, was named after the dyers and textile-makers who powered their machines on water-wheels in the Sorgue, one of which survives. Shaded by plane trees, crossed by little bridges, it is a pleasant place to dawdle over a beer or dinner—and hard to believe this Sorgue is the same stream that comes bursting like a bomb out of that other Petrarchan shrine, the Fontaine de Vaucluse.

    Rue des Teinturiers turns into Rue Bonneterie on its way to Avignon's shopping district and Place Pie, home of the ugly-duckling new **market**, although the produce inside is fit for a swan. Another evocative street, Rue Vieux Sextière, once site of the Jewish Ghetto, is the address of Avignon's 19th-century synagogue, while just beyond Place Carnot, **St-Pierre**'s flamboyant façade boasts a set of beautifully carved walnut doors (1551). Facing St-Pierre, Avignon's cosiest museum, **Musée Théodore Aubanel** (9–12, closed Sat, Sun and Aug) is dedicated to printing in Avignon, and to the romantic poet and Félibre Théodore Aubanel, whose family still owns one of Avignon's oldest publishing houses.

    From Place St-Pierre, Rue Carnot continues to another charming square, the Place des Carmes, dominated by the 15th-century façade of **St-Symphorien**, with a pretty cloister refurbished as a Festival venue. Visitors in the last century would continue from here along Rue Carreterie, out of the city gate and down the Lyon road to the **Cimetière St-Véran**, a romantic, shady park where John Stuart Mill and his wife Harriet are buried. Harriet died at the Hôtel d'Europe in 1858, a loss so devastating for the philosopher of utilitarianism that he lived in a house by the cemetery until he himself died in 1873. Another celebrated tomb belongs to Maurille de Sombreuil, who became a heroine during the Revolution when, to save the life of her father, the governor of the Invalides, she drank a goblet of human blood. Contemporaries noted that she always ordered white wine with her meals after that.

FESTIVAL

In 1946 Jean Vilar with his Théâtre National Populaire founded the **Avignon Festival**, with the aim of bringing theatre to the masses. Now rated among the top international theatre festivals in Europe, Avignon overflows in July and August with performances, by the Théâtre National in the Palais des Papes, and others throughout the city; the cinemas host films from all over the world, and churches are used for concerts (the **Maison Jean Vilar**, 8 Rue de Mons, tel 90 86 59 64, is the nerve centre and hosts exhibitions, films, and lectures the rest of the year). During the festival Avignon's squares and streets overflow with fringe (or 'Off') performers, who have their own HQ at 18 Rue Paul Saïn, tel 90 85 79 62.

SHOPPING

Pâtisseries, especially around Rue Joseph Vernet, sell Avignon's gourmand speciality, *papalines*, made of fine chocolate and a liqueur, *d'origan du Comtat* distilled from 60 herbs picked from the slopes of Mont Ventoux, and said to be a sure cure for cholera. For imaginative toys, try **Minute Papillon**, 18 Place de la Principale. Books in English, cultural exchanges, and Wednesday afternoon tea parties are open to all nationalities at the **Centre Franco Américain de Provence**, 23 Rue de la République, tel 90 85 50 98. **Markets**: produce market, Tues–Sun morning in Place Pie; second-hand goods on Sat in Place Crillon; flower market Sat morning and flea-market Sun morning in Place des Carmes; travelling market, Sat and Sun morning at Rempart St-Michel. Also, behind the Hôtel de Ville in Place des Puits-de-Boeufs, the **Maison du Pays de Vaucluse** has a large display of regional products and crafts.

ENTERTAINMENT AND NIGHTLIFE

Outside July and August, Avignon's best source of information on local events is the **Centre d'Action Culturelle**, 8 bis Rue de Mons, tel 90 82 67 08. Try to take in a performance by one of Provence's most talented theatre companies, **Le Chêne Noir**, 8 Rue Ste-Catherine, whose range covers the classics to the avant-garde (tel 90 33 84 23). The same theatre is also the home of the jazz club AJMI, tel 90 86 08 61, featuring live music every Thursday at 9 (membership cards available at the door). Avignon's oldest permanent company, the **Théâtre des Carmes**, performs in the restored Gothic cloister of St-Symphorien. Quality old and new films in their original language are shown at **Utopia Galante**, 15 Rue Galante, and **Utopia République**, 5 Rue Figuière, tel 90 82 65 36 for both. More spontaneous nightlife is concentrated in the bars in the southeast corner of town, especially around Place des Corps Saints and Rue des Teinturiers.

WHERE TO STAY   (postal code 84000)

Avignon's **hotel-finding/reservation service** is in the station (tel 90 82 5 81), though even that may fail you in July and August, when it's imperative to book ahead. Also note there are many other choices across the river in Villeneuve (see below). Oldest and still classically formal with its Louis XV furnishings, the ******Hôtel de l'Europe**, 12 Place Crillon, tel 90 82 66 92, was built in the 1500s, and converted to an inn in the late 1700s. Napoleon stayed here, as did the eloping Browning and Barrett. *****Palais des Papes**, Rue Gérard Philipe, tel 90 86 04 13, has the best views of the Palace, modern sound-proofed rooms and air-conditioning; or for even more quiet, the 16th-century **La Ferme Jamet**, Chemin des Bois on the Ile de la Barthelasse, (off Pont Daladier), tel 90 82 57 53, has rooms ranging from traditional Provençal in style to a gypsy caravan. Cheaper bets include the bright and charming *Mignon, 12 Rue Joseph-Vernet, tel 90 82 17 30, with small but modernized rooms; the friendly *Le Parc, 18 Rue Perdiguier, near the tourist office, tel 90 82 71 55; the quieter *Saint-Roch, with a delightful garden just outside the walls of Porte St-Roch at 9 Rue Paul-Mérindol, tel 90 82 18 63. Cheapest of the cheap is *Innova, near the station at 100 Rue Joseph-Vernet, tel 90 82 54 10, run by a jolly family with a dog, cat, and two canaries in tow. Otherwise, Ile de la Barthelasse has three **camping sites**, one of which, **La Bagatelle**, tel 90 82 63 50, has dormitory rooms in the summer.

EATING OUT
Avignon's gourmet bastion for the past 60 years, **Hiély** is a resolutely old-fashioned place, with a first-floor dining room, 5 Rue de la République, tel 90 86 17 07. The kitchen refuses to conform to any label, but never disappoints with its *tourte* of quail and *foie gras*, a legendary *cassoulet des moules aux épinards* and for dessert, *pudding aux fruits à crème vanille*, accompanied by carafes of Châteauneuf-du-Pape or Tavel; menus 200–300F. Just off Rue Bonneterie on Rue du Four-de-la-Terre, **Notre-Dame**, tel 90 82 34 12, draws its clients with its hearty Provençal atmosphere and cuisine: in summer try the refreshing *cassoulet d'été* (menu 120F). Popular for its reasonably priced and good food, **Entrée des Artistes** has the added advantage of its location in quiet Place des Carmes (tel 90 82 46 90, menu 100F); **Le Petit Bedon**, 70 Rue Joseph-Vernet, tel 90 82 33 98, is quickly becoming an Avignon institution for well-prepared dishes seldom found elsewhere, like *lotte au Gigondas*, the house speciality of angler-fish (lunch menu 90F, more in the evening). For under 100F: **Le Venaissin**, 16 Place de l'Horloge, tel 90 86 20 99 (get there early); the vegeterian/organic **Le Pain Bis**, 6 Rue Armand de Pontmartin, tel 90 86 46 77; **La Tâche d'Encre**, 22 Rue des Teinturiers, tel 90 85 79 71, has acceptable food, better-than-average atmosphere, and usually excellent live music Fri and Sat night, when you may want to book ahead. Fill up on late night titbits at **Tapas**, 22 Rue Figuière, tel 90 82 08 69, or try the *dim sum* at **Xuan**, Avignon's best Vietnamese restaurant at 6 Rue Galante, tel 90 86 03 75.

Around Avignon
If your pockets are deep enough, in easy driving distance of Avignon are three exceptional hotel/restaurants: ***Ermitage-Meissonnier**, Av. de Verdun, 30133 Les Angles (4 km west on D 900), tel 90 25 41 68, has only 6 luxurious rooms, but a glorious restaurant specializing in Provençal cuisine of the highest order—even the tomatoes taste better here, especially in the lovely garden (menus from 220–400F). ***Auberge de Cassagne**, 450 Allée de Cassagne, 84310 Le Pontet, 5 km north on the N 7, tel 90 31 04 18 has a pool, tennis courts, and access to a golf course; the food (fillet of red mullet with lime, followed by pear *croquant* in bitter chocolate) and wine cellar are perfect (menus from 190–300F). Five km east, on the N 107 (follow the Av. d'Avignon), ****Les Frênes**, 645 Av. des Vertes-Rives, 84149 Montfavet, tel 90 31 17 93, is a Relais et Châteaux member, its buildings set around a beautiful garden and pool; antiques furnish the rooms. Half-board mandatory in season, but the food, with

imaginative delights like salmon with truffles in a sweet and sour sauce is as marvellous as the setting (lunch menus from 200 F).

Villeneuve-lès-Avignon

In 586, on Puy Andaon, the rock that dominates Villeneuve-lès-Avignon, Casarie, a Visigoth princess-hermit died in the odour of sanctity (a smell like crushed violets, apparently). In the 10th century, Benedictines built the abbey of St-André to shelter her bones and lodge pilgrims on the route to Compostela. St-André soon became one of the mightiest monasteries in the south of France, and in 1226, when Louis VIII besieged pro-Albigensian Avignon, the Abbot offered the King co-sovereignty of the abbey in exchange for royal privileges. And so what was once an abbey town became a frontier fortress of the king of France, a new town (*ville neuve*) and a heavily fortified one, in case the pope over the river should start feeling frisky.

But Villeneuve was soon invaded in another way; wanton, squalid Avignon didn't suit all tastes, and the pope gave permission to his cardinals who liked it not-so-hot to retreat across the Rhône into princely *livrées cardinalices* (or palaces 'freed' from their original owners by the Curia). Though a dormitory suburb these days, Villeneuve still maintains a separate peace amongst its villas, well-fed cats snoozing in the sun, leisurely afternoons at the *pétanque* court and some amazing works of art.

GETTING AROUND/TOURIST INFORMATION

From Avignon, bus No. 10 runs every half-hour from the train station or Porte de l'Oulle to Villeneuve. Place Charles-David is the best place to park and has the Tourist Information as well, tel 90 25 61 33. Note that everything is closed Tues and in February.

Around Town

When Philip the Fair ratified the deal that made Villeneuve royal property, he ordered a citadel to be built on the approach to Pont St-Bénézet and be named after guess who. As times grew more perilous, this **Tour Philippe-le-Bel** was made higher to keep out the riff-raff, and now offers splendid views of Avignon, Mont Ventoux and on a clear day, the Alpilles (Nov–Mar 10–12 and 2–5; Apr–Sept 10–12:30 and 3–7:30, closed Tues and in Feb).

From here, Montée de la Tour leads up to the 14th-century **Collégiale Notre-Dame**, once the chapel of a *livrée* and now Villeneuve's parish church. From Villeneuve's Chartreuse (Charterhouse) it has inherited an elaborate marble altar of 1745, but the church's most famous work, a beaming, swivel-hipped, polychrome ivory statue of the Virgin carved in Paris out of an elephant's tusk *c.* 1320, has been removed to safer quarters in the nearby **Musée Pierre-de-Luxembourg** (same hours as Tour Philippe-le-Bel; adm), housed in yet another *livrée*.

The museum's other prize is the masterpiece of the Avignon school: Enguerrand Quarton's 1454 *Couronnement de la Vierge*, one of the greatest works of 15th-century French painting, commissioned for the Charterhouse (see below). Unusually, it portrays God the Father and God the Son as twins, clothed in sumptuous crimson and gold, like the Virgin herself, whose fine sculptural features were perhaps inspired by the ivory Virgin. Around these central figures the painting evokes the spiritual route travelled by the Carthusians through vigilant prayer, to purify the world and reconcile it to God. St Bruno, founder of the Order, saints, kings, and commoners are present, hierarchically arranged, while the landscape encompasses heaven, hell, Rome and Jerusalem, and local touches like Mont Ste-Victoire and the cliffs of the Estaque.

Other notable works in the museum include a curious 14th-century *double-faced Virgin*, the 'Eve' face evoking original sin and the 'Mary' face human redemption; Simon de Châlon's 1552 *Entombment*; and amid the uninspired 17th-century fluff, Philippe de Champaigne's *Visitation*.

La Chartreuse and Fort St-André

From the museum, take Rue de la République up to No. 53, the **Livrée de la Thurroye**, the best-preserved in Villenueve; a cardinal would maintain a household of a 100 or so people here. Further up the street and up the scale stands one of the largest charter-houses in France, the **Chartreuse du Val-de-Bénédiction** (Apr–Sept 9–12 and 2–6; Oct–Mar 10–12 and 2–5, adm). This began as the *livrée* of Etienne Aubert, who upon his election to the papacy in 1352 as Innocent VI, deeded his palace to the Carthusians for a monastery. For 450 years it was built and rebuilt, granted immense estates on either side of the Rhône by kings and popes, and in general lived rather high, even by Carthusian standards. In 1792, the Revolution forced the monks out, and the Charterhouse was sold in 17 lots; squatters took over the cells and outsiders feared to enter the cloisters after dark. Now mostly repurchased and restored, the buildings house the Centre Inter-national de Recherche de Création et d'Animation (CIRCA), devoted to a wide variety of arts, especially audio-visual and newer technologies; it hosts workshops, seminars, and exhibitions, both during the Avignon festival and at other times (tel 90 25 05 46).

Still, the sensation that lingers in the Charterhouse is one of vast silences and austerity, the hallmark of an order where conversation was limited (originally) to one hour a week; monks who disobeyed the rule of prayer, work, and silence ended up in the prison cells around the Great Cloister. Much of the art that once adorned the community buildings is now in the museum (see above), with the exception of 14th-century frescoes by Matteo Giovannetti and his school in the refectory chapel. In the church, the star attraction is **Innocent VI's tomb**, with an alabaster effigy under a fine Gothic baldachin. A hundred years ago this tomb was used as a rabbit hutch. Popes who took the name Innocent have tended to suffer such posthumous indignities: the great Innocent III was found stark naked in Perugia cathedral, a victim of poisoned slippers, while the corpse of Innocent X—the last of the series—was dumped in a tool-shed in St Peter's.

Gazing down into the Charterhouse from the summit of Puy Andaon are the formi-dable bleached walls of **Fort St-André**, built around the old abbey in the 1360s, the heyday of the 'Grandes Compagnies' (bands of unemployed soldiers, who roamed the countryside and held towns to ransom). The fort's stout round towers afford a famous vantage point over Avignon; the southwestern tower is called the Tour des Masques (sorcerers' tower), although no one seems to remember why. Jumbly ruins are all that remain of the splendid abbey of St-André, amid Italian gardens and writhing olives (same hours as the Charterhouse, adm).

Market Days: Place Charles-David, Thursday morning.

WHERE TO STAY/EATING OUT   (postal code 30400)
Villeneuve makes an attractive and quieter alternative to Avignon, and has some notable lodgings in its own right. The exquisite ****Le Prieuré, centrally located in Place du Chapître, tel 90 25 18 20, gives you the option of sleeping in the 16th-century priory, where the rooms are furnished with antiques, or in the more comfortable annex by the swimming-pool; gardens, tennis, and a remarkable restaurant that does delightful things with seafood and truffles are added attractions—gourmet lunch menus at 240F (closed Nov–10 Mar). At ***La Magnaneraie, 37 Rue Camp-de-Bataille, tel 90 25 11 11, you can choose between the old-fashioned rooms in a former silkworm nursery, or another modern annex; it too has been endowed with a pool, gardens, and Le Prieuré's rival for the best restaurant in town (menus 200F and up). For a less expensive sojourn into history, there's the 16th-century **L'Atelier, 5 Rue de la Foire, tel 90 25 01 84, with a walled garden in the centre of town, or the 17th-century **Résidence Les Cèdres, 39 Blvd Pasteur, tel 90 25 43 92, named after the ancient cedars that surround it, with a pool and a bungalow annex. Top budget choices: *Beauséjour, 61 Av. Gabriel Péri, tel 90 25 20 56, or the Hostel YMCA, by the river at 7 bis Chemin de la Justice, tel 90 25 46 20, with views of the Rhône and a pool to boot. For a reasonably priced meal, try La Mamma, in central Place Victor Bosch, tel 90 25 00 71.

To the north in Roquemaure, large gardens, old-fashioned rooms and delicious food combine to make a restful stay in the 18th-century **Château de Cubières, on the Route d'Avignon, 30150, tel 66 82 64 28.

Around Villeneuve, Through Rosé-coloured Glasses

Once you cross the Rhône into the Gard, the land takes on a more arid and austere profile, its knobby limestone hills and cliffs softened by crowns of silver olives and the green pin-stripes of vines, especially in the river bend north of Villeneuve along the D 976. The landmark here is Roquemaure, where Pope Clement V died his peculiar death (see p. 41) in its ruined castle, although it's not his ghost who haunts it, but that of a lovely but leprous queen who was quarantined in the tower. After she died, Rhône boatmen would see her on summer nights, flitting freely along the bank, dressed in white and sparkling with jewels. The D 976 continues west to the little village of Tavel, a place just as haunted—by wine fiends slaking their thirst on the pale ruby blood of the earth.

Tavel and Lirac
The sun-soaked, limestone pebbly hills on the right bank of the Rhône are as celebrated for their rosés as Châteauneuf-du-Pape is for its reds and whites. Tavel has the longest pedigree, a wine beloved of kings since the 13th century, when Philip le Bel declared: 'It isn't good wine unless it's Tavel'. By the 1930s, the vine stocks—grenache, cinsault, bourboulenc, carignan and red clairette—were so old that Tavel nearly went the way of the dodo. Since revived to the tune of 825 healthy hectares, the French have once again crowned it as king of the rosés, the universal, harmonious summer wine that goes with everything from red meat to seafood.

283

The French, however, may see what is ideal for summer drinking in a slightly different light and the rosé of Tavel may seem a little strong in alcohol to less acclimatized constitutions. Some growers add syrah and mourvèdre to give their Tavels extra body and colour, including the two best-known producers in the village, whom you can visit by ringing ahead: the de Bez family at the **Château d'Aquéria**, tel 66 50 04 56, and the prize-winning **Domaine de la Mordorée**, tel 66 50 06 12, where the talented Christophe Delorme also bottles a potent red Côtes-du-Rhône, Lirac, and Châteauneuf-du-Pape.

The Lirac district begins 3 km to the north of Tavel and encompasses four communes—Roquemaure, Lirac, St-Laurent-des Arbres and St-Geniès-de-Comolas. Its pebbly hills are similar to Tavel, and the *appellation* differs in the addition of two grape varieties—white ugni and maccabéo, and the fact that everything doesn't come up rosé: Lirac is making a name for its fruity whites, with a fragrance reminiscent of the wildflowers of the nearby *garrigue*, and for its well structured reds. Both 89 and 90 were fine years and can be sampled weekdays at **Domaine Duseigneur** at St-Laurent-des-Arbres, tel 66 50 02 57, and at **Château St-Roch** in Roquemaure, tel 66 82 82 59.

Between Avignon and Tarascon: La Montagnette

South of Avignon the Rhône curves to accommodate La Montagnette, a white mini-mountain sliced with valleys of market gardens and orchards of almonds and apricots, protected from the huffing and puffing of the mistral by hedgerows and poplars. Dominating this bijou landscape, **Barbentane** is a refined old town that so loved its *farandole* that a man who could not dance it would not be considered a fit husband. It is still defended by the 14th-century **Tour Angelica**, its medieval gates, and the arcaded **Maison des Chevaliers**, a lovely souvenir of the Renaissance. The **Château**, built in 1674 by the Marquis de Barbentane, the king's ambassador to Tuscany, would not look out of place in the Ile de France (open Easter–Oct, 10–12 and 2–6; other times Sunday only, adm): the furnishings are Louis XV and Louis XVI but the builder's acquired Italian taste permeates the other decoration. The enormous plane trees in the garden were brought over from Turkey by an earlier Marquis in the 1670s.

East of Barbentane, **Châteaurenard** is one of Provence's main wholesale fruit and vegetable markets, lording over a plain known as La Petite Crau, although it looks nothing like the rocky waste of the 'big' Crau (see p. 311). Two proud towers on its hill survive from its castle. This castle was first owned by Reinardus, a friend and ally of Charles Martel, who was killed below its walls fighting the Saracens; his wife Emma took over the command and fought bravely before dying of a broken heart, and her ghost haunts the **Tour de Griffon**. This now offers a little museum as well as great views over the Lubéron and Alpilles (10–12 and 2–6, closed Jan and Feb).

On the D 35 south of Barbentane, **Boulbon** was known as Bourbon until 1792, when the guillotine cut into the name's popularity. Still defended by 10th-century walls built into and onto the rocky escarpment overlooking the Rhône, Boulbon is best known for its unique June 1 *cérémonie du St-Vinage*, in honour of its patron saint Marcellin: the men of the village each bring a full bottle of wine to the saint's Romanesque chapel and hear the gospel in Provençal, after which the wine is blessed and God is toasted with a mighty swig. The bottle is then corked and for the rest of the year the blessed wine is used as a sovreign remedy for grave illnesses.

If you leave Barbentane by the D 35E, you'll arrive at the **Abbaye St-Michel-de-Frigolet**, founded around the year 1000 in the sheltered centre of La Montagnette (guided tours every hour at 10–11 and 2–6). The word Frigolet comes from the Provençal *férigoulo*, or thyme, a healthy, invigorating herb, for here the monks of Montmajour (see p. 300), enervated by the swamps, came for a cure—some of it in the form of a liqueur called *Le Frigolet*, on sale at the monastery. In 1632, Anne of Austria came here to its ancient Romanesque chapel of the Immaculée Conception to pray for a son, and soon after gave the world Louis XIV. In gratitude the queen sent the sumptuous gilt *boiseries* that frame 14 turgid Mignards. Another celebrity to pass through was the young Frédéric Mistral, who attended an improvised school here, where lessons were bartered for food; the stories and customs of these hills were to be a great source of inspiration in his writings.

In 1830, Mistral was born in **Maillane**, just to the east, and spent as much time as possible there until he died in 1914. The house he had built after 1876, now the **Muséon Mistral** (closed Mon and for lunch), was preserved as it was the day he died in 1914 'as sympathetic and as cosy as a coffin' as James Pope-Hennessy described it. Mistral's tomb, in the local cemetery, is modelled after the Pavillon de la Reine Jeanne at Les Baux, and decorated with a seven-pointed star and other Félibre symbols.

Market Days: Barbentane, Monday–Saturday. Châteaurenard, Saturday. Maillane, Thursday.

WHERE TO STAY/EATING OUT
In **Barbentane** (13570), ****Castel Mouisson** at the foot of the Montagnette in Quartier Castel-Mouisson, tel 90 95 51 17, is a typical Provençal hotel, with a pool and tennis (closed mid-Oct–Mar), while in the centre, ***St-Jean** (1 le Cours, tel 90 95 50 44) has decent rooms and a restaurant with a good 75 F menu. At **St-Michel-de Frigolet**, the Prémontrés monks run a hostel with 38 rooms for guaranteed quiet retreats for a day or two or even a month; write to the Service Hostellerie, Abbaye St-Michel-de-Frigolet, 13150 Tarascon, or tel 90 95 70 07 between 9 and 11 am.

Tarascon and Beaucaire

Few towns in the south of France are as determinedly frumpy as Tarascon and Beaucaire: most of the houses are not only unrestored but cry out for a lick of paint; garages outnumber crafts shops by ten to one; even the poodles look like real dogs instead of topiary hedges. Meanwhile the rival fairy-tale castles of Tarascon and Beaucaire muse at each other across the Rhône like the embodiments of a bi-communal Walter Mitty daydream, reminders of heroism, romance, international markets, man-eating monsters, and Alphonse Daudet's buffoonish anti-hero Tartarin, who never told a lie but, under the hot sun, was prone to imagine things. Provençal nationalists accuse Daudet (a native of Nîmes) of creating a stereotype that only heightened Paris's already smug attitude towards the Midi, to which Daudet replied that 'All Frenchmen have in them a touch of Tarascon'.

GETTING AROUND
Nearly every east-west **train** from Provence to Languedoc stops in Tarascon (tel 90 91 04 82). **Buses** run regularly between Beaucaire, Tarascon, and Avignon; other lines, from Tarascon's station, go to Arles, Boulbon, Nîmes, St-Rémy and Cavaillon. **Bike hire** in Tarascon: Cycles Christophe, 70 Blvd Itam, tel 90 91 25 85, and Motobecane, 1 Rue E. Pelletan, tel 90 91 43 32.

TOURIST INFORMATION
Tarascon: 59, Rue des Halles, tel 90 91 03 52.
Beaucaire: 24 Cours Gambetta, tel 66 59 26 57.

Tarascon and St Martha

All centuries have quirks that seem quaint to later generations: tulip-bulb speculation in the 18th, ladies' bustles in the 19th, muzak in the 20th. In the 11th and 12th centuries, it was a mania for the bodily parts of saints, a fad so passionate that a sure candidate for the inner circle, such as St Francis, had bodyguards from Assisi in his dying days to prevent rival towns from kidnapping him. If it had no fresh relics, every town with a saintly legend attached to it began digging for bones; and in Tarascon, *voilà*, in 1187 they just happened to stumble across the relics of St Martha. The pious 9th-century legend told how she found Tarascon bedevilled by a Tarasque, a man-eating amphibian whose ancestors are portrayed in Celtic sculpture chomping on human heads. Martha neatly tidied away the monster by showing it a Cross, before ordering it to the bottom of the Rhône, never to return.

The new-found relics attracted so many pilgrims that the 12th-century **Collégiale Ste-Marthe** was enlarged in the 13th and 16th centuries into a curious Romanesque/Gothic hybrid. The church was badly bombed in World War II, but even worse mischief had been done in the Revolution, when the great south portal of 1197 was shorn of its sculptures. Nowadays the chapels of the attractive five-aisled Gothic nave are filled with the lukewarm efforts of Mignard and Parrocel, masters of the Baroque fruitcake style, while in the crypt (part of the original 1197 church) there's a king-sized statue of Martha from 1400 and the slightly later and much more refined *effigy of Jean de Cossa*, Seneschal of Provence, attributed to Francesco Laurana.

The Château du Roi René
Rooted in a limestone rock over the Rhône, Tarascon's château gleams like white satin between the sun and water, a storybook feudal castle with crenellations and moat, named after the one character in Tarascon's history actually rounded out in flesh and blood, Good King René (guided tours daily except Tues: July–Aug 9–7; other months, tours at 9, 10, 11, 2, 3, 4, and 5, adm). René earned the 'Good' in his name for his good appetite and fondness for the good things of life, as well as the good sense to not let troubles or sorrows, of which he had many, get under his skin. He spent the last decade of his life (1471–80) surrounded by poets and artists in Tarascon, in this castle begun in 1401 by his father, Louis II of Anjou. After René's death and Provence's annexation to France, it underwent the usual conversion into a prison.

While the exterior is all serious business, the interior was designed with the good taste of René in mind—flamboyant and elegant and now, eloquently empty. In the courtyard there are busts of the King and his second wife, Jeanne de Laval; sculptural titbits and faded ceiling panels offer clues of the original decoration; graffiti by British sailors imprisoned here between 1754 and 1778 recalls the castle's later use. And taking in the precipitous views from the top terrace, you can see why no one ever tried to sneak up on it; or why, during the Revolution, Tarascon never needed to invest in a guillotine.

The Town

Tarascon's main street, the **Rue des Halles**, retains its medieval arcades. Walk halfway up it from the tourist office to the Franciscan **Cloître des Cordeliers** (1450s), now used for special exhibitions (10–12 and 2–5:30, summer 3–7, closed Jan and Feb). At the top of Rue des Halles stands the handsome **Hôtel de Ville** (1648); from here, Rue Proudhon leads to the **Musée Souleiado** (No. 39; open by appointment only, tel 90 91 08 80). Souleiado (a Provençal word for 'sun-ray piercing through clouds') is Provence's leading manufacturer of block-printed texiles, founded in 1938 by Charles Deméry to revive a 200-year-old Tarascon industry. The museum holds 40,000 18th-century fruitwood blocks—still the basis for all the company's patterns. Brought back to fashion in the 50s on such diverse backs as Bardot's and Picasso's, Souleiado's colour-drenched prints are again a hot fashion item.

Lastly, there's the so-called **House of Tartarin**, across from a Fiat garage at 55 bis Boulevard Itam (Oct–Mar 9–12 and 1:30–5; summer Apr–Sept 9–12 and 2–7). The modern Tarasconnais say they have forgiven Daudet for making them ridiculous, for in the age of Tourist Man he has also made them famous. Daudet claimed that the character of Tartarin was derived from his cousin, a big game hunter whom Daudet accompanied on a lion hunt in Algeria, but there's another version: in the original story, published as a newspaper serial, Tartarin was named Barbarin after an old Tarasconnais family—the head of which had rejected the author's suit for the hand of his daughter. The family threatened to sue if Daudet used their name in his novel, so he changed it to the fictional Tartarin, but got his own back by making the whole town the butt of his jokes. Inside are mementoes from the three Tartarin novels, and photos from the plays and films. The garden has been planted to fit the books' exotic flora and baobab tree, where Tartarin held court with his tall tales.

Also on display is the famous **Tarasque**, a moustachioed armadillo covered with red spikes. Scholars argue whether the monster is named after the town or vice versa; when King René founded the *Jeux et Courses de la Tarasque* in 1474, it was given a thick carapace to hide the men that made it walk, while fireworks blasted out of its nostrils and the people sang '*Lagadigadèu, la Tarasco, Lagadigadèu!*', or 'Let her pass, the Tarasque, let her dance'.

FESTIVAL

Nowadays the *Fêtes de la Tarasque* take place for five days around St John's Day (24 June), and include bonfires, costumes, bullfights, cavalcades, dances, opera (the *Miréio* of course), and—yes—someone dressed up like Tartarin.

WHERE TO STAY/EATING OUT (postal code 13150)
The best hotel in town, *****De Provence**, 7 Blvd Victor Hugo, tel 90 91 06 43, offers big rooms, big baths, colour TV and breakfast on your own balcony. More modest, though hardly less spacious, are the rooms at ****Le Saint-Jean**, 25 Blvd Victor Hugo, tel 90 91 13 87; it is connected to one of Tarascon's best restaurants, with the best value menu at 75F. Of the cheapies, try the recently restored ***Hôtel du Rhône**, by the station in Place Colonel Berrurier, tel 90 91 03 35. There are 60 beds in the well-kept **Auberge de Jeunesse** (youth hostel), 31 Blvd Gambetta, tel 90 91 04 08 (open Mar-Dec); lodgers can take advantage of the hostel's inexpensive bike hire. As for victuals, they're cheap, if not *cordon bleu*: **Brasserie La Tarasque** by the station is run by a patron with moustaches as big as Tartarin's and attracts the locals with a 50F menu; the prize for the best name goes to **Self du Roi René** near the Château at 10 Blvd Itam.

Beaucaire

Beaucaire can match Tarascon's stories tit for tat. It, too, was plagued by a river monster, called the Drac—a dragon in some versions, or a handsome young man—who liked to stroll invisibly through Beaucaire, before luring his victims into the Rhône by holding a bright jewel just below the surface. When the Drac became a father, he kidnapped a washerwoman to nurse his baby for seven years, during which time the woman learned how to see him when he was invisible. Years later, during one of his prowls through Beaucaire she saw him and greeted him loudly. He was so mortified that he was never seen again. Beaucaire was also the setting of one of the most charming medieval romances: of Aucassin, son of the Count of Beaucaire, and his 'sweet sister friend' Nicolette, daughter of the King of Carthage, whom Aucassin loved so dizzily that he fell off his horse and dislocated his shoulder, among other adventures.

But in those days Beaucaire was on everyone's lips. In 1216, during the Albigensian Crusade, the son of the Count of Toulouse recaptured the town from its French occupiers, who took refuge in the castle. As soon as word reached the cruel French leader Simon de Montfort, he set off in person to succour his stranded men and to teach Beaucaire a lesson, besieged the town walls, while his troops took up the fight from the castle, so that Beaucaire was sandwiched in a double attack. The fight lasted 13 weeks before the castle surrendered to Beaucaire and Simon admitted one of his very few defeats. In gratitude Raymond VI of Toulouse gave the town the right to hold a duty-free fair. But five years later Beaucaire was forced by treaty to become French along with the rest of Languedoc, and was stripped of all its rights and freedoms.

In 1464 Louis XI, eager to win Beaucaire to his side, restored its freedoms and fair franchise; soon its *Foire de la Ste-Madeleine* became one of the biggest in western Europe. For ten days in July, merchants from all over the Mediterranean, Germany and England would wheel and deal in the wooden booths of the *pré*, a vast meadow on the banks of the Rhône; by the 18th century, when the fair was at its height, Beaucaire (with a population of 8000) attracted some 300,000 traders, as well as acrobats, prostitutes, pickpockets, and sweethearts, who came to buy each other rings of spun glass, as a symbol of love's fragile beauty. The advent of the railway made the fair obsolete, and since then Beaucaire's economy has been dominated by wine, ranging from pretty good table plonk to the more illustrious AOC Costière du Gard. But if you come in the spring, you can try one last legacy of the great fair in Beaucaire's *pastissoun*, patties filled with preserved fruits introduced by merchants from the Levant.

Château Royal and Musée de la Vignasse
Louis XI's restoration of Beaucaire's rights paid off for a later Louis (XIII); in 1632, when the château was invested by the troops of the king's rebellious brother, Gaston d'Orléans, the loyal citizens forced them out. To prevent further mishaps Richelieu ordered Beaucaire's castle destroyed. But after demolishing the south wall, the shell was left to fall into ruins romantic enough for an illustration to *Aucassin and Nicolette*, its courtyard planted with Aleppo pines and irises (open Apr–Sept 10–12 and 2:15–6:45; Oct–Mar 10:15–12 and 2–5:15, closed Tues, adm). There are sweeping views of the Rhône from the 25-m **Tour Polygonale**. The **Musée de la Vignasse**, in the gardens (afternoons only; closed Mon and Tues) has finds from Roman Beaucaire (then clumsily called *Ugernum*) and mementoes from the fair, when thousands of brightly coloured cloths swung over the streets, each bearing a merchant's name, his home address and his address in Beaucaire; it was the only way in the vast, polyglot throng to find anyone.

From the Château, arrows point the way to the venerable **Place de la République**, shaded by giant plane trees, and the 1744 church of **Notre-Dame-des-Pommiers** (1744), which conserves, on its exterior transept wall (facing Rue Charlier), a 12th-century **frieze**, depicting Passion scenes in the same strong, dry relief as at St-Gilles-du-Gard. Nothing else indicated by the tourist signposts—Hôtel de Ville and other hotels you can't stay in—is as spectacular, though if it's a holiday, there's likely to be some dramatic bull follies in the **Arènes**. Beaucaire's *razeteurs* have the reputation as the most daring of all: statues of the most acclaimed *taureaux* they have faced greet visitors by the Rhône bridge and in Place Jean-Jaurès.

Around Beaucaire

Although little remains of Beaucaire's Roman incarnation *Ugernum*, the **Via Domitia**, by which it made its living transferring goods between the Rhône and Spain has survived in remarkably good nick in a place known as **Les Bornes Milliaires** (take D 999 1 km northwest past the train tracks, turn left 800 m, following the Enclos d'Argent lane). Nowhere else along the route have the milestones survived so well: these three, on the 13th mile between Nîmes and Ugernum, were erected by Augustus, Tiberius, and Antoninus Pius. Another curious sight, the vaguely spooky **Abbaye St-Roman-d'Ai-guille**, lies 4 km up D 999 (Apr, May, June, Sept 10–6, closed Mon and Tues; July and Aug, 10–7, closed Mon; other times Sat and Sun only, 2–5, adm) was founded in a cave in the perilous 5th century. In 1363 Pope Urban V made it a *studium*, a school open even to the poorest children. The abbey was converted into a castle in 1537, which in turn began to tumble down in the 1700s. Remaining are the subterranean cells and priory, and 150 rock-cut tombs in the necropolis on the upper terrace, from where the dead monks had better views than the live ones down below.

WHERE TO STAY/EATING OUT   (postal code 30300)
***Les Doctrinaires**, Quai Général de Gaulle, tel 66 59 41 32, was before the Revolution the home of the Doctrinaire fathers of Avignon, now metamorphosed into a

fetching, old-fashioned hostelry. Half-board is obligatory in season, but eating 'in', in the pretty courtyard, is particularly pleasant; the dishes are simple but well prepared, and rated tops in Beaucaire (menus from 100F). **Le Robinson, 2 km north on the Route de Comps, tel 66 59 21 32, has 30 rooms set in acres and acres of countryside, with pool, tennis, playground etc. and restaurant. Or for a real escape, hire a houseboat and make the leisurely loop down the Rhône-Sète canal to the Camargue, west to Aigues-Mortes and up the Languedoc canal past St-Gilles to Beaucaire. Two firms hire out house boats: Ancas Away, Quai Général de Gaulle, tel 66 58 66 71, and Connoisseur Cruisers, 9 Quai de la Paix, tel 66 59 46 08.

Part X

DOWN THE RHÔNE: THE ALPILLES, CRAU AND CAMARGUE

Arènes, Arles

The Rhône that flows so majestically from the Swiss Alps down half of France comes to a rather messy end in the Camargue, dithering indecisively through a delta of swamps, salt-pans and sand-dunes. And yet if all the chapters of this book had to compete in a talent show, this would be the one to beat. It has wild bulls, horses and pink flamingos; it has the cowboys, gypsies and the fancy dress of the Arlésiennes; it has Roman ruins, the best Romanesque art, and the most romantic stories, worthy of Sir Walter Scott; it has the sharpest mountains, a plain so uncanny that it took a myth to explain it, and the mistral-whipped landscapes painted by Van Gogh; it has the biggest bullring, France's only AOC hay (from Arles), and all the aluminium ore you could ask for.

St-Rémy-de-Provence and the Alpilles

GETTING AROUND
Though there are no trains, St-Rémy is a crossroads, surrounded by several big towns; consequently the **coach service** is slightly better than most places. All leave from Place de la République, across from the church: at least one a day to Arles, Tarascon, Cavaillon and Aix; more frequently to Avignon. You can easily walk to Les Antiques (see p. 293) and Glanum, but buses from St-Rémy to Les Baux are rare and inconvenient.

291

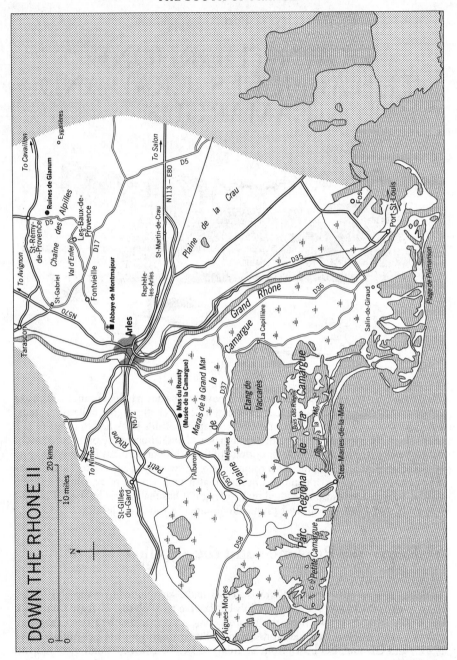

DOWN THE RHONE II

To Cavaillon
Eygalières
Ruines de Glanum
St-Rémy-de-Provence
D5
Chaîne des Alpilles
Les-Baux-de-Provence
Val d'Enfer
D17
To Salon
D5
N113 – E80
To Avignon
St-Gabriel
Fontvieille
N570
Plaine de la Crau
St-Martin-de-Crau
Raphèle-les-Arles
Abbaye de Montmajour
Arles
Tarascon
Grand Rhône
D35
D36
Fos
Port-St-Louis
Plage de Piémanson
Mas du Rousty
(Musée de la Camargue)
Marais de la Grand Mar
D37
Camargue
La Capilière
Salin-de-Giraud
Etang de Vaccarès
Bois des Rièges
Parc Regional de la Camargue
Digue à la Mer
Stes-Maries-de-la-Mer
Petit Rhône
N572
N Gilles-du-Gard
l'Albaron
D570
Plaine de la Mer
Méjanes
D58
Petite Camargue
Aigues-Mortes
To Nîmes

20 kms
10 miles

The latter is better connected to Arles, with four or five buses a day, stopping at Fontvieille.

The Alpilles are not too steep for **cycling** in most places; the Syndicat d'Initiative in St-Rémy has a list of bike-hire firms. You might enjoy a tour around the southern slopes of the Alpilles, near St-Rémy, looking for the spots where Van Gogh painted many of his famous landscapes.

TOURIST INFORMATION
St-Rémy (13210): Place Jean-Jaurès, on the way to Les Antiques, tel 90 92 05 22.
Les Baux (15320): Grand Rue, tel 90 54 34 03.

St-Rémy-de-Provence

It is only chance that finds little St-Rémy being called upon to start off this chapter, but it does its best to make a good first impression nonetheless. Enclosed by a garland of boulevards lined with plane trees, the town's tranquillity has attracted its share of the famous: Gertrude Stein spent years here, and Princess Caroline drops in for discreet visits (St-Rémy used to belong to the family). Vincent Van Gogh spent his tragic last year in the asylum, which during World War I was commandeered to hold interned Germans—the one who got Van Gogh's room was Albert Schweitzer.

Nowadays St-Rémy is home to a good many artists, and there are always exhibitions going on. The newest attraction is the bizarre-looking organ in the church of **St-Martin** on Blvd Marceau. Built only in 1983, it is said to be one of the finest in the world; the Organ Festival in August pulls out all the stops, as do the Saturday afternoon concerts in summer and autumn. The old attractions are two fine Renaissance palaces, both around Place Favier, behind the church, one street to the north: the **Hôtel Mistral de Mondragon** (1550), containing a museum of local folk life and arts, with a special section on Nostradamus, who was born in St-Rémy; and the **Hôtel de Sade**, with a small but interesting **Archaeological Museum** (in summer, guided tours at 10, 11 am and 3, 4, 5 pm; Oct–Mar, Sat and Sun only; adm). St-Rémy is the medieval successor to the abandoned Roman town of Glanum (see below); finds from Glanum on display here include architectural fragments, statues and reliefs of deities from Hermes to the Phrygian god Attis, Roman glass and jewellery

Les Antiques, and Van Gogh's Asylum

The Romans had a habit of building monuments and impressive mausolea on the outskirts of their towns, along the main roads. Just a 15-minute walk from the centre of St-Rémy, south on the D 5, stand two of the most remarkable Roman relics in France. They were here long before the D 5 of course; originally they decorated the end of the Roman road from Arles to Glanum, the ruins of which lie just across the D 5. The **Triumphal Arch**, built probably in the reign of Augustus, was one of the first to be erected in Provence. Its elegant form and marble columns show the Greek sensibility of the artists, far different from the strange Celtic-influenced arches of Orange and Carpentras. In the Middle Ages it inspired the creators of St-Trophime in Arles. Evidently, someone long ago carted off the top for building stone; the slanted tile roof is an 18th-century addition to protect what was left.

Next to it, the so-called **Mausoleum** was really a memorial to Caesar and Augustus, erected by their descendants in the early 1st century AD. There is nothing else quite like this anywhere, and it is one of the best-preserved Roman monuments. The form is certainly original: a narrow four-faced arch on a solid plinth, surmounted by a cylinder of columns and a pointed roof, 17 m above the ground; inside this are statues of Caesar and Augustus. The **reliefs** on the base are excellent work: mythological scenes including a *battle with Amazons*, a *battle of Greeks and Trojans* and a *boar hunt*. At the top of the arch, you can make out a pair of winged spirits holding a civic crown of laurel—the symbol of Augustus' new political order.

Just across the road from Les Antiques, a shady path leads to the monastery of **St-Paul-de-Mausole**, in a beautiful setting with gardens all around. Founded in the 900s, the complex includes a simple Romanesque church and a cloister with some interesting carved capitals. In 1810, the monastery buildings were purchased for use as a private hospital (it still is; no visits). This is the place Vincent Van Gogh chose as a refuge from the troubles of life in the outside world, in May 1890, not long after he chopped off the ear. He spent a year here, the most intense and original period of his career, painting as if possessed—150 canvases and over 100 drawings, including many of his most famous works, such as the *Nuit Etoilée* ('Starry Night') and *Les Blés Jaunes* ('Cornfield and Cypress Trees') The blueish mountains in the background of this work and many others are the Alpilles.

Glanum

Glanum began as a Celtic settlement—a proper town, really, under a heavy cultural influence from the Greeks at nearby Marseille. The Romans snatched it around 100 BC, under Marius, but not until the great prosperity of the Augustan empire did the city begin to bloom. Almost all of the ruins visible today (as well as Les Antiques) date from this period. In a prelude to the fall of the Empire, the Franks and Alemanni ranged throughout Gaul in the 250s and 60s. In one of their last hurrahs before the recovering Roman legions drove them out, they sacked Glanum in 270. After that, the townspeople relocated to a healthier and safer site, today's St-Rémy; silt washed down from the Alpilles gradually covered the city, and it passed out of memory until the 19th century, when some accidental finds alerted archaeologists to its presence. Excavations began in 1921, and have since uncovered a fascinating cross-section of Glanum, including its Forum.

More than Vaison-la-Romaine or anywhere else in France, this is the place to really feel at home in the Roman world. But you'll have to work for it; only the foundations remain, and recreating Glanum will require a bit of imagination (see the museum in the Hôtel de Sade first). From the entrance, to the left are the **Maison des Antes** and the **Maison d'Atys**, two typical wealthy homes built around peristyle courtyards. The latter had apparently been transformed into a sanctuary of Cybele and Attis; this cult was one of the most popular of the mystery religions imported from the east in imperial times.

Across the street are remains of a fountain and the **thermae** (baths), with mosaics, a *palestra* (exercise yard) and a *piscine* (pool). Next door is a building with an exedra that was probably a temple; altars to Silenus were found inside. In this part of the street the **sewers** have been uncovered. The **Forum** wasn't very impressive, by the standards of most Roman towns, and it is hard to make anything out today from the confusion of buildings from various ages that have been excavated. Beyond it, to the right, are foundations of temples; to the left are bases of another fountain and a monument. The street closes at a **gate** from Hellenistic times that was retained as the city expanded outside the original walls. Also retained was the **nymphaeum** beyond it, to the left; these decorated fountains were a common feature of Greek cities, built to allow travellers to refresh and clean up before entering the town.

WHERE TO STAY/EATING OUT

St-Rémy (13210) gets a heap of tourists, and consequently has a wide choice of places to stay; even for visiting the Alpilles, it will probably prove the most convenient base. Some of the hotels are exceptional: the ****Château de Roussan**, with lovely rooms in an 18th-century mansion, set in the middle of an extravagant park full of fountains and tree-lined avenues; some rooms are inexpensive, others up to 850 F, but book far ahead in any case for this one (3 km west of town, on the Rte de Tarascon, off the D 99, tel 90 92 11 63; closed Nov–Feb). Second choice, and a bargain for its three stars, is the *****Castelet des Alpilles**—rooms with a view in a somewhat more modest mansion, plus a simple restaurant with a garden terrace (on Place Mireille, near Les Antiques; requires half-board in season, tel 90 92 07 21, closed Nov–Mar).

Also near the ruins, the ***Auberge de Glanum** is family-run and has some surprising amenities for an inexpensive hotel: a pool and garden, and horses to ride, also a restaurant (46 Av. Van Gogh, tel 90 92 03 59; requires half-board; closed Jan). In the centre of St-Rémy, you'll enjoy the ingratiatingly old-fashioned ***Le Provence**, and its friendly management, on Blvd Victor Hugo (closed Oct–Mar; tel 90 92 06 27). Just down the street, the ****Hôtel des Arts** has rooms for the same rate; as the name suggests, lots of modern art (and artists) about, and a popular restaurant that specializes in steaks and frogs' legs (menus 80–90 F, 150–160 F, tel 90 92 08 50).

For an inexpensive lunch, you won't do better than **La Margarido** on Rue Jaume Roux in the centre of the old town; for a 90 F menu you'll get a generous salad buffet, and fish *au pistou* or other dishes to follow; also couscous.

Les Baux-de-Provence and the Chaîne des Alpilles

The ruins were nice, but there is an even greater treat ahead. The three twisting miles of the D 5 that take you from Les Antiques into the heart of the Alpilles are, in fact, one of the greatest sensual experiences Provence can offer. Van Gogh and cypresses, lushness and flowers are left behind; in a matter of minutes the road has brought you to another world. This world, incredibly, is at most 16 km across, and a stone's throw from the swamps of the Camargue and the sea. It is made of thin, cool breezes and brilliant light; its colours are white and deep green—almost exclusively—in an astringent landscape of limestone crags and patches of scrubby *maquis*.

From as early as 3000 BC, this exotic massif attracted residents. The Alpilles are full of caves, many of which were once inhabited. The Ligurians took advantage of its natural defences to found an important *oppidum* at **Les Baux**, a steep barren plateau in the centre of the massif, 11 km from St-Rémy. In the Middle Ages, this made the perfect setting for the most feared and celebrated of Provence's noble clans. The Seigneurs des

Baux are first heard of in the 900s. 'A race of eaglets, vassals never', as their slogan went, they never acknowledged the authority of the French king, the emperors, or anyone else, and their impregnable crag in the Alpilles allowed them to get away with it. They claimed to be descended from Balthazar, one of the magi at Bethlehem, and put the Christmas star on their feudal escutcheon.

Les Baux

The symbol was never a harbinger of glad tidings to their neighbours, however; for the next two centuries the lords of Baux waged incessant warfare on all comers, and occasionally on each other, gradually becoming a real power in Provence. They did it with flair, and the chronicles are full of good stories about them: one Seigneur once besieged the castle of his pregnant niece, and sent sappers to undermine her bedchamber. And they met memorable ends; one was stabbed to death by his wife, another flayed alive when he fell into the hands of his enemies. All the while, the family headquarters at Les Baux maintained a polished court where troubadours were always welcome. It ended with a bang in 1372, when an even nastier fellow took over the clan: Raymond de Turenne, a distant relation who was also a nephew of Pope Gregory IX. Taking advantage of confused times, in the reign of Queen Jeanne, this ambitious and bloodthirsty intriguer found enough support, and enough foreign mercenaries, to bring full-scale civil war to Provence, bringing it the same kind of misery to which the rest of France had become accustomed in the Hundred Years War.

When the last heir of Les Baux died in 1426, the possessions of the house were incorporated into the County of Provence. That isn't quite the end of the story; in the 1500s Les Baux began to thrive once more, first under Anne of Montmorency, who rebuilt the seigneurs' castle in the best Renaissance taste, and later under the Manvilles, who inherited it from her and made it a Protestant stronghold in the Wars of Religion. Cardinal Richelieu finally put this eternal trouble-spot to rest in 1632, demolishing the castle and sending the owners the bill for the job. Until the Revolution, the remains of Les Baux were, like St-Rémy, in the hands of the Grimaldis of Monaco.

A Million Visitors a Year
After the demolition, the village that surrounded the castle of Les Baux almost disappeared; Prosper Mérimée, in the 1830s, reported only a few beggars living among its ruins. But Provençal writers kept the place from being forgotten, men such as Mistral (born at Maillane, near St-Rémy) and Alphonse Daudet, whose famous windmill is just over the Alpilles (see below). In the last 50 years, Les Baux has become one of the biggest tourist attractions in France. The village below the castle has been rebuilt and repopulated in the worst way, and whatever spark of glamour survives in this tremendous ruin will definitely be extinguished by the ghastly inferno of trinket shops, bars and bad art that must now be crossed to reach it.

Even in the village, there are still plenty of ruins, and the first sight to greet you as you trudge up from the car park is an elegant carved Renaissance fireplace, open to the sky and standing next to a souvenir shop. The village has some attractions: along the main street, the Grande Rue, the **Fondation Louis Jou** features the works of this talented early 20th-century engraver, along with some of his predecessors (prints by Dürer among them) and early books. Further up the Grande Rue is the former **Protestant**

Temple of 1571. Nearby are two very refined 16th-century palaces: the **Hôtel de Manville**, behind the Temple, housing the *mairie* and a small museum about Les Baux and the Alpilles; and the **Hôtel des Porcelets**, with 18th-century frescoes of the *Four Seasons* on the ground floor, and a touristy, forgettable 'Museum of Modern Art' above.

Next to it, on Place St-Vincent, is the 12th-century church of **St-Vincent**, partly cut out of the rock; the modern stained glass inside was a gift of Prince Rainier. Also cut out of the rock is Rue du Trencat, behind the church; it leads to the entrance of the **castle ruins**, at the Tour de Brau, containing the ticket booth and a small museum of statues and architectural fragments found on the site (daily 9:30–5:30; in summer 8:30–8; adm).

Once inside, the ambience changes abruptly—a rocky chaos surrealistically decorated with fragments of once-imposing buildings. The path leads through this 'Ville Morte' (on the left are remains of the hospital and its chapel) to the tip of the plateau, where there is a monument to a Provençal poet named Charlon Rieu, and a grand view over the Alpilles. Turning back, the path climbs up to the chateau itself, with bits of towers and walls everywhere, including the apse of a Gothic chapel cut out of the rock, and the long eastern wall that survived Richelieu's explosives, dotted with finely carved windows. The only intact part is the **donjon**, a rather treacherous climb to the top for a bird's-eye view over the site—don't try it when the mistral is blowing.

An Infernal Valley and a Blonde Sorceress
Beneath Les Baux, on the western side, the **Pavillon de la Reine Jeanne** has nothing to do with the famous queen, but is a pretty Renaissance garden folly of 1581. The road that passes it will take you in another 3 km to the **Val d'Enfer**, the wildest corner of the Alpilles, a weird landscape of eroded limestone, caves and quarries. One thing the Alpilles has a lot of is aluminium ore—*bauxite*, a useless mineral until the process for smelting it was discovered in the last century. Now there are bauxite mines all over southern Provence; those to be seen here are exhausted, but Jean Cocteau took advantage of the landscape to shoot part of his *Orphée* here in 1950. Today the quarries host one of Les Baux's big attractions: the **Cathédrale des Images**, a slick show where thirty projectors bounce giant pictures over the walls; the theme of the show changes yearly.

Off the D 27A, near the crossroads for Les Baux, the **Col de la Vayède** holds scanty remains of the pre-Roman *oppidum*; the lines of the walls can be traced in some places, and there are bits of wall and no less than three necropolises, with small niches carved into the rock to hold the ashes of the deceased. On the side of the hill facing the D 27A, you can climb up a dirt path to see the mysterious relief called the **Trémaïe**. Neatly carved on a smoothed rock face are three figures and an effaced Latin inscription. It seems to be a Roman funeral monument, but local legend has it that the figures represent Marius, his wife, and a blonde Celtic sorceress named Marthe who helped Marius in his campaigns against the Teutones. Another relief, less well-preserved, can be seen a few hundred yards to the south. Finally, for hikers, there is the GR 6 trail, which traverses the best parts of the Alpilles from east to west. It passes right through Les Baux.

WHERE TO STAY/EATING OUT
Les Baux (13520), with its tourist hordes, isn't the most desirable place to stop over—and you'll have to pay a lot for the privilege. For a memorable splurge, though, the best (and dearest) of the luxury spots is ******l'Oustaù de Baumanière**; magical

surroundings in the Val d'Enfer, a restored farmhouse with all the amenities (even a golf course nearby) and a highly rated restaurant (two Michelin stars) with a spectacular terrace view; seafood is the star: salmon, *langoustines* and such, and there are sumptuous desserts and a formidable wine list of Provençal treasures; menus are at 540 and 650 F, but here you're just as well off choosing *à la carte* (tel 90 54 33 07).

Forget the luxury, and you can do just as well for half the price at the ****Mas d'Aigret. Some rooms have great views, others open onto the gardens; there is a pool, a restaurant as good as the Baumanière's; menus 160–210–280 F, and a tremendous bargain for lunch: 130 F (east of the village on the D 27A, tel 90 54 33 54, closed Jan–Mar). This is definitely the place to dine in Les Baux; the village itself has only a few tourist-oriented places, though there is a pleasant bar-*crêperie* on the Grande Rue, the Café de Musée. The only relatively cheap place to stay is in the village, the **Hostellerie de Reine Jeanne (tel 90 54 32 06; closed Jan).

 Coteaux des Baux-en-Provence
The AOC wine of the Alpilles is rosé, like most of Provence's vintages, but in recent years the reds of Les Baux have made a quantum jump in quality and attracted the most attention. This relatively new *appellation* comes under the heading of Coteaux d'Aix-en-Provence, and a majority of its growers are good environmentalists dedicated to growing grapes free from artificial fertilizers, pesticides and herbicides; the grapes that go into it include grenache, cabernet-sauvignon, syrah, cinsault, carignan and counoise. A good source is the charming Domaine de La Vallongue in Eygalières, tel 90 95 91 70, which uses traditional methods to create organic wines: fresh, fruity, fragrant rosés and intense reds, hinting at vanilla and spice; every year between 85 and 89 was a happy success. Mas Cellier in St-Rémy, tel 90 92 03 90, is a tiny estate, but one of the few vineyards in the region both owned and run by a woman, Dominique Hauvette, whose wines (also organic) have a warm, velvety quality, especially
the 88. In Les Baux itself, at the foot of the cliffs, visitors can take a didactic nature walk through the vines of Mas Ste-Berthe (tel 90 54 39 01) and learn all about the grapes. Some (ugni blanc, sauvignon, and grenache blanc) go into the white wine, while the sombre red, especially the 88, is excellent and still reasonably priced.

St-Gabriel and Fontvieille

The eastern half of the Alpilles is the more scenic, and if you're heading in that direction, lonely roads like the D 78 and D 24 make worthwhile detours that won't take you more than a few kilometres out of the way; Eygalières, on the D 24B, is a lovely village with a ruined castle.

Along the western fringes of the Alpilles, on the D 33, you will pass the canal port of *Ernaginum*, later called St-Gabriel, which flourished from Roman times until the Middle Ages. You won't see anything; the drying-up of the old canal doomed the city to a slow death, and Ernaginum has disappeared more completely than any ancient city of Provence, leaving only the impressive 12th-century church of St-Gabriel standing alone in open fields. There is little to see inside—and it's never open anyhow; the real interest is one of the finest Romanesque façades in the Midi. Very consciously imitating Roman architecture, it shows a stately portal with a triangular pediment, flanked by Corinthian columns. There are excellent sculpted reliefs on and above the tympanum: an *Annunciation*, *Daniel in the Lions' Den* and *Adam and Eve*, apparently just realizing they have no clothes on. Above it, a small Italianate rose window is surrounded by figures of the four Evangelists.

Eygalières

From here, the only village on the way to Arles is **Fontvieille**, best-known for the **Moulin de Daudet**, south on the D 33, a rare survivor among the hundreds of windmills that once embellished every hilltop of southern Provence. Alphonse Daudet never really lived here, but his *Lettres de Mon Moulin*, a collection of sentimental tales of the dying life of rural Provence in the late 1800s, is still popular across France today. The windmill has become a museum of Daudet, with photographs and documents. Two kilometres further south, there are sections of two Roman **aqueducts** that served Arles, along with vestiges of a **Roman mill**, unique in Europe. Unlike Daudet's charmingly folksy effort, this huge installation was a serious precursor to the Industrial Revolution, using the flow of the water to power 16 separate mills, along a stretch of canal over a kilometre long; nothing like it has been found anywhere else.

The Hypogeum of Castellet

On the D 17, at the crossroads with the D 82, you will find a very ruined castle that once belonged to the Counts of Provence. The surrounding area, a low, flat-topped hill called Castellet, contains one of the most unusual and least-known neolithic monuments in France. The **Hypogeum** consists of four covered avenues, carefully carved out of the rock or earth, under tumuli that have long since disappeared. They were made as collective tombs about 3500 BC or later, by the Ligurians or their predecessors, and probably also served as a kind of temple. Many have carvings, cup-marks and sun-symbols, inside or near their openings. The sites are not marked, and you'll be lucky to find their narrow, trapezoidal entrances in the undergrowth. All are within 200 yds of the D 17, three south of the road and one north.

From Castellet, you'll see another hill, the **Montagne de Cordes** about a half kilometre to the south. Like Castellet, this was an island in neolithic times. Nearby Montmajour (see below) was a third. The Cordes is private property, and you'll need permission from the owner (in the farmhouse on the slopes) to see another remarkable tomb-temple. The **Grotte des Fées** is also known as the 'Epée de Roland'; the tapering, 70-m tunnel has two small side chambers that give it the shape of a sword.

WHERE TO STAY/EATING OUT

Fontvieille (13990) has a surprising number of hotels and is only 11 km away from Les Baux. In the luxury class, there is the Relais et Châteaux' ******Auberge de la Regalido**, Rue Mistral, tel 90 54 60 22, in a restored mill with lovely gardens, including a restaurant that is a little temple of *haute cuisine* with prices to match, menus 240–400 F for excellent fresh seafood or roast pigeon with *morilles*. Less expensively, *****Le Valmajour** on the D 17, is a good bargain with a pool and tennis, and well-furnished quiet rooms (tel 90 54 62 23). Fontvieille also has the only budget rooms around the Alpilles, at the admirable

*Hostellerie de la Tour, 3 Rue des Plumelets (tel 90 54 72 21) and the more down-to-earth *Bernard (Cours Bellon; tel 90 54 70 35).

In Eygalières (13810), on the far eastern side of the Alpilles, the Relais du Coche is worth going out of your way for: a delightful, unpretentious inn, including a restaurant with good Provençal home cooking, 110 F lunch menu; 170 and 225 F for dinner.

Abbaye de Montmajour

Just before Arles, the D 17 passes one of the most important monasteries of medieval Provence. Founded in the 10th century, on what was then almost an island amidst the swamps, this Benedictine abbey was devoted to reclaiming the land, a monumental labour that would take centuries to complete. By the 1300s, the monastery had grown exceedingly wealthy, a real prize for the Avignon popes, who gained control of it and farmed it out, along with its revenues, to friends and relations. Under such absentee abbots, it languished thereafter, and its great church was never completed. To give some idea of its later decadence, an attempt to reform it in 1639 included importing new monks; the old crew refused to go, and sacked the abbey before they were chased out by royal troops. Montmajour became a national property not in the Revolution, but five years earlier. The 1786 'Affair of the Diamond Necklace' was a famous swindle that involved both Marie Antoinette and the great charlatan Cagliostro. One of the principal players was Montmajour's abbot, the Cardinal de Rohan; he got caught, and all his property, including the abbey, was confiscated. The abbey did service as a farmhouse, and its church as a barn, before restorations began in 1907.

Consequently, there isn't much to see. At the church entrance you'll notice the piers, built into the adjacent wall of the cloister, that would have supported the nave had it been completed. The interior is austere and empty, but gives a good idea of the state of Provençal architecture c.1200, in transition from Romanesque to Gothic. The most interesting part is the lower church, a crypt with an unusual plan, including a long, narrow nave and a circular enclosure under the high altar, with radiating chapels behind it; its purpose has not been explained. The cloister has some fanciful sculptural decoration; see if you can find the camel. Around the back of the church, you'll see a number of tombs cut out of the rock; these are a mystery too, and may predate the abbey. The mighty 26-m donjon was built in the 1360s for defence, in that terrible age when the lords of Les Baux and a dozen other hoodlums were tearing up the neighbourhood; next to it, the tiny chapel of St-Pierre (usually closed) was the original abbey church, built on the spot where St-Trophime of Arles (see below) had his hermitage.

STE-CROIX

A few hundred yards behind the apse of the church, in the middle of a farm, stands what was the abbey's funeral chapel, Ste-Croix. Don't miss it, even though you'll have to walk through the farmyard muck (it's visible from the road, near a barn). Few buildings show so convincingly the architectural sophistication of the Romanesque as this small work of the late 11th century, a central-plan chapel with apses along three sides and an elegant lantern on top. Some complex geometry and a mastery of proportions are built into this simple but perfect form, based on the Golden Section. Too much decoration would be superfluous, and there is only a discreet carved floral frieze along the cornice, along with Moorish-style interlocking arches.

Arles

Like Nîmes, Arles has enough intact antiquities to call itself the 'Rome of France'; unlike Nîmes it lingered in the limelight for another 1000 years to produce enough saints for every month on the calendar—Trophimus, Hilarius, Césaire and Genès are some of the more famous. Pilgrims flocked here for a whiff of their odour of sanctity, and asked on their deathbeds to be buried in the holy ground of the Alyscamps. Nowadays Arles holds the distinction of being the largest commune in France, ten times larger than Paris, embracing 750 square kilometres of the Camargue and Crau plains; it has given the world the rhythms of the Gypsy Kings, and the pungent joys of *saucisse d'Arles*, France's finest donkey-meat sausage.

In spite of all these trump cards, Arles is a torpid, conservative town in attitude and politics, very low in wicker café chairs once warmed by the distinguished bottoms of the Sartres and Cocteaus of the world. The essential Arles sits rather in the plain wooden chair that Van Gogh painted in his room in Place Lamartine, or as fussy old Henry James wrote, after initially taking a strong dislike to it: 'As a city Arles quite misses its effect in every way: and if it is a charming place, as I think it is, I can hardly tell the reason why.'

History

In 1975, the remains of a Celto-Ligurian settlement were uncovered near the Boulevard des Lices. It's hard to imagine what its builders thought in the 6th century BC, when Greek traders from Marseille arrived and began to dicker over prices. We know at least that the Greeks were pleased, and over the years they established the site as their principal 'counter' for dealings with the Ligurians, calling it *Arelate* ('near sleeping waters' or less poetically, 'bog town'). Business picked up considerably after Marius' legionnaires made Arelate a seaport by digging a canal to Fos (104 BC). In 49 BC, the populace, tired of getting bum deals from the wily Greeks, readily gave Caesar the boats he needed to punish and conquer Marseille for siding with Pompey. In return Arles was rewarded the spoils and received a population boost with a colony of veterans from the Sixth Legion. Most important of all, it got all of Rome's business that had previously gone through Greek Marseille. A bridge of boats was built over the Rhône, and the Colonia Julia Paterna Arelate Sextanorum was known far and wide for its powerful maritime corporations, called *utriculares* from their rafts that floated on inflated bladders.

At the crossroads of Rome's trading route between Italy and Spain and the Rhône, Arles grew rapidly, each century adding more splendid monuments—a theatre, temples, a circus, an amphitheatre, at least two triumphal arches, and a basilica. Constantine built himself a grand palace and baths as big as Caracalla's in Rome. In 395 Emperor Honorius made it the capital of the 'Three Gauls'—France, Britain, and Spain, and as late as 418 it was recorded that 'Arles is so fortunately placed, its commerce is so active and merchants come in such numbers that all the products of the universe are channelled there: the riches of the Orient, perfumes of Arabia, delicacies of Assyria...'

Arles was one of the last cities to fall to the Visigoths, only to become their capital in 476. The Franks inherited it in 536, and Saracen raids were frequent. But on the whole, the Dark Ages were not so dark in Arles; from 879 to 1036 it served as the capital of Provence-Burgundy (the so-called 'Kingdom of Arles'), a vast territory that stretched all the way to Lorraine. Most importantly, Arles was a centre of power for the new Christian religion. Several major Church councils convened here, including one back in 314 that condemned the heresy of Donatism (the quite reasonable belief that sacraments administered by bad priests had no value). Arles' cathedral of St-Trophime became the most important church in Provence; in 597 its bishop, St Virgil, consecrated St Augustine as the first Bishop of Canterbury and as late as 1178, Emperor Frederick Barbarossa was crowned King of Arles at its altar. After a busy career in the 11th and 12th centuries as a crusader port and pilgrimage destination, the city's special history ended in 1239 when Raymond Berenger, Count of Provence, evicted Arles' imperial viceroy. As the city declined even the Mediterranean abandoned it, leaving the former port stranded between feverish marshes and the rocky plain of the Crau, compressed in a time capsule of Roman monuments and ancient customs.

The Arles of Van Gogh

With the improved communications of the 19th century, Arles slowly resurfaced. The Roman amphitheatre was restored. The city's women, celebrated for their beautiful Attic features, inspired Daudet's story *L'Arlésienne* (1866) and Bizet's opera (1872). Its furniture makers invented what has become the traditional south Provençal style, more elegantly rococo than the heavy pieces of northern Provence. The Félibres made much of the city for the striking costumes the women continued to wear, for its bullfights and its *farandole*, a dance in 6/4 time dating back at least to the Middle Ages.

Vincent Van Gogh was a fervent admirer of Daudet, and it may well have been his stories that first brought him to Arles in February 1888. To his surprise, the city was blanketed with snow—a very rare occurrence and in a way, an omen. When the snow melted it revealed an Arles made mean and ugly by new embankments along the Rhône, cutting the city off from its life-blood (previously the flooding of the river had fertilized the countryside, like the Nile in Egypt). At the same time one of France's biggest railway lines was being installed by workers brought in from Belgium, housed in cheap ticky-tacky buildings. Arles had never looked shabbier. But Van Gogh stayed, found a room to rent in a poor neighbourhood by the station, and painted the shabby Arles around him: the *Café de Nuit* with its hallucinogenic lightbulb, *La Maison Jaune*, and *Le Pont de Langlois* (part of a ghastly irrigation project) with colours so intense in their chromatic contrasts they seem to come from somewhere over the rainbow.

Van Gogh's dream was to found an art colony at Arles, similar to the one at Pont Avenue in Brittany. He begged his overbearing friend Gauguin to join him, but when Gauguin finally arrived in October he found little to like in Arles, dashing Van Gogh's hopes. The tension between the two men reached such a pitch in December that the overwrought Van Gogh went over the edge and confronted Gauguin in the street with a razor. Gauguin stared him down and Van Gogh, despising himself, went back to his room, cut off his own ear, and gave it to a prostitute. Arles was scandalized, and breathed a sigh of relief when Van Gogh voluntarily committed himself to the local hospital, or Hôtel Dieu. In May 1889 he left for the hospital in St-Rémy.

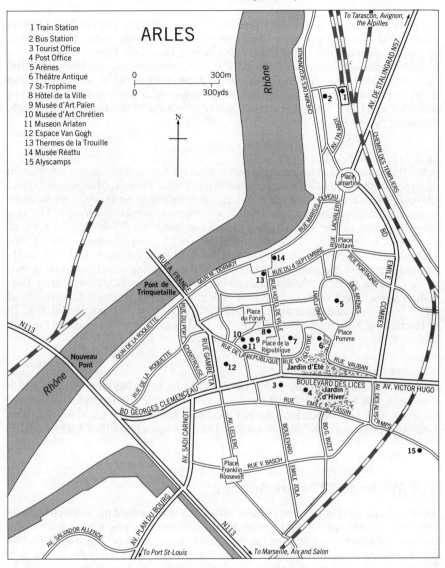

1 Train Station
2 Bus Station
3 Tourist Office
4 Post Office
5 Arènes
6 Théâtre Antique
7 St-Trophime
8 Hôtel de la Ville
9 Musée d'Art Païen
10 Musée d'Art Chrétien
11 Museon Arlaten
12 Espace Van Gogh
13 Thermes de la Trouille
14 Musée Réattu
15 Alyscamps

ARLES

303

Van Gogh's output in Arles was prodigious (from February 1888 to May 1889 he painted 300 canvases) but not a single one remains in the city today. His admirers, looking for the places he painted, have just as little to see: the famous bridge, yellow house, and café were destroyed in World War II or afterwards; only the clock in the Bar Alcazar in Place Lamartine remains as Van Gogh painted it in *Café de Nuit*. To make up for its belated appreciation of the mad, lonely genius who sojourned here, Arles has converted the Hôtel Dieu into a multi-media gallery called the **Espace Van Gogh**, displaying the works of others.

GETTING AROUND

Arles' **train station** is in the northern part of town on Avenue Talabot; (for information tel 90 82 50 50). Arles has frequent connections to Paris, Marseille, Montpellier, Nîmes, Aix-en-Provence, and to all the towns along the main line to Spain; there are frequent services to Avignon and Tarascon and a less frequent service to Orange. The **bus station** serving nearby towns is just across the street (tel 90 49 38 01). Cars de Camargue, from Rue J. M. Artaud, tel 90 96 36 25, have **coaches** to Salon, Aix, Marseille, Nîmes, Stes-Maries-de-la-Mer, Port-St-Louis, St-Gilles and Lunel, and in July and August, to Aigues-Mortes. Les Cars Verts, departing from Chemin de Bressy, tel 90 93 74 90, go to the Alpilles, Salin de Giraud, Avignon and the Nîmes/Arles/Carmargue airport. **Boat tours** of the Rhône or of the Camargue are run by Europaboat, tel 90 93 74 34. For a **taxi** day or night, tel 90 96 90 03. **Car hire:** Europcar, tel 90 93 23 24 or Interent Sté Last, tel 90 49 60 14, both in Blvd Victor Hugo. **Bike hire:** at the train station, tel 90 96 43 94; Dall'Oppio, Rue Portagnel, tel 90 96 46 83.

TOURIST INFORMATION

Esplanade Charles-de-Gaulle, south off the Blvd des Lices (tel 90 96 29 35), and in the station (tel 90 49 36 90). If you intend to see most of Arles' monuments and museums, stop here to purchase the 40 F **global ticket** to save money. Two-hour **Van Gogh tours** depart every Tues and Fri at 5. The **post office** is at 5 Blvd des Lices, tel 90 96 07 80.

The Arènes and Théâtre Antique

Despite the pictures in children's history books, Rome was ruined not so much by tribes of horrid Vandals, but by the latterday Romans themselves, who regarded the baths, theatres and temples they inherited as their private stone quarries. The same holds true of Arles' great monuments, except for the amphitheatre or **Arènes** (9–12 and 2–6; Nov–Feb until 4:30; June–Sept 8:30–7), all of 3 metres wider than its rival at Nîmes. As enormous as it is, it originally stood another arcade higher, and was clad in marble; like most public buildings in the Roman empire no expense was spared on its comforts. An enormous awning operated by sailors protected the audience from the sun and rain, and fountains scented with lavender and burning saffron helped cover up the stink of blood spilled by the gladiators and wild animals below. This temple of death survived in good repair because it came in handy. Its walls were tricked out with towers by Saracen occupiers and used as a fortress (like the theatres of Rome), and from the Middle Ages on it sheltered a poor, crime-ridden neighbourhood with two churches and 200 houses, built from stones prised off the amphitheatre's third storey. These were cleared away in 1825, leaving the amphitheatre free for bullfights, and able to pack in 20,000 spectators.

But a different fate was in store for the **Théâtre Antique**, just south of the Arènes (same hours): in the 5th century, in a fury usually reserved for pagan temples, Christian fanatics pulled it apart stone by stone. A shame, because the fragments of fine sculpture they left in the rubble suggest that the theatre, once capable of seating 12,500, was much more lavish than the one in Orange. Of the stage, only two tall Corinthian columns survived; nicknamed 'the two widows', and pressed into service as gibbets in the 17th and 18th centuries, they were also good at making widows. The most famous statue of Roman Provence, the *Venus of Arles*, lay buried at their feet until she was dug up in 1651 and presented to Louis XIV to adorn the gardens of Versailles. Tiers of seats have been rebuilt for modern performances and costume pageants, most of which take place in July.

South of the theatre runs the **Boulevard des Lices** ('of the lists'), where large cafés under the plane trees provide ringside seats for the rollicking Wednesday and Saturday markets. Since the 17th century the Boulevard has been the favourite promenade of the Arlésiens, where visitors like Van Gogh would go on Sunday to see the women dressed in their best costumes. On either side of the street are the **Jardin d'Eté** (with a bust of Van Gogh) and **Jardin d'Hiver** (where the 5th-century BC *oppidum* was uncovered).

Place de la République: St-Trophime

From Boulevard des Lices, Rue Jean Jaurès (the Roman *cardo*) leads to the harmonious **Place de la République**, an attractive square on the Roman model, with a fountain built around a granite **obelisk** that once stood in the *spina* (or barrier) of the circus. Overlooking this pagan sun needle is one of the chief glories of Provençal Romanesque, the church of **St-Trophime**.

The original church, built by St Hilaire in the 5th century and dedicated to St Stephen, was rebuilt at the end of the 11th century, and the great **Portal** added in the next. Inspired by the triumphal arches of Glanum and Orange, its reliefs describe the *Last Judgement*, mixing the versions of the Apocalypse and Gospel of Matthew. As angels blast away on their trumpets, the triumphant Christ sits in majesty in the tympanum, accompanied by the symbols of the four Evangelists, the 12 Apostles, and a gospel choir of 18 pairs of angels. Below, St Michael weighs each soul, separating the good from evil for their just desserts in the after-life—the fortunate in their long robes are delivered into the bosoms of Abraham, Isaac and Jacob, while the damned, naked and bound like a chain gang, are led off in a conga-line to hell: like all great Romanesque art, the figures on this portal seem to dance to an inner, cosmic rhythm. The large saints set back in the columned recesses below are, from left to right: Bartholomew, James the Minor, Trophime as bishop, John the Evangelist, Peter (over the man-eating lions), Paul, Andrew, Stephen (being stoned), James the Major and Philip. Van Gogh found it admirable but 'so cruel, so monstrous, like a Chinese nightmare, that even this beautiful example of so good a style seems to me to belong to another world and I am glad not to belong to it...'

After the sumptuous portal, the spartan nudity of the long, narrow nave is as striking as its unusual height (60 m). Aubusson tapestries from the 17th century hang across the top, and there are several palaeo-Christian sarcophagi along the sides. The best decoration, however, is by a Dutchman named Finsonius, who came down to Arles in 1610. Like Van Gogh, he stayed, mesmerized by the light and colour, and met a bad end, drowning in the icy Rhône in 1642. St-Trophime has three of his paintings: in the crossing, a beautiful *Annunciation* (1610), the *Stoning of St Stephen* over the triumphal arch in the nave, and on the right, a singular *Adoration of the Magi*, with nightmare architecture and animals in attendance.

THE CLOISTER
Around the corner in Rue du Cloître is the entrance to St-Trophime's cloister (9:30–12 and 2–7, until 4:30 in Jan and Nov; June–Sept 9–7, adm). No other in Provence is as richly and harmoniously sculpted as this, carved in the 12th and 14th centuries by the masters of St-Gilles. Because Arles was as anti-Revolutionary as a town could be, this masterpiece was spared the wanton vandalism that destroyed so much elsewhere.

The north gallery is the oldest, supported by two monumental pillars adorned with statues; those of *St Peter* and *St Trophime* on the northwest are masterpieces of the classically-influenced Arles school—even the foliage in the borders has a certain Corinthian air. The capitals in the Romanesque north and east galleries are carved with scenes from the New Testament, their figures moving to the same rhythms as those on the portal. The capitals of the more severe Gothic gallery to the south are carved with the *Life of St Trophime*, while on the west the capitals closely resemble the south gallery of Montmajour's cloister: note the *Magdalene* kissing Christ's feet, and *St Martha* with her Tarasque.

Hôtel de Ville et Musée d'Art Païen (Museum of Pagan Art)
Sharing Place de la République with the church of St-Trophime is Arles' palatial **Hôtel de Ville**, built in 1675 after plans by Hardouin-Mansart, architect of the Hall of Mirrors at Versailles; here, his virtuoso signature is in the remarkable flat vaulting of the vestibule. Facing the inner courtyard are remnants of older civic buildings: sections of the 12th–15th-century palace of the *podestats* (or prefects of the Holy Roman Emperor), and the town hall of 1500, with a Roman tympanum and bell tower modelled after the mausoleum of Glaunum.

Next to this, the former church of Ste-Anne (1620s) has since 1805 given shelter to the pagan statues and sarcophagi of the **Musée d'Art Païen** (9–12 and 2–4:30; summer until 6 or 7, adm). Nearly everything here was made in the Arles region, with the exception of the beautiful white marble *Hippolytus and Phaedra sarcophagus* (2nd or 3rd century AD), with its hunting scenes. Two exceptional mosaics brought in from nearby Roman villas show the *Rape of Europa* and *Orpheus* enchanting the wild beasts; there's a graceful but damaged dancing girl, a headless statue of Mithras, the god of the legionnaires, his torso decorated with signs of the Zodiac entwined by a serpent. The large statue of Augustus was found in the theatre, as was the Venus of Arles, represented here by a copy made before Louis XIV had it 'restored'. Although a fairly chaste specimen as marble love goddesses go, she earned from Théodore Aubanel the most ham-handedly erotic of all Félibre poems:

Laisso ti pèd toumba la raubo qu'à tis anco
S'envertouio, mudant tout ço qu'as de plus bèu:
Abandouno toun ventre i pountoun dóu soulèu!
Coume l'èurre s'aganto à la rusco d'un aubre,
Laisso din mi brassado estregne en plen toun maubre:
Laisso ma bouco ardènto e mi det tremoulant
Courre amouros pertout sus toun cadabre blanc!

(Throw to your feet the robe that around your hips
hangs, hiding all that is most beautiful about you:
Abandon your stomach to the kisses of the sun!
As ivy entwines the bark of a tree,
Let me in my embraces clasp all of your marble;
Let my ardent mouth and burning fingers
run lovingly over your body so white!)

Mothers in Arles use this armless Venus for their own ends. They bring their children to see her and warn: 'The same thing will happen to you if you keep biting your nails!'

Palaeo-Christian Art, Folk Art, and Art Art

Apart from the Lateran collection in the Vatican, no museum has a better collection of 4th-century Christian sarcophagi than Arles' **Musée d'Art Chrétien** (same hours as Musée d'Art Païen) housed in a former Jesuit chapel of the 1600s. Carved by Arlésien sculptors between the years 330 and 395, these remarkably-preserved tombs make a fascinating documentary of the newly victorious faith; as their pagan ancestors carved scenes from mythology, so these early Christians spared no expense to decorate their last resting places on earth with scenes from the Old and New Testaments. Nearly every figure of importance wears a Roman toga; in the **sarcophage de Trinquetaille**, discovered in 1974, the Three Magi sport Phrygian bonnets. A stair in the museum descends to a **Cryptoporticus**, a vast subterreanean barrel-vaulted double gallery of the 1st century BC, built as a foundation for the monumental structures of the Forum above. No one knows for sure what other purpose such underground galleries may have served—for storage, or perhaps, as on Rome's Palatine Hill, for cool promenades (several statues now in the pagan art museum were discovered here). During the last war it came in handy as an air-raid shelter.

The indefatigable Frédéric Mistral began his collection of ethnographic items from Provence in 1896, and in 1904, when he won the Nobel Prize, he used the money to purchase the 16th-century Hôtel de Castellane-Laval to house his **Muséon Arlaten** (9–12 and 2–5, closed Mon in winter; July and Aug until 7, adm—not on the global ticket). Mistral's aim was to record the details of everyday life in Provence for future generations, and out of respect for his memory, nothing, it seems, has been changed or dusted from the moment he arranged the exhibits and wrote out the little explanatory cards. The evolution of the traditional Arlésienne costume, one of Mistral's obsessions, is thoroughly documented, with the adjustments made to match fashion changes in Paris. The wearing of it declined along with the use of Provençal, in spite of the poet's folklore parades (the 'Festivals of Virgins') in Arles' theatre and his pronouncements that

307

the costume, 'in the shadowy transition of the centuries, lets us see a lightning flash of beauty!'

Most memorable and strange are the two life-size dioramas: a Christmas dinner at a *mas*, with a table groaning with wax food, and a visit to a new mother and her infant. The curious gifts of salt, a match, an egg and bread brought by the visitors symbolize the hope that the baby may grow to be (in the same order) wise, straight, full and good. The gallery of rituals has a prickly Tarasque retired from the procession at Tarascon, and a lock of golden hair discovered in a medieval tomb at Les Baux. One room is dedicated to the Félibrige, and another to Mistral himself, with the great man's cradle and cane. In the courtyard, a paved 'little forum' was uncovered, complete with an **exedra** cut with ten niches for statues.

To the north of the Muséon Arletan, the café-filled **Place du Forum** is the centre of modern life in Arles, watched over helplessly by a **statue of Frédéric Mistral**, moustachioed and goateed like his near-double, Buffalo Bill. Mistral himself attended its unveiling in 1909, thanking his admirers but regretting that they made him look as if he were waiting for a train. From here Rue Hôtel de Ville leads north to the ruins of Constantine's palace, of which only part of the baths, or **Thermes de la Trouille** remain (same hours as the Musée d'Art Païen).

Across the street on the banks of the Rhône stood the Priory of the Knights of Malta, built in the 14th century. The knights, who came from all over Europe, were divided into eight *Langues* or tongues, and this was the local headquarters of the *Langue de Provence*; the façade with gargoyles facing the river gives the best idea of its original appearance. After the Revolution a local academic painter named Jacques Réattu purchased the priory, and his daughter made it into the **Musée Réattu** (10–12:30 and 2–7, until 5 in winter, adm), the contents of which are so boring you may well wonder how Réattu and his mates stayed awake to paint them. In 1972, the museum was jolted awake with a donation of 57 drawings from Picasso, in gratitude for the many bullfights he enjoyed in Arles. Nearly all date from January 1971 and constitute a running dialogue the artist held with himself on some of his favourite subjects—harlequins, men, women, the artist and his model—and more unusually, a Tarasque. Other Picassos in the museum include a beautiful portrait of his mother Maria from the 1920s, donated by his widow Jacqueline, and a sculpture of a woman with a violin. There are more recent works by César and Pol Bury, and upstairs, an exhibition gallery devoted to photography.

The Alyscamps

One of the most prestigious necropolises of the Middle Ages (same hours as the Arènes), the Alyscamps owed its fame to the legend of St Trophime, a cousin of the proto-martyr St Stephen who became a disciple of St Paul. Paul sent Trophime to convert Gaul, where medieval hagiographers later confused him with a 2nd- or 3rd-century Bishop of Arles of the same name. The story has it that Trophime arrived in Arles in the year 46, and held secret meetings with his new converts in the lonesome Roman cemetery of Alyscamps (believed to be a corruption of *Elisii Campi*, or Elysian Fields), which according to Roman custom was built outside the city walls, along the Via Aurelia. Trophime eventually attracted quite a following, and before he died he gave a special blessing to the Alyscamps; Christ himself attended the ceremony, and left behind a stone imprint of his knee.

Burial in such holy ground was so desirable that bodies sealed in barrels with their burial fee attached were floated down the Rhône to Arles. Some rascals in Beaucaire took to robbing the dead of their coins as they floated downstream, but they were found out when the barrels miraculously returned upstream to the scene of the crime. At its greatest extent the necropolis stretched a mile and a half and contained 19 chapels and several thousand tombs, many of them packed five bodies deep. Dante mentions it in the *Inferno* (IX, 112) and it makes an appearance in numerous *Chansons de Geste*. Ariosto wrote how Charlemagne's peers, cut down in Roncevalles, were flown here and buried by angels.

The Alyscamps' mystique began to decline in 1152, when the relics of St Trophime were transferred to the cathedral. Grave-robbers pillaged the tombs, and the most beautiful sarcophagi were given away as presents to Renaissance potentates. Under Louis Napoleon the Alyscamps itself was dismembered by a railroad, a canal, factories, and a housing estate, leaving only one romantic, melancholy lane lined with empty mostly plain sarcophagi. Little holes of mysterious purpose are carved into the stone of many of them, similar to holes in other tombs from the megalithic era; they may have held tiny oil lamps. Of the 19 chapels, only the recently restored **St-Honorat** with its two-storey octagonal tower still stands, rebuilt in the 12th century by the monks of St-Victor in Marseille; in the apse are three Carolingian sarcophagi.

FESTIVALS AND ANNUAL EVENTS

Arles does its best to keep its visitors entertained. Easter is celebrated by a **Feria Pascale** with four days of bullfights, most of them Spanish *corridas* (for ticket reservations for Arenes events, tel 90 96 03 70). On 24 June, St John's Day, there are typical Arlésien dances in costume around bonfires, and the distribution of blessed bread. July is the busiest month, with a festival of music, dance and drama, the *Cocarde d'Or* bullfights, and most importantly, photography in the **Rencontres Internationales de la Photographie**, with over a dozen shows and workshops. The last bullfights of the year, on the second Sunday in September, coincide with the **Prémices du Riz**, or rice harvest.

SHOPPING

Besides the Wednesday and Saturday **market** in Boulevard des Lices, there are free tastings of Arles' donkey sausage at **La Cave du Saucisson d'Arles** at 11 Rue Réattu. You can surprise the folks back home by dressing in an authentic *gardian* costume (on sale at **Camille**, Blvd des Lices), or by decking yourself out in the shawls, lace, and *coiffes* of an Arlésienne at **L'Arélsienne**, 12 Rue Wilson. For colourful Provençal fabrics, try **Les Olivades**, 2 Rue Jean Jaurès or **Souleiado**, 4 Blvd des Lices.

ENTERTAINMENT

The most sociable bars in Arles are in Place du Forum; for lazy watching-the-world-go-by, plump for a chair in Place Voltaire or Boulevard des Lices. After dark, the liveliest place in Arles is **Le Méjean**, at Quai Marx-Dormoy, a complex that includes a book and record shop, art gallery, concerts, three cinemas and films in their original language (tel 90 93 33 56), also a bar and restaurant where you can eat for as little as 55 F a head.

WHERE TO STAY (postal code 13200)

Arles offers relief for the budget-bruised traveller, and charges less for more than you'll get in cities like Avignon or Aix. If you arrive without a reservation, the tourist office has a room-finding service for a small fee.

Expensive

The luxurious grand-daddy of hotels in Arles is ****Jules César (locally known as *Chez Jules*), Blvd des Lices, tel 90 93 43 20, occupying a former Dominican monastery with a Caesar-ish temple porch tacked on. The rooms are vast, air-conditioned and furnished with Provençal pieces; the pool is heated and the gardens beautiful. Its chief competitor, ****Nord Pinus, Place du Forum, tel 90 93 44 44, has some columns from a real Roman temple embedded in its façade. Once the favourite of the Félibres, poets, and literati like Stendhal, Mérimée, and Henry James, it now draws the top matadors and wealthy aficionados; the premises are comfortable and full of heavy dark furniture, bullfighting posters, trophies, and the mounted heads of famous bulls; weekend hunts in the Camargue and private boat excursions to the beach are some of its offerings.

Near the lively Place du Forum, the 12th to 18th-century home of the Comtes d'Arlatan has been converted into the charming ***D'Arlatan, 29 Rue du Sauvage, tel 90 93 56 66, with antiques and a garden; the ***Forum, at 10 Place du Forum, tel 90 93 48 95, in another old house, doesn't have as much charm but may win you over with its swimming-pool. Just north of Arles, a traditional farmhouse and 16th-century chapel are at the core of the ***Mas de la Chapelle, Petite Rte de Tarascon, tel 90 93 23 15; excellent service, a pool and tennis courts are some of the extras.

Moderate

Among the less expensive choices are **St-Trophime, 16 Rue de la Calade, tel 90 96 88 38, in an old house with a central court; **Diderot, in the centre of old Arles, 5 Rue Diderot, tel 90 96 10 30, with no-nonsense comfortable rooms; and **Calendal, 22 Place Pomme, tel 90 96 11 89, where rooms overlook a garden with palm trees.

Inexpensive

Best of the one-stars, *Gauguin, in Place Voltaire, just south of Place Lamartine, has simple but tidy rooms, some with balconies. Arles also has an Auberge de Jeunesse open year round at 20 Av. Maréchal-Foch, tel 90 96 18 25; bus from Place Lamartine.

EATING OUT

Lou Marquès (in the Jules César hotel) is Arles' elegant citadel of traditional *haute cuisine* (*croustillant de Saint-Pierre* and *carré d'agneau* with artichokes), with an excellent wine cellar (menus from 200 F). In Place du Forum, Le Vaccarès, tel 90 96 06 17, serves delicious renderings of Provence's finest dishes, using the freshest market ingredients (steamed *loup* with a citrus *compote*, *noisettes d'agneau*), to be washed down with the best wines from the Rhône valley (menus from 180 F). Set in a beautiful vaulted room from the 17th century, Le Tourne-Broche, 6 Rue Balze, tel 90 96 16 03, serves a selection of affordable menus from 90 F, including items like salmon terrine and *suprême de volaille*. Book to make sure of a table at the deservedly popular Hostellerie des Arènes, 62 Rue du Refuge, tel 90 96 13 05, which offers geniune southern homecooking—from a delicate *feuilleté de fruits de mer* to *daube* and homemade pastries (choose between two menus, 70 and 95 F).

Plaine de la Crau

Hercules, after completing his Tenth Labour, the theft of the cattle of Geryon, passed through Provence with the booty on his way back to Greece. He had some trouble with the native Ligurians, who apparently tried to pinch the cows. One thing led to another, and before long Hercules found himself in single-handed battle with the entire nation. As they advanced across the marshy plain, Hercules, armed only with his club, got down on his knees in despair at having nothing to throw at them. Zeus took pity on him, and sent down a shower of stones, with which the hero soon put the Ligurians to flight. This was an unaccountably important story in the mythology of the Greeks. They and the Romans put the Hercules of this battle in the sky; the northern constellation we know as Hercules they called *Engonasis*, the 'kneeler'.

The carpet of stones Zeus sent are still there for all to see, on the weird wasteland called the **Crau**, stretching from Arles to the Etang de Berre, between the Camargue and the Alpilles. The ancients found it fascinating, and many Greek and Roman writers attempted to explain it; Aristotle, a hopeless bird-brain at anything involving natural science, said the stones were formed by volcanoes, and 'rolled down naturally' to the low plain. In fact the rounded stones are alluvial deposits from the Durance, from long ago when the river followed this path into the Rhône delta.

The empty, wind-blown Crau is a major element of the Provençal mystique; Mistral, for example, dragged his poor Mireille across it before she met her sad end. Today it does its best to keep up a romantic appearance. Over 100,000 sheep make their winter home here, nibbling the tufts of grass between the stones before migrating in the old-fashioned way up to the Provençal Alps in May or June; the stone shepherd huts are still one of the few features of the Crau. The French, unfortunately, have been doing their best to make it disappear. Most of the northern part has been reclaimed for farmland. The rest is criss-crossed with railways, canals and roads, decorated with army firing ranges and the gigantic Istres military airport; there's even a dynamite plant. There are no good roads over the unspoiled parts of the Crau, and the only village, **St-Martin-de-Crau**, is a dismal spot, but you can still see something of the original effect along the N 568 (for Fos and Marseille) and the N 113 (for Salon), both east of Arles.

WHERE TO STAY/EATING OUT
On the edge of the Crau, and also convenient for a visit to Arles, the ***Auberge La Fenière** in **Raphèle-les-Arles** is an attractive, ivy-covered inn; nice rooms, some with air-conditioning, and a restaurant with an outdoor terrace which offers Camarguaise beef, duck with olives or salmon roulades (on the N 453, 6 km from Arles; tel 90 98 47 34).

The Camargue

To its handful of inhabitants, the Camargue was the *isclo*, the 'island' between the two branches of the Rhône. That river's course has taken many different forms over the millennia, as it gradually pushes its delta into the Mediterranean, but only the present one, with its two arms, could have created this vast marshland, France's salt cellar, its greatest treasure-house of water-fowl and home of some of its most exotic landscapes. The two branches, the *Grand* and *Petit* Rhônes, really build separate deltas, leaving the space in between a soupy battleground where land and sea slowly struggle for mastery.

GETTING AROUND

The only public transport to the centre of the Camargue begins at the Gare Routière in Arles: one or two buses a day each to Stes-Maries-de-la-Mer (via Albaron) and Salin-de-Giraud. There are also one or two SNCF trains to St-Gilles from Arles. St-Gilles has regular bus connections to Nîmes (five a day), a few to Arles and one to Lunel. Remember that the Camargue is really quite small—never more than 40 km from Arles to the coast. A serious hiker could see the whole thing in three days. It is perfect country for bicycling, and there are a few places in Stes-Maries-de-la-Mer to rent some wheels. Horses are even more popular; there are many places to hire one in Stes-Maries-de-la-Mer, or in Aigues-Mortes, the Ranch del Sol (tel 66 53 99 83) and St-Gilles, L'Etrier (tel 90 96 35 03). Boats are another possibility; Blue-Line (tel 66 87 22 66) and other firms in St-Gilles rent boats fit for a few days' trip through the Petite Camargue; at Stes-Maries-de-la-Mer and St-Gilles excursion boats make short cruises around the Camargue.

History

Ancient writers recorded the people of the Camargue living well enough, hunting boar in the swamp forests and actually raking fish out of the mud. Besides remarking on its curiosities (for the only thing remotely like it on the northern shore of the Mediterranean is the Cota Doñana, in southern Spain), the Greeks and Romans left it entirely alone. In the early Middle Ages, however, at least four monastic colonies were founded on the edges of the Camargue, not only to reclaim land but to collect that most precious of medieval commodities, salt. In this inhospitable country, all of them disappeared long ago; the most important was the Abbey of Psalmody, which became quite a power in Provence. Today only scant ruins can be seen, on a farm still called Psalmody north of Aigues-Mortes, in the region called the 'Petite Camargue' west of the Petit Rhône.

By the 1600s, the monks began to give way to cowboys. The new solid land built by the river was bought up by absentee owners, many from Arles, who created large ranches to exploit the two totem animals of the Camargue: the native black, longhorn cattle that thrive on salt grass no other cow would fancy, and who have always been the preferred stock for the Provençal bullfight; and another longtime resident, the beautiful white horse, believed to have been introduced by the Arabs back in the Dark Ages. A true cowboy culture grew up, a romantic image dear to the Provençaux, and especially to Provençal writers like Mistral. The cow-

Branding iron

poke was a *gardian*; a sort of rodeo game, with the cattle trying to escape from a circle of cowboys, was an *abrivado*; branding was called the *ferrade*. Interestingly enough, America's own first real cowboys were largely French, in the bayous of Louisiana and East Texas, and there must have been at least a few Camarguais *gardians* around to show them the tricks of the trade. Less romantically, from the *gardian*'s point of view, there were also plenty of sheep, which migrated each summer to the Provençal Alps or even further north, to the Vercors (many still do, and there are established transhumance trails throughout the Provençal countryside).

There are still a few score *gardians* in the Camargue today, keeping up the old traditions. Big changes have come to the swampland in the last century. As they did in the Crau, for a while the French threatened to dispose rationally of this inconvenient bit of land altogether. Dikes and drainage schemes went ahead, and large areas were turned into salt-pans and rice fields; the rice was first planted to desalinate the land, but after the loss of French Indochina it became big business. Fortunately, nature societies were able to secure the creation of a wildlife preserve around the heart of the Camargue, the Etang de Vaccarès, in 1928; the government finally joined the effort in 1970, making a Regional Park of the entire area.

Flora and Fauna

First and most spectacularly, there are the flamingos (*flamants roses*), a symbol of the Camargue; several thousand of them nest around the southern lagoons; the only others in Europe are found in Spain's Cota Doñana, and in Sardinia. Apart from these, probably no place in the Mediterranean has a wider variety of aquatic birds: lots of ducks, grebes, cormorants (white head and neck, with a black stripe that touches the eye), curlews and ibis (only a few, very dark, with long necks and the longest beaks of all). The beautiful Little Egret, white and long-billed, is a common sight, though they spend the winter in Africa, as does the avocet, a little black and white bird that looks like an aquatic magpie; there are also many Purple Herons, conspicuously striped on the head and breast. Not all are water birds; you may see an eagle or a majestic Red Kite (*Milan Royal*).

Besides birds, there isn't much; deforestation in favour of ranches destroyed most of the natural habitat for land animals, but there are still boars, and a few beavers, although you're more likely to see a blue frog. Trees are rare, although there are still small stands

Purple Heron

313

of umbrella pines and scrubby, pink-flowered tamarisks. Common plants include the purple-flowered *saladelle*, and the *salicorne*, which grows in tough clumps; people used to extract salt from them. Among the fauna, we nearly forgot the most important—the hard-drilling, inescapable Camargue mosquito; make her the prime consideration when you visit. If you're sensitive to mosquitoes, better not come at all, or scurry back to safety in Arles before twilight.

You may find the Camargue has been somewhat oversold. There are white horses indeed, as well as flamingos and bulls, but the photogenic landscapes that shine out from the pages of the Sunday magazines can be much less exciting when you're actually there. Most of the Camargue, in fact, could pass for East Anglia or the southern New Jersey shore. To really appreciate it, you'll have to spend some time, and penetrate into the most unspoiled parts, around the Etang de Vaccarès and south of it.

The Musée de la Camargue
It was an inspiration on the part of the Regional Park management, creating this museum in what not long ago was a working Camargue cattle and sheep ranch, the **Mas du Pont de Rousty**, 9 km southwest of Arles on the D 570 (daily exc Mon, 10:15–4:45; Apr–Sept, daily 9:15–5:45; adm). The buildings are well-restored and well-documented, giving a feeling of what life was like on the *mas* a century ago.

The museum proper is housed in the huge sheep barn. Didactic in the best French tradition, with slide shows and buttons to push, it won't let you leave without a thorough grounding in the geology, history and traditions of the Camargue. There are special exhibits on the *gardians*, on the fickle Rhône (you'll learn that 400,000 years ago it flowed past Nîmes), on Mistral's *Miréio*, and other subjects. Outside, there are marked nature trails leading deep into the surrounding swampy plain, the **Marais de la Grande Mar**.

About 4 km beyond the museum on the D 570, little **Albaron** was one of the first inhabited centres of the Camargue; a stout medieval tower survives, built to guard Arles from any attack or pirate raid up the Petit Rhône.

The Etang de Vaccarès
For all of us lazy motor tourists, the way to see the best of the Camargue is to take the D 37, a left turn 4 km south of the museum. After another 4 km, a side road leads to the **Domaine de Méjanes**, the closest thing the Camargue has to a dude ranch, owned by Marseille's Paul Ricard. It offers visitors horse riding and canoes, and on summer weekends the *gardians* put on shows of cowboy know-how, and occasionally bullfights. Call ahead, 90 97 10 62, for information. Further on, the D 37 skirts the edges of the **Etang de Vaccarès**, the biggest of the lagoons and the centre of the Camargue wildlife preserve. In some places you can see flocks of nesting flamingos year-round. Try not to disturb them; they're nervous enough with the flocks of migrating Germans and Dutchmen who come down to gape at them. A side road, the D 36B, leads all the way down to Salin-de-Giraud, passing the **Centre d'Information la Capillière** (daily 9–12, 2–7), with exhibits on the flora and fauna and earnest, intelligent guides to take you on fascinating nature walks around the edges of the lagoon.

At the end of the D 35 and D 36, the Grand Rhône meets its end in an anticlimax of factories and salt-pans; **Salin-de-Giraud**, with a tiny auto ferry (the *bac de Barcarin*), provides the last chance to cross the river before it reaches the sea. Salin is easily the most distinctive town in Provence. Founded by the Solvay company of Belgium around the turn of the century, it consists of neat, straight rows of brick houses with plenty of trees and greenery, the very picture of a contemporary 'company town' in Britain or America. The vast salt-pans, which provide almost half France's supply (*la Baleine* brand), extend towards the south and east. On the D 36D, almost at the mouth of the Grand Rhône, is another of the Regional Park's nature centres: **La Palissade**, in a park with white horses and bulls, offers a complete introduction to the Camargue, with audio-visual shows, a small aquarium, exhibits on flora and fauna, and guided walks through the area (weekdays 9–5; June–Sept open daily; adm).

If you really want to get away from it all, this part of the Camargue might be the place; the *salins* are barred from the Mediterranean by one of the longest and emptiest beaches in France, the **Plage de Piémanson** at the mouth of the Grand Rhône; the current is a bit treacherous for swimming.

With good local maps, determined swamp fans can hike the 40 km or so to Stes-Maries-de-la-Mer in summer, through the most unspoiled parts of the Camargue; a sea-wall, the **Digue de la Mer**, provides a crossing around the lagoons, and the only hazards are secluded beaches that have been taken over by bands of *naturistes*. You might even make it over to the **Bois des Rièges**, the only surviving forest of the Camargue, on a large island at the southern end of the Etang de Vaccarès. Though officially off-limits, as part of the nature preserve, it can sometimes be reached on foot in summer. Be careful though; this is the home of the Camargue's Abominable Snowman, the 'Bête de Vaccarès', a mysterious part-human creature first sighted in the 15th century; he became a celebrity in the 20s, when he provided both the subject and title for a popular novel by Provençal writer Joseph d'Arbaud.

East of the Rhône, it's an entirely different picture; a fifth of the Camargue's coast has been degraded into sprawling industrial areas, around **Port-St-Louis-du-Rhône** and the giant complex of **Fos**.

WHERE TO STAY/EATING OUT

Almost all of the accommodation in the area is in Stes-Maries-de-la-Mers (see below). But if you want to stay in the eastern or central parts of the Camargue, away from the tourists, there are some possibilities. One of these isolated spots, and also a good bet for lunch after visiting the Camargue museum, is ***Le Flamant Rose** in **Albaron** (13123); simple rooms and 75–120–150 F menus including a *salade fruits de mer* and stewed beef cowboy style—*boeuf à la gardienne* (tel 90 97 10 18).

Salin-le-Giraud (13129) doesn't even dream of attracting tourists. The family favourite restaurant is **La Saladelle** in the centre: a wide choice on 60–90–130 F menus, including more spicy *boeuf à la gardienne*, chops and fish, and seafood lasagne. And of course shakers of the local speciality on every table—all you can eat (tel 42 86 83 87). There's only one place to stay in the town, the simple and basic ***De La Camargue** on Blvd de la Camargue (tel 42 86 82 82).

Les-Saintes-Maries-de-la-Mer

Set among the low sand-dunes, jovial and lively Saintes-Maries-de-la-Mer has an open-armed approach to visitors that long predates any interest in the Camargue and its ecological balance. For this is one of Provence's holy of holies, and if you come out of season you become aware of the dream-like, insular remoteness that made it the stuff of legend.

The pious story behind it all was promoted to the hilt by the medieval Church: after Christ was crucified, his Jewish detractors took a boat without sails or oars and loaded it with three Marys—Mary Salome (mother of the apostles James and John), Mary Jacobe, the Virgin's sister, and Mary Magdalene, along with the Magdalene's sister Martha and their resurrected brother Lazarus, St Maximin and St Sidonius. As this so-called Boat of Bethany drifted off shore, Sarah, the black Egyptian servant of Mary Salome and Mary Jacobe wept so grievously that Mary Salome tossed her cloak on the water, so that Sarah was able to walk across on it and join the saints. The boat took them to the Camargue, to this spot where the elderly Mary Salome, Mary Jacobe, and Sarah built an oratory, while their younger companions went to spread the Gospel, live in caves, and tame Tarasques. In 1448, during the reign of Good King René (who was always pinched for money) the supposed relics of the two Marys were discovered, greatly boosting the local pilgrim trade. Les Saintes-Maries became, as Mistral called it, the 'Mecca of Provence'.

A few facts blazed the trail for the legend's ready acceptance. In the 4th century, a Roman writer described a settlement on this site called *Oppidum priscum Ra*. This lent its name to the first Christian church, Notre-Dame-de-Ratis, built over the site of a spring of fresh water—where a Gallo-Roman temple had been dedicated to three sea goddesses. *Ratis* was taken to mean raft (*radeau*), hence the connection not only with the Boat of Bethany but to ancient Egypt, where in the Book of the Dead the deceased sails in a boat without oar or sail, but with the image of Ra. Even the name Mary had a familiar ring to Provence's early Christians; not only for its resemblance to the word for mother (*Matre*) but to Marius, a local cult figure after his defeat of the Teutones, and who was advised by the blonde sybil Marthe (as pictured at Les Baux; see above).

Today Saintes-Maries-de-la-Mer is best known for the pilgrimage of Mary-Jacobe on 24 and 25 May. This attracts gypsies from all over the world, who have canonized Sarah as their patron saint. The reason seems to owe something to yet another co-incidence—the discovery of the relics coincided with a great convergence of gypsies in Provence in the 1440s, some of whom wandered up from North Africa and Spain, and others who crossed into Europe by way of Greece and the Balkans. The gypsies, however, claim that Sarah was not Egyptian at all, but one of their own, Sarah-la-Kâli ('the black' but also recalling the Hindu goddess Kali), who met the Boat of Bethany here and was the first of their tribe to be converted to Christianity. The Church obliged by 'discovering' the bones of Sarah in 1496.

GETTING AROUND

There are at least two buses daily from Arles (55 min), and many more options for exploring the Camargue itself. There's an hour-long cruise in the Petit Rhône from the end of March to the beginning of September on the paddle steamer Tiki III, tel 90 97 81 68; or hire a horse—the best way of exploring the trails (the tourist office has a list of stables, some offering tours for beginners). Camargue Safaris offer Jeep tours, tel 90 97 86 93; or you can pedal (although beware that in the heat or wind it can be hard going, and many bike trails peter off into sand). Hire a bike from La Vélociste, in Place des Remparts, tel 90 97 83 26 (open Sept–June); Delta Vélos, Rue Paul Peyron, tel 90 97 84

99 (open all year); and Camargue Vélo, 27 Rue F.-Mistral, tel 90 97 94 55 open Feb–Nov.

TOURIST INFORMATION
5 Avenue Van Gogh (13460), tel 90 97 82 55.

The Church

In 869, during the construction of a new church to replace the 6th-century oratory 'built' by the two Marys, the Saracens swooped down in a surprise raid and carried off the Archbishop of Arles, who just happened to be down to inspect the work. The pirates demanded a high ransom in silver, swords, and slaves for their hostage, and were dismayed when the bishop died on them—dismayed, but not so put out as to risk losing the ransom. The pirates tied his corpse in all its vestments to a throne and made off with the loot before the Christians realized the hostage was dead.

Faced with the threat of similar shenanigans, stones were shipped down from Arles at great expense to rebuild the church in 1130. The result is, along with St-Victor in Marseille, the most impressive fortified church in Provence: a crenellated ship with loopholes for windows in a small pond of white villas with orange roofs. Inside, along the gloomy nave, are wells that supplied the church-fortress in times of siege; pilgrims still bottle the water to insure their protection by St Sarah. In the second chapel on the left, near the model of the Boat of Bethany that is carried in the procession to the sea, is the polished rock 'pillow' of the saints, discovered with their bones in 1448. The capitals supporting the blind arches of the raised choir are finely sculpted in the style of St-Trophime. Under the choir is the **crypt**, where the relics and statue of St Sarah in her seven robes are kept; the statue has been kissed so often that the black paint has come off in patches. Here, too, is a *taurobolium*, or relief of a bull-slaying from an ancient Mithraeum, the bits scratched away long ago by women who used the dust to concoct fertility potions, along with photos and ex votos left by the gypsies. From April to mid-November, you can take a stroll below the bell tower, with views stretching across the Camargue that take on a magic glow at sunset (10–12:30 and 2:30–7).

This roof walk circles the lavish **upper chapel**, dedicated to St Michael, which in times of need served as a *donjon*. The coffer holding the relics of the Marys is kept here, except during the arcane *deus ex machina* rites unique to this church: during feast days the coffer is slowly lowered through a door over the altar after the singing of a special hymn, *Les Saintes de Provence*; the pilgrimage ends to the tune of *Adieu aux Saintes*, as the relics are slowly raised back into the chapel. In the 18th century this hocus-pocus had a reputation for curing madness, combined with the shock therapy of stripping the afflicted naked and throwing them in the sea. When Mistral attended the pilgrimage as a young man, a beautiful girl from Beaucaire abandoned by her fiancé dramatically flung herself across the altar just as the relics were being lowered, praying for the return of her lover. The girl made a considerable impression on Mistral and became the basis for his heroine Mireille, who arrives in Saintes-Maries-de-la-Mer to make a similar prayer and dies of too much sun and love in the upper chapel of this church, while the congregation in the lower church, like the chorus in a Greek tragedy, accuses the holy Marys: *Reino de Paradis, mestresso / De la Planuro d'amaresso* ('Queens of Paradise, mistresses / of the plain of bitterness . . .').

Around Les Saintes-Maries-de-la-Mer, and Pont de Gau

Mireille, in statue form at least, lives on in the main square north of the church, while to the south in Rue Victor-Hugo the **Musée Baroncelli** is devoted to zoology, archaeology and folklore. It is named after the Camargue's secular saint, the Félibre Marquis Folco de Baroncelli-Javon (1869–1943), a descendant of a Florentine merchant family in Avignon, who abandoned all at age 21 to live the life of a *gardian*. Baroncelli spent the next 60 years herding bulls, writing poetry, and doing all he could to maintain the Camargue and its customs intact. Although by trade he was a cowboy, his heart was with the Amerian Indians and other oppressed minorities; Chief Sitting Bull, in France with Buffalo Bill and his Wild West Show, smoked the peace pipe with the Marquis and named him 'Faithful Bird'.

FESTIVAL

The *Pélérinage des Gitanes*, 24–25 May. The gypsies began making the pilgrimage in numbers in the mid-19th century. In 1935, thanks to the intervention of the Marquis de Baroncelli, 24 May was especially set aside as St Sarah's day. Although the famous all-night candle vigil by her statue has been abolished by killjoys, her statue is still symbolically carried to the sea by a procession of gypsies, *gardians* and costumed Arlésiennes, where in imitation of ancient rainmaking ceremonies the statue is sprinkled with sea water while all are blessed by the bishop. Afterwards, the beaches and streets are alive with music and flamenco, *farandoles*, horse races and bullfights, attended by as many tourists as gypsies. The whole ceremony happens again, with considerably fewer gypsies and tourists, on the Sunday nearest 22 October for the other Mary, Mary Salome.

ENTERTAINMENT

There are other entertainments in Les Saintes: in the summer, nightly *Courses Camargues* in the bullring, guitars and buskers in the streets and miles of white sand beaches, including a *plage naturiste* 6 km to the east. At Pont de Gau, 4 km north, there's a **Centre d'Information du Parc de la Camargue** (9–12 and 2–6, closed Fri between Oct–Mar), and a **Parc Ornithologique** (8–sunset, Feb–Nov) with walks through the marshlands and aviaries containing some of the rarer birds.

Market Days: Monday and Friday mornings.

WHERE TO STAY   (postal code 13460)

There are a lot of choices in Les Saintes, but if you don't book during the summer or pilgrimages, you'll have to join the crowd on the beach. The really luxurious choices are all outside the centre, like the ******Mas de la Fouque**, 4 km on the Rte du Petit Rhône, tel 90 97 81 02, set in the midst of the Camargue with all possible comforts, its perfect serenity complemented by a garden, heated pool, golf, and tennis. The little pink *****Mas du Clarousset**, 7 km north on D 85A, tel 90 97 81 66, offers a fresh and simple decor. Each room has a private terrace, and there are extras—horses to ride, a pool, jeep excursions and gypsy music evenings in the excellent restaurants (menus from 220 F). Also there's the modern, laid-back cowboy-style *****L'Etrier Camarguais**, Chemin Bas-des-Launes, tel 90 97 81 14, offering large rooms in detached bungalows with a pool, tennis, lots of horses to hire. ****La Camargue**, 2 Rue Baptiste-Bonnet, tel

318

90 97 92 03, is just outside the centre of Les Saintes, and offers good value for the price, as does the newish seaside **Le Dauphin Bleu**, 31 Av. Gilbert-Leroy, tel 90 97 80 21. In the centre, *Le Delta, Place Mireille, tel 90 97 81 12, is one of the nicer cheapies. There's also an **Auberge de Jeunesse** on the Arles road in the hameau de Pioch-Badet, tel 90 97 91 72, open all year and fast to fill up in the summer.

EATING OUT
This is the place to try *boeuf gardian*, or bull stewed in red wine with lots of garlic; *bouriroun*, an omelette with elvers from the Vaccarès; *salade de télines*, made of tiny shellfish with garlic mayonnaise; or *poutargue*, Camargue caviar made from red mullet eggs. One of the best places to try the local products of land and sea is **Lou Mas du Juge**, over the Petit Rhône on D 85, tel 66 73 51 45, a friendly, family-run restaurant, specializing in fresh seafood (menus from 250 F). Elegant **Le Brûleur de Loups**, Av. Gilbert-Leroy, tel 90 97 83 31, has a terrace overlooking the beach and more delights from the sea, like a seafood mix in white Châteauneuf-du-Pape (menus from 130 F, cheaper for lunch). If you have a car, try the **Hostellerie du Pont de Grau**, on the Rte d'Arles, tel 90 97 81 53, with its jolly Provençal decor and a delicious *pot-au-feu de la mer* (menus from 90 F).

St-Gilles-du-Gard

West of Arles, the N 572 takes you through some of the drier parts of the Camargue; a drear landscape of canals and rice fields. After crossing the Petit Rhône, you're in the **Petite Camargue**, in the *département* of the Gard, approaching **St-Gilles**, the only town for miles in any direction.

TOURIST INFORMATION
Place Frédéric Mistral, tel 66 87 33 75.

History
In medieval times and earlier, St-Gilles was a flourishing port, much nearer the sea than it is now. Remains have been found of a Phoenician merchant colony, and the Greek-Celtic *oppidum* that replaced it, but the place did not really blossom until the 11th century. The popes and the monks of Cluny, who owned it, conspired to make the resting place of Gilles, an obscure 8th-century martyr, a major stop along the great pilgrim road to Compostela. The powerful counts of Toulouse helped too—the family originally came from St-Gilles. Soon pilgrims were pouring in from as far away as Germany and Poland; the port boomed with the onset of the Crusades, and both the Templars and Knights Hospitallers (who owned large tracts in the Camargue) built important commanderies. In 1116 the **Abbey Church of St-Gilles** was begun, one of the most ambitious projects ever undertaken in medieval Provence.

Destiny, however, soon began making it clear that this was not the place. As the delta gradually expanded, the canals silted up and St-Gilles could no longer function as a port (a major reason for the building of Aigues-Mortes; see below). The real disaster came with the Wars of Religion, when the town became a Protestant stronghold; the leaders of the Protestant army thought the church, that obsolete relic from the Age of Faith that

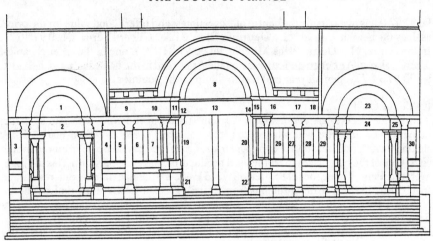

Façade of St Gilles-du-Gard

took 200 years to build, would look much better as a fortress, and they demolished nearly all of it to that end. It was rebuilt, in a much smaller version, after 1650. What was left suffered more indignities during the Revolution, and it is a miracle that one of the greatest ensembles of medieval sculpture has survived more or less intact.

The Church Façade
This is the masterpiece of the Provençal school of 12th-century sculptors, the famous work that was copied, life-size, in the Cloisters Museum in New York. Created roughly at the same time as the façade of St-Trophime in Arles, it is likewise inspired by the ancient Roman triumphal arches. Instead of Roman worthies and battle scenes, the twelve Apostles hold place of honour between the Corinthian columns. This is a bold, confident sculpture, taking delight in naturalistic detail and elaborately folded draperies, with little of the conscious stylization that characterizes contemporary work in other parts of France. In this too, the Romans were their masters. The scheme is complex, and worth describing in detail:

Left portal: tympanum of the Adoration of the Magi (1); beneath it, Jesus' entry into Jerusalem (2). Flanking the door, a beautiful St Michael slaying the dragon (3); and on the right the first four Apostles, SS Matthew and Bartholemew, Thomas and James the Lesser (4–7).

Central portal: tympanum of Christ in Majesty (8), with symbols of the Evangelists; underneath, a long frieze that runs from one side portal across to the other: from left to right, Judas with his silver (9); Jesus expelling the money-changers from the temple (10); the resurrection of Lazarus (11); Jesus prophesying the denial of Peter and the washing of the Apostles' feet (12); Last Supper (13); Kiss of Judas (14); arrestation of Christ (15); Christ before Pilate (16); Flagellation (17); Carrying the Cross (18). Left of the door, SS John and Peter (19); right of the door, SS James the Greater and Paul, with a soul-devouring Tarasque under his feet (20). Beneath these, at ground level, are small panels, representing the sacrifices of Cain and Abel and the murder of Abel (21); a deer hunt and Balaam and his ass, and Samson and the Lion (22).

Right portal: tympanum of the Crucifixion (23); beneath it, two unusual scenes: the three Marys purchasing spices to anoint the body of Jesus, and the three Marys at the tomb. To the left of this, the Magdalene and Jesus (24); to the right, Jesus appearing to his disciples (25). Left of the door, four more unidentifiable Apostles (26–29; note how the 12 represented here are not the canonical list; better-known figures like John the Evangelist and Paul were commonly substituted for the more obscure of the original Apostles). To the right of the door, Archangels combat Satan (30).

THE VIS DE ST-GILLES
The 17th-century interior of the rebuilt church holds little interest, but underneath it the original **crypt** or lower church survives (so many pilgrims came to St-Gilles that upper and lower churches were built to hold them). Behind the church, you can see the ruins of the **choir and apse** of the original, which was much longer than the present structure. Near it, the 'screw' of St-Gilles is a spiral staircase of 50 steps that once led up one of the church's bell towers. Built about 1142, it is a tremendous *tour de force*; the stones are cut with amazing precision to make a self-supporting spiral vault; medieval masons always tried to make the St-Gilles pilgrimage just to see it. Its author, Master Mateo of Cluny, also worked on the great church of Santiago de Compostela, where he is buried.

The Maison Romane
The rest of the town shows few traces of its former greatness. The medieval centre is unusually large, if a bit forlorn. Near the façade of the church, on Place de la République, is a fine 13th-century mansion, claimed to be the house of Guy Folques, who became Pope Clement IV. Today this 'Maison Romane' houses St-Gilles' **Musée Lapidaire**, with a number of sculptures and architectural fragments from the church, and collections of folk life and nature of the Camargue (daily 9–12, 2–6, later in summer; adm).

Market Days: Thursday and Sunday.

WHERE TO STAY/EATING OUT
In the Middle Ages scores of pilgrims, sometimes thousands, would stay over at **St-Gilles** (30800) every night; try it now and the innkeepers themselves will wonder why. Best choices are the ****Heraclée** on the Quai du Canal, not exciting but well-run (tel 66 87 08 59); and the venerable, determinedly old-fashioned ***Le Globe**, on Place Gambetta, with a restaurant to match: *boeuf à la gardienne* and other local favourites in a sweet provincial atmosphere (menus 50 F lunch, 90–130 F dinner; tel 66 87 30 41). Locals frequent **Lou Manescau**, just north of the centre at Porte de la Blanque, for simple dinners 75–110 F (tel 66 87 03 22).

Aigues-Mortes

Every French history or geography schoolbook has a photo of Aigues-Mortes in it, and every Frenchman, most likely, carries in his mind the haunting picture—the great walls of the port where St Louis sailed off to the Crusades, now marooned in the muck of the advancing Rhône delta. It is as compelling a symbol of time and fate as any Roman ruin, and as magically evocative of medieval France as any Gothic cathedral.

TOURIST INFORMATION

Place St-Louis, tel 66 53 73 00; they offer historical tours of the town, year round, beginning at the Porte de la Gardette.

Parking; there are signs around all the entrances to the town forbidding cars; these you may ignore, just as everyone else does. There will be no problem with driving around Aigues or finding parking, except perhaps in July and August.

History

In the 13th century, the Camargue was the only part of the Mediterranean coast controlled by France, a narrow strip wedged between the possessions of the Counts of Provence and the Kings of Aragon. To solidify the French hold on this precarious strip, and to provide a base for the Crusade he had always dreamt of undertaking, Louis IX (St Louis) began construction of a new port here in 1241, replacing grounded St-Gilles. Seven years later, it was complete enough to hold the 1500 ships that would carry Louis and his knights to the Holy Land. It was a grand occasion, with the banners waving and the entire army singing hymns on the decks of the ships; this Seventh Crusade though, was to bring Louis nothing but disasters at home and abroad. Louis also used Aigues-Mortes for his other Crusade, against North Africa (and the town was the last he saw of France—he died of the plague in Tunis in 1270). His successor, Philip III, finished Aigues-Mortes and built its great walls. Being the only French port, the town could monopolize all sea trade destined for northern France; in the late 13th century it was booming, with perhaps four times as many inhabitants as its present 4800, its harbour filled with ships from as far away as Constantinople and Antioch.

Aigues-Mortes means 'dead waters', and it proved to be a prophetic name. The sea deserted Aigues just as it had done at St-Gilles, and despite constant efforts to keep the harbour dredged, the port went into an inevitable decline after 1350. There were attempts to revive it in the 1830s, with the digging of a canal to the sea; unfortunately this came just at the time when the railroads and the new port of Sète were ensuring Aigues' final demise. At least the decline also allowed the works of Louis and Philip to survive undisturbed. Forgotten and nearly empty a century ago, Aigues now makes its living from tourists, and from salt; the half of France's supply that doesn't come from Salin-de-Giraud is collected here, at the enormous Salins-du-Midi pans south of town.

The Walls and the Tour de Constance

Romantic as it is, Aigues-Mortes is the perfect place to cast off some common misconceptions about the Middle Ages. The architecture has a very modern air: streamlined, businesslike and stripped down to the essentials, following a purposefully functional aesthetic that was always present in medieval architecture. The walls, over a mile in length, are nearly a perfect rectangle; Henry James described Aigues as ' a billiard table without pockets'. Inside the walls are no picturesque winding lanes, but broad streets that run as staight as a die—medieval 'new towns' tended to be as rectangular as those of the Romans or the Americans.

Though built in a uniform style along the entire circuit, the best parts are the east and south sides, where an empty wasteland has replaced the old port. On the south side, the spot where St Louis' men sang hosannas from the departing flagship is now occupied by the town's *cave coopérative* and bull ring.

The most impressive work of architecture in Aigues is the **Tour de Constance**, a huge cylindrical defence tower that guarded the northeastern land approach to the town (entry inside the walls on Rue Zola; daily 9–12, 2–6; adm—pick up a joint ticket for Carcassonne and Salses if you are going castle-touring further west). The interior consists of two vaulted, 12-sided chambers, with a circular stair that climbs between them and the 6-m thick walls. Both chambers are elegantly vaulted; the sophistication of every part of the structure, its sculpted capitals and pretty fireplaces, along with the insufficient number of slits for archers, makes one wonder whether it was really meant only as a defence tower. Neither would it be a very comfortable place as a residence. Originally called the 'King's Tower', it antedates the walls, being substantially complete when Louis first passed through in 1248; possibly it had some political or ceremonial purpose besides.

After the Crusades, the French kings began using this tower as a prison. The first inmates were important Templars, caught in the great Templar round-up of 1306. During the Wars of Religion the prisoners were Protestants, and most of them died here. After Louis XIV's revocation of the Edict of Nantes, the tower filled up with Protestants again, this time women only. One of them was Marie Durand, the teenage daughter of a minister who spent 38 years here in unspeakable conditions. She became a legend for her unswerving faith and her cheerful regard for the other prisoners. After so many years even the French courts had forgotten about her, but a sympathetic governor of Languedoc, on an inspection tour, was moved to release her in 1768. She left her credo behind, the one word *register* ('resist', in Provençal), chiselled into the wall where it can still be seen.

From the second floor, you can climb up to the roof, with a broad view over the Camargue; a *table d'orientation* points out landmarks on the horizon, claiming you can see as far as Nîmes and even Mont Blanc on a clear day. From outside the tower you can also get into the only part of the **walls** accessible to visitors, with less dramatic but charming views over the lagoons and into the Aiguemortains' back gardens.

Place St-Louis
A neatly rectangular square, just as Louis's surveyors planned it, this is still the centre of Aigues, not too overburdened with souvenir stands. On the southern side, the former **Capucin Monastery** of 1645 now houses the tourist office; the Capucins were little better than police spies, introduced here by the government after the Wars of Religion to keep an eye on the spiritually rebellious inhabitants. Across the square, **Notre-Dame-des-Sablons**—'Our Lady of the Sands' was built along with the town, and with the same no-nonsense approach to architecture. Light and airy, with a broad nave and aisles, it is a lovely church, even though a sacking by the Protestants deprived it of its original interior decoration.

Market Days: Wednesday and Sunday.

WHERE TO STAY/EATING OUT

Aigues-Mortes (30220) is well-served with accommodation, though almost all places are 250 F and upwards for a double room. At the top of the list is the gracious and welcoming *****St-Louis**, in a distinguished and beautifully furnished 18th-century building on Rue Amiral Courbet, just off Place St-Louis (tel 66 53 72 68; closed Jan–15 Mar). This establishment also includes a popular restaurant, **L'Archère**; best in town for steaks and seafood, with good homemade desserts: menus 100 F (lunch only), 140–180–210 F. On Boulevard Gambetta, ****Les Arcades** offers attractive rooms, some with television, and a good inexpensive restaurant: *taureau à la gardienne* and other local favourites on menus 100–175 F (tel 66 53 81 13).

The only budget-priced hotel is just outside the northern wall, on Boulevard Diderot: ***La Tour de Constance** (tel 66 53 83 50). For lunch, **Chez Laurette** has a filling 90 F menu, mostly seafood, with *fruits de mer* and *aïoli* for starters (Rue Alsace-Lorraine, behind the church; tel 66 53 62 67).

Part XI

NÎMES, THE GARD AND MONTPELLIER

Tour Magne, Nîmes

Nîmes

Built of stone the colour of old piano keys, Nîmes disputes with Arles the honour of being the 'Rome of France'—the Rome of the Caesars, of course, not of the popes: neither the Church (nor, for that matter, bossy old Paris) have ever gone down well in this mercantile, Protestant town. But after the passions of the Wars of Religion, Nîmes fell into a doze that lasted for decades. Travellers in the 1800s found it the quintessential dusty southern city; they came to marvel at the city's famous Maison Carrée, the best-preserved Roman temple in the world, and wrote that it was so neglected it looked as if it were dedicated to the goddess of sewage.

Much has changed, especially since 1983 when Nîmes elected as mayor a dynamo named Jean Bousquet, former head of Cacharel, Nîmes' fashionable *prêt-à-porter* firm. Bousquet has not only wakened Nîmes from its daydreams, but by devoting nearly 14 per cent of its budget to culture has begun to rival the ambitious efforts of upstart Montpellier, its chief rival in Languedoc. But what really makes the juices flow in Nîmes are its *ferias*, featuring top matadors from France, Spain and Portugal and a beautiful blonde *torera*, a native of Nîmes who learned her art at the city's Ecole Française de Tauromachie.

325

History

Geography dealt Nîmes a pair of trump cards: first, a mighty spring, the Fontaine, whose god Nemansus was worshipped by the first known residents, the Celtic Volcae-Arecomici, and second, a position on the main route from Italy to Spain, a trail blazed by Hercules himself during his Tenth Labour, as he herded the Geryon's cattle back to Greece from the Pillars that bear his name. The Romans paved his route and called it the Via Domitia, and made Celtic Nîmes into their Colonia Nemausensis. The Volcae-Arecomici Celts, unlike Asterix and Obelix, thought the Romans were just swell, and Augustus reciprocated by endowing Nîmes with the Maison Carrée, a sanctuary for the Fontaine, an aqueduct (the Pont du Gard) to augment the spring, and 7 km of walls. The Nîmois celebrated Augustus' conquest of Egypt, and the arrival of a colony of veterans from the Battle of Actium, by minting a coin with a crocodile chained to a palm, a striking image that François I adopted as the city's coat-of-arms in 1535.

Nîmes

Nîmes declined along with Rome; the city contracted and became a mere frontier post for the Visigothic kings of Toledo. After a brief Arab occupation in the 700s, Nîmes was ruled by Frankish viscounts, who regained some of the town's old prestige in the 11th century by dominating Narbonne and Carcassonne; the Roman amphitheatre was transformed into a fort, the *castrum arenae*, whose knights played a major role in urban affairs. Nîmes, like much of Languedoc, got into trouble with the Church in the early 13th century by taking up the Cathar heresy, although at the approach of the terrible Simon de Montfort the city surrendered without a fight.

Catholicism never went down well in Nîmes, and when the Protestant alternative presented itself in the 16th century, three-quarters of the population took to the new religion immediately, and bashed the other quarter's churches and prelates. The terror reached a peak with the 1567 massacre of 200 priests, monks, and nuns known as the *Michelade*, but continued off and on until the Edict of Nantes (1598); this brought Nîmes enough peace for its Protestants to set up a prosperous textile industry, and the city seemed happy to settle down comfortably as the Huguenot capital of the south.

Louis XIV spoiled everything by revoking the Edict in 1685; troops were quartered in the Huguenots' homes, forcing them to abjure their faith or face exile or slavery aboard the king's galleys. Nîmes and the Cévennes, the wild hilly region to the north, responded with the desperate war of the Camisards, tying up an important part of the French army by inventing many of the techniques used in modern guerrilla warfare. After the troubles, Nîmes went back to its second concern after religion: textiles. Its heavy-duty blue serge *de Nîmes* was reduced to the more familiar 'denim' in 1695, in London— where many of the Protestants went in exile—and it was exported widely. Some made it to California, where in 1848 a certain Levi Strauss discovered it to be perfect for outfitting goldrushers. Nîmes last made the headlines on 3 October 1988, when violent storms in the rocky hills of the *garrigue* brought down a torrent that engulfed the city in 8 ft of mud.

GETTING AROUND

Air Inter flies from Paris to Nîmes-Garons **airport**, 8 km from Nîmes along Rte de St-Gilles (A 54), tel 66 70 06 88. Nîmes' **train station**, at the south end of Av.

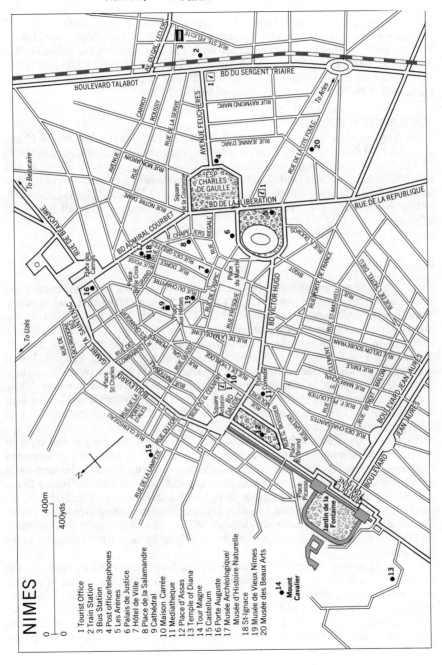

NIMES

0 ————— 400m
0 ————— 400yds

1 Tourist Office
2 Train Station
3 Bus Station
4 Post office/telephones
5 Les Arènes
6 Palais de Justice
7 Hôtel de Ville
8 Place de la Salamandre
9 Cathédral
10 Maison Carrée
11 Mediatheque
12 Place d'Assas
13 Temple of Diana
14 Tour Magne
15 Castellum
16 Porte Auguste
17 Musée Archéologique/
   Musée d'Histoire Naturelle
18 St-Ignace
19 Musée de Vieux Nîmes
20 Musée des Beaux Arts

327

Feuchères, is a kind of arcaded train-aduct that perfectly fits *la Rome française*, tel 66 23 50 50 (direct trains to Carcassonne, Montpellier, Arles, Orange and Marseille; TGVs in 5 hrs to Paris). The baggage area has a **bike hire**. The **bus station** is just behind in Rue Ste Felicité, tel 66 29 52 00; and has departures for the Pont du Gard, Uzès, St Gilles, Aigues-Mortes, Le Grau du Roi, La Grande Motte, Avignon, and Montpellier. **Car Hire**: Avis, 1 bis Rue de la République, tel 66 21 00 29.

TOURIST INFORMATION
6 Rue Auguste, near the Maison Carrée, tel 66 67 29 11 (Mon–Fri 8–7, Sat 9–12 and 2–5; Sun 10–12) and in the train station, which also has a hotel booking service (tel 66 84 18 13). One of their maps, *Nîmes sans obstacle*, describes access for the disabled. Also note: Nîmes has **synchronized opening hours of museums and monuments**: unless otherwise noted, they are mid-Sept–Feb 9–12 and 2–5; Mar–mid-June 9–12 and 2–6; mid-June–mid-Sept 9–7; closed Sun morn). Another pleasing note: **all have free admission**.

Les Arènes

Twentieth in size, but the best-preserved of the 70 surviving amphitheatres of the Roman world, the arena at Nîmes (late 1st century AD) is just a bit smaller than its twin at Arles (free guided tours, in English at 10:15, 11:45, 2:15, 3:45, and 4:30). Like the Maison Carrée, it escaped being cannibalized for its stone (the usual fate of Roman buildings) by being put to constant use—as a castle for the Visigoths and the knightly militia of the Frankish viscounts, who bricked up the arches facing the Palais de Justice and made them their headquarters—then after union with France, as a slum, where some 2000 people lived in shanties jammed into the arches, seats, and vomitoria. When restorers came in 1809 to clear it out, they had to shovel 20 ft of rubbish to reach the floor where the sands (*arènes*) were spread to soak up the blood of the men and animals who died here to amuse the crowd.

When new, the arena could accommodate 24,000 people, reaching or leaving their seats in only a few minutes thanks to an ingenious system of five concentric galleries and 126 stairways. Near the top of the arena are holes pierced in the stone for the supports of the awning that sheltered the spectators from sun and rain—an idea that mayor Bousquet revived in 1988, but with a mobile plexiglass and aluminium roof that from the air looks rather like a giant toilet seat, but allows the amphitheatre to host events year round. The event that has packed the crowds in since 1853 is the *corrida*, a sport always close to the hearts of the Nîmois—even in ancient times, judging by the two bulls carved over the main gate.

Wandering around the outside, note the curious Siamese-twin figure embedded in the wall of the Palais de Justice, known as the *Four-Legged Man*, made of ancient sculptural fragments pieced wrongly together long ago. You may also notice Rue Bigot, named after a 19th-century fable writer from Nîmes. The name is particularly pertinent to local attitudes in the Wars of Religion. 'Bigot', after all, comes from the Old French, and refers to the first religious intolerance to shake Nîmes—the conflict between the Catholicism of the Franks and the Arianism of the Visigoths, or *Bigothi*.

Crocodiles Galore

The *hôtels* in the historic centre—the area between Les Arènes, the Maison Carrée, and the cathedral—date mostly from the 17th and 18th centuries, when Nîmes' textile magnates and financiers enjoyed their greatest prosperity. Beginning at the Four-Legged Man, **Rue de l'Aspic** (which in French evokes vipers as well as jelly), is one of the candidates for the *cardo*, the shorter of the two main streets of a Roman town. Place du Marché opens up to the left, the city's most charming square and site of a fine new **crocodile fountain** designed by Martial Rayasse. Four more examples of the city's saurian emblem (donated by well-wishers to the city between 1597 and 1703) can be seen stuffed and dangling over the stair in the high-tech designer interior of the 18th-century **Hôtel de Ville**, to the right of Rue de l'Aspic. Around the corner, at 16 Rue Dorée, Nîmes' very own Académie meets behind the elaborate portal of the 17th-century **Hôtel de l'Académie**. This body was granted the same privileges as the Académie Française in 1682 by Louis XIV, and even today the Académiciens of Nîmes may sit with their fellows in Paris (though they are confined to the end of the table). The door is blazoned with the Académie's motto: *Nequid nimis* ('Nothing in Excess').

To the south, the amphibian community is represented in **Place de la Salamandre** named after François I's totem animal (many Renaissance rulers had similar emblems, used to represent them in works of art); François chose the salamander from the belief it could survive in fire—hence the first fabrics woven of asbetos were called 'salamander skins'. The salamander sculpture that once adorned this square now stands in the courtyard of the Archaeology Museum, but note the square's 17th-century **Hôtel de Chazelles**, another fine example of civic architecture.

To the north stands Nîmes' ragamuffin **Cathédrale Notre-Dame-et-St-Castor** which was consecrated in 1096 but completely flattened by rampaging Huguenots in 1597 and 1622, who spared only the campanile to use as a watchtower. Across the façade runs a vigourous frieze of the Old Testament (the scenes on the left, up to the *Death of Abel* are original Romanesque works while the others are a 1646 replacement). Lower down, and sadly damaged, are reliefs of Samson and the lions, and Alexander the Great being pulled up to heaven by a pair of griffons, coaxed by a piece of liver dangled over their heads—a favourite medieval fancy. There's another Romanesque frieze nearby, on the corner of Place aux Herbes and Rue de la Madeleine, this time adorning a rare, well-preserved 12th-century house (the **Maison Romane**).

Of course, more remarkable still is the state of that graceful little 1st-century BC temple known as the **Maison Carrée** just off the Via Domitia (Rue Nationale). The best preserved Roman temple anywhere, it was dedicated to the imperial cult of Augustus' grandsons, Caius and Lucius, known as the 'Princes of Youth'—their 'deification' a form of flattery to the emperor. Called 'Carrée' or square, because of its right angles and 'long' square shape (26 m × 15 m), its *cella* (or cult sanctuary) is perfectly intact, as are the Corinthian columns of the porch. Nîmes always found it useful for something, most notably as the meeting hall of the Consuls and least notably as a stable (at the time of writing, it's in a state of limbo, incongruously filled with giant examples of post-modern splotch art).

In his 1787 *Travels*, Englishman Arthur Young couldn't get enough of the Maison Carrée: 'What an infatuation in modern architects, that can overlook the chaste and elegant simplicity of taste, manifest in such a work and yet rear such piles of laboured foppery and heaviness as are to be met with in France.' One modern architect (and another Englishman), Norman Foster, has been given the chance to respond to Mr Young's gripe, on a site overlooking the Maison Carrée: to be known as the **Médiathèque**, a centre for contemporary arts and culture similar to Paris' Beaubourg. Visitors are invited to climb a viewing platform to examine the work in progress; four of the six floors will be underground.

Water, and Other Mysteries

A block north of the future Médiathèque is another recent project, the **Place d'Assas**, designed by Martial Raysse, as a kind of expiatory gesture, one imagines, to the two religions that went down in Nîmes without a fight: that of the Celts (the two figures in the central fountain represent the indigenous gods, 'Nemausa' and 'Nemausus') and the Cathars (the mysterious seven-pointed stars, the magic square ROTAS SATOR, and inscription LES NUAGES SONT SANS AGE). The statue at the west end, on the other hand, is of Ernest Denis of Nîmes, whose writing championed the founding of Czechoslovakia in 1918. Just north, in the irregular polygonal Square Antonin, is a 19th-century statue of Emperor Antoninus Pius (whose family was from Nîmes), holding his hand out, as the Nîmois say, to see if it's raining.

A short stroll to the west down Quai de la Fontaine is Nemausus' first abode, the great spring that originates in the karst caverns of the *garrigue*, to gush out at the foot of Mont Cavalier. It was domesticated as the **Jardin de la Fontaine** in the 18th century by Louis XV's Chief Military Engineer of Languedoc, Jacques-Philippe Mareschal, who marshalled the waters to flow in a neo-Roman nymphaeum below a maze of balustrades and urns. In ancient times a complex of temples and sanctuaries stood here, of which only the so-called **Temple of Diana** remains: a romantic enough ruin, perhaps once a library, with its niches, two corridors and barrel-vaulted nave, decorated with international graffiti from the 18th century.

Paths wind up among the flower beds and leafy arbours of Mont Cavalier to the oldest Roman monument in Gaul, the octagonal **Tour Magne**. No record of its origin or purpose has survived, though some speculate that it may have been a trophy dedicated to the opening of the Via Domitia, or a signal tower, or the mightiest of the 30 towers that once defended the city. Although 33 m high today, the tower is only two-thirds its original height; stairs spiral up to the viewing platform.

The Tour Magne made news in 1601, when a gardener named François Traucat read Nostradamus's prediction that a gardener would uncover an immense treasure buried in the earth. And as it was commonly believed that the Romans, like leprechauns, hid pots of gold in their ruins, Traucat decided the treasure must be buried under the Tour Magne. Henri IV gave him permission to dig (at his own expense, and with two-thirds of the loot going to the crown), but instead of finding gold, he found another large, pre-Roman tower around which the even larger Tour Magne had been built. No one could identify the rubble at the time, and the Consul of Nîmes, fearing that any more digging would undermine the Tour Magne, ordered the now bankrupt Traucat back to his garden.

Two hundred years later there was another discovery of something very rare, though not of gold, down below in Rue Lampèze: a round basin 5.5 m in diameter called the **Castellum**, where the water rushing in from the Pont du Gard was distributed in the city through ten pipes of lead. The only other one to survive is at Pompeii. Like so many things in Nîmes it was built under Augustus, and to him was dedicated the city's east gate on the Via Domitia (Rue Nationale), the **Porte d'Auguste**. Built in 15 BC, it had two large entrances for vehicles, and two smaller ones for pedestrians; you can still make out the outlines where bronze letters once told passers-by that the walls of Nîmes were the gift of IMP CAESAR DIVI F AVGVSTVS.

Nîmes' contemporary Caesar, Mayor Bousquet, hired Jean Nouvel (architect of Paris's Institut du Monde Arabe) to design a subsidized housing project known as **Nemausus I**. It's south of the station, off Av. du Général Leclerc, and looks like a pair of beached ocean liners from the future.

Museum Crawling

The former Jesuit college at 13 bis Blvd Amiral Courbet was, after the Edict of Nantes, diplomatically divided into a Protestant half and a Catholic half. Nowadays the division is between pot-shards and possums, the first half devoted to the **Musée Archéologie**, and the second to natural history. The former is filled with odds and ends for the expert, such as France's largest collection of ancient inscriptions (around the courtyard), but there are some crowd-pleasers as well: the 4th- to 3rd-century BC figure of the *Guerrier de Grézen*, in his curved hood-helmet and belt, and nearby, a rare Celtic lintel, the *Linteau de Nages* found near the *oppidum*'s spring (see Nages, below). The lintel has a frieze of galloping horses and human heads—favourite Celtic motifs, but rarely carved with such pizzazz. Upstairs is a fine collection of ancient glass and everyday Roman items, Greek vases, bronze figurines and miniature altars, some bearing the mallet of the Celtic god Sucellus, who the Romans adapted to their Silvanus.

The other half of the college is the charmingly old-fashioned **Musée d'Histoire Naturelle et de Préhistoire** (Natural History and Prehistory Museum), home to a collection of those mysterious menhirs-with-personality, the statue-steles. Carved with stylized faces, and sometimes with arms, a knife and a belt (*c.* 2000 BC), they are similar to those found in the Hérault, and also in Tuscany and Corsica. Large glass cases of scary masks and spears and turn-of-the-century photographs fill the ethnographic hall, and beyond, a brave little natural history collection features a beaver foetus, a wide selection of faded bats, two-headed lambs and kittens, pinecone-shaped animals called pangolins and an armadillo 'captured near the Pont du Gard'. Adjacent is the Jesuit church **St-Ignace** (1678), a fine piece of Baroque architecture with an unusal *mélange* of vaults and openings, now used for exhibitions.

Aficionados of bull-fighting can take in the memorabilia next door in a privately-run **Musée Taurin**, while for the **Musée de Vieux Nîmes**, follow Grand' Rue, behind the museums, north to Rue Lacroix. Housed in the handsome 1685 episcopal palace, it has an exceptional collection of 19th-century textiles and 500 print designs from Nîmes' wool and silk industries—a real eye-opener for anyone who thought paisley was invented in the 1960s. There are also 17th-century carved *armoires* and painted ones from Uzès, a Charles X billiard table, thousands of socks, a 19th-century bed supported by weight lifters, plus ceramics and curios.

The **Musée des Beaux-Arts** is on the other side of Les Arènes on Rue Cité-Foulc, in a charming 1907 building by a local architect, who chiselled the façade with the names

331

of Nîmes' painters and sculptors, and optimistically left plenty of room for future geniuses. In the centre of the ground floor is an enormous Roman mosaic of *The Betrothal of Admetus* surrounded by a frieze of scenes. Upstairs, look out for two Venetian paintings, an example of 15th-century retro in Michele Giambono's *Mystic Marriage of St Catherine*, and one of Jacopo Bassano's finest works, *Suzanna and the Elders* (1585), with a serene bunny rabbit in the corner. From the Lombards, we have a *sfumato* work by Leonardo da Vinci's follower Bernardino Luini, and an early 16th-century ex voto to St Catherine of Siena, who rescued the donor from the French just as she rescued the papacy from the same. As usual, it's the Dutch paintings, with their buxom wenches and oyster-slurping sessions that one would most like to be in, with the possible exception of Jan Asselyn's fierce portrait of a cow. Of the French offerings, the outstanding painting is Paul Delaroche's *Cromwell Looking into the Coffin of Charles I*, an 18th-century painting as memorable as its subject is odd.

FESTIVALS AND ANNUAL EVENTS
To find out what's going on in Nîmes, call the 24-hour info on 66 36 27 27. There are usually a couple of bullfights a month in the summer, but to see the best *toreros* come for the *Ferias* at Carnival time in February or the third week of September, and especially the 10-day *Feria de Pentecôte* (Whitsun), which draws even bigger crowds than Munich's Oktoberfest. As in Seville people open up their homes as *bodegas* to take the overflow of *aficionados* from the cafés and the drinking and music go on until dawn. A recent addition to the calendar are the *Mosaïques Gitanes*, a festival of gypsy music and dance, in mid-July, right before the Jazz festival.

ENTERTAINMENT
Opera, dance, and concerts take place continuously in July, Aug, and Sept. Reservations and tickets for events at Les Arènes are available from the Bureau de Location des Arènes, Rue Alexandre Ducros, tel 66 67 28 02. Films in their original language are shown at **Le Sémaphore**, 25a Rue Porte de France, tel 66 67 88 04. Nîmes also has a year-round indoor/outdoor water park, the **Parc Aquatique** with pools, slides, saunas, tennis, etc., located near the *autoroute* exit Nîmes-Ouest (Ville Active, 39 Chemin de l'Hostellerie, tel 66 38 31 00).

Nîmes' organic and farmers' **market** takes place on Tuesday and Friday on Blvd Jean Jaurès; on Monday along the same street there's a flower and flea-market.

WHERE TO STAY   (postal code 30000)
Expensive
Reservations are essential during the Ferias, but at other times the room-finding servive at the train station can usually book you a room. At the top of the line, there's the ****Hôtel Impérator Concorde**, Quai de la Fontaine (near the gardens) tel 66 21 90 30, a 19th-century dowager with a recent face-lift; a lovely garden, TVs, air-conditioning, and Nîmes' top restaurant to boot (see below). Other good choices in the centre include the ***Plazza**, 10 Rue Roussy (off Blvd Amiral Courbet), tel 66 76 16 20; an old house (with a private garage) converted into an air-conditioned hotel in 1988, with attractive retro furnishings; ***Le Louvre**, 2 Sq de La Couronne, tel 66 67 22 75, in a 17th-century hôtel with a pretty courtyard. If you have a car, it's a mere 8 km northeast

on N 86 to the charming ***L'Hacienda, a large farmhouse in the *garrigue*, converted into a hotel with an equally spacious swimming-pool, terraces, and a restaurant, Mas de Brignon, at Marguerittes (30320), tel 66 75 02 25.

Moderate
Next to the amphitheatre, the *toreros'* favourite is **Le Lisita, 2 Blvd des Arènes, tel 66 67 29 15, owned by an enthusiastic bullfighting fan who has given his rooms Spanish and rustic Languedocien furnishings, and plenty of personal touches; if there aren't any bullfights on, ask for the *toreros'* favourite rooms—19 or 28—with their iron beds. Another good choice, the delightful Art Deco **Royal is just off the esoteric Place d'Assas at 3 Blvd Alphonse-Daudet, tel 66 67 28 36, but reserve early in the summer because it fills up fast.

Inexpensive
Budget choices include the quiet *Des Voyageurs, 4 Rue Roussy, tel 66 67 46 52; *De la Mairie, 11 Rue des Greffes, tel 66 67 65 91, simple and in the historic centre, and the Auberge de Jeunesse, Chemin de la Cigale, on a hill 2 km from the centre (bus 20 from the train station), tel 66 23 25 04.

EATING OUT
Nîmes isn't exactly famous for its restaurants, but it has some delicious specialities: *brandade de morue* (pounded cod mixed with fine olive oil), a recipe said to date back to Roman times and *tapenade d'olives*, an appetizer made of olives, anchovies and herbs; *pélardons*, the little goat cheeses from the *garrigues*, are among the best anywhere. In the sweet category, the city is proudest of its *croquants Villaret*, almond biscuits cooked by the same family in the same oven since 1775, available at Raymond Villaret, 34 Rue Nationale. *Brandade* is often on the menu at Nîmes' top restaurant, L'Enclos de la Fontaine (in the aforementioned Hôtel Impérator, tel 66 21 90 30), although alongside the classics the chef cooks up imaginative, subtle dishes that melt in your mouth, like veal served with fresh fig *beignets*, which seem especially fresh served outside in the garden courtyard (menus from 200 F up). You can also eat out in a garden at Le P'tit Bec, 87 bis Rue de la République, tel 66 21 04 20, with a tempting selection of seasonal dishes (menus starting at 100F). For a vast choice of soups, stews and grills with a Catalan touch, try the rustic stone dining room of Lou Mas, 5 Rue de Sauve, tel 66 23 24 71, with a very reasonable 100 F menu, or for about the same price, dine on the fine cooking at La Belle Respire, in the unusual decor of Nîmes' former bordello, in the historic centre at 12 Rue de l'Etoile, tel 66 21 27 21. For half that, try the hot savoury pies and salads at the charming little Tarterie O Delices, by the cathedral in Place aux Herbes, tel 66 36 11 16.

Costières-de-Nîmes
Covering 24 communes between Beaucaire and Vauvert, the AOC Région des Costières-de-Nîmes rides the high terraces and hills of the Rhône, where the vineyards are planted amid round pebbles (*les grès*). Near Nîmes, the rough landscape is tempered by the sea, and although the district is best known for rosés, the reds (similar to Côtes-du-Rhône) and whites (made from clairette, grenache blanc, maccabéo, and malvoisie) are good, inexpensive, fresh young wines; the

reds are only aged two or three years at the most. The easiest place to get acquainted with them is near Nîmes' airport at the **Château de la Tuilerie**, Rte de St-Gilles, tel 66 70 07 52, which sells not only its own label but those from a score of Costières vineyards. Or try the medal-winning reds and rosés from the **Domaine des Goubins**, Chemin des Canaux, just outside of Nîmes, tel 66 84 39 93.

North of Nîmes: the Gard

Like most French *départements*, the Gard is named after a river—a river made famous by a feat of Roman engineering that symbolizes the South as boldly as the Eiffel Tower represents Paris. Here, too, is Uzès, *ville d'art* and the 'First Duchy of France'; Bagnols-sur-Cèze, with its exceptional little museum of modern art, and the natural charms and vineyards of the lower valley of the Cèze.

GETTING AROUND
STDG **coaches** link Nîmes, Uzès and the Pont du Gard 8 or 9 times a day; other buses frequently link the Pont du Gard with Avignon. In Uzès, you can **hire mountain and touring bikes** at Ets Payan, 16 bis, Av. Général Vincent, tel 66 22 13 94.

TOURIST INFORMATION
There is a tourist office on the Remoulins side of the Pont du Gard, tel 66 37 00 02, which dispenses information on the **canoe and kayak hire** available upstream at Collias.
Uzès (30700): Avenue de la Libération, tel 66 22 68 88.

Pont du Gard

By 19 BC, the fountain of Nemausus could no longer slake Nîmes' thirst and a search was made for a new source. The Romans were obsessed with the quality of their water, and when they found a crystal-clear spring called the Eure near Uzès, the fact that it was 50 km away hardly posed an obstacle to antiquity's star engineers. The resulting aqueduct, built under Augustus' son-in-law Agrippa, was like a giant needle hemming the landscape, piercing tunnels through hills and looping its arches over the open spaces of the *garrigue*, and all measured precisely to allow a slope of .07 centimetres per metre. Where the water had to cross the unpredictable, frequently flooding Gard, the Roman engineers knuckled down, ordered a goodly supply of 6-ton rock, neatly dressed, and built the **Pont du Gard**, at 48 m the highest of all Roman aqueducts, and along with the one in Segovia, the best preserved in the world. It is a brave and lovely sight, three tiers of arches of golden stone without mortar, some chunks protruding to support scaffolding for repairs: 'What better sign of faith in the immortality of their empire than the thought that one day they would have to repair the Pont du Gard?' wrote journalist Sanche de Gramont in his 1969 essay on the French. It's a good thing the Romans built it to last: nowadays the bottom tier has been expanded to take a road, and people regularly jump off it, boat under it, and walk along the top. You can fumble through the water channel, or brazen it out on the top-most tiles that covered it—but be warned! This top tier is no

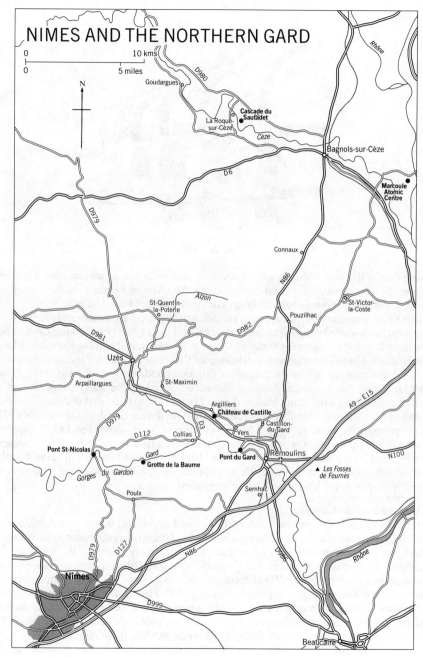

NIMES AND THE NORTHERN GARD

Pont du Gard

more than a few feet wide, and there are no guard-rails, not to mention the big gaps where tiles have been taken out to illuminate the channel beneath. If the mistral is huffing and puffing, you could easily go sailing off to meet your Maker.

Although the Pont du Gard is grand enough to take almost any number of tourists (it's the third most-visited site in France after the Eiffel Tower and Versailles) you can escape the crowds by exploring traces of the aqueduct to the south, in the hills of Sernhac. Here the Romans dug two impressive tunnels, one for the water and one for maintenance, still bearing the grooves left by the hammers that excavated them, stroke by stroke. The extraordinarily hard calcium deposits that accumulated in the water channels was a prized building material in the Middle Ages, chiselled out to build part of the walls of the fortified Romanesque church of **St-Bonnet-du-Gard**, near Sernhac. Other arches in a state of romantic ruin still stand in the vicinity of Vers, along the D 127 (by the level-crossing and down the white road a couple of hundred metres to the south); others are between Vers and Argilliers, just off the D 3, taking the side road that veers sharply on the left. One last curiosity in the neighbourhood are the **Fosses de Fournès**, a weirdly eroded lunar landscape east of Remoulins.

The Château de Castille
Along the main D 981 between the Pont du Gard and Uzès, just before Argilliers, a Romanesque chapel and a neoclassical colonnaded funeral chapel dedicated to St Louis mark the entrance to one of Languedoc's most charming oddities, the Château de Castille, the mania of its Baron (1747–1829) who was afflicted by a serious case of columnitis. He erected over 200 of them, of which only some 50 survive, incorporated into garden follies, porticoes and hemicycles inspired by Bernini. Some columns support an original domed *château d'eau* and there's a pyramid inspired by the 'needle' in the Roman circus at Vienne. Unfortunately, the estate isn't officially open, and you'll have to poke around and trespass to see the Baron's magic garden. In Argilliers' old cemetery (the thick clump of cypresses on the other side of the highway, 100 metres to the right),

the Baron erected a pair of funerary monuments that are still in good condition—a colonnade inspired by the temple of Paestum for his mother, and three columns arranged triangularly, surmounted by a ball with a crescent and a cross, dedicated to his eldest son.

From Argilliers, the D 3 heads south to **Collias**, where you can hire kayaks or canoes to paddle under the Pont du Gard, or take half- or whole-day trips into the steep-walled **Gorges du Gardon** (Kayak Vert, tel 66 22 80 76, or Le Tourbillon, tel 66 22 85 54). If you prefer to visit by land, a path from Collias descends into the gorge, passing by a medieval cave-hermitage. Alternatively, west 9 km on the D 112 is **Pont St-Nicolas**, so named for its pretty 13th-century bridge, built by a confraternity of voluntary bridge builders, the Frères Pontifes, who also helped St Bénézet build Avignon's famous bridge. From here take the scenic, serpentine *corniche* D 979 south, turning left for **Poulx**, where a trail leads into the gorge and its **Grotte de la Baume** (an hour's walk). Or take the same D 979 north to Uzès.

Uzès, the Premier Duchy of France

Few towns of 8000 souls have so bold a skyline of towers, or so little truck with the modern industrial world. Uzès seems to have been vacuum-packed when its wealthy, Protestant merchants of cloth and silk stockings packed their bags and left at the Revocation of the Edict of Nantes. 'O little town of Uzès', wrote André Gide (whose father was a Uzètien) 'Were you in Umbria, the Parisians would flock to visit you!' Now they do, more or less, ever since 1962, when Uzès was selected as one of France's 500 *villes d'art*, entitling it to dig into the historical preservation funds set aside by former culture minister André Malraux. Houses tumbling into ruin have been repaired, creating the perfect stage for films like *Cyrano de Bergerac* (the latest one, with Gérard Depardieu).

The de Crussols of Uzès, claiming a family tree that sent out its first shoots under Charlemagne, became the proud premier dukes and peers of the realm when the Duc de Montmorency forfeited the title by getting his head chopped off in 1632. Their grand fortified residence, the **Duché** can be visited (daily guided tours 9:30–12 and 2:30–6:30; winter until 5 and closed Mon; adm). Its oldest section, the rectagular *donjon* called the **Tour Bermonde**, dates from the 11th century (the fairy-tale crenellations were, inevitably, designed by Viollet-le-Duc after the originals were destroyed in the Revolution); a fine *escalier d'honneur* leads to views over the shimmering tiles of Uzès' rooftops. The Renaissance façade in the central courtyard, a three-layered classical cake of Doric, Ionic, and Corinthian orders, was constructed in 1550 and bears the motto of the dukes: *Ferro non auro* ('for iron, not for gold'). The interior is well stocked with period furnishings, complemented by wax dukes and duchesses decked out in 16th-century costumes.

Across Place du Duché is the attractive 18th-century **Hôtel de Ville**, while to the left of the Duché is a **Crypt**, believed to date from the 4th century, with some primitive bas-reliefs. Rue Boucairie leads from here to the **Hôtel du Baron de Castille**, its façade adorned with—guess what—columns, tall slender ones that don't conform to any classical order but which have a charm all their own. Beyond this, the 1671 **Ancien Palais Episcopal** was the seat of the powerful bishops of Uzès (64 bishops reigned here between the 5th century and the Revolution, when the bishopric was suppressed). A

Uzès

restoration attempt in the 1970s caused the interior to cave in behind the façade, although the right wing is in good enough nick to hold the eclectic collections of the **Musée Municipal** (afternoons mid-June to mid-Sept, closed Mon) with its fossils, pots, paintings, and memorabilia of the Gide family. Adjacent is the **Cathédrale St-Théodorit**, built in 1663 to replace the one burned in the Wars of Religion. The façade was redone in 1875, the better to match the stunning campanile inherited from the original, the 12th-century **Tour Fenestrelle**. Unique in France, this cylindrical six-storey gem is named after the rows of double-lit windows that encircle it, inspired by the towers of Ravenna and Lombardy. Inside the cathedral, the pride and joy is a splendid **organ** of 1670, the only one in France to have retained its original painted shutters. Recently restored, it is the centrepiece of the end-of-July festival, *Nuits Musicales d'Uzès*.

On the other side of St-Théodorit stands the small **Pavillon Racine**, named after the playwright and poet who, in 1661, at the age of 22 spent a year with his uncle, the Vicar-General of Uzès, during which time his family hoped he would forget his foolish love of poetry and turn to the priesthood. Just the opposite happened. The climate, the friendly welcome, and the inscrutable patois made a great impression on the young man, as did the food. The latter is celebrated in the Saturday market in the magnificently arcaded **Place aux Herbes**, which gives credence to Racine's tongue-in-cheek farewell:

> *Adieu, ville d'Uzès, ville de bonne chère,*
> *Où vivraient vingt traiteurs, où mourrait un libraire.*
>
> (Adieu, town of Uzès, city of good cheer/where twenty
> innkeepers may thrive, while one bookseller dies).

The Uzège
The countryside around Uzès—where fields of asparagus, cherry orchards, forests of truffle oaks and vineyards alternate with *garrigues*—is dotted with attractive old villages. You can walk from the Duché (or take the road towards Bagnols) into the **Vallée de**

l'Alzon and to the arcadian setting of the source of the Eure, where the Roman aqueduct began. Horse lovers, in July and August, can visit the 65 stallions at the national stud farm (Les Haras Nationaux d'Uzès, Rte d'Alès, Tues and Fri at 3; otherwise call ahead, tel 66 22 33 11). Near Arpaillargues, at Moulin de Charlier, the Musée 1900 has a collection of period cars, motorcycles, gramophones, movie posters, model trains, etc. The clay-rich soil north of Uzès has provided St-Quentin-la-Poterie with its vocation since the cows came home, and in some strange tangential way, inspired its most famous son, Joseph Monier (1823–1906) to invent reinforced concrete. Pots, cookware, and decorative ceramics are displayed in St-Quentin's Maison de la Terre and potters' workshops.

WHERE TO STAY/EATING OUT
A number of historic buildings in this area have been converted into inns, most luxuriously Relais and Châteaux' ****Le Vieux Castillon, in the heart of medieval Castillon-du-Gard, (30210), tel 66 37 00 77. The rooms are scattered on several different levels in the village, connected with each other by patios, tennis courts, with a stunning swimming-pool perched among the gardens, and an excellent restaurant, featuring dishes with truffles (the Gard produces 15 per cent of France's crop), *langoustines* and a wide variety of Côtes du Rhône wines (menus at 260 F and up, closed Jan and Feb). Another truffle specialist in Castillon, Serge Lanoix, Place du 8-Mai-1945, tel 66 37 05 04, serves some of the most refined and innovative dishes in the region, in an intimate dining room (so book ahead, menus at 130, 200 F and up). A five-minute walk from the Pont du Gard, ***Le Colombier, Rte du Pont du Gard, Remoulins (30210), tel 66 37 05 28, has ten comfortable rooms behind its broad awnings; Remoulins also has the cheaper, traditional **Le Moderne, Place des Grands Jours, tel 66 37 20 13, with meals from 70 to 150 F. At Collias (30210) the friendly ***Le Castellas, Grand'-Rue, tel 66 22 88 88, is spread out in two large houses, and has a good and stylish Art Deco restaurant (menus 140 and 215 F).

In the centre of Uzès (30700), ***d'Entraigues, 8 Rue de la Calade, tel 66 22 32 68, is a fine old hotel, fit for a duke; try to get a room near the top for the view. Just outside town, on the Nîmes road, **Emeraude, tel 66 22 07 50, has 66 spanking new and comfortable rooms, a swimming-pool and tennis courts and a restaurant (75 F menus and up). Back in town, **La Taverne 4 and 7 Rue Sigalon, tel 66 22 47 08, has recently renovated rooms, and the chance to dine out on a pretty garden terrace (starting at 80 F). The best food, however, is 6 km south in St-Maximin, in the charming garden terrace of L'Auberge de St-Maximin, tel 66 22 26 41, where they do wonderful things with asparagus and other local products (menus 100, 140 F and up). Or sleep and dine at the ***Marie d'Agoult, 4 km west of Uzès at 18th-century Château d'Arpaillargues, tel 66 22 14 48, named after the woman who inspired Liszt, and often stayed here in these delightful, antique-furnished rooms. There's a pool, tennis courts, and the garden restaurant serves a fine 130 F menu.

Bagnols-sur-Cèze

North of Uzès, where the river Cèze meets the Rhône, Bagnols-sur-Cèze is the traditional gateway—or exit—of Languedoc. Named by the Romans for its sulphur baths, Bagnols is nowadays more famous for its green beans (*les bagnolais*), and for the nearby nuclear power plant at Marcoule, the construction of which saw Bagnols' population quadruple. In spite of all the new building, the narrow lanes of the old town have changed little; every now and then you'll see the city's quaint emblem of three golden pots.

GETTING AROUND
Bagnols is on the main route between the north and Avignon, and takes nearly all **trains** except the TGV (tel 66 89 61 18). Buses link the town with Uzès, Avignon, and Nîmes. **Bike hire** shops: La Roue Libre, Av. Léon Blum, tel 66 89 91 79 and Vélos Tout Terrain, La Citadelle, tel 66 89 81 06.

TOURIST INFORMATION
Bagnols-sur-Cèze (30200): Esplanade du Mont Cotton, tel 66 89 54 61.
Goudargues (30630): Maison de la Cèze, Rte de Pont St-Esprit, tel 66 82 30 02.

A Museum That Rose out of the Flames

In Bagnols' central, arcaded **Place Mallet**, stands a tower erected by Philip le Bel, called the **Tour de l'Horloge**, and an 18th-century *hôtel* housing Bagnol's main attraction, the **Musée de Peinture** (10–12 and 2–6, summer 3–7, closed Tues, Feb, and holidays). Founded in 1854, the original museum burned down in 1924, having been rather embarrassingly set alight with fireworks by the local firemen during their annual ball. The curator then sent out a message to France's artists: 'I am the curator of a museum of naked walls. Help me fill them!' They did, making Bagnols the home of the first provincial museum of contemporary art. It includes top-notch paintings by Albert Marquet, with his famous Fauve *14 Juillet au Havre* (1906); Pierre Bonnard's *Fleurs des Champs*; Matisse's *La Fenêtre ouverte à Nice*, (1919); and works by Renoir, Van Dongen, Valadon, Maurice Denis, Paul Signac, Gauguin, Jongkind, and sculptures by Maillol and Renoir's student and mistress, Camille Claudel.

Besides calling on the local Côtes du Rhône vineyards (there's a fine belvedere over the region and the Rhône from the nuclear plant, if you don't mind getting close to the monster), there are some charming villages to visit. To the south, picturesque medieval **St-Victor-la-Coste** is clustered around a ruined château, and in the lower valley of the Cèze, there's **La Roque-sur-Cèze**, piled on its hill opposite a 13th-century bridge, with streets so narrow that cars are forbidden. La Roque overlooks the **Cascade du Sautadet**, where the water flows through a mini-canyon that looks as if it were clawed out of the rock by a giant bear. In the winter the Cèze pounds through it dramatically; in the summer, the waterfall becomes more like a playful fountain, and you can swim off pebble beaches and dive from the boulders. Further upstream, in green and shady **Goudargues**, where plane trees form a leafy roof over the canal, you can ask the tourist office about renting a canoe or kayak to journey down the Cèze, although this may be impossible in the high summer, when the flow is sometimes reduced to a trickle. Once, according to legend, a king of France came to cross the yet unnamed river during such a dry summer, and noted that it was '*très étroit*'. To which one courtly wit replied: 'Treize et trois font seize. Sire, seize (Cèze) sera cette rivière!' And so it was named.

Market Days: Bagnols, Wednesday and 2nd and 4th Friday of each month. Goudargues, Wednesday.

Côtes du Rhône Gardoise
Bagnols is the centre of Languedoc's Côtes du Rhône production (see p. 254), while three villages in the vicinity, Chusclan, Laudun, and St-Gervais take pride in bottling their own *Côtes du Rhône-Villages* as well as good red table wines. Try the **Cave des Vins Fins de Laudun** at Les 4 Chemins, N 86, near Laudun (tel 66 82 00 22); **Cave des Vignerons de Chusclan**, at Chusclan, tel 66 90 11 03, for bottled or petrol-pump *en vrac* wines; or the exceptional wines of **Domaine Ste-Anne**, at Les Cellettes in St-Gervais, tel 66 82 77 41, especially the 89 *Cuvée Notre-Dame* and a pure syrah *Côtes du Rhône*. The finest white Côtes du Rhône is made by **Luc Pelaquie** at **Laudun**, tel 60 50 06 04. Pelaquie's wine has a natural freshness that is unusual for such a hot area. It has great depth and will age well for several years. The 1990 is especially recommended.

WHERE TO STAY/EATING OUT   (postal code 30200)
In a large park, with tennis courts and a pool, ******Mas de Ventadous**, 69 Rte d'Avignon, tel 66 89 61 26, is **Bagnols'** most luxurious hotel, with rooms in individual bungalows around a 17th-century château, plus a bar and restaurant (half-board mandatory in season). *****Château de Courlorgues**, Rte de Carmignan, tel 66 89 52 78, is an attractive old mansion in a wooded park, equipped with pool and tennis. In Bagnols proper, ****La Ville**, 52 Av. Léon Blum, tel 66 89 61 32, has recently renovated rooms, each with a bath and TV. The best food in town, simple and perfect, is served in the equally simple white dining room of **Le Florence**, 16 Place B. Boissin, tel 66 89 58 24, (menu 155 F). In the heart of **La Roque-sur-Cèze**, La Hulotte, tel 66 82 78 60, features Provençal cusine and vegetarian dishes (130 F)

From Nîmes to Montpellier

There is a choice of three ways to do it: the *autoroute*, its parallel, the N 113, or the longest, prettiest, and most interesting route, along the back roads through Sommières.

TOURIST INFORMATION
Lunel (34400): Place des Martyrs, tel 67 71 01 37.
Sommières (30250): Place des Docteurs Dax, tel 66 80 97 98.

Fizzy Water, a Statue of Liberty, and a Celtic Oppidum

Just off the the N 113 at Vergèze, trendies may make a pilgrimage to the **Source Perrier**. Surprisingly, the vast complex was begun by an Englishman in 1903, and looks less like a

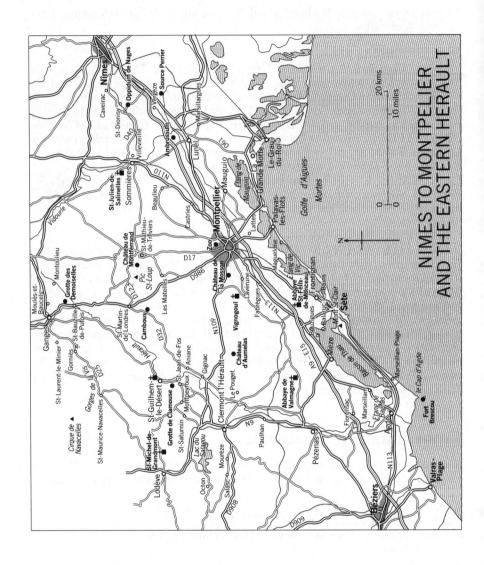

NIMES TO MONTPELIER AND THE EASTERN HERAULT

natural spring than an obsessively tidy aeroplane factory; ring 66 84 60 27 for the tour, to see the Indian-club-shaped green bottles come whizzing off the line in their billions, all guaranteed benzene-free.

The big town along this route is **Lunel**, and a peculiar place it is. Legend has it that Lunel was founded by Jews from Jericho under the reign of Vespasian. In the Middle Ages, at least before the expulsion of the Jews in 1306, it was their educational centre in France, with well-known schools of everything from medicine to the Cabbala. Today, the town is best known for its bullfights. Its landmark is a copy of the Statue of Liberty; its cops wear star-and-crescent badges just like those of New Orleans. It is the easiest town in Languedoc to get lost in, and probably the easiest in which to smash up your car. Be careful. Little remains of medieval Lunel: some bits of the Jewish schools on Rue Ménard, and a vaulted alley called the Passage des Caladons that once was part of a Templar commandery.

South of Lunel, the sweet and shady village of **Marsillargues** has an elegant Renaissance château. The rooms, with their marble and plaster relief decoration of the 1570s and later, are lovely, but empty; it's sad that this château, one of the few undamaged in the Revolution, should have lost most of its furnishings in a fire in 1936. The dungeons beneath belong to the original castle of the 1300s. The **Château de Teillan**, just across the river Vidourle from Marsillargues, has a large park with some fragmentary Roman ruins and a gigantic *pigeonnier*, part of a military supply centre from the 1600s (both châteaux open irregularly; ask at the *mairie* for a visit). North of Lunel, near the *autoroute*, fragments of a Roman bridge over the Vidourle stand at **Ambrussum**, a ruined town now undergoing fitful excavations; bits of Roman road, villas and public buildings have already been uncovered.

The alternative route to Montpellier begins with the D 40 from Nîmes, a winding, pretty route that passes through lush, hilly country and slumberous villages like Caveirac and St-Dionisy. Above the latter, off the D 737, is the 3rd-century BC **Oppidum of Nages**, 11 km to the southwest of Nîmes, one of the outstanding pre-Roman sites in the south (signposted from the village of Nages-et-Solorgues, where the *mairie* has the key, tel 66 35 05 26). Like Nîmes, Nages was built around a spring, entirely of dry stone, with a temple, and walls punctuated by a round tower; on top of the tallest, the *tour monumentale*, a cache of stones for slings was discovered. The streets, with their rectangular houses, are laid out in a tidy grid—long before the Romans introduced their waffle-shaped city plan. The first floor of Nages-et-Solorgues' *mairie* has been converted into a small **archaeology museum**, with finds from the site.

Sommières

Hidden under the cliffs of the Vidourle, in a part of the Gard where no one ever goes, Sommières has been spared the usual plagues besetting picturesque southern villages: the Parisians, the English, the trinket shops—it even has to do without a famous writer, since longtime resident Lawrence Durrell died in October 1990. Its streets and squares could be paintings by Maurice Utrillo: soft and pastel, well-worn and well-lived-in, with faded shop signs of a century ago and flowers under every window.

Sommières was a Roman town, and its reason for being has always been the **bridge** the Romans built in 20 AD. Its 17 arches have withstood the frequent floods of the Vidourle ever since; they carry road traffic today, and still look in mint condition; the top of the bridge was restored in 1715. Oddly, almost half of the bridge is now hidden inside the town; medieval Sommières expanded into the dry parts of the river-bed, and eventually an embankment was built. The **Tour de l'Horloge**, the entrance to the town, was built over the bridge's fifth arch in 1659.

Behind the bridge is the Place des Docteurs Dax, the lovely market square that everyone in Sommières still calls by its old name, the **Marché-Bas**. The arches of the bridge pass over the streets on the eastern side. In the old days, the square would be underwater every spring, and the market moved up to the **Marché-Haut** two streets away, now called Place Jaurès. These two are the heart of old Sommières, with its vaulted arcades and narrow streets. Sommières was an enthusiastically Protestant town, and was destroyed after a siege in 1622 during the Wars of Religion; most of what you see is from the 17th-century rebuilding, and little has changed since then. Rue de la Taillade is one of the most typical and attractive streets; from here steps lead up to the half-ruined **château**, worth the climb for its views up and down the valley of the Vidourle.

In the hills just above Sommières, **Vielleville** has a Renaissance château, remodelled by Louis XIII in 1622, while overseeing the siege of Sommières. Four kilometres north of the town, there is a restored 11th-century country chapel, **St-Julien-de-Salinelles**, in a lovely setting with an ancient cemetery.

Continuing towards Montpellier, there is only Castries to detain you, with a 17th-century **château**. Though wrecked in the Revolution, this castle came back into the possession of its original owners, the de Castries family, who restored it; the last count, who died in 1991, was the commanding officer at Dien Bien Phu when the Vietnamese captured a French army in 1954. Today it belongs to the Académie Française, which meets here once a year. The tour of the house and furnishings is not compelling, but there are lovely gardens, designed in the style of Le Nôtre, watered by an 18th-century aqueduct (daily exc Mon 10–12, 2–6; adm; closed Jan).

Market Days: Lunel, Thursday and Sunday. Sommières, Wednesday and Saturday.

WHERE TO STAY/EATING OUT

Close to the river in the centre of **Sommières** (30250), on Av. E. Jamais, the *****Auberge du Pont Romain** has nice rooms in a restored herbal distillery, with a pool, and a fine restaurant with a garden terrace, menus 150–220 F (closed Jan, Feb; tel 66 80 00 58). Less expensively, there is the **Hôtel du Commerce**, overlooking the river at 5 Quai Gaussorgues. Also in Sommières, you could watch the busy life of the Marché Bas pass by from an outdoor table at **L'Evasion** (except that by the time you're there, everyone else will be home eating lunch); the menu is none too complicated: medallion of veal, frog legs and pizza, too, around 95 F.

Even better, at **Beaulieu**, between Sommières and Castries, you can have *pistou* and duckling on a 90 F menu at the **Ferme Auberge La Clé des Champs**, (13 Chemin du Parc; tel 67 86 60 92, Thurs–Sun only). In **Castries**, L'Art du Feu offers refined cooking on bargain menus of 80 or 100 F; the house speciality is thin-sliced *aiguilletes* of beef or duck in delicate sauces (tel 67 70 05 97).

MONTPELLIER

If that town could suck as hard as it can blow, it could
bring the ocean to it and become a seaport.

Although this old saying originally referred to the brash, booming, braggart Atlanta of
the 1880s, it applies just as fairly to France's eighth city. The public relations geniuses in
Montpellier have managed to outdo even Atlanta: their beloved Montpellier is cocka-
doodled as the 'Technopole', the *Surdoué* (the Specially Gifted), the 'Synergetic Euro-
cité', the 'Capital of Southern Europe', rightful 'heir to the Florence of the Medicis', the
'French California', and indeed nothing less than 'the Rome of Tomorrow'. Unlike
Atlanta, Montpellier has actually sucked hard enough to get a port of its own (for
sailboats at least) by widening a puny river called the Lez, a feat that has given it a new
horn to toot: *Montpellier la Méditerranée*!

Until 1977 and the election of irrepressible Socialist mayor Georges Frêche, Montpellier was a pleasant, sleepy university backwater of fawn-coloured stone with a
population of 100,000, one that could put forth the modest claim that Stendhal found it
the 'only French city of the interior that doesn't look stupid' . Its population now
approaches 300,000, including the large staff of IBM and 55,000 university students
from around the world who come to study where Rabelais and Nostradamus learned
medecine. And despite the noise it makes, this is one live-wire of a city, politically one of
the most progressive in France, fun and friendly and decidedly low on poodles—you're
more likely to see synergetic, specially gifted dogs as big as bears.

History
Compared to its venerable Roman neighbours, Narbonne, Béziers and Nîmes, Montpellier is a relative newcomer, tracing its roots back a mere thousand years, to 985, when
the count of Mauguio bestowed a large farm at *Monspestelarius* on a certain Master
Guilhem. It was a fortunate site, near the old Via Domitia, and the newer *Cami Salinié*
(salt route) and *Cami Roumieu* (the pilgrimage route between St-Gilles and Compostela),
and it had access to the sea through the river Lez.

Guilhem's farm soon grew into a village of merchants, who made
their fortunes by importing spices from the Levant, especially spices
with medicinal uses taught them by their Arab and Jewish trading
partners, and by graduates of the medical school of Salerno; by the year
1000 they were training pupils in Montpellier. By the late 1100s, the
town was big enough to need a wall with 25 towers, shaped like an
escutcheon, or *écusson* (as the old town is still known). It lost its independence when Guilhem VIII failed to produce a son, and gave his only
daughter Marie to Pedro II of Aragon. Montpellier was her dowry, just
in time to spare the town from the horrors of the Albigensian Crusade. And when Marie
and Pedro's son, Jaime the Conqueror, divided Aragon between his two sons, Montpellier joined the kingdom of Majorca.

Montpellier

In 1220, the teachers of medicine formed a *Universitas Medicorum*, and began to attract
students from all over Europe; in 1250 it was supplemented by a *studium* of law, both of

which were given Pope Nicholas IV's seal of approval in 1289. Another impetus behind Montpellier's tremendous growth in the 13th and 14th centuries was dead bugs—dark red cochineal insects found on oaks in the surrounding *garrigues*, believed at the time to be grains, and used for dying cloth scarlet. The spice and gold-working trades thrived, especially after those mega-consumers, the popes, moved to Avignon.

In 1349 the Kings of Majorca sold Montpellier to France for 120,000 golden écus. A period of relative peace and prosperity continued until the 1560s, when the university academics and tradesmen embraced the Reformation. For the next 70 years much of what Montpellier had achieved was wiped out; churches and suburbs were destroyed, building and art came to a halt. In 1622 Louis XIII came in person to besiege the rebellious city and reassert royal authority; he built a citadel to keep an eye on the Montpellerains, then transferred the States-General of Languedoc here from Pézenas, with all its nobles, prelates and deputies, who proceeded to build themselves the patrician *hôtels* that still dominate the old city.

Putting its merchant republic days behind it, Montpellier settled down to the life of a university town and regional capital. The Revolution passed without kicking up much dust; a far bigger crisis for Montpellier occurred in the 1890s, when phylloxera knocked out the wine-making industry the city had come to depend on—an economic blow from which it only began to recover in the 1950s. With the French mania for categorizing, Montpellier now pigeon-holes its economy into five 'poles': *Eurodmédecine*, including its numerous labs and pharmaceutical industries, *Héliopolis* (tourism), *Informatique* (IBM has been here since 1965), *Agropolis* (it boasts the first European research centre of agronomy in hot climates, among other institutes), and *Pole Antenna* for its role as the telecommunications centre of Languedoc. Meanwhile, the city teasingly threatens to tax the balconies of its residents to pay for the ambitious 'follies' of Mayor Frêche, follies that are the envy of the nearly every other city in France.

GETTING AROUND

The city's **airport**, Montpellier-Fréjorgues is 8 km southeast of the centre on D 21 (tel 67 65 60 65); Dan-Air flies direct to London (tel 67 65 88 88), and UTA to New York, once a week (tel 67 58 56 56). Air Littoral, tel 67 65 49 49, serves Nice, Marseille, Perpignan, and Barcelona. Other destinations are served by Air France, tel 67 92 48 28 and Air Inter, tel 67 65 01 66.

The **train station** is in Place Auguste-Gilbert, tel 67 58 50 50. You can race there from Paris in 4 hours and 40 min on the TGV, or catch direct trains to Avignon, Nîmes, Marseille, Nice, Perpignan, Narbonne, Agde, Lunel, Sète, and Carcassonne. The station is linked by an escalator with the **coach station** in nearby Rue du Grand St-Jean (tel 67 92 01 43), which has buses to Nîmes, La Grande Motte, Béziers, Aigues-Mortes, etc; every 20 min bus No. 17 trundles down to the sea at Palavas. For a taxi any time of day or night, tel 67 58 10 10 or 67 58 74 82. Brand name **car hire** firms are at the airport, or try Budget at 6 Rue J.-Ferry, tel 67 92 69 00; City, 25 Rue du Grand St-Jean, tel 67 58 34 78, or a less expensive used car from A.D.A., 8 Blvd Berthelot, tel 67 58 10 15.

TOURIST INFORMATION

Allée du Tourisme, Le Triangle, just off the Place du Comédie, tel 67 58 67 58. Also in the station, tel 67 22 08 80. They have a hotel reservation service, and offer tours of the city centre, in English on Mondays. Or ask for the walking tour brochure of Ecusson that lists all the *hôtels particuliers* open to the public.

A Place Named Comédie

The various personalities of Montpellier all come together in the lively, café-lined **Place de la Comédie**, locally known as *l'Oeuf*, or the Egg, due to the shape it had in the 18th century. Now flattened into an omelette, the centre is watered by the fountain of the *Three Graces* (1796), while along one side stretches the waist-level trough of a modern fountain, where three bronze stooges gesticulate frantically, presumably because they forgot their trousers. Other ornaments of the square include a doppelgänger of the Paris Opera, and various 19th-century larded bourgeois buildings with domes reminiscent of bathyspheres, while opposite looms a modern glass-and-steel semi-ziggaurat, the **Polygone**, a shopping mall and town hall complex. Walk through this to see one of the jewels in the Euro-Cité's crown: **Antigone**, a mostly moderate-income quarter with housing for 10,000 people, and shops and restaurants, all designed by Barcelona architect Ricardo Bofill in 1979. Bofill understood just what a Rome of Tomorrow needs: Mannerist neo-Roman arches, cornices, pilasters, and columns as big as California redwoods, built around the squares of the 'Golden Number' and the 'Millennium' that link Montpellier to its newly dredged-out Tiber, the Lez. But does Antigone work? On a bad day it looks like the surreal background to a De Chirico painting, as troubling as the Antigone of myth; on a good day, it seems like a delightful place to live, especially for kids, who can play football in the monumental Place du Nombre d'Or and still hear their parents call them in for lunch.

To the north of Place de la Comédie extends the **Esplanade Charles de Gaulle**, replacing the city walls demolished by Louis XIII after the siege of 1622, the better to keep Montpellier at the mercy of the cannons of his new citadel. In the 18th century the Esplanade was planted with rows of trees and became Montpellier's chief promenade; among its monuments is a rare survival of 1908, the **Cinématographe Pathé**, a little cockerel-emblazoned palace from the magical early days of cinema (now renamed the Rabelais Cultural Centre, it often shows foreign films). The north end of the Esplanade is closed by the mastadonic **CORUM**, 'the House of Innovation' designed by Claude Vasconi, another of Georges Frêche's Euro-Cité showcases, encompassing the Opéra Berlioz and two smaller congress halls.

Musée Fabre

On Boulevard Bonne Nouvelle, between the Cinématographe and CORUM, in the fastness of a former Jesuit College, the Musée Fabre was long the main reason for visiting Montpellier, with one of the most important collections of art in provincial France (open 9–5:30, until 5 Sat and Sun, closed Mon, adm). In the front courtyard, a large arch built into the wall is decorated with two mossy look-alikes of Michelangelo's *Day* and *Night*, although instead of moping in opposite directions, these two statues lean amorously towards each other—fittingly enough, for this museum was founded on a Florentine romance. François Xavier Fabre (1766–1837), a pupil of David, was in Florence at the outbreak of the French Revolution, where he became a close friend of the

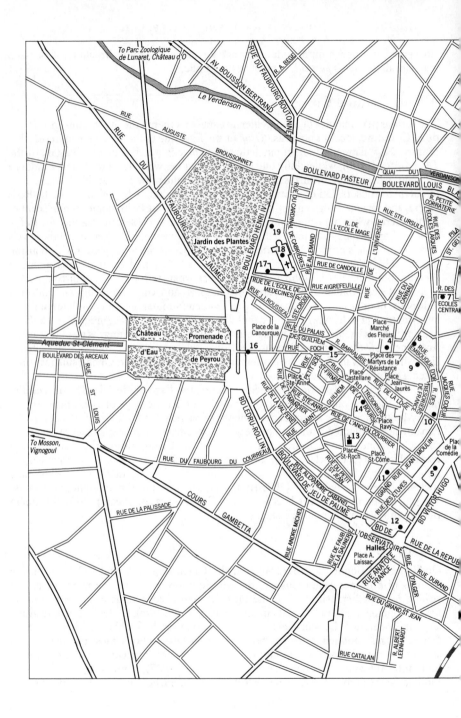

To Parc Zoologique
de Lunaret, Château d'O

AV. BOUISSON BERTRAND

RUE DU FAUBOURG BOUTONNET

R. A. BÉGÉ

Le Verdenson

RUE
DU

RUE
AUGUSTE

BROUSSONNET

FAUBOURG

BOULEVARD PASTEUR

QUAI   DU   VERDANSON

BOULEVARD   LOUIS   BLA

R. PETITE
CORRATERIE

RUE STE URSULE

RUE DES
ÉCOLES LAÏQUES

PILA

ST. GE

RUE DU CARDINAL DE CABRIÈRES

R. DE
L'ÉCOLE MAGE

RUE DE
L'UNIVERSITÉ

19

Jardin des Plantes

18

BOULEVARD HENRI IV

RUE ALLEMAND

RUE DE CANDOLLE

DE

17

ST-JAUMES

RUE DE L'ÉCOLE DE
MÉDECINES

RUE AIGREFEUILLE

RUE DU
CANNAU

R. DES

RUE DE

ÉCOLES
CENTRA

7

RUE J.J. ROUSSEAU

STE-CROIX

Place de la
Canourgue

RUE DU PALAIS
DES GUILHEM

Place
Marché
des Fleurs

4

8

Château

Promenade

BOULEVARD DES ARCEAUX

Aqueduc St-Clément

d'Eau

de Peyrou

16

RUE
FOCH

R. BARRALERIE

15

Place des
Martyrs de la
Résistance

RUE
EMBOUQUE D'OR

9

RUE
JACQUES COEUR

RUE DES

RUE DU
PETIT SCEL

RUE
ST-FIRMIN

Place
Castellane

Place
Jean
Jaurès

RD TRÉSORIERS
DE FRANCE

TRÉSORIERS
DE FRANCE

Place
Ste-Anne

RUE DE LA LOGE

BD LEDRU-ROLLIN

RUE STE-ANNE

RUE DE L'ARANDIER

RUE DE LA VALFÈRE

SAINT GUILHEM

RD TRÉSORIERS
DE LA BOURSE

14

Place
Ravy

10

RUE DE L'ANCIEN COURRIER

RUE
FOCH

To Mosson,
Vignogoul

RUE DU FAUBOURG DU COURREAU

BOULEVARD ALEXANDRE DE JEU DE PAUME

RUE ALEXANDRE CABANEL

13

Place
St-Roch

RUE DU PETIT
ST-JEAN

Place
St-Côme

Plac
de la
Comédie

11

GRAND RUE JEAN MOULIN

5

COURS

RUE DE LA PALISSADE

GAMBETTA

RUE ANDRÉ MICHEL

RUE DES ÉTUVES

12

BD DE

BD VICTOR HUGO

RUE DE FAUB
DE LA SAUNERIE

L'OBSERVATOIRE

Halles
Place A.
Laissac

RUE DE LA REPU

RUE ANATOLE
FRANCE

RUE
D'ALGER

RUE DURAND

RUE DU GRAND ST-JEAN

RUE CATALAN

R. ALBERT
LEENHARDT

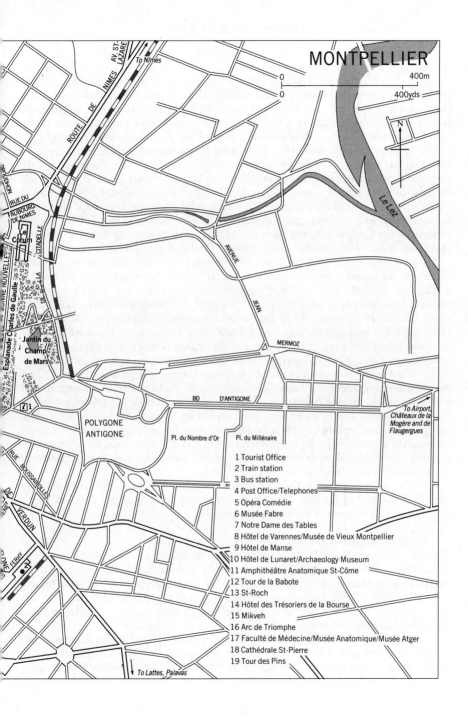

MONTPELLIER

0   400m

0   400yds

N

To Nîmes

AV. ST-LAZARE

NIMES

ROUTE   DE

RUE DU FAUBOURG DE NIMES

CITADELLE

DE   LA

BOULEVARD HENRI

Le Corum

BONNE NOUVELLE

Esplanade Charles de Gaulle

Jardin du Champ de Mars

Le Lez

AVENUE

JEAN

MERMOZ

1

POLYGONE ANTIGONE

BD   D'ANTIGONE

Pl. du Nombre d'Or   Pl. du Millénaire

To Airport, Châteaux de la Mogère and de Flaugergues

RUE

BOUSSAIROLLES

DE   VERDUN

JULES FERRY

1 Tourist Office
2 Train station
3 Bus station
4 Post Office/Telephones
5 Opéra Comédie
6 Musée Fabre
7 Notre Dame des Tables
8 Hôtel de Varennes/Musée de Vieux Montpellier
9 Hôtel de Manse
10 Hôtel de Lunaret/Archaeology Museum
11 Amphithéâtre Anatomique St-Côme
12 Tour de la Babote
13 St-Roch
14 Hôtel des Trésoriers de la Bourse
15 Mikveh
16 Arc de Triomphe
17 Faculté de Médecine/Musée Anatomique/Musée Atger
18 Cathédrale St-Pierre
19 Tour des Pins

To Lattes, Palavas

Countess of Albany, the merry widow of Bonnie Prince Charlie, and her lover the Italian dramatist Vittore Alfieri. When Alfieri died in 1805, he left the Countess his library and paintings. Fabre in turn inherited the Countess's affections, and when she died in 1824, she left everything to her young man from Montpellier. A year later, Fabre donated the lot to his native city; the valuable Alfieri and Albany libraries are now in the adjacent **Gutenburg Médiathèque**, in a building formerly (and more simply) known as the Hôtel de Massilian, where Moliére played in the *Ballet des Incompatibles* in 1655.

The Musée Fabre has six levels. The penalty for touring it from the bottom up is to start with the compost of the 17th century, when sunlight was an abomination, and people who paid for paintings liked bloody hunting scenes of boars goring dogs, and only the hard-drinking Dutch seemed to have any fun (works by Ruysdael, Jan Steen, David Teniers, and a good Rubens portrait). The next floor up, formerly the Jesuits' kitchen, is devoted to ceramics: apothecary vases made in Montpellier in the 1600s, faience portraits of the Caesars (like the nasty Galba, with veins protruding from his face and neck), and finest of all, a 16th-century plate by Orazio Fontana of Urbino.

The next floor up contains the bulk of Fabre's donation, and although much of it is overblown and unintentionally hilarious, there are some gems: a lush *Mystic Marriage of St Catherine* by Paolo Veronese, that explains why 'Veronese green' is such a popular colour in France; a self-portrait by Bernini; Magnasco's *Fondaco dei Turchi* set in Venice, where wraith-like creatures flit in the cavernous darkness; a Florentine *tondo* of the *Virgin and Child* by a talented follower of Botticelli; a 16th-century Lombard *Leda and the Swan*, with Leda wagging a coy finger at the brazen bird. From Naples, there's an anonymous Caravaggiesque *Ecce Homo*; from Spain, a Ribera and a pair of Zurbaráns, *St Agatha* carrying her breasts on a plate and the *Angel Gabriel*, who looks as if he can't find the right address; and from England, landscapes by Richard Parkes Bonington and Joshua Reynolds' famous *Infant Samuel in Prayer*. Fabre himself (*St Sebastian* and *The Death of Narcissus*) proves to be a romantic in his art as in his life; more influential, though, was Jean-Baptiste Greuze, who seems to have invented the simpering genre of big-eyed kid pictures they sell in supermarkets. On that side of the coin, there's Rigaud's portrait of *Louis XIV*, all curls and steel, and the cool, pubescent crispness of Houdon's celebrated statues of the *Four Seasons* (1785).

Fabre's *cabinet* on the fourth floor contains portraits of Alfieri, Canova, and of Fabre himself at the end of his life. The other outstanding work here is Louis Gauffier's snapshot-like *Views taken at Vallombreuse*, painted in 1796.

THE GOOD NARCISSIST OF MONTPELLIER

The superb collection on **Floor 5** was donated by the museum's other great benefactor, Alfred Bruyas (1821–77). Born into a Montpellier banking family, Bruyas resolved the frustration of not being able to paint himself by befriending many of the artists of his day and asking them to paint him—there are 24 portraits of the red-bearded patron in this museum alone, lined up one after another, including examples by Delacroix and Alexandre Cabanel of Montpellier (1823–89). Four are by Gustave Courbet (1819–77), who became Bruyas' friend, and whose works are the highlight of the museum. Two paintings were pivotal in Courbet's proto-Impressionist discovery of light: the *Baigneuses*, which caused such a scandal in the Salon of 1853 that Napoleon III ordered it removed, and the delightful, sundrenched *Bonjour, Monsieur Courbet* (1854), in which the jaunty Courbet, strutting down a country lane with easel and paints strapped to his back meets who else but Alfred Bruyas.

Other paintings on this floor cover the artistic movements on either side of Courbet: Elisabeth Vigée-Lebrun's refined *La Grande Duchesse Elisabeth Alexeïevna* (1798); the cold classicism of Ingres' *Stratonice* (1866) and David (the clean, unbloodied *Dead Hector*), paintings that stand as the antithesis of the warm exotic romanticism of Delacroix's *Mulatress* and *Algerian Odalisques* (1849) or the melting landscapes of Corot. From southern painters of the period there are big historical and exotic scenes and landscapes, including Jules Laurens of Carpentras' *Blue Mosque of Tauris in the Snow*. The gloomy young romantic Théodore Géricault (1791–1824) is represented by an unidealized *Portrait of Lord Byron* and a surreal *Study of arms and legs*, cannibal leftovers painted in a medical school while students dissected the corpses.

Floor 6 is dedicated to painters from Montpellier. Eugène Castelneau (1827–94) painted bright landscapes around Languedoc, like the *Vue du Pic Saint-Loup* (1859). Alexandre Cabanel (1823–89), who studied in Rome, left his best work in Montpellier, including the pre-Raphaelesque *Albaydé*, *La Chiarruccia* and *Self-portrait at age 29*, before he went off to paint fashionable portraits in Paris. Best of all is the short-lived early Impressionist Frédéric Bazille (1841–70), a friend of Renoir and Monet, whose best works glow with the strong sun of Languedoc: *Les Remparts d'Aigues-Mortes* and *La Vue du Village* (Castelnau, now engulfed by Montpellier). The museum's few more recent works are here, too: Berthe Morisot's *L'été*; a jolly Fauvist Desnoyer, *Les Joutes à Sète*; *Nature morte portugaise* by Robert Delaunay; *Fernande Olivier* by Kees Van Dongen; and Nicolas de Staël's painting of *Ménerbes*, which if it really looked like that, wouldn't attract so many tourists or disciples of Peter Mayle.

Into the Ecusson

There is nothing as compelling as the Musée Fabre in Montpellier's historic centre; much was lost in the Wars of Religion, and even the many 17th- and 18th-century *hôtels particuliers*, as stuccoed and ornate as many of them are inside, show mostly blank walls to the street. But few cities in the south of France manage to be as pleasant and lively without gaggles of tourists; instead Montpellier has students to keep the city on its toes.

One of the major crossroads of the Ecusson is Place Notre-Dame, under the cool gaze of the neoclassical **Notre-Dames-des-Tables** (1748), originally the chapel connected to the Jesuit college (now the Musée Fabre). In front passes the old pilgrims' route, the *Cami Romieu*, now Rue de l'Aiguillerie, where St Roch was arrested as a spy (see the plaque by Rue de Pila-St-Gély), and where Montpellier merchants and innkeepers cashed in on passing pilgrims. Residential *hôtels* went up later; nearby **Rue du Cannau** has some of the flashiest 17th-century models, while in Place Pétrarque, the **Hôtel de Varennes'** façade (1758) conceals a pair of Gothic halls, one a depository for architectural fragments salvaged from medieval Montpellier. Upstairs, there's a pair of small museums devoted to the good old days: **Musée de Vieux Montpellier** (Mon–Fri 1:30–5), with portraits of notables, and plans and views of the city from the 1500s on; and **Musée du Fougau** ('the Foyer' Wed and Thurs 3–6:30), founded by the local Félibres to preserve the arts and traditions of old Montpellier.

351

Around the corner, at 4 Rue Embouque-d'Or, the 1670 **Hôtel de Manse** is famous for its richly decorated openwork staircase, designed by Italian architects—a stair that became the prototype for a score of others in Montpellier, including the one in the nearby **Hôtel de Lunaret**, at 5 Rue des Trésoriers-de-France. This was originally the residence of the famous merchant and financier Jacques Coeur, whose motto was 'flies can't enter a closed mouth'. In 1441 he was appointed a treasurer of Charles VII, and charged with obtaining royal subsidies from Languedoc. Reasoning that the wealthier the land, the easier it is to tax, Coeur became one of Montpellier's greatest benefactors, among other things building a merchants' exchange and dredging the outlets of the Lez to make them navigable; this town-house originally had a tower so high that he could scan the sea and its traffic. His career ended abruptly in 1451, when he was accused of poisoning the king's mistress, Agnès Sorel; he escaped prison in 1454 and died in Chios, fighting the Ottomans for the Pope. In the last century, Montpellier erected a statue of him on Rue Jacques Coeur, at the side of the *hôtel*.

Although much renovated since Jacques Coeur's day, most of the *hôtel's* contents predate him, as it's now the **Musée de la Société Archéologique**. Although you may have to arrange your schedule to fit theirs (guided tours Mon, Wed, Fri at 2:30), it has its rewards—Greek vases, dolmens, funeral steles and other prehistoric finds from the Hérault; an excellent collection of Romanesque sculpture salvaged from the 11th-century version of Notre-Dame-des-Tables and from surrounding abbeys, especially St-Guilhem-le-Désert and Fontfroide; the rock-crystal seal of King Sancho of Aragon; 14th-century Parisian ivories, and three 12th-century Islamic funeral steles discovered in Montpellier, a rare relic of the city's cosmopolitan spice trading days; from Jacques Coeur's day, two fine paintings, an anonymous Catalan *SS. Apolline and Guilhem* and, from the Clouets' workshop, *Gabrielle d'Estrées and her sister in their bath*. A major collection of 16th- to 18th-century faience made in Montpellier rounds things off, together with a grand ceiling painting of 1660, *Justice discovering Truth with the help of Time* by Jean de Troy, the city's top interior decorator of the age. A plaque in Rue des Trésoriers-de-France recalls that another of the city's colourful cast of characters lived here: that great wanderer Rabelais, who enrolled at Montpellier's medical school in 1530, at the age of 40, and became a doctor as well as a priest, although he later wrote that 'the calling was far too tiresome and melancholy a one', and that 'physicians always smelled of enemas, like old devils' (*Pantagruel*, 1532).

To the south, Rue Jacques Coeur becomes Grand Rue Jean Moulin, one of Montpellier's most elegant streets. On weekdays you can drop in at the Chamber of Commerce and Industry at No. 32 to see the **Amphithéâtre Anatomique St-Côme**, built in 1757 with funds left by Louis XV's surgeon, François Gigot de Lapeyronie, and of a classical elegance that belies its function. Turn left at the foot of Grand Rue Jean Moulin for the **Tour de la Babote**, a recently-restored medieval tower topped by an astronomical observatory in 1741.

Western Quarters: St Roch to the Jardin des Plantes

Despite its Protestant leanings, Montpellier's fame in heaven's closed circle hinges on Roch, the pious son of a wealthy merchant, who was born around 1350 and abandoned all of his worldly goods to make the pilgrimage to Rome in 1367. On his way home, he came to an Italian village decimated by plague; after curing a number of victims with the sign of the Cross, Roch went down with the disease himself, and retreated to the country where no one could hear his groans. Nourished by a friendly dog who stole food for him from its master's table, Roch recovered and returned to Montpellier, so ravaged and changed by his illness that he wasn't recognized, and was thrown into prison as a spy, where he died in 1379. Only then did his grandmother recognize him by a birthmark in the shape of a cross. News of Roch's reputation as an intermediary against the Black Death reached plague-torn Venice, and even though he had yet to be canonized, Venetians disguised as pilgrims stole his bones and built the magnificent Confraternity of San Rocco in his honour—one of the wonders of the lagoon city.

As patron saint of Montpellier, St Roch came through for his home town in the cholera epidemics of 1832 and 1849, and finally a church of **St-Roch** was built, in Viollet-le-Duc's Ideal Gothic, in the medieval quarter of the Ecusson. Rue Voltaire leads up to the socializing centre of the neighbourhood, Rue de l'Ancien Courrier and Place Ravy. Here, too, is the largest and one of the most handsome residences in old Montpellier, **Hôtel des Trésoriers-de-la-Bourse** (1631–93) on the street of the same name (No. 4), with a fine interior garden courtyard.

From the centre of the Ecusson, Rue Foch was sliced out as a grand Paris-style boulevard, just missing a rare Jewish ritual bath, or **Mikveh**, at 1 Rue Barralerie (to visit contact the tourist office). Dating from *c.* 1200, it was part of the synagogue in the midst of what was then a large, active Jewish quarter. Since the late 17th century, however, this loftiest edge of Montpellier has been devoted to tons of mouldy fol-de-rol glorifying Louis XIV, beginning with an **Arc de Triomphe** (the triumphs referred to include digging a canal, wrestling the English lion to the ground and conquering heresy—with the Revocation of the Edict of Nantes, a nasty piece of bigotry that went down like a lead balloon in Montpellier). Beyond stretches the **Promenade du Peyrou**, a nice park spoiled by an equestrian statue of his megalomaniac majesty as big as the Trojan Horse: the story goes that the sculptor was so mortified to discover he had forgotten the king's stirrups that he committed suicide. It was brought down laboriously from Paris in 1718, fell into the Garonne en route, whence it was rescued and brought here, only to be smashed to bits in the Revolution—a fact that didn't prevent the erection of the present copy in 1838. At the edge of the promontory stands the far more elegant **Château d'Eau**, an open temple designed by Jean Giral to disguise the reservoir of the **Aqueduc St-Clément** (1771) snaking below in curious perspective, a triple-tiered work inspired by the Pont du Gard that brings in water from the river Lez. The Promenade is about to undergo an upheaval: American architect Richard Meier has been charged with adding an 'Espace Pitot' to the area, whatever that might be.

The waters feed the unicorn fountain in the nearby **Place de la Canourgue**, a charming 17th-century square shaded by nettle trees (*micocouliers*). It looks down on the medieval monastery college of St-Benoît, built by papal architects from Avignon and (since 1795) the **Faculté de Médecine**, housing an enormous medical library, and a **Musée d'Anatomie** (Mon–Fri 2:15–5) with an important collection of mummies, bodily parts, ancient and modern medical instruments, and more. There's also the **Musée Atger** (1:30–4:30, closed Sat, Sun, and school holidays), with a hoard of drawings mostly by southern French artists like Rigaud, Fragonard and Mignard but also by Flemish, Dutch, German and Italian schools of the 15th–18th centuries, including some remarkable sketches by Giambattista Tiepolo. Adjacent, the former monastic chapel has been Montpellier's **Cathédrale de St-Pierre** ever since the see was transferred here from Maguelone in 1563, although its status didn't spare it the usual depredations in the Wars of Religon and the Revolution. The cathedral's greatest distinction is its unusual porch, supported by two conical turrets. The best paintings are 17th-century canvases in the transepts, by Montpellier's own Sébastien Bourdon, a Huguenot who painted himself among the heathen in the *Fall of Simon Magnus* and Jean Troy's *Healing of the Paralytic*.

Boulevard Henri IV, running alongside the Faculté, descends to the tree-topped **Tour des Pins**, a last vestige of the medieval walls. Nostradamus wrote that Montpellier would perish with the pines that once grew here, a prediction the city thumbed its nose at by replacing them with cypresses. A plaque on the tower commemorates the birth in 1208 of Jaime (Jacques) the Conqueror, son of Marie and Pedro of Aragon. Beyond lies the lovely **Jardin des Plantes**, the oldest botanical garden in France, founded by a decree of Henri IV in 1593 to instruct students on native and exotic plants used for healing. It has several magnificent 400-year-old trees, exotic succulents, plants from the *garrigues*, and an *orangerie*; near the latter, in a spot celebrated for its exquisite melancholy, there's a marble plaque with the inscription *Placandis Narcissae Manibus*. The Narcissa in question is said to be the consumptive 18-year-old daughter of the poet Edward Young (best known for his *Night Thoughts*, illustrated by Blake). In 1734 he brought Narcissa to France, hoping the warm climate would cure her; instead the exertion of travelling killed her, and she was buried either in Lyon, or here 'in the garden she loved'—a story that made this a favourite rendezvous for romantic students like Paul Valéry and André Gide. At the highest point of the garden is the Tree of Secrets, its trunk pitted with niches where lovers would leave *billets d'amour* for one another.

The Montpellier Follies

Montpellier, one of the fastest growing cities in France, is spreading its tentacles to suck in all that surrounds it, and has already gobbled up a number of 18th-century châteaux and gardens that were the country retreats of its elite (before setting out, check hours at the tourist office; some places can only be visited on the office's *Les Folies* tour). One of the oldest is 3 km east of Antigone on the D24, the **Château de Flaugergues** (guided tours, July and Aug Tues–Sun 2:30–6:30, otherwise telephone ahead, tel 67 65 79 64, adm). Begun in the 1690s, the place is impressively filled with 17th- and 18th-century furnishings, tapestries, and a collection of optical instruments. A bit further east (take D 172), **Château de la Mogère** is a refined *folie* of 1716, with period furnishings, family portraits, and in the garden a delightful Baroque *buffet d'eau*, a fountain built into a wall (guided tours, daily 2:30–6:30 Pentecost–end of Sept; other times Sat, Sun and holidays only, adm).

North of Montpellier, on the road to Mende, the **Parc Zoologique de Lunaret** (open all day) has exotic and regional fauna, wandering with as few fences as possible amid woodlands and *garrigues*. The 1750 **Château d'O** (northwest, on the road to Grabels), now used for receptions and theatrical performances, is famous for its park, decorated with statues taken from the gardens of the **Château de la Mosson** (1729), which lies to the south, just off N 109. La Mosson was the most opulent of all the follies until the

Revolution and its conversion into a soap factory; after decades of neglect the city of Montpellier acquired it in 1982 and is restoring it. It has a lovely oval Venetian-style music chamber and a poignant seashell and pebble *buffet d'eau* in the garden, now stripped of its ornaments.

From Mosson, take D 27E/D 5E and turn towards Pignan for the remarkable 1250 church of the Cistercian **Abbaye St-Martin-du-Vignogoul**, open by request to the custodian, (closed Wed am). Believed to be the first attempt at Gothic in Languedoc, the church is small is size but grand in vision, a lofty, single-naved, pint-sized cathedral decorated with a trefoil arch, finely sculpted capitals, still more Romanesque than Gothic, and a unique polygonal choir, lit by a row of bull's-eye windows.

FESTIVALS

The city hosts four annual festivals: theatre in early June, during the **Printemps des Comédiens** at Château d'O, tel 67 61 06 30; dance performances of all kinds, including whirling Dervishes, films, and workshops at the **Festival International Montpellier Danse** from the end of June to the start of July; all-star music to suit every taste from opera to jazz during late July through August at the **Festival de Radio France et de Montpellier**; and in October, the **Festival International du Cinéma Méditerranéen** (info for the last three from 7 Blvd Henri IV, tel 67 61 11 20).

SHOPPING

At Espace Mosson, at La Paillade, there is a **flower market** on Tues and a **flea-market** on Sun morning, when free buses link it every 20 min with Square Planchon. Daily food **markets** take place in Place J. Jaurès, Halles Castellanes, Halles Laissac and Plan Cabannes; on Tues and Sat there's an **organic market** at Aux Arceaux, by Rue Marioge. The tourist office has a large display of wine, *confits* and other regional products; antique shops cluster around Place de la Canorque; or for something really special, pick up a bottle of 'Eau de Montpellier' (no kidding) for your sweetie-pie at G. de Guidais, 51 Rue de la Méditerranée. A good selection of reasonably-priced English books and videos, and the latest lowdown on Montpellier are available at Steve Davis' **Bookshop**, 4 Rue de l'Université, tel 67 66 09 08.

ENTERTAINMENT

To find out what's going on in the new Rome, pick up a copy of the free weekly *Sortir Montpellier* or the monthly *Edito*; or visit FNAC, in the Polygone, which has tickets for most events. For a babysitter, try AGEM, 5 Rue Croix-d'Or, tel 67 60 57 23, or CROUS, 2 Rue Monteil, tel 67 63 53 93.

During the year, there are performances at the CORUM (tel 67 67 67 61), home of **L'Orchestre Philharmonique de Montpellier** and **Montpellier Danse**, an internationally renowned company under its innovative choreographer/director Dominique Bagouet. The old **Opéra Comédie** (tel 67 66 00 92) still puts on opera and theatrical performances; popular singers and comedians often crop up at **Zénith**, Rt de Mauguio, tel 67 64 50 00.

Films in their original English crop up on Wednesdays at the **Ciné-Club des Anglicistes**, Université Paul Valéry, Amphi A (for information contact the tourist office at 67 58 67 58); at **Gaumont**, Place de la Comédie, tel 67 52 72 00; and at the **Cinémathèque Jean-Vigo**, 20 Rue Azéma, tel 67 42 35 42. *The* place to stop for a coffee: **Café Bibal**, 4 Rue Jacques-Coeur.

WHERE TO STAY
(postal code 34000)
Montpellier is well-endowed with hotels, especially two-star hotels for small business travellers that double well enough for pleasure travellers as well. At the top of the line, there's the antique-furnished ******Métropole**, 3 Rue Clos-René, tel 67 58 11 22, between the train station and Place de la Comédie, with a quiet garden courtyard and air-conditioning. If you have a car, the most charming place to stay is *****Demeure des Brousses** (a few minutes from either the city or the sea at Rte des Vauguières, 4 km east of town on D 24 and D 127E, towards the Château de la Mogère, tel 67 65 77 66) an 18th-century ivy-covered *mas*, surrounded by a vast park of shady trees, furnished with antiques and an excellent restaurant to boot. Another gem requiring your own transport, *****La Maison Blanche**, 1796 Av. de la Pompignane (off the route to Carnon) tel 67 79 60 25, has 38 rooms in a big, balconied house that escaped from the French quarter of New Orleans, here surrounded by a 5-hectare park. Within the Ecusson, *****Noailles** offers lots of classy 17th-century stone-built atmosphere next to Place Notre Dame (2 Rue des Ecoles Centrales, tel 67 60 49 80). ****Parc**, 8 Rue Achille Bège, tel 67 41 16 49, north of the Jardin des Plantes, is in an 18th-century *hôtel particulier*, fitted out with air-conditioning, TVs, etc. More central (just off Rue Foch) the ****Palais**, 3 Rue du Palais, tel 67 60 47 38, has comfortable rooms in a recently restored building; ****Nice** manages to be very pretty and flowery on a dull street near the station (14 Rue Boussairolles, tel 67 58 42 54). The cheaper choices aren't brilliant, but off Grand Rue Jean Moulin, there's the ***Majestic**, 4 Rue du Cheval Blanc, tel 67 66 26 85, and closer to the station, the ***France**, 3/4 Blvd de la République, tel 67 92 68 14. The **Auberge de Jeunesse**, 2 Impasse de la Petite Corraterie (at the bottom of Rue des Ecoles Laïques), tel 67 79 61 66, has functional dorm rooms (take bus 5 from the station).

EATING OUT
Montpellier isn't celebrated for its cuisine, but prosperity, as always, is encouraging newcomers to have a go, especially the three young men who opened **Le Jardin des Sens**, 11 Av. St-Lazare (off the N 113 towards Nîmes; bus 4), tel 67 66 25 23, and have made their garden pavilion a bastion of imaginative cuisine, with a light, fresh touch—delicate courgette blossoms filled with scallops, fillet of *loup*, duck with pine-nuts, spinach and cream, superb desserts, and the best wines of Languedoc (menus at 130, 190, 300 F), book ahead as space is limited. Another temple of fine cooking (complete with columns) is **Le Chandelier**, 3 Rue Leenhardt (off Rue du Grand St Jean, near the station, tel 67 92 61 62), featuring well-polished versions of the classic French repertoire (lunch menus at 120 and 170 F, dinner considerably more).

Lively Rue des Ecoles Laïques, with its reasonably priced restaurants is Montpellier's Latin Quarter, where the colours, smells and live music from the Turkish, Greek, Spanish and Tunisian restaurants collide in gleeful discord. At No. 1, **Le Vieil Ecu**, tel 67 66 39 44, has good French food, served in the old chapel or on the terrace (85 F menu). **Ramses**, at No. 22 has delicious Egyptian food and vegetarian specialities, in a micro-Pharaoh's palace (78 F menu); nearby **Yakonsoga**, up on Rue de l'Aiguillerie specializes in seafood and has live jazz on Fri nights (80 F). **Les Puits Ste-Anne**, near the church of Ste-Anne at 9 Rue de l'Amandier, tel 67 60 82 77, offers a vast choice for its 40 F menu, or you can splurge and get an extra course from an equally long list for 69 F, with wine. Or dine outside in the monumental heart of Antigone's Place du Nombre d'Or, at the **Brasilian Grill**, with black beans (*feijoado*) and a grill for 60 F.

NIGHTLIFE
Most nightclubs are to the south of the Ecusson. On weekends there's live jazz, African, or Caribbean music at **Le Doyen**, 13 Rue du Grand St Jean, tel 67 58 05 30; **Cotton Pub**, 9 Place Laissac, tel 67 92 21 60; at **La Pleine Lune**, 28 Place R. Salengro, tel 67 58 03 40; and with flamenco, blues, and country at the new **La Movida**, 2 bis Rue Legendre Herail, tel 67 92 15 39. Or dance to South American/Caribbean music at **Sax'aphone**, 24 Rue Ernest Michel, tel 67 58 80 90, or **Le Boksop**, 24 bis Rue Boyer, near the bus station. French rock bands are the main fare at **Rockstore** disco, 20 Rue de Verdun, tel 67 58 70 10, while on the other side of the coin, the **Centre Culturel Irlandais**, 10 Rue du Berger, tel 67 66 22 66, is responsible for spreading Irish music in deepest, darkest Languedoc.

Part XII

THE HÉRAULT

St-Guilhem-le-Désert

France isn't the sort of country that allows itself to be neatly dissected for the benefit of geographers and travel writers. So it is only for convenience's sake that the rugged *garrigue* of the upper Hérault, the green hills of the Espinouse and the flat expanses of the Béziers coast are combined together in a single chapter. In this *département*, some 150 km across at the most, the diversity is tremendous: a microcosm of France, from mountain forests of oak and pine, limestone *cirques* and *causses*, to the endless beaches of the coast and the delicious rolling hills around the Canal du Midi.

For devotees of rural France, this seemingly innocuous area may be the ultimate find. Just enough tourists come for there to be plenty of country inns and *fermes-auberges*, though in most villages foreigners are still a novelty. The food is good; and there's enough wine to make anyone happy—that's an understatement. The Hérault is the most prolific wine-producing region. It can be a perfect alternative to overcrowded and overpraised Provence: just as beautiful, more real and relaxed, full of things to see—and considerably less expensive.

GETTING AROUND
Except along the coast, public transport is rudimentary at best; the coastal SNCF line runs from Montpellier through Frontignan, Sète, Agde and Béziers on its way to Narbonne and Perpignan, with as many as 22 trains a day. The only train service in the interior is from Béziers northwest to the Espinouse, taking a roundabout route through Bédarieux, Lamalou-les-Bains, Olargues and St-Pons on its way to Castres in the Tarn; a few trains daily at most. St-Pons is also connected by bus to Béziers, via St-Chinian. Coach lines from the *gare routière* in Montpellier have regular services to Gignac,

358

Clermont l'Hérault and Lodève, less regularly to other villages in the *département*; there are additional buses to some tourist attractions (like St-Guilhem-le-Désert) in the summer.

North of Montpellier: the *Garrigue*

On a map, you'll notice lots of blank space in this region, a *pays* without a name. It is a geographer's textbook example of *garrigue*, a dry limestone plateau with sparse vegetation where nothing thrives, and even sheep and vines can only just get by. *Garrigue* is an old Occitan word for the holly-oak, and these scrubby would-be trees grow everywhere, along with thyme and lavender-scented *maquis*. The windblown landscapes are as romantic as anything in Provence, though sombre. The few villages seem timid, closed into themselves.

TOURIST INFORMATION
Ganges (34190): Av. du Mont-Aigoual, tel 67 73 66 40.

Pic St-Loup

One of the most typical and attractive of these villages, **Les Matelles**, lies on the borders of the *garrigue* north of Montpellier. The narrow back roads north of here are especially pretty, including the D 1/D 122 west from St-Mathieu-de-Tréviers; this scenic high road of the *garrigue* passes below the ruined **Château de Montferrand**, a long climb but one that offers a memorable view. Montferrand was one of the first castles to fall to the Albigensian Crusade, but the real damage was done by Louis XIV, as part of his general royal policy of cleaning up unnecessary and possibly dangerous castles. The view takes in **Pic St-Loup**, just up the road, the lone, striking exclamation point of the *garrigue*. This is a folded mountain; the lines of stratification are clearly visible. Even so it seems incredible that the pressure of the earth would push one small patch up to such a height—650 m. A path leads to the summit. The Pic's steep slopes make it a favourite spot for hang-gliding.

St-Martin-de-Londres, 7 km up the D 986 from Les Matelles, is a surprise package. Passing the tiny, densely-built village on the road you would never guess it conceals one of the most exquisite medieval squares anywhere, picturesquely asymmetrical and surrounded by houses that have not changed for centuries. The ensemble has a **church** to match, an architecturally sophisticated 11th-century building with a rare elliptical cupola. A recent restoration, clearing out the dross of a brutal 19th-century remodelling, has uncovered some charming fragments of the original decoration: St Martin on horseback, carved Celtic spirals and neo-Byzantine capitals. *Londres* is a local place-name, and has nothing to do with the big town on the island.

South of St-Martin, in a military zone just off the D 32, a 5000-year-old settlement was discovered at **Cambous** in 1967. For anyone interested in Mediterranean pre-history, this will be a fascinating place to visit. With considerable intelligence and dedication, the archaeologists have made the site into a veritable recreation of ancient life for the benefit of visitors. They have reconstructed one of the communal houses of this 'Fontbouisse civilization', a long stone building with a thatched roof, and gathered together enough artefacts and explanations to make you feel entirely at home among the Fontbouissians. These peaceful folk knew both farming and husbandry, and were just learning about copper tools. They also had a well-developed cultural life, as evidenced by their geometrically-decorated pottery and stone statue-steles (open Jul–15 Sept daily exc Tues, 9–12, 2–6, the rest of the year Sat and Sun only; adm).

From St-Martin, the main D 986 leads northwards towards the Cévennes. From the village of St-Bauzille-de-Putois, there is a steep side road to the **Grotte des Demoiselles**, a cave discovered in 1889 that has one of France's most spectacular displays of pipe-organ stalactites and stalagmites (daily 9:30–12, 2–7; adm). **Ganges**, just up the road, is the only real town in this region, and quite a pleasant one, closed in between the river Hérault and *maquis*-carpeted hills. Once this town was famous for silk stockings. The farmers of the region would raise silkworms in their bedrooms—the delicate creatures needed the cosiest place in the house. Ganges still makes stockings, but now they're nylon. Like most of the Cévennes, this was and remains a mostly Protestant area, and Ganges' only sight is the imposing, peculiar seven-sided Protestant 'temple', built in 1850.

Ganges makes a good base for exploring the natural wonders of this pretty region, between the *garrigue* and the Causse du Larzac. The **Gorges de la Vis** can be followed on the D 25 west of town, passing a waterfall and a 17th-century château (at St-Laurent-le-Minier). The route through the gorges is 34 km long (one-way only); the best parts, after Madières, can only be reached on foot. If you go the whole route, there's a real curiosity at the end, the **Cirque de Navacelles**. A *cirque* looks like a deep lunar crater, though it is in fact a loop dug deep into the limestone of the *garrigue* by the meandering river Vis long ago. There are many in the *causses* and *garrigues* of the Midi, and this is the most striking, with steep, barren walls and a rocky 'island' in the centre; various points along the D 713 offer views down into the *cirque*.

Market Days: Ganges, Tuesday and Friday mornings.

WHERE TO STAY/EATING OUT

St-Martin-de-Londres (34380) hardly seems big enough to support one restaurant; actually there are a few good ones: **Les Muscardins** offers fancy terrines and *pâté*, game dishes, formidable desserts and a selection of the best regional wines (good value on a choice of four menus from 120–300 F, 19 Route des Cévennes, tel 67 55 75 90). Just south of town on the D 986, the **Mas de Loup** exerts itself for a roast leg o'mutton on Sundays; the rest of the week you'll have to get by with *escargots* or frogs' legs (120 F). If you're staying in this region, you'll have to make do with the no-frills **Hôtel des Touristes** on the D 986 (tel 67 55 01 15).

For lunch, after a trip to the Grotte des Demoiselles, there is home cooking at the **Ferme-Auberge Mas Domergue**, 5 km to the east on D 108 at Montoulieu (summer only, call ahead, 67 73 70 88). Open all year, 7 km east of Ganges on D 999 at a place called Moules et Baucels (34190), the **Ferme-Auberge Domaine de Blancardy** has homemade *confits* and *pâté*, also some rooms, in a distinctive old *mas*; they can arrange horses, hang-gliding and other activities (tel 67 73 94 94 or 67 73 13 13).

Ganges itself (34190) has only simple food and accommodation; the ****Hôtel de la Poste** is inexpensive and comfortable (8 Plan de l'Ormeau; tel 67 73 85 88). For dinner, just south of town in Cazilhac, the **Auberge des Norias** offers trout *cévenole* and other mountain favourites (120–150 F; Route de Lodève, by the bridge, tel 67 73 55 90). If you're staying around the Cirque de Navacelles, there are some surprising luxuries in the wilderness; the ******Château de Madières** (34190) is an impressive, rustic castle begun in the 1100s, completely modernized inside; posh and expensive, with restaurant (in the centre of Madières, tel 67 73 84 03). A more reasonable choice would be the ***Hôtel des Gorges de la Vis** at **Gorniès** (34190); at least stop for the restaurant, where river crayfish and game dishes are the specialities (dinner 110–160 F, tel 67 73 85 05).

 Coteaux du Languedoc
By the time Caesar conquered Gaul, the vineyards in the hills and the great plain of Languedoc (north and west of modern Montpellier) were already well established, thanks to the Greeks. Amphorae full of wine sent back to Rome met with such fervent demands for more that the winemakers back in Italy went to court to curtail the competition—history's first round of the great French-Italian wine battle. The Gauls won this one, perhaps because they hired the oratory of Cicero.

Zoom ahead to the 18th century, when the Canal du Midi made it easy to ship wine to northern Europe and the New World through Bordeaux. The region boomed; American presidents were proud to serve the wines of Languedoc at the White House. But boom turned to bust in the phylloxera epidemics of the 1880s. In the subsequent depression, recovery was hastened by grafting, and vintners, in response to the increased demand of the new industrial society, set their sights on the mass production of a soul-less wine dubbed *bibine du Midi*, competing with tankers of high-octane plonk from Algeria, and graded as if it were crude oil, by its alcohol content—as French rotgut is to this day.

All of this is only worth mentioning to help the newcomer better savour the revelation that now awaits in the bottles of Coteaux du Languedoc (AOC since 1963). The post-war return to Gallo-Roman techniques and craftsmanship have so improved matters that French oenophiles predict the *appellation* will be *the* wine of the next decade. A huge confusing region that takes in pockets from Lunel to Narbonne-Plage, it has been divided into 12 specialized micro-areas (*terroirs*) and three *crus*. The Pic St-Loup area produces red wines of character that can take considerable ageing (such as the 87 of **Domaine de La Roque**, at Fontanès, tel 67 55 34 47). Or try the melting reds of the **Cave Coopérative les Coteaux de Montferrand**, at St-Mathieu-de-Tréviers, tel 67 55 20 22. Just west of Montpellier, at Lavérune, **Château St-Georges d'Orques**, tel 67 27 60 89, produces fine red wines with a scent of dried herbs.

The Valley of the Hérault

TOURIST INFORMATION
St-Guilhem-le-Désert (31450): At the *mairie*, tel 67 57 42 50.
Gignac (31450): Place Général Claparède, tel 67 57 58 83.
Clermont-l'Hérault (34800): Place Jean-Jaurès, tel 67 96 23 86.

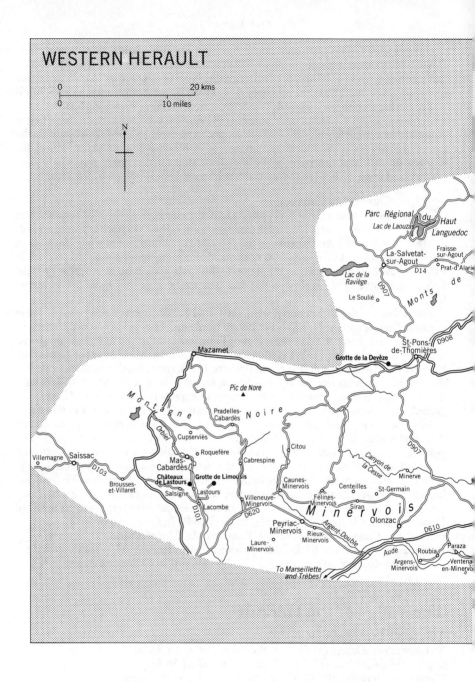

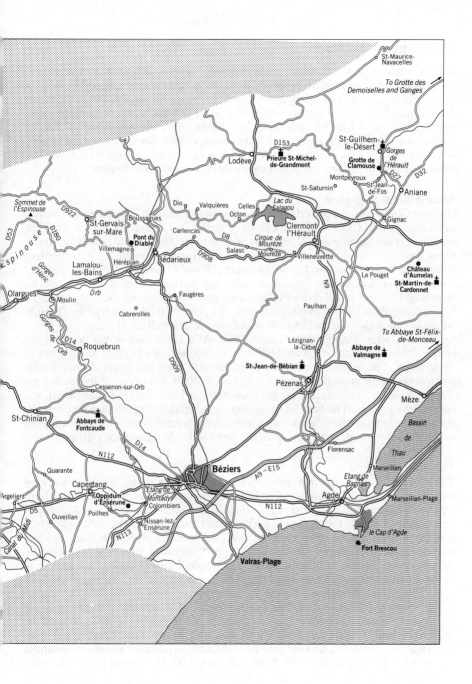

St-Guilhem-le-Désert

'Desert' might seem a little unfair to this rosemary-scented jumble of *garrigue* around St-Guilhem, northwest of Montpellier; there are plenty of green, shady spots for a picnic, and even forests of pines. But 'desert', in French or English, originally meant *deserted*, and this is still as lonely a region as it was when the hermit St Guilhem came here, in the reign of Charlemagne. Little has changed since. Besides being a delightful place to visit, St-Guilhem is a living history lesson, evoking the time when the 'desert' was a troubled frontier between Frank and Saracen, and later, when it became a key cultural outpost in the process of making the Midi Christian and French.

Saint William Pug-nose

Guilhem Court-Nez, the powerful Frankish Count of Toulouse, Aquitaine and Orange, was a grandson of Charles Martel, cousin, liegeman and friend to Charlemagne. For over thirty years, he campaigned from the Atlantic to the Alps, mostly against the Arabs, whose great wave of 8th-century expansion through Spain had washed up as far north as Poitou and Narbonne. Another of Guilhem's friends was Benedict, the monastic reformer from Aniane (see below); Benedict too had once been a warrior, and he convinced Guilhem to follow his example and renounce the world. Guilhem spent the last six years of his life in a humble cell here, at a place near the gorges of the Hérault, originally called Gellone, and was canonized soon after his death in 812.

And soon after that, pilgrims began to visit. As a vanquisher of the heathen, St-Guilhem was a popular saint with the Spaniards, and with northerners on their way to Compostela. The original community of hermit cells grew into a wealthy monastery; construction of the great abbey church began about 1050. Already in decline during the Wars of Religion, it was sacked by the Protestants in 1569—its celebrated library was burnt in the process. The final indignity came not during the Revolution, surprisingly, but a decade before, when clerics from Lodève and other towns succeeded in having the monastery suppressed, apportioning its treasures and holy relics among themselves.

The Abbey Church

The little village of St-Guilhem is stretched on the edge of a ravine. Its one street being too narrow for traffic, a parallel road and car park has been built on the other side; from here you'll have a good view of its rugged stone houses and their gardens, little changed from medieval times. From the car park you can cross over to the abbey church, a remarkably grand and lovely specimen of Lombard architecture, with its blind arcading and trademark cross-shaped window. The best part, the broad, arcaded apse, recalls the contemporary churches of Milan or Pavia. The façade, facing an ancient, colossal plane tree in the village square, is somewhat blighted by an ungainly tower of cheap stone, built in the 1300s more for defence than for bell-ringing.

The interior, lofty and dark, has lost almost all of its original decoration. Some fragments of frescoes survive in the side chapels, and niches in the pillars around the choir once held the relics of St-Guilhem and a bit of the True Cross, a gift from Charlemagne. The rest has been removed to the adjacent **cloister** and the **museum** in the restored refectory (daily, 8–12, 2:30–6:30, Sun 8:30–11, 2:30–6; adm). There are some real treasures of 12th-century sculpture here, including the sarcophagus of St

Guilhem and the church's altar, in marble and enamel inlay. The cloister itself is largely ruined, and most of its capitals have ended up at the Cloisters Museum in New York.

On the village's main street, some modest Romanesque palaces survive from the 1200s; at the opposite end, facing the D 4 at the entrance to the village, the church of **St-Laurent** has another fine apse like that of St-Guilhem; it looks a bit sad and confused now, housing the offices of the *mairie*. More medieval relics can be seen along the Hérault: medieval mills, for grain and for oak bark (used in tanning leather), set near the modern trout hatcheries by the river; and 4 km to the south, a massive stone bridge of

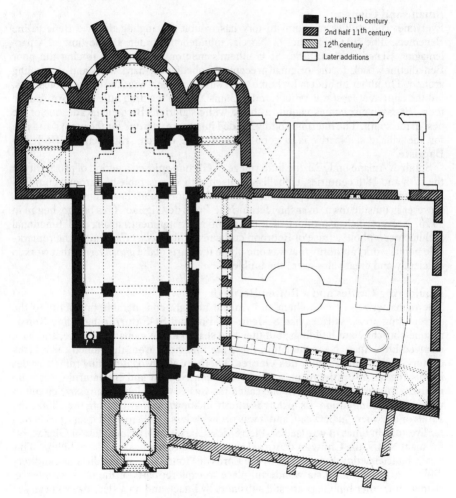

1st half 11th century
2nd half 11th century
12th century
Later additions

Church plan of St-Guilhem Le Désert

1030, the **Pont du Diable**. The hills around St-Guilhem make interesting exploring on foot: a ruined castle and other fortifications, and the **Rue du Bout du Monde**, a road that leads from the back end of the village to a lovely spot with a flowing spring. The steep **Gorges de l'Hérault** extend on both sides of the village, and can be followed on the D 4.

With all this eroded limestone about, you would expect caves, and there are several. The most impressive, just to the south, is the **Grotte de Clamouse**, one of the big tourist attractions of the Hérault (daily 9–12, 2–6; continuously in July and August; Sun only in winter, 2–6; guided tour; adm).

Aniane and Gignac

Everyone who studies medieval history has trouble untangling the two Benedictine Benedicts. The first, Benedict of Norcia, founded the order. In the time of Charlemagne, Benedict of **Aniane**, St Guilhem's mentor, reformed it, forcing the poor Benedictines back to the original precepts of obedience, hard work and no fooling around. The abbey he built in his home town was thoroughly wrecked by the Protestants, but the church at least was rebuilt under Louis XIV. In the drab little village of Aniane today, **St-Sauveur** comes as quite a shock, with its glorious Baroque façade, one of the best in the south. The interior is oddly divided into two parts: one for the monks and one for the villagers. Nearby is a good Romanesque church, 12th-century **St-Jean-Baptiste**.

South of Aniane on D 32, the little village of **Gignac** enjoyed a period of prosperity in the 17th and 18th centuries, embellishing itself with an ensemble of Baroque churches and palaces to go with its pretty medieval Tour de l'Horloge; its best-known monument, however is outside town, over the Hérault: the **Pont de Gignac**. This bridge, begun in 1776, is every inch a product of the Age of Enlightenment, strong and functional architecture without a trace of Bourbon curlicues. The *Ponts et Chaussées*—the remarkable public works authority that was one of the few parts of the *ancien régime* that worked efficiently and creatively—were the builders.

Mouldering Castles and a Rotten Borough

The monasteries of St-Guilhem and Aniane brought considerable prosperity to the surrounding areas. Villages like **St-Jean-de-Fos** and **St-Saturnin** have fine Romanesque churches and buildings; but they also shared in the monastic decline, and have changed little since. Near the latter, there are fine views from the ruined early 11th-century castle on the **Rocher des Vierges**. There are also two fascinating ruined castles in this region. **Montpeyroux**, a village between St-Jean and St-Saturnin, grew up around a mysterious abandoned pile called the Castel Viel, a long, impressive circuit of walls with nothing inside. Its history is utterly unknown; it may be from the 1000s, the 1500s or anywhere in between, and it was probably less a military post than a protection for livestock in times of war (see St-Pierre-des-Clars, p. 404). Southeast of Gignac, off the main N 109, the **Château d'Aumelas** occupies a romantically isolated hilltop. This castle, built sometime before 1036 by the Lords of Montpellier, is on a dirt track and very difficult to reach, but it's a wonderful place to explore; parts of the noble residence, chapels and other buildings are still substantially intact, and on a clear day you can see the Mediterranean from its walls.

The castle is located in one of the biggest completely blank spots on the French map. It is part of a real, old-fashioned rotten borough, a commune without a town and hardly any inhabitants; it does have a mayor, who has a say in deciding representatives to the French Senate—two centuries after the Revolution, such things are still common in rural France (wilder anachronisms are not unknown; this commune still seems to owe some sort of feudal dues to the British crown, by way of their ancestors in the House of Orange—Aumelas is that noble house's place of origin). Another attraction in this 'Commune d'Aumelas', south of the château on a rocky track, is a beautiful and austere Romanesque church, **St-Martin-de-Cardonnet**, set amidst the ruins of the monastery that once surrounded it. To the west, back towards civilization on the D 139, **Le Pouget** is home to the colossal **Dolmen Gallardet**, just south of the village.

Clermont-l'Hérault

Not to be confused with Clermont-Ferrand, home of the insufferable, eminently deflatable Michelin man, this Clermont is a peacefully bovine and prosperous town, living off the wine and table grapes of this more fertile part of the Hérault valley. Its medieval centre, on a hilltop, is large and well-preserved, including a tall and graceful Gothic church, **St-Paul**, begun in 1276. The **castle** around which the town grew up is also in good shape, including the gates, prisons and keep. Clermont has the big weekly market in this region, every Wednesday.

West of Clermont, you leave the green valley for more peculiar landscapes, around the **Lac du Salagou**, a large man-made sheet of water surrounded by hills that is much more natural-looking and attractive than most artificial lakes; it has become a popular recreation spot, well-stocked with fish and surrounded by camping-sites and picnic spots. Circumnavigating it, you'll pass some singular cliffs and weirdly eroded rock formations, and also the village of **Celles** on the water's edge, now almost completely abandoned. The oddest bits lie to the south, in the **Cirque de Mourèze**, a long, stretched-out *cirque* with the dusty village of Mourèze and its ruined castle at the centre. In this pocket badlands, surreal rock formations pop up everywhere; they are old, familiar friends to the people of Mourèze, who have given them names like the 'frog' and the 'sphinx'.

Between the Cirque and Clermont lies **Villeneuvette**, founded only in 1670. The 'little new town' was a manufacturing centre for *londrins*, printed linen cloth. Louis XIV's minister Colbert oversaw its development, and after the Revolution it passed into the hands of a pious textile magnate named Casimir Maistre. Though the works are now closed (since 1954) Villeneuvette is still the very picture of an old French paternalistic company town. The manufacturies remain—behind the gate with the big inscription *Honneur au Travail*—along with some of the workers' housing, school, church, warehouses and gardens. Lately, artists and artisans have been recolonizing the place, and there are art galleries and handicraft shops.

North of Clermont, the N 9 heads into the *causses* of deepest France, passing **Lodève**, a comfortable, somewhat isolated town wedged between two rivers. Like Clermont-l'Hérault, Lodève has a Gothic church as its chief monument; **St-Fulcran**, named after a 9th-century bishop who became the city's patron, was begun in 1280, and turned into a fortress during the troubles of the Hundred Years War. Lodève was a Roman town, and its **Musée Municipal** on Rue Cardinal Fleury has finds from that age, along with dinosaur bones and fossil trilobites. This area's peculiar geology has made it a rich mine for palaeontologists. Another sort of mine—France's biggest uranium deposit, can be seen to the southeast, a gigantic and eerie open pit near the village of St-Martin.

East of Lodève, a narrow but very pretty country road, the D 153, takes you 9 km to the **Priory of St-Michel-de-Grandmont**. The Order of Grandmont, founded in the Limousin in the 1100s, was a monastic reform movement like that of Cluny or Cîteaux; it faded away five centuries ago and no one even remembers it today. This priory is its only surviving monument, gradually restored by private owners over the last century. The Bec family, who own it now, support a troupe of rare Rhove goats; part of the goatherds' job is to give guided tours of the place (15 Jun through Sept, otherwise Sun only; 3 pm; adm). The austere church and cloister, begun in the 12th century, are remarkably well-preserved, but the real attraction here is a group of outlandish **dolmens** in the grounds, colossal works shaped like cèpe mushrooms, dating from about 2000 BC.

Market Day: Clermont-l'Hérault, Wednesday.

WHERE TO STAY/EATING OUT

In **St-Guilhem** (34150), rooms are unfortunately scarce; if you're stuck in town try the *****Taverne de l'Escuelle** on Rue Val de Bellone (tel 67 52 72 05). There is a comfortable motel with a pool at Aniane (34150), the ****Hostellerie St-Benoit**, which also has a good restaurant, menus 80–200 F (on the road to St Guilhem, tel 67 57 71 63, closed Jan, Feb). For lunch in St-Guilhem, climb up a block from the main street to the *crêperie*/restaurant **Trois Voutes**: lamb in a cream garlic sauce is good, also stuffed haunch of rabbit (menus 100, 150 F).

Try to be around **Gignac** at dinner-time; the **Ferme-Auberge Le Pélican** does a wonderful 90 F menu—stuffed *pintade* (guinea-hen) and homemade desserts (at Domaine du Pélican, tel 67 57 68 92). Or for something a little more ambitious, **Capion**, in town on the Blvd de l'Esplanade. Run by the same family for almost a century, this popular restaurant with an outdoor terrace eschews simple local cooking in favour of complex seafood fantasies like salmon *à trois façons* (prepared three different ways). There is an outdoor terrace, and also a ****hotel** with eight simple rooms (tel 67 57 50 83, menus 150–300 F).

Clermont-l'Hérault (34800) will be the most likely place to find a room in this region if you haven't booked ahead: there are four modest hotels, including the well-kept and sympathetic *****Terminus**, in the centre on the Allée Roger Salengro (tel 67 96 10 08). The best of the restaurants is **L'Arlequin**, in the medieval centre, on Place St-Paul: smoked trout, *confits*, and good Faugères wine, in a refined candle-lit room (good bargain, with 80 and 110 F menus, tel 67 96 37 47).

In **Villeneuvette**, ****La Source** makes a refreshing stopover for summer visitors to the mountains, a rural retreat with a pool and tennis (open Easter to 1 Oct, tel 67 96 05 07, with an impressive restaurant, specializing in salmon and truffles, 140–240 F menus). Around Salagou and the Cirque de Mourèze, the **Ferme-Auberge de la Vallée du Salagou** offers a filling 66 F menu, with grilled lamb or steaks and wine from nearby Octon (west of Mourèze to Salasc, continuing west on the D 8, tel 67 96 15 62).

The Northern Fringes: Monts de l'Espinouse

If you continue along the northern fringes of the Hérault, you'll get an idea of what France is like for the next hundred miles northwards, through Aveyron and Lozère into the Auvergne—rough canyons and rough villages, an occasional dusting of snow, trout streams and chestnut groves. The natural beauty of the Espinouse did it little good in former times; even forty years ago, this was a poor area, losing its population rapidly to the cities. The creation of the Parc Régional du Haut Languedoc in the 60s has made all the difference; *tourisme verte*, as the French call it—hiking and canoeing or just relaxing under the pines—increases every year. It's no strain on the kind and hospitable folk in the villages, and right now the Espinouse is as happy and content as a patch of mountains can be.

TOURIST INFORMATION
Bédarieux (34600): Rue St-Alexandre, tel 67 95 08 79.
Lamalou-les-Bains (34240): tel 67 95 70 91.
Olargues (34390): tel 67 97 71 26.
St-Pons-de-Thomières: on the N 112 (Av. de Castres), tel 67 97 06 65; for the Parc Régional, there is a **Maison du Parc** on Rue du Cloître, tel 67 97 02 10.

Bédarieux and Lamalou-les-Bains

The only big road in this region, the D 908, runs west from Clermont-l'Hérault across the base of the mountains, following the valleys of the Orb and the Jaur. The first town on the way is **Bédarieux**, a humble enough agricultural centre. Humility stops, however, with Bédarieux's famous son, the 19th-century painter Pierre-Auguste Cot, one of the kitsch-realist artists so popular with the academicians, the sort that made the Impressionist revolution necessary. They've named the main square after him, and you can see his work (including an incredible *Prometheus in chains*) in the town's **Maison des Arts**, along with some fossils, railroad memorabilia and exhibits recreating country life and costumes in the old days.

Lamalou-les-Bains, 10 km further west, is a sort of museum in itself. A thermal spa since the 1600s, Lamalou made it big when the railroad came through in 1868. The prosperity of the next three decades—dukes and counts, famous actresses, even a Sultan of Morocco checked in for the cure—built it into a sweet little resort of *Belle Epoque* hotels and villas, cafés and a casino. Today Lamalou is bidding to become fashionable once again. Its restored 19th-century centre makes a perfect setting for the big event on its calendar: an important festival of operettas (and opera) that lasts throughout the summer. Inside the cemetery, on the eastern edge of town, is an exceptional Romanesque church with a sculpted portal and apse, **St-Pierre-de-Rhèdes**.

Market Day: Lamalou-les-Bains, Tuesday.

GETTING AROUND

Either of these towns is a good base for exploring the eastern half of the Espinouse. North of Bédarieux, the upper valley of the Orb starts out plagued by industry and power lines, but you can escape into the hills on either side, to **Dio** or to **Boussagues**, both delightful medieval villages with ruined castles. Persevere northwards, and you'll come to the **Gorges de l'Orb**, ending in a big dam and artificial lake at Avène. East of Bédarieux, there's another pretty village, **Carlencas**, famous for chick-peas; to the south is **Faugères**, centre of a small wine region (see below). And to the west, towards Lamalou, you can visit a 300-year-old bell foundry, one of the few left in France, at **Hérépian** (Fonderie Granier, on the D 908). From here there is another medieval detour, north on the D 922 to **Villemagne**. Villemagne-*l'Argentière* it was, in the 1100s when a Benedictine abbey here looked after a rich silver mine, owned by the Trencavels of Béziers and Carcassonne. Most of the abbey and its fortifications are in ruins, and the parts that are left still, are sadly neglected: two lovely churches, Romanesque **St-Grégoire** and Gothic **St-Majan**, along with a richly decorated 13th-century building believed to have been the mint, the **Hôtel des Monnaies**. Just to the north of Villemagne is a humpbacked medieval bridge called, like that of St-Guilhem and so many others, the **Pont du Diable**—it must have been hard for the medieval peasant imagination to see how such things could stand up without divine or infernal aid.

Continuing west from Lamalou, at Moulin, the Orb turns south, away from the road; there's a choice of directions and of scenery: the **Gorges d'Heric** to the north, a hiker's paradise with no roads, and the **Gorges de l'Orb** to the south, leading towards **Roquebrun**. Sheltered by the mountains, this village grows mimosas and likes to call itself the 'Little Nice'. And south of Roquebrun, it's a clear shot along to Béziers and the sea, with nothing to detain you along the way—except **Cessenon**, and we only mention this village, set among the cypresses of the Orb, for the story of its name. On some obscure occasion, the Devil (the same one who built all the bridges) appeared to the village bell-ringer while he was doing his job. Like any downstairs tenant, he must have been bothered by the noise. He shouted 'CESSE!'. And the bell-ringer replied 'NON!'.

The Parc Régional du Haut Languedoc

The loveliest village of the Espinouse, **Olargues** is dominated by two medieval monuments, a striking 11th-century bell tower, set up above on a hill, and a humpbacked bridge. The next town is **St-Pons-de-Thomières**, the little capital of the Espinouse, surrounded by forests. St-Pons probably gets more snow than anywhere in Languedoc east of the Pyrenees, and it has a decidedly Alpine air about it. Its landmarks are its **cathedral**, with a Romanesque portal and a tremendous 18th-century organ, and its **Musée Préhistorique** (May–Sept, daily 10–12, 3–6; otherwise Wed, Sat, Sun 2–5; adm). Never suspecting they were in a future Regional Park, Neolithic people made St-Pons and the Espinouse one of their favourite haunts in France; archaeologists go so far as to speak of a *civilisation saintponienne*. This museum documents their career comprehensively, but the star attractions are the **statue menhirs,** the true cultural totems of this part of the Mediterranean, similar to those found in the Gard, in Tuscany and in Corsica, from 3000 BC to Roman times.

St-Pons is the perfect base for visiting the **Parc Régional du Haut Languedoc,** spread over a wide area of the Espinouse, on the borders of the Hérault, Tarn and Aveyron. It's an extremely well organized park; all you need do is travel up the D 907–D 169 to the **Maison du Parc** at Prat-d'Alaric, a restored farm with exhibits and presentations on the park and the life and traditions of its inhabitants (open regularly in July and August, 9–12, 2–6, otherwise check first at the Maison du Parc in St-Pons). There is a wide choice of hiking trails in the mountains, through wild areas that have, among other things, what is said to be the largest population of *mouflons* in Europe. From Prat-d'Alaric, the valley of the Agout spreads across the heart of the park; the roads that follow it, the D 14 and D 53, make a delightful tour, through picturesque villages like **La Salvetat-sur-Agout** and **Fraisse-sur-Agout,** and continuing on towards the summit of the Espinouse (1113 m). A little further on—over the Lauze pass on the D 180—there is a stone enclosure, a vestige of a Roman army camp, and beyond—on the D 922—**St-Gervais-sur-Mare,** full of medieval and Renaissance buildings; an enjoyable short walk from St-Gervais takes you to the ruined village of Neyran, with a 12th-century church.

Market Days: La Salvetat, Thursday and Sunday.

Much closer to St-Pons, there is the **Grotte de la Devèze,** another gorgeous cave of delicate stalactites and shining crystals (Mar through Sept, daily guided tours at 1; otherwise call 67 97 03 24). To climb down from the Espinouse, there is the choice of the D 907 out of St-Pons towards Minerve, or the N 112 for Béziers and the Canal du Midi (see below). On this route, you'll pass through **St-Chinian** and its wine region; about 9 km east of that village is the Romanesque **Abbey of Fontcaude.**

Faugères and St-Chinian

It's the mix of limestone and schist in this beautiful mountainous corner of Languedoc that creates the dark, beefy red wines of Faugères and St-Chinian. The French currently view these wines as the ascendant stars of the country's lesser known regions. This is borne out by the concentration of talented winemakers to emerge from the area. The wines require a few years in the cellar to reveal their true personalities; AOC Faugères has a high percentage of syrah, as well as grenache, old carignan stock, and mourvèdre grapes—the 86 is ready to drink now, but look upon the excellent 88s as a future investment. Pick up a few bottles at **Domaine Gilbert Alquier,** Rte de Pézenas, in Faugères, tel 67 78 06 09; **Château des Estanilles,** in Cabrerolles (call ahead, tel 67 90 29 25), which produces delightful variations in all three colours (including a fine white Coteaux de Languedoc of macabeu and grenache); and in Laurens, the **Cave Coopérative de Laurens,** tel 67 90 28 23, where the wines are aged in oak casks and the prices are as refreshing as the wine itself.

St-Chinian encompasses 20 villages, but you can try nearly all the labels of fruity, dark cherry red St-Chinian (especially the 88s and 89s) at St-Chinian's **Maison des Vins**, tel 67 38 11 69. Or visit the **Château Moulinier**, Rue de la Digue in St-Chinian, tel 67 38 14 21, or **Château Cazals** in Cressenon, tel 67 89 63 15; here the complex 89 is the best buy.

WHERE TO STAY/EATING OUT

The *Belle Epoque* survives in **Lamalou-les-Bains** (34240), at the ****Hôtel Mas**, across from the casino on Avenue Charcot: furnishings and murals circa 1900, and a restaurant that will please anyone fond of wild mushrooms—cèpes and morels in everything, 80–190 F, tel 67 95 62 22. Between Olargues and St-Pons, on the D 908, the *****Domaine de Rieumégé** (34390) is a 17th-century estate with an excellent restaurant in its restored grange: seafood, *boeuf en croûte* and a big wine list (menus 100–200 F). Also 12 nice rooms, pool and tennis—and a separate farmhouse with its own pool for a big splurge, tel 67 97 73 99.

There are plenty of nice places to stay around **St-Pons**—out in the country, with friendly proprietors who can help you get started with mountain sports or hunting or whatever you want to do in the Parc Régional. At **Riols**, to the north, the ****Auberge de Cabaretou** is an old coach-stop, thoroughly modernized with 10 lovely rooms, and a good, simple restaurant with a vaulted dining hall and outside terrace, 120–180 F (tel 67 97 02 31). Also near Riols, on the Route de Lizame, the **Ferme-Auberge St-Aulary** would fit the same description, with a few rooms in a wooded setting; the restaurant is exceptional, with an outdoor terrace and home-cooking: trout *en papillote* and duck, and venison when they have it (90 F menu; tel 67 97 01 93). To do the Espinouse in style, there is the *****Hôtel Château de Ponderach**, expensive and beautifully furnished rooms, some with individual terraces, with restaurant; 180–220 F (Route de Narbonne, south of St-Pons; tel 67 97 02 57). In St-Pons itself,there is the simple and adequate ***Bel Horizon** (Route d'Artenac; tel 67 97 01 31).

Up in the park, 6 km from La Salvetat at **Le Soulié**, the **Ferme-Auberge La Pagnérié-le-Haut** offers a 70 F menu with homemade *pâtés* and plenty of home-raised poultry (tel 67 97 26 65). And in **Fraisse-sur-Agout**, there's the hotel-restaurant ***Auberge de l'Espinouse** (Rue des Frènes; tel 67 97 63 10), with outdoor dining and mountain specialities plus some seafood—including *écrevisses* (freshwater crayfish), a popular item in these parts.

The Hérault Coast: La Grande Motte to Agde

West of the Camargue, the lagoons continue for another 80 km, dotting the coast like beads on a string. Unlike the Camargue, almost all of this coast is easily accessible by car; there are beaches and resorts in abundance, and attractions like salty Sète and medieval Maguelone and Agde. Only a few kilometres from the walls of Aigues-Mortes, the Hérault coast begins with a bang, with an uncanny skyline of tall holiday ziggurats, a resort town straight from science fiction. (See map p. 342).

TOURIST INFORMATION
La Grande Motte (34280): Place du 1 October, tel 67 56 62 62.

La Grande Motte

At the same time as the Fos complex was going up on the eastern edge of the Camargue, something even stranger was happening on the west. It almost seems as if France's planners wanted an appropriate book-end to Fos's weird mill furnaces and refinery towers. Making the Languedoc resort plan in 1963, they decided that one of the new holiday towns was to be boldly modernist, and they picked the 'big lump', an empty swath of sand on the Gulf of Aigues-Mortes for the experiment.

Jean Balladur, the original architect, and his successors gave them more than they bargained for. La Grande Motte looks like no other resort in the world: its hotels and apartments rising in colourful triangles and roller-coaster curves, its public buildings in jarring, amoeboid shapes like a permanent 60s World's Fair. The 'modernism' of the Motte is more surface than substance; there are no real innovations in architecture or design. The buildings themselves, like all the experiments of the kitschy 60s, already look a bit dated. But La Grande Motte is a great success as a resort, a proper city with room for almost 90,000 space-age holidaymakers, and it continues to grow despite its high prices.

The fun starts at **Point Zéro**, the name Balladur whimsically gave the central square on the waterfront. In season little 'train' tours around the town start from here. The first clutches of ziggurats (the Grande Mottois prefer to call them *pyramides*) rise to the west, around the marina; to the east are the outlandish buildings of the civic centre, including the Mairie and congress hall. Another of Balladur's creations, the **Porte de St-Jean** on the edge of town, includes a sort of sun clock that marks the summer solstice. Beyond that, the planners ensure you will be entertained to death, with broad beaches, golf courses, marinas, a casino and all the rest. The complex has expanded to envelop the old fishing village of **Le Grau-du-Roi**, just to the east.

For you fogies, a more old-fashioned beach holiday can be spent at **Palavas-les-Flots**, 15 km down the coast. Built around a narrow canal full of boats, Palavas is an endearingly humble resort where grocery clerks from Montpellier come to flash their polyester in the frowzy waterfront casino. It has a wonderfully casual air about it, and some 8 km of good beaches. Inland, towards Montpellier, you can visit Roman necropolises and a small archaeological museum in the village of **Lattes**.

Maguelone

To balance La Grande Motte, a town without a history, here we have a history without a town. Maguelone, 4 km from Palavas, may have begun as a Phoenician or Etruscan trading post. It prospered under the Romans and Visigoths, becoming the seat of a bishop. After that the history is obscure. Old maps show the place as 'Port Sarrasin', suggesting Arab corsairs were using it as a base in the 700s, and there is a record of Charles Martel coming down from Paris to chase them out, destroying the town in the process.

Maguelone still had one attraction—salt—and the rights were still owned by a powerful and progressive multinational, the Church. In the 1030s, when demand was high, a cleric named Arnaulf oversaw the town's rebuilding and added a monastery. The enterprise prospered; Urban II, the first of many popes to visit (1096), called Maguelone the 'second church of Rome', and gave its restored bishops special privileges. Later, Maguelone became a papal holding, a key base both politically and ideologically in the difficult 12th century. It gradually dwindled after that, and the see moved to Montpellier in 1536. Maguelone passes out of history with Mehmet Effendi, the Turkish ambassador, who had to spend a few weeks in quarantine here in 1721; he seems to have enjoyed it, and he left a letter with the seal of the Sublime Porte thanking the monks for their hospitality.

Though almost no trace of the town remains today, the impressive **cathedral** was saved from ruin and restored in the 1870s (open daily, 10–6:30, until 8 in summer). Built, and built well, by Lombard masons in the 1170s, it is an austere building. The main decorative feature—reliefs around the main portal—show Christ in Majesty with the four Evangelists; below are Peter (with the keys) and Paul (with a sword). Inside, there are fragments of the bishops' tombs, inscriptions and furnishings, and you may climb the bell tower for views down the coast.

Except at the height of summer, Maguelone makes a peaceful place to escape to; there are plenty of beaches around it, a bit rocky but good for sea shells. The lagoons in this stretch of coast, from La Grande Motte to Frontignan, are rich in waterfowl (you may see flamingos) but little else. Most are stagnant and lack oxygen; decomposing water plants in hot summers cause a phenomenon called the *malaïgue*, making the air smell like rotten eggs. From Maguelone, you'll need to backtrack to Palavas and continue around the landward side of the lagoons, rejoining the coast at **Frontignan**, an industrial town with a good 12th-century church.

WHERE TO STAY/EATING OUT

The bad news about **La Grande Motte** (34280) is that you can't stay there; all the hotels in the centre are overpriced to the point of absurdity, excepting the simple *****Copacabana**, a bit far from the action on the Route des Plages (tel 67 56 51 01; closed 15 Sept–15 April). ****Hôtel Altéa** is the splashy status address on the Big Lump, looming over the marina like a concrete refugee from Miami Beach; charmless and soberingly expensive, but a chance to meet that segment of the fast crowd who choose to avoid the Riviera (Rue du Port; tel 67 56 90 81). Restaurants in La Grande Motte can seem a bit formal and indifferent. **Chez Fabrice**, on the marina (tel 67 56 75 93; menus 145 F and up), is a splurge for elaborate seafood; they specialize in *langoustes* and several different varieties of *bouillabaisse* and other fish stews.

Palavas (34250), on the other hand, could not begin to affect any pretensions: watch the Montpellier grocery clerks, freshly cleaned from the casino, drift into **La Maguelone** on Rue Maguelone for pizza or paella (about 70 F). Palavas has some gratifying, no-nonsense seafood joints, worth a detour: **La Maison du Pêcheur**, on the canal; a 90 F menu or more for serious shellfish and lobster, (tel 67 68 01 68; Quai Cunq); or **L'Escale**, north of the canal on the seafront: *sèche à la rouille* for starters, or extravaganzas like the mixed shellfish plate they call *panache de coquillages*—the bill can go up to 300 F before you recover your reason (Blvd Sarrail, tel 67 68 24 17). Palavas has plenty of inexpensive, undistinguished hotels; for something special, go inland a bit, to **Lattes** (34970) and the ****Mas de Couran**, set in a beautiful park, with swimming-pool and restaurant, menus 110–210 F (Route de Fréjorgues; tel 67 65 57 57).

Sète

After the glitzy candy-land of the Côte d'Azur, and the empty spaces that follow, you may have despaired by now of finding anything really *Mediterranean* on these shores, some place where sea, sky and people's lives fit together; you can find it almost anywhere along the coast of Spain, Italy or Greece, but in southern France it is as rare as snowmen. Just in time, there's gritty, salty, workaday Sète, France's biggest Mediterranean fishing port. What could be more romantic? In Sète, you can stroll along the Canal Maritime and watch businesslike freighters carry French sunflower and rape-seed oil to every corner of the globe, along with dusty cement boats, gigantic tankers of Algerian natural gas (if one ever goes off, it will take the whole town with it) and Algerian wine (marginally less dangerous), and rusty trawlers jammed full of woebegone sardines. After that, perhaps a leisurely tour of the city's artistic monuments. Go ahead and try; in this infant city, younger even than Boston or New York, there isn't a single one.

For entertainment, there are the sailors' bars, or you might try one of the **boat tours** (along the Quai de la Résistance) through the Bassin de Thau, with a stop at an oyster farm. Or take in an American football match, and watch the Sète Praetorians joust with the dreaded Bastia Black Heads from Corsica. If you can stand a little modern madness, Sète will be great fun. It's an attractive town, laced with canals, and livelier and more colourful than any place on the coast, save only Marseille.

TOURIST INFORMATION
60 Grand Rue Mario Roustan; tel 67 74 71 71.

Along the Grand Canal

The city's arms show a field of *fleurs-de-lis* with a whale—*cetus* in Latin—one of the possible explanations for the name, which is first mentioned in a Carolingian document of 814. In 1666, Louis XIV's minister, Colbert, began construction of the port, the terminus for the Canal du Midi (see p. 383), which was begun in the same year. In 1673 the new town was declared a free port. The first English came to visit in 1710, occupying the city during the War of the Spanish Succession. Little has happened since. Despite its booming port, Sète never grew into a major city; hedged between Mont St-Clair, the lagoons and the sea, there simply isn't room.

Sète should be the twin city of Livorno (Leghorn) in Italy. Both grew up at the same time; both have canals (Sète likes to call itself the 'Venice of Languedoc') and a winsome architectural anonymity. And they have both made their offbeat contributions to modern culture; Livorno was the birthplace of Modigliani, Sète of the poet Paul Valéry, and the late singer-composer Georges Brassens.

The bustling centre of Sète is its 'Grand Canal', the **Canal de Sète**, lined with quays where the ambience ranges from boat-yards and ship chandlers to banks and boutiques.

375

A block west, on Place Aristide Briand in front of the Mairie, Sète has what is undoubtedly the **world's biggest cast-bronze octopus**, writhing over a modern fountain. At the southern end of the canal, the **Vieux Port** handles most of the fishing fleet, as well as offering tourist fishing boats and excursions around the Thau lagoon. If you see a particularly sleek-looking sailboat (or perhaps a catamaran) it may be France's next entry in the America's Cup; the boatyards for this serious but as yet frustrated national cause are right here, on the Môle St-Louis. From the Vieux Port it's a bit of a climb up to the **Cimetière Marin**, celebrated in a famous poem by Paul Valéry, who was buried here in 1945. The adjacent **Musée Paul Valéry** contains exhibits on the poet, and on the history of Sète, as well as a good collection of modern paintings (daily exc Tues, 9–12, 2–6). Further out in the harbour, **Fort St-Pierre**, much damaged in World War II, was built in 1710 to keep out the pesky English.

Bassin de Thau

Rising above the city, **Mont St-Clair** used to be the Sunday promenade of the Sètois; it still has fine views up and down the coast, though much of the hill has been covered by suburban developments. Beyond this extends the Bassin de Thau, one of the largest lagoons along the Mediterranean shore. There have always been salt-pans here, though today most of the lagoon has found a more lucrative employment as a huge oyster and mussel farm (you can learn more than you ever cared to know about the business at the 'Musée de la Conchyliculture' in Bouzigues, north of Sète).

There are two roads south from Sète; taking the coastal route you'll pass 15 km of unbroken, nearly perfect **beaches**. Since there is no room for development, this is your best chance on the entire coast to find some peacefully empty beach space, even in the height of summer. At the southern end, the beach piles up into an expanse of partly overgrown dunes, near the small resort of Marseillan-Plage.

The other, longer route, passes around the back of the lagoon. Along the way, it takes in the 11th- to 13th-century Benedictine (later Cistercian) **Abbaye St-Félix-de-Montceau**, accessible on a white road from the village of Gigean. Romantically ruined on its hilltop site, with a view over the lagoon, the abbey includes both a Romanesque and a Gothic church, as well as some of the outbuildings, abandoned after a sacking by mercenaries in the Hundred Years War. Further south, there are the two ancient lagoon ports of **Mèze** and **Marseillan**, still making a go of it as fishing villages, though nowadays the money comes from the less romantic chores of oyster farming.

Abbaye de Valmagne

It might try the patience of some readers, dragging them on another detour, to another ruined abbey—but this is the best one of all (8 km north of Mèze on the D 161; guided tours; in summer daily exc Tues, 3–6 pm, the rest of the year Sun afternoons only). Valmagne was an early Cistercian foundation, begun in 1138 and financed by Raymond Trencavel. Being one of the richest houses, it also gradually became one of the most decadent; the records mention a 16th-century Florentine abbot named Pietro da Bonzi, who built himself a palace on the site, plus a French garden with a statue of Neptune, and who threw the best dinner parties in Languedoc. Thoroughly trashed in the Revolution, the abbey has survived only by good luck; one owner proposed to dismantle it to provide building stone for a new church in Montpellier, but the canons there found the price too high. For the last century, the vast **church** has served as the biggest wine cellar in the Hérault, with some of the best fruity red AOC Coteaux de Languedoc and a traditional lemon-coloured white (June–Sept, Wed–Mon 2:30–6:30, or ring 67 78 06 09, also see below, p. 381).

Valmagne is not your typical Cistercian church. St Bernard would have frowned on architectural vanities like the porch, the big bell towers (these may have been later additions, for defence) and the sculpted decoration—grapevines, representing less the scriptural 'labourer in the vineyard' than the real vineyards that made Valmagne so rich. Its size is astonishing: a 130-m nave, and great pointed arches almost as high as Narbonne cathedral's. Most of the work is 14th-century, in a straightforward but sophisticated late Gothic; note how the nave columns grow slightly closer together towards the altar, a perspective trick that makes the church seem even longer (St Bernard wouldn't have fancied that either). The relatively few monks who lived here would hardly have needed such a church; here too, architectural vanity seems to have overcome Cistercian austerity.

Both the chapter house and the refectory are well preserved, around a pretty **cloister** that contains the loveliest thing in the abbey, an octagonal Gothic pavilion with a tall flowing fountain inside, a fantasy straight from a medieval manuscript or tapestry; an 18th-century poet, Lefranc de Pompignan, named it right: a *fontaine d'amour*.

Agde

If Sète is a brash young upstart, Agde has been watching the river Hérault flow down to the sea for some 2500 years. Founded by Greeks from Phocis, not long after Marseille, its name was originally *Agatha*, after *Agatha Tyche*, the 'good spirit' of popular Greek religion, usually portrayed carrying a cornucopia; the people of Agde are still called *Agathois*. In medieval times it was an important port, despite occasional visits by Arab sea-raiders. The last few centuries have left Agde behind, but it is still a good town, and a grey one—built almost entirely of volcanic basalt from nearby Mont St-Loup. With the massive new tourist development at nearby Cap d'Agde, this lovely town does not get much peace in the summer; in parts of the old quarter there are almost as many restaurants as houses.

TOURIST INFORMATION
Agde (34300): Rue J. Roger, tel 67 94 29 68.
Cap d'Agde: Av. des Sergents, tel 67 26 38 58.

The tiny old quarter is defined by its walls, now largely demolished for a promenade; a bit of the old ramparts remains, near the river, resting on Greek foundations (now below street level). Overlooking the Hérault, Agde's stern basalt **Cathédrale St-Etienne** was begun about 1150. Its fortress-like appearance is no accident; Agde's battling bishops used it as their citadel (the outworks have been demolished); previous cathedrals had been wrecked in battles, once at the hands of Charles Martel himself. Inside, the only original feature is the 12th-century marble altar.

From the quay along the Hérault, Rue Chassefière leads into the *bourg*, or medieval addition to the city, passing an unusual relic, a little stone fountain engraved 'Napoléon

Bonaparte, Premier Consul, 1799'—declaring Boney's seizure of power, and the end of the constitutional republic. Nearby on Rue de la Fraternité, the **Musée Agathois** is one of the best of the South's town museums, encapsulating nearly everything about Agde's history and traditions in a few well-arranged rooms: archaeological finds, religious art, exhibits of costume, dances and festivals, an old-fashioned kitchen and fishermen's gear (daily exc Tues, 10–12, 2–6; adm). Behind the museum, Agde's market shares Place Gambetta with the church of **St-André**, where important Church councils were held in the days of the Visigoths; of the present building, though, the oldest part is the 12th-century tower. Another church, **St-Sever** on Rue St-Sever, contains a fine Renaissance painting of Christ on wood, a little the worse for wear from having been thrown into the Hérault during the Revolution.

A Suspicious Saint and a Synthetic Resort

The road to Cap d'Agde, only 4 km away, passes the ancient, extinct volcano **Mont St-Loup**, its top disfigured by communications pylons. Agde's black basalt comes from here. Whoever St Loup, or 'Holy Wolf', might have been is not clear (though there is a northern saint by that name, a 5th-century bishop of Troyes). *Loup* is also the name for the sea-bass, the favourite fish in Agde's restaurants. **Cap d'Agde**, built around a small harbour, is the biggest beach playground in all Languedoc, and another triumph of French holiday efficiency. Like La Grande Motte, it began in the 60s as a planned resort fostered by the government, and it looks it: a freshly built 'traditional' centre, with plenty of parking, broad boulevards, and everything in its place. Typically, the plan even accommodated the *naturistes*; the camp called **Héliopolis** on the northern edge of town, towards Marseillan, has become the biggest nudist colony in Europe, with a futuristic semicircular central building that includes shops, banks, even a *naturiste* supermarket.

Cap d'Agde may not be what you came to Languedoc for, but there's plenty to do: a first-rate golf course and other sports facilities (they'll be hosting the Mediterranean Games in 1993); a wildlife sanctuary at the nearby **Etang de Bagnas**, with many rare waterfowl (purple heron, grand bittern) for twitchers to scrutinize; boat trips to **Fort Brescou**, a 1586 fortress on a volcanic island at the mouth of the Hérault, long used as a political prison by the French kings; a Casino, a Luna Park and the inevitable **Aqualand**, with big water-toboggans. One surprising attraction is the **Musée de la Clape**, a fine, small archaeological collection; the star of which is the *Ephèbe d'Agde*, a Hellenistic bronze of a boy, recently discovered in the bed of the Hérault (daily exc Mon, 9–12, 3–6; 9–12, 2–7 in summer; adm).

WHERE TO STAY/EATING OUT

For a night's flop in **Sète**, nothing less than the *****Grand Hôtel** will do. Right on Sète's 'Grand Canal', it almost deserves its name, with plenty of the original decor from the 1920s. If you can't swing the Danieli in Venice, this will do fine; nice people and very reasonable rates (17 Quai Maréchal de Lattre de Tassigny; tel 67 74 71 77). Plenty of other electric signs beckon from the Canal and its surrounding streets: no harm will come to you at ****Le Brise-Lames** (tel 67 74 33 48; June–Sept only) or ****Les Abysses** (tel 67 74 37 73), both on Quai Général Durand.

Sète has lots of seafood, of course, but as part of the total experience you should take in a place called the 'Golden Spot', or 'Gold Rush', or some such American nonsense, located on the Canal de Sète, to watch harried cooks churn out mountains of *frites* while trading insults and banter with the Sètois (the sandwiches aren't bad, really). Or for lunch with the dock-hands, try **La Péniche**, simple stuff (55 and 80 F menus) on an old barge in the harbour (on the Montpellier road). For quality seafood, try **La Palangrotte**, on the lower end of the Canal de Sète (Rampe Paul Valéry): grilled fish, and several styles of fish stew, including the local *bourride sètoise* (menus 120–300 F, tel 67 74 80 35). Another possibility, on Promenade Marty, just above the Canal de Sète, is **Le Hostal**, a splurge for stuffed mussels and paella or *parillade* for about 150–200 F.

You won't regret stopping over at **Agde** (34300) if you're passing anywhere nearby. It's a sweet town, and the hotels and restaurants are as good as you'll find on the coast. First choice is ****La Galiote**, a 19th-century imitation castle exactly in the centre, on Place Jean Jaurès. Some of the rooms overlook the river; there's a bar full of English beer, and an excellent restaurant—75–170 F menus; seafood or roast lamb with thyme, and alcoholic ices between courses (tel 67 94 45 58). Second choice is across the square: **Le Donjon**, with old-fashioned and comfortable rooms, though as with its neighbour there may be some difficulty finding a place to park (Place Jean Jaurès; tel 67 94 12 32).

Rue Jordan is the exotic restaurant street in Agde: starting with **La Candela**, a cosy new establishment offering coconut chicken and other specialities from the French Indian Ocean *département* of Réunion (70 and 160 F menus); continue down the street (in summer at least) and you'll find Greek and Vietnamese places, and even Mexican. For pizza, in the centre, **Pizzeria Scarpio** on Quai du Chapitre, offers wide choice of pizzas in the evening and a 50 F lunch menu.

Pézenas

The area inland from Agde, behind the Bassin de Thau, is one of the duller stretches of the Hérault, a rolling plain dotted with a score of agricultural villages—up-to-date and businesslike rather than picturesque and cosy; on the back roads you may pass fewer cars than tractors, gleaming, air-conditioned beasts that look more like some sort of lunar excursion module. Right in the centre is **Pézenas**. If Carcassonne (see below) is Languedoc's medieval movie-set, this town has often been used for costume dramas set in the time of Richelieu or Louis XIV. Few cities in France have a better ensemble of buildings from what the French (rather over-enthusiastically) used to call the 'Golden Age'. Even when the cameras aren't rolling, it is all too easy to imagine moustachioed musketeers and *grandes dames* with laced bodices and perfumed gloves strolling its elegant streets. In summer, the Piscénois live out a lingering *ancien régime* fantasy, with festivals, concerts and exhibitions called the *Mirondela dels Arts* that lasts from mid-June clear into September.

History

Roman *Piscenae* was known for spinning wool, the best in Gaul. In the 1200s, it became a possession of the French crown and renewed its prosperity by royally chartered merchants' fairs. Later, the troubles of Béziers and Narbonne in the Albigensian Crusade and the Hundred Years War would prove lucky for Pézenas. Besides draining off trade and commerce from those cities, the royal town replaced Narbonne as seat of the Estates-General of Languedoc after 1456. The royal governors of the region followed in

1526, bringing in their wake a whole wave of wealthy nobles, clerics and jurists, who rebuilt Pézenas in their own image, with new churches, convents, government buildings and scores of refined *hôtels particuliers*. For the next two centuries they remained, preferring their little aristocratic town to decaying Narbonne or to Montpellier, full of untidy industry and Protestants. All this came to an end with the Revolution, but Pézenas has done its best since to keep up its monuments, while making a discreet living from agriculture and tourism.

TOURIST INFORMATION
Place Gambetta, tel 67 98 11 82.

And the Tourist Information office is the place to start. They offer a brochure with a detailed walking tour of the town and its 70-odd listed historical buildings. From the Renaissance through to the 1700s, Pézenas really did develop and maintain a distinctive architectural manner; this can best be seen in the *hôtels particuliers*, with their lovely arcaded courtyards and external staircases. It was an eclectic style, incorporating elements as diverse as Gothic vaulting and Italian Renaissance balustrades: tasteful, if not ambitious. Nonetheless, the architects were ambitious men who could go to extremes to attract clients. One of them, a certain Monsieur Thomas, made his name building a country house near here—starting with the roof, and working his way down to the foundations.

The tourist office was also once the shop of a barber named Gély. Molière spent some seasons in Pézenas in the 1650s, when his troupe was employed by the governor, the Prince de Conti. He liked passing the afternoons in Gély's salon, doing research for his comedies—watching the comings and goings of the town and listening to the conversations. Across Place Gambetta, the former government palace, the **Maison Consulaire** has been rebuilt so many times since the 1200s that it is a little museum of Pézenas architecture. Around the corner on Rue Alliés, the **Musée de Vulliod-St-Germain** contains memorabilia of Molière and his time in Pézenas, along with collections of tapestries, faience, paintings and the bric-à-brac of Pézenas' past (daily exc Tues and Wed, 10–12, 2–5; in summer exc Tues, 10–12, 3–6; adm).

West of Place Gambetta are some of the best streets for peeking inside the courtyards of the *hôtels*: Rue Sabatini, Rue François-Oustrin (the **Hôtel de Lacoste**, with an elegant staircase, is at No. 8); Rue de Montmorency, and especially **Rue de la Foire**, the status address of the old days, with a number of palaces including the Renaissance **Hôtel de Carrion-Nizas** at No. 10. Just down the street, note the charming relief of child musicians at No. 22. At the northern end of the street, a left takes you into Rue Emile-Zola, with the **Hôtel de Jacques Coeur** (the famous merchant of Montpellier; see p. 352), at No. 7, with an interesting allegorical sculpted façade. It faces the **Porte Faugères**, a 1597 remnant of the town walls, and the nearby entrance to the small **Jewish Ghetto**.

The broad **Cours Jean-Jaurès**, site of the Saturday market, divides Pézenas in two. It too has its palaces: an especially good row of them at Nos. 14–22, including the **Hôtel de Grasset**. The Cours leads into Place de la République, and the church of **St-Jean**, with profuse 17th- and 18th-century marble decoration that proves Pézenas' artistic instincts were much sounder in secular matters. South of the Cours, there are more palaces: the **Hôtel de Malibran** and **Hôtel de l'Epine**, with a lavish sculptural façade, both on Rue Victor Hugo; the **Hôtel Montmorency**, the Pézenas home of one of 16th-century France's most illustrious noble houses, on Rue Reboul; and best of all, the **Hôtel d'Alfonse** on Rue Conti, with a delightful courtyard loggia on three levels, built in the 1630s.

Market Day: Saturday.

WHERE TO STAY/EATING OUT

Pézenas (34120) could be a major tourist attraction if it really wanted, but places to stay and restaurants of any quality are both a bit lacking. The ****Genieys**, at 9 Av. Aristide Briand, is outside the historic centre, but it is the only good hotel in town, with a restaurant known for its seafood (menus 60–220 F, outdoor terrace; tel 67 98 13 99). For a modest lunch with the postmen of Pézenas, try **Chez Jean**, by the Post Office on Place du 14 Juillet; 70–90–160 F menus, although the postal set prefers a simple beefsteak with shallots.

More Coteaux du Languedoc
One of the best pockets of this AOC label (see p. 361) is here. Pézenas is the home of some excellent wines, especially those of the **Prieuré de St-Jean de Bebian**, tel 67 98 13 60, and its amazing 'black' 88. For a unique golden-hued clairette wine from the fragrant thyme-covered slopes to the north, try the **Château St-André**, Rte de Nizas at Pézanas, tel 67 98 12 58. Pomérols, near Pézenas, is the centre of a traditional but obscure, miniscule growing area on the west shore of the Bassin de Thau called Picpoul de Pinet, producing an unsual soft white wine with sea-green highlights that goes well with freshwater fish; try some at the **Cave Coopérative Les Costières**, in Pomérols, tel 67 77 01 59. In Lézignan-la-Cèbe, just north of Pézenas, the **Vignobles d'Ormesson**, tel 67 98 23 80, is run by a count devoted to perfecting his white and red Vins de Pays d'Oc that have surpassed not a few proud AOC labels: especially a red called L'Enclos made of merlot and cabernet-sauvignon and the dry white O. d'Ormesson.

Béziers

This city's history is succinct; a rude interruption and a second chance. Béziers is older than the Romans; its site, a commanding, defensible hill on a key part of the Mediterranean coast, seems promising, but Béziers' long career has produced little distinction and only one famous anecdote. In 1209, at the beginning of the Albigensian Crusade, a large number of Cathars took refuge in the city and were besieged. When the besiegers offered the Catholics a chance to leave the city, they refused. The troops stormed the city, and found that the entire population had taken refuge in the churches. The crusaders' ayatollah, the Abbot of Cîteaux, had ordered the massacre of all the Cathars. Asked how to distinguish them from the Catholics, he replied 'Kill them all, God will know his own.' From all accounts, that is exactly what happened; in his report to Rome, the papal legate bragged that some 20,000 people were put to death.

Not surprisingly, Béziers languished for centuries. The second chance came in the 1660s, with the building of the Canal du Midi (see below). A new Béziers has grown up since then, a busy port and industrial town of some 90,000, known best for its crack rugby squad. Approaching it from the surrounding plains, you'll see its heroic hilltop skyline from miles away, crowned by its impressive cathedral; seen from inside, unfortunately, Béziers will not sustain your initial expectations, a pigeon-grey city with plenty of traffic and its mind firmly on its business.

GETTING AROUND
Béziers is on the main coastal rail line, and it's easy to get to Narbonne, Sète, Montpellier or points beyond, with trains never more than two hours apart. The other line from the city heads north for Castres, passing through Bédarieux and St-Pons. The *Gare Routière* is on Place Jean Jaurès (tel 67 28 23 85), with regular connections to Pézenas (and to everywhere the trains go), and less regular ones to villages of the eastern Hérault. City buses run from here to nearby Valras, the popular lido of the Bitterois.

TOURIST INFORMATION
27 Rue du 4 Septembre; tel 67 49 24 19.

The Cathedral
The modern centre is the **Allées Paul Riquet**, a broad promenade of plane trees named after the city's great benefactor, the builder of the Canal du Midi. Besides a statue of Riquet, there is a pleasant outdoor theatre, built in the 19th century. From here, any of the streets to the west will take you up to the top of the hill and the medieval centre.

Someone must have been left in Béziers after 1209, for the city spent the next two centuries working on its grandiose **cathedral**, replacing the original building that was wrecked in the sack. Its grim, fortress-like exterior, similar to Narbonne's, seems a foreign presence, the citadel of an occupying force—a perfect symbol for the Church Militant that had made the rebuilding necessary. The inside is more graceful, in clean, warm ashlar masonry with plenty of stained glass; it creates a light and airy effect, especially in the apse, where large windows of blue and white decorative glass (behind a dreadful Baroque altar) are the prettiest feature in the church. In two of the chapels (2nd right and 2nd left) there are fragments of some Giottoesque frescoes, and at the west front, a magnificent organ almost as good as the one in Narbonne. Architectural fragments from the earlier church can be seen in the beautiful vaulted **cloister**, a work of the late 1300s.

Behind the cathedral, the **Musée des Beaux Arts** includes a collection of Greek vases, some 17th-century Italian works (a Guido Reni and a Domenichino) and a large number of 18th and 19th-century French paintings (open 9–12, 2–6, except Mon and Sun morning). Another museum, just around the corner on Rue Massol, the **Musée du Vieux Biterrois et du Vin** divides its space between local archaeological finds and displays on the history of wine. If you have time for two more churches, the Gothic **Madeleine** north of the cathedral and the markets, on Place de la Madeleine, was one of the sites of the massacre of 1209; **St-Aphrodise** was Béziers' cathedral in the 8th century. 'St-Aphrodise', if it isn't Aphrodite herself, would be the legendary first bishop, who rode into Béziers one day on a camel (now the city's symbol). The Romans naturally chopped off his head and threw it into a well—but the water rose miraculously to the surface, floating the head with it. Aphrodise fished it out and carried it under his arm to the site of this church, and then disappeared into the ground. It's more likely that pagan Aphrodite had a temple on or near this site. Almost nothing remains of the original building, but a 4th-century sarcophagus has been recycled for use as a baptismal font.

Market Day: Friday (flowers and antiques).

WHERE TO STAY/EATING OUT

Béziers (34500) is not necessarily a convenient place to stay; getting in and out of it is a problem, and parking is murder. But if you want to do it in relative style, without much expense, there is the ****Imperator** at the best location in town, the Allées Paul Riquet (No. 28, and there's a garage, tel 67 49 02 25). Less expensively, down the street is the ****Club Hôtel des Allées** (46 Alées Paul Riquet, tel 67 76 44 37).

For a good lunch bargain, try **Le Bistrot des Halles**, between the Madeleine church and the markets on Place Madeleine; the 95–120 F menus often include smoked salmon, and homemade desserts (tel 67 28 30 46). *Hai nostalgia d'Italia?* Then betake yourself to **La Storia**, Rue de l'Argentière behind the post office—the real thing, from ham and melon or *carpaccio antipasti*, through to the pasta and *saltimbocca alla Romana* (tel 67 28 18 11; menus 110, 140 F). In the same area, on Rue Viennet, for a walk on the wild side, **Aladin** with Italo-Tunisian stabs at couscous and spaghetti (100 F or more).

The Canal du Midi

The best thing to do in Béziers is go west, for one of Languedoc's best-kept secrets. The waterways of other parts of France are well-enough known; this one, one of very few in the south, remains serene and relatively unburdened by tourism, planted its entire length with parallel rows of great plane trees (not just for decoration; they hold the soil, and help keep the canal from silting up). However shady and idyllic, Paul Riquet's canal is also an early monument of economic planning, from the days of Louis XIV's great minister Colbert, when everything in France was being reformed and modernized (and Louis was blowing all the profits on Versailles and his endless wars). Riquet was a local baron, the state's Tax Farmer (*fermier-général*) for Languedoc (a wonderful system; *ancien régime* tax farmers bought rights to collect taxes in a region, and got to keep any amounts above the sum expected by the government). He conceived the idea for the canal and sold it to Colbert, then saw through its construction with remarkable single-mindedness, inventing ingenious tricks to get the canal over the highest stretches, paying a third of the expenses himself, and even sacrificing his daughters' dowries to the cause. From 1666, as many as 12,000 men worked on the project, which required over 100 locks, and runs for 235 km. It was completed 39 years later; Riquet died just a few months before the opening.

No one has shipped any freight on the Canal du Midi for years, but it is still kept up for the benefit of holiday-makers. Some of the locks are tended. At others you'll have to figure out the mechanism yourself; it isn't hard. You can take a slow cruise from Béziers all the way to Toulouse, or just rent a rowing-boat or canoe in one of the villages and spend a drowsy day under the plane trees.

GETTING AROUND

Forget about buses and trains; you'll need a car to get around here; it's also one of the most pleasant corners of the south for bicycling. For a small boat on the canal, ask at any of the villages or for a motor cruiser try the modern but not-too-stylish ones available from a firm called **Rive de France** in Colombiers, southwest of Béziers along the canal, tel 67 37 12 60. There are other firms in Capestang (**Bateliers du Midi**, tel 67 93 38 66), and Homps, south of Olonzac (**Croisières du Soleil**; tel 68 91 38 11). *La Belle Isaure* is the only horse-drawn boat still in use on the canal; it cruises regularly between Béziers and Poilhes in the summer (tel 67 92 17 22). If you plan to spend a lot of time around the Canal, write ahead for complete information to: OTSI, 15 Blvd Pelletan, BP 142 11012 Carcassonne Cedex.

TOURIST INFORMATION

Nissan-lez-Ensérune (34440): tel 67 37 82 21.

The canal connects Sète on the Mediterranean with Toulouse—where it still flows right past the central railway station—and thence to the Atlantic, by way of the river Garonne. The best parts of it are west of Béziers, where it passes through a score of lovely old villages, fitting so well into the landscape that it seems to have been there all the time. Pick it up just outside Béziers, at the **Ecluses de Fonséranes**, just off the N 113 for Narbonne. This is a series of eight original locks, a watery stair that facilitated the biggest drop in altitude along the canal's length. No one road follows the canal for long; with a good map and some careful navigation you can stay close to it, on the back roads through **Colombiers**, first of the canal villages, then to **Nissan-lez-Ensérune**, a busy place with a 14th-century Gothic church and a small museum of religious art and archaeological finds. The latter come from the forested hill to the north. You will already have noticed this landmark in the flat countryside; signs from Nissan will lead you up to it, and to the remains of one of the most important pre-Roman towns of southern Gaul, the **Oppidum d'Ensérune**.

Oppidum d'Ensérune

The site is a relic of the time when these coasts were first coming into the mainstream of Mediterranean civilization (daily exc Tues; 9–12, 2–6:30 Apr–Oct, otherwise 10–12, 2–5; guided tours; adm). First settled in the 6th century BC, it began as a fortified trading village under Greek influence, closely connected to Marseille. By 250 BC it may have had as many as 10,000 people, though later in that century it was wrecked, possibly by Hannibal, on his way to Italy during the Punic Wars. Under Roman rule it revived again, refounded as a Roman colony, but in peaceful, settled times it could not survive. The cramped, difficult site was good for defence; when this was no longer necessary, people and trade gradually moved down to the plains and the coast, and Ensérune was largely abandoned by the 1st century AD.

Not much remains of the town: the foundations of the wall, cisterns and traces of habitations can be seen. The excellent **museum** in the centre of the excavations has a collection of ceramics, including some fine Greek and Etruscan works, along with local pieces that show the strong influence of the foreigners. Just outside the town, where an ancient column with an unusual, trapezoidal capital has been re-erected, you can take in one of the oddest panoramas in France, a gigantic surveyor's pie, neatly sliced. This was the **Etang de Montady**, a roughly circular swamp reclaimed in the 13th century, when the new fields were precisely divided by drainage ditches radiating from the centre.

Canal Villages

Most of these have at least one restaurant, some have guest houses and boat rentals; all of them are agreeable spots to while away an afternoon. From Nissan, the D 37 takes you to **Poilhes**, a sleepy, lovely village built around one of Paul Riquet's graceful brick canal bridges. **Capestang**, the next one, has a landmark visible for miles around: the tall, unfinished Gothic **Collégiale St-Etienne**, a monument to unfulfilled ambition, like Narbonne Cathedral, which indeed may have been the work of the same architect. A detour south of Capestang, and just west of the village of Ouveillan, will take you to an unusual and almost completely forgotten medieval monument, the **Grange de Font-calvy**. A testament to the wealth of the Cistercian order, this was a key stronghold of Fontfroide Abbey (see p. 405), a fortified barn of considerable architectural sophistication, 20 m square, with ogival vaulting.

Quarante

All along, the lands around the canal have been packed full with vineyards. Further west, this continues, but the countryside becomes greener and lusher, with some of the cosiest landscapes in the Languedoc. **Quarante** isn't on the canal, but it is worth a 4 km side trip, north on D 36/D 37E, for its severe and dignified Romanesque church, the **Abbatiale Ste-Marie**, built between 982 and 1053. The *Trésor* contains a marble sarcophagus of the 3rd century, decorated with angels and portraits of the deceased, and a remarkable example of Montpellier silversmithing from the 1440s, a very leonine bust of *St John the Baptist* with almond eyes and a Gallic nose—the artist must have thought John was a Frenchman. Quarante also has a pretty picnic-ground and park (with a pool), in the grounds of the Château de Rouière.

Back on the canal, the string of villages continues: **Argeliers, Ventenac-en-Minervois, Paraza, Roubia** and finally **Argens-Minervois**, a once-fortified village with a ruined castle. The canal at this point runs parallel to the River Aude, and in places the two are only a few hundred feet apart. Near Roubia, the canal passes over a small stream on the **Pont-Canal de Répudre**. Paul Riquet designed this too; it is the oldest canal bridge in France. Further west comes **Homps**, with another ruined castle, built by the Knights Hospitallers, and then a long, empty stretch (very scenic, though), leading towards Marseillette in the Minervois, and then **Trèbes**, a big village where there are several locks and another canal bridge.

Market Days: Capestang, Wednesday and Sunday mornings.

WHERE TO STAY/EATING OUT

Can you dine well under the *platanes* of the Canal? Indeed; most of the villages have at least one place with a garden terrace overlooking it; and as you get closer to Minervois, there will also be some chances for wine-tasting on the banks, as at the **Château de Ventenac** at Ventenac, and the **Domaine de Sérame**, a lovely *mas* outside Argens-Minervois.

Poilhes (34310) is the place to stop along the Canal, a village relaxed to the point of coma. Imaginitive *haute cuisine* is represented here with **La Tour Sarrasine**; pigeon stuffed with *foie gras*, steaks in a sauce of wine and marrow—a memorable dinner, if a bit dear, menus at 160–290 F (tel 67 93 41 31). Less expensively, **La Romaine** is located right on the canal, with good if somewhat fussy cooking (a *casselote d'escargots* or an *entrecôte* with Roquefort sauce), 100 F menu. They also rent boats. In nearby **Nissan** (34440), *****L'Acropole** is a sweetly old-fashioned and very inexpensive stop, right on the market square (7 Place du Marché, tel 67 37 01 50). In **Colombiers,** you can stop over at the **Via Domitia**, with colour TV and air-conditioning. The local dining isn't so up-to-date—but the lace-curtain **Chez Dédé** isn't bad, with a 60 F lunch menu, in the village centre.

At **Le Somail**, a tiny hamlet on the D 926 east of Paraza, *****Le Poivre Vert** has rooms overlooking the canal and a good restaurant with French and Indian cooking (tel 68 46 28 15; 110–130 F menus). In **Paraza**, there will be less ambitious cooking but a terrace with a canal front view, at **Le Coup de Foudre** (mostly grilled meats, 90 and 110 F).

The Minervois

This is a *pays* with plenty of character, though not many people. With typical French irony, the Minervois suffered grievously from poverty and rural depopulation throughout this century—then, just when everyone was gone, vintners improved the quality of their Minervois wines; they have become increasingly popular across France, and the region's prosperity has returned. The Corbières, just across the Aude (see below), tells much the same story. And in other ways, too, the Minervois is a prelude to the Corbières: the sharp contrast of tidy, lovingly cared for vineyards with ragged, wild country and outcrops of weird, eroded limestone, the sense of strangeness and isolation—in a region of France that has been inhabited for more or less 200,000 years.

TOURIST INFORMATION
Olonzac (34210): Mairie, tel 68 91 21 08.
Minerve (34210): Mairie, tel 68 91 22 92.
Rieux-Minervois (11160): Place de l'Eglise, tel 68 78 13 98.

The Minervois do love their region, and truly welcome visitors from faraway places. An women's association called **Les Capelles du Minervois** conducts individual tours of the region's sights, coupled with dinner and visits to wine cellars; call Mme Vidal at 68 91 17 17 for details. In Olonzac, call **Evasion-balades** (mornings) on 68 91 15 47 to arrange nature walks on the back trails.

From the Canal to Minerve

Olonzac, just north of the Canal, is the centre of the wine district and the closest thing the eastern Minervois has to a town. To the northwest, some of of the most civilized landscapes in the Minervois lie around the village of **Siran**, with three little-known attractions: to the east, an impressive dolmen called the **Mourel des Fades** ('fairy dolmen') and the 12th-century country church of **St-Germain-de-Cesseras**, with a beautifully sculpted apse. Both are signposted off the D 168. Another country church, the **Chapelle de Centeilles** north of Siran, is a unique survival, entirely covered inside with frescoes from the 13th to the 15th centuries: the *Resurrection of Christ, SS George and*

Bernard, a *Tree of Jesse*, amidst a profusion of geometric and floral borders; there is also a fragment of Roman mosaic, found nearby. The church is only open on Sunday afternoons, which is just as well, since any other day the frantic post-lady of Siran would probably smash up your car with her ancient Renault on the way—it's happened before.

From Olonzac, the narrow D 10 will take you up into the heights of the Minervois, to **Minerve**, a town as old as any in Languedoc. Minerve is a natural place for a defensible settlement, on a steep rock between two rivers, but that does not explain why the area around it should have been so popular for so long. Traces of habitation dating back 170,000 years have been found in its caves; Neolithic dolmens abound. The Celts and the Romans built the town itself, and in the Middle Ages it was a feudal stronghold with a Cathar slant. Minerve accepted refugees from the sack of Béziers in 1209; Simon de Montfort followed them, and took the town after a two-month siege, followed by the usual butchery.

Minerve today counts little over a hundred inhabitants; nothing has been done or built since Unspeakable Simon's visit, and the medieval relic on its dramatic site has become a peaceful and unambitious tourist attraction, with potters, artists and souvenir stands filling the spaces left by all the folks who moved to the cities in the last 80 years. Parts of the walls are still in good nick, but all that is left of the château is a single, slender, octagonal tower; the Minervois call it the 'candela'. There are narrow medieval alleys, gates and cisterns, a simple 12th-century church, and a small **museum**, across from a *caveau de dégustation* of Minervois wines.

The real attractions are out in the country. A short walk from town, there are **'natural bridges'**—really more like tunnels, eroded through the limestone by streams. To the west extends the **Canyon de la Cesse**, and determined hikers can seek out a collection of caves and dolmens north of this, at Bois Bas, off the D 147.

The Seven-Sided Church of Rieux-Minervois

West of Siran, the Minervois flattens out into the valley of the Argent-Double ('silver water'; *dubron* was a Celtic word for water, and the Romans made it *Argentodubrum*). On its banks you will find the village of Rieux, and one of the most uncanny medieval monuments in France.

The seven-pointed star is the recurring mystic symbol of the Midi. The Cathar castle at Montségur, in Ariège, was laid out to subtly fit inside its angles; the Félibres of Provence used it as part of their emblem and it has been a recurring theme in folk art. Just what it means has never been adequately explained; neither has anyone ventured an explanation for the presence in this unremarkable Minervois village of what may be the only seven-sided church anywhere. Dedicated to the Virgin, the church was built sometime in the late 12th century, exactly when, why and by whom no one knows. A medieval scholar would have cited Scripture: *Wisdom has built her house; she has set up her seven pillars* (Proverbs 1:9), also recalling that the Divine Wisdom was identified (at the time) with the Virgin Mary. Clearly, this temple opens a deep vein of intellectual medieval mysticism, full of geometry and allegory and not entirely recoverable by our minds. Its builders, pressed to explain why the central heptagon around the altar has four squat pilasters and three columns, might have mumbled something about the 'Marriage of Heaven and Earth'—the foursquare world and the spiritual triangle. Modern investigators have also discovered various series of ley lines based on this site; according to

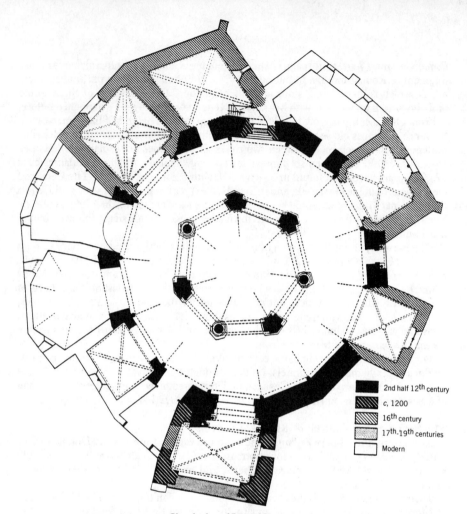

2nd half 12th century
c, 1200
16th century
17th-19th centuries
Modern

Church plan of Rieux-Minervois

them the line of the midsummer sunrise passes from an altar inside the church, through a (now closed up) window and begins an alignment that goes as far as Minerve and St-Guilhem-le-Désert, passing several chapels dedicated to St John along the way.

The ambition of the builders of this church, and their resources, are seen in the sculptural detail inside, entrusted to the Master of Cabestany. Most of the fanciful carved capitals are by his workshop, while the Master himself is believed to have done the capitals with the reliefs of *Daniel in the Lions' Den* and the *Assumption of the Virgin*. Building in heptagons certainly must have tried the patience and mathematical know-how of a 12th-century mason; we can admire their careful work, especially the seven-sided belfry, directly over the altar, and the tricky toroid vaulting that connects the heptagon with the 14-sided exterior wall. Over the centuries, a number of chapels have

388

been built along the edges of the church; its exterior aspect, along with the original portal, are now lost.

The marble for Rieux's church came from **Caunes-Minervois**, just up the Argent-Double, which is also the source of the marble for the Paris Opera and parts of Versailles. It is rare for good stone in so many tints, from green to pink to reddish-orange, to occur in one place. The quarries, neatly geometrical excavations around Caunes, make an unusual sight. Over the centuries they have made Caunes more prosperous and open to the world than its Minervois neighbours. Its streets show some modest palaces, such as the **Hôtel d'Alibert** on the main square, along with the former abbey church of **St-Pierre-et-St-Paul**, a hotchpotch of Gothic, Romanesque and later styles, conserving some odd capitals from the Carolingian original. North of town, the D 620 leads past the marble quarries into the narrow and scenic **Gorge de l'Argent-Double**, passing the village of **Citou**, with a high ruined castle.

Minervois

Rough and arid, protected from the cold winds of the north by the mountains, the sunburnt region of AOC Minervois stretches from Carcassonne almost to St-Chinian. Its glories are supple but powerful red wines, dominated by mourvèdre, grenache, syrah and carignan, with a lingering bouquet reminiscent of the *maquis* that has long been one of the gems of Languedoc—one that requires many patient years in the cellar to reach its best. Along with Fitou, Minervois is the region's wine that has built the best reputation for itself in recent years; it can be found in shops all over France, and is also widely available in British supermarkets.

At Laure-Minervois, taste the dark, exquisite 88 Cuvée Alexandre at **Château Fabas**, on the Rieux road, tel 68 78 17 82; also try the **Cave Coopérative de Peyriac-Minervois** at Peyriac, tel 68 78 11 20, where the star is the **Tour St-Martin 88**, although the 89 has an excellent future as well, if you can bear to wait ten years. If you're passing by the Canal du Midi, you can stop in to try some Minervois wines right by the canal at two spots: the **Domaine de Sérame**, an old *mas* just outside Argens, or the **Château de Ventenac**, at Ventenac. Another estate worthy of mention is **Château de Paraza**, high above the canal (Paraza, 11200, Lezignan, tel 68 43 20 76), run by the enterprising M. de Girard. The white wines of Minervois are amongst the revelations of recent years, they are both clean and packed with character. Good examples are to be found at **Château La Grave** at Badens, tel 68 79 16 00, and Château de Paraza (see above).

Market Days: Laure-Minervois, Sunday. Rieux-Minervois, Sunday.

WHERE TO STAY/EATING OUT

The only hotel in **Minerve** (34210), the *****Relais Chantovent**, has just seven rooms; also a fine restaurant with a terrace overlooking the gorges, serving truffles and *cèpes*, and some seafood (menus 80–200 F, tel 68 91 14 18). Just outside Minerve, on the road to Olonzac, the **Restaurant les Alliberts** serves up *boeuf en daube* and Minervois wines for 120–160 F (tel 68 91 22 95).

A typical Minervois lunch-break, in **Olonzac** for example, may be had at the **Restaurant le St-Louis**, on Place de la Citadelle: stewed chicken, half the village for company, and a slowly ticking clock *chez grand-mère* (60 F). In the village of **Félines-Minervois**, above Rieux in the hills, there is somewhat fancier fare at **Lou Caminaire**—grilled chops *aux sarments de vigne* (grilled over vine shoots) are the speciality. The ****Logis de Merinville** is a dignified stone inn in the centre of **Rieux-Minervois** (11160), with lovely rooms and a restaurant (Av. Georges Clemenceau; tel 68 78 12 49; closed Jan). Just to the west, in a restored farm complex outside **Peyriac-Minervois**, the *****Château de Violet** is the Minervois's luxury resort; elegant, sumptuously furnished, with pool and gardens (Route de Pepieux, tel 68 78 10 42, a bit expensive for its rating, it also has a restaurant with 180–260 F menus).

The Montagne Noire

Even wilder than the Minervois, if not as unusual, the Black Mountain is a 30 km-wide stretch of peaks, taller than their neighbours and difficult of access until modern times. Its slate-roofed villages have a solemn air, and their people are bent to serious mountain pursuits—mining and quarrying, logging and paper-making. In the old days they scratched iron and copper out of the mountain; this still continues, along with a bit of silver and gold—the deposits at Salsigne, discovered a century ago, yield a ton of gold each year. The trees are even more important; you'll see plenty of chestnut groves, some planted in the Middle Ages when chestnuts were a mountain staple, and also stands of foreign intruders—Scots pine and Douglas fir, important to the lumber business.

All the routes into the mountains follow narrow parallel valleys leading up from the river Aude; the first is the Argent-Double, from Caunes (see above). Next comes the Clamoux (on the D 112), with equally impressive **gorges**, north of Villeneuve-Minervois; further north it passes **Cabrespine** with its lofty castle (Simon de Montfort slept here), on the way to **Pradelles-Cabardès**, where the people used to make a living by shipping ice down to the cities of the valley. Their sunken ice chambers are still a feature of the landscape. Above Pradelles looms **Pic de Nore**, at 1200 m the highest point of the Montagne Noire—so naturally a TV tower has been stuck on top.

Châteaux de Lastours

The next valley, that of the Orbiel (D 101) is the most populous of the region, and perhaps the most beautiful. It also contains the region's landmark, the **Châteaux de Lastours**—not one, but four castles, in various states of picturesque ruin, all on the same hilltop. The Lords of Cabardès, bosses of the Montagne Noire before the arrival of de Montfort in 1211, built the first of them, the castles of Cabaret and Quertinheux; the two between these, Surdespine and Tour Régine, were added by the French kings in the 13th century. Remember the Drac, in Beaucaire? Apparently after his embarrassment there he took refuge in the Hérault. The legendary knight Roland himself was on his trail near Lastours, and his horse left a hoof-print in a great boulder near the Châteaux, a place still called the *Saut de Roland*.

Salsigne, with its gold mine, lies just to the west of Lastours. To the east is a remarkable cave, the **Grotte de Limousis**, with unique formations of gleaming white aragonite crystals, one of which, called the *Lustre* (chandelier) is over 9 m across (daily 10–12, 2–5:30; adm). Further up the valley are two of the most beautiful and unspoiled villages of the region: **Roquefère** and **Mas-Cabardès**; north of Roquefère a 5-km detour will take you up to a high, lovely **waterfall** at a place called Cupserviès. Mas-Cabardès has some half-timbered houses and a 16th-century church with a rugged octagonal belfry. In the village centre, note the pretty, carefully carved stone **cross**, a typical decoration of Montagne Noire villages. This one was a 16th-century gift of the weavers' guild; with its abundance of water, this region had a thriving textile trade (like nearby Carcassonne) before the black-hearted English Industrial Revolutionaries started underselling them in the 1700s.

Further west, the crown of the Montagne Noire is dotted with artificial lakes, part of a big hydroelectric scheme. In the valley furthest west, that of the Vernassonne, is **Saissac**, another lovely village, built over a ravine and surrounded by forests. Saissac too has its ruined fortress, and a 3-m **menhir**, just to the north off the D 4. To the south, the 13th-century **Abbaye de Villelongue** has little artistic interest, but it is one of the better-preserved medieval monastic complexes in Languedoc (summer daily exc Tues, 2–6 pm; guided tour).

For regions to the west and south, see below, Carcassonne and Castelnaudary, p. 406. North of Pic de Nore, the Montagne Noire descends to rolling hills, in a vast forested area that is part of the Parc Régional du Haut Languedoc. Beyond the boundaries of this book, in the Tarn, there are two large and businesslike towns, worth a detour if you are interested in the Cathars or Spanish art. **Mazamet** has the **Cathar Museum**, with a full exposition of the cult and their demise. **Castres**, a decidedly non-charming city, offers its **Musée Goya**, with a wonderful collection of important works by the Spanish magician, left to the city by a local artist.

WHERE TO STAY/EATING OUT

Accommodation up here will be rudimentary, partly because Carcassonne (see next chapter) is close enough for the Montagne Noire to be an easy day trip. But you'll always eat well. The **Ferme-Auberge Ai Mouli** at **Cabrespine** (tel 68 26 14 10; menus 65–300 F) is certainly out of the way, unless you're going to see the caves. But it's worth the detour if you're fond of trout—it's a trout farm, and they do them a dozen different ways. Also duck and lamb, and game dishes in season. There's more trout, and a wide selection of seafood, at **La Cascade**, beautifully set on a little lake just outside **Brousses-et-Villaret**, between Mas-Cabardès and Saissac (Lac des Rochers; tel 68 26 51 73, 80 F or more). It's also a hotel with eight inexpensive rooms.

Among other hotels, there is the *****Pic de Nore** in **Pradelles-Cabardès** (11380), tel 68 26 16 85, with a simple restaurant; north of Mas-Cabardès, at **Les Martys** (11390), the **Auberge des Martys** (tel 68 26 52 08). Closest to Lastours, at **Lacombe-du-Sault** (11310), there is **La Galaube** (tel 68 26 51 23), and at **Saissac**, also small and inexpensive, the **Montagne Noire** on Av. Maurice Sarrault (tel 68 24 46 36).

At **Villemagne**, 7 km west of Saissac (11300), the Occitan flag flies proudly above the ******Castel de Villemagne**, a restored country house begun in the 14th century. The proprietors are as passionate about keeping up the atmosphere of the place as they are about their land's history and customs; the seven rooms are as lovely and comfortable as you'll find anywhere; good company and a good bargain (tel 68 94 22 95).

Part XIII

NARBONNE, CARCASSONNE AND THE CORBIÈRES

Fragment of marble, Narbonne Museum

This southern corner of Languedoc, mostly in the *département* of the Aude, is famous for two things—wine and castles—and it has more of them than any other part of France. Western Languedoc traditionally fills an ample bay of the EC wine lake, and provides the raw materials for much of the *vin ordinaire* on French tables. After centuries of complacency, it is also beginning to produce some really good wine. The castles, on the other hand, are strictly AOC. Before the border with Spain was definitively drawn in 1659, this was a hotly contested region for a thousand years, disputed first by Visigoths and Saracens, and finally by Madrid and Paris. The French determination to hold it has left us Carcassonne, queen of all medieval castles, cloud-top Cathar redoubts like Aguilar and Quéribus, and over a hundred others, in every shape, colour and style known to military science.

Seldom does the Midi offer a greater jumble of landscapes, with wild mountain gorges just an hour's ride from sandy coastal lagoons where the tramontane blows your hat off in the spring; in greenness the region ranges from the lush Aude valley to the scrubby plateau of Opoul, where the French Army enjoys its desert training.

NARBONNE

Narbonne gave birth to the last of the troubadours, Guiraut Riquier (d. 1292). A melancholy soul, like many men of his time, Riquier never seemed to earn his lady's affection, or the appreciation of his patrons, and he grew to a bitter old age watching his world unravel. *Mas trop suy vingutz als derriers*—'but I was born too late', he mourned in one of his last songs. If he had lived longer, he would have seen his own proud city become a symbol for the eclipse of the Midi and its culture. Narbonne, Languedoc's capital and metropolis since Roman times, suffered some outrageous fortune in the decades after Riquier's death, enough trouble to plunge it into a centuries-long decline. The symbol for Narbonne's own particular eclipse is its majestic, unfinished cathedral, the arches and truncated columns of its skeletal nave haunting the square in front of the plain brick façade thrown up when ambition died.

Fortunately, the Narbonne of today has no interest in melancholy whatsoever. Thanks to roads and railroads, trade has come back for the first time since the Middle Ages. The local economy is still largely fuelled on plonk—the bountiful vineyards of the Corbières and other nearby regions. The city is also finding a new vocation as an industrial centre, and its outskirts have developed accordingly. With a population of only 45,000, Narbonne can nonetheless sometimes fool you into thinking it a metropolis. With its impressive medieval monuments, boulevards and lively streets, it is quite a happy and contented town—one of the Midi's most agreeable urban destinations—with an excellent museum, and the best cathedral in the south.

History

Colonia Narbo Martius, a good site for a trading port along the recently-built Via Domitia, began by decree of the Roman Senate in 118 BC. The colony rapidly became the most important city of southern Gaul, renowned for its beauty and wealth. Under Augustus, it was made the capital of what came to be known as the province of *Gallia Narbonensis*. After 410, it briefly became the headquarters of the Visigoths, and continued as their northernmost provincial capital until the Arab conquest of Spain in the 8th century; the Arabs took Narbonne, but could not hold it, and Pépin the Short reclaimed it for the Frankish Kingdom in 759.

In the 12th century, Narbonne entered its second golden age. Under a native dynasty of viscounts, the city maintained its independence for two centuries and began its great cathedral (1272). The famous Viscountess Ermengarde, who ruled for five decades after 1134, managed the ship of state with distinction while presiding over a 'court of love' graced by troubadours such as Bernart de Ventadorn. The troubled 14th century was murder on Narbonne, however. As if wars and plagues were not enough, the harbour began to silt up; finally even the river Aude decided to change its course and desert the city, ruining its trade. By the end of the century, the city had shrunk to a mere market town, albeit one with an archbishop and a very impressive cathedral.

Stagnation continued until the present century, despite the efforts of the indefatigable Paul Riquet in the 1680s; though his Canal du Midi met the sea further north, Riquet began a branch canal, the Robine, that followed the old course of the river through Narbonne. Powerful interests in Béziers and Sète, however, kept it from being completed until 1786; the man who finally saw it through was Narbonne's last archbishop, an Irishman named Arthur Dillon, an important figure in the city's history. Only in the last

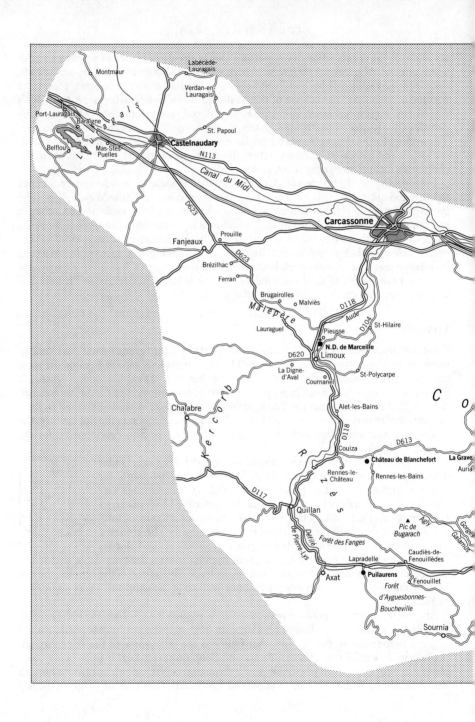

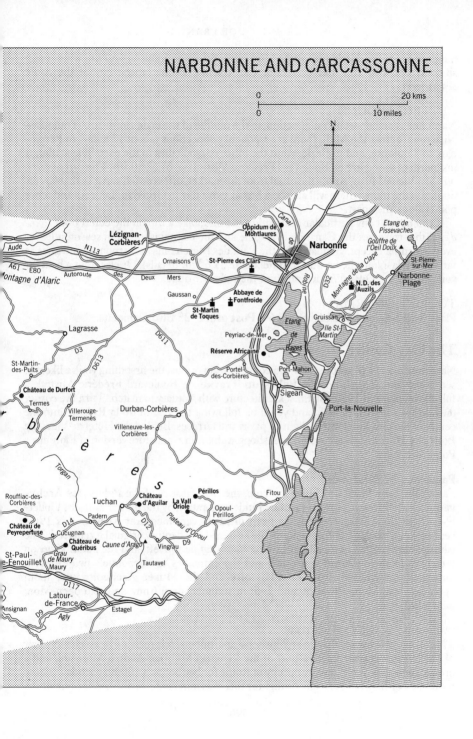

NARBONNE AND CARCASSONNE

0   20 kms

0   10 miles

N

Etang de
Pissevaches
Oppidum de
Montlaures
Gouffre de
l'Oeil Doux
St-Pierre-
sur-Mer
Narbonne
Canal de la
Aude
N113
Lézignan-
Corbières
Ornaisons
St-Pierre des Clars
Montagne de la Clape
Narbonne-
Plage
A61 – E80
Autoroute
des
Deux
Mers
Gaussan
N.D. des
Auzils
Montagne d'Alaric
St-Martin
de Toques
Abbaye de
Fontfroide
Robine
Lagrasse
D611
Peyriac-de-Mer
Etang
de
Bages
Gruissan
Ile St-
Martin
St-Martins-
des-Puits
D3
D613
Réserve Africaine
Portel-
des-Corbières
Port-Mahon
Château de Durfort
Sigean
Termes
Villerouge-
Termenès
Durban-Corbières
Port-la-Nouvelle
b
i
è
r
e
s
Villeneuve-les-
Corbières
Torgan
N9
Rouffiac-des-
Corbières
Tuchan
Château
d'Aguilar
Périllos
Fitou
La Vall
Oriole
Opoul-
Périllos
Padern
D14
D12
Plateau d'Opoul
Château de
Peyrepertuse
Cucugnan
Château de
Quéribus
Caune d'Arago
Vingrau
D9
St-Paul-
e-Fenouillet
Grau
de Maury
Maury
Tautavel
D117
Latour-
de-France
Ansignan
D9
Agly
Estagel

hundred years has Narbonne started to revive, thanks to industry and the wine trade; since World War II it has overtaken Carcassonne as the largest city of the Aude *département*.

GETTING AROUND
Narbonne is an important rail junction, in the middle of the main Bordeaux–Toulouse–Nice route across the Midi; there are frequent connections (about 12 a day) to Perpignan, to Toulouse, and to Beziérs and the other coastal cities to the east. The station is just north of the centre on Boulevard Frédéric Mistral (tel 67 62 50 50). The *gare routière*, on Quai Victor Hugo, across the canal from the market, offers coach services that largely duplicate the trains; there will also be a bus or two a day to Gruissan, Leucate and other points along the coast.

If you haven't any particular destination in mind, take a trip on the **canal boat** (*coche d'eau*) that traverses the Canal de la Robine and the coastal lagoons; in season it leaves every morning except Monday from the Pont des Marchands in Narbonne, and goes as far as Port-la-Nouvelle on the coast (tel 68 32 31 60 for details). Or else, rent a boat for yourself, on the Quai d'Alsace north of the railway bridge.

TOURIST INFORMATION
Place Roger-Salengro, tel 68 65 15 60. **Post office**: 25 Blvd Gambetta.

The City Centre

Narbonne is a city of surprises. If you come by train or bus, the first thing you're likely to see is the gargantuan, horrific **Palais du Travail** on Boulevard Frédéric Mistral, a full-blown piece of 1930s Stalinist architecture with statuary to match. Turn the corner on Rue Jean Jaurès, though, and you'll be following the **Canal de la Robine** into the centre of the city, lined with delightful parks and terraces. Behind the Hôtel de Ville, the **Pont des Marchands** is covered with shops, a charming miniature version of Florence's Ponte Vecchio.

Palais des Archevêques
Facing the busy Place de l'Hôtel de Ville, the twin façades of the **Palais des Archevêques** were blessed with a romantic Gothic restoration by the master himself, Viollet-le-Duc, in the 1840s; opinion has been divided ever since over whether this 19th-century fancy was an improvement on the austere 13th-century original it replaced. The passage between the two buildings (the *Palais Neuf* on the left, and the *Palais Vieux* on the right) leads to a small courtyard, and the entrances to Narbonne's two excellent museums, the **Musée d'Art et d'Histoire** and the **Musée Archéologique** (both open daily exc Mon, 10–11:50 and 2–5; in summer, until 6 pm, and also open Mon; joint adm).

THE MUSÉE D'ART ET D'HISTOIRE
This museum occupies the old archbishops' apartments; it is reached by an elegant stair of the 1620s, decorated with a bust of the Venetian historian Andrea Morosini, and a bronze capitoline Wolf, sent by the city of Rome for Narbonne's 2000th birthday. These reminders of Italy are perfectly fitting, for this museum could easily pass for one of the

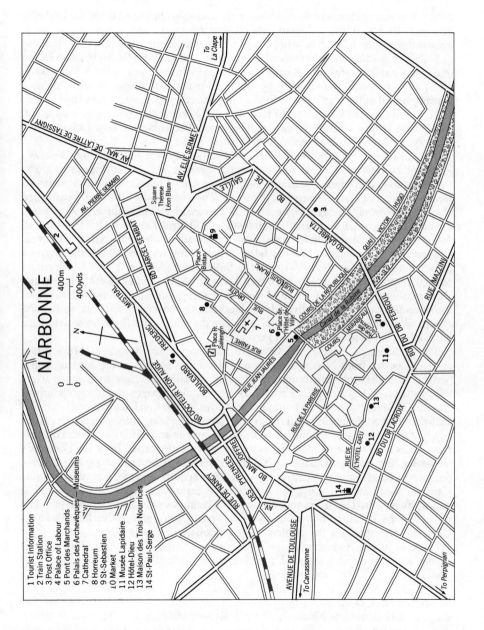

NARBONNE

1 Tourist Information
2 Train Station
3 Post Office
4 Palace of Labour
5 Pont des Marchands
6 Palais des Archevêques — Museums
7 Cathedral
8 Horreum
9 St-Sebastien
10 Market
11 Musée Lapidaire
12 Hôtel-Dieu
13 Maison des Trois Nourrices
14 St-Paul-Serge

great aristocratic galleries of Rome. Most of the collection belonged to the archbishops; they must have acquired a Roman taste on sojourns there. The sumptuous rooms of these princes of the Church have been well-preserved, beginning with the chapter house or **Salle des Audiences**, where there is a portrait of the redoutable Archbishop Dillon (the last of the line—his period of office was rudely interrupted by the Revolution in 1792) and an *equestrian Louis XIV* by van der Meulen—a pompous, quite offensive portrait, typical of the Sun King's use of art as political propaganda. Louis slept here in 1642, in the adjacent **Chambre du Roi**. The 1632 ceiling frescoes are by local talent, the Rodière brothers: harmless *Muses* that look more like nursery-school teachers. Note the floor, a restored Roman mosaic in a labyrinth pattern.

The third room, the **Grande Galerie**, contains some of the best paintings: a gloomy landscape by Gaspard Dughet and an intense *St Jerome* by Salvator Rosa (both artists were favourites in Rome), a Canaletto and, among many Dutch and Flemish pictures a *Wedding Dance*, by Pieter Bruegel the Younger. The 16th- and 17th-century enamelled plaques come from Limoges, with portraits of French kings and an illustration of one of the most bizarre of all hagiographies, the story of *St Ursula and her 11,000 Virgins*, all demure and cute in their little boats, ready to sail off and be martyred by the Huns. Opposite these, a collection of lovely faience apothecary jars from Montpellier makes a proper introduction to the next room, the **Salle des Faïences**. These 18th-century painted ceramics come mostly from well-known French centres like Moustiers and Varange, though many are from cities such as Marseille and Montpellier, where the art has since died out. Typically divided in subject matter between neoclassical scenes and *chinoiserie*, some of these are very good (note also the bridal chest, from Moustiers, for a hint of the 18th-century approach to eroticism).

The archbishops' chapel, the **Oratoire**, harbours a few surprises: 14th-century carved alabaster from Nottingham, an odd Byzantine icon from the Aegean, and a perfect, incandescent 15th-century Florentine *Madonna*; though anonymous (once falsely attributed to Piero della Francesca) it gracefully upstages everything else in the museum. The rest of the apartments are a grab bag: Archbishop Dillon's library, with his well-thumbed St Augustine, and his dining room, appetizingly decorated with plaster reliefs of the archepiscopal dinner. You will encounter an *azulejo* tile floor from Portugal, King François I's vinegar pot, Beauvais tapestries with scenes from La Fontaine's fairy-tales, and more good painting: a luscious Veronese (the *Anointing of King David*), portraits by Nattier and by Venice's favourite 18th-century celebrity portraitist Rosalba Carriera, a sprinkling of native and foreign followers of Caravaggio, and a tortured *St Andrew* by Ribera. The last room contains 19th-century works, many by local painters: two by Monfried, Gauguin's teacher, two pretty paintings on glass by Narbonne's Henri Cros, and something for the gentlemen—a wanton nudie by Abel Brye.

Come in July or August, and they'll let you up into the 13th-century *Donjon Gilles Aycelin*, a Gothic defence tower with a collection of medieval sculpture, and good views from the top.

MUSÉE ARCHÉOLOGIQUE

It is only luck that made Nîmes the 'French Rome', while none of Narbonne's monuments have survived; the ambitious viscounts and archbishops of medieval Narbonne obviously had a greater appetite for recycling old building stone. There is, however, no shortage of remaining bits and pieces, and the best of them have been assembled here: reliefs from Narbonne's three triumphal arches and the gates of its walls, milestones from the Via Domitia, funeral monuments, and a model of a Roman house. The **Chapelle de la Madeleine**, where Greek and pre-Greek ceramics are displayed, retains some fragments of its original 14th-century frescoes; it also offers the best view of the apse and buttresses of the adjacent cathedral, which is almost completely surrounded by buildings.

Christianity seems to have come late to Narbonne; the first bishop, Paul, is recorded in the 3rd century; nevertheless there are some Christian sarcophagi, and an unusual reliquary in the form of the Church of the Holy Sepulchre in Jerusalem. The products of other faiths here are more interesting: a Greek statue of a *drunken silenus*, altars dedicated to Cybele and Attis, and an *image of Priapus*, that mythological embarrassment, this time at least keeping it decently covered.

The parts of the Archbishops' Palace not used for museums house Narbonne's city hall. In the courtyard of the Palais Vieux, you will see a 9th-century bell tower from the original cathedral. In the Palais Neuf, the 1628 Hall of the Synods has original Aubusson tapestries. Now a reception room for the city, it was once the political centre of the region; Narbonne's archbishop had the right of presiding over the *Etats-Généraux*, or parliament, of Languedoc, though that body moved to Pézenas in 1456.

Cathédrale St-Just

This can be entered through the fine 14th-century **Cloister**, near the entrance to the museums, a Gothic quadrangle with leering gargoyles. A better way, though, is to circumnavigate the huge bulk of the cathedral and palace complex towards the west front, and the **Cour St-Eutrope**, a spacious square that occupies the unfinished third of the cathedral itself. On every side rise truncated pilasters, walls and bases of arches, witness to medieval Narbonne's ambition and the 14th-century disasters that stopped it cold.

This is the third church to occupy the site; the first was a basilica from the reign of Emperor Constantine, the second a Carolingian rebuilding of 890 AD. The present church was begun in 1272, at the height of the city's fortunes. Funds were hardly lacking; the cornerstone was sent by Pope Clement IV, a former Archbishop of Narbonne, and he probably contributed a little more besides. To extend the new cathedral to its planned length, it would have been necessary to rebuild a section of the city wall; in 1340, a lawsuit over this broke out between the city and the Church, a good, old-fashioned French lawsuit, just what was needed in those bad times to put an end to construction forever.

Just the same, this two-thirds of a cathedral is by any measure the finest in the Midi, the only one comparable to the magnificent Gothic structures of the Ile-de-France. The short nave, in fact, heightens the exuberant verticality of the 40-m apse and choir, exceeded in height only by those of Amiens and Beauvais. Throughout, the structural lines are accented with ribbing or with protruding stone courses, as if the builders wanted to leave a gentle reminder of the extraordinary technical skill that made such a building possible. The whole is done in a clean and elegant stone, grey perhaps, but a grey that here bids to be included among the colours of the spectrum.

Inside, most of the best features are in the ambulatory and its chapels. Near the altar, facing the chapels, are two remarkable archepiscopal tombs: the **Tomb of Cardinal Briçonnet** (1514), with a decorative mix of Renaissance refinement and ghoulish, grinning skeletons, typical of that age. The other, the **Tomb of Cardinal Pierre de Jugie**, is an exquisite Gothic work of 1376; though much damaged, some of the original paint remains. The ambulatory chapels are illuminated by lovely 14th-century glass: the *Creation* (left chapel), the *Infancy of Christ* in the centre, and *SS Michael, Peter and Paul* (right chapels). Some faded original frescoes can be seen in the far right chapel, and also around the main altar. The central **Chapelle de la Vierge** has something really special, unique polychrome reliefs of the late 1300s. Ruined and covered in a Baroque remodelling of 1732, these were rediscovered in the last century, and currently they are being restored and replaced. On the upper band (left to right): an *Annunciation* and *Kings of France*, the *Presentation at the Temple*, *Palm Sunday* and *Crucifixion*. Lower band: *Purgatory, Hell* and *Limbo*. Hell, as always, fired the artists' imaginations the most; in the mouth of the inferno, the damned screech and howl while the Devil prepares his cooking pots and knives.

The side chapels have little to see but tapestries; in the first right is a 16th-century polychrome *Entombment of Christ* from Bavaria. Almost the entire west wall is covered by a spectacular **organ**, a mountain of carved wood and statuary that took over a hundred years to complete (1741–1856).

CATHEDRAL TREASURY

It's closed almost all the time in winter (only open Saturdays, 2:15–4; but open daily in summer, 9:30–11:30 and 2:30–5:30; adm), and the entrance is in a tiny door in the right ambulatory chapel. Many visitors miss it altogether. Arranged in a domed chamber with odd acoustics, formerly housing the cathedral archives, the collection includes medieval reliquaries, books and a 10th-century carved ivory plaque. Also the most outlandish of all Narbonne's surprises, two early 16th-century Flemish tapestries, unlike any others you're ever likely to see. Originally a set of ten, belonging to Archbishop François Fouquet, eight-and-a-half have disappeared, probably ending up as insulation, mattress-stuffing and a bed for the dog. The half-tapestry that remains depicts Adversity, from an *Allegory of Prosperity and Adversity*. Amidst a landscape of shipwrecks and earthquakes you will notice Cleopatra, Antiochus Seleucis and other celebrities of antiquity who met bad ends (all conveniently labelled), while Vulcan grinds out strife on his forge and a grinning Penury exults over the unfortunates. Part of the centrepiece also survived (on the left), dominated by an uncanny Goddess of Fortune on horseback, her face veiled.

The other tapestry, much better preserved, is a strange account of the *Creation*. The seven days of Genesis are arranged in tableaux, each with figures of the Holy Trinity, represented as three crowned, bearded old men. The iconography is unorthodox in the extreme; the symbolism throughout seems to hint at some concealed vein of medieval mysticism. In any case, the artists who created it produced a true *tour de force*, filling every corner with delightful naturalistic detail—a forest, the firmament, spring flowers, the Kingdom of the Sea—as intricate and lovely as any tapestry ever made. Bring the children, and see if they can spot the elephant.

Roman Narbonne

There isn't much of it. The centre of the ancient city, north of the Cathedral, is a dowdy, blank-faced quarter, with a newly-formed neighbourhood development group trying to interest people in fixing up the many abandoned houses. Small signs on the street corners direct you to the only Roman monument left—a warehouse or **Horreum**, on Rue Rouget de Lisle (daily 2–6; adm). Typical of the state-run warehouses of any Roman city, this is the only complete one anywhere. Just a small part has been excavated, a maze of tiny chambers; the original structure was over 152 m long. Among the ancient fragments displayed in the various rooms is a charming relief of bear-trainers and their bears, bathing together. To the west, on Rue de l'Ancienne Porte Neuve, the **Maison Vigneronne** is a 17th-century powder-house (in the middle of the city!) converted into a museum of wine and its cultivation. From the Place de l'Hôtel de Ville, Rue Droite runs northwards, roughly following the route of the Roman main street; it ends at **Place Bistan**—the former Forum, though nothing remains but some re-erected columns and a modern mural painting. One block east is the 15th-century Flamboyant church of **St-Sébastien**, built over the (apocryphal) birthplace of the saint himself. A favourite of artists across southern Europe (usually depicted stuck full of arrows) Sebastian was always a popular saint, for the belief that he could intercede against the plague, like St Roch of Montpellier.

The Bourg

This is Narbonne's medieval extension across the river (now across the canal). Cross over by the bridge in the **Promenade des Barques**, the elegant park along the canal. On the other side, the city's covered **market** is a rare sensory experience even by French market standards. The Narbonnais take great pride in it, and it recently won an annual award as the best in France. Behind it, the deconsecrated 13th-century church of Notre-Dame-de-Lamourguier now houses the **Musée Lapidaire**, a large collection of architectural fragments from ancient Narbonne, displayed more or less at random (daily exc Mon 10–11:50, 2–6; open Mon in Jul and Aug; adm). The fragments are here thanks to François I; on a visit, he recommended to the Narbonnais that they incorporate the vast heaps of antique rubble lying about into the new walls they were building. The walls themselves thus became an open-air museum, much commented on by travellers, until they were demolished in the last century and the old bits assembled here.

Follow the boulevards west, along the course of the demolished medieval walls; the modern city hospital on Boulevard Dr Lacroix incorporates the old one, the **Hôtel-Dieu**, with a grand Baroque chapel decorated by Narbonnais painters of the 1780s. Behind this, the **Maison des Trois Nourrices** on the street of the same name is the best surviving example of a Renaissance palace in the city; the 'three nurses' are the three classical caryatids holding up the main window.

Narbonne's other ancient church, the **Basilique St-Paul-Serge**, was first built in the 5th century, and dedicated to the first bishop of Narbonne. The present building was begun in 1229, an imposing monument that was one of the first in the south to adopt the new Gothic architecture. Three early Christian sarcophagi remain from the first church, an introduction to the catacomb-like **cemetery-crypt** beneath (daily exc Mon 10–12, 2–6; adm). This subterranean necropolis was begun in the time of Constantine. Such burials were not peculiar to the Christians. In Rome, pagan and Christian catacombs exist side by side; parts of this one are decorated with pagan symbols, raising the intriguing possibility that this cemetery was for a time a non-denominational one.

Market Day: Outdoor market on Thursday.

WHERE TO STAY   (postal code 11100)
But for the lack of parking and a bit of street noise, **La Dorade** would be perfect. Narbonne's old 'Grand Hôtel', with marble telamones holding up the balcony, this establishment is still well kept, centrally located overlooking the canal, and a good bargain (44 Rue Jean Jaurès, tel 68 32 65 95). Another gracious old establishment, a bit fancier and more expensive, is the ***Hôtel du Languedoc at 22 Blvd Gambetta, tel 68 65 14 74.

Most of the inexpensive places are around the station, especially on or around Av. Pierre Semard. **Will's Hôtel is not run by a Will, and the present owners can't imagine who Will might have been, but it is still a comfortable and extremely friendly place (23 Av. Pierre Semard, tel 68 90 44 50).

EATING OUT
As you might expect after a tour of their wonderful market, the Narbonnais are a gastronomically fastidious lot; their restaurants reflect this, with a minimum of pretension. Authentic Languedoc, its wines and ingredients, finds its apotheosis at **La Reverbère**. Expensive, lavish and highly rated, it excels in seafood spectaculars like the lobster 'in four episodes'; the extensive cellar has an emphasis on Corbières and other Languedoc wines (4 Pl. des Jacobins, south of the canal, menus from 240 to 475 F, tel 68 32 29 18).

Great stuffed dolls hang from the ceiling on garden swings, and the rest of the decor is cutesy to excess; if you order less than a half litre of wine, you'll get it in a baby bottle. Nevertheless, **L'Ame des Poètes** comes with the highest recommendation. They're absolutely nuts, but they try hard, and cook with verve and imagination (90 and 110 F menus, 19 Av. Pierre Semard, near the station, tel 68 32 73 70). Le Goût en Train occupying a vaulted medieval cellar, is a wine bar with a modest restaurant that makes good use of the local brews, in dishes like *estouffade au Corbières*. It's on Rue Fabre, opposite the cathedral, tel 68 90 61 29, about 80–120F).

For Chinese-Vietnamese cooking, very correct and tasty too, try **La Baie d'Along**, on Place Bistrin in old Narbonne; 90 F menu, though you may want to splurge for the elaborate starters, tel 68 65 58 83. Le Castel, with a wide choice of pizzas, also has steaks and chops with good salads, on Blvd du Dr Lacroix (150 F at most, much less for pizza).

Narbonne's Coast

The coastal road cannot follow this complicated shoreline, a miasma of marshes and lagoons; some detours on the backroads will be necessary to see it. One big obstacle is the mouth of the Aude, northeast of Narbonne; this pretty and amiable river comes all the way from the high Pyrenees to meet an inglorious end in a boggy landscape called (literally) 'Piss-cow Swamp'. South of here, one of the rare fishing villages in these parts, St-Pierre-sur-Mer, has been swallowed up by the bright modern resort of **Narbonne-Plage**. Just to the north is Languedoc's answer to the Fontaine de Vaucluse, a 'bottomless' pool called the **Gouffre de l'Oeil Doux**—the 'sweet eye', always full of pure, fresh water, though only a mile from the sea. Beyond Narbonne-Plage, the landscape rises into the **Montagne de la Clape**, once an island and still a world in itself. Parts are lush and pine-clad, others rugged and desolate, reminiscent of a Greek island; on the lower slopes are vineyards that produce small quantities of a very good wine (see below). It's a great place for hiking, though much of it is also inaccessible by car. Near the top, the chapel of **Notre-Dame-des-Auzils** has a fascinating collection of sailors' ex votos—ship models, paintings and the like, many over a century old (open Sun afternoons, and daily in summer, 3–6); the nearby marine cemetery has exceptional views over the coast.

Most of those sailors came from **Gruissan**, south of La Clape. One of Narbonne's ports in the Middle Ages, Gruissan today is surrounded by lagoons and salt-pans; the charming village is set in concentric rings around a ruined 13th-century castle, built to defend the approaches to Narbonne. Its tower, the 'Tour de Barbarousse', possibly takes its name from a visit by the famous Turkish pirate-admiral Barbarossa; in the 1540s the Ottoman sultan's fleet was briefly based in Toulon, helping the French against the Holy Roman Emperor Charles V. To Gruissan's fine beaches the government has added a pleasure marina, resulting in one of the more agreeable resorts on these coasts. Gruissan's other landmark is the *Plage des Pilotis*, where neat rows of beach cottages hang in the air. The sea regularly covers the sand here, and over a century ago people began the habit of building their holiday retreats on stilts.

To go further south, you'll have to return to Narbonne, and circle around the Etang de Bages et de Sigean. This broad lagoon, with its many islands and forgotten, half-abandoned hamlets, is especially rich in waterfowl, including a few flamingos, as well as cormorants, egrets and herons. **Boat trips** can be arranged through the Cercle Nautique des Corbières, tel 68 48 42 62, starting from the dock of a vanished medieval village, Port-Mahon, near Sigean. Wildlife of an entirely different sort coexists peacefully nearby at the **Réserve Africaine** north of Sigean, a big zoo and drive-through safari park with the only white rhinoceroses, most likely, in all Languedoc.

When the builders of the Canal de la Robine laid out their coastal port in 1820, they gave it the strikingly original name of **Port-la-Nouvelle**. Now France's third-largest Mediterranean port, it is a gritty, no-nonsense town of Communist stevedores, where the most prominent restaurant is called 'Le Chicken Shack', and where the waterfront promenade takes in a panorama of shiny oil tanks. It has good beaches, and for a long time it was also a resort; there are, incredibly, still some holiday motels in town. If you didn't fancy the palms and ice-cream of La Grande Motte or Cap d' Agde, a day on the beach here, watching cement barges and tankers sail past, might be just the thing.

WHERE TO STAY/EATING OUT

Gruissan (11430), still a real fishing port, is understandably a good place for seafood. For a worthwhile splurge, there is the popular **La Marée**, in the centre of the village on Av. Azibert, with an extremely wide choice, and interesting starters like squid *au vermouth*, 200 F at the most (tel 68 49 16 26). If you're staying over, the **Hôtel Corail** on Quai Ponant in Gruissan Port is perfectly acceptable though unremarkable— but it has a fine restaurant, specializing in *bouillabaisse* (closed Nov through Jan, tel 68 49 04 43, several menus from 90–160 F).

Narbonne-Plage (11100), like Gruissan, is hardly an up-market resort. Hotels are generally two-stars and all of a piece. The **Hôtel Bureau de la Clape** is a wonderful address from which to write home (closed Nov–Easter, on Rue des Flots Bleus, tel 68 49 80 15), but a slightly better choice is the **La Caravelle**, close to the beach (closed Oct–Easter, Av. Front de Mer, tel 68 49 80 38). Good seafood with no frills can be had at **Restaurant L'Oasis** on Av. Front de Mer (tel 68 49 97 66, menus 70–140 F).

Wines of the coast

Winemakers around here like to say that these are the oldest vineyards of France. There is no proof, but it is likely that the Romans of *Colonia Narbo Martius* brought the vine here at a very early date. Most of the coastal area is part of the **Corbières** wine region (see below, p. 415), but it is also the home of three exceptional wines, little-known because the areas are so small and produce so little. The sunny Montagne de la Clape, in soil and climate, is a totally separate entity; the **Coteaux de Languedoc-La Clape**, a rarefied red concoction of syrah, grenache, and carignan, high in alcohol and very fragrant, the perfect wine for a leg of lamb; there's a soft, floral white La Clape as well, dominated by bourboulenc. La Clape's winemakers tend to be small operators—gentlemen vintners who are intensely proud of their wine, and ready to bend your ear about it for hours. You'll see signs for the vineyards on the D 32–D 168 route around the mountain; among the best are the award-winning 88 and 89 reds of Jacques Boscary's **Château Rouquette-sur-Mer**, off the D 168 southwest of Narbonne-Plage in Gruissan, tel 68 32 56 53; **Château de Pech Redon**, Rte de Gruissan in Narbonne, tel 68 90 41 23 (especially the 89 red), and for whites, **Domaine du Fraisse**, at Autignac, tel 67 90 23 40.

In the deep red soils skirting the western borders of the Etang de Bages et de Sigean, south of Narbonne, there is a really obscure *appellation* called **Quatourze**, a noble variation on Corbières made along the back roads around Bages and Peyriac-de-Mer. And further south near the border with Roussillon, is the smaller of the two regions that produce **Fitou** (see p. 415); stop just outside the town of Fitou itself for a taste at the **Coopérative de Fitou**, on the N 9, tel 68 45 71 41.

Around Narbonne: Abbaye de Fontfroide

Some attractions within a short drive of the city: 11 km to the north, the **Oppidum de Montlaures**, the site of a pre-Roman town, similar to the Oppidum d'Ensérune (see p. 384) and set on the same sort of hilltop; nearby are a number of freshwater springs in the rock. Better, take the N 113 west from the city, and turn south on the D 613. The first sight, to the left, is a derelict, frequently-overlooked castle. For all its impressive walls, **St-Pierre-des-Clars** has been quite forgotten. In its grounds, Roman coins with the images of Pompey and Brutus have been found, but the present building probably dates from the late 12th or 13th century. The purpose of this ineffably romantic ruin was probably to protect sheep in wartime. This is not as daft as it may sound; after iron, sheep were the most valuable commodity of the Middle Ages, the wool-on-the-hoof that made the banking fortunes of so many medieval cities. This corner of the Corbières was as rich and overcrowded a pastureland as any. It helped finance Narbonne's cathedral. In more settled times, in the 1500s, the city of Narbonne petitioned the king to demolish the fortress; cities always felt a little nervous about nearby castles that might fall into the hands of an unfriendly faction or foreign invader. This explains the gaps torn in the outer wall and the ruined *donjon*, of which one lofty wall has steadfastly, inexplicably, refused to fall. Despite the wild roses and other prickly nuisances, it's a good ruin to explore; no one will mind if you do.

Three km further down the D 613, you'll see another ruined castle in the distance, madly perched on a perpendicular cliff. A perfect introduction to the fortified wilderness of the Corbières (see below), **St-Martin-de-Toques** was gradually built between the 10th and 13th centuries, and occupied until the 1600s. Someone, somehow, has got a crane up to it, and restorations are underway. A little further along, a marked side road leads to the **Abbaye de Fontfroide** (Apr-Sept, daily 9–12 and 2:30–6, rest of the year daily exc Tues, 9:30–12 and 2–5; adm, mandatory guided tours, generally on the hour).

When the tour reaches the monks' refectory, the guide will take pains to point out that the fireplace is a recent addition; heating of any kind was a little too posh for medieval Cistercians. On the other hand, after inspecting the lavish church and grounds it is hard to believe the monks were giving much away to the poor—a typical medieval enigma: power and wealth, without the enjoyment of them. One of the most important Cistercian abbeys in the south, Fontfroide was founded in 1145, on the site of an earlier Bene-dictine house. Until its suppression in 1791, it was one of richest and most influential of all Cistercian houses. It was largely in ruins when a local family, the Fayets, bought it early in this century; they have been fixing it up a little at a time ever since—an example of the kind of shoe-string private restoration that has saved so many French monuments, neglected by a traditionally stingy national government.

The best part of the tour is Fontfroide's lovely 13th-century **cloister**; its style of broad arches, inset with smaller ones, was much copied in later cloisters in Languedoc. The 12th-century **church** impresses with its proportions and Romanesque austerity; follow-ing Cistercian custom simple floral patterns constitute the only decoration. The art of making stained glass, once one of France's proudest achievements, had nearly died out by the 19th century. There has been a modest revival in our own century; one of its first productions was the excellent set of windows here, a *Last Judgement* and *signs of the zodiac* done in the 20s. More glass can be seen in the **dormitory**—fascinating abstract collages of old fragments, brought here from northern French churches wrecked during World War I. Behind the cloister is a nursery of roses where medieval varieties are grown by a local firm.

To protect the produce of its vast estates, the Abbey maintained a network of fortified farms and storehouses all over the region. The most impressive one is near Capestang (see p. 385); the closest, 8 km west of Fontfroide, is called the **Château de Gaussan**. Followers of Viollet-le-Duc restored it in the last century, with plenty of neo-Gothic ornament and frescoes inside.

From Narbonne to Carcassonne

The *Autoroute des Deux Mers* and the N 113 follow this corridor inland, across the coastal plain and the valley of the Aude. There is nothing especially interesting along the way, unless you make some detours, or take the back roads following the Aude and the Canal du Midi (for areas to the north, see above, **Canal du Midi**, p. 383, and **Minervois**, p. 386; for south, see below, **Corbières**, p. 413).

CARCASSONNE

Standing before the great eastern gate of the walled city, the writer had his notebook out and was scribbling furiously. It was market day, and rustic villeins in coarse wool tunics were offering hung pheasants and great round cheeses from their wooden carts. Geese honked from cages made of twigs and rushes, while pigs and hounds poked about in the cobbled gutters. 'This is medieval indeed', the writer mused—just then the director and his entourage appeared over the drawbridge. 'Lovely, everyone, but we'll want more sheep; lots more sheep!'

Plenty of obscure costume-dramas have been shot here, drawn by Viollet-le-Duc's romantic restoration. Even without pigs in the gutters, Carcassonne is the Middle Ages come to life. Not the real Middle Ages, perhaps—Carcassonne is one of a kind—but the realm of medieval legends, a perfect pastel watercolour from some turn-of-the-century book of fairy-tales. The people of the city do their best to heighten the medieval atmosphere every August for the two-week festival called the *Médiévales*, with artisans in costume, music and even jousts under the walls. Reality intrudes in the history of the place. Today a dour manufacturing town, Carcassonne was once the strategic key to the Midi; the castle built here by St Louis was a barrier greater than the Pyrenees to invading armies.

History

After running north down from the Pyrenees, the river Aude makes a sharp right turn for the sea, thus conveniently providing not only an easy natural route across the mountains, but also one across the 'French isthmus', between the Mediterranean and the Atlantic. The river's angle, one of the crossroads of France since prehistoric times, is an obvious site for a fortress; there seems to have been one nearby since the 8th century BC. The Tectosage Gauls occupied the site of the present *cité* in the 3rd century; a century later the Romans established a fortified veterans' colony on it called *Carcaso*, which gradually grew into a town. With the coming of the Visigoths, in the Germanic invasions of the 5th century, Carcassonne began to assume its present role, as a border stronghold between France and Spain—the Frankish and Visigothic kingdoms. The action started as early as 506 AD, when the Frankish King Clovis unsuccessfully besieged the town.

Arabs from Spain arrived about 725, one of the high-water marks of the Muslim tide in Europe. Pépin the Short chased them out 30 years later. Not that the Franks could hold it either. With the collapse of the Carolingian Empire, local viscounts attained a *de facto* independence. From 1084 to 1209 Carcassonne enjoyed a glorious period of wealth and culture under the Trencavels, a family who were also viscounts of Béziers and Nîmes. Under them the cathedral and the Château Comtal were begun. Simon de Montfort, realizing the importance of the town, made it one of his first stops in the crusade of 1209. The last viscount, Raymond-Roger Trencavel, was no Cathar, but a gentleman and a patriot, determined to oppose the planned rape of Languedoc by the northerners. His famous declaration is still remembered today: 'I offer a town, a roof, a shelter, bread and my sword to all the persecuted people who will soon be wandering in Provence'.

Unfortunately, Trencavel allowed himself to be tricked outside the *cité* walls on pretence of negotiation; he was put in chains, and the leaderless town surrendered soon after. Raymond-Roger died in prison three months later, probably poisoned by Montfort, who declared himself viscount and used Carcassonne as his base of operations until his death in 1218. His son, Amauri, ceded the town and the rest of Montfort's conquests to King Louis IX. The last of the Trencavels, Raymond-Roger's son and heir, also named Raymond, fought to reclaim his lands until 1240, without success despite popular revolts. Under Louis and his son, Philip III, the outer walls were built, making the entire town into the greatest fortress in Europe, the impregnable base of French power in the south. No attempts were ever made on it; even the Black Prince, passing through in 1355, declined to undertake a siege.

When France gobbled up the province of Roussillon in 1659, this mighty bastion no longer had any military purpose, and it was allowed to fall into disrepair. While the lower town, with its large textile industries, prospered until English competition ruined the trade in the 1800s, the *cité* gradually decayed into a half-abandoned slum. It was the writer Prosper Mérimée, France's Inspector-General of Historic Monuments in the 1830s, who called attention to this sad state of affairs. Viollet-le-Duc, fresh from sprucing up Narbonne, got the huge job of restoring the *cité* in 1844; work continued, according to his plans, for the rest of the century.

Today's Carcassonne has a split personality: up on its hill, the pink towers of the lovingly restored *cité* glitter like a dream. No longer entirely impregnable, its 750 inhabitants are invaded by over 200,000 visitors each year, while down below, the grim, workaday *Ville Basse* gets on with the job.

GETTING AROUND

From the SNCF station, on Av. du Maréchal Joffre at the northern edge of the Ville Basse, there are regular connections to Narbonne (11 a day), and from there to all the coastal cities; also a few trains down the Aude valley to Limoux, Quillan and from there to Perpignan (tel 67 48 50 50). You can rent bicycles and scooters at the station—and also boats; the station is right on the Canal du Midi.

The *gare routière* is a few streets south of the rail station, on Boulevard de Varsovie. There are several a day to Narbonne and Castelnaudary, three to Toulouse, and a rare few to outlying towns liike Limoux or Foix; also a daily coach to Barcelona. Some buses to villages in the Montagne Noire and Minervois leave from the Café Bristol ᵻn front of the rail station. To get up to the *cité* from the town, take the No. 4 city bus from the rail station or from Place Gambetta near the tourist office.

TOURIST INFORMATION
Place Gambetta, in the centre of the Ville Basse; tel 68 25 07 04. Also in the *cité* (summer only), just inside the Porte Narbonnaise. **Post office**: Rue Jean Bringer in the Ville Basse, and Rue Trencavel in the *cité*.

The Walls of the Cité

Haute Ville

Most visitors come in through the back door, by the car parks and the bus stop, at the **Porte Narbonnaise**. This is not the best introduction to the impressive military sophistication of Carcassonne's defences. It's probably the weakest point along the walls, though there may have been outworks that have since disappeared. Still, it looks strong enough, with two stout rounded bastions on the inner wall from which to mow down any attackers so fortunate as to get through the outer wall.

Between the two walls, you can circumnavigate Carcassonne through the open space called **les Lices**, the 'lists', where knights trained, and where tournaments were held. The **outer wall** is the work of Louis IX; note how it is completely open on the inside, so that attackers who stormed it would have no protection from the defenders on the **inner wall**. Parts of this date back to the Romans—wherever you see large, irregular blocks without mortar, or layers of smaller stones interspersed with courses of thin brick; the ground level within the lists was slightly lowered by the French, so you will often see their rectangular stones, either smooth or rusticated, beneath Roman work, where they had to underpin the towers.

To the right of the Porte Narbonnaise, the first large tower is the mighty **Tour du Trésau**. Beyond it, the northern side of the inner wall is almost completely Roman, begun in the 1st century and rebuilt in the imperial decline of the 4th century, like the walls of Rome itself, with the characteristic rounded bastions used all over the Empire. Near the second-last of them is a Roman postern gate. The walls to the left of the Porte

Narbonnaise were almost completely rebuilt under Philip III, a long stretch of impressive bastions culminating in the great **Tour St-Nazaire**.

Atop both the inner and outer walls, almost everything you see today—the crenellations, wooden galleries (*hourds*) and pointed turrets that make up Carcassonne's memorable skyline—is the work of Viollet-le-Duc. As in all his other works, the pioneer of architectural restoration has been faulted for not adhering literally to original appearances. This is true, especially concerning the pointed turrets and northern slate roofs, but Viollet-le-Duc worked in a time before anyone could have imagined our own rigorous, antiseptic approach to recreating the old. His romantic, 19th-century appreciation of the Middle Ages made possible a restoration that was not only essentially correct, but creative and beautiful. Viollet-le-Duc *improved* Carcassonne—and he would have been the first to admit it.

Château Comtal

Approaching the *cité* from the western side, above the river, you pass the Gothic church of **St-Gimer**, ascending to the **Porte d'Aude**. In the old days, you couldn't come empty-handed; the *cité* has no natural source of water, and commoners from the Ville Basse had to bring up two buckets each time to get in. The Porte d'Aude was the ultimate discouragement for an attacker, employing every trick in the medieval bag. Note, for example, how the approach comes from the right; to protect themselves, soldiers on the way up would have to keep their shields in their right hand, making it difficult to do anything else. The winding path made it impossible to use a battering ram on the gate, and attackers would be under fire from the walls the entire way; there is another gate inside, and if anyone got through the first they would find themselves trapped in a box, under fire from all sides.

The defences are strongest on the western side because here, the *cité's* three lines of defence—the outer and inner walls and the citadel, the **Château Comtal**—are closely compressed. Probably the site of the Roman governors' palace,it was rebuilt by the Trencavels for their own palace, and expanded by King Louis IX. Most of it now houses the **Musée Lapidaire** (daily exc Sun, 9:30–12:30 and 2–5; 9–7 in summer; hours may vary at certain times of year; adm). The collection includes ancient and medieval fragments: from Roman inscriptions and milestones to Merovingian sarcophagi, laughing monster faces on corbels from the cathedral, and country roadside crosses (in local folklore, erroneously believed to be tombstones of the Cathars). Old prints and paintings give an idea of the half-ruined state of the *cité* before Viollet-le-Duc went to work on it, with houses half-filling les Lices and windmills along the walls.

Two medieval works saved from the town's churches are especially worth a look: an unusual 15th-century English alabaster of the *Transfiguration*, and an excellent sculpted altarpiece, with a host of expressive faces in attendance. In one of the halls, faded 14th-century frescoes of battle scenes have been discovered, in a stylized manner oddly reminiscent of ancient Cretan art.

The entrance to the museum is also the base for **guided tours** of the walls and towers (usually on the hour, schedule posted at the entrance) which begin with a room-sized model and continue, in fascinating, excruciating detail, through an advanced course in medieval military architecture. Louis' builders laid as many traps for invaders inside the walls as without—for example the stairways where each riser is a different height. Be careful.

Basilique St-Nazaire

In 1096 (the year after he declared the First Crusade), Pope Urban V visited here, giving his blessing to the beginning of the works. The building took shape as an austere, typically southern Romanesque church, and stayed that way until 1270. The French conquerors had more ambitious plans for the cathedral, and rebuilt the transepts and choir in glorious, perpendicular Gothic. The best features can be seen from outside: two tremendous rose windows and a tall apse with more acres of windows. Inside, you'll see them illuminated by fine 16th- and 17th-century stained glass, with a *Tree of Jesse* and *Life of Christ*.

In the right aisle, you can pay your respects to the devil himself, at the **Tomb of Simon de Montfort**, marked by a small plaque. Understandably, Montfort is no longer present; six years after his death, his descendants took him back up north where there would be less danger of desecration. There is some good medieval statuary around the choir, including the 1266 **Tomb of Bishop Radulph**.

The Ville Basse

Before Louis IX, the *cité* was surrounded by long-established suburbs. In 1240, these were occupied by Raymond Trencavel, son of the last viscount. With the help of the townspeople, he besieged the *cité* and nearly took it. Louis pardoned the rebels, but did find it necessary to knock their houses down, to deprive any future attackers of cover. To replace the old *bourg*, he laid out a new town across the river; this *Ville Basse* has gradually replaced the *cité* as the centre of modern Carcassonne.

Descending from the Porte d'Aude, you'll pass some streets of houses that managed to creep back despite the royal decree. Rue Trivalle, with a pair of elegant Renaissance *hôtels*, leads down to the long, 14th-century **Pont Vieux**. At the far end, there once was a sort of triumphal arch, as can be seen in the old prints in the Château Comtal. Now there remains only the chapel of **Notre-Dame-de-la-Santé**, built in 1538. The Ville Basse proper begins two streets further down, with a circle of boulevards that replaced the old walls. Inside is a grid of streets as strictly rectilinear as Aigues-Mortes'. The plan contributes

Ville Basse

much to the general drabness of the Ville Basse. At the north and south ends of it are two huge, mouldering Gothic churches: **St-Vincent** and **St-Michel**, both begun under Louis IX, and both on Rue Dr Tomey. St-Michel was restored by Viollet-le-Duc, and serves as co-cathedral along with St-Nazaire.

Market Days: in Place Carnot, on Tuesday, Thursday and Saturday.

WHERE TO STAY   (postal code 11000)
Stay in the *cité* if you can, though it won't be cheap. The ******Hôtel de la Cité**, in a pretty garden right under the walls, occupies the former episcopal palace, grandly restored in 1909: marble baths, a pool, the works (Place de la Cathédrale, tel 68 25 03 34, closed

Jan–Mar). A little less posh, another charming old mansion of the *cité* houses the ***Hôtel du Donjon, with a small garden and a fine restaurant (Rue du Comte Roger, tel 68 71 08 80). For anything cheaper, you'll be outside the walls; one of the closest to the *cité*, and one of the best is the **Hôtel du Pont Vieux (32 Rue Trivalle; tel 68 25 24 99).

All of the rest are down in the Basse Ville, near the train station or around Blvd Jean Jaurès. Some are real dives, as in any industrial town, but most are respectable enough; the *Hôtel Central, on Blvd Jean Jaurès, is one of the cheapest, but quite nice (tel 68 25 03 84).

A luxury alternative to staying in the *cité* is the ****Domaine d'Auriac, south of town on the Rte St-Hilaire: a stately, ivy-covered 18th-century mansion set in a large, immaculately kept park. There's a pool, tennis, and even a golf course close by. Also an elegant and highly-rated restaurant, featuring some seafood but mostly traditional dishes of the Aude, such as pigeon, which you can get here with truffles (tel 68 25 72 22, dinner 220–400 F, rooms the dearest in the region, 600 F and up for a double).

EATING OUT

In the *cité*, the restaurant of the Hôtel du Donjon (see above) dedicates itself to the best of Languedoc cooking—even the humble *cassoulet* reaches new heights (110 F menu, tel 68 71 08 70). More ambitiously, and expensively, the Auberge du Pont-Levis has an outdoor terrace near the Porte Narbonnaise, and specializes in *langoustines* in various guises (tel 68 25 55 23, menus 160–280 F). Less expensive places can be found in the *cité*, but as you might expect in such an intense tourist zone, none are anything special.

Down in the Ville Basse, Le Relais de l'Ecluse is another temple of Languedocien *confits* and *cassoulet*; also some seafood (tel 68 25 08 96, in the Terminus Hôtel at 2 Av. Maréchal Joffre, menus 80–240 F). A good square meal with no frills can be had at the Restaurant Pont Neuf (14 Av. Arthur Mullot, 70 F menu). Around the corner on the Allée de Bezons, refined Vietnamese cuisine is to be found at Le Dragon d'Annam, (tel 68 25 29 07, 110–150 F). And in most of Carcassonne's *pâtisseries* you can satisfy your sweet tooth on the local favourite, *boulets de Carcassonne*, made with peanuts and honey.

Castelnaudary, Famous for Beans

TOURIST INFORMATION
Cours de la République, tel 68 23 05 73.

To be right, a *cassoulet* requires four things: it must be 'white beans from Lavelanet, cooked in the pure water of Castelnaudary, in a casserole made of clay from the Issel, over a fire of furze from the Black Mountain'. Every French book ever written on the area mentions this, so we felt obliged to pass it on. The clay pot of *cassoulet* in Castelnaudary's kitchen is the town's Eiffel Tower, its Acropolis, its very identity. Having finally penetrated to Deepest France, what you find is not always what you might expect. Here, the precious insight into the folk soul is a cherished mess of beans, lard, goose grease and miscellaneous pork parts. Back in the 1570s, Castelnaudary's *cassoulet* was prescribed to Queen Margot as a cure for sterility, unfortunately without success. Today, all over central France, housewives are torn between making their own, or succumbing to the

411

allure of *canned cassoulet*; any good supermarket will stock at least six brands. The children prefer frozen fish-fingers, until they grow up and become traditionalists.

With *cassoulet*, the charms of Castelnaudary (northwest of Carcassonne, off the N 113) are nearly exhausted. There is the 14th-century church of **St-Michel**, with a tall steeple that dominates the city; the **Moulin de Cugarel**, a restored 17th-century windmill; an archaeological museum, and the port and turning basin of the Canal du Midi.

Market Day: Monday.

The Medieval Lauragais

Castelnaudary is the metropolis of a region called the **Lauragais**, a mostly flat expanse of serious farming of the humbler sort: beans, of course, barley and pigs, and in some villages a substantial chicken-plucking trade. In the Middle Ages, **St-Papoul**, 8 km east of Castelnaudary on the D 103, was the centre of the Lauragais and the home of its bishop. An abbey had been here since the time of Charlemagne; in 1317 Pope John XXII turned the abbot into a bishop and the monks into canons—the better to keep an eye on local heretics. In decline for centuries, this forgotten town still has some of its walls and half-timbered houses, as well as a fine Romanesque **cathedral**—from the 14th century, a typically archaic building in a region that disdained the imported Gothic of the hated northerners. Though remodelled in trashy Baroque inside, the exterior has remained largely unchanged, including a beautiful apse with carved capitals attributed to the Master of Cabestany (*Daniel in the Lions' Den* and other scenes of that prophet). Other good Romanesque churches with carvings can be visited west of Castelnaudary at **Mas-Stes-Puelles** and **Baraigne** (take the D 33 and D 218 from Castelnaudary) and at **Montmaur**, north of the D 113 on the D 58; the latter two preserve examples of small circular roadside crosses, like those in the Carcassonne museum. In medieval times this region had hundreds of them; almost all have been destroyed or moved.

West of Castelnaudary, the Canal du Midi loses most of its tranquillity, as both the *Autoroute des Deux Mers* and the N 113 move in to keep it company on the way to Toulouse. On the borders of the *département*, at **Port-Lauragais** the canal passes its highest point. Figuring out how to cross it was Paul Riquet's biggest challenge; he solved it by an elaborate system of smaller canals and reservoirs, carrying water to the locks from as far as 50 km away, in the Montagne Noire. Near Port-Lauragais there is a large obelisk in Riquet's honour (erected by his descendants in 1825, the year the canal finally turned in a profit!) and a small museum-cum-information centre about the canal, accessible from the autoroute.

South of Castelnaudary are more reminders of the Cathars and their oppressors. **Fanjeaux**, on the D 119, began its career as *Fanum Jovis*, from an ancient temple of Jupiter; from that you can guess that the town, like almost all the sites dedicated to the god of thunder and storms, is on a commanding height, with a wide view over the Lauragais plains. Fanjeaux gained its fame in 1206, when St Dominic himself came from Spain to live here as a missionary to the heretics—quite peacefully and sincerely, though his Dominican followers would be the Church's chief inquisitors and torture-masters for centuries to come. They bequeathed Fanjeaux a 14th-century Gothic church, in the former Dominican monastery; a better work, the parish church of 1278, has a *trésor* full of unusual old reliquaries. St Dominic founded a monastery in nearby **Prouille**, which has become a pilgrimage site. South of Fanjeaux, on the way to Limoux, the villages are often laid out on a circular or even elliptical plan: Ferran, Brézilhac and La Digne, among others. They are medieval new towns; no one knows why the medieval planners decided here to depart from their accustomed strict rectangularity, and there are few villages like them anywhere else in France.

WHERE TO STAY/EATING OUT
The choice in **Castelnaudary** (11400) is the family-run, remodelled but still a bit old-fashioned ****Hôtel Fourcade**; even if you're not staying, its restaurant is the best in town, the place to experience gourmet *cassoulet* or many less folkloric treats (14 Rue des Carmes, tel 68 23 25 95, menus 80–280 F).

One of the Aude's few *fermes-auberges* is run by the Cazenave family, at the Château de la Barthe in **Belflou** (11410) on an artificial lake off the D 217, west of Castelnaudary; home cooking and a pleasant room at bargain rates (tel 68 60 32 49). Five kilometres from St-Papoul, in **Verdun-en-Lauragais** (11400), the ***Hôtel Sanègre** occupies a restored farmhouse, with a garden and a good, simple restaurant (tel 63 74 11 79).

The Corbières

Among other things, the Corbières may be France's most underestimated wine region. Thanks to the vineyards it has finally found its vocation. This scrubby, mountainous area, where landscapes range from classic Mediterranean to rugged Wild West, has been the odd region out since ancient times. As a refuge for disaffected Gauls, it was a headache to the Romans. In the Middle Ages, sitting astride the boundaries of France and Aragon, it was a permanent zone of combat. Local *seigneurs* littered the landscape with castles in incredible, impregnable mountain-top sites. Some of these became the last redoubts of the Cathars; nearly all of them are ruined today. For anyone with clear lungs and a little spirit, exploring them will be a challenge and a delight. Amidst the lonely landscapes of limestone crags and hills carpeted in *maquis*, the vineyards advance tenaciously across every dusty, sun-bleached hectare of arable ground. It doesn't take many men to tend them, and villages are few and far between.

GETTING AROUND
SNCF rail lines make a neat square around the Corbières—they define its boundaries almost exactly, but none of them ventures inside the region. The only useful one is from Carcassonne, following the Aude valley and then turning east through the Fenouillèdes, stopping at Limoux, Alet-les-Bains, Couiza, Quillan and St-Paul-de-Fenouillet on its way to Perpignan.

Don't count on buses either. There are some regular services from Perpignan's *gare routière* up the Agly valley to Maury, St-Paul and Quillan, and one a day through the heart of the Fenouillèdes to Sournia. If you're driving keep the tank full. The Corbières is the badlands of France, and its unique fascination comes from traversing spaces as empty as central Anatolia with all the specific charms of France close at hand. There are only a few good roads; here are two possibilities for a quick tour: from Narbonne, the D 613/D 3 passing Fontfroide and Lagrasse, then south on the scenic D 212, rejoining the D 613 and ending up in Couiza. Alternatively, the N 9/D 611A/D 611/D 14/D 10/D 7 from south of Narbonne passes the best of the wine country, the castles of Aguilar, Peyrepertuse and Quéribus, and the Gorges de Galamus, ending up on the main D 117 route for Perpignan.

TOURIST INFORMATION
Lezignan-Corbières: Place Marcelin Albert, tel 68 27 05 42.
St-Paul-de-Fenouillet: tel 68 59 00 26.

Lagrasse

The northern part of the Corbières has more monasteries than castles. The greatest of these was the Abbey of Fontfroide, just west of Narbonne (see p. 405). Continuing in that direction on the D 613/D 3 takes you to **Lagrasse**, a walled medieval village that grew up around a Benedictine abbey founded in the 8th century and chartered by Charlemagne himself. Some of the houses date back to the 14th century, while the walls and the graceful arched **Pont Neuf** are from the 12th. The bridge leads to the **Abbey**, partly in ruins and partly the restored home of a Byzantine Catholic monastic community (daily 8–12 and 4–8, guided tours).

Southwest of Lagrasse, in one of the remotest corners of the Corbières, there is a remarkable country church at **St-Martin-des Puits**. The oldest part, the choir, was built in the 900s, and the nave has some still older capitals, recycled Merovingian pieces. The fanciful frescoes all around are 12th-century (ask at the mayor's house for the key).

Aguilar and Quéribus

The humble, two-lane D 611 and D 14 were the medieval main routes through the Corbières, connecting with the passes over the Pyrenees to Spain. Castles occur with the frequency of petrol stations on a motorway; before the kings of France asserted their authority, one wonders how many times the poor merchants had to pay tolls. Even the landscape is suggestive of castles, with limestone outcrops resembling ruined walls and bastions, and upright cypresses standing sentinel above. All of the real strongholds are in ruins today; the first, one of the smaller models, is at **Durban-Corbières**, in the centre of the wine-growing region; it was built by the kings of Aragon. **Tuchan**, another typically stark and dusty Corbières village, has no less than three ruined castles; the best of them, the impressive **Château d'Aguilar** saw plenty of action: Simon de Montfort stormed it in 1210, but the French had to take it again from rebellious barons 30 years later; over the next 200 years the Spaniards knocked at the gate with regularity (always open; a short climb from the end of the signposted road).

West of Tuchan the landscapes become higher and wilder. **Padern** has another castle, ruined despite rebuilding work in the 18th century, so does **Cucugnan**. Both these towns offer scenic detours—from Padern, north through the **Gorges du Torgan**, and from Cucugnan, south through the spectacular **Grau de Maury**, the Corbières' back door. Its landmark is obvious from a distance, the picture-postcard **Château de Quéribus**, balancing nonchalantly on a slender peak, a half-mile in the air over the gorge. Quéribus was the last redoubt of the Cathars; a small band of bitter-enders held out against the French for months here in 1255. Probably the best maintained of the Corbières castles, it's also the most difficult to reach—a 30-minute vertical climb.

Corbières, and Some Others

The Corbières has a singular micro-climate, swept by the tramontane and with a sparse, irregular rainfall. Under its vines and *maquis* lies a geological jigsaw puzzle of Liassic, Triassic, Urgonian and who-knows-what-other kind of rocks, not to mention the Urgo-Aptian debris and Villefranchean scree. There are as many variations of soil, often giving wine from one village a completely different character to that of its neighbour. Wine has always been made here—the land isn't good for much else—but only recently have producers really tried to exploit its unique possibilities. The results have been more than encouraging. Corbières red (mostly carignan, grenache, and cinsault) varies widely in price and quality: from some of the best 8 F *appellation contrôlée* plonk you'll ever taste, to truly excellent, estate-bottled wines costing seven times as much. Always, though, it will be dark ruby red, full-bodied and intense. There is also white and rosé Corbières, although you won't often see them; good rosé (as well as red) comes from **Château La Baronne** near Fontcouverte (tel 68 43 90 20).

The Corbières is a stronghold of the village cooperative cellar, and has been ever since the troubles in 1907. There are nevertheless a number of strictly private producers. Along the D 611A, you may visit **Château Gléon**, west of Portel, tel 68 48 28 25, a lovely estate behind an old stone bridge, which makes a fine, very traditional red and a striking Corbières white, based on malvoisie. Nearby, the vast **Château Lastours**, Portel-des-Corbières, tel 68 48 29 17, set among the *garrigues* and canyons where motor-heads train for the Paris-Dakar rally. Château Lastours has grown wine since the 12th century, and was revived in 1970 by a group in Marseille to produce Corbières and special *cuvées* according to the most modern methods, and at the same time to offer employment and independence to the mentally handicapped (try the concentrated 88 Cuvée Ermengarde or the Cuvée en fûts 86).

The stretch of D 611 between Villeneuve and Tuchan is the heartland of one of Languedoc's finest wines, **Fitou**; strong and fragrant with the scent of the *garrigue*, dominated by carignan (mixed with grenache and syrah), it was the first AOC-designated wine in the region (1948). It isn't sold until after a year or more of maturation, and after five years or longer in the bottle takes on a spicy, wild aroma. The Cave Pilot, or **Cave de Villeneuve-les-Corbières**, tel 68 45 91 59, sells an excellent and reasonably priced 88 Fitou, aged in oak, as well as Corbières. At the **Château de Nouvelles**, tel 68 45 40 03, on a side road north of Tuchan, try the complex 13.5% Fitou 85, and come back in 1995 to buy the 88, which promises to be fantastic. The very best of the bunch is **Château L'Espigne** at Villeneuve-les-Corbières, tel 68 45 91 26. This ancient estate was originally a 'Moulin à l'Huile'. It is planted with 80-year-old vines that produce tiny amounts of grapes, resulting in wines of enormous concentration and complexity.

In the valley of the Agly, just over the boundary between Languedoc and Roussillon, the wine scene changes completely. Like most of Roussillon, the area around Maury and Estagel produces sweet dessert and aperitif wines called VDNs, or *vins doux naturels* (see Rivesaltes)—but it makes what many consider the best of them, **Maury**. Like its chief rival Banyuls, Maury is made from grenache noir, but it has a distinctive character of its own, a more consistent colour and spicy, leathery aroma, especially as it ages (1983 was a great year); a fragrant well-aged Maury Chabert is one of the few French wines that goes well with curries. Most of the 40,000 hectalitres produced each year pass through Maury's village cooperative, on Av. Jean Jaurès in Maury, tel 68 59 00 95.

Château de Peyrepertuse

Castles atop mountains will be nothing new by now, but nowhere else, perhaps, is there a bigger castle atop a taller, steeper mountain. If the air is clear, and you know where to look for it, you can see Peyrepertuse from any bit of high ground as far as the coast. From Cucugnan, it is an unforgettable sight, a white, limestone cliff rising vertically up to the clouds, crowned by a stretch of walls and towers over 275 m long. Close up, from the bottom of the cliff, you can't see it at all.

Probably begun in the 10th century, Peyrepertuse was expanded to its present dimensions by St Louis in the 1240s. As important to the defence of France's new southern border as Carcassonne, Peyrepertuse was intended as an unconquerable base, big enough to hold a large force that could come down and attack the rear of any Aragonese invader. As you will see when you climb up to it, attacking the place would be madness; no one ever tried. The vertiginous road to the castle starts from the village of Duilhac; from the car park it's an exhausting 20-minute struggle up to the walls (hours and adm, are posted but there's no gate and you can come at any time; outside summer months the keeper is a friendly orange cat). The entrance leads into the **Château Vieux**, the original castle, rebuilt by St Louis. Here you'll discover one of Peyrepertuse's secrets; the castle may indeed be long, but conforming to its narrow site, it is in places only a few yards across. Nearly everything is in ruins; the keep is still in good shape, and a large cistern and the ruined chapel can be seen directly behind it.

Further up is a vast open space that held most of the barracks and stores; and above this, Louis added yet another citadel, the **Château St-Georges**, with another keep and chapel. Take a map up with you; from here you can pick out almost every landmark in the Corbières.

Do you need more castles? North of Peyrepertuse, in the wildest, least-travelled part of the Corbières, there are at least four more, starting with one at **Auriac**, an old copper-mining village; nearby, at La Grave is an unusual 9th- to 12th- century country church, the **Chapelle de St-André**. A bit further north, castles at **Termes** and **Durfort** are less than 5 km apart. Both the strongholds of local barons, both were besieged and taken by Simon de Montfort under the pretext of the Albigensian Crusade. Montfort also conquered the much better-preserved castle at **Villerouge-Termenès**, 14 km to the east (10–6 in summer), the venue for a festival in August—medieval concerts and cooking, all in honour of Guillaume Bélibaste, the last Cathar *parfait*, who was burned here in 1321.

There are no easy roads in any other direction from Peyrepertuse, but if you're heading west, rejoin the main route by way of the D 7 and the white cliffs of the **Gorges de Galamus**, the most impressive natural wonder of the Corbières.

The Plateau d'Opoul

The southern border of the Corbières is a long rocky wall, crossed by the Gorges de Galamus and the Grau de Maury. Near the sea it spreads into a petite plateau, one of the most barren and isolated places in France. Don't be surprised to find tanks and suchlike growling across your path. The western half of the Plateau d'Opoul is one of the French army's zones for manoeuvres, the closest France can get to desert conditions. Most of the time, however, you won't see anyone at all, save old farmers half-heartedly trying to keep their ancient Citroëns on the road, on their weekly trip to the village to get a goose or a haircut. The village is **Opoul-Périllos**, a cosy place that shuts itself off from the surrounding void. It is a relatively new settlement; its predecessor, **Périllos**, is an eerie ruined village higher up on the plateau, now inhabited only by praying-mantises, with another castle nearby. Both castle and village have enormous stone cisterns. Water was always a problem here—indeed, everything was a problem, and the 14th-century Aragonese kings who built both village and castle had to bribe people with special privileges to live on Opoul. Today there are vineyards, but until very recently the only real occupation was smuggling. Near the castle, a rocky side-road leads west into the most desolate part of the plateau; at a spot called La Vall Oriole, you'll see a massive, lonely limestone outcrop with a door at the bottom (locked). Sometime in the early Middle Ages, this rock seems to have been hollowed out by a community of cave-dwelling monks, like the famous ones of Cappadocia in Turkey. There are no records, and no one knows anything more about it.

Tautavel and the Fenouillèdes

Descending from Opoul to the southwest, the D 9 passes through some romantically empty scenery towards **Tautavel**, a pretty village under a rocky escarpment. Through-out Europe, prehistoric man picked the unlikeliest places to park his carcass. Around Tautavel, human bones have been found from as far back as 680,000 BC, making 'Tautavel Man' a contender for the honour of First European; the only older finds come from Isernia, an equally unpromising spot in southern Italy. Back then, the climate was quite different, and Tautavel Man had elephants, bison and even rhinos to keep him company. Palaeolithic bones have become a cottage industry—over 430,000 have been found, the best being displayed in the village's **archaeological museum**, which shares a car park with the wine cooperative and a stand selling honey perfumed by the Opoul *maquis*. A statue has been erected to Tautavel Man north of town, at a site called the Caune de l'Arago; it may not do him justice.

From Tautavel, the D 9 continues south into the valley of the Agly, joining the D 611 and finally the D 117 west , the main route inland from the coast to Foix and the Ariège. This road passes **Maury**, a village famous for its dessert wines (and quite prosperous

417

from them, too) and St-Paul-de-Fenouillet, better known for almond cookies. The next village, **Caudiès-de-Fenouillèdes**, has become something of an art centre, especially in the summer. To the north, you will see the Pic de Bugarach, the highest crag in the Corbières. Three kilometres to the south, the hamlet of Fenouillet is guarded by three more ruined castles, all within a few hundred yards of each other (for the crow, anyhow). Beneath them, the simple medieval chapel of **Notre-Dame-de-Laval** has a wonderful polychrome wooden altarpiece, dated 1428; this naive masterpiece (recently badly repainted) includes scores of carefully carved figures below scenes from the *Life of the Virgin*. Higher into the mountains, there's yet another mountain-top castle to climb (about 20 min): **Puilaurens**. Even Simon de Montfort couldn't get into this one; its fortifications were the most complete and sophisticated of any in the region.

The Fenouillèdes

The Agly valley and the mountains around it make up the **Fenouillèdes**—or *Fenouillet*, in Catalan, the northernmost region of medieval Catalunya. Though equally mountainous, its scenery makes a remarkable contrast to the dry and windswept Corbières. Here, limestone gradually gives way to granite, the true beginning of the Pyrenees. Much of it is covered by ancient virgin forest, broken by quick-flowing streams and scenic ravines. The best parts are the **Forêt d'Ayguesbonnes-Boucheville** southwest of Fenouillet, and the **Forêt des Fanges**, in the steep mountains behind Puilaurens Castle. The D 619 south from St-Paul-de-Fenouillet is the only good road through the Fenouillèdes (and it isn't much), passing through Sournia on the Desix river, the only real town. Along the way, be sure to stop at Ansignan to see the **Roman aqueduct**, a rustic version of the famous Pont du Gard. An arcade of 168 m, with 29 arches, carries it over the Agly; it is still in use, carrying water to the vineyards. The question is why the Romans built it, with no nearby towns for it to serve. It is unlikely that agriculture on the coastal plains was ever so intensive as to merit such a work. One possibility is an important patrician villa—such things were often cities in themselves—but no traces of one have been discovered.

Market Days: Lagrasse, Monday. Lezignan-Corbières, Wednesday. Tuchan, Thursday.

WHERE TO STAY/EATING OUT
For tourism, the Corbières is utterly virgin territory. Not only will you have trouble finding a petrol station, but accommodation of any kind is scarce—the price you pay for experiencing the least-touristed corner of the Midi. Most people visit by day-tripping across, hopping between the four corners of the region: Carcassonne, Narbonne, Perpignan and Quillan. But if you want to spend some time exploring, there are some possibilities. **Lagrasse** (11220) gets a few visitors for the abbey, and there are simple hotels; try the **Hostellerie Charlemagne**, 10 Blvd de la Promenade (tel 68 43 10 89). In **Tuchan** (11350), the whitewashed **Hostellerie du Mont Tauch** is as quiet a stop as

you'll find anywhere, and it has the only restaurant in town (tel 68 45 40 14). If you're stuck, ask around; there are often rooms over a café in the larger villages.

For a luxury base on the northern edge of the Corbières, there is the *****Relais du Val d'Orbieu**, north of Fontfroide Abbey in the village of **Ornaisons** (11200). A modernized *mas* among the fields north of the village, it has tennis and a pool and all the amenities, including an excellent restaurant, but seems a bit dear for its rating (on the D 24, tel 68 27 10 27). **Lezignan-Corbières** (11200), halfway between Carcassonne and Narbonne on the autoroute, has a number of inexpensive hotels, among them the ****Le Derby** on Av. Clemenceau (tel 68 27 00 02). The town has one good restaurant, **Le Patio**, on the outskirts, along the N 113 (best for seafood, tel 68 27 42 23, menus 80–180 F) and a popular, better-than-average pizzeria on the main street, the **Stromboli** (43 Cours Lapeyrouse).

Near Peyrepertuse and Quéribus, the closest rooms are in **Maury** (66460), at the ****Auberge de Mas Camps**, east of town on the D 117 (tel 68 29 10 51); and in **St-Paul-de-Fenouillet** (66220), ***Le Chatelet**, is pleasant and a good bargain (on the D 117, tel 68 59 01 20). Right under the castle at Puilaurens, at **Lapradelle** (11140), is the modest **Hôtel du Château** (tel 68 20 54 39).

In, **Estagel** (66310), near Tautavel on the D 117, if you're passing by at lunchtime try the grandmotherly **La Petite Auberge** with *choucroute* and a mixed grill called *grillade Catalan* (65 F menu; on the D 117 in the village centre). In **Tautavel** (66600) itself, by the museum and wine co-op, **Le Pied Jaloux** is a laid-back roadside inn that offers local wines, *civet de sanglier* (stewed boar) and an interesting French attempt at chilli (90 F menu).

The Valley of the Upper Aude

TOURIST INFORMATION
Limoux: Promenade du Tivoli, tel 68 31 11 82.

Near the castle of Puilaurens, the D 117 joins the course of the Aude, passing northwards through a spectacular canyon, the **Défilé de Pierre-Lys**. The *pays* that begins here is called the **Razès**, a sparse, scrubby, somewhat haunted region, the back door to the Corbières. As *Rhedae*, it has been known to history since the time of the Visigoths. **Quillan**, the first town after the canyon, makes its living from manufacturing shoes; it has an odd, perfectly square castle from the 1280s. The Razès' biggest town, gritty and peculiar **Couiza**, makes even more shoes, and plastic panelling too. Its landmark is the imposing Renaissance château of the Ducs de Joyeuse, who made nuisances of themselves on the Catholic side during the Wars of Religion. You can't visit; their descendants still live here.

Rennes-le-Château

Whatever is haunting the Razès, it resides here, in a woebegone mountain-top village above Couiza that is possibly familiar to more people in Britain and America than Carcassonne. The ancient capital of the Razès, Rennes-le-Château is claimed to have had a population of 30,000 before it was definitively sacked by the Aragonese in 1170 (3000 would be closer to reality). The fun began in the 1890s, when the young parish priest, Berenger Saunière, began spending huge sums of money on himself and on embellishing his church. The story, and the speculation, hasn't stopped unfolding since. Is Jesus Christ buried here, along with his wife Mary Magdalene? Did Saunière find the treasure of the Visigoths, the Merovingians, the Cathars, or the Templars? The first and best account in English of this strange business came with the 70s bestseller *Holy Blood, Holy Grail*. Oceans of hogwash on the subject, in French and English, have appeared since. The origin of all this is Jesus' problematical but well-publicized western European tour, an escape from Israel after a faked crucifixion. It has been a recurring theme in French and English legend from the beginning ('And did those feet in ancient time' etc.). Here, the idea is that Jesus came to Gaul with Mary Magdalene (see p. 316), and that their descendants were the Merovingian kings of France, deposed in the 8th century by a shady deal between the popes and Carolingians. Supposedly, the blood line has survived to this day, sustained by an enduring secret society that has included among its leaders Leonardo da Vinci, Botticelli and Sir Isaac Newton.

In a nation addicted to secret conspiracies, preferably with a medieval pedigree, every sort of shadowy religious cult and fantastico-political faction has got its oar in, from neo-fascists to neo-Jews, along with monarchists, satanists, dilettante Cathars and dress-up Templars. Plenty of people are convinced there is still more treasure in the area, and the authorities have had to post 'No Digging' signs everywhere.

With its few dusty streets, spectacular views over the Aude valley, and a super-abundance of mangy dogs, Rennes-le-Château is an unsurpassed vortex of weirdness. It has two businesses: a snack bar called the 'Asmodeus', and an occult bookshop with a sign in the window advertising '666 different titles about the Cathars'. Relics of Berenger Saunière can still be seen: the mansion he built, and nearby a peculiar small tower called the **Tour Magdala** (Saunière's rusting Citroën is still parked out the back). The 12th-century **church**, dedicated to Mary Magdalene, was expanded and embellished by Saunière, with some outlandish carvings on the portal, along with another carved stone that may have been a Visigothic altar.

From the belvedere edges of the village, you can see a number of towers, fortresses and other ruins, their origin and purpose a matter of conjecture; the largest of them, the **Château de Blanchefort**, was probably wrecked by Simon de Montfort. Down in the valley, **Rennes-les-Bains** is a small spa in business since the time of the Romans.

Alet-les-Bains

Continuing down the Aude, **Alet-les-Bains** is one of the most beautiful and best-preserved medieval villages of Languedoc. A small spa since Roman times, Alet owes its prominence to the popes, who made it a bishopric in 1318. Alet's two jewels are the 14th-century church of **St-André** with frescoes and a fine west portal, and the nearby Benedictine **Abbey**, wrecked in the Wars of Religion but still impressive. The narrow streets of the village itself are an equal attraction, with a score of 13th- and 14th-century buildings such as the colonnaded house called the **Maison Romane**.

Limoux

Before its right turn at Carcassonne, the Aude traverses a lovely, modest stretch of country, the **Limouxin**. Most of the roads here are still graced with their long arcades of plane trees—there isn't enough traffic yet to threaten them. Even before you notice the vineyards, the civilized landscapes suggest wine. As you approach **Limoux**, where some very large wineries crowd the roadside, you'll see that wine is quite a big business. Limoux is an attractive town, with a medieval bridge across the Aude, the **Pont Neuf**; this meets the apse and steeple of **St-Martin**, a good piece of Gothic, if anachronistic— though the church was begun in the 1300s, most of the work is from three centuries later. The centre is the pretty, arcaded **Place de la République**; around it the streets of the old town make a pleasant stroll. Rue Blanquerie, named for the tanneries that once were Limoux's main business, is one of the streets with 15th- and 16th-century houses, like the 1549 **Hôtel de Clercy**, with a lovely and unusual courtyard of interlocking arches. Limoux's **Mairie** is on the Promenade du Tivoli, a broad boulevard that replaced the town walls. The building includes the **Musée Petiet**, with 19th-century paintings left by the Petiet family (the building was once their home). The collection would not be remarkable, save for the work of one of the Petiets themselves—Marie Petiet, a talented, neglected artist of the 1880s. A woman painter, and a woman's painter, her work brings a touch of magic to very domestic subjects, nowhere better than in the serene, luminous composition called *Les Blanchisseuses* (the washerwomen).

In the sculptured countryside around Limoux, you can combine picnics and piety with a tour of three sites. The chapel of **Notre-Dame-de-Marceille**, just to the northeast, houses a 'Black Virgin', an icon from the 11th century; still a popular pilgrimage site, it has a collection of ex votos from as far back as the 1700s. To the east, an exceptionally pretty side road (the D 104) takes you to **St-Hilaire** an abbey founded in the 8th century; its Benedictine monks invented the bubbly *blanquette de Limoux* (see below). A graceful, double-columned Gothic cloister survives, along with the Romanesque abbey church, containing the tomb of St Sernin, the patron of Toulouse; the tomb is a work of the Master of Cabestany. South of St-Hilaire, the monastery of **St-Polycarpe** is just as old, though not as well preserved. Its Romanesque church retains some bits of early frescoes and Carolingian carved altars.

Southwest of Limoux, you may venture into one of the most obscure *pays* in all France. Very few Frenchmen, even, have heard of the **Kercorb**, a region that has plenty of sheep and plenty of trees. It is known for its apple cider, and little else. **Chalabre**, an attractive village of old stone houses with overhanging windows, is its capital.

Market Days: Quillan, Wednesday. Couiza, Tuesday and Saturday. Chalabre, Saturday. Limoux, Friday.

Blanquette de Limoux

Available in many corner shops of London or New York, *Blanquette de Limoux* may already be familiar under the Aimery label and others, popularly recognized as the poor man's champagne. The Limouxins wouldn't care to hear it put that way; they would point out that their Blanquette was the world's first sparkling wine, produced at least since 1531, when it was first recorded—long before anyone ever heard of champagne. Blanquette, made from mauzac, chenin and chardonnay, does have a little less character than its celebrated rival—softer, sweeter and a bit lacking in sparkle; but such comparisons are invidious, and you should certainly give it a try while you're here. Locals like to drink it as an aperitif, with little cakes called *fogassets*, made with pepper.

You'll have little trouble finding Blanquette (along with the other, non-classified *vins de pays*, white and red) on the roads around Limoux, starting with the big firm **Aimery-Les Arques**, north on the D 118, which welcomes visitors (tel 68 31 14 59); they also produce an excellent slightly less sparkling wine called *Crémant de Limoux* like the extra-brut Sieur de Limoux. Best of the smaller producers are **Domaine de Fourn**, north on the D 104 at Pieusse, tel 68 31 15 03, where you can choose between traditional and modern wines like the pure Mauzac Brut du Cinquantenaire; and the **Maison Antech**, at Domaine de Flaissan on the D 118 towards Carcassonne, tel 68 31 15 88, producer of several special *cuvées* and a fine Crémant called Chanterac.

Northwest of Limoux, you'll find an estimable but little-known VDQS red wine called **Côtes de la Malepère**, obscure only because it is produced in such a small area, but the closest one in Languedoc to Bordeaux—hence the use of varieties like cot, merlot and cabernet franc . You'll find it around Malepère, Brugairolles, Malviès and Lauraguel: one of the best in recent years is the 1988 from **Château de Malviès**, tel 68 31 14 41.

WHERE TO STAY/EATING OUT

Quillan (11500), the only town of any size for a long way in any direction, is a comfortable base for the eastern Corbières; accommodation is simple, at the ****Hôtel Cartier** at 31 Blvd Charles de Gaulle (closed mid-Dec–mid-March, tel 68 20 05 14) or less expensively, the ***Terminus**, just down the street at No. 45 (tel 68 20 05 72). Most of the other hotels and restaurants are in this area, around the bus and train stations; also on Charles de Gaulle, at No. 25, there's good mountain cooking—trout and salmon, even boar—at **La Chaumière**, a very gratifying place and good value too (tel 68 20 17 90, menus 70–180 F).

The only hotel in **Alet-les-Bains** (11580) is an unusual one; the ****Hostellerie de l'Evêché**, as the name implies, was once the bishop's mansion. Plain and inexpensive, it nevertheless has a huge, pretty garden (tel 68 69 90 25, closed Oct–Mar). An alternative outside town is the **Domaine de Coursilhac**, another simple and very inexpensive country inn, with a restaurant (tel 68 69 91 09).

In **Limoux** (11300), the **Maison de la Blanquette** on the Promenade du Tivoli is run by the Aimery company; besides sampling their wines, you should try the restaurant they run on the premises (tel 68 31 01 63, closed in Oct); it offers home cooking and an emphasis on the local specialities, from Limoux's *charcuterie* to *confits* to the people's choice, a variation on *cassoulet* called *fricassée* (the Limouxins are very proud of it; Limoux even has an *'Association pour la Promotion de la Fricassée'*). South of Limoux, just off the D 118 at Cournanel, the ***Auberge de la Corneilla** is an inexpensive find; an unpretentious, restored farmhouse with nice rooms, and a nice garden and pool (tel 68 31 17 84). If you would rather stay in town, there is the ****Grand Hôtel Moderne et Pigeon** on Place Général Leclerc (tel 68 31 00 25).

Part XIV

ROUSSILLON

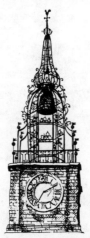

Bell tower, Perpignan

Crossing the Agly river, bound for the southernmost angle of the French hexagon, you'll begin to notice a certain non-Gallic whimsy in the names of the towns. The further south you go in Roussillon the stranger they become: Llivia, Llous and Llupia, Eus and Oms, Molitg, Politg and Py. You'll also notice that some malcontents have decorated all the yellow diamond 'priority road' signs with four red stripes, making them into little escutcheons of the long-ago Kingdom of Aragon. On your restaurant table, impossibly sweet wines and peculiar desserts will appear, and you may begin to suspect that you are not entirely in France any more.

You are in fact among the Catalans, in the corner of Catalunya that, for military considerations in the 17th century, was destined to become part of France. Like the other captive nations of the Hexagon—the Bretons and Corsicans, for example—most of Roussillon's people have rationally decided that being French isn't such a terrible fate after all. Catalan is spoken by relatively few, but this culturally passionate people stays in close touch with the rest of Catalunya, across the border in Spain, and in the squares of many mountain villages they still do a weekly **sardana**, the national dance and symbol of Catalan solidarity.

Perpignan is the capital; around it stretches the broad Roussillon plain, crowded with the dusty, introverted villages that make all that sweet wine. The real attractions are on the periphery: Collioure and the delectable Côte Vermeille on one side, and on the other valleys that climb up into the Pyrenees. The scenery is tremendous, even an hour's drive from the coast; among the pine forests and glacial lakes you can visit Vauban fortresses, ride the famous Little Yellow Train, and get an introduction to the surprising architectural and sculptural monuments of Catalunya's brilliant Middle Ages.

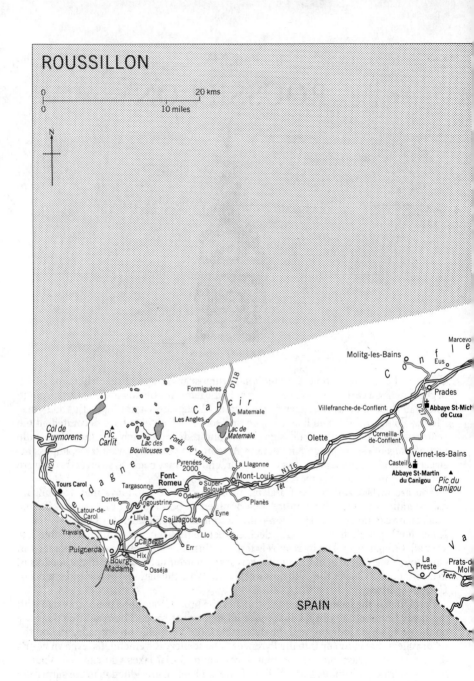

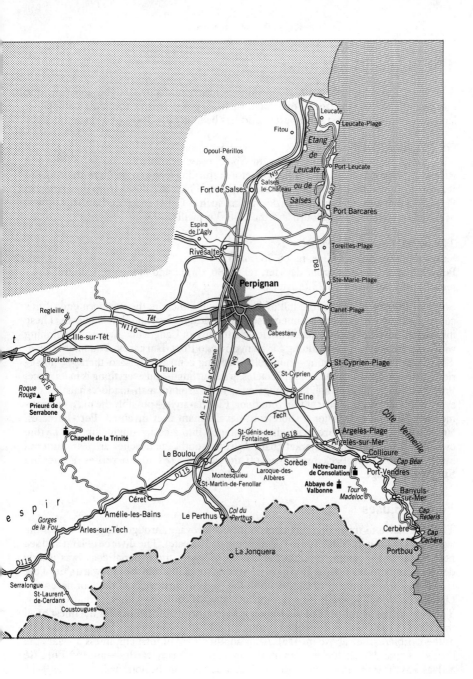

The Roussillon Coast

A geographical oddity, this run of coastline is nearly perfectly straight, and runs due north–south for 40 km, from Port Barcarès to Argelès. It isn't the most compelling landscape, but it is almost solid beach, and has been greatly developed since the 40s.

GETTING AROUND
The coastal railway from Narbonne to Spain passes through Leucate, Salses and Rivesaltes, dipping inland for Perpignan before returning to the coast; there are frequent services to Elne, and then Collioure and Cerbère. There are buses from the station in Perpignan to resorts where the train doesn't go, such as Canet and Port-Barcarès, as well as frequent services to Collioure and the Côte Vermeille.

TOURIST INFORMATION
Salses (66600): Rue G. Clos, tel 68 38 66 13.
Port-Barcarès (66420): Front de Mer, tel 68 86 16 56; and at Centre Culturel Cocteau/Marais, tel 68 86 18 23 (Easter to Sept).

South of Port-la-Nouvelle, the hill of **Cap Leucate** anchors the northern end of this coast, with new government-planned resorts at Leucate-Plage and Port-Leucate. These initiate perhaps the most animated but least attractive of Languedoc's resorts, beginning with Port-Leucate and continuing for 8 km down to **Port-Barcarès**. You might like it. There's a place for everything—minigolf, shopping centres, 'thalasso-therapy', horse-riding, model airplanes, folkloric spectacles, windsurfing—and everything is in its place. Port-Leucate is mostly holiday bungalows, built around man-made canals so that everyone can park their boat at the front door, Florida-style—possibly the most environmentally harmful design for a shorefront development ever invented. Port-Barcarès' landmark is a beached Greek freighter revamped into a casino-nightclub, the **Lydia**, owned by a Japanese supermarket chain. Further south, the beaches are less cluttered but harder to reach; back roads lead off the coastal D 81 to **Torreilles-Plage** and **Ste-Marie-Plage**.

Fort de Salses

The alternative to traversing this inferno means a voyage through the back end of the lagoon, the **Etang de Salses** (also called Etang de Leucate). The divorce of land and sea here is startlingly complete. Until the last few decades the malarial coast was utterly deserted, and no one in the region gave it a second thought; from the landward side of the lagoon in a few minutes you can be up in the rugged, dusty hills of the Corbières and Opoul (see above) where it is hard to believe any sea could be within a hundred miles. The only village on this side of the lagoon is **Fitou**, justifiably famous for the finest of all the wines of Languedoc-Roussillon (though most Fitou wine comes from a nearby area of the Corbières; see above, p. 415). After another 7 km of total emptiness appears the last, lowest, and least spectacular of all this region's many castles—but the **Fort de Salses** was the most important of them all (guided tours on the hour daily exc Tues 9–11 and 3–5; 9–12 in summer).

Built in 1497 by Ferdinand the Catholic, first king of united Spain, Salses was the last word in castles for its time, the masterpiece of a great military architect named Ramiro Lopez. Set squarely on the French-Spanish border, Salses was meant to guard Perpignan and the coastal road. It did not have a chance to do so until 1639, and sadly it was not up to the task. The Spaniards, caught by surprise, had only a small garrison at Salses; nevertheless, it required 18,000 Frenchmen and a month's siege to take it. The same year, a Spanish army spent three months winning it back. Both sieges were serious operations; the locals still go out cannonball-hunting for fun in the surrounding hills. When France acquired Roussillon in 1659, Salses no longer had a role to play. It has spent time as a political prison and a powder-house, and probably would have been demolished long ago had someone thought of a way to do it cheaply.

At first glance, Salses looks strikingly streamlined and modern. It is a product of a transitional age, when defenders were coming to terms with the powerful new artillery that had made medieval castles obsolete. Salses is all curves and slopes, designed to deflect the cannonballs; its walls are not only incredibly thick (9 m on average), but also covered with heavy stone barrel-vaulting to protect the walkway at the top. The tour guides are almost as merciless as Carcassonne's. They'll drag you from the elegant central court into the kitchens, the stables, the keep and barracks until they are completely satisfied that you have acquired a proper appreciation for the cleverness of Señor Ramiro Lopez, a true architect with an eye for both the aesthetic and the practical. Note how the officers' quarters were made as a fortress-within-a-fortress; most of the troops were usually Catalans, of doubtful loyalty to the Spanish crown.

The region around Salses and **Rivesaltes**, to the south, is famous for its inexpensive sweet wines, sold throughout France. Rivesaltes was the home of Marshal Joffre, and has a small museum dedicated to him and the Battle of the Marne. In nearby **Espira-de-l'Agly** stands the impressive fortified Romanesque church of Ste-Marie, built in 1136 as part of a monastery by the bishops of Urgel in Spain (powerful Catalan clerics whose successors, along with the presidents of France, are still the joint tributary lords of Andorra). The fortifications, including the squat, striped bell tower, were put to the test many times in the Hundred Years War. The businesslike exterior has one fine carved portal, but the lavish interior still comes as a surprise, with polychromed marbles and elaborate altarpieces from the 16th century. The church actually predates the village, which was founded in 1381 by a bishop of Urgel after the monastery was moved to Perpignan.

Rivesaltes and Côtes du Roussillon

Catalans have a notoriously sweet tooth, and some 90 per cent of the dessert wine (vin doux naturel) of France comes from this *département*, spilling over into the Corbières to the north. Mostly from grenache, muscat or maccabeu grapes, these are made simply by stopping the fermentation at the right moment, leaving more sugar in the wine; usually a small amount of pure alcohol is added at the same time. Since the 13th century, Rivesaltes has been known for its fruity muscat, a wine to be drunk young, with sorbets or lemon tarts. Its AOC status, awarded in 1972 along with other Rivesaltes red and white aperitif wines covers 99 communes in the eastern Pyrenees. Try some at Rivesaltes itself at the **Domaine Cazes**, 4 Rue Francisco-Ferrer, tel 68 64 08 26; the talented brothers Bernard and André Cazes not only produce one of the finest Rivesaltes reds (the rich, perfumed Vintage 86) and Muscat (the elegant 89), but also an aromatic dry white Vin de Pays des Côtes Catalanes and red Côtes-du-Roussillon. In the past few wine writers ever had anything good to say about this old *vin de pays*, but as in Languedoc, a number of producers like the Cazes brothers have been exerting themselves to create notable, individualistic wines from fine blends of syrah, carignan, grenache, and mourvèdre. Côtes du Roussillon is made all over the *département*, often in village cooperatives that also produce Rivesaltes or sweet muscat, but there are a few good estates to visit. In the hot corner around Perpignan, **Domaine Sarda-Malet** (Chemin de Ste-Barbe, tel 68 56 72 38 puts out two labels of red; the white to be drunk after a few years, and a black label 88, itself nearly black in colour. Or visit the **Château de Jau** on the D 117 in Cases-de-Pène, tel 68 38 91 38, with a fine 88 red, and a wonderful, inexpensive red *vin de pays*.

Canet to Argelès

Back on the coast, **Canet-Plage** has long been the favourite resort of the Perpignanais. After taking a beating in the last war, it has been rebuilt without much distinction. It does have three **museums** to amuse the bathers on rainy days: one of antique cars, one of ship models, and one of toys (the Musée du Jouet, a fun collection with exhibits from as far back as ancient Mesopotamia). There is also an **Aquarium**, where the star attraction is that impossibly unlovely living fossil from the depths of the Indian Ocean, the coelacanth (daily exc Sun afternoon and Tues, 10–2, 2:30–6:30; adm).

St-Cyprien-Plage looks just like Canet; it stays in competition with two museums of its own: an exhibit of Catalan art and crafts, and the **Fondation Desnoyer**, with a small collection of lesser works by some big-name Impressionists and Modernists. Both of these are in the old town of St-Cyprien, 3 km from the beach. St-Cyprien has invested a lot in sports facilities: including two golf courses and a big tennis centre. After St-Cyprien, **Argelès-Plage** is the next big resort, largely given over to campers.

Elne and Its Cathedral

Between these last two resorts, set a little way inland atop a steep hill, the citadel of **Elne** has guarded the Roussillon plain for at least 2700 years. Its ancient name, *Illiberis*, is said to come from the Iberians. Hannibal sojourned here on his way to Italy, waiting to negotiate an alliance with the Celts to guard his rear. The name-change came in the time of Constantine, to *Castrum Helenae*, after the Emperor's mother, St Helen, legendary discoverer of the True Cross. Through the Middle Ages, and until the 1500s, Elne remained the most important city in Roussillon and seat of the archbishops. Now a mere village of some 6000 souls, having lost its honours and status to Perpignan, Elne still has an equally good **Cathedral**.

This is a fortified church, and it has a wonderful stage presence, with its crenellated roof-line and stout, arcaded tower. Inside are some early sculpted capitals from the building's earliest history (1069), and some fine tombs, especially that of Ramon de Costa (1310), one of the church's benefactors. In a chapel on the right is an Italianate 14th-century altarpiece of St Michael. The **cloister** is perhaps the best in the Midi, and also the best-preserved. Capitals and pillars are decorated with imaginative, exquisitely-carved arabesques and floral patterns. The four sides were completed in different periods; that closest to the cathedral is the earliest, from the 1100s, and its capitals show the influence of the sculptors of St-Michel-de-Cuxa (see below). Note the capital carved with mermaids, spreading their forked tails in a rather suggestive pose. This mysterious symbol is found in hundreds of medieval churches, especially in Italy; it has occasioned much discussion, including the claim that it represents the survival into the Middle Ages of a secret Dionysian dancing cult. The west and north sides are 13th century, the east side a century later, with expressive scenes from the Old Testament on many capitals. Adjacent to the cloister is a **museum** of the city's history and archaeology (cloister and museum daily exc Sun 10–11:45, 2–5:45; adm).

Market Days: Monday, Wednesday and Friday.

WHERE TO STAY/EATING OUT
Port-Barcarès and its homogeneous fellows to the south are a little too young and raw, and too commercial to have produced many places of distinction. For dinner, though, try **Barcarès** village (66420) and **Les Almadies** on Rue Vauban; good couscous and seafood (90 and 110 F, tel 68 86 38 17, closed in winter). One of the class resort hotels in the area is the ***Plage des Pins** at **Argelès-sur-Mer** (66700); modern rooms between the pine groves and the beach, with a pool and tennis courts (on the Allée des Pins, tel 68 81 09 05). Another is the ***Mas d'Huston** in **St-Cyprien**, adjacent to the resort's golf course, also with a pool and tennis, and an excellent restaurant (closed Dec and Feb, tel 68 21 11 33).

The Côte Vermeille

For anyone with the determination to follow France's long Mediterranean coast all the way to the end, there is a lovely surprise. After Argelès, the shoreline changes dramatically, climbing into the Pyrenees and a delicious southern world of crystalline rock, olive trees and uncanny sunlight, a 30 km prelude to Spain's famous Costa Brava. Forgive yourself for cynically thinking that the name 'Vermilion Coast' might have been cooked up by tourist promoters—of course it was, just like the 'Côte d'Azur', 'Costa Smeralda' and all the rest. They're lucky they grabbed the name before someone else did. The red clay soil of the ubiquitous olive groves does lend the area a vermilion tint, but as far as colours go that is only the beginning. Every point or bend in the Mediterranean coast is a sort of meteorological vortex, given to strange behaviour: the Fata Morgana at the southern tip of Italy, the winds of the Mani in the Peloponnese or the glowing, subdued light of Venice. The Côte Vermeille gets a particularly strong dose of the tramontane, but also a remarkable mix of light and air, inciting the coast's naturally strong colours into an unreasonably heady and sensual Mediterranean spectrum. Henri Matisse spent one summer here, at Collioure, and the result was a milestone in the artistic revolution called Fauvism.

TOURIST INFORMATION
Collioure (66190): Place Mairie, tel 68 82 15 47.

Port-Vendres (66660): Port de Plaisance, tel 68 82 04 93.
Banyuls-sur-Mer (66650): Av. de la République, tel 68 88 31 58.

Collioure

If the tourists would only leave it in peace, Collioure would be quite happy to make its living in the old way, filling up barrels with anchovies. As it is, the town bears their presence with admirable grace. In its way, Collioure is unspoiled—a remarkable claim for a place with 2500 inhabitants and 16 hotels. Mediterranean France's one civilized and practically perfect resort has all the requisites: a castle, a pretty church by the sea, three small beaches, a shady market square with cafés. It does *not* have a casino, a miniature golf course, or a water slide. Unaffectedly beautiful, with no pretensions of ever becoming another St-Tropez, Collioure has found the best of all possible worlds.

History
It's hard to believe, looking at the map, but in the Middle Ages this village was the port for Perpignan; with no good harbours on the dismal and (then) unhealthy coast to the north, Perpignan's fabrics and other goods had to come to the Pyrenees to go to sea. In the 14th century Collioure was one of the biggest trading centres of Aragon, but nearly the whole town was demolished by the French after they took possession in 1659. They weren't angry with the Colliourencs; the town was merely in the way of modernizing its castle's fortifications. Our own century has no monopoly on twisted military logic. Collioure had to be razed in order that it could be better defended.

The population moved into the part that survived, the steep hillside quarter called the Mouré, where they have made the best of it ever since. Collioure was discovered in 1905 by Matisse. Many other artists followed, including Picasso, but it was Matisse who was most inspired by the place, and who put a little of Collioure's vermilion tint into the colourful splash of his first Fauvist experiments. He painted views of the town, its church and its rooftops, but you won't see them here; all are in private collections, or in the Hermitage in Leningrad.

Castle and Church
Collioure (or as the locals call it, *Cotllures*) is a thoroughly Catalan town, and the red and yellow striped Catalan flag waves proudly over the **Château Royal**, dominating the harbour (daily 2:30–7:30 in summer; irregularly in winter). With its outworks it is nearly as big as the town itself. First built by the Templars in the 13th century, it was expanded by various Aragonese kings. The outer fortifications, low walls and broad banks of earth, were state-of-the-art in 1669, when they were begun. The great Vauban, Louis XIV's military genius, oversaw the works and the demolition of the old town. Collioure's fate could have been even worse; Vauban had wanted to level it completely, and force everyone to move to Port-Vendres. The older parts of the castle have been restored, and are open for visits, along with a small collection of modern art.

From the castle, cross the small stream called the Douy (usually dry) into the **Mouré**, the old quarter that is now the centre of Collioure. There is an amiable shorefront, with a small beach from which a few anchovy fishermen still ply their trade; at the far end you'll see Collioure's landmark, painted by Matisse and many others: the church of **Notre-Dame-des-Anges**. The Colliourencs built it in the 1680s to succeed the original church destroyed by Vauban; they chose the beach site to use the old cylindrical lighthouse as a bell tower. On entering, you'll pass a neatly handwritten, hysterical missive from the parish priest, who must be hard beset in summer: 'No Dogs! Not even in the Corridor! *They do not know where they are.*'

The best thing about the church is that you can hear the waves of the sea from inside, a profound *basso continuo* that makes the celebration of mass here a unique experience. The next best are the **retables**, five of them, done between 1699 and 1720 by Joseph Sunyer and others. Catalan Baroque at its eccentric best, influenced by the Spanish Churrigueresque, often concentrated its finest efforts on these towering constructions of carved wooden figures, dioramas of scriptural scenes with intricately painted stage-drop backgrounds. Sunyer's are especially lifelike. The compositions are intense and operatic—some of the figures are even seated in boxes, while the rest seem ready to burst into song (in Catalan, of course) at any moment.

The second of Collioure's beaches lies right behind the church; really an old sand-bar that has become part of dry land, it connects the town with a former islet, the **Ilôt St-Vincent**, crowned with a tiny medieval chapel. A scenic footpath called the **Sentier de la Moulade** leads from near the church along the rocky shore north of Collioure. High above, you'll see **Fort Miradoux**, the Spanish King Philip II's addition to Collioure's defences, and still in military use.

Port-Vendres and Banyuls-sur-Mer

Few of us, probably, give any thought to anchovies and how they are apprehended in the open sea. It isn't, in fact, a terribly difficult operation. The diabolical Catalans have boats called *lamparos*, with big searchlights. They sneak out on warm summer nights, when the normally shy anchovies are making their promenade, and nab the lot. After spending a few months in barrels of brine, the unfortunate fish reappear, only to be stuffed into olives, a Catalan favourite. Much of this doubtful business goes on in **Port-Vendres**. This is a *real* fishing village, modern-style, with none of the charm of Collioure; before 1962 it had a growing trade with Algeria, and it would still like to be a port when it grows up. Louis XVI's government had big plans for developing Port-Vendres, all of which were scuppered with the Revolution; some grandiose neoclassical buildings remain from this programme, around the central Place de l'Obélisque, along with a 300-m obelisk, decorated with propaganda reliefs celebrating poor Louis' glorious reign.

From here, the coast juts out eastwards, with a picturesque small promontory called **Cap Béar**, topped by another of this area's many Baroque-era fortresses. There are many isolated beaches in the vicinity, though they are hard to reach; most are south of the cape, including the one at Paulilles, near an abandoned dynamite factory (a mildly historic one, because it belonged to Alfred Nobel, inventor of dynamite and plywood, who used the profits to finance his Prizes).

Banyuls-sur-Mer (*Banyuls de la Marenda* in Catalan) is the next town along the picturesque coastal N114, a sleepy resort with beach and mini-golf right at the centre. The heart of the Banyuls wine region (see below), it is also the home of the Fondation Arago, an oceanographic laboratory affiliated to the University of Paris. They run an excellent **Aquarium** displaying Mediterranean species (daily 9–12 and 2–6, until 10 pm in July and August; adm). Aristide Maillol, perhaps the best-known French sculptor of the last century after Rodin, was a native of Banyuls. He contributed the town's War Memorial, on the waterfront; other examples of his work can be seen in many towns along the Côte Vermeille, and in Perpignan.

If you don't care to go to Cerbère, or to Spain, there is an alternative to retracing your steps along the coast—an extremely scenic route through the mountains back to Collioure, along the steep and narrow D 86. It begins from the back of Banyuls, beyond the railway overpass, and climbs through ancient olive groves on the lower slopes of the **Monts-Albères**. Several abandoned fortresses come into view, though none are especially easy to reach. This border region rivals even the Corbières for quantity of castles; from one spot on the D 86 you can see seven of them at once. There is also a ruined monastery, the Abbaye de Valbonne, on the heights to the west; the track to it begins at the pilgrimage chapel of **Notre-Dame-de-Consolation**. A little before this, the **Tour Madeloc** is the climax of the trip, with tremendous views over the coast in both directions, as far as Agde on a clear day. This was a signal tower, part of the sophisticated communications network that kept the medieval Kings of Aragon in close contact with their borders.

Banyuls

A naturally sweet wine, usually served as an aperitif or with desserts, Banyuls (AOC since 1936), according to legend, was first made by the Templars in the 11th century, from the dark grenache grapes grown on the rocky red terraces of the Côte Vermeille. A fine old Banyuls is claimed to be the only wine that can accompany chocolate desserts, but a cheap young bottle will hardly do justice to a Mars bar. Collioure, Port-Vendres, Cerbère and Banyuls are the only places allowed to wear the AOC label, and 80 per cent of their wine, as well as the delightful red wines of Collioure pass through the **Cellier des Templiers**, a large concern centred in Banyuls; they are happy to receive visitors at their *cave* near the Mairie or at their cellar in a 13th-century former Templar commandery (where you can also see a film on the wine) located west of town on the D 86 (tel 68 88 31 59). The **Cave de l'Etoile**, 26 Av. de Puig-del-Mas in Banyuls (tel 68 88 00 10) is a cooperative where everything is done lovingly in the old-fashioned way; up the same street, at the private **Domaine de la Rectoire** (tel 68 88 13 45), the bottle of choice is Cuvée Léon Parce 88.

Cerbère, and Beyond

You may well have already been here, but Cerbère won't bring back any pleasant memories—being herded from one train to another in the middle of the night (because Spanish railways still use a different track gauge) under the gaze of Senegalese soldiers with submachine-guns and impossible customs men who do their best to make this seem like an old Hitchcock spy film instead of one of the busiest, most unexciting border rail-crossings in the EC. No one has ever seen Cerbère in daylight, but you might give it a try. The coast here is at its most spectacular, and there are a few pebble beaches, never crowded. With its two small hotels, Cerbère is a miniscule resort, with a World's End air about it, and plenty of cops standing around drinking coffee; it's hard to imagine there are still many smugglers around to chase, but old habits die hard.

There is a lot to be said for pressing on even further, into Unoccupied Catalunya (the signs at the border still say 'Spain' for courtesy's sake). **Barcelona**, the most vibrant and creative city in Europe today, is only two hours by train from Cerbère. **Girona**, with its exquisite medieval centre and unique cathedral, is half the distance. If you liked the Côte Vermeille, continue south for more of the same in the **Costa Brava**, often overcrowded though still nice (especially the northern parts). And if you can manage only one unambitious day trip into Spain, try **Figueres**, a short hop by train or a pleasant 50-km drive along the C 252; the Salvador Dalí Museum here, in the artist's home town, is an unforgettable attraction, the 'temple of surrealism', where you may water the plants in the garden by feeding pesetas into a Cadillac.

Market Days: Collioure, Thursday.

WHERE TO STAY/EATING OUT

In **Collioure** (66190) town centre, ***Casa Païral** is the place for an agreeable stay; a dignified, Mansard-roofed palace a few streets from the shore; a wide choice of rooms, from the simple to the luxurious and expensive; also a pool and enclosed garden (Impasse des Palmiers, tel 68 82 05 81, closed Nov–April). The pink and jolly **La Frégate** (34 Quai de la Amirauté, tel 68 82 06 05) is on the busiest corner of Collioure, but still quiet enough; it has a good restaurant (mostly seafood; menus from 90 to 160 F). Dinner on the Côte Vermeille need not necessarily include anchovies, but the rest of the local catch merits your attention. In Collioure, **La Marinade** on Place 18 Juin (closed Jan, tel 68 82 09 76) serves delectable seafood from simple *sardines en papillote* to an elaborate Catalan *bouillabaisse*; menus at 100 and 170 F.

In **Banyuls** (66650), a satisfying and moderately-priced seafood dinner can be had at the restaurant of the *Hôtel La Plage, at the centre of the beach strip; various set menus at 130 F including *sole meunière*, grilled salmon, or a Catalan mixed grill called a *parillade*. For lunch, the lace-curtained neighbourhood lunch favourite is **Chez Rosa**; not much seafood, but roast pork, chicken and mushrooms and such, and quite tasty (Rue St-Pierre; 65 F menu). Just down the street, the snack bar **Casa Miguel** reminds us of the proximity of Spain with good tapas, mostly seafood.

The choice spot in **Cerbère** (66290) is the **Hôtel la Vigie, on the N 114 just south of the centre, built on the sea cliffs, with a fine view (tel 68 88 41 84, also has a restaurant).

Perpignan

PERPIGNAN DEAD CITY is the slogan the local anarchists write on the walls, and if that's slightly premature, you can't help wondering about a town named after a reactionary murderer, one that has let its most beautiful Gothic monument become a hamburger franchise, and which highlights its tourist brochure with a photo of its trucking terminal. And how can any city of 114,000 support 23 foxtrot academies?

There's a little craziness in every Catalan soul. In *Perpinyà* (as its residents call it), this natural exuberance is rather suppressed by French centralization. While grateful for

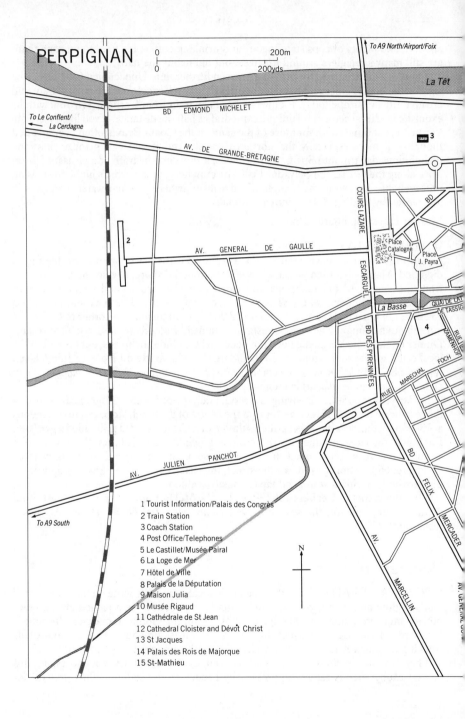

PERPIGNAN

0		200m
0		200yds

To A9 North/Airport/Foix

La Têt

BD EDMOND MICHELET

To Le Conflent/
La Cerdagne

3

AV. DE GRANDE-BRETAGNE

COURS LAZARE

BD

2

AV. GENERAL DE GAULLE

ESCARGUEL

Place
Catalogne
Place
J. Payra

La Basse

QUAI DE LA
DE TASSIG

4

BD DES PYRENNÉES

RUE

MARECHAL

FOCH

RUE
DAMENRIOT

AV. JULIEN PANCHOT

AV.

1 Tourist Information/Palais des Congrès
2 Train Station
3 Coach Station
4 Post Office/Telephones
5 Le Castillet/Musée Pairal
6 La Loge de Mer
7 Hôtel de Ville
8 Palais de la Députation
9 Maison Julia
10 Musée Rigaud
11 Cathédrale de St Jean
12 Cathedral Cloister and Dévot Christ
13 St Jacques
14 Palais des Rois de Majorque
15 St-Mathieu

To A9 South

N

BD

FELIX

MERCADER

AV.

MARCELLIN

AV. GENERAL

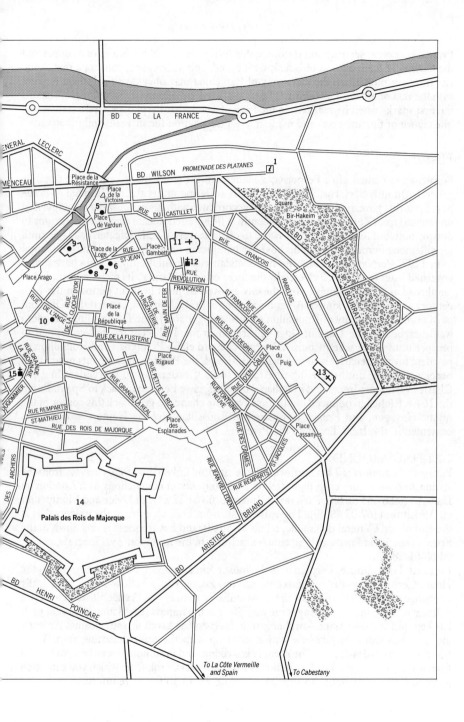

French economic security and *croissants*, this former capital of the Kings of Majorca and the Counts of Roussillon is obviously a bit bored, and its livelier spirits hope that as the EC frontiers melt away, the electricity of Barcelona may once again galvanize it along with the rest of greater Catalunya. The king of kookiness himself, Salvador Dalí, set off the first sparks when he realized, in the back of a taxi, that Perpignan's train station was 'the centre of the universe' and made it a hot destination for surrealist pilgrimages.

History

Perpignan is named after Perperna, a lieutenant of the great 1st-century BC populist general, Quintus Sertorius. While Rome was suffering under the dictatorship of Pompey, Sertorius governed most of Spain in accordance with his astonishing principle that one should treat Rome's provinces decently. The enraged Senate sent out five legions to destroy him, but his army, who all swore to die if he were killed, defeated each one until the villainous Perperna invited his boss to a banquet in the Pyrenees and murdered him.

In 1197, Perpignan became the first Catalan city granted a municipal charter, and governed itself by a council elected by the three estates or 'arms'. Its merchants traded as far abroad as Constantinople, and the city enjoyed its most brilliant period in the 13th century when Jaime I, king of Aragon and conqueror of Majorca, created the Kingdom of Majorca and County of Roussillon for his younger son Jaime II. This little kingdom was absorbed by the Catalan kings of Aragon in the 14th century, but continued to prosper until 1463, when Louis XI's army came to claim Perpignan and Roussillon as payment for mercenaries sent to Aragon. Besieged, the Perpignanais ate rats rather than become French, until the King of Aragon himself ordered it to surrender. In 1493 Charles VIII, more interested in Italian conquests, gave Perpignan back to Spain. But in the 1640s Richelieu pounced on the first available chance to grab back this corner of the mystic Hexagon, and French possession of Roussillon and the Haute Cerdagne was cemented in the 1659 Treaty of the Pyrenees.

GETTING AROUND

Perpignan's **airport** is 7 km northwest of the city, and linked by aerobus *navettes* from the station an hour before each flight (tel 68 54 54 66); direct connections with London on Dan-Air (tel 67 65 88 88); Paris on Air Inter (tel 68 61 22 24); and Nice and Montpellier on Air Littoral (67 65 49 49). The **railway station**, Dali's 'centre of the universe', is at the end of Av. Général de Gaulle, tel 68 35 50 50, and has frequent trains down to the Spanish border at Portbou. The **coach station** is to the north, on Av. Général Leclerc, tel 68 61 28 98.

Le Petit Train Jaune: Perpignan is the most popular place to begin a journey into the Haute Cerdagne by way of the scenic narrow-gauge 'Little Yellow Train', practically unchanged since 1910. One of the most unlikely railways in France, it was entirely a political project, meant to bring some new life into the impoverished mountain valleys. It has kept puffing ever since—probably only tourism has saved it from closing. An early morning bus from Perpignan's station links up with the train departing from Ville-franche-Vernet-des-Bains. The scenery is striking, and in summer it can be appreciated from topless carriages. The last station is La-Tour-de-Carol, from which you can catch a bus to Andorra or return to Perpignan: tel 68 35 50 50 for more information.

TOURIST INFORMATION
By the red British phone box (Lancaster is Perpignan's sister city), inside the Palais des Congrès, Place Armand-Lanoux, tel 68 66 30 30. **Post office**: Rue Dr Zamenhof.

Le Castillet

When Perpignan's walls were destroyed in 1904, its easy-going river-cum-moat, La Basse, was planted with lawns, flower-beds, mimosas and Art Nouveau cafés. Only the fat brick towers and crenellated gate of **Le Castillet** were left upright, for memories' sake; built in 1368 by Aragon to keep out the French, it became a prison once the French got in, especially during the Revolution.

In 1946, a mason broke through a sealed wall in Le Castillet and found the body of a child, which on contact with the air, dissolved into dust; from the surviving clothing fragments the corpse was dated to the end of the 18th century. And ever since, people have wondered: could it have been Marie-Antoinette's son, the dauphin Louis XVII? After all, the child buried in the Temple in Paris was known to be a substitute, and there have always been rumours that the Revolutionaries used the Dauphin as a secret bargaining chip in dealing with his Bourbon relatives in Spain.

Along with this mysterious ghost, Le Castillet houses a cosy museum of Catalan art and traditions, the **Musée Pairal** (9–12 and 2–6, summer 9:30–12 and 2:30–7, donation), with items ranging from casts of Pau (Pablo) Casals' hands to a kitchen from a Catalan *mas*, complete with a hole in the door for the Catalan cat.

Loge de Mer to the Musée Rigaud

From Le Castillet, Rue Louis Blanc leads back to Place de la Loge, where the cafés provide a grandstand for contemplating Aristide Maillol's voluptuous bronze *Venus* and Perpignan's most beautiful building, the Gothic **Loge de Mer**, or Llotja, built in 1397 by the king of Aragon to house the exchange and the Tribunal de Mer (*Consolat de Mar* in Catalan), a branch of the Barcelona council founded by Jaime I to resolve trade and maritime disputes. This proud and noble building of ochre stone, with its Venetian arches and loggia and ship-shaped weathercock, fell on hard times—but Perpignan takes good care of its monuments. The city rented the Llotja to a fast food chain, and now it looks very much the beggared pasha, flipping out Quick Burgers.

The neighbouring 13th-century **Hôtel de Ville** has been spared the Llotja's humiliation, probably because it still serves its original purpose: on Saturday mornings, its courtyard fills with blushing brides posing for photos by Maillol's allegory of the Mediterranean (as a naked woman, of course). The Hôtel is built of rounded river pebbles and bricks in the curious layer-cake style of medieval Perpignan; three bronze arms sticking out of the façade are said to symbolize Perpignan's three estates, or *bras*. To the right, the **Palais de la Députation Provinciale** (1447) is a masterpiece of Catalan Renaissance, formerly the seat of Roussillon's parliament and now housing dismal municipal offices. In Rue Fabrique d'en Nabot, the street facing the palace, is the **Hôtel Julia** (No. 2), a rare survival of a 1400s town house, with a Gothic courtyard.

South from the Députation, Rue de la Cloche d'Or leads to Rue de l'Ange and the **Musée Rigaud**, named after Perpignan's own Hyacinthe Rigaud (1659–1743), court painter to Louis XIV (9:30–12 and 2–6, summer 9:30–12 and 2:30–7, free). Hyacinthe, master of raising the insipid and mediocre to virtuoso heights, is well represented, most famously in his portrait of the *Cardinal de Bouillon*, complete with *putti* wallowing in very worldly loot. All the hyper-sensitive theft alarms, however, are around the *Retable de la Trinité* (1489) by the Master of Canapost, painted for the 100th anniversary of the Consolat de Mar and showing, underneath, a fanciful scene of the sea lapping at the base of Perpignan's Llotja. Drawings by Picasso, Dufy, and Maillol are upstairs (with photos of Picasso eating a paella in this very building, the 18th-century Hôtel Lazerme). The ground floor holds an excellent collection of Hispano-Moorish ceramics.

Cathédrale de St-Jean and the Dévôt Christ
Just east of Place de la Loge unfolds Place de Gambetta, site of Perpignan's pebble-and-brick cathedral, topped by a lacy 19th-century wrought-iron campanile. Begun in 1324 but not ready for use until 1509, the interior is a success because the builders stuck to the design provided in the 1400s by Guillem Sagrera, architect of the great cathedral of Palma de Majorca. Typical of Catalan Gothic, it has a single nave, striking for its spacious width rather than its soaring height.

The chapels, wedged between the huge piers, hold some unique treasures, the oldest of which is a mysterious marble **baptismal font** (first chapel on the left). Pre-Roma-nesque, perhaps even Visigothic in origin and carved from the drum of a Roman column to look like a tub bound with a cable, it bears a primitive face of Christ over an open book. Further up the left aisle, the massive organ was decorated in the 15th century with painted shutters and sumptuous carvings (undergoing restoration at the time of writing). On the pendentive under the organ is carved a Moor's head—a common Catalan conceit symbolizing wisdom, taken from the Templars, who exerted a powerful influence over the Catalan kings, especially their pupil, Jaime the Conqueror. Beyond the Moor's head, in an 11th-century chapel from the original cathedral, is a pawn-shop window of dingy reliquaries, and the effigy of the cathedral's founder, Jaime's son Sancho, his feet resting on a Chinese lion.

The cathedral is proudest of its exquisite retables: on the high altar, the marble *Retable de St-Jean* carved in a late Renaissance style in 1621 by Claude Perret; at the end of the left crossing, the **Retable des Stes Eulalie et Julie** (1670s); in the apsidal chapels, the painted wood *Retable de St-Pierre* (mid-1500s) and to the right, the lovely, luminous *Notre-Dame de la Mangrana*, (1500)—its name 'of the pomegranate', in Catalan, from the original statue of the Virgin, which held a pomegranate to symbolize fertility.

A door in the right aisle leads out to a 16th-century chapel constructed especially to house an extraordinary wooden sculpture known as the **Dévôt Christ**. Carved in the Cologne region in 1307, this wasted Christ, whose contorted bones, sinews and torn flesh are carved with a rare anatomical realism, is stretched to the limits of agony on the Cross. Almost too painful to behold, it comes straight from the gloomy age when Christendom believed that pain, contemplated or self-inflicted, brought one closer to God. An object of great veneration, the Perpignanais claim that when the Christ's bowed head sags another quarter inch to touch His chest, the world will end.

Another door leads to the **cloister** (1302), used from the beginning as a cemetery and recently cleared of offices belonging to the Gendarmerie. There are some fine bas-reliefs on the tombs. A door from the cloister leads into the striking 15th-century **Salle**

Capitulaire, its complex ogival vaulting attributed to Guillem Sagrera. Also worth a look (to the left of the cathedral's façade), is Perpignan's oldest church, **St-Jean-le-Vieux** (1025), converted into an electrical generating station in 1890. But its Romanesque door is worth a look for its very different view of Jesus, the imperious and typically Catalan *Majestat* (Christ in Majesty)—though his stern air is softened by the two slug-like *putti* on his shoulders.

Quartier St-Jacques

The piquant neighbourhood south of the cathedral, built on the slopes of Puig des Lépreux (Lepers' Hill) was once the *aljama*, or Jewish quarter of Perpignan. In its happiest days, in the 13th century, it produced a remarkable body of literature—especially from the pen of the mathematician and Talmudic scholar Gerson ben Salomon (author of the philosophical *Gate of Heaven*), as well as rare manuscripts and calligraphy, all now in Paris. After the Jews were exiled, the quarter was renamed St-Jacques, and inhabited by workingmen's families and gypsies, and most recently by Algerians. The church of **St-Jacques** contains a handsome painted statue of St James the Greater in pilgrimage gear (1450) and more fine retables, especially the 15th-century *Notre-Dame de l'Espérance*, featuring a rare depiction of the pregnant Virgin. In the early 1400s, while the fire-eating Dominican preacher St Vincent Ferrer was in Perpignan to advise in the dispute between Antipope Benedict XIII and Rome, he founded in this church the confraternity of the Holy Blood (*de la Sanch*) to bring religious comfort to those condemned to death. As in Seville, the confraternity reaches a wider audience during Holy Week, dressed in spooky hoods and bearing a procession of holy floats (the *misteri*, one of which is the Dévôt Christ) while singers wail dirges from the crowd.

The Palace of the Kings of Majorca

Enclosed in a vast extent of walls, originally medieval and later enlarged by Vauban, the Palais des Rois de Majorque (entrance in Rue des Archers, open 9–12 and 2–5, summer 9:30–12 and 2:30–6, adm), is the oldest royal palace in France, begun in the 1270s and occupied by Jaime II after 1283. Yet for all its grandeur, only three kings of Majorca were to reign here before Roussillon and Majorca were reabsorbed by Aragon.

A rectangle built around a mastodonic but elegant Romanesque/Gothic courtyard, the palace is now a favourite venue for events, exhibitions and dancing the *sardana*. The **Salle de Majorque**, or throne room, with its three vast fireplaces, and the double-decker chapels in the **donjon**, with the queen's chapel on the bottom and the king's on top, both conserve enough of their original decoration to hint at the splendour of the Majorcan court. The sacristy was the entrance to a network of underground passageways that connected the palace to its enormous 45-m deep wells, which also afforded Jaime II an escape from his fierce and unwelcome older brother, Pedro III of Aragon. The palace once stood in the midst of what the archives call 'Paradise'—partly enclosed terraced gardens of delight, inspired by Moorish examples on Majorca. A few traces can still be seen to the right of the mightiest tower, the **Tour de Homage**.

On the way down from the palace, at Rue des Archers and Rue Remparts Mathieu, you can tour the Rois de Majorque ceramic workshops; the grid of narrow streets further down, around the church of St-Mathieu, is on a plan designed by the Templars, although most of the buildings date from the 18th century.

Cabestany

Of all the villages ingested by Greater Perpignan, none is as celebrated as Cabestany (*Cabestanh*), 4 km to the southeast. It produced a great Romanesque sculptor known as the Master of Cabestany who worked as far afield as Tuscany, and left on his hometown church a **tympanum** of the *Dormition and Assumption of the Virgin*, from where she sends her girdle down to St Thomas.

Cabestany was also the home of the troubador Guilhem de Cabestanh, who wrote some of the most popular love poems of the age. He is most famous for a legend so popular that a version of it reached Boccaccio (*Decameron*, Day 4; 9). Guilhem loved and was loved by the wife of a knight, one Raymond of Castel-Rossello (now ruined, 4 km east of Perpignan). Raymond learned of this, ambushed Guilhem, murdered him, and cut out his heart, which he gave to his cook to prepare with plenty of pepper. The lady ate it all, and praised the dish. 'I am not surprised', said her husband, 'As you loved it so well when it was alive'. And he told her what she had eaten. But the lady kept her sang-froid. 'Sir', she said, 'You have given me such an excellent thing to eat that God forbid any other food should again pass my lips'. Then she leapt out of the window to her death.

ENTERTAINMENT

On Tuesday and Thursday evenings from June to September, the Perpignanais dance *sardanes* in Place de la Loge. The second week of September sees a major international show of photo-journalism called **Visa Pour l'Image** attracting photographers from around the world. **Markets** take place daily in Place de la République, and Saturday and Sunday mornings in Place Cassanyes.

WHERE TO STAY   (postal code 66000)

Located in a 16th-century building in the centre, ***Hôtel de la Loge on Place de la Loge, 1 Rue Fabrique d'en Nabot, tel 68 34 54 84, has recently renovated rooms, some with TV and air-conditioning. In a private residence from the same period, with the added plus of a pool, the **Athéna, 1 Rue Queya (near Musée Rigaud), tel 68 34 37 63, has charming, quiet rooms looking out over the patio. Less expensive choices are clustered near the station: **Le Helder, Av. Général De Gaulle, tel 68 34 38 05, has some inexpensive rooms; at *Le Berry, 6 Av. Général de Gaulle, tel 68 34 59 02, they're even cheaper. The **Auberge de la Jeunesse** is near the bus station, on Blvd Edmond Michelet.

EATING OUT

Long Perpignan's finest restaurant, **Le Chapon Fin**, 18 Blvd Jean Bourrat (near the ancient plane trees in Promenade des Platanes), tel 68 35 14 14, is also one of the prettiest, decorated with Catalan ceramics. But it's the *tartare de saumon* and ravioli stuffed with scallops and its excellent list of Roussillon wines that keep its clients coming back for more, even all the way from Spain (menus 190 F and up; closed Sat eve and Sun). Another refined gourmet oasis, **Le Bourgogne**, is hidden near the bus station, at

63 Av. Marcel Leclerc, tel 68 34 96 05, where you can indulge in quail in pineapple sauce and a devastating *millefeuillle au chocolat* (menus 180 F and up; closed Sun eve and Mon). More reasonable choices include the 75 F seafood menu at **L'Huîtrière**, 12 Rue Pierre Rameil (near Place de la Résistance, tel 68 35 56 42); or **Les Expéditeurs**, 19 Av Marcel Leclerc (paella, *cassoulet*, etc, 70 F); or, for Alsacienne specialities, **Chez Grandmère**, 18 Av. Général de Gaulle, tel 68 34 60 35 (menus at 55 and 100 F).

West of Perpignan: Pyrenean Valleys

There are two important ones: the **Conflent** (the valley of the river Têt) and the **Vallespir** (of the river Tech), sloping in parallel lines toward the Spanish border. Don't think that this butt end of the Pyrenees consists of mere foothills; in between the two valleys stands snow-capped **Canigou**, one of the most imposing peaks of the chain. The *muntanya regalada*, 'fortunate mountain' of the Catalans, is one of the symbols of the nation, wreathed in bonfires from the surrounding villages every year at the summer solstice; it is also the subject of one of the best-known Catalan folksongs. Legends and apparitions abound on Canigou. Fairies and 'ladies of the waters' are said to frequent its forested slopes. King Peter I of Aragon climbed it in 1285, and met a dragon near the top.

GETTING AROUND
Coach and train service is probably better here than in any other rural region in this book—only it won't help you see rural monuments like St-Michel or Serrabone. Using Perpignan as a base, it's possible to see quite a bit of the Conflent and Vallespir; from the *gare routière* there are 10 or 12 buses a day to Prades and Villefranche-de-Conflent, and a few of these continue on to Font-Romeu and Latour-de-Carol. There's also the Little Yellow Train from Villefranche to Latour, with bus connections from there to Andorra and Spain (see above, p. 436). For the Vallespir, there are frequent, convenient daily buses to Arles-sur-tech and Amélie-les-Bains-Palada, with a few pressing on further up the valley to Prats-de-Mollo.

TOURIST INFORMATION
Prades (66500): 4 Rue Victor Hugo, tel 68 96 27 58.
Vernet-les-Bains (66820): tel 68 05 55 35.
Villefranche-de-Conflent (66500): tel 68 92 22 96.

From Perpignan to the Conflent

The Têt, before passing through Perpignan, washes a wide plain packed full of vineyards and fat villages. The fattest, **Thuir**, puts up signs all over Roussillon inviting us over to see the World's Biggest Barrel, in the cellars of the famous aperitifs Byrrh and Dubonnet—wine mixed with quinine, a popular drink invented here a little over a century ago. At **Ille-sur-Têt**, an attractive village at the gateway to the mountains, neglected art from churches all over Roussillon has been assembled in an old hospital, the **Centre d'Art Sacré**, with exhibitions on various themes and periods, changing every six months or so. The D 2 northwest of Ille takes you to some surprising scenery, including eroded 'fairy chimneys' called the **Orgues d'Ille**, as well as a forgotten ruin of the 12th century, the fortified church of **Régleille**. It looks like a castle at first sight—a typical example of a monastic church, in an area without any castles, that grew into a fortress to protect not only the monks, but the population of the village; Ille was located here before its population drifted to the present site.

Prieuré de Serrabone

Seeing the finest medieval sculpture in Roussillon requires a detour of 13 km, most of it hairpin turns, starting from the D 618 in the Têt valley, at Bouleternère, and ending in a lofty, barren spot on the slopes of a mountain called Roque Rouge. The spare shape and dark stone of Serrabone's church are not promising, making the surprise inside that much the greater. The best efforts of the 12th-century Catalan sculptors were concentrated on the **tribune**, in rose marble from Canigou. Perfectly preserved in its isolated setting, this includes a fantastical bestiary and plenty of Christian symbolism, set in a lush, brilliant garden of floral arabesques. Note the small figure of the Virgin; a narrow window allows a ray of sunlight to illuminate it only one day each year—the Feast of the Assumption on 15 August. The style of these capitals will become familiar if you spend much time in the Conflent; like most of the works in the region, Serrabone's was done by the school of artists that grew up at St-Michel-de-Cuxa (see below). There are more of these capitals in the south gallery (daily 9–12 and 2–6; adm).

Further south, if you have the patience for another 14 km of narrow and difficult roads, you'll pass the ruins of the **Château de Belpuig** and, below it, the **Chapelle de la Trinité**, with more sculpture of the same school, including a *Majestat* (ask at Serrabone if you can get in).

Prades, St-Michel and the Canigou

Prades is known in connection with the famous music festival founded by Pablo Casals, but few people could place it on a map. Casals, in exile after the Spanish Civil War, spent much of the 40s and 50s here, in the one safe corner of his beloved Catalunya, and from the beginning his festival attracted many of the world's greatest musicians. Prades has a small museum dedicated to Casals, and a church with another incredible Baroque altarpiece by Joseph Sunyer and a fine Romanesque bell tower. It is a typically grey and taciturn Catalan town, with little to recommend it save the **festival** (beginning of August) and the fact that it is the only large town near the delights of Pic du Canigou—the nearest of which, a few kilometres up through orchards and Pyrenean forests, is **St-Michel-de-Cuxa**, one of the most important monasteries of medieval Catalunya (daily exc Sun afternoon, 9:30–11:50 and 2–5; adm). Besides fostering its school of sculptors, St-Michel kept its hand in politics on a European scale; one of its abbots, Olida, was a leading force behind the 'Truce of God' of the 1030s, giving nascent Western civilization a little breathing space by limiting the endless warfare of the feudal lords. Even in its reduced, semi-ruined state, the scale is impressive; this is indeed one of the great monastic centres from which medieval Europe was planned and built; when it was new, in the 11th century, it would have been a marvel—nothing like it for a hundred miles in any direction.

The coming of the French Revolution found St-Michel already in a state of serious decay. Looted and abandoned, the abbey suffered greatly in the last century; one of the two bell towers collapsed, and much of the best sculptural work was carted off to the Cloisters Museum in New York. Now restored, St-Michel is occupied once again, by a small community of Benedictine monks who are ever happy to sell you some of their peach marmalade. St-Michel is happiest in August, when it hosts concerts of the Pablo Casals festival.

While much of the inspiration for early medieval architecture in Languedoc came from north Italy or France, Roussillon was heavily influenced by nearby Spain. Here the obvious Spanish feature is the more-than-semicircular 'Visigothic' arches in the nave. This style, which goes back almost to Roman times, never became too popular in Christian Europe, though the Muslims of Spain adopted it to create the architectural fantasies of Seville and Granada. Other notable features of St-Michel include the massive and extremely elegant bell tower, and an unusual circular crypt, built in the 11th century under a building that was later demolished. The crypt is covered by toroid barrel-vaulting, with a mushroom-like central column almost unique in medieval architecture. Antonio Gaudí used similar columns in his work in Barcelona—a fascinating piece of Catalan cultural continuity; Gaudí could not have got the idea here, since the crypt was discovered and excavated only in 1937. In the cloister, you can see the galleries and capitals that managed to avoid being carted off to Manhattan, illustrating St-Michel's distinctive style of capital, as seen at Serrabone and many other Catalan churches: monsters from the medieval bestiary in the corners, intertwined with men on the four faces.

St-Martin-du-Canigou

The D 27, the narrow road that snakes around the lower slopes of Canigou, is an exceptional drive through the mountain forests; after St-Michel-de-Cuxa, it takes in **Vernet-Les-Bains**, a quiet spa that seems to have changed little since the 1920s. The hot sulphuric waters are good for your rheumatism and respiratory problems. Three kilometres further into Canigou, **Casteil** is a wooded resort with a small museum of mountain life and plenty of picnic grounds; it is the base for visiting Canigou's other great medieval monument, the abbey of **St-Martin-du-Canigou**—a taxing though lovely half-hour walk up from the town (daily exc Tues, tours at 10, 11:45 (12 on Sun), 2:30, 3:30, 4:30, adm).

A monkish architect named Sclua designed this complex, begun in the early 11th century by a count of the Cerdagne named Guifred. Sclua was a designer ahead of his time; he made his monastery a rustic acropolis, spectacularly sited with views around Canigou and the surrounding peaks, and arranged as a series of courtyards and terraces on different levels. The church, with its immense, fortress-like bell tower, has two levels, an upper church dedicated to St-Martin and a lower crypt for a certain obscure subterranean Virgin Mary: *Notre-Dame sous-Terre*. Some good capitals can be seen in the cloister, heavily restored in the early 1900s, and medieval tombs, including Count Guifred's, survive in the upper church. But on the whole St-Martin, with a history of decline and decay similar to that of St-Michel, retains little of its original glories.

To complete the tour of Romanesque Canigou, there is another 11th-12th-century church in the village of **Corneilla-de-Conflent**, with more good sculpture. Side roads to the west, in the valley of the Rotja, can take you to several more, including rare 10th-century churches in the tiny villages of Fuilla and Sahorre. Not all the area's attractions are on Canigou. Northeast of Prades, in the empty, largely forested Pyrenean foothills, **Eus** has won classification as one of the 'most beautiful villages in France'. Eus is an ambitious place and claims to have 'the most sunshine of any *commune* in France'. Spilling down its steep hillside, as you see it from the Têt valley, it is an elegant composition. Close up, you'll see plenty of cement-mixers; restoration has taken over since Eus won the award. The parish church has some elaborate 17th-century polychrome retables. Closer to Prades, on the D 14, is a huge and glorious Belle Epoque spa, now a little forgotten, set in the forest under a hilltop village, **Molitg-les-Bains**.

Villefranche-de-Conflent

Some villages have their own ideas for welcoming visitors. This one casually points cannons down at you as you pass along the N 116, by way of an invitation to drop in. Villefranche, the most logical place from which to defend the Têt valley, has had a castle at least since 1092. In the 17th century it took its present form, as a model Baroque fortress-town, rebuilt and re-fortified by Vauban. Almost nothing has changed since, and Villefranche remains as a fascinating historical record, a sort of stage set of that era. The old machinery for closing the western gate, the Porte d'Espagne, seems to be in good working order, and the old barracks still stand, on Rue St-Jacques. Tours of Vauban's **walls** are offered in summer, and if you have sufficient puff and military curiosity, there's a steep climb up to **Fort Liberia**, dominating the valley and long used as a prison.

In the centre, the church of **St-Jacques** survives from the pre-Vauban Villefranche, a fine 12th-century building with the familiar capitals from the workshop of St-Michel-de-Cuxa. Vauban built its walls and tower into his wall to help with the defence. For all its grim purpose, Villefranche is a lovely town, lately attracting much restoration and a number of artists and artisans; many of these have their shops on Rue St-Jacques—woodcarving and wrought-iron, and at No. 42 excellent ceramics in striking patterns. Outside town, some of the Pyrenees' most peculiar stalactites await your inspection at the **Grottes des Canalettes**.

Market Day: Prades, Tuesday.

WHERE TO STAY

Villefranche (66500), though tiny, makes the best base for visiting this region. Open all year, the attractive and inexpensive ****Le Vauban** is inside the walls on Place de l'Eglise (tel 68 96 18 03). There are also a few inexpensive rooms at the **Auberge St-Paul** restaurant (see below). **Prades** (66500) has only the ***Hôtel Hostalrich**, all grey paint and 50s neon; some rooms with balconies from which to observe the throbbing street life below (on the N 116 in the centre, tel 68 96 05 38, avoid the restaurant). In the warmer months, **Casteil** (66820) makes a delightful base for exploring the environs of Mont Canigou. Here, ****Le Catalan** is a simple and inexpensive place with surprising amenities—a heated pool, a playground for the kids and pet kangaroos (open June through September; tel 68 05 54 08).

EATING OUT

We picked up a couple of young hitch-hikers, and discovered they were studying to become cooks. Perfect, we thought, and tried a conversational opener by asking them about the local specialities. After a long silence, one of them volunteered: 'Anchovies'. 'How do you grow them, up here in the mountains', we asked. His friend broke in: 'Well, there's tomatoes, too...'

After one or two really foul meals, we began to understand. As with Venice or Malta, total indifference in the kitchen is a major part of the Catalans' charm. Near the coasts they will occasionally excel with seafood, but up here visitors are on their own. Travellers on a budget may be hard pressed finding something more enticing than a hotel-room picnic. **Prades** is certainly no paradise for dining; the one decent place in town is Spanish: **El Patio**, with paella and grilled fish, Andalusian-style (in the centre, facing the church; 115–200 F). You'll do better in **Villefranche-de-Conflent**, at the lovely **Auberge St-Paul** on central Place de l'Eglise. Down from Canigou they get the basic ingredients for mountain surprises like *filet mignon de sanglier* (boar) and beef with rare morel mushrooms; good value for 100 and 150 F menus (tel 68 96 30 95).

The restaurant at **Le Catalan** in **Casteil** is the best bet around Canigou (June through September; roast boar and mountain trout on 115 and 135 F menus). One of the best choices for splurge here would be **Le Grangousier**, with a garden terrace overlooking the lovely village of **Eus** and a rarefied cuisine: seafood spectaculars like *délice* of lobster stuffed with morels (110 and 140 F menus, tel 68 96 28 32).

The Cerdagne

This is as close as we get, in this book, to the heart of the Pyrenees, but it's far enough for the real thing: mountain rhododendrons and blue gentians, hordes of skiers, bears, and snow on top until May or June. The Cerdagne (*Cerdanya* in Catalan), was an isolated and effectively independent county in the Middle Ages; from the 10th century its counts gradually extended their power, becoming eventually Counts of Barcelona— the founders of the Catalan nation. In spite of this heritage, the Cerdagne was split between Spain and France in the 1659 Treaty of the Pyrenees. The building of the Little Yellow Train, in 1911, brought the French Cerdagne into the modern world (see p. 436); skiing has made it rather opulent today. And besides skiing, you can see a mysterious triangular church, warm up at the world's largest solar furnace, visit the highest railway station in France—and circumnavigate Spain in less than an hour.

TOURIST INFORMATION

Mont-Louis (66210): Rue du Marché, tel 68 04 21 97 (summer only).
Les Angles (66210): Av. Mont-Louis, tel 68 04 42 04.
Font-Romeu (66120): Av. Emmanuel-Brousse, tel 68 30 02 74.
Bourg-Madame (66760): Place de la Mairie, tel 68 04 55 35.

Mont-Louis and the Capcir

The gateway to the Cerdagne, on the main N 116, is **Mont-Louis**, another work of Vauban's and the highest fortress in France, named after Louis XIV. The army still resides here, though only to look after a pioneer **solar furnace**, built in 1953 and used, not for generating power, but for melting substances for scientific experiments; the huge mirror generates temperatures up to 6000 degrees. It shares the small space inside the walls with some 200 residents and plenty of cafés and tourist shops. A 7 km detour up into the mountains is **Planès**, and its unique triangular 11th-century church. Like the seven-sided model at Rieux-Minervois, this one has occasioned much speculation; some have claimed it as the centre of a network of ley-lines.

The road to Planès is a dead end, but there are better choices from the big crossroads at Mont-Louis. To the north, D 118 carries you to the isolated plateau of the **Capcir**. It's a perfect place to get away from it all—after a road was built into the Capcir in the last century, almost the entire population deserted it, tired of scratching a living from land that would only support a few cows. They left behind beautiful pine forests, and a score of little lakes carved out long ago by Pyrenean glaciers. Skiing has brought the Capcir back to life since the 60s, and the government has transformed the landscape with a number of dams and artificial lakes.

On your way into the Capcir, don't miss the church of St-Vincent in **La Llagonne**, only 3km from Mont-Louis. The centuries have left it in peace, with a remarkable collection of medieval art, including an altarpiece and painted baldachin (12th- and 13th-century) and a excellent polychrome *Majestat*. Further north, **Les Angles**, **Matemale** and **Formiguères** are the main ski centres. This region is great for hiking. The best parts lie to the west, on the slopes of the 2921-metre **Pic Carlit**; there you will find the sources of both the Têt and the Aude (above the D 60, in the Forêt de Barrés). Tiny glacial lakes are everywhere, collected in groups like the **Etangs de Carlit**, west of Lac des Bouillouses along a hiking path that leads to the summit of Carlit.

Font-Romeu

The western road (D 618) will take you through more pine forests to **Font-Romeu**; along with its new satellite towns, Super-bolquère and Pyrénées 2000, this is one of the biggest ski resorts in France. Font-Romeu grew up after 1910, around a now-closed 'Grand Hôtel'; it prospers today partly by its excellent sports facilities, often used for training France's Olympic teams. Stamped from the same mould as every other continental ski resort, it has plenty of fake Alpine chalets, innumerable pizzerias, and 260 snow machines to help out when the weather isn't cooperating. But no other resort has the World's Largest **Solar Furnace**, the successor to the one in Mont-Louis. With its curved mirror, covering an entire side of the nine-storey laboratory building, it reflects the Pyrenees beautifully while helping scientists work out all sorts of high-temperature puzzles (exhibit, open daily). Above the town, the pilgrimage chapel of **Notre-Dame-de-Font-Romeu** contains an exuberant altarpiece by Joseph Sunyer.

Another solar experiment can be seen at **Targasonne** west of Font-Romeu on the D 618; this big mirror was built to generate electricity, but hasn't quite worked as well as intended. The glaciers that reshaped the Capcir were busy here too, leaving a strange expanse of granite boulders called the **Chaos**. The Cerdagne is famous for its

Romanesque churches and chapels, testimony to the mountain Catalans' prosperity and level of culture even in the very early Middle Ages. One of the best of the churches is St-André, at **Angoustrine**, west of Targasonne, with fragments of 13th-century frescoes representing the months of the year. To the west, **Dorres** is a lofty *village perché* with another church, this one from the 11th century.

The Vallée du Carol

From the village of **Ur** (with yet another richly decorated Romanesque church), you can make a northern detour into the Vallée du Carol, the western edge of Roussillon. **Latour-de-Carol** is a romantic name for another great border rail-crossing most of us have blinked at in the dark; the name does not come from Charlemagne, as most people think, but the Carol river, though the Frankish emperor may have passed by here, with Roland and Oliver, on his way to fight the Moors. Latour's church has more work by Joseph Sunyer. The best church in the area, however, is the Chapelle St-Fructueux in the miniscule village of **Yravals**, above Latour-de-Carol—with a wealth of medieval art inside, and a magnificent mid-14th-century altarpiece of St Martha, by a Catalan named Ramon Destorrents. The painting, showing an Italian influence, includes all the familiar scenes of the saint's life (see Tarascon), including what must be the highest and most westerly Tarasque of all Tarasques.

Further up this scenic valley, you'll pass the tower of the ruined 14th-century castle that gives Latour its name. The trees give out as the tortuous road climbs to the pass of Puymorens. From here, if you have a sudden hankering for some tax-free Havanas, or a new phonograph, it's only 40 km to the Pyrenean Ruritania, the Principality of **Andorra**.

Llivia, Llo and Eyne

Bourg-Madame is the crossing point for Spain; just across the border lies Puigcerdà, with a 14th-century church and the best ice-hockey squad on the Iberian peninsula. The N 116 will take you northeast from here, back to Mont-Louis, completing your circumnavigation of Spain—or at least the tiny Spanish enclave of **Llivia**, left marooned by accident in the Treaty of 1659. The treaty stipulated that Spain must give up the *villages* of the Cerdagne, and everyone had forgotten that Llivia had the legal status of a city; it had been a Roman *municipium*, the capital of the Cerdagne in ancient times. Llivia's unlikely attraction is a 17th-century pharmacy, one of the most beautiful and best-preserved in Europe.

East of Bourg-Madame, more Catalan Romanesque churches can be visited: at **Hix**, an impressive edifice of 1177, built when the town was the residence of the counts of the Cerdagne, and at **Caldégas**, where the frescoes include a hunting scene with falcons. **Osséja**, south of Hix, is home to an international competition for sheep-dogs every July. Further east, along the N 116, road signs will startle you with town names like Llo and Err; linguists say they're Basque, evidence that the Basques lived here in remote times. **Llo** has a church with a lovely sculptured portal; from here there are opportunities for hiking, southwards into the narrow **Gorges du Sègre**. Even better, come to nearby Eyne in May, late enough to avoid the skiers from the big resort called Eyne 2600, and just in time for a spectacular display of wildflowers in the Vallée d'Eyne, climbing up to the Spanish border.

447

MOUNTAIN ACTIVITIES

Canigou and the Capcir are exceptional places for **hiking**. The tourist office in Vernet-les-Bains has all the information and sells trail guidebooks for Canigou (they also know where non-hiking types can rent a jeep). Hôtels in sports-oriented Font-Romeu can set you up with just about anything from *pétanque* to squash; there's also a (nine-hole) golf course and a school of **hang-gliding**. The other **golf course** in the region is in Saillagouse. The best **market** in the area is the Sunday morning spread in Puigcerdà.

WHERE TO STAY/EATING OUT

If you're staying at the crossroads town of **Mont-Louis** (66210), make sure you get a room with a view at the ****Le Clos Cerdan**, on a cliff overlooking the valley; modern but comfortable (on the N 116, tel 68 04 23 20, closed Nov). **Font-Romeu** (66120) has any number of modern places that cater to the ski crowd, like the ****Clair Soleil**, on the Route L'Odeillo, also with a view, and a swimming-pool (open except May and Nov-Dec, tel 68 30 13 65). The bargain choice around Font-Romeu is the cosy and family-run **La Capeillette** (route de Bolquère in Odeillo, tel 68 30 11 15).

Country inns unconcerned with the skiing business are somewhat rare. Llo, above Saillagouse, has the ivy-covered *****Auberge l'Atalaya**; tranquillity is assured in this setting, close to the wildflowers of the Vallée d'Eyne and infinitely far from anything else, with a pool and an excellent restaurant (tel 68 04 70 04). Also in this area, the *****Auberge d'Eyne**, on the Route des Pistes in Eyne: an unpretentiously cosy country inn, in a restored farmhouse (closed late Dec-mid Jan; tel 68 04 71 12). In this very holiday-oriented area almost all the hotels have restaurants of their own; taking full or half-board is usually a better bargain, and worth it in places like the Auberge l'Atalaya or the Auberge d'Eyne, where the restaurants are better than anything else you'll find nearby.

The Vallespir

The valley of the Tech, the southernmost valley of Roussillon, and of France, winds a lonesome trail around the southern slopes of Canigou. Known for its mineral waters since Roman times, it traditionally made its living from these and from ironworking, the basis of Catalan prosperity in the Middle Ages. When the iron gave out, there was smuggling. Today, as smugglers have become superfluous, the Vallespir lives by tourism, with some francs on the side from cherries and cork oak—the *primeurs*, the first cherries in the French market each year, and the *grand cru* corks that have kept the best champagne bubbly for centuries.

TOURIST INFORMATION

Céret (66400): Av. Clemenceau, tel 68 87 00 53.
Prats-de-Mollo (66230): Place le Foiral, tel 68 39 70 83.

Le Boulou and St-Martin-de-Fenollar

From Perpignan, you reach the Vallespir by the A 9, getting off at **Le Boulou**, a truck-stop known to every European TIR jockey. The ancient Roman teamsters knew it too. Le Boulou has been fated by geography as an eternal transit point; just co-incidentally it has a fine Romanesque church with a portal sculpted by the Master of Cabestany, portraying the *Nativity*. East of Le Boulou, **St-Génis-des-Fontaines** was one of the important early medieval monasteries of Roussillon. Its church has a remarkable carved lintel from about the year 1000, with a *Majestat* and stylized apostles shaped like bowling-pins; the cloister was dismantled and sold off in 1924, one of the final scandals of France's traditional lack of concern for its medieval heritage. The best of it ended up in the Pennsylvania University Museum in Philadelphia.

The A 9 and N 9 continue south into Spain, passing **St-Martin-de-Fenollar** and its 12th-century church, with some of the most unusual and best-preserved frescoes in the Midi. Nine-tenths of all early medieval painting is lost to us, and this is a rare example of the best of what is left: brilliant colours and a confident stylization, with an imagery untroubled by the dogma of later religious painting, as in the *Nativity*, where Mary lies not in a stable, but in a comfortable bed under a chequered baldachin.

Hannibal entered Gaul through **Le Perthus**, the last, or first stop in France. As a fitting book-end to this long volume, archaeologists have recently uncovered here a monumental pedestal, probably from a monument of Augustus similar to the one at La Turbie near the Italian border.

Céret

Back in the valley of the Tech, the D 115 streaks from Le Boulou to Céret, centre of the optimal cherry-growing region suspended between the Pyrenees and the sea. Céret found its artistic destiny at the turn of the century as the 'Mecca of Cubism', thanks to Picasso, Braque, Matisse, and others. As an artists' colony it continued until 1940, harbouring refugees like Cocteau and Dufy. Today, some of their works can be seen at the **Musée d'Art Moderne** (daily exc Mon, 10–12, 2–3, summer until 6; adm). Céret also has a war memorial by Maillol, and an elegant medieval bridge across the Tech. In summer there are occasional **bullfights** in the arena.

Amélie-les-Bains and Arles-sur-Tech

Sulphurous waters, good for your rheumatism, have been the fortune of Amélie-les-Bains since ancient times; a Roman swimming-pool with a vaulted roof has been uncovered, and the spa still does a grandstand business, with over 30 hotels in the area. Arles-sur-Tech, a curious old village and the ancient capital of the Vallespir, offers some even curiouser hagiography in its 11th- and 12th-century church of Ste-Marie, originally the centre of an important monastery. Dark Age Arles-sur-Tech got by with an anonymous saint—an empty 4th-century sarcophagus known as *Ste-Tombe*—until the dreaded *simiots* came to town, ape-like monsters that trampled the crops and violated the women. In despair, the abbot of Ste-Marie went to the pope asking for some holy relics. This was in 957, when demand for saints' bones was at its historic high, and the best the pope could offer was a pair of Persian martyrs named Abdon and Sennen. The abbot brought them back in a false-bottomed water-barrel, to fool the Venetians and Germans and any other relic thieves, and they dealt with the *simiots* as efficiently as if they had been the bones of St Peter himself.

The story is portrayed in a 17th-century retable, in the chapel where Abdon and Sennen's relics are kept. The *Ste-Tombe* is also present. It fills continually with a mysterious liquid. The same phenomenon can be seen at the tomb of St Nicholas at Bari, in Italy; both are credited with miraculous cures, and the faithful often keep a phial of it in the house. Besides all this, there is the 1304 *Tomb of Guillem Gaucelme*, a local baron whose effigy rather conspicuously lacks a nose; modern speculation suggests a bizarre cancer. Ste-Marie has some well-preserved 12th-century frescoes, discovered recently behind the church organ, and a pretty marble cloister of 1262. Arles-sur-Tech is the last redoubt of the valley's famous medieval iron industry; the last working mine in Roussillon is above the town at Batère. You can take the mining road up the mountain for the view, but a better excursion would be to the steep **Gorges de la Fou**, along the D 44 to the northwest.

Continuing up the valley, just south of the D 115, the hilltop village of **Serralongue** has a church dating from 1018, and one of the only surviving examples of a Catalan *conjurador*; this is a small, square pavilion with a slate roof, and statues of the four Evangelists facing the four cardinal directions. When a storm threatened, the priest would go up to the *conjurador* and perform certain rites facing the direction of the storm, to avert its wrath. A detour further south, on the D 3, will uncover **St-Laurent-de-Cerdans**, famous for making espadrilles, and **Coustoges**, which has a lovely early 12th-century church with carved portals; few ever see it, in this isolated village, the furthest south in continental France.

Some towns just ask for it. As if having a name like **Prats-de-Mollo** weren't enough, this tiny spa advertises itself as the 'European Capital of Urinary Infections'. Prats-de-Mollos's other claim to fame is a European record for rainfall, 33 inches in 16 hours on 15 October 1940. The baths are really at **La Preste**, 8 km up in the mountains; Prats-de-Mollo itself is an attractive village, with remains of its old walls and medieval buildings that recall the days when this was a little textile manufacturing centre, specializing in Catalan bonnets. This is as far as we go; the Spanish border is 14 km away.

Market Days: Céret, Saturday. Arles-sur-Tech, Wednesday. Ille-sur-Têt, daily.

WHERE TO STAY/EATING OUT
Even with the baths, tourism has still failed to make much of an impact on this out-of-the-way valley. Neither in accommodation or in cuisine are you likely to find anything worth writing home about. But it can be pleasant enough. A typical example is ****Les Glycines** in **Arles-sur-Tech** (66150), a simple, modern hotel on Rue Joc de Pilota; the restaurant has a garden terrace (mostly seafood, and a good choice of dinner menus from 85 to 200 F; tel 68 39 10 09; closed Jan). **Amélie-les-Bains**, as modest a spa as you'll find, has dozens of budget hotels; one good one that does not require full board is ***La Pergola** on Av. du Vallespir (closed Jan, tel 68 39 05 71).

A posher stop, in **Céret** (66400), is the *****Terrasse au Soleil**, a restored and modernized *mas* on Route Fontfrède, with a view, a heated pool and tennis court (closed Jan-Feb; a bit dear, especially on full-board pension, tel 68 87 01 94). Also in Céret is **Les Feuillants**, recently opened but probably already the best restaurant in the Vallespir; Catalan cooking with *haute cuisine* ambitions, amidst startling 30s decor, tel 68 87 37 88.

GEOGRAPHICAL, ARCHITECTURAL, AND ARTISTIC TERMS

Abbaye: abbey.
Anse: cove.
Arrondissement: a city district.
Auberge: inn.
Aven: a sink-hole (a pre-Gallic word).
Bastide: a taller, more elaborate version of a *mas*, with balconies, wrought-iron work, reliefs, etc; also a medieval new town, fortified and laid out in a grid.
Beffroi: tower with a town's bell.
Borie: dry-stone shepherd's hut with a corbelled roof.
Buffet d'eau: in French gardens, a fountain built into a wall with water falling through levels of urns or basins.
Cabane: a simple weekend or holiday retreat, usually near the sea; a *cabane de gardian* is a thatched cowboy's abode in the Camargue.
Calanque: a narrow coastal creek, like a miniature fjord.
Capitelles: the name for *bories* in Languedoc.
Caryatid: column or pillar carved in the figure of a woman.
Causse: rocky, arid limestone plateaus, north of Hérault and in the Bas Languedoc.
Cave: cellar.
Château: mansion, manor house or castle.
Chemin: path.
Chevet: eastern end of a church, including the apse.
Cirque: a round natural depression created by erosion at the loop of a river.
Cloître: cloister.
Clue: a rocky cleft or transverse valley.
Col: mountain pass.
Côte: coast; on wine labels, *côtes, coteaux* and *costières* mean 'hills'.
Cours: wide main street, like an elongated main square.
Couvent: convent or monastery.
Crèche: a Christmas crib with *santons*.
Donjon: castle keep.
Ecluse: canal lock.
Eglise: church.
Etang: lagoon or swamp.
Félibre: member of the movement to bring back the use of the Provençal language.
Ferrade: cattle branding.
Gardian: a cowboy of the Camargue.

451

Gare: train station (SNCF).
Gare routière: coach station.
Garrigues: irregular limestone hills pitted with caves, especially those north of Nîmes and Montpellier.
Gisant: a sculpted prone effigy on a tomb.
Gîte: shelter. *Gîte d'etape*: basic shelter for walkers.
Grande Randonnée (GR): long-distance hiking path.
Grau: a narrowing, either of canyon or a river.
Halles: covered market.
Hôtel: any large building or palace; a Hôtel de Ville is the city hall.
Mairie: town hall.
Manade: a *gardian*'s farm in the Camargue.
Maquis: Mediterranean scrub.
Marché: market.
Mas: a farmhouse and its outbuildings.
Motte: a hammock, or a raised area in a swamp.
Oppidum: pre-Roman fortified settlement.
Pays: region.
Pont: bridge.
Porte: gateway.
Predella: small paintings beneath the main subject of a retable.
Presqu'île: peninsula.
Restanques: vine or olive terraces.
Retable: a carved or painted altarpiece, often consisting of a number of scenes.
Rez-de-chausée (RC): ground floor.
Santon: a figure in a Christmas nativity scene, usually made of terracotta and dressed in 18th-century Provençal costume.
Source: spring.
Tour: tower.
Transi: in a tomb, a relief of the decomposing cadaver.
Tympanum: sculpted semicircular panel over a church door.
Vieille ville: historic, old quarter of town.
Village perché: hilltop village.

CHRONOLOGY

BC

c. 1,000,000	First human presence, near Menton; use of bone as a tool
c. 450,000	Tautavel Man in northern Roussillon
c. 400,000	Discovery of fire, as at Terra Amata in Nice
c. 60,000	Neanderthal hunters on the Riviera and around Ganges
c. 40,000	Advent of *Homo sapiens*; invention of art
c. 8000	Invention of the bow
c. 3500	Development of Neolithic culture; first villages built
c. 2000	First metallurgy; copper and tin at Vence and Caussols
c. 1800– 1000	Worship at Mont Bégo, at Tende, and Vallée des Merveilles incisions
c. 800	Celts begin to occupy Languedoc
c. 600	Greek traders found Marseille
c. 380	Celtic invasions in Provence
218	Hannibal and elephants pass through region on the way to Italy
125	Roman legions attack Celto-Ligurian tribes that threaten Marseille
122	Founding of *Aquae Sextiae* (Aix)
118	Founding of Narbonne and *Provincia*, the first Roman province in Gaul
102	Marius and his legionaries defeat the Teutones
49	Marius' nephew, Julius Caesar punishes Marseille for its support of Pompey
14	Augustus defeats Ligurian tribes in the Alpes Maritimes

AD

46	Arrival of the Boat of Bethany at Stes-Maries-de-la-Mer (traditional)
310	Emperor Maximian captured at Marseille by son-in-law Constantine
314	Constantine calls Church Council at Arles
410	Honorat founds Lérins monastery
413	Visigoths conquer Languedoc
476	Formal end of Western Roman Empire
535	Provence and Languedoc ceded to the Franks
719	Arab invasions in Languedoc
737	Charles Martel defeats Arabs and crushes anti-Frank rebellions in Arles, Avignon and Marseille
759	Pépin the Short adds region to his Frankish empire
812	Canonization of St-Guilhem, Languedoc's warrior saint
855	Creation of the kingdom of Provence for Charles the Bald, third son of Lothaire
879	At the death of Charles the Bald, the Duke Viennois Boson proclaims himself king of Provence
c. 890	More Arab raids and invasions
924	Magyars (Hungarians) sack Nîmes
946	Lords of Cerdagne become Counts of Barcelona; beginning of Catalan nation
949	Conrad of Burgundy inherits Provence and divides it into four feudal counties
979	Count William defeats Saracens at La Garde-Freinet, proclaims himself Marquis of Provence

985	Montpellier founded
1002	First written text in Occitan
1032	Death of Rudolph II, king of Burgundy and Provence, lands bequeathed to Holy Roman Emperor Conrad II
1084	Trencavels rule Carcassonne and Béziers
1095	Occitans join First Crusade under Raymond of St-Gilles, Count of Toulouse and Marquis of Provence; William of Aquitaine writes first troubadour poetry
1112	Marriage of Douce, duchess of Provence, with Raymond-Berenger III, Count of Barcelona
1125	Provence divided between the houses of Barcelona and Toulouse
1137	Catalunya unified as Kingdom of Aragon
1176	Pierre Valdo of Lyon founds Waldensian (Vaudois) sect
1186	Counts of Provence make Aix their capital
1187	Discovery of relics of St Martha at Tarascon
1208	Albigensian Crusade begins
1209	Sack and massacre at Béziers by Simon de Montfort
1213	Battle of Muret; Montfort defeats Count of Toulouse and King of Aragon
1229	French annex Carcassonne and eastern Languedoc
1246	Charles I of Anjou weds Béatrice, heiress of Provence, beginning the Angevin dynasty
1248	St Louis embarks on Seventh Crusade from Aigues-Mortes
1255	Fall of Quéribus, the last Cathar stronghold
1266	Battle of Benevento gives Charles of Anjou the Kingdom of Naples
1272	Narbonne Cathedral begun
1274	Papacy acquired Comtat Venaissin
1276	Division of Aragon; Kingdom of Majorca founded with capital at Perpignan
1280	Relics of Mary Magdalene 'discovered' at St-Maximin-la-Ste-Baume
1286	First meeting of the Etats de Provence
1289	The school of medicine in Montpellier becomes a university
1295	The death of the 'last troubadour', Guiraut Riquier
1297	Francesco Grimaldi the Spiteful, merchant-prince of Genoa, conquers Monaco (but is forced to abandon it in 1301)
1303	Boniface VIII founds University of Avignon
1309	Papacy moves to Avignon
1327	Petrarch first sees Laura
1340s	Siennese painters bring International Gothic style to Avignon
1344	Kingdom of Aragon reunited
1348	Jeanne of Naples and Provence sells Avignon to the Pope; the Black Death strikes the South
1349	Jews expelled from France and take refuge in Comtat Venaissin
c. 1350	First paper mills in the Comtat Venaissin
1362	Election of abbot of St-Victor as Pope Urban V
1360s	The *Grandes Compagnies* ravage the countryside
1363	The Grimaldis recover Monaco and hold it still
1377	Papacy returns to Rome
1380	Louis I d'Anjou adopted by Jeanne of Naples
1388	Regions of Nice, Barcelonnette and Puget-Théniers secede from Provence, join County of Savoy
1464	Founding of the Fair of Beaucaire
1481	Charles du Maine, Count of Provence, leaves Provence to the King of France

1492	Union of Aragon and Castile (Ferdinand and Isabella); end of Catalan independence.
1496	Military port founded in Toulon
1501	French create Parlement of Aix to oversee Provence
1524	Provence invaded by the imperial troops of Charles V
1525	Jews in the Comtat Venaissin compelled to wear yellow hats
1539	Edict of Villars-Cotterêts forces use of French as official language
1540	Parlement of Aix orders massacre of Waldensians in the Lubéron.
1559	Completion of the canal between the Durance and Salon
1560	First Protestant synod in Languedoc
1562	Beginning of Wars of Religion: Protestant assembly at Mérindol
1577	First soap factory (Prunemoyr) founded in Marseille
1590–92	Carlo Emanuele of Savoy invades Provence
1598	Edict of Nantes ends the Wars of Religion
1603	Royal college founded at Aix
1639	Last meeting of the Etats de Provence before the Revolution
1646	Jews confined to ghettos
1650	Molière moves to Pézenas
1659	Treaty of the Pyrenees; French annex Roussillon
1666	Digging begins on the Canal du Midi; founding of Sète
1680	Louis XIV enters rebellious Marseille
1685	Louis XIV revokes Edict of Nantes
1702–4	The War of the Camisards
1707	Toulon unsuccessfully besieged by the English and Duke of Savoy
1720–21	100,000 die of plague, mostly in Marseille
1731	Principality of Orange incorporated into France
1752	Last Protestant persecutions
1766	Tobias Smollett publishes his *Travels*, enticing the British to Nice
1779	Roman mausoleum and palace of the counts demolished, at Aix
1784	Hot air balloon goes up in Marseille
1787	The Edict of Tolerance
1790	France divided into *départements*
1791	France annexes Comtat Venaissin
1792	Volunteers from Marseille sing *La Marseillaise* to Paris
1793	Revolutionary tribunal in Marseille; Siege of Toulon makes Bonaparte famous
1795	Massacres in Marseille and Tarascon
1800	Marseille population around 100,000
1815	Napoleon escapes Elba and pops up again near Juan-les-Pins
1820	First signs of tourist industry at Hyères
1830	Revolution bring Louis Philippe to power
1831	Lord Brougham begins the vogue for wintering in Cannes
1839	Inauguration of Marseille–Sète railroad; birth of Cézanne
1840–8	Prime Ministry of Guizot, Protestant liberal from Nîmes
1844	Viollet-le-Duc begins restoration of Carcassonne
1851	Louis Napoleon's coup ends Second Republic; armed resistance in the south
1854	Founding of the Félibrige at the Château de Fontségugne
1859	Mistral publishes *Miréio*
1860	Plebiscite in County of Nice votes for union with France
1861	The prince of Monaco sells Roquebrune and Menton to France
1865	Silkworm industry destroyed by disease

1868–90	Phylloxera epidemic devastes vines
1869	Opening of Suez Canals brings boom times to Marseille
1888	Stephen Liégeard gives the Côte d'Azur its name
1888–90	Van Gogh in Provence
1900	Population reaches 500,000 in Marseille, 20 per cent of which is Italian
1904	Frédéric Mistral wins the Nobel Prize for Literature
1906	Colonial *Exposition* at Marseille
1907	Climax of farm protests; Languedoc occupied by the army
1911	Diaghilev signs contract to bring the Ballets Russes to Monte Carlo
1924–5	Scott and Zelda Fitzgerald raise hell on the Riviera
1928	Creation of the Camargue Regional Park
1930	D.H. Lawrence dies in Vence
1930s	Marcel Pagnol films his *Marius, Fanny* and *César* trilogy in Marseille
1939	Founding of the Cannes Film Festival
1942	Sinking of the fleet at Toulon
1943	Formation of the Maquis resistance cells
1944	American and French landings around St-Tropez; Provence liberated in two weeks
1945	Creation of the Institut d'Etudes Occitanes
1947	Val de Roya incorporated into France
1956	Bardot and Vadim make *And God Created Woman* in St-Tropez
1962	Independence of Algeria: tens of thousands of French North Africans (*pieds-noirs*) settle in the south
1965	Last silk weaving company closed
1966	Steelworks founded at Fos
1968	Big resort development plan begins in Languedoc
1970	Completion of Paris-Lyon-Marseille autoroute
1982	Regional governments created
1988	Floods in Nîmes

LANGUAGE

A working knowledge of French will make your holiday more enjoyable, but is hardly essential in the most visited parts of the south—the Côte d'Azur and resorts of Languedoc, the cities, and heartland of Provence where you can always find someone working in travel offices, banks, shops, hotels, and restaurants who speaks at least rudimentary English. Venturing into the less-travelled hinterlands may well require an effort to recall your school French: a small travel phrase book and English-French dictionary can come in handy. On either end of the coast you can try out your Italian or Catalan.

Even if your French is brilliant, the soupy southern twang may throw you a curve. Any word with a nasal *in* or *en* becomes something like *aing* (*vaing* for *vin*). The last vowel on many words that are silent in the north get to express themselves in the south as well (*encore* becomes something like *engcora*). What stays the same is the level of politeness: use *monsieur, madame* or *mademoiselle* when speaking to anyone, from your first *bonjour* (and never *garçon* in restaurants!) to your last *au revoir*.

Many of the restaurants in this book don't translate their menus, so we've included the decoder below; try the section on regional specialities (pp. 28–30) if an item isn't listed below.

Deciphering French Menus

Hors d'oeuvre et Soupes	Starters and soups
Assiette assortie	Mixed cold hors d'oeuvres
Bisque	Shellfish soup
Bouchées	Mini vol-au-vents
Bouillon	Broth
Consommé	Clear soup
Crudités	Raw vegetable platter
Potage	Thick vegetable soup
Velouté	Thick smooth soup, often fish or chicken
Vol-au-Vent	Puff pastry case with savoury filling

Poissons et Coquillages (Crustacés)	Fish and Shellfish
Aiglefin	Little haddock
Anchois	Anchovies
Anguille	Eel
Barbue	Brill
Baudroie	Anglerfish
Belons	Rock oysters
Bigourneau	Winkle
Blanchailles	Whitebait
Brème	Bream
Brochet	Pike
Bulot	Whelk
Cabillaud	Fresh cod
Calmar	Squid
Carrelet	Plaice
Colin	Hake

Congre	Conger eel
Coques	Cockles
Coquilles St-Jacques	Scallops
Crabe	Crab
Crevettes grises	Shrimps
Crevettes roses	Prawns
Cuisses de grenouilles	Frogs' legs
Darne	Thin slice of fish
Daurade	Sea bream
Ecrevisse	Freshwater crayfish
Eperlans	Smelt
Escabèche	Fish fried, marinated, and served cold
Escargots	Snails
Espadon	Swordfish
Flétan	Halibut
Friture	Deep fried fish
Fruits de mer	Seafood
Gambas	Giant prawns
Gigot de mer	A large fish cooked whole
Grondin	Red gurnard
Hareng	Herring
Homard	Lobster
Huîtres	Oysters
Langouste	Spiny Mediterranean lobster
Languoustines	Dublin Bay Prawns
Limande	Lemon sole
Lotte	Monkfish
Loup (de mer)	Sea bass
Maquereau	Mackerel
Merlan	Whiting
Morue	Salt Cod
Moules	Mussels
Oursin	Sea urchin
Pageot	Sea bream
Palourdes	Clams
Poulpe	Octopus
Praires	Small clams
Raie	Skate
Rascasse	Scorpion fish
Rouget	Red mullet
Saumon	Salmon
Saint-Pierre	John Dory
Sole (à la meunière)	Sole (with butter, lemon and parsley)
Stockfisch	Stockfish (wind-dried cod)
Telline	Tiny clam
Thon	Tuna
Truite	Trout
Truite saumonée	Salmon trout

Viandes et Volaille	Meat and Poultry
Agneau (de pré salé)	Lamb (grazed in fields by the sea)
Ailerons	Chicken wings
Andouillette	Chitterling (tripe) sausage
Biftek	Beefsteak
Blanc	Breast or white meat
Blanquette	Stew of white meat, thickened with egg yolk
Boeuf	Beef
Boudin blanc	Sausage of white meat
Boudin noir	Black pudding
Brochette	Meat (or fish) on a skewer
Caille	Quail
Canard, caneton	Duck, duckling
Carré	The best end of a cutlet or chop
Cervelles	Brains
Châteaubriand	Porterhouse steak
Cheval	Horsemeat
Chevreau	Kid
Civet	Stew of rabbit (usually), marinated in wine
Confit	Meat cooked and preserved in its own fat
Contre-filet	Sirloin steak
Côte, côtelette	Chop, cutlet
Cuisse	Thigh or leg
Dinde, dindon	Turkey
Entrecôte	Ribsteak
Epaule	Shoulder
Estouffade	A meat stew marinated, fried, and then braised
Faisan	Pheasant
Faux filet	Sirloin
Foie	Liver
Foie Gras	Goose liver
Frais de veau	Veal testicles
Fricadelle	Meatball
Gésier	Gizzard
Gibier	Game
Gigot	Leg of lamb
Graisse	Fat
Grillade	Grilled meat
Grive	Thrush
Jambon	Ham
Jarret	Knuckle
Langue	Tongue
Lapereau	Young rabbit
Lapin	Rabbit
Lard (lardons)	Bacon (diced bacon)
Lièvre	Hare
Maigret (de canard)	Breast (of duck)
Marcassin	Young wild boar
Merguez	Spicy red sausage
Museau	Muzzle
Navarin	Lamb stew with root vegetables

459

Noix de veau	Topside of veal
Oie	Goose
Os	Bone
Perdreau (perdrix)	Partridge
Petit salé	Salt pork
Pieds	Trotters
Pintade	Guinea fowl
Porc	Pork
Poularde	Capon
Poulet	Chicken
Poussin	Baby chicken
Queue de boeuf	Oxtail
Ris (de veau)	Sweetbreads (veal)
Rognons	Kidneys
Rôti	Roast
Sanglier	Wild boar
Saucisses	Sausages
Saucisson	Dry sausage, like salami
Selle (d'agneau)	Saddle (of lamb)
Steak tartare	Raw minced beef, often topped with a raw egg yolk
Suprême de volaille	Fillet of chicken breast and wing
Tête (de veau)	Head (calf's)
Toro	Bull's meat
Tortue	Turtle
Tournedos	Thick round slices of beef fillet
Travers de porc	Spare ribs
Tripes	Tripe
Veau	Veal
Venaison	Venison
Légumes, herbes, etc.	**Vegetables, herbs, etc.**
Ail	Garlic
Algue	Seaweed
Aneth	Dill
Artichaut	Artichoke
Asperges	Asparagus
Aubergine	Aubergine (eggplant)
Avocat	Avocado
Basilic	Basil
Betterave	Beetroot
Cannelle	Cinnamon
Céleri (-rave)	Celery (celeriac)
Cèpes	Wild dark brown mushrooms
Champignons	Mushrooms
Chanterelles	Wild yellow mushrooms
Chicorée	Curly endive
Chou	Cabbage
Choufleur	Cauliflower
Choucroute	Sauerkraut

Ciboulettes	Chives
Citrouille	Pumpkin
Coeur de palmier	Heart of palm
Concombre	Cucumber
Cornichons	Gherkins
Courgettes	Courgettes (zucchini)
Cresson	Watercress
Echalote	Shallot
Endive	Chicory
Epinards	Spinach
Estragon	Tarragon
Fenouil	Fennel
Fèves	Broad beans
Flageolets	White beans
Fleure de courgette	Courgette blossoms
Frites	Chips (French fries)
Genièvre	Juniper
Gingembre	Ginger
Girofle	Clove
Haricots (rouges, blancs)	Beans (kidney, white)
Haricots verts	Green (French) beans
Jardinière	With diced garden vegetables
Laitue	Lettuce
Laurier	Bay leaf
Lentilles	Lentils
Maïs (épis de)	Sweet corn (on the cob)
Marjolaine	Marjoram
Menthe	Mint
Mesclum	Salad of various leaves
Morilles	Morel mushrooms
Moutarde	Mustard
Navet	Turnip
Oignons	Onions
Oseille	Sorrel
Panais	Parsnip
Persil	Parsley
Petits pois	Peas
Piment	Pimento
Pissenlits	Dandelion greens
Poireaux	Leeks
Pois chiches	Chick-peas
Pois mange-tout	Sugar-peas
Poivron	Bell pepper
Pomme de terre	Potato
Primeurs	Young vegetables
Radis	Radishes
Raifort	Horseradish
Riz	Rice
Romarin	Rosemary
Safran	Saffron

Salade verte	Green salad
Salsafi	Salsify
Sarnette	Savory
Sarrasin	Buckwheat
Sauge	Sage
Seigle	Rye
Serpolet	Wild thyme
Thym	Thyme
Truffes	Truffles

Fruits, Desserts, Noix	**Fruits, Desserts, Nuts**
Abricot	Apricot
Acajou	Cashew
Amandes	Almonds
Ananas	Pineapple
Banane	Banana
Bavarois	Mousse or custard in a mould
Biscuit	Cake
Bombe	Ice-cream dessert in round mould
Bonbons	Sweets, candy
Brebis	Sheep cheese
Brioche	Light sweet yeast bread
Brugnon	Nectarine
Cacahouète	Peanut
Cassis	Black currant
Cérise	Cherry
Charlotte	Custard and fruit in almond biscuits
Chausson	Turnover
Chèvre	Goat cheese
Citron	Lemon
Citron vert	Lime
Clafoutis	Berry tart
Coing	Quince
Compote	Stewed fruit
Corbeille de fruits	Basket of fruit
Coupe	Ice cream
Crème anglaise	Custard
Crème Chantilly	Sweet whipped cream
Crème fraîche	Sour cream
Crème pâtissière	Thick cream pastry filling made with eggs
Dattes	Dates
Figues (de Barbarie)	Figs (prickly pear)
Fraises (de bois)	Strawberries (wild)
Framboises	Raspberries
Fromage (plateau de)	Cheese (board)
Fromage blanc	Yoghurty cream cheese
Fromage frais	Similar to sour cream
Fruit de la passion	Passion fruit
Gâteau	Cake
Génoise	Rich sponge cake

462

Glace	Ice cream
Grenade	Pomegranate
Groseilles	Red currants, gooseberries
Lavande	Lavender
Macarons	Macaroons
Madeleines	Small sponge cakes
Mandarine	Tangerine
Mangue	Mango
Marrons	Chestnuts
Merise	Wild cherry
Miel	Honey
Mirabelle	Mirabelle plum
Mûres	Mulberry, blackberry
Myrtilles	Bilberries
Noisette	Hazelnut
Noix	Walnuts
Oeufs à la neige	Meringue
Pamplemousse	Grapefruit
Parfait	Frozen mousse
Pastèque	Water melon
Pêche (blanche)	Peach (white)
Petits fours	Tiny cakes and pastries
Pignons	Pine-nuts
Pistache	Pistachio
Poire	Pear
Pomme	Apple
Prune	Plum
Pruneau	Prune
Raisins (sec)	Grapes (raisins)
Reine-clande	Greengage
Sablé	Shortbread
Savarin	A filled cake, shaped like a ring
Tarte, tartelette	Tart, little tart
Tarte Tropezienne	Sponge cake filled with custard and topped with nuts
Truffes	Chocolate truffles

Cooking terms, miscellaneous, snacks

Addition	Bill
Aigre-doux	Sweet and sour
Aiguillette	Thin slice
A l'anglais	Boiled
A l'arlésienne	With aubergines, potatoes, tomatoes, onions, and rice
A la châtelaine	With chestnut purée and artichoke hearts
A la grecque	Cooked in olive oil and lemon
A la périgordine	In a truffle and foie gras sauce
A la provençale	Cooked with tomatoes, garlic, olive oil
Allumettes	Strips of puff pastry
A point	Medium steak
Au feu de bois	Cooked over a wood fire

Au four	Baked
Auvergnat	With sausage, bacon, and cabbage
Baguette	Long loaf of bread
Barquette	Pastry boat
Beignets	Fritters
Béarnaise	Sauce of egg yolks, shallots and white wine
Beurre	Butter
Bien cuit	Well done steak
Bleu	Very rare steak
Bordelaise	Red wine, bone marrow and shallot sauce
Broche	Roast on a spit
Chasseur	Mushrooms and shallots in white wine
Chaud	Hot
Chou	Puff pastry
Confiture	Jam
Coulis	Strong clear broth
Couteau	Knife
Crème	Cream
Crêpe	Thin pancake
Croque-monsieur	Toasted ham and cheese sandwich
Croustade	Small savoury pastry
Cru	Raw
Cuillère	Spoon
Cuit	Cooked
Diable	Spicy mustard sauce
Emincé	Thinly sliced
En croûte	Cooked in a pastry crust
En papillote	Baked in buttered paper
Epices	Spices
Farci	Stuffed
Feuilleté	Flaky pastry
Flambé	Set aflame with alcohol
Forestière	With bacon and mushrooms
Fourchette	Fork
Fourré	Stuffed
Frais, fraîche	Fresh
Frappé	With crushed ice
Frit	Fried
Froid	Cold
Fromage	Cheese
Fumé	Smoked
Galantine	Cooked food served in cold jelly
Galette	Flaky pastry case or pancake
Garni	With vegetables
(au) Gratin	Topped with crisp browned cheese and breadcrumbs
Grillé	Grilled
Hachis	Minced
Hollandaise	A sauce of butter and vinegar
Huile (d'olive)	Oil (olive)

Marmite	Casserole
Médaillon	Round piece
Mijoté	Simmered
Mornay	Cheese sauce
Nouilles	Noodles
Oeufs	Eggs
Pain	Bread
Pané	Breaded
Parmentier	With potatoes
Pâte	Pastry, pasta
Paupiette	Rolled and filled thin slices of fish or meat
Pavé	Slab
Piquante	Vinegar sauce with shallots and capers
Pissaladière	A kind of pizza with onions, anchovies, etc.
Poché	Poached
Poïvre	Pepper
Quenelles	Dumplings of fish or poultry
Raclette	Toasted cheese with potatoes, onions and pickles
Salé	Salted, spicy
Sanglant	Rare steak
Sel	Salt
Sucré	Sweet
Timbale	Pie cooked in a dome-shaped mould
Tranche	Slice
Vapeur	Steamed
Véronique	Green grapes, wine, and cream sauce
Vinaigre	Vinegar
Vinaigrette	Oil and vinegar dressing

Boissons	**Drinking**
Bière (pression)	Beer (draught)
Bouteille (demi)	Bottle (half)
Café	Coffee
Chocolat (chaud)	Chocolate (hot)
Demi	A third of a litre
Doux	Sweet (wine)
Eau (minérale)	Water (mineral, spring)
Eau de vie	Brandy
Gazeuse	Sparkling
Glaçons	Ice cubes
Infusion (or tisane)	Herbal tea
Lait	Milk
Moelleux	Semi-dry
Pichet	Pitcher
Pressé	Fresh fruit juice
Pression	Draft
Sec	Dry
Sirop d'orange/de citron	Orange/lemon squash
Thé	Tea
Verre	Glass
Vin blanc/rosé/rouge	Wine white/rosé/red

465

FURTHER READING

Ardagh, John, *France Today* (Penguin, 1987). One in Penguin's informative paperback series on contemporary Europe.

Barr, Alfred, *Henri Matisse: his Art and his Public* (Museum of Modern Art, New York, 1951).

Bishop, Morris, *Petrarch and His World* (Chatto & Windus, 1964).

Bonner, Anthony, *Songs of the Troubadours* (Allen & Unwin, 1973). An excellent introduction to the life and times of the troubadours, with translations of the best-known verses.

Cézanne, Paul, *Letters*, (London, 1941).

Cook, Theodore A., *Old Provence*, (London, 1905). A classic traveller's account of the region, out of print and hard to find.

Daudet, Alphonse, *Letters from my Windmill* (Penguin, 1982). Bittersweet 19th-century tales of Midi nostalgia by Van Gogh's favourite novelist.

Dumas, Alexandre, *The Count of Monte Cristo*, many editions; romantic fantastical tale of revenge, much of it set in Marseille and the Château d'If.

Durrell, Lawrence, *The Avignon Quintet* (Faber, 1974–85); lush wartime sagas that take place in Avignon and around.

Fitzgerald, F. Scott, *Tender is the Night*, many editions. 1920s Riviera decadence based on personal research.

Ford, Madox Ford, *Provence: From Minstrels to the Machine* (Allen & Unwin, 1935). A lyrical pre-war view of the region.

Fortescue, Winifred, *Perfume from Provence* (1935). Poor, intolerable Lady Fortescue's misadventures with the garlicky peasants near Nice.

Giono, Jean, *To the Slaughterhouse, Two Riders of the Storm* (Peter Owen, 1988). Giono is a major 20th-century novelist of Provence, whose deep pessimism contrasts with the sunnier views of his contemporary Pagnol.

Goldring, Douglas, *The South of France* (Macdonald, 1952). Travels and comments by another English resident.

Gramont, Sanche de, *The French: Portrait of a People* (Putnam, New York, 1969). One of the funnier attempts at the favourite French intellectual pastime: national self-analysis.

Greene, Graham, *J'Accuse: The Dark Side of Nice* (Bodley Head, 1982). The late Graham Greene, resident of Antibes, discovers the mafia connections and graft in the government of discredited mayor Jacques Médecin.

Hugo, Victor, *Les Misérables*, many editions. Injustice among the galley-slaves and basis for the hit musical.

Ladurie, Emmanuel Leroi, *Love, Death and Money in the Pays d'Oc* (Scolar, 1982).

Lugand, Jacques, Robert St-Jean and Jean Nougaret, *Languedoc Roman*, (Zodiaque, 1975). The best of Languedoc's Romanesque architecture, with plans, lots of photos and an English translation.

Lyall, Archibald, *Companion Guide to the South of France* (Collins, 1978). Personal, well-written but dated guide of the entire Mediterranean coast.

Mayle, Peter, *A Year in Provence* and *Toujours Provence* (Sinclair Stevenson/Pan, 1989 and 1991). The entertaining bestsellers on ex-pat life in the Lubéron.

Mistral, Frédéric, *Miréio* and *Poème de la Rhône*, epic poems by the Nobel prize-winning Félibre, widely available in French or Provençal.

Morris, Edwin T., *Fragrance: The Story of Perfume from Cleopatra to Chanel* (Charles Scribner & Sons, 1984).

Pagnol, Marcel, *Jean de Florette* and *Manon of the Springs, The Days were too Short* (Picador, 1960). Autobiography by Provence's most beloved writer.

Petrarch, Francesco, *Songs and Sonnets from Laura's Lifetime* (Anvil Press, 1985).

Pope Hennessy, James, *Aspects of Provence* (Penguin, 1952). A fussy but lyrical view of the region in the 40s and 50s.

Raison, Laura, compiler, *The South of France: An Anthology*, (Cadogan, 1985).

Smollett, Tobias, *Travels through France and Italy*, (London, 1776). The irrepressible, grouchy Tobias 'Smellfungus' makes modern travel writing look like advertising copy.

Stendhal, *Travels through the South of France*, (London, 1971).

Süskind, Patrick, *Perfume*, (Penguin, 1989). Thrilling and fragrant murder in the 18th-century perfume industry in Grasse.

Van Gogh, Vincent, *Collected Letters of Vincent Van Gogh*, (New York, 1978).

Vergé, Roger, *Cuisine of the Sun*, (London, 1979). The owner of the Moulin de Mougins tells some of his secrets of nouvelle Provençal cooking.

Whitfield, Sarah, *Fauvism* (Thames and Hudson, 1991). A good introduction to the movement that changed art history.

Worwood, Valerie, *Aromantics* (Pan, 1987), an amusing look at aromatherapy.

Wylie, L., *Village in the Vaucluse* (Harvard University Press, 1971). The third edition of a very readable sociologist's classic based on the village of Roussillon.

Zeldin, Theodore, *France 1845–1945* (Oxford University Press, 1980). Five well-written volumes on all aspects of the period.

GENERAL INDEX

Page numbers in *italics* refer to illustrations;
page numbers in **bold** refer to maps

INDEX OF ARCHITECTS, ARTISTS, MUSICIANS AND WRITERS

See also Artists' Directory, pp. 65–9